Library of
Davidson College

The Road to Europe

PETER LANG
New York • San Francisco • Bern • Baltimore
Frankfurt am Main • Berlin • Wien • Paris

David W. P. Lewis

The Road to Europe

History, Institutions and Prospects of European Integration, 1945-1993

PETER LANG
New York • San Francisco • Bern • Baltimore
Frankfurt am Main • Berlin • Wien • Paris

337.4
L673r

Library of Congress Cataloging-in-Publication Data

Lewis, David W. P.
  The road to Europe : history, institutions and prospects of European
integration, 1945-1993 / David W.P. Lewis.
    p. cm.
  Includes bibliographical references.
  1. Europe—Economic integration.   2. European Federation.
3. Europe 1992.   I. Title.
HC241.L44   1993   337.4—dc20   91-16050
  ISBN 0-8204-1640-1 (hdk)   CIP
  ISBN 0-8204-2113-8 (pbk)

Die Deutsche Bibliothek-CIP-Einheitsaufnahme

Lewis, David W. P.:
The road to Europe : history, institutions and prospects of European
integration, 1945-1993 / David W. P. Lewis.—New York; Berlin; Bern;
Frankfurt/M.; Paris; Wien: Lang, 1993
   ISBN 0-8204-1640-1 (hdk)
   ISBN 0-8204-2133-8 (pbk)

Maps and charts by Thomas Brandt.
Cover photo by Søren Gregersen.

Cover design by James Brisson.

The paper in this book meets the guidelines for permanence and
durability of the Committee on Production Guidelines for
Book Longevity of the Council on Library Resources.

© Peter Lang Publishing, Inc., New York 1993

All rights reserved.
Reprint or reproduction, even partially, in all forms such as microfilm,
xerography, microfiche, microcard, offset strictly prohibited.

Printed in the United States of America.

96-0835
ACZ-1437

Contents

To the members of Freshman Seminar 93, Fall 1990, who helped to set me on this road to Europe

Thomas Scott Altholz
Gregory George Asaf
Alissa Lauren Beaudet
Janette E Chakeres
Jaymes Scott Choy
Sean Jason Denham
Robin Beth Epstein
Susan Jameson Gleeson

Benjamin Winters Graves
Stephanie Greene
Sara Kathryn Guben
Michael Lamolino
Brett Alan Perlmutter
Joseph Edward Pratt
Elizabeth Ann Robinson
Jeremi Arthur Roth

David John Shepley

List of Maps and Charts

Foreword

Down the ages, the rise and fall of empire, interspersed with war, has been the stuff of history and the lot of men. Peoples who considered themselves civilized cultivated their new beginnings in the soil of stricken societies and biodegradable cultures. Violence and untimely death were the twin harrow blades of growth.

Following two world wars more widespread and more deadly than any which had gone before, and even as the two remaining superpowers faced off in a confrontation threatening society with nuclear annihilation, the second half of the twentieth century has seen a new type of international society emerge. The union of Europe has become an empire without an emperor, a commonwealth without colonies, where international expansion is achieved by consent of the governed, committed not to the practice of war but to its proscription. Like the facets of a finely-cut jewel, diversity of cultures is here celebrated, each true to itself in the mirror of the whole. There are of course, horrendous setbacks, like the suicide of Yugoslavia, Europe's greatest conflict since 1945, but even these can teach us watchfulness and tolerance.

As the Council of Europe discovered a new mission and a new vigor; as the European Community faced in 1993 the most important deadline since its birth; as the great flat stone of communism was lifted from the east and the continent made whole again, Europe seemed a tale worth telling.

There are many books on European union; and many more on aspects of European institutions. This is perhaps the first to encompass the sweep of history over half a century from a holistic inter-institutional and, it is hoped, objective viewpoint; objective not as to the outcome, for the building of Europe needs faith, hope, charity, commitment, patience, forgiveness, humor, but as to the process itself and the role of each of the players.

In studying the achievements of the past decades and the projects of the millennium, it is important to know "what" and "how", more vital yet to understand "why". Thus do even our setbacks become building blocks, ideally not in Europe alone but among emulators across the earth.

A word about the organization of the book. It was decided to place the storyline at the head of the work, followed by a description of institutional structures. It is possible, however, for those who so wish, to read section III before section II. A greater challenge was presented by the necessary choice between chronology and continuity of subject matter in the historical account. Coherence has been my main concern here. Recent events are discussed in greater detail than those which preceded them. To assist with the work's reference function a detailed datelist, an index and a glossary of acronyms have been included.

With a subject so vast choices had to be made. Two are obvious. Only passing reference is made to the extensive contribution of non-governmental organizations (NGO's) to European unification. Their role has been important not only in specific sectors, such as the protection of Europe's cultural and environmental heritage, but also in shaping public opinion in general. Whereas IGO's represent all the citizens, NGO's, while frequently defending the general interest in a highly professional manner, are usually composed of an unpaid and highly committed membership. To do them justice another book awaits an author.

Another subject accorded only passing reference here, precisely because it is so vast, is the extensive partnership developed between the European Community and former colonial territories and protectorates, the so-called ACP countries, and the multilateral assistance extended to other developing nations. In an official visit to Senegal the Commission President, Jacques Delors, assured his listeners that the Community would not neglect its responsibilities in this domain, despite the newly-added burden of aid to eastern Europe.

I thank those who have shared with me this road to Europe and made it possible — my family, especially my wife Avril; Debbie Russo, Brigitte Mignot, my sister Audrey Hereford, whose patience triumphed over bad handwriting and outlasted second thoughts and rewrites; Tanya Atwood, who contributed a finely crafted chapter on monetary union; Thomas Brandt, for clear attractive maps; Lehigh University, which granted study leave in spring 1992 to make sense of a continental cascade of events; Christopher Myers of Lang Publishers, for faith and encouragement.

I thank also the College of Europe in Bruges, Belgium, for teaching me European objectivity before it was fashionable or, at least, the balancing of biases; and for nurturing the fire of a mission which has accompanied me not only through several professions, down four decades and in five countries of residence but also across two continents, that Europeans and North Americans might know, understand and tolerate each other better and never become the *frères implacables* of the twenty-first century. The Rector Emeritus of the College of Europe, holder of the Charlemagne Prize for services to the European cause, has honored this book with a preface.

In a historical synthesis of this breadth it is hard to thank all those who have contributed source material. Nevertheless, special appreciation is due to the Council of Europe and especially my former colleague, now Deputy Director of Education, Culture and Sport, Maitland Stobart; to the European Community in Brussels and Peter Doyle of the EC Delegation in Washington; to the information services of Western European Union, GATT and EFTA in Geneva and OECD and ESA in Paris; and not least to Mikhail Gorbachev for providing such spectacular copy: never in the history of human peacemaking has so much been achieved so rapidly by (allegedly) so hesitant an individual! Let my inspiring mentor Marie-Joseph Lory and his wife Marthe, my dear friends Michel and Monique Roche in Paris and Guy and Paulette Aureau in painterly Provence also know that their friendship, hospitality and encourage-ment are not forgotten.

David W. P. Lewis
Bethlehem, Pennsylvania
Saint-Rémy-de-Provence,
France, 1990-1992

Preface

by H. Brugmans

One day, Dr. Joseph Retinger, the Anglo-Polish secretary of the European Movement, said to me: "The integration of this Continent is not an economic enterprise, as some people seem to think. It is an historic movement, aiming at the rebirth of a civilisation".

This remark struck me, since it corresponded to a vision of what was going on. Of course, "a Europe without internal frontiers" remains one of the most striking features of contemporary affairs. But the "founding fathers", such as Robert Schuman, did not exclusively or even mainly think in terms of industrial and commercial growth. They dreamed of a reconciliation between nations that had fought each other so bitterly only a few years ago. They dreamed of peace and renewal, not just of a closer co-operation between those active in the economic professions—managers, bankers and trade unionists. They wanted to see more friendly diplomatic relations between countries, but above all, they considered the era of totally "sovereign" States as waning. These States had been the expression, lately, of modern Democracy and Nationalism and, consequently, the major political forces of the XIXth century. The so-called "Great War" of 1914-1918 had closed that period.

For the last time, pacifists and socialists of all countries had forgotten their solemn declarations. They had accepted uniforms and weapons, in order to fight those whom they sincerely considered as the enemies of their fatherland. They had rushed to the frontiers, in order to make them safe for the future. Anti-militarists became patriots overnight. The unanimous enthusiasm was short-lived. The endless struggle in parallel trenches could only provoke doubts, and the wish to end this war and all wars to come. The Nation still remained a decisive point of reference, but when President Wilson stressed that the peace treaty should include the organisation of an inter-national League, his initiative was greeted with great expectation, all over the world. National security was no longer enough. Permanent peace would henceforth be guaranteed only by collective action.

A few years later, Black Friday announced another message, equally important for the future. A recession could not be stopped by protectionist measures, taken by governments. The disease was no longer a national catastrophe but a collective one, a sign of world-wide crisis. Just as no national army or navy could protect their citizens any more, no deflationist policy, decided by "sovereign" nations, could cure the disease that had fallen upon all like an economic earthquake.

Unfortunately, the League of Nations, located in Geneva, Switzerland, proved to be as inefficient as the States. Since it had no "teeth" it could not break the impact of Japanese and Nazi-German imperialists, nor could it transform international economics into a realm of prosperity and well-ordered production. In other words, the League too had become obsolete. It could, no doubt, achieve progress in such matters as education and social legislation, but in matters like defense planning, it had to admit the limits of its power.

The same was true in the field of international affairs. A fervent patriot like Francois Mitterrand, France's President during two terms, declared recently that his country was no longer what it used to be at the beginning of the century. In those early days, even when the Geneva League was in operation, the "great powers" were almost exclusively located in the heart of Europe. Today, by contrast, only countries with a population well above a hundred million inhabitants, could still claim to be "great". The modern world functions on the scale of united continents, larger and more powerful than even united Germany. If the Europeans wanted to be heard, they should coalesce their strengths and "speak with one voice" (as the phrase runs).

Finally, we all become more and more concerned about the ecological future of mankind. Even in Britain, separated from the Continent by the Dover Straits, the direct impact of acid rain is considerable. Winds do not respect borders however venerable. A change of climate , a hole in the ozone-layer, remain immediate dangers for all mankind. Here again, for the first time in history, the concept of "humanity as a whole" becomes more than an idealistic dream of universal brotherhood: it starts to be tangible task, to be neglected at our peril.

All this seems so evident that it would seem only reasonable to set up structures and institutions capable of handling this post-XIXth century situation.

But it seems to be the fate of the human race, *not* to be guided by reason alone. In Europe, in particular, traditional feelings of national identity are so strong that each new step in the right historic direction is met with hesitation and distrust. For millions of people, the national State remains much more than just a sociological instrument for handling problems. To many, it seems to embody the concept of a fatherland. What is operational in practice consequently becomes a sentimental issue. Each progress seems to be an attempt to desacralise the "amour sacre de la patrie", as *La Marseillaise* sings. France, Germany, Italy and so on, mean much more to the "common man" than a theory of European Union, indispensable as it may be.

So the road to economic and political union is a fairly long one, studded with mistakes, setbacks and disappointments. For instance, in 1954, the French Assembly rejected the Treaty for a common European Defense as anti-national and thereby immoral. Feelings of a similar kind wake up at present, as the creation of a common European currency is at stake. However, for the European Federalists it is consoling to remember the remark of a French philosopher: "Slowly but surely the world achieves the dream of the wise".

In the beginning, the European drive towards "something like the United States of Europe" (to quote Churchill's Zurich-speech in 1946) was popular in America. At long last, the Europeans had become wise enough to realise that

Federal Union offered the solution to their problems. That enthusiasm, however, did not last, since the progress towards unification became slower and slower. Moreover, a European "Common Market" appeared to many as a protectionist fortress.

But quarrels about the Common Agricultural Policy should not obscure either our Atlantic solidarity, or the historic achievement of more than one federalistic break-through. We need each other in issues to come and feel now closer together than yesterday, but only because our union is a means to overcome ancient inferiority-complexes. The stronger we get, the more equal to America, as we cease to be the "poor relations", asking for aid.

European Federalism is, like things important usually are, a problem of moral *consciousness*. It was a moral issue to shake hands with former enemies; a moral issue to lay our future in the hands of a collectivity; a question of morality, to believe that, as Europeans, we have so much in common as members of an all-embracing group, claiming its place under a common sun.

This account by Dr. David Lewis, who was my student in Brugge many years ago, provides the reader with a guidance that may be trusted. Things are on the move. New problems will arise as we proceed. But they will be better understood by virtue of Lewis's explanations, since the future, concretised in the present, is the fruit of a conflictual past. Here is Ariadne's thread through the European labyrinth.

Brugge (B), December 1992
H Brugmans
Former Rector of the College of Europe

The Road to Europe

I

INTRODUCTION

The Road to Europe

The long short road from Aachen to Maastricht

Like most European cathedrals, the cathedral of Aachen, a German city close to the Dutch and Belgian borders, has miraculously survived the ravages of war. In this place Charlemagne, patriarch of the Holy Roman Empire, crowned in Rome on Christmas Day 800, sage of the Song of Roland, was laid to rest in his own Palatine Chapel in the year 814. Today the city of Aachen awards each year a prestigious prize in his name. The prize is presented to a public figure having rendered exceptional service and inspiration to the cause of European unity. The symbolism is puissant, for Carolus Magnus was emperor of Europe. After division of the Empire upon his death, many hundreds of years would pass before Europe was united once again. The new empire would be founded not only on geography and history but also on freedom, an empire where the people are sovereign, an empire without an emperor. . . Moreover, lest there should be any doubt about the eastern marches of the new empire, in 1991 the Charlemagne Prize was awarded to Vaclav Havel, playwright president of Czechoslovakia.

Some thirty kilometers from Aachen, westwards across the flat green countryside of Limburg, the southernmost province of the Netherlands, stands a frontier town astride the Meuse, where two thousand years ago the Romans threw a bridge across the river, *trajectum ad Mosam*, the city of Maastricht.

The journey from Aachen to Maastricht takes less than an hour by road. Despite its brevity, it is a truly international journey—you can even travel through Belgium. Yet from the deathbed of an emperor to the birthplace of a Treaty of Union, it has taken eleven centuries to travel the Road to Europe. Most of those eleven centuries were consumed in conflict, in the rise of dynasties and the fall of prophets, in blind alleys and false starts; indeed, most of those thirty kilometers have been travelled in the last fifty years.

Not that the green valley of the Meuse is the Promised Land, nor Maastricht the New Jerusalem, nor even a European Oz at the end of a yellow-brick road. The Treaty of European Union, signed on February 7, 1992, is itself presented as an evolutionary document. Its entry into force on January 1, 1993, assuming ratification by all twelve participants, is a new beginning. If the Road to Europe appeared actually to have reached its goal, it would be but another blind alley. Economically, politically, but above all socially and culturally, Europe is a dynamic process. More important, because more true, more quintessential than the United States of Europe is the united state of Europe, a State of mind.

The builders of Europe may be likened to those medieval journeymen masons who raised the cathedrals, building upon the foundations set by their forbears and laboring in faith that after them the task would be carried forward from generation to generation with no hope of ever seeing the finished product. But the cathedrals were actually completed, spires thrusting skywards, whereas Europe reserves surprises round the bend of the road, in the fold of the hills. Although recently the vista has been fertile there are often arid tracts to cross. Yet as we progress from sunrise to sunrise, new horizons open before us, offering new challenges, new achievements, fresh hope. While this book purports to explain much, therefore, it does not offer one central definition, a straightforward answer to the question, "What is Europe?" Mikhail Gorbachev claimed in Strasbourg a common European home; Vaclav Havel, on receiving the Charlemagne Prize, spoke of his country, after years of oppression, finally coming home to Europe. If a home is a place where unity in diversity is cherished, this comes close to a definition. Robert Schuman spoke of banishing war; . . . but when the swords have been beaten into plowshares, they are subject to the Common Agricultural Policy! For Europe, too, is "Eurocracy" and nuts and bolts; a standard for quince paste; certificates of origin. (HRH Prince Charles recently rose in defense of French cheeses in all their unpasteurized magnificence.) Those who all their lives have paid tribute to the European dream of unity, human rights and democracy, have also failed to agree on a permanent home for Europe's parliament.

Europe today is a product of enlightened self-interest, of quiet progress, of marathon negotiations and stopping the clock to strike a deadline deal. Sometimes, more than failure, men have feared success, the entry into a new world, albeit one anchored in the old. Luck, vision, determination, skepticism and trust, courage within and danger without have combined to create new institutions and political procedures never before conceived, much less brought to fruition.

For each observer, each player, there is a spatial Europe (but how big?), a numerical Europe (how many?), a political Europe (how decisional?), a Europe of cultures and languages, of nations and regions and minorities, a Europe of trade and aid, an environmental Europe (nature knows no frontiers), a Europe of shame, a Europe of pride, a Europe of the past, a Europe of the future . . .

Much has been written of January 1993 opening a new era for Europe, a fresh challenge to the world. In the narrow sense, however, while it may affect everyone indirectly, the Treaty of European Union concerns directly only twelve of Europe's fifty or so countries and governments. For the foreseeable future there will be layers of Europe or, to change the metaphor, an inner core and outer concentric circles. But just as the six have become twelve, so also have the Council of Europe's original ten become twenty-seven. When the curtain was lifted and the Wall fell, a new outer ring was added . . . to the dynamism of Europe's members corresponds a necessary adaptability of structure. The Treaty of European Union recognizes this. It is a vast document, but much of it is devoted to the amendment of earlier treaties. It leaves the door open to new membership.

In reality, then, the much heralded threshold of January 1993 is a technical staging post along a road that Europeans have long been travelling and will continue to travel for the forseeable future. This is not to diminish its importance — certainly the most significant event in European unification since 1957 — but rather to emphasize its inevitability, an inevitability that John Major of Britain was quick to recognize. Maastricht builds upon the Single European Act (SEA), which in turn arises out of the experience of the European Economic and Atomic Energy treaties (EEC, EURATOM). These extended the experience of the European Coal and Steel Community (ECSC). The ECSC was a new approach for those dissatisfied with the Council of Europe formula, and so back again to the defunct League of Nations.

Diversity enhances unity
A "variable geometry" of institutions has gradually merged standards and procedures while preserving national and regional cultures. Yet awareness of a common heritage is a driving force behind Europeans' yearning for union. This itself is a major achievement, for "common heritage" is not necessarily evident to Norwegians and Italians, to British and Czechs . . . although two world wars, both of which started in Europe, were important negative unifiers. In 1940 flyers of many nations fought a common enemy in the Battle of Britain. Men and women learned what they shared when they were about to lose it. They also learned that "Europe" reposed more on values than on geography.

Alike as peas?
The fact remains that European unity cannot be achieved without respect for diversity. No family can "spare" a child. No Europe worth the name can "spare" a Van Gogh, a Cervantes, a Beethoven, a Comenius, a language or a folk-dance. As a bulwark of democratic values diversity enhances unity. If Europe were only a paradise of salesmen and consumers, we would seek in the name of efficiency to be as alike as peas in a pod. As standards are set and procedures merged, national and regional cultures must be protected. In most cases they are: the Brussels Commission threatens neither the throne of Denmark nor the House of Windsor nor yet the town square democracy of Switzerland. It may make the trains run on time; but Hitler did that too. In working for a necessary standardization, whether in the size of windows, the description of blood plasma or the mutual recognition of diplomas, we must know where to draw the line before bureaucracy becomes the master instead of the servant. (Here the much denigrated "Brits" have played a valuable role.) Today, everyone has sauerkraut and fish and chips and, of course, McDonalds; but France, *Dieu merci*, is still France.

As frontiers disappear, minorities find new living space. Governments collaborate to build the Airbus, but also subsidize translations of Icelandic short stories. Europe may one day have an elected president, but, let us hope, no single minister of education or culture. Working in nine languages which, with accessions from Eastern Europe, may multiply further, the European Community has decided to pay the price.

Europe at three levels
This book will certainly not answer all questions but it does attempt to make some sense out of a plethora of interacting forces and a jungle of institutions. One major rectification is that while the European Community and its Common Market are at the heart of the process, and are proving a powerful magnet, they do not yet and indeed may never meet everybody's needs or conceptions of unity. Furthermore, in recent years the whole process has been immensely complicated by a necessary disunion in the eastern half of the continent. Our study pays considerable attention to this phenomenon and to its impact on a unification process which until recently was centered largely on western and southern Europe. In the process of reintegrating "East" and "West" an old institution, the Council of Europe in Strasbourg and a relatively new one, the Conference on Security and Cooperation in Europe, are playing immensely valuable roles. The very fact that the membership of CSCE, Council of Europe and EC overlaps is evidence that their purposes are complementary and distinct.

With surprising perseverance, the Council of Europe continues, after over four decades as the "mother" of European institutions, to enfold all the factions and to promote human and social rights, environmental protection and cultural cooperation. More than a hundred Council of Europe conventions have made it easier for people to work in any member country with equal recognition of professional qualifications, health services and pension rights, and to feel themselves to be citizens of Europe. The Council is now opening its doors to new members from the East—to Czechoslovakia, Hungary, and Poland and soon no doubt to the Baltic states and others. The fact that it has few decision-making powers outside the human-rights field is being turned to advantage, making it easier to join as a first step for East European countries seeking eventually to enter the European Community.

Born as a prolongation of a "Helsinki process" intended, ironically enough, in Soviet eyes, to consecrate post-war European frontiers (a sort of latter-day Yalta) in exchange for greater respect for human rights in the Eastern bloc, the CSCE was in the first instance consensual in character and unstructured in its operation. It rapidly became apparent, however, that there was a need for a comprehensive organization, bringing together East and West, which, unlike the Council of Europe, had competence for security problems and also included Canada and the United States. Thus the CSCE is European in its focus but Atlantic-European-Asian in its membership. As such it places all-European cooperation in a world context. Today the CSCE has a secretariat in Prague, related structures in other central European cities and is developing a European "security council" function. It boasts a membership of some fifty countries, all of them established or emerging democracies.

Birth of a superpower? American misgivings
Not everyone shares an idealistic vision of the new Europe, especially those who watch from outside. Americans in particular are in two minds. Officially, they have supported the Western European "integration process" both as a bulwark against totalitarianism and as a trading partner for the industrialized world. Americans should look back before they look ahead, and take pride in their post-war foreign policy. The Marshall Plan of 1947 restored Europe's devastated economies, while the Atlantic alliance guaranteed its peace. With American support, Western Europe flourished, the Berlin Wall was breached, the Iron Curtain lifted. Today, however, Americans are anxious as they anticipate the final fruit of their labors. Already traumatized by virulent competition from Japan, they do not want to fight a trade war on both Pacific and Atlantic fronts. Moreover, they wish to retain influence in Europe but are unwilling to continue to pay a major share of European defense.

Defense, the equivocal dimension
In seeking to present a holistic view of the process of European integration, we may not concentrate on economic, political and social factors to the exclusion of security concerns. It has been said that military force, or the threat of it, is the ultimate expression of a political objective which cannot be achieved by other means. Defense of western Europe since 1945 has played a complex role in the integration process. The North Atlantic Treaty Organization provided the shield behind which integration could proceed, including the incorporation of the western half of Germany. At the same time, until the collapse of the Soviet Union, the dominant role played by the United States in European defense made it clear that "Europe" was not a free-standing political entity, a nascent superpower in its own right. Symptomatic of the friction this caused between Europe and America and also within Europe were France's withdrawal under de Gaulle from NATO'S integrated military command and periodical accusations that the British, with their English language, were too close to the United States and not sufficiently committed to Europe. (de Gaulle, hardly a supranationalist himself, knew how to play both sides of an issue).

Inevitably, then, defense issues played an equivocal role in the integration process. The failure of the potential short cut to a political unification, the European Defence Community (EDC) in 1954 can be ascribed to differences of outlook between the United Kingdom and France. On the other hand, out of defeat came new approaches resulting a few years later in creation of the European Economic Community (EEC). To meet the defense issue, Western European Union (WEU), was set in place, mainly to bring the Federal Republic into the western military fold. Its relationship to NATO remained ambiguous for years and is only now being clarified through its assimilation into the structures of the European Community. Europe today pays lip-service to Atlantic solidarity but, now that the nuclear threat has receded, is clearly tempted by the notion of demonstrating her maturity by managing her own defense. Ultimately, the US budget deficit may well decide the issue for both parties. During the Cold War, Atlantic defense made European unification possible while at the same time setting limits upon it.

To return to 1954, the EDC failure did have its positive aspects. It caused a return to the brilliant strategy of Monnet, Schuman and Adenauer, the integration of Europe by economic sectors. Thus the EEC and EURATOM were born and eventually merged with the European Coal and Steel Community to create a single European Community. The EC has been strengthened further by the Single European Act (SEA) of 1986 and the Maastricht Treaty of 1992. It is difficult today to state whether it is economic integration or joint institutional structures (Commission, Parliament, Court of Justice, Council of Ministers, European Council "summits") which have played the greater role in bringing Europe together.

Impact of world events

The world was watching; but it also was not without influence on events. Europeans know that they do not function in a vacuum. History has shown a correlation between progress in European integration and crises in world affairs. The Berlin blockade, Korean War, Suez crisis, Berlin Wall, Prague Spring, Afghanistan, glasnost, the Persian Gulf War, Yeltsin on a tank, the Yugoslavian conflict, all proved admirable stimuli to rapprochement in Western Europe. External shocks usually spur unification but sometimes the response is more complex. After the Hungarian uprising and Suez crisis of 1956, for instance, France headed toward Europe but the UK turned back to her increasingly illusory "special relationship" with the US. In 1990-1991 the Gulf War forged a coalition of East and West yet demonstrated that Western Europeans do not yet speak with a single political voice. The lesson was brought home (literally!) when the Community failed to act effectively and in concert to stop the Yugoslav conflict. (The EC held a so-called peace conference under Lord Carrington's chairmanship, but it was former US Secretary of State Cyrus Vance and the Security Council which stemmed the fighting and sent peacekeepers.) Legal niceties about "internal affairs" provided a convenient fig leaf for Europe's political nakedness. The EC has also turned a blind eye to Northern Ireland's shameful conflict. Germany, Japan and now Europe have learned that while economic power is essential to political influence, it does not guarantee it.

The European cuckoo

The fact remains that it is the economic aspect, the impact of European integration on world trade, which currently most concerns Europe's Atlantic partners, Canada and the United States. Some leaders of government and industry are fearful that the powerful new economic bloc will become protectionist in its trade policy. There was talk of a trade war with "Fortress Europe" as the Europeans refused to bow to American demands over agriculture in the GATT "Uruguay Round" negotiations. Just as Japan has threatened US competitiveness on the Pacific Rim, a "European Germany" or, worse a

"German Europe" is seen by some to loom on the Atlantic Rim, competing both inside America and in the restructuring of Central and Eastern Europe. (Germany has already carved out a privileged position by leading all comers in aid to the former Soviet Union.) An eventual all-European market of half a billion people could prove unstoppably cost-effective in the rest of the world. Some Americans are wondering whether they have spent four decades nurturing a European cuckoo in the American nest: there is a grain of truth and a mountain of misperception in this scenario. For those same four decades Western Europe was America's front line against communism and the strengthening of the "European pillar" of the Atlantic Alliance strengthened the Alliance as a whole.

Others, it is true, see the US problem differently: America should look more to herself than to others for answers; to deficit reduction, to improvements in US productivity, to reduction of health cost overheads, to arresting social decay in the cities, to revamping education and honing foreign language skills. To be number one abroad you must be number one at home. These things are necessary, of course, but America and Europe will continue to need each other in the "post-Soviet" world.

Meanwhile, Europe continues to reorganize herself economically. Recently the rival, albeit unevenly matched twelve-nation European Community (EC) and seven-nation European Free Trade Area (EFTA) agreed to merge their forces in a nineteen-nation European Economic Area (EEA) stretching from the Arctic to the Mediterranean, a vast market of 380 million consumers. Austria, Finland, Sweden, Turkey, Cyprus and even little Malta have applied to join the Community. Switzerland hesitates. Poland, Czechoslovakia, Hungary, and Lithuania have already become linked through Association Agreements. In response to this trend, trading groups are emerging in North America (NAFTA), in the southern cone of South America, in the Baltic, around the Black Sea, among Turcic-speaking and Muslim republics, in South-East Asia (AFTA) . . . Whether this development will result in protectionist blocs or global free trade remains to be seen.

Breaking the agricultural log-jam
The most intractable problem threatening the harmony of Atlantic relations is agriculture. Every country protects its farmers on economic, cultural and political grounds. Europe's farms are small by American standards, its countryside more diverse and heavily populated. The Community's Common Agricultural Policy (CAP) has not yet moved beyond price supports and export subsidies and the EC has difficulty envisaging a free and open market. However, the pressure for CAP reform has proved as strong inside the EC as it is from outside. Agriculture simply costs too much. Not that the US is innocent: each side seems to be waiting for the other to blink first. The Europeans are unwilling to reveal their hand completely (at national or international levels) unless the US shows signs of flexibility in other sections of the economy. (The vote in Congress in favor of "fast track" negotiation with the EC and in NAFTA was certainly helpful.) As the heavyweights battle it out they will still

need GATT to referee the struggle, interpreting the rules and keeping the fight clean. We shall take an early look at GATT'S contribution to the liberation of world trade. Meanwhile, the EC/US agreement signed in December 1992 marks a major step forward (not withstanding French objections) and goes far to avoid a world-wide trade war.

All is not bleak for North American exporters. The removal of the last obstacles to trade in Western Europe in 1993 will create a unified and standardized market for American products, reducing unit costs and facilitating marketing for American producers from Dublin to Dresden. The Community has welcomed US investments, mergers and joint ventures; they enable US business to leapfrog the tariff wall. Improved living standards resulting from more efficient economic units increase the demand for imports. Peace in Europe means new opportunity for US industry and a smaller military bill, providing some relief for the US deficit. In GNP percentage terms Europe's third-world development assistance is higher than that of the US. All of this scarcely adds up to "Fortress Europe" isolation. The North American Free Trade Agreement (NAFTA) among Canada, Mexico and the US is a tribute to and a potential extension of the European Economic Area. GATT did not permit creation of trade blocs to foster trade wars of continental proportions.

Europe's socialists and conservatives alike support her unification, even as they differ on how to bring it about or what it should look like. Here too there are frequent misunderstandings. "Federalism" for some implies a heavy central bureaucracy sapping national powers. For others it means decentralization. European union must not destroy democracy but defend it through a tiered system of decision-making and cooperation at the appropriate level: the new in-word is subsidiarity. Local and regional authorities have an important role. They even join together across national boundaries to seek greater autonomy from their own national governments! The forging of a Celtic axis among the people of Europe's "Atlantic bow" is a case in point.

Toward the last frontier
Europe never ceases to amaze the traveller for her dazzling diversity. There is therefore something equally miraculous about the unification achievements of the last half-century. After two world wars, in which even the winners were losers, and the collapse of several empires, Europe's pioneers found within their own borders an inspiration for fresh concepts and structures. The new frontier would be no frontiers at all. The new Europe will be a cornerstone of any "new world order": there can be no going back.

For the close observer, however, especially the public officials so disparagingly called Eurocrats, progress gets bogged down in technical detail and seems frustratingly slow. Europe did not spring from a Philadelphia Convention of 1787; and even Americans fought a Civil War before their union was complete. The fruit of both vision and compromise, passion and patience, the European Union is emerging as a pragmatic yet dynamic reality with several levels of membership, commitment and decision-making authority which leave national entities firmly in place. Europe is seeking a third way between confederation and a unitary state.

Amid the ruins of 1945, Europe's federalists resolved not just to achieve economic reconstruction but to prevent another war by building a new political union. Thus every action which promoted greater unity, whether opening up trade, cleaning up the Rhine or labelling blood plasma, acquired a political context. Europeans wanted to contain communism and avoid being squeezed between two superpowers. They sought peace and a seat at the table when Europe's fate was discussed. Today they have not only occupied that seat but shaped it to their needs. Some distancing from friends, even close friends like America and Canada, was not only inevitable but necessary. Atlantic ties were not less strong than European ties: like cousinage and brotherhood, they were of a different order.

As for Europe's responsibilities in the Third World, a number of far-reaching aid and trade conventions have been negotiated with Europe's former colonies and developing nations. With South Africa's final emancipation, Africa must find new leadership within herself. An African democracy is slowly emerging, with new challenges for Europe's cooperative assistance. The entry of Spain and Portugal into the Community has raised the latter's consciousness of responsibilities and opportunities for cooperation with Latin America. Europe is thus indirectly repaying the debt owed for US assistance in the nineteen-forties and fifties.

As Western Europe scrambled to unite, in recent years the East has been disuniting. Inevitably, the puzzle must be reassembled, but on a freewill basis. Today, European unification is beginning to seal reconciliation between East and West. There is a moral imperative for Europe to come together. Will the new Europe ultimately stretch from the Atlantic to the Urals, as Charles de Gaulle, albeit a lukewarm internationalist, envisioned?

Does Europe's unification — geographical, instrumental, spiritual — teach us anything about the feasibility of an Atlantic Union or even of a world government? For the United States, are such notions impossible dreams or nightmares to be avoided? America would have to play a leading role but could not expect to dominate. Could the US renounce not only nuclear riposte but its Security Council veto? How long will it remain in the American interest to be more equal than others? Europe's step-by-step approach, both cautious and daring, merging traditionalist and federalist models, offers food for thought. Europe today needs a new Monnet, a young Konrad Adenauer, a latter-day visionary who can rise above the tug and haul of nations to loft a new holistic view of Europe — beyond our grasp, perhaps, not our reach. The task is unfinished and will ever remain so, for the Road to Europe is a road to the future. We have far to travel; so let us begin.

II

WINDING ROAD: AN HISTORICAL OVERVIEW

1

Survivors and Visionaries
(1945-1948)

For a thousand years or more, men have dreamed of uniting Europe. What stave and scimitar, chariot and battering rams, horse and Heinkel, Caesar, Charlemagne, Henry, Louis, Napoleon, Briand and Hitler failed each in his own way to achieve, what Yalta failed to prevent, may yet be voted into being by the peoples of the Continent. Where the sword failed the ploughshare, the microchip and the ballot box may, indeed must succeed. An empire without an emperor, this continental union will be the first to come into being without the use of force.

After the costly and harrowing experience of the First World War, a few men of vision sought peaceful change for Europe's nationalistic climate of international relations. While America stood on the sidelines, declining to join the infant League of Nations, Count Coudenhove Kalergi, the Austrian leader of the Pan-European Movement, proposed in 1923 the creation of the United States of Europe. Six years later, addressing the assembly of the League of Nations on September 29, 1929, the French foreign minister, Aristide Briand, backed by his German counterpart, Gustav Stresemann, sought the establishment of a European Union under League of Nations auspices. However, the economic depression of the thirties swept aside these dreams in a brusque return of nationalism and illusions of empire. Hitler and Mussolini rose to power. Under the threat of a second global conflict, men of such diverse backgrounds as Léon Blum, Eduard Benes and Count Sforza clung to the hope that European unity might avert hostilites. Yet the deadly civil war in Spain fuelled ideology and nationalism and, with the unchecked rape of Abyssinia by Italy, the League of Nations expired in feckless impotence.

As the Nazi *Blitzkrieg* rolled across the plains of Europe and south towards Paris Winston Churchill, in a glorious futile gesture, on June 17, 1940, offered common citizenship to France and Britain. The proposal was cut short by the fall of the French government and advent of the Vichy regime. Only after Europe had been once again devastated by war and divided into zones of influence under the hegemony of newly emergent superpowers, the United States of America and the Soviet Union, did the futility of incessant European rivalry become apparent.

Winston Churchill's vision

As they fought to the death in the bunkers of Berlin, Adolf Hitler and Joseph Stalin became the catalysts of a new European community. Although the boundaries of the pre-war nation states were largely re-created in the west,[1] the Soviet Union retained Estonia, Latvia and Lithuania, absorbed large portions of East Prussia and Poland and acquired Moldavia from Romania. Yugoslavia's boundary with Italy remained in contention. Moreover, western and eastern forces were face to face across the Elbe. The Yalta conference of the Great Powers had split Europe into zones of ideological influence and set the stage for half a century of ideological confrontation. The cry went up in Europe "Never again!" but it echoed though a continent newly-divided.

One man above all others emerged from the smoke of war with the moral authority to propose a new order; the fact that he was no longer Prime Minister of Britain gave this talented amateur artist the freedom to paint a broad canvas. Speaking in Zurich, Switzerland, on September 19, 1946, Winston Churchill proposed the reconciliation of France and Germany and, on this foundation stone, creation of the "United States of Europe"[2] and establishment of a "Council of Europe".

Four months later, on January 16, 1947, a provisional United Europe Committee was set up in London. In view of subsequent foot-dragging by successive United Kingdom governments *vis-à-vis* European unification, these early initiatives formed across the Channel should not be forgotten.

By 1947 the post-war euphoria engendered by hopes of a new era in Europe have largely evaporated. Security concerns re-emerge as the Soviet Union consolidates its hold on Eastern Europe from the Baltic to the Black Sea. In response to this threat France and the United Kingdom[3] enter into a defensive alliance, signed, with heavy symbolism, at Dunkirk on March 4, 1947. This is the first step towards the collective security arrangements resulting in the creation of the North Atlantic Treaty Organization in April 1949.

Trade and aid

Another major concern in 1947, related to the new threat from the east and the rebuilding of Europe's political institutions, is the economic weakness of the European democracies. Just as "lend-lease" from the United States had given a vital boost to Britain's war effort in the dark days of 1940 and 1941, so now American help was needed to "win the peace". In a speech at Harvard University in June 1947, General George Marshall proposed an economic plan for Europe. For the United States this was a gesture of enlightened self-interest: without assistance from the great democratic partner across the Atlantic, European democracy was liable to wither under communist influence. Furthermore, America herself needed strong trading partners.

Meanwhile, negotiations were going forward at world level to promote the free flow of trade. Pending creation of a world-wide organization an interim treaty, the General Agreement on Tariffs and Trade, was negotiated in 1947 and entered into force on January 1, 1948. A case of *le provisoire qui dure*, the GATT agreement, based on the "most favored nation" principle (whereby, subject to specific exceptions, trading partners are accorded equal treatment), is not only still in force but acquiring new signatories every year. GATT rules are monitored by a small secretariat located in Geneva, Switzerland; the "world-wide organization" proved unnecessary.

At European level, the first comprehensive cooperation agreement was signed in Belgium on March 17, 1948. The Brussels Treaty is significant for a number of reasons. It is a multilateral agreement expanding the Franco-British Treaty of Dunkirk to bring together five countries: Belgium, France, Luxembourg, Netherlands and, not least, the United Kingdom. Secondly, it provides for a wide range of cooperation: not only collective self-defense but also economic, social and cultural cooperation. Thirdly, being signed in Brussels, it inaugurates the role of the smaller countries as "honest brokers" among the larger powers such as France and the United Kingdom and providing an insurance against both domination or stalemate. [4]

The European Movement

The Brussels Treaty went further, however timidly, in setting up a study committee on European Union. This cautious governmental initiative was strengthened two months later from an unexpected source. A European Congress was convened in The Hague, Netherlands, from May 7-10, 1948. This historic event owed its existence to the initiative not of governments but of private citizens, under the leadership of former resistance fighters — *les maquisards* — from all the countries recently under Nazi occupation, including Germany itself. The European Federalist Movement was born.

The Hague Congress proposed not only a European Union and appropriate governing institutions but also, significantly if more modestly, a post-graduate College of Europe to train the administrators and opinion-shapers of the new Europe. The College opened its doors two years later in Bruges, Belgium, thanks to the combined efforts of a Spanish free-thinker, philosopher Don Salvador de Madariaga, a Belgian Capuchin, Antonius Verleye and a Dutch socialist educator, Hendrik Brugmans, who became its Rector. Official support was soon forthcoming and for many years now the College has enjoyed the rare distinction of receiving direct financing from several governments. Today many of its alumni hold key positions in national governments and international bodies. Responding to changes in eastern Europe the College recently set up a sister institution in Poland.

Meanwhile, things were not proceeding too smoothly on the economic front. The countries of western Europe and even Czechoslovakia had responded enthusiastically to General Marshall's proposal in his speech at Harvard on June 5, 1947, of American aid for Europe. Unfortunately, however, their plans were uncoordinated, sometimes even contradictory: a coordinating agency was manifestly needed. Thus did a convention for European economic cooperation come to be signed by seventeen countries in Paris on April 16, 1948. Although the United States was not a member of the new Organisation for European Economic Cooperation (OEEC), it enjoyed observer status and, more importantly, set up in Washington a coordinating agency for assistance to Europe, the European Co-operation Administration.

The OEEC headquarters was established at the Château de la Muette in Paris. European economic recovery was finally under way but the shadow of the Soviet Union grew longer after the communist take-over in Prague and the forced withdrawal of Czechoslovakia from the Marshall Plan. Now, as so often in later years, the European unification movement in Western Europe was spurred on as much by world events as by its own inner dynamism.

Be it noted that on January 8, 1949, under Soviet leadership, Albania, Bulgaria, Czechoslovakia, Poland, Romania and the USSR established the Council for Mutual Economic Assistance (CMEA, more frequently known as COMECON). However, this was far removed from being an "Eastern Marshall Plan". The headquarters were in the capital of the superpower and the Soviet Union was the primary beneficiary of the "mutual" economic assistance it provided, much of which was little more than a disguised form of war reparations.

Stormclouds in the East

As we have seen, Britain and France entered into a defensive alliance at Dunkirk on March 4, 1947. Despite the many jokes, more or less well-founded, about Anglo-French rivalry, this was a natural conjoining. Although United States troops were still present in Europe, in their occupation zones of south-western Germany, Berlin and Austria their liberation task was over and their future intentions uncertain. Dunkirk, symbolic Dunkirk, provided a setting for the two major powers of western Europe—powers with the privileges and responsibilities of UN Security Council membership—to come together in a mutual defense pact against a revival of German aggression. "Never again" were Nazi boots to reverberate on the bridges of the Rhine; "never again" were British "tommies" to stand around a shrinking perimeter in the dunes, backs to the Channel...

As the ink dried on the parchment, the world turned. Within months the fundamental incompatibility of the Western and Soviet systems had become apparent. The free elections promised at Yalta for the countries of eastern Europe never took place. Two years of endeavors by the Council of Foreign Ministers of France, the United Kingdom, the United States and the USSR to draft peace treaties with the Axis powers finally broke down on Soviet intransigence. On December 15, 1947, Ernest Bevin, British Foreign Secretary, declared to the American Secretary of State George Marshall:

> I am convinced that the Soviet Union will not deal with the West on any reasonable terms in the foreseeable future: and that the salvation of the West depends upon the formation of some form of union, formal or informal in character, in Western Europe, backed by the United States and the Dominions—such a mobilisation of moral and material force as will inspire confidence and energy within, and respect elsewhere.[5]

As we have seen, Belgium and the Netherlands were invited in January 1948 to adhere to the Treaty of Dunkirk. Joined by Luxembourg, they did so in March. However, by the time it was signed, the Brussels Treaty was as much or more a gesture of collective defense against a real threat from the Soviet Union as against any putative aggression from a renascent Germany. Perceptive as ever, Belgian Foreign Minister Paul-Henri Spaak considered the new defense treaty virtually meaningless unless it were conceived with the Soviet Union in mind. This in turn implied United States backing.

The US position was delicate. Americans had been schooled since George Washington's day against "entangling alliances". The United States had stood aloof even from the League of Nations. The Marshall Plan for European reconstruction had not yet received congressional approval. On the other hand, it was evident that, unlike the Marshall Plan, in military matters the United States could not operate from the outside. The Republican chairman of the Senate Foreign Relations Committee, Senator John Vandenberg, understood not only the international issue but also its relationship to internal American policies in this presidential election year. In the Vandenberg Resolution of June 11, 1948, the Republican-controlled Senate advised the Democratic President, Harry Truman, to sign such a treaty, including Scandinavia on the northern flank and Italy on the southern, since a system limited to the central sector would have been strategically meaningless and, furthermore, could have impeded US supply lines across the "stepping stones" of Greenland (Danish territory), Iceland and the Azores (Portuguese territory).

The stage was set for NATO. On April 4, 1949, by virtue of a treaty whereby an attack on one member is considered an attack upon all, the United States and Canada became inextricably linked, for an indeterminate period, with the defense of European democracy.[6] The Treaty covered all the territory of the member states, including Algeria (legally part of France) and "the occupation forces of any Party in Europe". The latter phrase was a device for including western Germany, as defined by British, French and American zones of occupation, without that country, still without a peace treaty, being a party to the Treaty itself.

The Treaty has kept the peace and survived over forty years of sometimes factious partnership. Today the communist threat has faded in the east; the Alliance is being reshaped to meet fresh responsibilities and new realities.

Notes

1 Belgium acquired Eupen and Malmédy from Germany and France recuperated Alsace-Lorraine. The status of the Saar was left in abeyance.

2 In 1943, to forestall the possibility of a Stalinist takeover in Eastern Europe, Churchill had advocated landings from North Africa in Greece rather than Sicily.

3 Britain's official name is "United Kingdom of Great Britain and Northern Ireland". "Great Britain" includes England, Scotland and Wales, that is all the territories governed from Westminster, together with the two Bailiwicks of the Channel Isles and also the Isle of Man, which enjoy a certain autonomy as dependencies of the Crown (for instance, Guernsey, Jersey and the Isle of Man opted to remain outside the European Community). The term "British Isles" is a geographical notion including the Republic of Ireland. To refer to the UK as "England" is as erroneous as calling the Netherlands "Holland".

4 The Grand Duchy of Luxembourg, with its modest population of 300,000, its strategic location at the conjunction of Belgium, France, the Federal Republic of Germany and, almost, the Netherlands, will later develop its "European vocation" to its own benefit and that of Europe as a whole, beginning with the ECSC treaty. With Europe's highest standard of living (above that of Switzerland), Luxembourg is referred to characteristically as "the smallest of the big countries." There is a book to be written about the little countries of Europe. Their role in European integration has grown in recent years with developments in Central and Eastern Europe and, in the West, the Danish rejection of the Maastricht Treaty of European Union (TEU). Asked when visiting the Avignon festival whether he believed in a European cultural identity, the Mexican Nobel literature prize winner Octavio Paz replied: "I do not believe in the identity of Europe. I believe in its plurality. I am for a Community Europe but also for a diversified Europe. Plurality gives great things to the European nation. In Greece the world was plural; so also the Renaissance in Italy, composed of small states of which we are all the cultural descendants. Long live the small nations!" (*Le Figaro*, July 20, 1992). The conciliation of economic and political unity and cultural diversity will be a major theme of this book.

5 Reported by Theodore C. Achilles in *NATO's Anxious Birth* by André Staercke and others, Hurst, London, 1985, p. 30. Bevin expressed similar views to Georges Bidault, French Foreign Minister, and in the House of Commons on January 22, 1948.

6 The original signatories of the North Atlantic Treaty were Belgium, Canada, Denmark, France, Iceland, Italy, Luxembourg, the Netherlands, Norway, Portugal, the United Kingdom and the United States. Greece and Turkey acceded to the Treaty in 1952, the Federal Republic of Germany in 1955 (with a reconstituted German military force, the *Bundeswehr*) and Spain in 1982.

2

Fits, Starts and Misfits (1949-1954)

On January 28, 1949, spurred by the Hague Congress, the consultative council of the Brussels Treaty decided to establish a permanent institution specifically designed to promote European unification. Events moved quickly. On February 16 British Foreign Secretary Ernest Bevin proposed Strasbourg, capital of Alsace, in Eastern France, as the seat of the Council of Europe. The choice of this city of some 300,000 inhabitants on the bank of the Rhine, which here forms the border between France and Germany, was intended to symbolize the reconciliation of former foes (even though Germany, still under occupation status, would not be able to join the organization until 1950). On May 5 of the same year, the statutes of the Council of Europe were signed in St. James's Palace, London. There were ten founding governments: Belgium, Denmark, France, Ireland, Italy, Luxembourg, Netherlands, Norway, Sweden and the United Kingdom. To meet the needs of the neutral states defense questions were excluded from the Council's terms of reference; there were no other limitations.

The inaugural session opened in the Alsatian capital on August 9, 1949. The atmosphere was exciting enough, yet some ambiguity reigned. For the cautious, led by the United Kingdom and Scandinavia, this was just another step towards the diplomatic consensus that was to bring harmony to a reinvigorated Europe. For the federalist idealists — some would call them impractical dreamers — the inauguration of the Council of Europe, and more particularly of its unique parliamentary assembly, marked the beginning of a new era. Although the Consultative Assembly (now called the Parliamentary Assembly) had very little power, it rapidly established itself as the keeper of the European conscience. At its very first session it proposed the European Convention on Human Rights. Greece and Turkey were invited to join (no European cultural torch could burn aloft without nourishment from the Hellenes). One year later a newly democratic Germany, albeit truncated by the Iron Curtain, was welcomed back into the consort of European nations.

Of pioneers, philosophers, preachers and early eurocrats

Europe today both engenders and feeds upon a vast bureaucracy. The thinkers and doers of early days fade into history. Talented, idealistic, polyglot, these exotic enthusiasts were held hostage to a dream and oft suffered the indignity of not being taken seriously. May they not be forgotten.

... Don Salvador de Madariaga: small, bent, silver-haired, slow of hand and quick of mind; yearningly agnostic; like Casals and Picasso, a voluntary exile from Franco's Falangist Spain (how proud he would be today). A founder of the College of Europe in Belgium's canal city, Bruges, whether expounding to the world's statesmen in the columns of the *Neue Zürcher Zeitung* or rapping with students into the small hours, bestriding a reversed dining chair in a dorm. Here was a man who believed that European union would give a surge to the tide of freedom in his native Iberia ...

... Antonius Karel Verleye, OFM, tall, serene, imposing in the brown, roped robe of the Capuchins, who knew that by putting Europe together he could put Belgium together also—the Walloons, Flemings, Bruxellois, even the German-speaking minority of Eupen and Malmédy ... He raised the funds to found a Christian-European study center, Centrum Rijckevelde, in Flanders' fields, built step-gabled of warm rose brick with a dovecote in the eaves. Here, at a crossroads of Europe's history, poplars and still waterways stretch their perspective lines to a horizon of low white cottages and windmills ...

... Hendrik Brugmans, Dutchman, resistance fighter, socialist, author and speechmaker, Minister of Education, Professor of French, Rector of the College of Europe, for whom cultural history is buried treasure, friend of statesmen and mentor of young minds—rarest of mortals, a believer in people, in clean politics, in the logic of paradox, in changing one's mind, in a new society of peace, intolerant only of intolerance ... who in years beyond the normal span found peace and joy with a young poetess ...

... I.B.F. Kormoss, émigré Hungarian, who removed his shoes to eat his brown-bag lunch and invented the cartography of European integration ...

... Leons Paklons, the smiling Latvian, who built Western Europe's first modern-day European library ...

... Marie-Joseph Lory, professor of history, raconteur of Europe's false starts and setbacks, whose sense of humor carried him through a lifetime of teaching missed opportunities between the two world wars and tolerance to former foes.

... Maurice Le Lannou, professor at Lyon, Bruges and the *Collège de France*, geographer—human geographer, as he always insisted—who demonstrated on field trips that frontiers strangle and distort regional economies and tended the flame of Europe in university aulas and the columns of *Le Monde* ...

Beside still canal waters, guarded by silent swans, Bruges the silted trader, daughter of the Middle Age, crossroads of great powers, dreams in her northern mists of a new peaceful Europe. Belfries toll the hours.

At another continental crossroads, in Strasbourg, beside Europe's river, where France and Germany meet, bureaucracy soon set in during those early days of the Council of Europe secretariat. Nine to six, with two hours for lunch (*cuisine française oblige*). Yet this was no normal paper-mill. Fire was there, stirred in the Information Directorate by Paul M.G. Lévy, a tall, ascetic Christian Jew with hare lip, ulcer, stentorian voice and large, graceful hands, who whipped to action a devoted, faithful crew of inspired scribblers, speakers and, as we would now say, spin-doctors ready to talk continental from road signs to blood donations and threatened species to space exploration . . .

. . . Deputy Director Solf, former *Offizier* of the *Wehrmacht*, whose mustachioed military bearing belied a mild manner and avuncular conversation, made a perfect *Chef de Protocole*. His office floor was littered with newspapers — German, French, English — since the first task of the day was to review the press, marking cuttings for the Secretary General's briefing. Solf rhymed with golf . . .

There was Aydin Sinanoglu, whose name means brightness, a smiling, irascible bear of a Turk, with flailing arms . . . Hugh Beesley, correct, efficient Cambridge cool, a good man with a blue pencil, a sense of style and carefully penned handwriting (no loops). Had he not believed in European rainbows he might have hunted spies. He rarely lost his temper except with Louise "Timi" Timiriaseff, a petite, fiery Russian émigrée with auburn hair and nut-brown eyes. She wrote a good piece and didn't like her prose carved up.

But now the Assembly is in session. Limousines slide through. Flags sprout. The Information Directorate explodes, its corridors jostling with the press. Office hours are forgotten; people grab a sandwich in the Press Bar, opened up for the occasion, or wait outside closed committee-room doors. "Europe" is a new subject: even the process is news. Students hired from out of town on sought-after short-term contracts work with a head-set in a "fishbowl" overlooking the Assembly hall, summarizing speeches and proceedings into a microphone for typing and posting in the press corridor. Highly strung interpreters burst from their cubicles. Typewriters clatter and shuttle (soft-shoe micros have not yet been invented). Journalists waylay politicians with leading questions, hoping to jog loose a quote; or besiege the 'phones to make their deadlines in a dozen languages. Who cares that this novel Assembly has the power only to recommend? The dreamers are afoot; Europe is a-building.

Serge Nabokov, dapper, polka-dot bow-tied look-alike of a more illustrious cousin, hammers out copy for Reuters, impervious to the din. Lunch breaks for him are gnaw-bone affairs: "When you work for a news agency there's always a deadline somewhere in the world". Every home-town journal has a favorite son, "our man in Strasbourg," whose speech in the European arena on anything at all is good for a couple of paragraphs. For many, to be honest, the speech is made for the coverage, not the coverage for the speech. Sound bites took longer in those days: sound snacks, perhaps.

At a blue-hazed ministerial press conference (everybody smokes) the world can turn on a phrase. Here, in a few incisive phrases, institutions are born. Rotund and smiling interpreter André Kaminker, a twinkling hairless heavyweight somewhere between Pickwick and Telly Savalas, works his consecutive magic, remembering word for word five or more minutes of speech-making, reproducing even the gestures. His daughter, French film star Simone Signoret, will inherit and redirect his talent.

Fernand Dehousse, ponderous Belgian Assembly president, struggles to "rationalize" European institutions which seem to pop up like mushrooms ...

Somewhere in the corner of the bar old Liam O'Mahoney strokes a white beard and tells tall tales for whiskey shots as young Oliver Crawford, who has lost two front teeth to undernourishment, works and reworks his avant-garde novel; nobody quite understands why they are there. They suck up the atmosphere and contribute to it ... Europe already has her hangers-on.

... Inside the Assembly hall the parliamentarians adopt another report, ... a voice-drone cuts in momentarily as swing doors flap open, ... another resolution, ... a recommendation to ministers, ... another directive to the multinational secretariat ... (600 then, 900 now) ...

... Upstairs in Personnel, red-maned Mr. Gudfin Gudfinsson of ancient Viking stock, sole Icelandic staff member, draws a salary larger than his tiny country's contribution to the entire organization ... Of course since those days Liechtenstein has joined.

Finally, the Assembly suspends its session and the press corridors fall silent. The post office with its extra territorial Council of Europe stamps puts up the shutters. Alsatian cleaners move in to sweep up order papers and discarded leads zipped from typewriters and crumpled to the floor.

The parliamentarians have dispersed for a leisurely dinner at the Restaurant de l'Orangerie behind the children's zoo in the park; or to La Wantzenau for plump, golden-crisp corn-fed young chicken; or, in May, to Hoerdt for generous platefuls of finger-thick white asparagus and fine slices of *jambon du pays*, washed down with pale-green astringent Riesling, the semi-sweet reasonableness of Gewürztraminer or the heady bouquet of Tokay.

Back at the *Maison de l'Europe*, outside every door but never stepping across the threshold, the French CRS police, a national guard, stand protecting the extra-territorial privileges of the Council of Europe, as they have stood all day and all evening, ram-rod erect; and will stand, all night, under the stars.

From such inspired chaos a new continental order was decanted. Today they do it with Regulation EC/1738 (93) 59, sub-section 3 (g), in nine languages.

Schuman's pragmatic dream

It rapidly became apparent, however, that the hybrid character of the Council of Europe — a parliamentary assembly reporting to a ministerial committee with no real powers — and the ambiguity of political intentions upon which it rested, was not going to satisfy the "federalists". On May 9, 1950, backed by the visionary Jean Monnet, French foreign minister Robert Schuman went further, proposing the pooling of coal and steel production by France and Germany. For Schuman, himself a German-speaking Lorrainer, born in Luxembourg, who had been a citizen of both countries, this was designed in the first place as a confidence building measure. The amalgamation of basic heavy industry would make war impossible, or at least considerably more unlikely, between the two major powers of "continental" Europe. For the longer term, Schuman understood that European unification could not occur without both reconciliation between France and Germany and a measure of supranational authority delegated to a new type of international executive. The idea was to build Europe by sectors, with the pill of supranationalism coated with the sugar of economic development. Something for everyone: a pragmatic dream. Although addressed in the first instance to the new Germany, the French proposal was open to membership by other countries. It is difficult today to say which aspect of the "Schuman Plan" was more significant — the economic or the political.

As this important proposal was under consideration it was given a nudge from the other side of the world. Students of the process of European unification have observed that progress has been uneven. However, threats to world peace from outside western Europe have frequently had a catalysing effect. The Berlin blockade of 1948 had been one such event. Now, on June 25, 1950, North Korean forces attacked the Republic of South Korea.[1] Here was a spur to European unification and the organization of western defense. "If it can happen in Korea, on the eastern perimeter of the Soviet Union, it can happen in Europe," went the thinking. UN intervention in South Korea was made possible only by the temporary boycott of the UN Security Council by the USSR — a mistake the Soviets would not repeat.

In addition to West Germany, Italy and the three Benelux countries (whose economies were already in process of unification) accepted the French invitation. As the United Kingdom and the neutral countries stood aside, the "Two" rapidly became the "Six". Negotiations opened in Paris on June 20. By April 18, 1951, the European Coal and Steel Community was in place. Its High Authority was invested with powers legally independent of those of the founding governments, including the authority to levy financial resources. On January 1, 1952, the ECSC levy became the first European tax. Albeit limited to a single, if basic, sector, the supranational toe was in the European door.

European defense and the German question

While establishment of the North Atlantic Treaty Organization in Washington on April 4, 1949 had assured western Europe's military security, it had given rise to almost as many political problems as it solved. As its "Atlantic" title and membership suggest, the alliance was based on the "twin pillars" of North America and Europe. With superior Soviet forces poised on the Elbe, the defense of Western Europe was inconceivable without North American assistance. Moreover, since Soviet supply lines were on land whereas US and Canadian participation required the crossing of three thousand miles of ocean, the presence of US and, to a lesser extent, Canadian forces in Britain and on the continent of Europe was essential to the credibility of the NATO deterrent. This was important, since NATO's primary strategy was one of dissuasion (a concept which would resurface later in the debate over nuclear "first strike" capability).

However, whereas the North American "pillar" had only two components, the European "pillar" was a veritable mosaic. If the countries of Western Europe could not be defended without America, could they become "Europe" with America? Could Europe afford to ignore responsibility for organizing its own defense? Were the two pillars of equal political stature? [2]

Another issue of immense strategic and geo-political importance was the status of Germany. Defeated in war, truncated of half its territory (the rest absorbed into the Soviet Union and Poland or established as a puppet communist regime, the German Democratic Republic), the western part of Germany nonetheless represented the forward defense line for Western Europe. Wanting a peace treaty (upon which as we have seen the occupying powers had failed to agree), "West" Germany, composed of the occupation zones of Britain in the north, the United States in the center and south-east, France in the south-west,[3] was not even a party to the NATO treaty. The political "battle lines" were forming between those who, on the one hand, feared the rearming of even a diminished Germany and those who, on the other, felt that Germany could be more effectively monitored from within the fold than outside it and considered the Soviet threat to be more imminent. Led by Konrad Adenauer, former mayor of Cologne, the West Germans themselves saw their security and even putative German reunification in terms of political and military integration with the western powers. (The astonishing events of 1989 and 1990 bear witness to Adenauer's farsightedness).

Relieved of the responsibilities of office, Winston Churchill, a member of the United Kingdom delegation to the Consultative Assembly of the Council of Europe, could permit himself a vision of a new Europe to which he might not have subscribed as a head of government. On August 11, 1950, the Assembly adopted his proposal to create a European Army.[4] It was not long before this far-reaching suggestion found an echo in government circles. On October 24 French Premier René Pleven advanced a plan for just such an army, including German "contingents",[5] within the framework of NATO. The French Assembly approved the idea two days later. It was not yet clear, however, whether such an act of military union was to be directed against the Soviet threat or against Germany, for in the NATO ministerial council only three days later France opposed German rearmament. Both the political and the military aspects of the problem were referred to the Permanent Representatives and to the military Committee, respectively, for further study.

Realpolitik — to use a German word — soon pressed its own clarification on the situation. On December 19, 1950, NATO opened discussions, the "Petersberg negotiations", with the Federal Republic on a possible German contribution to the defense of Western Europe. One day later the Consultative Council of the Brussels Treaty powers decided to merge the military organization of the western union into NATO.

EDC: pragmatic dream II

Yet on February 15, 1951, looking for another supranational solution, the French Government convened a conference in Paris on setting up a European Army. These deliberations superseded the Petersberg negotiations which were accordingly suspended on July 8. The new threat from the east was pushing Europeans and Atlanticists together.

It was rapidly becoming clear that German rearmament was unavoidable and that it could best take place in a European context. The "European army" would strengthen the European pillar of the Atlantic alliance. With United States support but without American participation, the Europeans were putting their European "house" in order. As a supremely political instrument a European Army was only conceivable if controlled by a European Defence community with supranational powers of decision. The federalists, of course, were delighted: for them Europe's military integration was a short cut to political union. On the other hand, it must be recognized that the practical problems were enormous; and that the measures taken so far had been more political than technical. Little consideration had been given to the coordination of different types of equipment or how a multilingual command structure would function on the battlefield.

On July 24, 1951, the Paris Conference approved an interim report to governments, recommending the creation of a European Army. The NATO "Supremo", General Eisenhower, agreed to cooperate in working out the military problems. Progress was rapid and by May 27, 1952, the six governments which had signed the ECSC Treaty were ready to sign into being a European Defence Community. This community was to put in place a single European High Authority, with a unified command structure in charge of integrated units of French, Belgian, Dutch, Italian, Luxembourg and German troops. All German forces would be placed under the Defence Community, but the other member countries would continue to have national forces outside the integrated command. Such was the "Pleven Plan", in fact the brainchild of the extraordinary European visionary Jean Monnet who, although considered the "Father of Europe" never held political office. [6]

France's military policy for Europe still remained ambiguous. The French wanted the Allies to commit to a "forward defense" at the frontier between the two Germanys but had still not conceded that this implied the rearmament of a sovereign Federal Republic. In December 1953, John Foster Dulles, United States' Secretary of State in Eisenhower's Republican Administration, told the NATO foreign ministers in Paris that an "agonizing reappraisal" of American commitment to NATO might become unavoidable unless the political issues surrounding Europe's defense were quickly resolved.

To be fair, the French Government had much on its plate. Things were going badly in Indo-China. A conference to negotiate an end to the colonial war was convened in Geneva in April but Dien Bien Phu fell in May. A month later Pierre Mendès-France came to power with a promise to get rapid agreement on an armistice. Although Dulles withdrew from the Geneva negotiations, refusing any deal with the communists, on July 21, 1954, Mendès-France secured an agreement to partition Viet Nam at the 17th parallel and to retain Cambodia and Laos. Given the circumstances, this was hailed as a considerable achievement.

Fresh from this success, the French Premier decided to brave the "unholy alliance" of the French Gaullists and Communists against the EDC Treaty. However, despite the Premier's pleas, the Belgians and Dutch refused to water down the text and the British remained aloof. Turning a deaf ear to the pleadings of Dulles (who had helped him so little over Viet Nam) Mendès France decided to allow a free vote in the French Chamber. On August 30, 1954, four years of effort to create a European Defence Community went down to defeat in the same assembly in which it had been proposed.

Nordic cooperation

While the defense drama was being played out in Western Europe among the Six and Britain, the North had been organizing her own cooperation. Politically the Nordic nations ran the gamut from NATO membership (Denmark, Norway and, albeit without armed forces of its own, Iceland) to two "shades" of neutrality: a sturdily independent Sweden and a Finland held prisoner by geo-politics as a too-close-for-comfort neighbor of the Soviet Union. Culturally and philosophically, however, these nations shared values firmly anchored in the West.

It was not surprising, therefore, that on March 4, 1952, all the Scandinavian states except Finland joined to create the Nordic Council (NC). Not only did these countries share cultural traditions but history and protestant Christianity. Even their languages were close enough to permit mutual comprehension, at least between Norwegians, Danes and Swedes. Joined by Finland in 1955 (subject to discretion as regards discussions on foreign policy and defense), the Nordic Council notched up numerous achievements in the ensuing decades: a common labor market, suppression of frontier formalities, harmonization of legislation (especially social security and health insurance). Agreements were signed on cultural exchanges (1971), communications and transport (1972) and environmental protection (1974). The Nordic Council could claim, not without pride, that in some sectors it had moved more rapidly forward than the European Communities.

For political reasons, however, Finland blocked a proposal for a Nordic common market (NORDEK), although the national economies were also not sufficiently complementary. The proposal was abandoned when Denmark entered the EC in 1972. Today, with Sweden and Finland in the Brussels antechamber and Norway facing yet another reappraisal, the Scandinavian nations have conceded that their cooperation in the Nordic Council and even in EFTA has not sufficed to counteract economic isolation, now seen as a recipe for recession.

The Nordic Council may continue to play a significant role if it broadens its horizons to form a bridge between East and West as a "Baltic Council". Baltic

Cooperation was on the agenda at the fortieth anniversary meeting in Helsinki, in March 1992. Estonia, Latvia, Lithuania ... and St. Petersburg were watching; Germany too, with Chancellor Kohl the first foreign guest speaker in the history of the Council.

An EDC substitute: Western European Union

Back in 1954, following the EDC defeat, it was now evident that there were no short cuts to European political union. Nevertheless, the military threat remained. The "balance of terror" made nuclear war unlikely but did not deter, and may indeed have fostered, conventional conflicts around the perimeter of the Eurasian communist heartland. Such indeed was the understanding of those countries (Australia, France, New Zealand, Pakistan, Philippines, Thailand, United Kingdom, United States) which met in Manila on September 6 to set up the South-East Asia Treaty Organization (SEATO). In Europe the issue of German rearmament remained unresolved. With revealing speed—within one month of the EDC defeat in Paris- a Conference of Nine (the six plus Canada, the United Kingdom and the United States) met in London on September 28 to seek an alternative to the European Defence Community. Their decisions were endorsed in Paris on October 22 at a conference bringing together the Federal Republic of Germany and the three western occupying powers (France, United Kingdom, United States). The occupation regime of the Federal Republic was terminated. West Germany was admitted to the western alliance, subject to limits on its arms production. The United Kingdom undertook not to withdraw its troops unilaterally from continental Europe (a commitment which, had it been given earlier, might have saved the EDC). The Federal Republic was invited to join NATO. The Brussels Treaty of 1948 was modified to admit West Germany and Italy and to create the Western European Union (the Six plus the United Kingdom). In addition, France and Germany agreed on a European Statute for the disputed territory of the Saar, with a provisional administration under WEU auspices. [7]

WEU was a much weaker organization than the European Defence Community would have been, being modelled on the Council of Europe rather than the ECSC. Indeed, Jean Monnet resigned from the presidency of the ECSC High Authority in protest at WEU's non-supranational character. Although WEU was given a considerable measure of authority to inspect and control armaments production, its powers were and remain today essentially consensual. There was no High Authority, as in ECSC, and no majority voting other than on purely procedural matters. Politically, for the time being at least, the traditionalists had won. Another organization had been slipped into the alphabet soup of European integration with minimal transfer of power by national governments.

On the other hand the outcome was far from negative. With the advent of the WEU Assembly European military cooperation acquired an official parliamentary dimension. [8] European governments had an organization of their own which, albeit in many ways overshadowed by the North Atlantic Council, was not subject to the vagaries of United States politics. The United States, moreover, ever desirous of strengthening the European pillar, had been midwife to its birth. Perhaps more importantly, after refusing to join the ECSC, the United Kingdom was for the first time associated specifically with the Six in a joint venture. Most significantly, "West Germany" finally became a sovereign federal republic integrated not only territorially but politically into the western alliance, both Atlantic and European. The "house" of the European Defence Community was in ruins but Western European Union had saved much of the furniture.

Today, a new configuration of European security, superseding the Yalta agreements, has arisen from the unification of Germany, general dissolution not only of the Warsaw Treaty Organisation but of the USSR itself, arms reductions and the increasing importance of the Conference on Security and Cooperation in Europe (CSCE). WEU is about to acquire a modest facelift through its absorption into the European Community. As for the politicians in Washington, with the European cuckoo growing in the Atlantic nest they are still debating America's role in European security; and the price-tag.

Notes

1 After several decades of Japanese occupation, Korea had been partitioned at the end of the second world war. The north became Communist under Soviet influence. U.S. forces occupying Japan exercized influence in the south, without succeeding in instilling true democracy.

2 It is interesting to note that whereas the Secretary General of NATO has always been a European, the Supreme Commander of NATO forces has always been an American. It should be further noted that, claiming world-wide responsibilities, Britain and France committed only a portion of their military forces to NATO command. As to the debate on America's role in "Europe", discussion endures today.

3 The Canadians had an airbase at Lahr, in the French zone. Berlin as former capital, Austria and Vienna were similarly divided into occupation zones.

4 It required a personality of Churchill's stature to make such a proposal, considering the declared neutrality of member countries such as Sweden, and the fact that defense matters are specifically excluded from the charter of the Council of Europe.

5 The term "contingents" conveys an evident ambiguity and betrays French hesitation: military "forces" but not yet a new German "army".

6 For a detailed account of events leading up to the EDC plan, see Cook, Don, *Forging the Alliance, NATO 1945-1950*, London, Secker and Warburg, 1989.

7 It will not appear so strange that the provisional Saar administration should be entrusted to a military body such as WEU if one remembers, firstly, that West Germany was emerging from a regime of military occupation; and, secondly, that the "pragmatic dreamers" were trying to turn a disputed territory into the first territorial expression of the new Europe.

8 The "NATO parliamentarians" are an unofficial body not provided for in the North Atlantic Treaty. The WEU Treaty provides for parliamentary representation through an Assembly consisting of national delegations to the Consultative Assembly of the Council of Europe.

3

New Beginnings (1955-1960)

On May 5, 1955 — Europe Day in Council of Europe countries — the occupation regime in West Germany ended ten years almost exactly after it had begun on May 8, 1945. One day later Western European Union was officially constituted with headquarters in London and an assembly secretariat in Paris. The Federal Republic of Germany entered the North Atlantic alliance. The German parliament recreated the German army, on a volunteer basis, on July 22.

Meanwhile, on May 7 the USSR had renounced its wartime treaties with France and the United Kingdom. One week later the USSR brought the Warsaw Pact into being with the signing of a mutual defense treaty with Albania,[1] Bulgaria, Czechoslovakia, the German Democratic Republic, Hungary, Poland and Romania. The military division of Europe was finally sealed — the single bright spot being the signing of the State Treaty confirming Austria's neutrality and ending four-power occupation.

As on previous occasions the most resolute of the "Europeans" seemed to react to world events by favoring closer integration. On June 1 and 2, 1955, the foreign ministers of the Six, recovering from the EDC setback, decided to extend the successful integration of the ECSC to the whole economy. The conference charged a committee of experts under Paul-Henri Spaak of Belgium to draft a general economic union and a nuclear energy union. Again fearing loss of sovereignty, the United Kingdom remained aloof.

We can now see that this was a major blunder on Britain's part. For eighteen years she had to endure the Communities from without instead of helping to shape them from within. Historians may judge however, that it was a blessing in disguise, making possible a more sure-footed start to the new concept of Europe than would have been possible among seven or more partners with widely-differing visions of how to proceed. The Little Europe of the Six went ahead with putting its house in order.

Saarlanders true to themselves

On October 23, in a referendum administered by WEU, the electorate of the Saar overwhelmingly rejected the proposed European statute (by 423,434 votes to 201,973), opting to become a *Land* of the Federal Republic of Germany on January 1, 1957. France, which had originally laid claim to the Saar, suffered the first inkling of the power of a renascent, democratic Germany. The result seemed like a setback at the time, but probably facilitated the progress of the European Community. With the hindsight of today's Europe we may also aver that it was the first demonstration that peoples are unwilling to put their cultural identity at risk in the achievement of European union. It is one more indicator of the importance of cultural roots in setting in place the European mosaic. The Saarlanders felt themselves not so much anti-European as first and foremost German. They wanted to be Germans in Europe rather than somewhat amorphous Europeans in Germany.

The Six received the Spaak report on May 29, 1956 and decided to negotiate creation of a European Economic Community (EEC) and a European Atomic Energy Community (EURATOM). Losing no time, they opened negotiations in Brussels on June 26. [2]

There was now growing concern among the European traditionalists, led by the United Kingdom, and to a lesser degree in the United States and Canada, that Western Europe would become divided against itself. A common external tariff would be introduced by the new "customs union" of the Six against the rest of the world. OEEC, of which all the countries principally concerned in this unfolding drama were members, therefore decided to set up a study group for creating a free trade area, which would permit free trade in industrial products without committing participants to a common external tariff and centralised decision-making institutions. [3] The chairman of the committee was Reginald Maudling of the United Kingdom. The Maudling committee was condemned to failure since at the time the two concepts appeared mutually exclusive, politically as well as economically. (Today the enlarged European Community and the European Free Trade Association have largely overcome technical and political obstacles and have set up a single nineteen-nation European Economic Area).

Britain, France and the Suez fiasco

Once again world events had a catalysing effect. On October 31, 1956, France and the United Kingdom, in collusion with Israel, invaded Egypt to call a halt to President Gamel Abdul Nasser's nationalization of the Suez Canal. Ironically, tragically, this event coincided with and distracted western attention from the anti-communist uprising in Hungary. The West turned a deaf ear to Hungarian pleas for assistance and, after a few days of euphoria in the streets of Budapest, the movement was crushed by Red Army tanks. Krushchev's "revision" of Stalinism, seen by many as a forerunner of Gorbachev's glasnost and perestroika, did not extend to self-determination for the satellite countries of Eastern Europe.

It is said that we are condemned either to learn from history or to repeat it. In January, 1991, Soviet troops took control of Vilnius, capital of Lithuania, while the world's attention was riveted on the new world order imposed by "smart bombs" over Baghdad. Unlike the Gulf War, the Anglo-French action in the Fall of 1956 not only failed to gain United States' support but attracted its loud condemnation. President Eisenhower was in the final stages of a re-election campaign in which world peace had been a major theme. He and

Secretary of State Dulles not only publicly denounced the British and French but went so far as to impose a veto against them in the UN Security Council. Britain and France were eventually forced to withdraw without achieving their objective: the canal remained nationalized (although now out of commission for years). Moreover, President Nasser became the first Arab leader to demonstrate that it was possible to win politically while losing militarily. Anthony Eden resigned as Britain's Prime Minister and was succeeded by Harold Macmillan, while Nasser became the undisputed leader of the entire "Arab nation".

The fiasco consummated, the crisis blew itself out. Britain and France learned that even acting in consort they could no longer afford imperialist adventurism. In the aftermath, however, they reacted in different ways. Britain under Macmillan turned once again to its "special relationship" of language and culture with the United States. France, albeit under Socialist leadership with Guy Mollet as Premier, decided to build her own atomic bomb. Don Cook neatly explains the link between the two:

> The French were now well into their Algerian War, and they felt after Suez that there was ample evidence that French interests, European interests, were not always going to be the same as American interests- and to defend one's own interests would require possession of the ultimate weaponry of military power.[4]

France's other reaction, however, was equally important. Britain had turned to the United States; France sought consolation and strength in Europe, finding no incongruity in at one and the same time asserting nationalist independence through nuclear armament and relinquishing a measure of sovereignty to a European economic authority. For the French it was more important than ever to build up Europe. As the ill-fated and short-lived Franco-British alliance fell apart, France redoubled her efforts to negotiate economic union for the Six. Meeting in Paris on February 20, 1957, the Six decided upon the conditions associating overseas territories (former colonies and protectorates not, of course, including Algeria, still considered part of France) with the EEC, an important step for development assistance.

"Forget the bananas"

As luck would have it, the French premier Guy Mollet, the Foreign Secretary Christian Pineau and German Chancellor Konrad Adenauer, on a visit to Paris, had been together in Mollet's office when Anthony Eden telephoned from London to say that, under US and Soviet pressure (the two superpowers being united for the occasion), the UK was withdrawing her forces from Suez. The effect on the French and German leaders was immediate, pushing them into each other's arms.

The French were nevertheless very cautious. France had proposed the EDC and France had failed to ratify it. How was a new "supranational" project to be presented to the fragile Fourth Republic Chamber of Deputies whose parties had been rent within their own ranks by the EDC debate? Since not one but two treaties were under negotiation, the strategy adopted was to highlight the less threatening of the two, the EURATOM treaty, each time a report was presented on the progress of the Spaak working party (laboring quietly, away from the public eye in a Nice hotel overlooking the surf). Thus to allay fears and calm sensitivites did EURATOM become a smokescreen for the more significant common market project. Finally the Spaak working party came out of the shadows and submitted its proposed texts (which carried no political commitments) to the ministers of the Six gathered in Venice in June 1956. It was the moment of truth. Now the Six would have to negotiate in earnest; and under the spotlight. Mollet had given his representatives, Christian Pineau and Maurice Faure, Secretary of State for European Affairs, a free hand.

Contrary to what one might imagine, the Germans were not the most enthusiastic of delegations. They haggled over details such as giving up traditional African suppliers of bananas in order to grant preference to French colonies. Finally however, Adenauer called upon his delegation to "forget the bananas and build Europe."

Maurice Faure, who told this story on France Culture radio on April 6, 1992, in a program marking the 25th anniversary of the Rome treaties, also drew a moral. It was essential, he said, for the Maastricht Treaty of European Union to be ratified so that the new members now lining up at the door clearly understood that they were committing themselves to a political conception of Europe and not merely to a trade agreement. Otherwise there was a danger of European union being irreparably diluted by enlargement.

Modern history made in ancient Rome

Thus did the grandiose ceremony in Rome one month later mark one of the great dates of European history. On March 25, 1957, before a vast crowd of dignitaries, the Six signed the EEC and EURATOM agreements. Between July and December the six parliaments ratified the treaties, which entered into force on January 1, 1958. Brussels was selected as "provisional" headquarters. The first commission presidents were Walter Hallstein of Germany for the EEC and Louis Armand of France for EURATOM. On March 19, 1958, the European Parliamentary Assembly of the Six opened its first session, electing Robert Schuman as its president. The pace of progress did not let up. In July the EEC Council of ministers adopted social security provisions for migrant workers, an essential element of the free movement of labor which must accompany removal of barriers to trade and competition. The same month a conference of the Six at Stresa, in northern Italy, laid the groundwork for a European market in agriculture. (The provisions of the EEC treaty are in many cases less precise than those of the more narrowly defined ECSC treaty. Measures for the agricultural market were only outlined in the EEC Treaty. While this may at first sight appear as a weakness, in practice it accorded more latitude and hence more power to the Commission and favored the development of "Community law".)

1958, then, proved to be the year of the Six. It was rounded out on December 15 by the inevitable, indeed preordained failure of the OEEC free trade area negotiations. As the first 10% reduction of customs tariffs and 20% increase of quotas (quantitative restrictions to trade) became effective on January 1, 1959, a "two-speed" Europe was facing deep economic division.

The British dilemma

It is possible today, with historical perspective, to view Britain's role in Europe more dispassionately then was the case a few years ago. She came out of the Second World War with immense prestige. Continental Europe had hopes of leadership from Britain's parliamentary democracy. In fact, the British respected their commitments to the letter; they simply made fewer commitments. Democracy, after all, holds sacred the right of dissent. Britain, of course, was not "outside" Europe. The United Kingdom was a founder-member of the Council of Europe and played a leading role in Western European Union, OEEC and NATO. The fact remained that, albeit by her own decision, the United Kingdom was facing a major trading bloc of some three hundred million people, including the main western European powers of France, West Germany and Italy. She could not accept the relinquishment of sovereignty involved in delegating important powers to a High Authority or a European Commission; but neither could she afford to stand completely aside from the process of European economic integration and the competitive edge provided to the Six by an expanded "home" market. The United Kingdom therefore took the lead in seeking out like-minded partners willing to establish conditions of free trade without supranational institutions, free movement of labor or a common external tariff. In her own case, the latter would put an end to or at least seriously impinge upon the "imperial preferences" enjoyed by countries such as Canada, Australia and New Zealand in their trade with the United Kingdom, "mother country" of the Commonwealth.

The European Free Trade Association

The first exploratory meeting between governmental officials took place in Oslo in February, 1959. A sense of urgency reigned among the heterogeneous group of negotiators from Austria, Denmark, Norway, Portugal, Sweden, Switzerland and the United Kingdom, as the EEC's common external tariff began to be felt. The Convention establishing the European Free Trade Association (EFTA) was drafted in record time, initialled in Stockholm on November 20, 1959, and signed in the same city on January 4, 1960. Following ratification by the seven parliaments, it entered into force on May 3, 1960.

Geopolitical considerations made the position of Finland even more sensitive than that of officially neutral countries such as Austria, Sweden and Switzerland. Finland had not even become a member of the Council of Europe. Consequently, the Finns did not sign the Stockholm Convention as a founder-member of the Association. However, an Association Agreement between the EFTA countries and Finland was signed less than a year later, on March 27, 1961, and entered into force on June 26 of the same year. In effect, Finland managed to have it both ways, saving appearances *vis-à-vis* her powerful neighbor, the Soviet Union, while enjoying the benefits of a western European trading partnership.[5]

EFTA was founded as a reaction to the EEC but not as its rival. EFTA countries would have preferred the Maudling Committee negotiations to succeed, producing a single trading bloc for all members of the OEEC. The Preamble to the EFTA Convention seeks early "removal of trade barriers and the promotion of closer economic cooperation between the members of the Organization for European Economic Co-operation, including the members of the European Economic Community". However, things did not work out that way. EFTA was ultimately a British creation. Although Britain had the right to adopt a cautious approach to Europe, she institutionalized the cleavage by fostering another economic organization as an alternative to the EEC.

In keeping with the spirit of its creation, EFTA bureaucracy was kept to a minimum, with a small secretariat in Geneva. Decisions were taken consensually without recourse to supranational institutions. Members' world-wide trade links were preserved by omitting the harmonization of tariffs and quotas with non-member countries.

Despite the importance of agriculture for members' national economies, this sector was to all intents and purposes excluded from the Stockholm Convention. In a modern industrial society every country affords some form of price support to its agriculture due to its economic, political and cultural significance. Agriculture equates with the face of the landscape, with regional identity, with the very land itself. Farmers, although small in number, are resilient, self-reliant, naturally conservative, politically influential. EFTA governments wished to retain control over their policies in this sector and to avoid submitting them to rules of harmonization and free competition.

Iceland

It is not surprising that, although the other Nordic Council members took part from the beginning of the sixties, Iceland did not join EFTA until the end of the decade. The economy of Iceland depended almost exclusively on exports of fish and fishery products, which could not benefit fully from EFTA's industrial free trade provisions.[6]

Iceland applied for membership in November 1968. The application was accepted in December 1969 and the membership entered into force on March 1, 1970. Iceland also acceded to the Agreement between Finland and EFTA. The Nordic countries were no longer divided by trade barriers.

Iceland's trade in fishery products came under the appropriate provisions of the Convention (Articles 26 to 28) and she was granted special terms for her small and sensitive industrial economy, being allowed ten years for the progressive elimination of tariffs. Iceland was encouraged to diversify and develop her industrial economy. In particular, the five Nordic countries established an interest-free Industrialization Fund with a capital of fourteen million dollars refundable over fifteen years, beginning in 1980. (If this figure seems low, it must be remembered that Iceland's population is under 200,000. On the other hand, it is burdensome for the "smallest of the big countries", such as Iceland and Luxembourg, to maintain the state apparatus necessary for playing a meaningful international role.)

Returning to 1960, we find that creation of the European Free Trade Association has in no way slowed progress in the EEC. On May 11 the Community's ministerial Council set up the European Social Fund. One day later it decided to speed up the integration process by accelerating the time-table for reduction of tariffs and quotas between member countries. The central structures of the European Community, inadequate as they may appear to some (particularly as regards the limited powers of the European Parliament), overbearing towards national governments to others, are in place to stay.

OECD replaces OEEC

Europe's North American partners followed these family tiffs with forebearance. At the end of 1960 an important development took place at Atlantic level. Following months of study the member countries of the Organisation for European Economic Cooperation — including, significantly, members of both EEC and EFTA — agreed to important changes in their institution. First, they recognized that the original purpose of OEEC, namely to coordinate and promote the rebuilding of the European national economies with fourteen billion dollars of American assistance, had been achieved. The existence of EEC and EFTA, involving as they did the dismantling of protective measures, testified to this fact. A democratic Europe of two trading blocs was unquestionably less divided than a Europe of fifteen or sixteen uncoordinated economies. Secondly, it was evident that the strength of the North Atlantic Alliance depended not a little on coordination of North Atlantic and Western European trade relations. Canada and the United States could not, as the saying goes, "sit idly by" as two European trade groups promoted intra European trade and one of them, the European Community, set up common external trade tariffs against them. Finally, and not least, the gross imbalance of the "North-South" relationship between developed and underdeveloped countries — the "haves" and the "have nots" — was becoming not only a moral responsibility but also a threat to world peace almost as sensitive as the "East-West" dichotomy.

To meet these new priorities the eighteen OEEC members, Canada and the United States replaced OEEC by the Organisation for Economic Cooperation and Development. Substitution of "Development" for Europe in the title illustrates the change of membership and of emphasis.

The convention setting up OECD in succession to OEEC entered into force on September 30, 1961. A month later, on October 28, Yugoslavia became an associate member of the restructured organization. As a Communist state adhering firmly to its political and economic independence of the Soviet bloc

(Yugoslavia was a founder-member of the "non-aligned" nations) it thus became the first Communist state to achieve formal links with the capitalist economic system. In subsequent years, with the accession of Japan, Finland, Australia and New Zealand and the addition of an agency for monitoring oil supplies and consumption, OECD will become, with its twenty-four member countries, the principal institution for the coordination of economic policy in the industrialized world.[7]

Notes

1 Albania withdrew from the Pact in 1968 after siding with China against the Soviet Union. Diplomatic relations with the USSR were not restored until July 31, 1990.

2 The choice of Brussels was no doubt due to the influence of Spaak. However, as a small, central, bilingual country, Belgium was a natural, if not neutral meeting ground for the six. Still today it serves as the principal albeit unconfirmed seat of the European Community.

3 For discussion of the notions of customs union and free trade area, see the chapters on GATT and EFTA.

4 Cook, Don, *op. cit.,* p. 262.

5 The Association Agreement gave Finland essentially the same rights and obligations as EFTA members. Finland participated in the subsequent timetable acceleration for the abolition of import duties. On January 1, 1986, as glasnost relaxed tensions in Finno-Soviet relations, Finland became a full member of EFTA. For a detailed account of Finnish policy in the context of East-West confrontation and glasnost by a prominent Finnish diplomat, see Jakobson, Max, *Finland: Myth and Reality*, Helsinki, Otava, 1987.

6 Even today the figure remains above seventy per cent. In December 1991 Iceland gave notice of withdrawal from the International Whaling Agreement, claiming that its provisions were too strict and that some countries cheated under the guise of "research killings". Iceland has no difficulty selling whalemeat to Japan.

7 A notion of the extent of the current challenge from the EC and the Pacific Rim to US trading supremacy may be gathered from the following figures, collated by GATT:

Leading exporters in 1991
(in billions of dollars)

USA	422	Hong Kong	98
Germany	403	CIS	78
Japan	315	Taiwan	76
France	217	China (PRC)	72
UK	185	Sth Korea	72
Italy	169	Switz'l'd	62
Neth'l'ds	133	Spain	60
Canada	129	Singapore	59
Bel./Lux.	117	Sweden	55

4

Family Feuds (1961-1970)

Meanwhile, the Council of Europe in Strasbourg was pursuing its role of *Dachorganization*, a "roof organization" bringing together in its Consultative Assembly representatives of all parties and countries for wide-ranging political debates. In 1961 the European Social Charter laid down basic standards and principles in a previously somewhat neglected field. Comparable and reciprocal social rights and protection not only bring home the value of unification to the individual citizen but are also basic to fair economic competition. The European Convention on Human Rights was gaining world-wide respect as the only text of its kind embodying effective machinery, the Commission and the Court, to guarantee the rights enunciated.

In East-West relations two events brought successive shocks to the euphoric atmosphere of the first few months of John F. Kennedy's presidency. On April 12 the Soviet Union achieved with Major Yuri Gagarin man's first orbital flight in space. Two days later, with the tacit support of the United States government, Cuban exiles were defeated on the beaches of the Bay of Pigs in their attempt to destabilize the Castro regime in Cuba. The United States was beginning to learn the lesson which would finally be brought home in Viet Nam and, for the Soviet Union, in Afghanistan: there are limits to the influence of all nations, even superpowers.

First summit of the Six

The European Communities of the Six continued to grow in strength. Europe needed the American shield yet did not want to feel obligated always to march in the direction pointed by the American sword. Growing economic strength would provide some political leeway. Indeed, from inside the Six voices would soon be heard criticizing the United Kingdom for excessive political subservience to the United States.

A major step was taken on the political front (pundits may differ as to whether it was truly a step forward) when de Gaulle hosted the first "summit" meeting of the Six in Paris on February 10 and 11, 1961. The meeting was significant for a number of reasons.

The Treaties of Rome had entered into force only six months before General de Gaulle was called out of retirement on July 1, 1958, following the crisis in Algeria, to head the French Government. One may speculate that had he returned to the political arena a few months earlier he would not have acceded to such an extension of "supranationality". Now the General's attitude was ambiguous. While honoring the letter of the treaties he nevertheless sought to downplay renunciations of sovereignty. One way to do this was to convene meetings of the Six outside the legal and administrative framework of the Community. He advocated a limited integration of *l'Europe des patries*, the Europe of the Fatherlands, a position which stood somewhere between the traditional British view and that of the committed federalists. (Given de Gaulle's antipathy to the influence of what he called *les Anglo-Saxons*, the UK and the US, in Europe, one might today ironically assert that the French president's view of Europe was to be most closely emulated by that of Britain's Margaret Thatcher . . .)

On the other hand, while jealously guarding France's independence (and proceeding with the Socialist Guy Mollet's decision to build a nuclear *force de frappe*), de Gaulle saw the value to the Six of coordinating their policies in order to give Europe sufficient independence of posture between the two superpowers.

France proposes a union of states

Thus, the meetings of heads of government inaugurated by de Gaulle (with France alone sharing government between head of state and prime minister: under the new French constitution the head of state played a powerful political role) could be variously interpreted for their own ends by advocates of all political tendencies within the Six. At a second summit, held in Bad Godesberg, Federal Republic of Germany, on July 18, France put forward a plan for a union of European states involving close cooperation at a technical level but no true merging of sovereignty. The proposal was refined into a draft treaty for an indissolvable union (but not a federal merger) known as the Foucher Plan. It was submitted by France on November 2, 1961, revised and then finally rejected by France's European Community partners on January 18, 1962.[1] President de Gaulle in turn firmly rejected the principle of supranationality on May 15. Five of his cabinet ministers, including Pierre Pflimlin, former premier and mayor of Strasbourg, resigned in protest.[2]

The fact that de Gaulle put forward the Foucher Plan, however controversial it proved, and that it would be thwarted by a coalition of smaller countries, demonstrated that the European Community had by 1961 established its viability. While arguments might continue on the speed and direction of further integration, it was now evident that the Common Market was not going to fade away. On July 9, 1961, Greece signed a treaty of association with the EEC without first joining EFTA. More importantly, it was becoming clear to the United Kingdom that the European Free Trade Association could not provide the economic and political "clout" essential to a major European power. Quietly, Britain had concluded that the "open sea" was no longer an option and that on "the continent" half measures would not suffice. Her Majesty's Government was preparing a major policy reversal. The postwar experience had failed to provide bluebirds over the white cliffs of Dover. The proud islanders would finally cross the Channel to Brussels and ask to join the

Davidson College Library

European Communities. Today, they even have a tunnel and the island is no more . . .

Ireland and the EEC

The Gaels beat them to the punch. On July 31, 1961, the Republic of Ireland applied for Community membership. This surprising development requires explanation.

In a relationship not unlike that existing between Canada and the United States, Ireland has always been dominated — historically, politically, geographically — by the United Kingdom. Although the southern part of the island revassalized by Cromwell has been an independent republic since 1921, it has always maintained a "love/hate" relationship with its larger neighbor. Irish citizens can move easily between the Republic and the United Kingdom. The economies of the two countries are closely interwined. Although not a member of the British Commonwealth, Ireland enjoyed trade preferences with the United Kingdom similar to Commonwealth preferences long before the drafting of the General Agreement on Tariffs and Trade (see Part III). For years the Irish *punt* was tied to sterling, the British pound. Yet, fearing renewed dominion, Ireland had remained neutral during the Second World War and steadfastly denied safe haven to all belligerents in the Battle of the Atlantic.

When it became evident, however, that Britain was preparing an application to join the European Communities, Ireland, not even a member of EFTA, could ill afford to see a common external tariff strung out against her through the waters of the Irish Sea. The neutral Irish had been enthusiastic "cultural Europeans" in the Council of Europe. Putting the best face on the situation and with a colorful gesture of defiant if harmless independence, they entered their bid before the British themselves. The UK applied for membership on August 9, 1961, followed by Denmark one day later.

Denmark between Brussels and the Baltic

Like Ireland's, Denmark's decision was not an easy one. The country had suffered greatly under Nazi occupation and many of her citizens were not keen to see such a close *rapprochement* with the Federal Republic. Moreover, Denmark worked closely with other Scandinavian countries in the Nordic Council. Of these, Sweden was traditionally neutral and Finland was constrained by its *Realpolitik* with respect to the Soviet Union. Denmark might well have been "satisfied" with its membership in the Council of Europe and EFTA.

On the other hand, apart from the presence in Denmark of a strong current of European "federalist" thinking, there were strong arguments in favor of EEC membership. Principal among these was the fact that trade with other EFTA countries could in no way balance Denmark's trade with the United Kingdom, particularly since a major portion of this was in the agricultural sector (notably dairy products and bacon). To put it succinctly, Denmark could not afford to see the British breakfast (the best meal of the day, say some) taken over by the Irish and the French. On August 10, 1961, Denmark too knocked on the door of the European Commission in Brussels.

British balancing act in Brussels

The United Kingdom's application to join the European Communities was taken up on November 8, 1961. It had been decided to deal first with the British application, as the one most likely to give rise to major difficulties because of Britain's world-wide connections and the fact that adjustments requested by a country of over fifty million inhabitants would have the greatest impact on the existing member states and Community institutions. For her part, the United Kingdom had to negotiate within marrow margins: if it "gave away the store" the British Government would encounter serious opposition at home and from traditional Commonwealth trading partners. The negotiations dragged on for over a year until Britain's application was summarily vetoed by General de Gaulle on January 14, 1963, during one of his celebrated press conferences, magnificently staged amid the golden baroque splendor of the Elysée ballroom yet quite unpredictable as to their content. On this occasion the failure to observe diplomatic niceties served only to exacerbate the snub.

Although Charles de Gaulle's followers had bitterly opposed creation of the European Economic Community we have seen that when he returned to power he saw it as a useful means of extending French influence. During his early years in power he encouraged its development. Yet de Gaulle never subordinated Community interests to those of France, much less those of another state. Did not his memoirs begin with the memorable phrase: "I have always adhered to a certain conception of France...."? For de Gaulle France was a great power, to be respected rather than liked. To quote one of his celebrated aphorisms, a great nation has no friends, only interests.

Britain had certainly been remiss in standing aloof from the Community in its formative stage. Did she, however, deserve the Gaullian off-handedness she now endured? The French President had a number of reasons for his action. At a psychological—some would say petty and personal—level he had never forgotten the humiliation of his experiences in England during the war, as an exiled army officer, officially in rebellion, fighting his way back to the conference table and to recognition for his country, after the famous "Declaration of June 18, 1940", from the "Anglo Saxons" Winston Spencer Churchill and Franklin Delano Roosevelt.

However, there were more immediate concerns. De Gaulle was certainly irritated by the protracted haggling at the conference table in Brussels. More significantly, he feared that the British so-called "special relationship" with the United States would provide a Trojan horse of undue American involvement within the Community. Finally, de Gaulle had developed a special relationship of his own with Chancellor Adenauer and between France and Germany. Closer ties with West Germany were a cornerstone of de Gaulle's European policy, sealed in the Franco German Treaty of Friendship concluded on

January 22, 1963, only one week after the veto of Britain's entry, and followed up by twice-yearly Franco-German "summits" which continue today. Ernest Bevin's vision that European union be built upon Franco German reconciliation was coming true ... at Britain's cost. The treaty provided for coordination of the two countries' policies in foreign affairs, defense, information, youth exchanges and cultural affairs. The Franco-German *entente* has indeed been essential to progress within the European Community. France's partners, while shocked at both the manner and the substance of the French action, were certainly not willing to put at risk all that had been achieved.

Even as negotiations with the United Kingdom were proceeding, agreements among the Six had continued apace (some even saw in this a lever to press the British into concessions). As early as January 14, 1962, following a marathon negotiation which had "stopped the clock" — a backdating device — the EEC Council decided to institute the second stage of the common market effective January 1, 1962, earlier than required. At the same time — in fact, in a trade-off — the principles of a European agricultural policy (PAC) were adopted, including market support and export subsidies not provided in the industrial sector and of questionable GATT validity. A European orientation and price guarantee fund (FEOGA), to be financed from import levies, was also agreed. On March 7, 1962, the EEC concluded a tariff agreement with the United States. Following seven hard years of a conflict which had brought de Gaulle back to power, France agreed to Algerian independence at Evian on March 18. A Europe/Africa trade agreement was signed in Brussels on April 11, an African aid agreement hammered out on June 26. The European agricultural policy entered into force on July 30. Movement of capital was freed within the Six on December 8 and, to round out a memorable year, the EEC and Associated States, mostly former colonies, signed a convention of cooperation on December 20. President de Gaulle's press conference veto of British (and by implication Irish and Danish) membership in January 1963 did nothing to slow this frenetic pace. As we have seen, the Franco German friendship treaty, signed only days later, suffered no delay. On May 4, the EEC Council gave its approval to the agreement with Associated States. On July 20, what came to be known as the Yaoundé Convention on EEC/African cooperation was signed by seventeen African countries and Madagascar. A second agricultural "marathon", from December 16 to 23, settled policy on milk, meat and rice.

Meanwhile, Japan's entry into OECD as the first "non Atlantic" member, on April 28, 1964, marked that nation's re-emergence as a major industrial power.

A constitutional crisis

Agriculture had by now become the primary element of EEC negotiation, policy and financing. Its importance to all members, and particularly to France, was such that it rapidly became the keenest point of friction among the Six, culminating in a major institutional crisis. 1964 was a slow year for

Europe. Not until December 15 did a third marathon negotiation, coming a full year after the second, achieve agreement on the Mansholt plan for cereal prices. On March 31, 1965, the EEC Commission put forward proposals for financing the common agricultural policy, including vesting supranational powers in the Commission to raise levies (as was already the case with the High Authority of ECSC). The alternative was to finance the policy on an annual basis, through a budget voted by the ministerial Council, with all the political pressures this procedure would involve when such huge interests were at stake.

On June 15, 1965, France opposed the Commission's proposals. When no solution was found President de Gaulle provoked an institutional crisis by walking out and boycotting Council meetings for six months.[3]

Behind the immediate policy differences lay a deeper conflict of conception as to how European unification should proceed. These philosophical and political differences opposed Professor Walter Hallstein, German President of the EEC Commission, and French President Charles de Gaulle.[4] Hallstein's supranational concept of European unification was incompatible with de Gaulle's "Europe of the Fatherlands" approach. The breaking point might have come over several issues, not least the French President's rejection of British membership. In fact, it proved to be the decision-making process within the Council of Ministers which led to the dislocation.

As we have seen, de Gaulle had in general respected France's treaty commitments and the functioning of Community "machinery". The walk-out was occasioned by his refusal to accede to majority voting (particularly where France was obviously in the minority) over such fundamental issues as the common agricultural policy, France's contribution thereto and extension of the budgetary powers of the European Parliament.

France's "empty chair" policy came to an end only with the so-called Luxembourg compromise of January 29, 1966. The Five had found that they could not operate "Europe" without France, and the "compromise" was really a concession to de Gaulle. Notwithstanding the majority voting procedures in the treaties, in an agreement to disagree without holding up the work of the Community, it granted France, and by implication all member states a right of veto when their "very important interests" were concerned. The compromise was made weaker still by the fact that a state in effect defined its own very important interests. The agreement at least brought France back into the negotiating process, but Dr. Hallstein rightly concluded that the Commission's powers had been undermined and submitted his resignation. History proved Hallstein right inasmuch as abuse of the procedure slowed Community decision making and the pace of integration. Although it helped the United Kingdom to enter the Community, allowing the Government to "play down" supranationality to the British public, the Thatcher administration eventually agreed with its partners to put an end to the practice when they signed the Single European Act on December 4, 1985.

Agricultural policy rules were agreed on May 11, 1966. On the same date the Six agreed to speed up dismantling of trade barriers, targeting a customs union by July 1, 1968. In Geneva, EFTA was making noteworthy progress on industrial goods. Abolition of tariffs between EFTA countries was achieved on December 31, 1966. In February 1967 first steps were taken to harmonize EEC turnover taxes, an important component of product cost and therefore of trade competition. These measures led to introduction of a common value added tax system (VAT) in 1970, although governments remained free to determine the level of imposition.

De Gaulle's second veto

With the internal difficulties of the Six smoothed over, the moment seemed propitious for the UK and her associates to move again to join the Communities (or "Community" as they became with the merger of the three executives on July 1, 1967). Denmark and the United Kingdom applied on May 10, 1967, Ireland the next day. A new applicant, Norway made the move on July 21. The Six were therefore facing the prospect of rapidly becoming "the Ten". However, negotiations never got under way. President de Gaulle made it clear on November 27, again in a press conference, that he had not changed his view.

Following failure of the second attempt to enlarge the European Community, 1968 proved a quiet year for European integration. The final adjustment to external tariffs put the customs union in place on July 1. On July 26 a cooperation agreement was concluded between the EEC and Kenya, Uganda and Tanganyika.[5] Thus EEC cooperation with the developing world was extending beyond the recent colonies of member states. On July 29 the free circulation of workers, an essential element of a customs union, was achieved eighteen months ahead of schedule.

If 1968 was relatively quiet in Western Europe, it was a critical year in Eastern Europe. On January 19, 1968, the United States and the Soviet Union achieved the first major step towards armaments control, if not disarmament, in the shape of the nuclear non-proliferation treaty. If there was an ephemeral hope that this tentative softening in the deep freeze of the Cold War would also relax the Soviet grip on Eastern Europe, disillusion came swiftly and brutally. On August 20 Soviet tanks, supported by troops from East Germany, Poland, Bulgaria and Hungary, turned the clock back on Alaxander Dubcek's "Prague Spring". The Czechs would have to await another twenty-one years their glasnost and their perestroika. Hampered by the "balance of terror", but also by the Yalta agreements on spheres of influence, the West limited itself to verbal condemnation ... Nevertheless, protected by geography (beyond Yugoslavia) little Albania dared on September 20 to leave the Warsaw Pact, accusing the latter not of behaving in too Stalinist a fashion, but rather of not being ruthless enough. Closed in behind her mountains, Enver Hoxha rejected all reform and aligned himself with the People's Republic of China. Over two decades later, under Hoxha's successor Ramiz Alia, Albania would be the last East European state to embark on political reform.

Gaullian exit

1969, too, was a quiet year for European integration. On January 28 Finland joined OECD. July 29 saw a new Yaoundé Convention signed between EEC, African and Malagasy states. However, the year ended with a political earthquake. Upon losing a national referendum over a relatively minor administrative issue, President de Gaulle resigned in April 1969 and retired in haughty but dignified silence to Colombey-les-deux-Eglises. He was succeeded within a couple of months by his former premier, Georges Pompidou. This modified the political climate in Paris.[6] On December 1 and 2, at the regular summit conference of the Six, in The Hague, President Pompidou lifted French opposition to EEC enlargement. At the same time, the Six agreed to move from the transitional to the final phase of implementing EEC mechanisms by adopting definitive rules for agriculture and preparing direct levy of EEC resources. The French had always felt that Community rules and procedures gave an "edge" to the Federal Republic by emphasizing the industrial common market over agriculture. Now France's farmers were granted a greater opportunity to supply Europe's needs. At the same time, Community principles were safeguarded by putting all the major "machinery" in place before enlargement negotiations commenced. It is a matter for scholarly debate whether the delay in entry of the United Kingdom and other postulants into the Community was advantageous or disadvantageous to the building of Europe.

Be that as it may, on June 30, 1970, negotiations were formally opened between Denmark, Norway, the United Kingdom and Ireland, on the one hand, the European Community on the other, on the terms of their accession to the three Community treaties. A new era was opening in the economic, social and political integration of Western Europe.

Notes

1 The larger states—and particularly Gaullist France—thought that they should effectively direct the Community's foreign policy. The smaller Benelux countries feared domination and wanted a more equal say.

2 Nevertheless, the summit meetings of the Six launched by France eventually acquired secretariat services of their own within the Brussels bureaucracy, albeit outside the strict jurisdiction of the treaties, and came to be known as the European Council. Finally, "institutionalized" in 1986 under the Single European Act and in 1992 under the Treaty of European Union (see Part III, the Institutional Framework), the Council now meets twice yearly under rotating chairmanship. The ambiguity deliberately created by Charles de Gaulle has been resolved and the Europe of the Twelve—twice as many as in 1961—has finally endowed itself with an institutional framework capable of setting European foreign policy.

3 It should be noted that French deputies of all parties remained in the European Parliament, which continued to function normally.

4 Dr. Hallstein had been a close aide and confidant of Konrad Adenauer. His name was previously associated with the Hallstein Doctrine, under which the Federal Republic refused to have diplomatic relations with any government recognizing the East German regime (DDR). Hallstein had been the leader of the West German delegation to the Schuman Plan conference (1950) leading to ECSC. He enjoyed much support in his early years at EEC but his supranational beliefs now opposed him to de Gaulle's nationalistic approach to Europe.

The "very important interests" dragon raised its head one more time in May 1992 in the French National Assembly, when Gaullist traditionalists jibbed at ratifying the Maastricht treaty.

5 These countries had been German colonies until the Treaty of Versailles which put an end to the first World War, and thereafter League of Nations and United Nations protectorates under British administration until their independence.

6 The referendum proposed elimination of the Senate and granting of greater powers to the regions. The real issue, at least for the voters, was de Gaulle himself. The French Senate was (and remains) a rather unsatisfactory patronage institution and few voters were opposed to increased regional powers (since instituted under President Mitterrand). Historians still argue whether de Gaulle anticipated defeat and in fact engineered the whole thing to provide himself with a dramatic and heroic exit. The secret is well kept under a simple tombstone in the churchyard at Colombey ... As for Pompidou, he is still the only French statesman to have managed the difficult transition from the Hôtel Matignon, the prime minister's office, to the Elysée Palace. While preserving the Gaullian heritage Pompidou soon established himself as his own man, a situation not unlike that of John Major in post-Thatcherite Britain.

5

A Dysfunctional Parallel in the East
(1949-1992)

We interrupt our narrative of Western European integration to take a closer look at parallel efforts in the East bloc to organize economic cooperation. Superficially, the situation behind the line of demarcation agreed at Yalta may appear to mirror that of the West: small European nations devastated by war (and in several instances radically dismembered) under the potential hegemony of a victorious superpower and in need of its assistance. In fact, however, both politically and economically, widely different paths were followed.

Writing in 1988, before the major political upheavals which characterized the end of the eighties in Eastern Europe, Adam Zwass showed how hard it was for planned economies such as those of the Soviet Union and Eastern Europe before economic perestroika to develop multilateral trade relations and achieve economic integration. [1]

As a former counselor in the COMECON secretariat in Moscow, Zwass asserts that the reforms introduced by Gorbachev will leave unchanged many of the command mechanisms of a planned economy; that the growing "self-awareness" of the smaller countries is likely to result in divergence rather than convergence of interests. Convertible currencies are seen to be essential among the new mechanisms to be developed.

The unequal face-off between Europe's two largest economic communities, the EC and COMECON, might in Zwass' opinion long persist, since, unlike the EC, COMECON cannot regulate the trade relations of its members. [2] Zwass concedes, however, that it might be possible to restructure the organization into a genuine commonwealth with equal rights and obligations and a democratic executive.

We now know that this view proved too optimistic: the Organisation for International Economic Cooperation (OIEC) proved stillborn. East Germany is already well integrated into the EC; the Baltic states and several eastern European countries have signed association agreements with the Community (and also with EFTA) as a prelude to full membership, anticipated around the turn of the century.

Origin of COMECON

How did this muddled state of affairs come about? The Council of Mutual Economic Assistance, variously referred to as COMECON and CMEA, was founded on January 8, 1949, by seven countries: Albania, Bulgaria, Czechoslovakia, Hungary, Poland, Romania, and the Soviet Union. (The organization was further internationalized by the accessions of Cuba, Vietnam and Mongolia. Finland became an associate member on June 8, 1973, the only country to be directly associated with both eastern and western economic groups.)

The purpose of the organization was set out in the final communiqué of the founding conference as being "to organize a closer economic cooperation between the people's democracies and the Soviet Union". Although the communiqué goes on to speak of "equal rights", this formulation clearly sets the USSR apart as "more equal", to borrow George Orwell's phrase, than the other members. The declared means of cooperation, "exchanging economic experience and providing mutual technical assistance as well as assistance in raw materials, foods, machinery and equipment", clearly does not amount to economic integration. The lack of currency convertibility and of a credit and capital market and the state monopoly of the means of production not only isolate COMECON from world markets but also impede economic exchanges within the group.

Far from seeking to integrate the economies of Europe, the Soviet Union sought through COMECON to isolate the Soviet bloc from the reconstruction of Europe proposed by the US in the Marshall Plan. We may recall that moves by Czechoslavakia, Hungary and Poland to join the Plan were quickly squelched by Stalin. The countries of Eastern Europe were compelled to refuse the extended hands of US officials such as Harry White, author of the Bretton Words project, and Henry Morganthau, Secretary of Commerce. The statement issued by Tass, the Soviet news agency, when announcing the establishment of CMEA, made this policy clear. It confirmed the refusal of the founding nations to "submit themselves to the dictatorship of the Marshall Plan, which would have violated their sovereignty". At the same time the new organization stressed the principle of equality among its members, with decisions requiring the consent of all. The majority principle was clearly repudiated. So much for theory: in practice Soviet hegemony was both evident and painful. The countries of Eastern Europe were compelled not only to undertake alone the rebuilding of their economies but also in some cases to pay reparations to the Soviet Union. GDR payments to the Big Brother were four times larger than Marshall Aid received by the Federal Republic, itself four times larger than the GDR! Clearly, the focus of economic relations was not the group as a whole, but the Soviet Union.

Progress was slow even within COMECON's own administration. Not until December 14, 1959 — a decade after its first meeting — did the Council adopt its executive and procedural statutes; even then they were amended several times thereafter. On December 15, 1961, the COMECON Assembly, meeting in Warsaw, adopted its Basic Principles of the International Socialist Division of Labor, including "steady elimination of historical differences in the levels of economic development" of its member countries.

The organization remained ineffective for many years. In 1962 General Secretary Kruschchev made strenuous efforts to restructure COMECON and inject life into it, notably with the proclamation of the Basic Principles by first party secretaries. However, COMECON could not overcome its fundamental flaws. Adam Zwass has convincingly brought to light that centralized planning and political domination at the national level are no recipe for mutually bene-ficial economic integration, especially where one country accounts for seventy per cent of the total community product.

Despite Soviet hegemony, CMEA members were not entirely submissive. Romania declined to participate in a number of projects which it considered unrealistic. Moreover, while maintaining a strongly totalitarian system, Roma-nia objected politically to foreign (meaning Soviet) intervention in internal affairs. Consequent upon this policy, Romania pursued a number of indepen-dent links with the West, such as the exchange of ambassadors with the Fed-eral Republic (1967) and her refusal to join the Warsaw Pact in invading Czechoslovakia to suppress the Prague Spring (1968). In 1961 Albania was expelled from both COMECON and the Warsaw Pact and four years later refused Leonid Brezhnev's invitation to rejoin. [3]

Before the combined onslaught of East European political emancipation and West European economic strength, the Council for Mutual Economic Assistance finally faced the reality of Eastern Europe's rush to the free mar-ket. On January 5, 1991, the Executive Committee announced its dissolution and a decision to set up a more market-oriented body, the Organization for International Economic Cooperation. It is amusing to speculate on the private thoughts of the Cuban delegate to that meeting.

The Soviet planners proved to be whistling in the dark. After that first brave announcement OIEC was overtaken by events and has not been heard of again. With recognition of the Baltic states and a determined bid for full independence by the Ukraine, the Soviet Union's own dissolution was, ironically, hastened by the failed August *coup*. The more developed, more democratic northern tier of the former satellite ring—Poland, Czechoslovakia, Hungary— strengthened their links to the EC through a form of association approximating that of EFTA countries and actually became full members of the Council of Europe, followed shortly by Bulgaria.

COMECON's collapse brought a new set of economic challenges which could not be explained by the world economic crisis or Soviet disintegration alone. German reunification contributed to the process even before CMEA formally came to an end in June 1991. The former GDR had been a major trade partner not only for the Soviet Union (11%) but also for most East European countries. Currency union between the two Germanys brought a switch to hard currency and major shifts in trade patterns. German imports from COMECON countries dropped some 30% in 1990. At the same time a rate of DM 2.34 to the ruble favored GDR exports, which rose by 8%.

The State Treaty of May 18, 1990, between the two German states guaran-teed existing contractual obligations with CMEA countries "taking into account the realities of the currency and economic union" and "with respect for market economy principles." However these commitments have been implemented only to a limited extent. The severe recession in eastern Germany in 1991/92 was caused in part by the drop in trade with former CMEA partners, especially the ex-USSR. Eastern European countries and the USSR (now the CIS) must pay off their debts to the new Germany in hard currency, unless these are forgiven as a form of economic assistance.

As newly independent nations in Eastern Europe achieve democratic stability, it becomes increasingly clear that political independence is no substitute for economic integration. New groupings are beginning to emerge from the former COMECON trading unit. Estonia, Latvia and Lithuania are looking for stronger links across the Gulf of Bothnia with Scandinavia; eleven "sovereign republics" from the core of the former USSR are groping towards a form of economic union in the Commonwealth of Independent States (CIS). Poland, Czechoslovakia (be it as one nation or two) and Hungary are looking west. Things are even more difficult in the south, where Albania, Bulgaria and Romania remain preoccupied by internal reforms. The break-up of Yugoslavia creates a flashpoint for the whole region. Danube Basin, Black Sea and Turcic-speaking groups have also been launched on agitated economic waters.

COMECON offers us a paradoxical casebook. Both the highly centralized, state-controlled economies of which it was composed and Soviet domination stood in the way of balanced and effective economic cooperation while at the same time holding the organization together. Once it became clear that military force would no longer be employed to back up political control the whole system unravelled.

Although OIEC proved stillborn, the countries of Eastern Europe, including the former Soviet republics, know they cannot afford to stand alone. The West should not gloat, however, about the superiority of its system. There have always been several concepts of European unification. A system fixated is a system condemned. In the move for closer economic, cultural and social ties in Western Europe the political balance mechanism clearly remains to be fine-tuned. After half a century of division the road to Europe must integrate the two halves of the continent.

Notes

1 Zwass, Adam, *The Council for Mutual Economic Assistance: the thorny path from political to economic integration*, M.E. Sharpe, Inc., Armonk (N.Y.) and London, 1988, p. 269. Zwass refers to COMECON as the CMEA.

2 Zwass, *op. cit.,* p. xii.

3 For a discussion of COMECON's relations with the European Community, see Part III, Chapter 7.

6

Communities I (1971-1986)

Back in mid-1970, as the third attempt to negotiate enlargement of the European Communities got under way, events on the broader European and world stages reminded Western Europe's statesmen yet again that they were putting their house in order none too soon.

The origins of glasnost: east-west confidence building

For thirty years European divisions had become ever more entrenched. Peace in Europe had offered no brave new world. The meeting on the Elbe between United States and Soviet troops was negated by the European carve-up at Yalta, where a perceptive Churchill had been unable to counterbalance a devious and triumphant Stalin facing a death-smitten Roosevelt. Western Europe was able to hold back the Communist tide through the resolve of NATO, confrontations like the Berlin blockade and the economic strengthening produced by the Marshall Plan. However, she was shown incapable of reaching beyond the Elbe, as was evidenced by western inaction during the Hungarian uprising of 1956 and the Prague Spring of 1968. Nuclear stand-off escalated towards President Reagan's "evil empire" speech and the strategic defense initiative of the eighties. Of all the countries entered by Soviet troops in 1945 only Austria, after years of four-power occupancy as a post-*Anschluss* portion of the Third Reich, managed to slip the noose at the price of constitutional neutrality. At the northern end of the Iron Curtain, Finland had had to cede land to provide a buffer zone for Leningrad in exchange for a precarious independence.

It is commonplace to ascribe the extraordinary chain of events in Europe and the Soviet Union in the late eighties to the steadfastness of the Atlantic alliance, to economic weakness in the USSR and above all to the marvellous emergence in Moscow in March 1985 of a man of extraordinary courage and vision, Mikhail Gorbachev. We can now see, however, that the first intimations of possible changes extend as far back as 1969. In December of that year the Federal Republic of Germany, under the leadership of Willi Brandt, who had spent many years on the "front line" of the Cold War as mayor of Berlin, embarked on negotiations with the Soviet Union leading to the signature in Moscow on August 12, 1970, of the Soviet-German non-aggression Treaty. At the same time the Federal Republic sought to normalize relations with Poland and to come to an understanding with the German Democratic Republic.

Treaties were signed with Poland on December 7, 1970, and the GDR on December 21, 1971. Supportive of an *Ostpolitik* designed to face realities and reduce tensions, the three western Berlin occupation powers, France, the United Kingdom and the United States, on March 26, 1970, began talks with the Soviet Union designed to supplement the Quadripartite Agreement on Berlin. As a holdover from the end of World War II, the whole "occupied" and divided city was a monument to the souring of relations among the victors. Since the USSR objected to the incorporation of West Berlin into the FRG, occupation status in the British, French and US sectors provided a protective constitutional fiction. Occupation status and procedures were not ended but they were eased. The supplementary Agreement was signed on June 3, 1972.

The improved atmosphere in East-West relations created by these contacts made it possible for the NATO Council to declare at its Rome meeting of May, 1970, its willingness to enter into "exploratory contacts" to establish the "feasibility" of convening a broad conference, open to all interested countries, on European security and cooperation, and on the principles which should govern relations between states, including the renunciation of force. The proposal was prickly with precautionary language but the opening was real.

The first move had actually come from the East: Moscow was willing to give something in exchange for the recognition of frontier changes imposed in Eastern Europe at the end of the war. Western suspicion of Soviet motives is highlighted by the insistence on preliminary "talks about talks": contacts to establish the feasibility of convening a conference! However, the importance which NATO governments attached to their initiative was underlined by the Council's decision to forward the proposal, through the foreign minister of the host-country, Italy, to other interested parties, including neutral and non-aligned governments. The breadth of the proposed conference was thereby clearly signalled. A quarter century after the end of World War II a general peace settlement was finally being envisaged.

Talks about talks about talks

At the same time countries members of NATO's integrated military structure—all except France—invited Warsaw Treaty countries and the other governments concerned to undertake exploratory talks on mutual and balanced force reductions (MBFR), skirting the question of whether arms build-ups are the cause or the consequence of tension. A further relaxation of eye-ball to eye-ball politics was achieved when signature of the treaty on limitation of anti-ballistic missile systems (ABM Treaty) followed during President Nixon's visit to Moscow in May 1972. The ABM Treaty was designed to reduce the temptation to undertake a first strike by restricting defense against a counter-strike. This was not yet disarmament (a downward spiral) but at least it set limits on the upward spiral of the armaments race. Moreover, almost as important as the limitation on multiple warheads was the principle of mutual control and reciprocal verification which it implied.

Talks about talks about talks paid off. Meeting in Bonn on May 30 and 31, 1972, NATO countries agreed to enter into multilateral discussions to prepare a conference on security and cooperation in Europe. A Finnish proposal that the talks be held in Helsinki—as neutral a venue as one could imagine—was accepted. This highly political initiative of all-European security discussions offered acknowledgement that a new approach to the arms race was required: NATO had deterred war but it had not guaranteed peace. Doubtless the notion was dawning in NATO circles that if one side can win a war it takes all sides to win the peace.

Midnight sun and a ray of hope

Multilateral preparatory talks for a possible conference on security and cooperation in Europe opened in Helsinki on November 22, 1972. The name of this clean-lined Nordic capital on the shores of the Baltic opposite Estonia was rapidly to become synonymous with *détente*. With her western market economy and her eastern geo-political realities, Finland offered an ideal meeting ground. The Finns have not forgotten that in the Second World War, amid their own lakes and forests, they found themselves fighting the Russians in the south and the Germans in the north. In a war of words a new and more promising cliché was about to emerge—the spirit of Helsinki.

After months of delicate discussions and referrals back to governments, the western allies were satisfied that the Soviets were serious and not merely seeking propaganda advantage. Negotiations concluded on June 8, 1973, with a proposal to convene the conference under three headings or "baskets"— security; economics, science and technology, including the environment; and humanitarian issues, including human rights.

The conference itself finally opened at the level of foreign ministers on July 3, 1973. Responding to NATO's diplomatic initiative of May, 1970, all thirty-four European states except Albania and Andorra[1] plus Canada and the United States, participated.

Equally noteworthy is the emphasis on confidence-building measures and non-military cooperation. The breadth of the agenda suggested a realization among participating governments that if armaments suffice to keep nations apart, it requires cooperation over common problems to bring them together. Perhaps for the first time in many years, the armaments race was seen as the consequence of distrust rather than as its cause. The Conference on Security and Cooperation in Europe (CSCE), embryo of a new and broader European community, would make it possible to move from arms limitation to arms reduction. Disarmament might not be an impossible dream if the notion of common or reciprocal security could one day replace the prickly stand-off of opposing alliances. Twelve years before Mikhail Gorbachev rose to power the Iron Curtain had let through a chink of glasnost.

Further consultations went forward in Geneva during 1974 and 1975. The Conference promulgated its Final Act on July 21, 1975. The Act is more of a beginning than an end. At once a simple constitution, a process and a program, it was followed over the next fifteen years by some thirty specialized meetings, culminating in conferences of heads of governments in Paris in November 1990 and again in Helsinki in July 1992.

From Six to Nine

In the renewed negotiations with applicant countries launched in mid-1970, a fresh negotiating technique was employed by the European Communities. Instead of open discussions round the table, the Six came to a common position on each item before ushering in the United Kingdom delegation. (Once again, negotiations with the British, regarded as pivotal, preceded discussions with the other applicant countries). Political will and goodwill overcame serious obstacles. Transitional provisions were negotiated both for the United Kingdom and for the latter's traditional trading partners, especially Australia and New Zealand, which after UK entry would find themselves separated from their British customers by the common external tariff. Steps were also initiated with EFTA to avoid re-erection of dismantled trade barriers in industrial goods when the new entrants moved from one group to the other.

The key ratification of Community enlargement came promptly. On April 23, 1971, a referendum of the French electorate resulted in a lopsided approval of 68.3 percent. Britain, it seemed, was no longer *la perfide Albion*. On October 28 the House of Commons approved United Kingdom entry by 356 votes to 244, with 22 abstentions. The Labour Party, in oppositon, was not satisfied with the terms of entry. However, in a national referendum the Norwegian electorate rejected accession by a majority of some eight percent. Newly-discovered North Sea oil and the long memory of Swedish domination bolstered Norway's proud independent stance. She felt more comfortable in EFTA, although there are signs today that after Austria, Sweden and Finland have applied to join the EC, spelling the end of EFTA, opinion may be moving on the issue.

Accession treaties for Denmark, Ireland and the United Kingdom were signed on January 22, 1972. As the midnight chimes of Big Ben ushered in the New Year on January 1, 1973, the Six triumphantly confirmed their success by becoming Nine.   Traditional party-goers splashing in the fountains of Trafalgar Square seemed blissfully unaware that anything other than the date had changed.

The bridesmaids of EFTA

With the long-drawn-out yet nonetheless dramatic fifty per cent increase in Community membership one could be forgiven for dismissing the rest of Europe as irrelevant periphery. This would not be the case today, with our fifty-one nation CSCE perspective. Frontiers may have shifted in the East but we have essentially restored our conception of Europe to its pre-war definition (and one de Gaulle never lost sight of) from the Atlantic to the Urals. Yet even on January 1, 1973, although the champagne corks were surely not popping in Stockholm, Vienna or Lisbon, the EFTA rump was not bereft of achievements.

Let us remember that the Stockholm Convention had reiterated the objective of OECD's Maudling Committee (however impossible that may have been) to set up a wider European solution to the question of economic integration. The issue was not the desirability of the latter but the degree of commitment considered necessary to achieve it.

Throughout the nineteen-sixties EFTA countries had continued their efforts to find an acceptable solution. At a meeting of EFTA ministers in London in June 1961, it was agreed to try a bilateral approach. Thus the applications of Denmark and the United Kingdom (Ireland too, of course, but she was not a member of EFTA) were made with EFTA's consent. More particularly, for our present concern, on December 15 of the same year Austria, Sweden and Switzerland applied to the EEC for negotiations under Article 238 of the Treaty of Rome, which provides for associate membership. On May 2, 1962, Norway presented its demand for accession to the Community (subsequently renounced in the national referendum) and on May 18 Portugal informed the EEC of its desire to enter into negotiations. [2]

In the ensuing years, as we have seen, several attempts were made to arrive at arrangements appropriate for each country, but it was only after Community enlargement that EFTA countries received satisfaction. Thus it could be argued that the triple marriage of January 1, 1973 was in fact a good day for the bridesmaids of EFTA.

The free trade agreements

The summit of the Six in The Hague at which President Georges Pompidou had lifted the French veto on Community enlargement had also decided that membership increase should not involve re-erection of tariff barriers in Europe. Thus remaining EFTA countries were accepted as exceptions to the common external tariffs of the enlarged Community; indeed agreements with non-candidate countries should, it was asserted, wherever possible enter into force on the day enlargement took place.

No less than fourteen agreements were negotiated. The seven remaining members of EFTA were Austria, Finland, Iceland, Norway, Portugal, Sweden and Switzerland. Each negotiated an agreement with both the Economic Community and the Coal and Steel Community. These agreements were made applicable to future EC members; they have therefore since been extended to Greece, Portugal and Spain on a fully multilateral basis. [3]

In most cases the progressive reduction of import duties reached zero on July 1, 1977. Three and a half years after Community enlargement virtually all trade in industrial products among the sixteen countries involved was free of duty. The European free trade system was completed by an EFTA free trade agreement with Spain, concluded on June 26, 1979, which complemented an EEC agreement with Spain dating back to 1970.

Even though a legalistic mind could claim that such an arrangement infringed the GATT most-favored-nation rule (see Part III), the creation of such a vast open market not only promoted intra-European trade but also stimulated economic activity throughout the world. As for the United States, although some sectors of the American economy might have had their reservations, there is no doubt that the White House welcomed avoidance of an economic split in western Europe. For the US, political gains undoubtedly counterbalanced possible economic losses.

Housekeeping for new residents

With the notable exception of the Yom Kippur war, in which the Egyptian attack against Israel on October 6, Judaism's most holy day, was rapidly repelled, bringing Israeli forces across the Suez canal, 1973 proved a fairly quiet year as the European countries adjusted to their new arrangements. On January 5 Francois – Xavier Ortoli of France succeeded Sicco Mansholt of the Netherlands as President of the EC Commission. History will credit Mansholt, who served as Commissioner for Agriculture before becoming President, with two major achievements during his stewardship: the European agricultural policy and Community enlargement. On January 15 the first Council of the Nine was held in Brussels. Adjustments were also being made within the Brussels and Luxembourg bureaucracies. Vacancies were reserved for nationals of the new member countries.[4] Moreover, translation and interpretation services were adjusted from four official languages (Dutch, French, German, Italian) to seven, adding Danish, English, and even, officially at least, Irish Gaelic. Greek, Portuguese and Spanish have since joined the list. Clearly EC countries are prepared to sacrifice cost and efficiency to preservation of national cultures and identity. This issue is further discussed in Part IV.

On the broader European scene – one cannot yet speak of a community – tensions were being eased. May 1972 had been a fruitful month with the Moscow SALT and ABM agreements between the US and the USSR and the NATO proposals for CSCE and MBFR talks. These were strengthened in June by the new Quadripartite Agreement on Berlin. SALT II and the CSCE exploratory contacts followed in November. CSCE talks continued, first in Helsinki, then in Geneva, for the rest of the year. CMEA also expanded her ranks, welcoming Cuba as a full member on July 19 and Finland as an associate member in June 1973. Despite the Yom Kippur war (or perhaps because of it) the US and the Soviet Union opened MBFR talks in Vienna on October 30.

To round out the year, in Copenhagen a summit meeting of EC countries (still convened technically outside the Community framework) agreed in principle to meet more frequently. This was confirmed a year later when the heads of government (for France, head of state and government) formalized the European Council and decided to meet three times a year.

Cultivating Europe's vegetable patch

1974 opened with a three-day agricultural "marathon" of the Nine. Such intensive negotiations have occurred from time to time because the common agricultural policy (CAP), often referred to by its French acronym of PAC, involves annual price agreements. The mechanisms of the CAP are very different from those of the common market in industrial goods. Even today, Community agricultural policy is not yet synonymous with free market forces.

It has been observed elsewhere that the Treaty of Rome is much less explicit and detailed on agriculture than on industrial goods. Furthermore, the PAC provides for variable levels of external market protection (levies) which are related to contemporary world prices. The basic principles of the policy are set out in Article 39 of the Treaty of Rome. They include:

   (i)   increased productivity through technical progress and the best use of all the factors of production, in particular manpower;
  (ii) a fair standard of living for the agricultural community;
 (iii) stabilization of markets;
 (iv) guaranteed supplies;
  (v) reasonable prices to consumers.

It is clear from the foregoing that social and political imperatives are here impinging upon the free flow of market forces. The principles set in the Treaty of Rome have been fleshed out by means of directives and regulations enacted by the Council since 1960 and by implementing regulations drafted by the Commission. In fact, the CAP owes its origins to the conference in Stresa, Italy, which took place in July 1958, six months after the Treaties of Rome (EEC and EURATOM) entered into force. The main principle set out at Stresa was the gradual coming together, known as approximation, of agricultural prices in member states. In a true common market this happens as a result of free market forces; however, since governments apply for their agriculture various forms of price support which, for political, economic and social reasons related to preservation of the farming community they could not easily forego, an artificial and therefore political time-table had to be devised. As production costs were in general higher in the Community than in the other major producing countries, prices had in many cases to be set above the world market level to guarantee Community production. The aim was balance rather than self-sufficiency. The Stresa conference also recommended improvement of agricultural structures.

It is important to understand that Europe's agricultural structures differ markedly from those of the other main producers. In the late nineteen-fifties the Community's 17.5 million farmers had only 65 million hectares (one hectare [ha] equals some 2¼ acres) from which to feed 150 million people. The US had over 400 million ha to feed 200 million inhabitants and the USSR 600 million ha for 250 million citizens. At 100 ha the average American farm was almost twenty times larger than its European counterpart. The American farmer could feed fifty inhabitants, his European counterpart ten. The US was

a net exporter; the European Community met only 85% of its food requirements.[5]

In December 1960, the Council of Ministers adopted the principles for
common management of the market, known as "Green Europe" (the fisheries
policy would be dubbed "Blue Europe"). In 1962 the first steps were taken
towards a structural policy. In 1968 a Commission memorandum led to structural directives, issued by the Council in April 1972. The purpose of these
directives is to modify the agricultural sector of the economy where supply and
demand call for permanent change. Financial solidarity is also an essential
principle of the CAP. Policies cost money. A common fund, the European
Agricultual Guidance and Guarantee Fund (EAGGF, more commonly known
by its more pronounceable French acronym, FEOGA) was set up.

Thus it may be said that the EC's common agricultural policy rests on the
twin pillars of prices and markets on the one hand and stuctural change on the
other. In the policy's application three principles can be established: the
single market, Community preference and financial solidarity. The single
market implies, of course, the free movement of products from one member
country to another. Community preference implies protection of the internal
market against cheap imports and excessive price fluctuations on the world
market. Financial solidarity implies the sharing of costs by all members and
the provision of funds where they are required, regardless of the product or
member country where such expenditure is incurred. These principles and the
problem of the Community's relations with third countries will be developed in
later chapters.

Labour's historic commitment: the UK referendum

Perhaps the most extraordinary non-issue of the entire process of European
unification is whether it benefits the left or the right, labor or management,
socialism (as understood in western Europe, not to be confused with the pre-
communist socialism of Marxist dogma) and conservatism. Across Europe
nationalism proved a much greater obstacle to union than political dogma,
always excepting the extremes of communism on the left and fascism on the
right. Things were somewhat different in Britain. There was some truth to the
notion of the islander mentality (one recalls London's apocryphal newspaper
headline "Fog in the Channel: Continent isolated") and even today some of
those feelings remain with respect to the Channel Tunnel. Successive governments were tempted to play to these fears. It seemed as though the most anti-
European party was neither the Labour Party nor the Conservative Party as
such, but whichever of the two happened to be in power. The Liberal Party,
chronically under-represented on account of the United Kingdom's single
member constituency system of election favoring the two main parties, was
always the most European-minded. It is fair to say that, over the years, the
Conservative Party grew to be more "pro-Europe" than Labour, particularly in
the eighties, after moderates in the Labour Party, led by Roy Jenkins, a former

Minister who had served as Commission President in Brussels, broke away to form the Social Democrats.[6]

Although while in opposition Labour had voted in 1971 against UK accession to the Treaties of Paris and Rome, upon becoming Prime Minister once more in the national elections of February 28, 1974, Harold Wilson applied a softer policy. Labour claimed that it was the conditions of Britain's accession which had led to the 244 hostile votes, not the principle of membership. The Labour Government would renegotiate the Treaty of Accession and submit the results to a national referendum. Negotiations continued for half a year. Changes agreed were more appearance than substance, enabling the Westminster government to keep its promise to go to the people. The result surprised almost everybody: the United Kingdom electorate approved continued Community membership by 67.2% to 32.8%, a strong majority of two to one.

The first all-European forum

The log-jam was also breaking on the all-European front. Two months after the British referendum, on August 1, 1975, the Final Act of the Conference on Security and Cooperation in Europe was signed in Helsinki by thirty-five nations. At first the US approach to CSCE had been skeptical. Henry Kissinger, amongst others, was convinced that the Conference would be a short-lived experiment. Undue emphasis on individual human rights cases slowed progress. The Americans, who were induced by the Helsinki Final Act to recognize the status-quo of Europe's eastern frontiers,[7] were reluctant to hand the Soviet Union a propaganda victory. Nevertheless, the CSCE's low-key approach (no permanent secretariat and decision-making by consensus) proved its worth, culminating in the Paris peace conference of November 1990, at which a reunified Germany finally "made peace" with the rest of Europe.[8]

Consolidation of Europe of the Nine

Meanwhile the western world was not standing still. On April 25, 1974, a military coup in Portugal shattered the long-standing corporatist dictatorship. On July 23 Richard Nixon became the first American president to resign in office, being succeeded by Vice-President Gerald Ford, himself a replacement for Spiro Agnew.

In December, the second European Community summit of the Nine made important decisions. The heads of state and government formally established themselves as the European Council and proposed the election by direct suffrage of members of the European Assembly (a measure foreseen in the EEC Treaty but without a deadline). The European Regional Development Fund (ERDF/FEDER), designed to assist underdeveloped areas ill-equiped to meet the challenge of the free market, was launched on this occasion.

On May 31, 1975, the European Space Research Organisation and the European Launcher Development Organisation, formed in the sixties with slightly differing memberships to promote a European counterpoint to NASA (using a lauch site in Kourou, French Guiana) were merged to form the European Space Agency, with eleven member countries. [9]

Greece joins the European Community

July 27, 1976, marked the opening of membership negotiations between Greece and the European Community. Discussion moved forward without major impediment. The Treaty of Athens was signed on May 8, 1979. On January 1, 1981, Greece became the tenth member country, strengthening the ranks of the smaller countries and also of members with Mediterranean interests. Because of the importance of agriculture to the Greek economy, Greece was allowed seven years to phase in the Common Agricultural Policy. Five years were allowed for other trading and financial adjustments, including ECSC participation. It is of particular note that the accession of Greece more than doubled the Community's merchant fleet. Greece received five votes where a qualified majority was required, 24 parliamentary seats and a seat on the European Court in Luxembourg.

Portugal and Spain

A generous EFTA initiative to help its economically weakest member came to fruition on April 7, 1976, upon creation of the Industrial Development Fund for Portugal, with a capital of 84.6 million Special Drawing Rights, equivalent at the time to one hundred million dollars. Capital was provided by all EFTA countries, with the largest contributions coming from Sweden (30%) and Switzerland (25.509%). After six years these contributions bear interest at 3%, guaranteed by the Portuguese government.

The Fund was set up for twenty-five years and continues to operate even though Portugal is now an EC member. Interest paid on the capital is available for relending. The loans have helped considerably to reduce unemployment. The IDF has assisted a wide range of industries in all nineteen districts of continental Portugal as well as the Azores and Madeira.

Despite this assistance, Portugal finally decided that its interest would be better served by belonging to the Community. Since the independence of Angola, Mozambique and the Cape Verde Islands, Portugal had been reduced to the status of a peripheral European nation, almost as remote as Ireland. With Spain as its only geographical neighbor, it needed unrestricted access to the heartland of Europe for its agricultural and fisheries products. It had a long-standing "special relationship" with Britain, now inside the Community's common tariff wall, and was a full member of NATO, whereas EFTA was now composed mainly of neutral nations. On March 28, 1977, Portugal applied for membership in the European Community.

Spain followed suit on July 28. Clearly, the two applications from the Iberian peninsula would be taken together, resolving Portugal's sense of isolation. On the other hand, with her thirty-eight million people, her 505 thousand square kilometers of which 276 were devoted to agriculture, the most vulnerable economic sector inside the Community, it was evident that negotiations would not be easy for Spain. It would take nine long years for Portugal and Spain to become, on January 1, 1986, the eleventh and twelfth members of the European Community, markedly altering its economic, cultural, geographic, and even religious balance. Today Spain is one of the most dynamic countries in the EC.

Fisheries

As though in anticipation of the Iberian applications, on January 1, 1977, the Community declared a 200-mile fishing zone around its coasts. The traditional concept of territorial waters provided a three-mile limit. With exploitation of the sea-floor this was extended to twelve (allowance always being made for free passage through narrow channels such as the Straits of Dover). The notion of the continental shelf as "territory" gained adherents. However, issues such as marine pollution, oil exploration and depletion of fishery resources have overlaid the notion of territorial waters (now accepted as twelve miles) with that of sovereign economic zones, wherein a nation must allow free passage but may regulate its economic interests. Growth of the EC from the original six to a more ocean-oriented nine increased the importance of fisheries ("Blue Europe") as an aspect of agricultural policy. Blue Europe policy was finally set by the Ten, after six years of negotiation, on January 25, 1983 and is further discussed under that dateline.

In January 1977, Roy Jenkins (UK) succeeded France's François-Xavier Ortoli in the presidency of the European Commission. Six months later the customs union between the Six and the three new members was achieved with the elimination of the final stage of tariff barriers. On December 31 the transitional period for aligning agricultural prices was also completed.

Snakes and tunnels: sliding towards a European currency

An important step in the building of Europe was made at the European summit in July 1978. France and the Federal Republic of Germany proposed the European Monetary System (EMS) to replace the "snake in the tunnel" mechanism of limited currency exchange rate fluctuation.

A national currency is not necessarily the appropriate standard for individuals, companies or governments to conduct business in a customs union, since its value can be unilaterally set or influenced by the monetary authorities of the issuing country. It also costs money to change money without adding value to the product offered for sale. A common unit of value acceptable to both trading partners is desirable, not only to determine rights and obligations in a contract but also to preserve future value. The changing value of a "floating" currency reflects both economic factors and speculation; it is difficult to distinguish the two. Ultimately, then, a unified market needs a unified currency. Could one imagine California and Pennsylvania having different currencies?

Civilizations have long sought stable units of measure, from cowrie shells to gold. An unreliable "measure" does not measure anything.

The counter arguments are that a currency is a symbol of national sovereignty; that the international rate of a currency reflects a national economic situation; and that control of a currency is an important lever of national economic policy.

The member countries of the Community enjoy equal rights but employ different currencies. From the earliest days the Six needed a common measure for drawing up budgets, settling claims and, a few years later, setting common prices for agriculture under the CAP. The European Payments Union (EPU), set up in 1950 to facilitate post-war economic recovery under OEEC auspices, had selected the American dollar not merely on account of the strength of that currency but also because it was itself "pegged" to gold at $35 an ounce,[10] ensuring a stable unit of measurement. This measure was adopted by the Six, so that at the outset the Communities's unit of account (u.a.) and the United States dollar were of identical value.

This situation changed abruptly in December 1971 when the US devalued the dollar and again in March 1973, when it was decided to allow US dollar exchange rates to float. Conversion of the European u.a. into national currencies now became highly theoretical, with the rate "on paper" bearing only a limited relationship to daily fluctuations.

On April 21, 1975, the Community therefore decided to create a basket-type unit of account composed of specific quantities of the members' nine currencies, with shares apportioned according to the economic importance of each currency. However, although the share of each currency providing a basis of calculation remained fixed, each currency was permitted to fluctuate within upper and lower limits—the so-called "snake in the tunnel". Consequently, the value of the European unit of account (EUA), set daily at a fixed hour, fluctuated in relation to "real" currencies not only because of changes in other currencies but also on account of small changes in its own component currencies. Nevertheless, creation of the relatively stable EUA made it possible for a single accounting system to be adopted within the Community. The confusion caused during the seventies by the existence of different units of account (some geared to IMF parities, others to daily fluctuations) was gradually ended.

The European Monetary System (EMS) put forward at the Bremen summit was agreed in December 1978 and inaugurated on March 13, 1979. The European unit of account was retained but a review clause was added and the EUA renamed the European currency unit (ECU). Today the ECU is used for all Community operations, including relations with ACP (Yaoundé and Lomé convention) countries. Although an English acronym, the letters ECU spell the name of an old French coin, the *ecu*, introduced by Louis IX, and the designation is acquiring universal acceptance. The ECU has also been introduced into the private sector for savings accounts, international checking and the floating of loans in the financial market. The last country to join the EMS was the United Kingdom, which did not become a member until October 8, 1991.

Each currency is permitted a limited margin of fluctuation, set for most countries at 2.5%. When repeated price support fails to correct excessive deviation, the Community may make official adjustments.

In 1970 a study group led by Pierre Werner, Prime Minister of Luxembourg, formulated four conditions for monetary union: irreversible currency convertibility, elimination of rate fluctuation, locking of parities, liberalization of capital movements. The ECU contributes to a stable trading climate for intra-Community trade. Today the Community is well on the way to adopting a European currency.[11]

When is a parliament not a parliament? Europe's first elections

When the ECSC treaty was negotiated the Council of Europe's Consultative Assembly was taken as a model for the parliamentary arm of the Community institutions. The notion that international cooperation was no longer the business of governments alone and that a parliamentary control mechanism beyond the national level was required was thereby confirmed. For the federalists, however, this was only half a loaf, half a victory. European democracy, they declared, could not be assured without direct expression of the *vox populi*.

The federalists got another opportunity when the atomic energy and common market treaties were negotiated half a dozen years later. Although no agreement was reached to make direct elections coincide with the inception of the new treaties, provision was made in the Treaty of Rome for eventual direct elections. The federalists had another quarter loaf.

Equivocations about the role of the Assembly persist even today. "The Assembly" is the name used in the treaties and the one employed for official regulations and directives. However, the parliamentarians call themselves the "European Parliament". (The Consultative Assembly of the Council of Europe has also "raised" its title, to "Parliamentary Assembly", filling as it were the "vacancy" left by the European Parliament's name change. Such semantics clearly represent an attempt on the part of the parliamentarians to improve their image and enhance their function. "Parliamentary" is a step up on "consultative" and a "parliament" more prestigious than an "assembly").

In 1960, less than two years after the Rome Treaty came into force, the European Parliament—we give the Assembly the courtesy of using the name it has selected for itself—drew up a convention for direct elections but it was not followed up by the ministerial Council. We have noted that the December 1974 summit produced agreement in principle to hold direct elections. In January 1975, Parliament drafted a new convention. At the end of 1975 the European Council set direct elections for 1978. In July 1976 it decided upon the number and distribution of seats. The instruments for the election of members of the European Parliament by direct universal suffrage for five-year terms were signed by the Council on September 20. Finally, some twenty years after the Treaty of Rome provision, Europe's first direct elections took place. The electorates of the nine member countries chose 410 members to the reconstituted Parliament between June 7 and 10, 1979. In order to guarantee equality of influence all the results were promulgated at the same time. [12]

France, the Federal Republic, Italy and the United Kingdom elected 81 members (MEPs) each, the Netherlands 25, Belgium 24, Denmark 16, Ireland 15, Luxembourg 6. The highest turn-out at the polls was in Italy, with 86%, the lowest in the United Kingdom (32%), where few well-known personalities were standing. The election was generally fought on a national manifesto, but the Liberals adopted a common platform in all countries except Ireland.

The first elected Parliament was called to order on July 17, 1979, and itself elected Simone Veil of France at its President. Each new member country subsequently held Euro-elections upon joining the Community. (Greece elected 24 in 1981; Portugal and Spain 24 and 60, respectively, in 1986). The European Parliament now has 518 members. At the next election Germany seeks to add 18 to reflect reunification. Members meet in political groups regardless of nationality, the Socialist Group being the largest.

A number of other significant events took place in 1979. As we have seen, the European Monetary System integrated Community accounting on March 13. Greek accession negotiations were concluded with the Treaty of Athens on May 8 and the second Lomé convention was signed with fifty-eight ACP countries on October 31. EFTA concluded its trade agreement with Spain on June 26.

Outside Western Europe, Presidents Carter and Brezhnev signed the second strategic arms limitation agreement (SALT II) in Vienna (June 18); the People's Republic of Yemen became an observer at COMECON; the 444-day hostage crisis began in Teheran (November 4); and on December 27 the Soviet Union invaded Afghanistan or, as was asserted, responded to a call for assistance from a friendly government, as the US had done in Viet Nam.

No velvet gloves for *La Dame de Fer*

For the Community's internal relations, however, the most significant event of 1979 was undoubtedly the Dublin summit of November 29 and 30. Mrs. Margaret Thatcher of the United Kingdom was proving a doughty negotiator and had gained grudging admiration in European circles, especially Brussels and Paris, as *la Dame de Fer*. The Iron Lady's contempt for the Brussels bureaucracy, the "Eurocrats", could only be compared (*quelle ironie!*) with that of de Gaulle, who distrusted both Brussels and London.

The British Prime Minister's basic complaint was that the United Kingdom contribution to the Community budget was far in excess of the benefits received. Although the Community system is not based on a formal "profit and loss" accounting for each member, there was some basis for the complaint since the statistics showed all other members achieving a net gain. The other closely related issue was the common policy for agriculture. Food production was eating up the budget.

Britain had long fed her island multitudes (with a surface area half that of France for a comparable population of up to fifty-six million) through traditional trade links based largely on "Commonwealth" formerly "Imperial" preference tariffs for the import of staples such as wheat from Canada and meat from Australia and New Zealand. Admirably supplemented by a small but efficient domestic farming community in the United Kingdom, these countries provided the British with food both cheap and plentiful. When the United Kingdom joined the Community and accepted the CAP, all this changed. The new outlets "on the continent" for Britain's farmers had no bearing on the progressive imposition of tariffs on imports from Britain's traditional suppliers: on the contrary, since European farmers now had easier access to Britain's table. True, the British housewife found her supermarket stocked with a new array of French cheese, Italian tomatoes and olive oil and German sausage at generally lower though still CAP-controlled prices, while retaining her Danish butter and bacon which had entered the market at the same time; but her overall food bill rose sharply. Moreover the extra costs did not remain in the British Treasury to provide tax-relief—they had to be paid over to the Brussels Commission. Here they were used to subsidize excessive production and storage (a *Butterberg*, or butter mountain, as the German called it); the wholesale uprooting of overproducing, low-grade vinestocks (some of which were replanted a few years later to qualify for a new "cash crop"...) and similar extravagances which the Iron Lady found outrageous. She did have a point: two-thirds of the EC budget, much of it "supplied" by levies on UK food imports was being devoted to implementation of the agricultural policy.

At the Dublin meeting of the European Council, held under Irish presidency (the chairmanship of the ministerial bodies of the EC rotates at six-monthly intervals), Mrs. Thatcher called for reduction of the United Kingdom's contribution to the Community budget. Without espousing all the British arguments, the newly elected Parliament, seizing an opportunity to flex its muscles, agreed that the CAP was getting out of hand and rejected the Community budget proposed by the Commission. These issues were taken up again at the Luxembourg summit of April 27 and 28, 1980. For the first time the European Council broke up in deadlock. Fortunately, the shock was salutary: cooler counsels prevailed. On May 30 the Council of Ministers agreed to a two-thirds reduction in the UK contribution (the burden being shared among other members in varying degrees). In a complementary measure the Council raised agricultural price guarantees a relatively modest 5%, a British concession. Two squeaky wheels on the European chariot, one British, the other largely French, had been judiciously oiled.

Stirrings in the East

Meanwhile, seminal events were taking place in Eastern Europe. President Tito of Yugoslavia died on May 4, 1980. On August 31, the Gdansk Agreements recognizing the Polish trade union *Solidarnosc*, Solidarity would eventually prove to have been the first step in shaking Communism's hold on Eastern Europe. A humble, devoutly Catholic electrician was emerging in a leadership role which would sweep him into presidential office ten years later.

In another event deeply impinging upon the situation in Eastern Europe, the ESCE follow-up conference opened in Madrid on November 11.

Moreover, a new convulsion was seizing that epicenter of political crisis, the Middle East. On September 22 Iraq attacked Iran, principally to claim exclusive control of the Shatt-al-Arab waterway, the Tigris-Euphrates outlet to the sea, in a bitter war which would end in stalemate after eight years of conflict. Although Iraq's Saddam Hussein was the aggressor, the West tended to support him because of the US hostage crisis in Iran and fear of the spread of Islamic fundamentalism. Such political opportunism would prove costly in 1990 when Iraq invaded Kuwait . . .

Manifest crisis

Europe, however, had crises enough nearer home. As the Dublin compromise cobbled up the green sleeve of agricultural policy, steel was coming apart at the welds. In fact, the steel industry had been in trouble for some years. This was a world-wide phenomenon, not to be attributed to the ECSC as an institution. On the contrary, the existence of the Coal and Steel Community offered hope of a holistic approach to resolution of a crisis which was both structural and cyclical, *structurelle et conjoncturelle*.

Three years previously, in November 1977, the Community had recognized the existence of a serious problem in coal and steel. On that date European commissioner Etienne Davignon of Belgium put forward a plan for restructuring a steel industry assailed by a general economic downturn — not quite a recession — in the free economies of the industrial world. Now, however, on October 30, 1980, the Community declared a "manifest crisis" in the steel industry, as provided in the ECSC Treaty itself. The downturn in steel was a crisis of capitalism, as real in the United States as it was in Europe. The measures employed to combat it were classical, but for the first time the level of reaction was international, indeed supranational.

The causes were obvious: the rise of new, more competitive producing countries, like Korea; a weakening in demand occasioned by the global economic crisis; the growing propensity to economize an expensive commodity such as steel by using other materials (plastics, fiberglass). At the same time, world production capacity had continued to rise as a result of the sixties' boom (investment planning and production are usually "behind the curve"). Now the industry was faced with excess capacity, downward pressure on prices, a lag in machine-tool design and financial losses preventing the industry from financing its own restructuring. Only a few small producers of highly specialized steels escaped the *crunch*.

Public authorities could not disregard the problem. To permit the demise of the steel industry would be tantamount to ringing the economic knell of entire regions and to depriving Europe of its autonomy for the production of a whole range of goods: cars, refrigerators, even bridges . . . Conversely, however, it would overburden the economy — and infringe GATT's fair trade regulations — to pursue indefinitely a policy of high prices and subsidized production for steel. Moreover, a purely protectionist approach would elicit reprisals even more harmful to overall employment and eventually run down the production base.

The only reasonable strategy, therefore, was to modernize and restructure the industry at the level of the Community as a whole, so as to conserve the trading advantages offered by a single European market. The policy adopted by the Commission was harsh yet, far from seeking to effect multiple shutdowns, sought to salvage as many jobs as possible. The aim was to enable the industry to become competitive once more and to shake off all public subsidy by 1986.

The principal elements of this policy were as follows:

— A system of production quotas for each firm, accompanied by a minimal or suggested price structure.
— Understandings with major external producers to reduce the negative impact of imports on the Community market. These measures made it possible to balance supply and demand and halt the fall in prices while preserving the market shares of firms. This artificial system was of course considered transitory, with free competition to be restored as soon as possible.
— Supervision of restructuring undertaken by member countries. The Commission saw to it that national projects were in conformity with overall Community objectives. Government assistance which did not contribute to capacity reduction, modernisation and competitiveness was disallowed.
— Financial assistance from Community sources designed to facilitate the necessary changes. These funds were used for research, new technology, development of replacement industries, partial unemployment and short hours, early retirement programs, etc.

The plan balanced economic and social responsibilities. Today Europe's steel industry is leaner, stronger, more competitive. The US steel industry entered a similar crisis around the same time. It did not enjoy the benefits of intergovernmental intervention and industry-wide coordination which were available in Europe, however. Left almost exclusively to market forces as required by pure capitalist doctrine, its recovery has been slower. As late as 1992 Bethlehem Steel was still "downsizing".

The road to disarmament: building down through joint political action

1981 opened with further enlargement of the European Community, Greece becoming the tenth member on January 1, and closed with prospective enlargement of NATO, Spain applying for membership in December. However, most of the year's historical highlights concern individuals. On January 6, Gaston Thorn of Luxembourg succeeds Roy Jenkins as President of the European Commission. January 20 marks the opening of Republican Ronald Reagan's presidency, May 10 that of Socialist François Mitterrand of France. The two enjoyed a close relationship, which shows that ideology counts for less when political rivalry is not an issue. 1981 also marks three assassination attempts—on Reagan (March 30), on Pope John Paul II (May 13) and the tragically successful assault on Egyptian President Anwar Sadat for having dared to make peace with Israel (October 6).

Undoubtedly the most portentous event of the year, however, was not recognized as such at the time: the opening on November 30, 1981 of US—Soviet negotiations for a treaty to eliminate intermediate-range missiles (INF). Many will recall the pacifist protests in England and West Germany when the cruise missiles were deployed to upgrade the Western arsenal in the face of a formidable array of similar weapons in Eastern Europe. Despite or because of this Western deployment—we'll leave that gnawbone to the pundits—the climate was already changing, thanks in large measure to CSCE and the Helsinki Final Act. When the Treaty had been signed six years later, on December 8, 1987, a prominent Soviet spin-doctor, Vladimir Baranowsky, was to write:

> It may prove a turning point in Soviet-American relations and East-West relations in general, and in a broader sense, in the evolution of world politics as a whole. The treaty not only signals the end of a complicated and highly tense state of international political development . . . What is also important is that the world has gained its first practical experience in implementing a fundamentally new approach to security whereby political means prevail not military ones, and joint actions in the search for solutions to security problems enjoy unconditional priority over unilateral ones. [13]

"Unconditional" or not (the US President who signed INF for Europe's defense policy was also quietly developing SDI—"Star Wars"—for American defense), Baranowsky is correct in pointing out that disarmament negotiations were moving from limitation to reduction, from unilateral albeit collective security to a multilateral approach. The INF Treaty would open the way to actual troop withdrawals.

Negotiating Europe without the Europeans

As the two teams of delegates shook hands over the long polished table in Geneva and clicked open their briefcases on the morning of November 30, 1981, the world moved to a post-containment concept of security. The process of *décrispation* started by Willi Brandt's *Ostpolitik* and the Helsinki process moved forward another notch. Four years before Mikhail Gorbachev burst upon the international scene there began to emerge a structure of common security, whereby both East and West took account of each other's security needs in formulating security policy.[14] This move from build-up to build-down certainly enhanced the security of Europe and facilitated the 1989 breakaway of Eastern Europe from Soviet and Communist domination. However, it must also be noted that, while these negotiations were taking place in Europe and about Europe (being the only theater where intermediate-range nuclear weapons were deployed, with the possible exception of the Sino-Soviet border which was not under discussion), the European powers and Western European Union were notable for their absence from the negotiating table. Economically Europe was taking charge of her destiny; militarily and therefore politically she still had a long road ahead.

On December 2, 1981, Spain continued its political rehabilitation after the Franco era by applying for membership of NATO. However, it did so under arrangements similar to those in force for France, joining the political activity without integrating any of its forces into the military command structure. The Spanish Prime Minister gave this undertaking in order to achieve a majority in a national referendum on the issue. However, it should be noted that arrangements continued with the United States with respect to the use of certain military bases by American air and naval forces, a fact not overlooked in the 1990 Gulf War build-up. Spain became the 16th member of the Atlantic Alliance on May 30, 1982.

Solidarity setback

1981 closed with an important development in Eastern Europe. On December 13 General Jaruzelski declared martial law in Poland in order to suppress the activities of the Solidarity union led by Lech Walesa and to stave off threatened military intervention from the Soviet Union. History will judge the enigmatic figure of Jaruzelski, seen by some as a Communist autocrat, by others as a Polish patriot who managed to avoid overt Soviet interference by walking a fine line of limited independence.

Lion's tail's last flick?

The Spring of 1982 was marked by an anachronistic colonial war in the South Atlantic between Argentina and the United Kingdom. On April 2 the governing Junta in Buenos Aires invaded the Falkland Islands which, with South Georgia, constitute a British colony claimed by Argentina as the Islas Malvinas (named after the sailors from Saint-Malo who discovered them). The conflict ended with a British victory and ceasefire on May 14. European opinion generally favored the British position, although there were divisions in Italy owing to that country's strong ties to Argentina through emigration. After the conflict and its 900 deaths British Prime Minister Margaret Thatcher received a rousing welcome in Stanley, there being no doubt about the 1800 Falkland citizens' attachment to their British status. Some good did come of the loss of life: in Buenos Aires the Junta resigned and democracy returned to Argentina.

Europe was going through a quiet period. On February 23 Greenland's small population of some 45,000 people of Inuit extraction voted by a 52% majority to withdraw from the European Community. This was possible because Greenland is a self-governing region of Denmark. Greenlanders have managed to preserve their language and a variety of distinctive customs. They have a remarkable culture, as may be seen in their colorful national costumes and wood-and bone-carving skills. It was from Greenland that Leif Ericsson discovered the North American continent in the year 1000, but Greenland's Icelandic Viking settlements died out mysteriously many centuries ago.

Greenland has substantial trade with North America as well as Europe. With such a specialized economy, based largely on fishing and tourism, the Greenlanders felt they had only marginal involvement in EC affairs. Following their withdrawal they negotiated a fishing agreement with the Community. (For comparable reasons, when the United Kingdom joined the Community, the self-governing Channel Islands and the Isle of Man had voted to remain outside).

May was marked by further tension between Margaret Thatcher and her Community colleagues over agricultural policy. On May 19 the annual fixing of prices under the Common Agricultural Policy took place over British objections. Mrs Thatcher's discontent was assuaged a week later, on May 24, in a barely concealed *quid-pro-quo* when the United Kingdom contribution to the EC budget was once more reduced. However, the Ten spoke with a single voice on June 22 when they vigorously denounced United States' trade policy and protectionist measures.

The end of 1982 saw two important changes of political leadership. After an impressive win by the Spanish Socialist party in national elections, Felipe Gonzalez became Prime Minister of Spain. Young, handsome, forward-looking he was greeted as the symbol of a new era. One of his first acts, a gesture of European reconciliation, was to open the frontier with Gibraltar, closed since 1969, to pedestrians on December 15. Despite many difficulties, including terrorism from both the right-wing Falangist old guard and Basque separatists, Gonzalez has largely fulfilled his promise. Spanish democracy has been consolidated, regional culture (including the Catalan language in the northeast) recognized and economic infrastructure, particularly the road system, strengthened. A decade later Gonzalez had earned recognition for his country: 1992 was the year of Spain for Europe, with Olympic Games in Barcelona, a world exhibition in Seville, the Ibero-American summit and the Columbus quincentennial. Even the *Tour de France* started in Spain!

In the Soviet Union the death of Leonid Brezhnev on November 10 provided the initial opening for systemic evolution. Despite his secret police background Yuri Andropov showed signs of understanding that changes were necessary, but, dying fifteen months later, had no chance to initiate significant reform.

Ocean Blue

1983 opened with a significant achievement: agreement on a fisheries policy for the Community, commonly known as Blue Europe. The importance of fisheries, a subsidiary but significant aspect of agriculture, to the Community increased with the accession of Denmark, Ireland and the United Kingdom. New issues arose when Greece joined the Community, but these were fairly

limited because Greek fishermen ply their trade only within the Mediterranean. In 1983 both Portugal and Spain were EC applicants; it was therefore
important to the Commission to reach a Community position before negotiations with the Iberian countries were complete. Thus Portugal and Spain were
constrained to accept the policy in principle, although transitional arrangements were agreed.

In fact, the new members have most of the fishing grounds within the 200-
mile limit which is now the accepted world standard even though Chili was
criticized for inaugurating it. The policy covers both fishing quotas and methods, imposed for reasons of stock conservation, and regulates trade between
states. The United Kingdom, for instance, came under political pressure to
resist the unrestricted landing of catches by foreign trawlers, particularly in
Scotland. The election of Scottish Nationalist Winifred Ewing to the European Parliament did not go unnoticed. One recalls the "Cold War" of 1975-76
between Iceland and Britain, caused precisely by Iceland's extension of fishing
limits (and which Iceland won by using gunboats to cut trawl nets) as a
reminder how sensitive this sector of the economy can be. While this particular dispute was crucial to Iceland's economy, fisherman everywhere risk their
lives daily in this ancient profession and are a proud and independent breed
who often feel unappreciated.

Why was a fisheries policy necessary in the first place? Immediately after
World War II European fishing enjoyed a golden age because, since activity
had been largely abandoned during the conflict, fish stocks were abundant.
The war had also caused the public to accept fish as an important source of
food.

As in the case of agriculture, the Treaty of Rome of 1957 set out only the
framework of a common policy. It took until 1970 to spell out three components. The principle of free access to Community fishing grounds for all member countries was asserted, thereby respecting the Treaty principle of non-discrimination against Community citizens. Secondly, a common market in fish
was established, including price support mechanisms and measures to protect
the EEC market. The purpose of this action was to guarantee a fair standard
of living for members of the industry, to stabilize markets and to guarantee
supplies to consumers at reasonable prices. Finally, the policy sought to modernize infrastructure and to provide equal terms of competition by coordinating national structural policies, using financial intervention as necessary.

Fundamental changes in the industry necessitated an updating of this policy
in 1983. The first of these changes was the introduction of the 200-nautical
mile (370 km) exclusive fishing zone by Atlantic countries such as Iceland,
Norway and Canada. These limits were later endorsed by a new Convention
on the Law of the Sea. The action was significant because most commercial
fish species inhabit the continental shelf. The Community negotiated on
behalf of its members both to strengthen their hand and to ensure impartiality.

The extension of fishing limits had an economic and scientific basis: regres-
sion of fish stocks had been observed due to overfishing by foreign trawlers in

European waters and to technical progress in methods. Certain problems were endemic to the industry itself: variety of fish, fluctuation in catches, a perishable product, competition from imports and the constraints of biological conservation essential to management of a renewable resource. These problems became more acute in 1986 when the accession of Portugal and Spain doubled the number of fisherman, increasing fishing fleet tonnage by 65% and total catches by 30%. These figures also show that Iberian entry exacerbated problems of productivity (lower among the new members) and equal competition.

The revised policy, which cost only half of one per cent of the Community budget, addressed access and the conservation and management of stocks, market organization, structural changes and international relations.

With respect to access and management, the Community zone was set at 200 nautical miles from Atlantic and North Sea coasts, but member countries were allowed to reserve limits up to twelve miles for their own fleets and for boats with traditional rights. Fishing for potentially endangered species north of the United Kingdom was made subject to a Community licence system. Atlantic fish stocks were to be conserved by setting total allowable catches (TAC's). Other measures, such as minimum net guage (protecting small fish) and obligatory logbooks, could be applied by a member country or the European Commission on a non-discriminatory basis.

Organization of the market was introduced in 1970 and revised in 1981. It included marketing standards of quality, size and packing, common rules and guide prices for the main species. Under certain conditions fishermen are compensated by the EAGGF for withdrawn catches. Conversion and storage subsidies can be paid to avoid catch destruction. Exports can be promoted by export refunds which compensate for the difference between Community and world prices, although such practices are closely monitored by GATT.

As with other economic sectors, such as farming and steel production, a structural change policy promotes permanent change where required, including reduction of fishing capacity, construction and modernization of boats and development of new fishing grounds. Through the European Social Fund fishermen may be assisted to qualify for alternative employment.

In Spring 1992, as the tenth anniversary of Blue Europe approached, Manuel Marin, the competent EC Commission vice-president, warned member states that Community waters were being dangerously overfished, especially in the North Sea and to the west of Scotland. Meeting in Luxembourg in April the ministerial Council decided to undertake a thorough reform of fishing policy.

On paper, the TAC system is ideal but many fishermen exceed their allowance and member governments often fail to enforce the rules. The Commission proposes introducing a licensing system for each boat and fleet reduction inducements. The pillar of the reform will be stricter monitoring (including surveillance by satellite) and penalties. Policing of the scheme will still lie with national authorities but the Commission insists on oversight privileges. To this big stick the Commission suggests adding the carrot of Community funding to promote economic restructuring in regions heavily dependent on fishing. Given the tripwires and pitfalls of Green Europe—the Common Agricultural Policy—the ministers deserve credit for undertaking to tackle the problems of Blue Europe.

With respect to third-country relations, the Commission negotiates fishing agreements and conservation management in international waters with non-member countries. Agreements have been signed with Norway, Sweden and the Faeroes (a semi-autonomous part of Denmark, like Greenland outside the EC); Canada and the US; and a number of African countries. The latter exchange fishing rights for development assistance. We have noted that an agreement with Greenland followed its withdrawal from the Community in 1985.

As for multilateral relations, the Community respects the Law of the Sea Convention and other conventions. It participates in a number of bodies set up to manage marine resources.

Star Wars: effective defense or *pi* in the sky?

On March 23, 1983, President Reagan announced a new policy for military research, labelled Strategic Defense Initiative (SDI). The concept was to deter nuclear attack from the Soviet Union by building a new line of defense in space against missile attack, based on laser technology and anti-missile missiles. The policy was criticized by the Democrats on several grounds: unreliability, cost and the risk of producing not greater but less stability in the "balance of terror". It was also noted that the policy could undermine the strategic arms reduction talks, in progress at Geneva since June 30, 1982. In Europe, various opinions were voiced. "Star Wars", as the policy was dubbed after the film of the same name, was seen by some as a unilateral initiative increasing the possibility of a pre-emptive strike by the Soviet Union, which could drag Europe into a global conflict. SDI addressed intercontinental missile defense between the US and the USSR, Europe being too close to the frontline to have the time to react effectively. The relative success of anti-missile Patriots against Iraqi Scuds have since caused some revision of this view. The urgency of SDI has declined in recent years and the Bush administration gave it a lower profile than Reagan's. With the break-up of the Soviet Union, once the question of "whose finger on the button?" has been resolved, SDI may be phased out all together. (At their 1992 Washington summit Bush and Yeltsin proposed a multilateral approach). The main concern in Europe at the time was that SDI testing should not undermine the SALT treaties; and that the transition to "common security" launched through the Helsinki process and INF progress unimpeded.

Political declarations on European union from the EC summit in Stuttgart (June 19) and the European Parliament (September) proved premature but helped prepare opinion for the Single European Act of 1986.

Turkey and Europe

1983 closed with the formation of a civilian government in Turkey after years of military rule, following parliamentary elections under a new constitution. Although a member of the Council of Europe since 1949, Turkey's relations with the movement for European unification have been delicate for a number of reasons. Geo-politically, the country is important to the West as an anchor of NATO's southern flank, as a bridge to the Middle East and, more recently, as a link to the Turcic ex-USSR republics. On the other hand, only a small western portion of Turkey actually lies in Europe. Since the reforms of Attaturk in the thirties Turkey has been officially a lay country (the eastern equivalent of separation of church and state) but remains 98% Islamic in faith. (The vibrant Jewish Ladino minority in Istanbul is the exception which proves the rule). The traditional hostility between Greece and Turkey, exacerbated by the occupation of Northern Cyprus by Turkish forces and establishment in the seventies of a Turkish Republic of Northern Cyprus, recognized only by Turkey, has also inhibited harmonious relations between Turkey and Europe. In the Consultative Assembly of the Council of Europe, mindful that an undemocratic Greek regime was at one point expelled from the organization, there have been frequent expressions of unease at the "undemocratic" character of Turkish government and its ruthless suppression of Armenian and Kurdish dissent. After the restoration of her own democracy, Greece not only rejoined the Council of Europe but also became the tenth member of the European Community. Now Turkey's entry into the Community is subject to Greek veto. This is unlikely to be lifted until the Cyprus problem, issues of territorial waters and free passage in the Aegean Sea and the status of the Kurdish minority have been settled. The Turkish retort that there is also unspoken reluctance in some quarters to accept an Islamic culture with only a geographic toehold in Europe into the Community's Judeo-Christian "western" culture may also have some validity.

"1984"

The totalitarian nightmare predicted by George Orwell's allegorical novel ("some are more equal than others") did not come to pass in regions protected by the policy of containment. In fact there was a trend for the better in the Soviet Union itself, fostered by frequent changes in the leadership. On February 9, 1984, President Yuri Andropov died after barely more than a year in office. His successor, Konstantin Chernenko would fare no better.

On April 18, at the Geneva Conference on Disarmament, a multilateral meeting which had been going on for years under UN auspices, Vice-President George Bush presented a US draft treaty banning the development, production, stock-piling and use of chemical weapons (an extension of earlier agreements forbidding their use). The proposal included on-site inspection to ensure compliance.

Western European Union, so often overshadowed by NATO, came back into its own in June, when the ministerial council abolished limits imposed upon the Federal Republic of Germany for the production of conventional weapons. Western governments had been trying to square the circle of German rearmament for years. Many structures had been imposed on the former enemy, as was also the case with Japan. (This would come to the fore during the Persian Gulf conflict of 1990-91, when both countries declared themselves constitutionally prevented from sending combat forces abroad and a year later with respect to Yugoslavia). As a mark of growing confidence in German democracy, but not least out of economic need, the governments of WEU now gave the Federal Republic full-partner status in the military aspects of WEU in addition to the political role it had enjoyed for many years.

Four months later WEU again made the headlines with its Rome Declaration setting out political aims and institutional reform, discussed in Part III, Chapter 4.

EC Research

The early months of 1984 were marked by developments in one of the less well-known sectors of Community cooperation, scientific research. On February 28 a research program in information technology (ESPRIT) was adopted by the ministerial council. On April 9 EURATOM launched a controlled nuclear fusion known as JET at its research institute at Culham, near Oxford, a modest yet significant development in the search for a cheap and plentiful source of fuel. (EURATOM has no provision for or interest in the military applications of nuclear research). Further progress in scientific cooperation was to be made the following year.

The second European elections were held on June 14 and 17, 1984 (MEP's serve five-year terms). Conservative parties enjoyed relative success and Pierre Pflimlin of France was elected President of the European Parliament at the opening of the new term on July 24. Monsieur Pflimlin, who, as his name suggests, is of Alsatian origin, is a right-of-center moderate Catholic. He has enjoyed a remarkable political career, having served as Mayor of Strasbourg, where the assemblies of the Council of Europe and the EC have their home, several ministerial posts, Prime Minister of France just prior to De Gaulle's return in 1958, President of the Parliamentary Assembly of the Council of Europe and finally President of the European Parliament.

In world affairs, the United Kingdom divested herself of another remnant of empire by reaching agreement with the PRC on the return of Hong Kong and the New Territories to China in 1987. Welcomed in Europe and the US as a piece of *Realpolitik* which fostered better relations with the PRC, the accord got a mixed reception in the UK and Hong Kong itself, where many thought the colony's citizens should have been granted the right of abode in Britain. President Ronald Reagan was elected to a second term on November 6. The year closed with the signing of another cooperation agreement between the Community and ACP countries (Lomé III) in Togo on December 8.

New star in the east

On March 11, 1985, Soviet Communist Party General Secretary Konstantin Chernenko died in Moscow, the third national leader to expire in two years, opening the way for the rise to power of a little-known Russian, Mikhail Gorbachev.

Until its break-up, the Soviet Union was the largest country in the world — over 230 million citizens spread through eight time zones and two continents. There were fifteen republics and many autonomous regions, of which Boris Yeltsin's Russian Republic (still the biggest country) is greater in surface area than all the other ex-Soviet republics combined and is home to some seventy per cent of the population.

No assessment of Eastern Europe, from Poland south to Bulgaria, is possible without taking into account the free debate and new economic approaches — glasnost and perestroika — fostered by leaders like Mikhail Gorbachev and Eduard Shevardnadze. Few people anticipated — certainly not Gorbachev himself — that these policies would lead to the dissolution of the Soviet Union.

Human rights again

The Council of Europe was overshadowed by the advent of the ECSC and, even more so, after 1958, by the EEC. Closer to conventional diplomacy, dependent largely on consensus, the Council of Europe also presents a more disparate image, with broader membership and a field of competence covering everything except defense. Its activities are rarely headline-grabbing spectaculars. They nevertheless provide many of the nuts and bolts of integration and, not least important, foster a community of values which respects cultural diversity. It is therefore worthy of note that on March 19, 1985, the eighth protocol to the European Convention on Human Rights was signed in Vienna, extending even further the basic rights and fundamental freedoms guaranteed to any resident — not just citizens — of the participating countries. The Council of Europe now has over 150 international conventions to its credit, all ratified by national parliaments, which, taken together, constitute a considerable measure of social and legal integration.

Eureka! (Research II)

April 1985 saw a major extension of European cooperation among the Nine. Since 1958 the EURATOM Treaty, least known of the European *troika*, has provided a major basis for Community research in the peaceful uses of atomic energy. Now President Mitterrand proposed new fields for technology development under the ingenious name of EUREKA which, apart from suggesting "Europe" also means "I have found it" in Greek.

France's initiative elicited an immediate response from her partners. There was a little negotiation over the actual list of projects, followed by approval in principle at the Milan summit in June. A feature of this proposal is that it is not limited to EC member countries. In November, at Hannover in the Federal Republic, eighteen participating countries adopted the EUREKA "charter" and ten projects.

Presenting its program of work for 1991 to the European Parliament, the EC Commission emphasized the importance of research and technology in the building of Europe:

> The Community will be there where it's all happening, in the free market, where the industrial fate of Europe is decided—by big industry but also by small business—from microelectronics to biotechnology, satellite telecommunications . . . and high-definition television. Links with the EUREKA initiative will be strengthened . . . Attention will be focused on the following: the contribution made by research and technology to the other policies such as the environment, agriculture or development aid, for example the use of space data; taking account of the needs of society, for example the application of information and telecommunications technology to the elderly or disabled; basic research in high-performance computing [15] and the development of environmental models.

Single European Act

1985 closed with a major step forward in European cooperation. By signing the Single European Act (SEA) the nine EC governments were moved by the "will to continue and strengthen the unification process undertaken on the basis of the Treaties establishing the European Communities" and "to transform relations as a whole among their states into a European Union, in accordance with the Solemn Declaration of Stuttgart of 19 June 1983". They accordingly added a fourth treaty to Community constitutional structures, updating and extending the other three. The Single European Act (SEA)—a singular name indeed!—strengthened the treaties, restored qualified majority voting and established formal political cooperation by incorporating the meetings of heads of state and government, the European Council, into the Community structure.[16] One of the least noticed yet interesting provisions of the SEA is the extension of the European legal system. At a date to be agreed courts of first instance will be set up to deal with routine cases of Community law. The European Court of Justice in Luxembourg, first created under ECSC but with its docket now overburdened with cases from all three treaty sectors, thereby assumes the functions of an appeals court.

The SEA was ratified by all twelve countries in February 1986 and entered into force on July 1, 1987. In providing for the elimination of all obstacles to a single market by December 31, 1992, the Single European Act captured American imaginations more than any Community initiative since the signing of the Rome treaties in 1958, being perceived as both an achievement and an economic threat. As we have seen, however, European union concerns much more than trade, and more nations than those twelve who are currently members of the European Community.

Notes

1 The Principality of Andorra is located in the Pyrenees mountains between France and Spain. Its official languages are Catalan and French. Founded in 1278, it has maintained its independence and its neutrality through allegiance to two coprinces, the Bishop of Urgel in Spain and the French head of state, whether king, emperor or president. Thus by a quirk of history the Socialist François Mitterrand is a prince of another country! Today fewer than 20% of Andorra's 50,000 inhabitants are Andorran citizens. As the EEC eliminates its border controls, the tiny, rich, tax-free haven of Andorra is being pressed to conform. (This is a problem for other micro-states also: Monaco, Liechtenstein, San Marino). In 1990 President Mitterrand and Bishop Juan Marti Alanis issued the country's first penal code. Divorce, abortion, and trade unions are still banned. If Andorra is not represented in the CSCE it is because it still has no diplomatic representation independent of France and Spain. On April 7, 1992, in a national election, Andorrans voted to change the constitution and end feudal rule so that the country might join international organizations.

2 The Portuguese application, not officialized until March 28, 1977, had to await Spain's before receiving serious consideration.

3 The dates of entry into force were as follows:

	EEC	ECSC
Austria	01.01.1973	01.01.1974
Finland	01.01.1974	01.01.1975
Iceland	04.01.1973	01.01.1974
Norway	07.01.1973	01.01.1975
Portugal	01.01.1973	01.01.1974
Sweden	01.01.1973	01.01.1974
Switzerland	01.01.1973	01.01.1974

For 1974 ECSC Agreements, tariff cuts began 04.01.1973. The Austrian EEC FTA replaced an Interim Agreement in force since 01.10.1972. Dates listed American style (month, day, year).

4 To the credit of EFTA it should be noted that nationals of the three former members retained their posts within the Secretariat in Geneva.

5 *A Common Agricultural Policy for the 1990's*, Office for Official Publications of the European Communities, fifth edition, Luxembourg, 1989, p. 14.

6 The attempt was not successful: eventually the Social Democrats themselves split, half joining with the Liberals to form the Liberal and Social Democratic Party (today called Liberal Democrat). Nevertheless, under Neil Kinnock, Labour renounced its left-wing doctrinaires and became more "pro-Europe" than Margaret Thatcher.
   Proponents of European union drawn from across the political spectrum must of course combine their talents and conciliate their viewpoints in the Brussels administration. Each government tends to nominate commissioners of its own political persuasion. Thus the current President of the Commission is the highly respected French Socialist Party member and former finance minister Jacques Delors. A few doors down the corridor on the 13th floor of the EC headquarters on Rue de la Loi is the office of UK Conservative Party member, former home secretary (interior minister) and minister for trade and industry, Sir Leon Brittan. Sir Leon is the commissioner responsible for free market competitiveness, strongly opposed

to turning the EC into Fortress Europe. He has charged many top firms, including Renault, Alfa Romeo, Air France and Britain's Imperial Chemical Industries with violating the EC rules on monopolies. He has threatened to take ten governments to the European Court if they do not end their state gas and electricity monopolies. For such action Sir Leon needs Commission support whatever the political color of the commissioners. He has conciliated the need for regulations (and therefore bureaucracy) with the free market ethic.

7   With the notable exception of the Soviet assimilation of the Baltic states in 1940.

8   It is ironical that this Paris meeting, not originally scheduled in the carefully managed CSCE plan, was added to the list of CSCE events to discuss German reunification. Such was the pace of events that by the time the conference opened a reunified Germany (a full member of NATO) was present in a dominant peacemaking role.

9   Today there are thirteen full members and two associated states. See Part III, Chapter 10 and map.

10 The official determination was 0.88867088 gram of fine gold for one US dollar.

11 The respective weight of each currency in the ECU is based on its economic strength, as measured by GDP, share of EC external trade and its quotas under Community short-term monetary support arrangements.
    Current percentage shares are as follows: B-7.6, DK-2.45, D-30.1, GR-0.8, EIR-1.1, E-5.3, F-19.0, I-11.0, L-0.3, NL-9.4, P-0.8, UK-13.0. The EC Commission calculates the rate of the ECU daily, using the individual exchange rates recorded at 2:30 PM. The rates thus obtained are published in the Official Journal and used in EC transactions. This official rate may vary slightly from ECU quotations on national foreign exchange markets. For further discussion see Part II, Chapter 10 and Part IV, Chapter 3.

12 For this reason France used a single-ballot proportional procedure, based on national lists, instead of its usual two-round constituency-based method. France and Germany employed a 5% hurdle to combat fragmentation into splinter groups. In general, national systems were retained, with the UK using the "first-past-the-post" single-member constituency procedure (except in Northern Ireland, where the list procedure guaranteed proportional representation of the Catholic minority). Not a single Liberal was successful in the UK but a Scottish Nationalist, Mrs Winifred Ewing was elected. Anti-Market candidates did poorly everywhere except Denmark, where 5 were elected.

13 Baranowsky, Vladimir, "The Treaty on the Elimination of Intermediate-Range and Shorter-Range Missiles", in Institute of World Economy and International Relations, USSR Academy of Sciences, *Disarmament and Security: 1987 Yearbook*, Moscow, Novosti, 1988, p. 58.

14 For a detailed analysis of this change see Lucas, Michael R., *The Western Alliance after INF: Redefining US policy towards Europe and the Soviet Union*, Lynne Rienner Publishers, Boulder and London, 1990, p. 3 *et seq.*. The topic is developed further in our historical narrative at the point where the treaty is signed (1987).

15 In March, 1991, Japan proposed joint development of high-speed computers as the need for transnational cooperation in "hitech" reached a new, intercontinental level.

16 The Single European Act (SEA) includes provisions amending the existing treaties and others which are added to them, in particular European political cooperation for which the SEA itself provides the constitutional basis.
    Title I establishes the European Council of Heads of State or Government as a permanent body and provides that they shall meet at least twice a year.
    Title II concerns amendments to the existing Treaties and is accordingly divided into three chapters. The section on the ECSC extends the legal functions of the Treaty by allowing for the setting up, at some future date, of a court of first instance, subject to a right of appeal to the existing Court of Justice on points of law. Actions brought by member states

and Community institutions would continue to be heard by the Court of Justice. This provision recognizes both the heaviness of the caseload of the Court and its success in establishing Community jurisprudence. Chapter II of Title II deals with provisions amending the EEC Treaty. It first raises the role of the European Parliament from "consultation" to "cooperation" in certain fields of competence. The Parliament's impact on the decision-making process is modestly strengthened. A lower court to supplement the Court of Justice is envisioned, as for the EEC Treaty. In its second section, the Chapter amending the EEC Treaty sets December 31, 1992, as the deadline for establishing the internal market "without internal frontiers in which the free movement of goods, persons, services and capital is ensured". The second section also makes provisions on the harmonization of laws, in particular tax law, and on voting in the ministerial Council by qualified majority. There are also subsections on monetary capacity (preparation of institutional changes, based on EMS and ECU experience—in other words, movement toward a single currency), on social policy (health and safety of workers) and on economic and social cohesion (funds for redressing regional imbalances through regional development). A complete subsection is devoted to institution of Community action to "preserve, protect, and improve the quality of the environment, ... to protect human health, ... to ensure a prudent and rational utilization of natural resources".

A short chapter of Title II is devoted to amending the EURATOM Treaty. This again provides for future creation of a court of first instance. This fourth Chapter allows for majority decisions (instead of unanimity) on the Community's system of raising its own resources.

Title III of the Act concerns cooperation with respect to foreign policy, an important new dimension of Community activity. There is specific reference to "consistency", to "common positions", and to extending such joint policy making to "European security". This is the first hint of the EC possibly impinging upon the prerogatives of WEU and NATO, developed further at Maastricht in 1991. The presidency of European Political Cooperation is to be held by the country presiding (for a six-month term) over the EC Council. This explains the prominent role of Luxembourg during political action over the Gulf crisis of 1990-91.

Communities II (1986-1988)

On January 1, 1986, both of Western Europe's trading blocs increased their membership.

Finland became a full member of the European Free Trade Association. Thanks in large measure to a balanced foreign policy and to Mikhail Gorbachev's conciliatory stance, Finland was finally free to abandon the transparent fiction of associate status and to move from under the geopolitical shadow cast by her huge southern neighbor ever since the Soviet Union forced the frontier north of Lake Lagoda in 1940.[1]

Ten to twelve: the Iberian connection

On the same day as Finland joined EFTA, Portugal and Spain became members of the European Community, thereby doubling the original membership of six.

Despite its Latin and African ethnicity, Portugal is more of an Atlantic nation than a Mediterranean one. Nevertheless, her EC accession influenced the geopolitical balance of the Community, as did that of Spain, by strengthening the southern, Latin tier.

A few statistics will provide a profile of the new members. With 504,800 square kilometers Spain is a large country by European standards, stretching from the Atlantic to the Mediterranean, from the Pyrenees to Africa (enclaves of Ceuta, Melilla and off-shore islands), together with the Balearic Islands and the West African Canaries.[2] The population of 39 million represents a density of slightly over 75 to the square kilometer. Some 18% are employed in agriculture (much higher than existing EC members), 34% in industry.

Writing in KPMG Peat Marwick's special EC edition of World in 1989, three years after Spain's entry, Manuel Fraga Iribarne, president of the right-wing Popular Party (significantly, not a partner in the government) made this positive assessment:

> Spain's entry into the EC has produced dramatic results for our country. With approximately 5 percent annual growth rate for the past three years, the Spanish economy is one of the fastest growing in the world. Foreign investment, primarily represented in the financial services and construction-related industries, has also increased dramatically, totaling $5.2 billion for 1988. And it's expected that 1992 will bring even greater potential for growth.
>
> While Spain is not the richest country in the EC, neither is it the poorest. We are in an excellent position to take advantage of the single-market opportunities with our young and plentiful labor force, though these young people will require technical training to compete with the rest of the world.

Apart from giving added importance to agriculture and Mediterranean issues, Spain's entry into EEC provided an important channel for strengthening relations with Islamic North Africa (Morocco, Algeria, Tunisia, Libya and Mauretania), commonly known as the Maghreb. France has strong ties in this region also, but they are rendered more delicate by the legacy of the Algerian war of independence. Spain is motivated to strengthen relations because she feels vulnerable on account of her North African enclaves, because of historical ties and because of the pressure of Arab immigration from the south, which is switching from France to Spain. 1492 is not known to Spaniards only for Columbus' voyage to the Americas. This is also the date both Arabs and Jews were driven from Spain after eight centuries of relatively harmonious cohabitation. (On March 30, 1992, 500th anniversary of the Jewish expulsion, King Juan Carlos made a gracious and historic apology by repealing the ordinance). Today, Spaniards continue to look south as well as west and north. Spain is thriving inside the Community; she is also making a unique contribution to Europe's role on the Mediterranean's southern rim.

Just as the US works to raise living standards in Mexico in order to relieve legal and illegal immigration pressure across the Rio Grande, Spain tries to develop the nations across the Straits of Gibraltar. In a policy of enlightened self-interest she has taken the lead in mobilizing Community aid to North Africa. As a first step, Italy, Portugal and France have joined Spain in a "4 plus 5" regional forum with the five countries of the Arab Maghreb Union, a nascent North African common market. Furthermore, Spain's commercial interests in North Africa are growing. Morocco is Spain's second-largest trading partner (after France) and the state oil company, Repsal, is exploring for gas in Algeria.

The Gulf War gave Spain the chance to broker the split between the Maghreb countries and Western Europe. France sent troops; Italy sent ships; Spain only allowed US B1 planes to use an airfield as a stopover point. The measured response sought to conciliate ties to north, south and west, while respecting Security Council resolutions. This policy paid off when Madrid was chosen as the site of the first Arab-Israeli negotiations in 1991.

Portugal is less developed, more rural, even more agricultural. With an area of 92.1 million sq. km. including Madeira and the Azores, both Portuguese provinces (not to be confused with former colonies in Africa and the South China Sea), the country has a population of just over ten million people, representing a density of 104 to the sq. km., a third higher than Spain's. Over a quarter of the Portuguese are employed in agriculture, which, with the possible exception of Greece, gives the country the highest percentage in the Community. It can thus be understood that each accession to the EC alters the balance of political and economic concerns. The redistribution of weighted votes also dilutes the clout of the four major member countries.

The first day of 1986 was also an important milestone for another European organization. In Western European Union new agencies were established for arms control and disarmament.

The Chunnel

On January 20, 1986, meeting in Lille, France and the United Kingdom, countries which General de Gaulle once described to the British Ambassador as always at war unless united against a common enemy, decided to build a tunnel under the Channel. This new project follows many attempts, the latest of which was cancelled by Britain in the seventies' recession for reasons of cost. Accordingly, it was now agreed that the project would be financed entirely by the private sector. There are two rail tunnels, one for each direction, linked to a smaller, central service and safety tunnel. The Channel Tunnel, known as the "Chunnel", gives a great boost to the economies of northern France and Belgium, already one of the most densely populated and intensively industrial regions of Europe. More importantly, perhaps, it breaks down British insularity as the new blue TGV slides into London and even more "Brits" head for holiday spots "on the Continent". Let's hope that the French will have the delicacy not to name one of their sleek high-speed locomotives William the Conqueror! For North American exports depressed European entry points like Liverpool and Manchester will save shipping costs and at the same time permit the British north-west to experience economic revival.

On March 20, having won parliamentary elections, Jacques Chirac, leader of the neo-Gaullist right-wing RPR party, became Prime Minister of France under Socialist President Mitterrand in the first cross-party cohabitation of the Fifth Republic.

By far the most important European events of this late winter season, however, took place in national parliaments, with the ratification on February 17 (nine countries) and February 28 (three countries) of the Single European Act. The urgency of the environmental provisions of that Act seemed to be confirmed two months later when the nuclear meltdown at Chernobyl in the Ukraine provided a lesson for the world, even as certain self-satisfied voices proclaimed that "such a disaster could not happen in our country".

Reykjavik's hot springs give Europe the shivers

A jolt of another type was provided in the fall of 1986 by the hastily-prepared Reagan-Gorbachev summit in Reykjavik, Iceland. When General Secretary Gorbachev proposed sweeping nuclear disarmament the West was caught unawares. The Europeans suspected that a deal was being made over their heads. Even though Ronald Reagan demurred, they feared a unilateral withdrawal of US nuclear protection from Europe; and they discovered overnight that it was easier to advocate disarmament than to implement it. The change from build-up to build-down, albeit fostered by "the spirit of Helsinki", implied a vulnerable inertia at the U-turn. The third CSCE follow-up conference, held in Vienna, provided some consolation, but Europeans started thinking once again about the need for a degree of European defense autonomy as a post-NATO insurance policy.

Murmurs of US budget deficits and the consequent cuts in defense expenditure thereby implied remain muted to the end of the Reagan presidency but swell rapidly under his successor. Reykjavik is a half-success in the sense that it highlights the danger of cracks in Western solidarity and points once more to the necessity of a common approach to security issues: nobody wants to sing in the rain without a nuclear umbrella. All of this of course is a tonic for the heretofore moribund Western European Union.

The Reykjavik summit was ill-prepared because it was hastily convened. Both major players seemed in need of a diplomatic success on the world stage. Spin-doctors and pundits managed to paint a positive picture even as Iceland's thermal springs ran cold. Gorbachev was hailed as a daring innovator who called the West's bluff; Reagan was praised for his prudence and for standing firm. In back rooms, however, experts settled down to the foundation work which should have preceded the conference. As though to show the world that the Icelandic hiatus in US-Soviet relations had not caused permanent damage, the two superpowers moved to resume their MBFR talks in Vienna on January 29. A concerned Europe got into the act: 1987 would be the year of re-linking European and superpower security. The French and the British, of course, were both smug and insistent about their own independent nuclear deterrents.[3]

Kaleidoscopic defense communities: reviewing image and substance

Realisation that confidence-building steps had to precede sweeping reduction in the nuclear umbrella led to direct talks between NATO and the Warsaw Pact (WTO) in neutral Vienna in February, 1987.

WEU claimed a political role in August by coordinating minesweeping operations in the Persian Gulf, made necessary by the Iran-Iraq war. The initiative seemed ridiculously puny, yet constituted the first operational move by the organization. The limited WEU comeback continued in October, when its Ministerial Council adopted a policy statement on European security interests. Despite ritual protestations that the Atlantic Alliance was rock solid, the strengthening of NATO's European pillar sent out slightly ambiguous signals which persist today. WEU was caught in a state of institutional tension between the need to maintain Atlantic solidarity in NATO and a desire for a distinctive European identity. The policy statement, known as the Hague platform, sought to define criteria for European security and WEU responsibilities in western defense, arms control and disarmament.

Writing in the *Frankfurter Allgemeine Zeitung* on April 19, 1991, Günther Gillesen put the European dilemma succinctly:

> The crucial question is always the same: does "Europe" want to pursue defense policy mainly within or beyond the confines of the Atlantic alliance? If the answer is plainly the latter, as in Paris, or partly so, as in Bonn, on France's account, the consequence must surely be that the Americans will be elbowed out of joint consultations and out of Europe. That would mean the end of American participation in the Helsinki process and the end of European disarmament. But if European defense is to stay within NATO, which is Lon-

don's aim in resurrecting the WEU, the very least to which WEU expansion can be expected to lead is duplication of organisation, of command structures, of intended uses and of control over pact forces.

The failure of the European Defence Community in 1954 demonstrably showed that control over its armed forces is the last power a sovereign state is going to cede to a supranational institution.

And France, despite its fine words about Europe, is likely to be even more reluctant to do so than Britain.

Until such time as supranational control is established, European defense policy can only be pursued on a cooperative basis, with integration of military command structure as the most that can be expected . . .

No amount of cooperation between European Community countries, either among the Twelve or among the nine WEU member-states, is going to accomplish more than can be achieved in NATO with the Americans. If the European Community countries are having difficulties with "European defense" or with political union, they are difficulties they are having with each other and not with the United States.

In the four years between the period under discussion and this article, the role of WEU was scarcely clarified. This intractable issue is further discussed in Part III, Chapter 4.

Defense issues were however moving significantly on other fronts. Following assent to the Intermediate-Range Nuclear Forces (reduction) Treaty (INF) by the Warsaw Treaty Organization, Gorbachev and Reagan signed the Treaty eliminating land-based intermediate-range nuclear missiles on December 8, 1987, at their Washington summit. They also agreed on reciprocal measures to monitor nuclear explosions at test sites and pledged deep cuts in strategic arms while seeking a formal agreement in line with the 1972 ABM Treaty.

Rounding out two active years in the rethinking of defense measures set in train by Gorbachev's conciliatory approach (itself triggered in part by economic pressures back home) the December NATO Council meeting in Brussels mirrored WTO action by welcoming INF. As part of this process, Belgium, the Federal Republic of Germany, Italy, Netherlands and the United Kingdom signed bilateral agreements permitting on-site inspection of missile bases.

Although 1987 was characterized by reappraisal of defense policies, it also saw important developments in the European Community. The European Parliament selected Conservative Sir Henry Plumb as its first British president in January. The same month US and Community officials signed an agricultural agreement permitting US corn sales to Spain. This concession temporarily lifted the common external tariffs by which Spain was bound following her entry into the EC and acceptance of the Common Agricultural Policy. It also signalled to the US that Community enlargement did not signify increased protectionism.

Tentative trade tentacles creep east

Like the Council of Europe, NATO and WEU, the Community was also beginning to look east. It would have preferred to negotiate bilateral trade agreements. As a concession to the Soviet Union, however, talks were opened through the Council for Mutual Economic Assistance. The two organizations met in Geneva on March 18, 1987.

The main obstacle to normal trade relations between the Community and Eastern Europe was COMECON's insistence that it deal with the Community on behalf of its members. The Community was prepared to establish a limited working relationship with COMECON but insisted that in parallel there should be trade agreements with any of its members who wanted one.

Contacts between the Community and Eastern Europe had begun in the early 1970s but, at Soviet insistence, these were initially channelled through COMECON. The Community made a first offer in 1974 to conclude a series of trade agreements with the individual countries and repeatedly restated this willingness. Only Romania responded; an agreement was signed in 1980. Limited accords on steel and textiles were signed with a number of other East Bloc countries.

The Community resisted the multilateral approach for several reasons. COMECON was clearly seeking to reinforce its international legitimacy by creating formal links with the EC. More importantly, the Community considered that COMECON did not have the structure or authority to be an equal partner. As discussed earlier, the organization was seen to be politically and economically dominated by the Soviet Union. The degree of economic integration and shared decision-taking within the organization was more limited than that in the Community. As a result, the COMECON administration had no authority to negotiate on trade or other issues on behalf of its members.

By 1986, exports from the EC to COMECON still accounted for a mere 7% of the EC's external trade, the bulk of it with the Soviet Union. After Mikhail Gorbachev came to power, COMECON signalled its readiness to accept the Community's double approach, agreeing to the principle of a framework agreement with the Community but leaving trade matters to be negotiated by its individual members. Thereafter the pace accelerated.

The agreement between the two organizations, signed in Luxembourg on June 25, 1988, took the form of a Joint Declaration under which formal relations between the two where established. The two sides undertook to cooperate in areas where they were competent and where there was a common interest.

This vague framework declaration opened the way for negotiation of the individual trade agreements. These were concluded with the Soviet Union and all the East European countries. The first to sign an agreement was Hungary in September 1988, to be followed by Czechoslovakia (December 1988), Poland (September 1989), the Soviet Union (December 1989) and East Germany and Bulgaria (both May 1990). The initial, limited agreement with Czechoslovakia was updated in May 1990. [4]

The rapid pace of events in Eastern Europe forced the EC to develop additional responses. These so-called first-generation trade agreements were modest instruments with which to meet the challenge of helping the emergence of democracy and market economies. As we have seen, the Council for Mutual

Economic Assistance was dissolved in January 1991, effective April 1, and several former members now enjoy substantial association agreements with the Community.

1988: a year of politico-military redeployment

The European Community continued to take steps towards putting its agricultural house — or should one say garden? — in order. On February 13, responding to constant prodding from Margaret Thatcher who, although a difficult partner, proved a valuable watchdog against financial and bureaucratic excesses, the Brussels European Council summit agreed on revision of Community financing, deciding in particular to set limits on agricultural expenditure. Doubtless lack of progress in lowering world tariffs through GATT's Uruguay Round was also a factor. May was marked by developments on the social front. In the Council of Europe Europe Day (May 5) saw the signature of a protocol to greater Europe's Social Charter. A week later, in Stockholm, Jacques Delors proposed a charter of workers' rights for the Twelve, eventually approved at Maastricht by all except the United Kingdom. In June EC finance ministers adopted a plan for freeing up movements of capital from one member country to another. Since World War II governments had protected their currency, their trade and their balance of payments by imposing financial controls, sometimes of draconian severity.

August brought the stalemate end of the Iran-Iraq war (although Iraq claimed victory). In November San Marino joined the Council of Europe. George Bush (or was it Willie Horton and the image packagers?) defeated Michael Dukakis for the US presidency.

The revival of WEU was further enhanced by the November accession of Portugal and Spain, a natural consequence of their entry into the EC. Military affairs were in the news again when Mikhail Gorbachev electrified Europe on December 7 by announcing unilateral reduction of conventional forces in Europe (and on the Chinese border) to the UN General Assembly. Although pushed by economic pressures at home, the Soviet leader enhanced his reputation for risk-taking and new thinking and placed the ball squarely in the western court. While conserving his diplomatic "cool", George Bush was clearly impressed.

Notes

1   Finland has a population of 4,900,000 and a surface area of 338,000 sq. km. (130,085 sq.mi.). Forest products are very important but the economy is diversified (mining, steel, electronics, plastics, chemicals, textiles, printing, design and shipping are prosperous). The official languages are Finnish and Swedish (the latter an 8% minority enjoying equal status). Finland, a member of the 5-nation Nordic Council and of the Council of Europe, OECD and GATT, has played a crucial role in the establishment of CSCE as a bridging organization between the opposing camps of NATO and WTO. See Jakobson, Max, *Finland: Myth and Reality*, Otava, Helsinki, 1987.

2   Spain claims sovereignty not only to the two enclaves but also to all Morocco's Mediterranean off-shore islands, uninhabited but important for fishing and perhaps, one day, mineral rights.   Morocco resents these historical anomalies just as Spain resents the "occupation" of Gibraltar (4 sq.km.) by its 27,000 mixed-blood awkwardly independent British subjects.

3   The United Kingdom and France have consistently refused to link their modest nuclear deterrents to US-Soviet and US-Russian nuclear disarmament negotiations, at least until the forces of dissuasion reach more equitable proportions.   In Britain the Labour Party was rethinking the policy of unilateral nuclear disarmament which threatened to keep the party out of power for two decades.

4   The present review of EC-CMEA relations is based on *The European Community and its Eastern Neighbours*, EC Office for Official Publications, Luxembourg, 1990, pp. 7, 8.

8

Eastern Horizons:
Return of the Nations (1989-1992)

Under one roof? Gorbachev's "House of Europe" speech

On May 5, 1989, the Council of Europe in Strasbourg celebrated its fortieth anniversary. However, one of the principal events of the anniversary took place two months later, on July 6, when at the conclusion of a state visit to France Mikhail Gorbachev visited the House of Europe in Strasbourg to address the Parliamentary Assembly of the Council of Europe on the theme of the European Home. As her troops began to head east, the Soviet Union was looking to the western horizon for partnership.

The Soviet President began by evoking Europe's triple duty to humanity: a sense of historical responsibility, realization of the acuteness and urgency of problems and awareness of the opportunities offered. He warned against attempts to "overcome socialism": in fact, competition between different social systems was benefical if directed at creating better material and spiritual conditions for all people. The reference to spirituality was a concession to changing times, yet little could he know that the acceleration of history would discredit not only the Soviet Communist Party but the whole Soviet Union only two years later. Socialism would not be overcome: it would disintegrate from within.

Gorbachev did not claim to provide a detailed blueprint for the European home but called rather for a restructuring of the international order in Europe, replacing balance of forces by balance of interests:

If security is the foundation of a common European home, multifarious cooperation is its superstructure.

Gorbachev accepted the Council of Europe's offer of "guest status" in the Assembly but suggested going further: to join some of the international conventions (ecology, culture, education, broadcasting) and envisaged the opening of a general consulate in Strasbourg. He also viewed a "vast economic zone" from the Atlantic to the Urals as "possible though not immediate". Gorbachev ended on a warning note that European integration should preserve rather than destroy cultural diversity:

Theater stages, cinema and television screens, exhibition halls and publishing houses are flooded with commercial pseudo-culture which is alien to Europe. A contempt of national languages begins to be displayed. All this calls for our joint attention and joint efforts in the spirit of respect for all genuine national values.

This involves sharing experience in preserving our cultural heritage, measures to acquaint European peoples with the specific features of each other's modern culture, and collective assistance in language studies. This work may likewise include cooperation in preserving monuments of history and culture, co-production of movies and of television and video films popularizing the achievements of national cultures and the best works of art in the past and present.

The restructuring of Soviet foreign policy, declared President Gorbachev, will have a salutary effect on the whole of the world process. How the world had turned: the Assembly responded with a standing ovation.

Back in Moscow, Gorbachev explained to the Supreme Soviet on August 1 why he had elected to address the Council of Europe assembly. In the words of the official Soviet translation:

I think it is too early fully to appreciate our delegation's visit to Strasbourg. Figuratively speaking, we visited Western Europe in all its present unity. Strasbourg is one of the centres of West European integration in the economic, political, parliamentary, legal, cultural and other spheres. My address to the parliamentary assembly of the Council of Europe began a dialogue at the highest level with a political organization which unites 23 countries and is most representative of Western Europe. It is also the oldest of its kind: last May it celebrated its 40th anniversary. Apart from that body, Strasbourg is the seat of the European Parliament which unites 12 countries. Its members were also invited to our meeting.

I admit that the reception we were accorded there, the response to the ideas we outlined in our statements and talks, and the willingness to discuss with us practical, specific aspects concerning the problems of Europe's development — all this came as a surprise of sorts to our delegation. Strasbourg became for us convincing proof of the viability and promise of the European process.

The Council of Europe can become one of the pillars of the European home and a body in which to work jointly on important initiatives. We should scrutinize not only the declaration we have been given, but also the Council of Europe's conventions concerning culture, education, ecology, television, etc. and decide which of these we can join.

This statement went far to illustrate the importance of the "powerless" but not uninfluential Council of Europe in the constellation of European institutions. Shortly thereafter the Assembly admitted Soviet parliamentary observers to its deliberations.

Three months later the world turned again as the Berlin Wall was breached. On "different social systems" the peoples of Eastern Europe gave their modulated yet astonishingly concordant response.

East European disintegration: seeking the magic moment

It is difficult to find a historical parallel for the changes which took place in Eastern Europe in 1989 and 1990. In their speed, their depth and their unexpectedness they are unique. There were portents, of course, but their significance had been consistently underrated. The NATO-WTO talks on conventional force reductions; WTO approval of the INF Treaty in 1987; Gorbachev's announcement of unilateral conventional force reductions in

1988: all these pointed to the fact that the Soviet Union no longer had the will or the wherewithal to maintain its military grasp on Eastern Europe. Another pointer was the completion of the Soviet withdrawal from Afghanistan in February, 1989.

With the hindsight of history, analysts will argue over the actual "magic moment" which launched the ripple through the domino line. The wire clippers on the Austro-Hungarian border which sent refugees fleeing west in May 1989 will certainly qualify as an irreversible moment of change. However, we have already looked much farther back to the Helsinki CSCE conference of 1975 (designed, ironically enough, in Soviet eyes to confirm the *status quo*) and to the death of Leonid Brezhnev on November 10, 1982, both of which provided openings for changes in the Soviet Union.

A — Central Europe struggles free

Poland the key

It is reasonable to believe, however, that the search for the true origins of change in Eastern Europe began in 1989 on the chilly Baltic coast, in that historic, ephemerally "free" city of Danzig, dominating the pre-war Polish corridor to the sea, where echoed still the first shots of the Second World War. In 1945 Danzig became Gdansk as the frontiers of Poland, forever squeezed between two major European powers, Germany and the Soviet Union, were moved west, with part of Poland annexed by the Soviet Union, and parts of Germany passing to Poland. East Prussia was divided between Poland and the Soviet Union.

Negotiation held in February 1989 between opposition and governmental representatives, with the participation of the Catholic Church, failed to achieve re-establishment of the Polish trade union, *Solidarnosc* or Solidarity, which had been formed in Danzig in 1981 under the leadership of an electrician named Lech Walesa ... The economic situation in Poland continued to deteriorate. Finally the government acknowledged its need for Solidarity's cooperation: on April 5 agreement came not only to legalize the union but also to hold open elections.

The situation in Poland was unique for two reasons: the unofficial yet persistent role of the Church in national life throughout more than four decades of Communist rule; and creation of Solidarity as the first opposition trade union among the so-called proletarian regimes of Eastern Europe. After the union was registered on April 17 many members who had gone underground re-emerged. One month later, on May 17, the government granted official recognition to the Catholic Church as well.

As the price of compromise, the April 1989 agreement had reserved a large number of seats to the Communists in the lower house of the national parliament. As a result, the free elections of June 4 resulted in an overwhelming victory for Solidarity's candidates without giving them a majority. In the upper house, where the Communists had no reserved seats, the opposition took every seat except one. We say "Solidarity's candidates" because it was unclear whether the movement had now become a political party or remained a trade union. Such philosophical issues were submerged by the overriding concern to wrest power from the Communists.

Solidarity moved cautiously so as to avoid a military crackdown. On July 18 parliament elected the Communist leader, General Wojciech Jaruzelski, President of Poland by a single vote majority, an outcome engineered by Solidarity to promote a soft transition. He was succeeded as head of the Communist party by Miezyslaw Rakowski.

Eleven days after his election, President Jaruzelski invited Solidarity to join a coalition government. The union was hesitant to commit itself to addressing Poland's horrendous economic problems without a free hand and a lower house majority. However, after deciding not to take the post himself, Lech Walesa proposed Solidarity intellectual Tadeusz Mazowiecki, who was first nominated by the President then elected by the parliament on August 24, 1989. His rise from membership of a banned organization to the premier's office had taken less than five months.

In November solidarity leader Lech Walesa visited the United States, receiving a tumultuous welcome, including an opportunity to address a joint session of the Congress. Moving closer to the European union movement, Poland signed the European Cultural Convention on November 16, as a first step towards applying for full membership in the Council of Europe in January 1990.

January 29, 1990, was a historic date for Poland: the Communist Party voted to disband. However, the decision was not unanimous. The Social Democratic Party (SDP) was formed to replace the Communist Party but a hardline breakaway group, led by Tadeusz Fiszbach, founded the Union of Social Democracy. This political fragmentation would also strike Solidarity and culminate in the indecisive elections of 1991, when no group exceeded fifteen percent of the vote. Freedom of ideas, it seems, proved a headier wine than political pragmatism.

Poland made further progress on the European front in February when the EC Commission proposed associate status for the former East European "satellite" nations. An even more pressing issue for Warsaw, however, was the future status of Germany and the frontier question. Poland demanded a role in German unity talks to ensure that the post-1945 Oder-Neisse line was ratified by all parties. On the other hand, Poland was well aware that Soviet troops were still stationed in the GDR. To avoid a dangerous power vacuum, the Poles somewhat surprisingly called for a reunited Germany to remain in NATO.

Meanwhile the nation was suffering from the government's "cold turkey" move to a free market system, so much so that in April the solidarity convention in Gdansk criticized the shock therapy. Finance minister Leszek Balcerowicz responded that there was no slowing down, much less going back. The nation must take her medecine and stay the course.

On May 27 Solidarity supporters notched up resounding victories in Poland's local elections.

Following surprise elimination of Prime Minister Mazowiecki by Edward Tyminski, a Polish-Canadian businessman, in fall primaries (after a falling out with Lech Walesa), Walesa was elected President of Poland by universal suffrage on December 9, 1990. Mazowiecki resigned from the premiership. He was replaced by Jan Krysztof Bielecki. President Jaruzelski left office gracefully on December 22 amid mixed "traitor/hero" assessments. (Two years later he would be touring the West, picking up speaking fees to defend his role). It was a climatic conclusion to an eventful political year in eastern Europe's most populous nation.

Poland's disengagement from eastern political and economic structures continued early in January 1991 when CMEA, the East European economic body also known as COMECON, was dissolved (see map). The replacement Organization for International Economic Cooperation would prove still-born, overtaken by events in the Soviet Union itself and by EC association moves. To facilitate the reform process, Poland signed a cooperation agreement with Czechoslovakia and Hungary a month later. At the same time Poland concluded a three-year cooperation agreement with the International Monetary Fund, a move which opened the door to technical and financial assistance but also implied an international commitment not to let up on the rigors of the move to a market economy. Marian Krzaklewski replaced Walesa as Solidarity leader. These moves to strengthen ties with the West culminated in the president's second visit to Washington in March.

Poland's policy of watchful conciliation with the "new" (reunified) Germany finally paid off on June 17 when the German-Polish Treaty of Friendship and Cooperation was signed in Bonn by Chancellor Kohl and Premier Bielecki. A finishing touch came in July when the Warsaw Pact (WTO) was finally dissolved.

Democratic orgy

With Europe's attention focused on events in the Soviet Union (the August coup), and Yugoslavia (civil war), Poland was doubtless happy to be out of the headlines during the summer and fall of 1991. However, the spotlight returned with the national parliamentary elections of October 27, the first fully free parliamentary vote, since the Communist Party had previously been guaranteed a large number of seats in the lower house or Diet. Over fifty groups—one could hardly call them national parties with names like Beer Drinkers' Union—contested the election in an orgy of democracy. Solidarity alone split into seven competing groups. Given the difficulty of forming a viable coalition, Walesa even suggested serving as premier himself—a notion which fell on deaf ears.

Finally, on November 8 Walesa called on Poles to set aside their differences and himself set an example by proposing Bronislaw Geremek as premier. Geremek is a member of the Democratic Union which headed the polls with a scant 12% of the vote! Not less significant in the Polish context are his Jewish origins and the fact that the Democratic Alliance had been in conflict with Walesa himself. Poland has had an uneasy relationship with the Jews. Only a tiny Jewish minority survived the Holocaust and the communist government's 1968 anti-semitic campaign. During the 1990 presidential election Walesa was himself criticized for remarks against Polish Jews. He subsequently apologized and appointed a committee to ease tensions. In the general election an anti-semitic group failed to win a seat. Now Walesa was going a step further.

On December 6, 1991, the strains of the rush to a market economy finally proved fatal to the Bielecki administration. Blocked by the parliament, Walesa reluctantly nominated former Solidarity lawyer Jan Olszewski, a critic of the free market reforms, as prime minister and the candidate of the center-right coalition. Nevertheless, himself in need of parliamentary support, Olszewski asked Bielecki's finance minister, Leszek Balcerowicz, who had spearheaded the reforms, to stay on in the government. Without actually turning back, Poland had now entered a period of more moderate economic and structural evolution.

Walesa speaks out

Lech Walesa's second address to the Council of Europe parliamentarians in February 1992 was very different from the first, when he had been courted and flattered with a human rights award. Poland was now a full member of the organization and the Polish president spoke as the sharp-tongued politician concerned about the welfare of his people, accusing the West of flooding Poland with consumer goods without investing in the country's economic infrastructure. He was clearly applying pressure on the West's point of moral weakness: the irresistible temptation to make a quick and easy buck.

Walesa did not stop here, however, declaring that Europe was still divided because of economic disparities. "The vision of a single Europe has faded greatly", he declared. Western Europe had become an exclusive club, closed to Eastern Europe. He did not hesitate to remind his listeners of their moral debt to Poland: "It is the Polish revolution which broke down the walls of the Kremlin . . . It is you who turned a profit".

The tongue-lashing was doubtless salutary, reminding self-satisfied free-marketeers who prided themselves on having won the Cold War that they did not do it alone: and that, as Soljenitsin has been telling the West for twenty years from behind the walls of his self-imposed *gulag* in New Hampshire, not everything in the western paradise is worthy of emulation.

The Olszewski government soon ran into trouble. On February 28 and again on March 5, 1992, the Diet rejected the government's economic program by 171 to 138, with 38 abstentions. In seeking to soften the "shock therapy" applied for several years, Olszewski seemed to be caught between a restless citizenry and an unstable coalition of small parties. Olszewski's center-right government attempted to recapture authority by challenging Walesa on defense and foreign affairs. However it overstepped the mark by its decision to release the names of politicians alleged to have collaborated with the Communist secret police. On June 4, 1992, it fell to a no-confidence motion by 261 – 149 votes.

As Polish democracy matures it will have to learn to accept political compromise in order to build broader-based, more viable groupings. However, the austerity program will have to stay in place if Poland hopes to continue to enjoy IMF support and to aspire to Community membership by the turn of the century.

Hungary

Hungary had long since acquired the reputation of being the mildest of the Eastern European regimes, perhaps on account of her historical ties to Austria, when parliament voted on January 11, 1989, to permit creation of political parties outside the Communist system. (In Hungary as in Poland docile "fellow travelling" parties nominally independent of the Communist Party but in fact subservient to it had existed for some time). A month later, on February 12, the Communist Party itself endorsed the multi-party system. In Moscow the Hungarian conversion was interpreted positively, for in April Gorbachev ordered withdrawal of units of the armed forces stationed in the country.

Doubtless in this television age the breaching of the Berlin Wall on November 9, 1989, will live in history as the most spectacular event of the Eastern European reform. In fact, however, the wall was broken through only after it had lost its significance as a political and economic barrier. The domino line actually began to tumble six months earlier on May 2, 1989, when a stunned world learned that Hungarian troops were applying cutters to the electrified fence set up along the Austrian border in 1956. People began to move freely, not simply as refugees, from East to West, but in both directions. In the relative economic well-being of Hungary there was no great flight to the West and the very option to travel seemed to ease certain pressures. The significance of the event lay rather in the chance it offered East Germans to join their brothers in the Federal Republic (no other East European country having such a western partner waiting with open arms) without risking life and limb in a minefield, under the glare of a searchlight on a barbed wire fence or swimming a canal in the sights of machine guns. [1]

In Hungary, nevertheless, events moved rapidly. After the wire-cutters it took only a week for Janos Kadar, who had been in power since his installation by the Soviets after the 1956 uprising and who in recent years had mellowed considerably, to be summarily ousted by his own party. Attention was distracted for a while by the spectacle of members of the Hungarian minority fleeing the Ceausescu regime in Romania, from one east European country to another. The final break with the past came when, on June 16, 1969, the Communist Party conceded after nearly thirty years that former premier Imre Nagy had been illegally executed for his role in the 1956 uprising. In a ghoulish search of the unmarked graves of executed dissidents, Nagy's remains were identified and on June 16 reburied in Budapest with full honors. Communist history was rewritten with his official rehabilitation on July 6. The Party was excluded from the proceedings. History added her own ironical touch: Janos Kadar died the same day.

From that moment intellectual dissidence swelled to political opposition. On September 10 Hungary suspended her undertaking to block passage of East Germans "vacationing" in the country to flee to the West: the flood gates were open. Nine days later government and opposition agreed on free elections. In anticipation of this event the Communist Party under Karoly Gross disbanded and reformed as the Socialist Party. As in Poland, an orthodox minority remained faithful to Marxist principles, although even this group changed its name, to Hungarian Socialist Workers Party. The former Communists wanted the elections to be held as soon as possible, before the opposition could organize itself. However, in a November referendum—the first free one in an eastern European country—the voters themselves rejected the government's timetable, forcing abandonment of a plan to elect the first president of the new republic while the Socialists controlled the government. It had taken a bare ten months to brush aside the old communist structures introduced by Kadar in 1956.

On October 2, the interim president, Matyas Szüross, declared Hungary an independent, new republic under a new constitution based on the rule of law and immediately began to make overtures to the West. She joined Poland in signing the European Cultural Convention of the Council of Europe on November 16, opening the way to full participation in that body's cultural and educational activities, and applied for full membership on the same day.

Pursuing Hungary's feelers to the West, the foreign minister suggested on February 24 that his country join the political arm of NATO. This bold proposal did not evoke a positive response, the West being doubtless mindful of Soviet sensibilities. The Soviet Union certainly welcomed warmer relations with the West, but not at any price.

These rapid changes in Hungary's political climate culminated in free elections on April 8, 1990. Availability of consumer goods had not been matched by political liberalization. The electorate was unforgiving. The Socialists (former Communists) were swept from power in a Conservative victory.

In May the Conservative-dominated parliament agreed upon writer Arpad Goncz (Free Democrat) as president and Josef Antall became prime minister. The Soviet Union bowed to demands that its troops be withdrawn and on June 26 parliament voted withdrawal from the Warsaw Pact. On November 26 Hungary became the 24th member country of the Council of Europe and signed the European Convention on Human rights the same day. Thus did the "mother" of Western European institutions become the first to extend her representation to the former Communist bloc.

President Goncz explained to Council of Europe officials his view of the significance of the event:

> Hungary's admission is one of the salient events of post-war European history. It is proof that our continent's ideological division is disappearing and that we share the same interpretation of democracy and human rights. There are several reasons why Hungary was the first ex-socialist country to join the Council of Europe. For one thing, a peaceful process of reform has been going on in Hungary for several years, resulting in a change of regime without bloodshed or major social conflicts. Secondly, we are ahead of the other former socialist countries in democratising our legislation. Lastly, we were the first country to hold

entirely free parliamentary and local elections, a fundamental condition of membership of the Council of Europe. [2]

To the credit of the Parliamentary Assembly, it should be noted that it had never accepted being confined to the representation of half of Europe; and had produced reports on the situation in what it euphemistically called "non-member countries" for forty-five years. November 26, 1989 was a day of great satifsaction to the members of an institution so often dismissed as devoid of power and influence.

Land reform in Hungary presents problems of a type which assail all the eastern economies seeking to emerge from a totalitarian system: where to begin and how to change part of the system while the rest stays in place. In many Hungarian villages the State cooperative remains the principal employer and the central unit of social life. A law adopted by the national parliament in January 1992 sets the end of the year for completing privatisation of agricultural cooperatives. The main issue for some 1200 units, representing over ten percent of the labor force and two-thirds of the nation's arable land, is the redistribution of land among employers, municipalities and dispossessed original owners or their heirs. Added to the ownership question is the danger of farms being broken up into inefficiently small units: farmer owners have claimed pieces of land as tiny as one hectare.

Given the uncertainties of restructuring and ownership some farmers held off spring sowing. Meanwhile, in the context of western European overproduction prices fell. To make things worse the demise of COMECON had shut off outlets to the east and turned off the subsidy tap. The outcome of all these pressures was that cooperatives were frequently in deficit when offered for sale to a private sector itself still deficient in wholesalers, distribution networks and financial infrastructures.

Going for the gold: a business update
July 1992. At the other end of Europe the Olympic Games are in full swing. Hungarian swimmers are doing well. Which central European country will win the gold medal for economic restructuring? Between Czech and Slovak scission and Yugoslav disintegration western investors are increasingly backing Hungary. An American has bought Gundel, Budapest's most celebrated restaurant. *Crédit Lyonnais* has hung out its shingle on the Vörosmärti in the heart of the business district. Austrian Julius Mainl has bought the Közert shopping chain ... Foreign investment exceeds 3.9 billion dollars. Hungarians welcome the vote of confidence, even if Costa Rican bananas are pushing aside Hungarian apples and not all the sausages for sale were made at home. In short, the market economy has arrived. The pragmatic Hungarians are ahead of the politically fragmented Poles and the culturally fractured Slovaks and Czechs.

Bankruptcy laws, a central bank and accounting systems have given the market place a viable infrastructure but, as Erik Izraelewicz reports (*Le Monde*, July 28, 1992) some bad habits are also being picked up from the West. Principal among these is the dual society, with its underground economy (and related tax losses to the state), irrational distribution of government and private ownership and gross discrepancies between rich areas in the capital and west and poor ones in the east.

By mid-1992 some twenty per cent of state industry had been privatized. The government made an attempt to speed up the process; but sale of assets requires a client able and willing to buy. Like the rest of Europe, Hungary was in its third year of recession, which did not favor the process.

Nevertheless, these problems should not mask Hungary's achievements. Even a dual economy *à l'italienne* borrows from the West. The forint is strong; loans are being paid off. For once the industrialized nations may not have to choose between generosity and profitable investment.

The Czech and Slovak dominoes
Although living standards were relatively high in Czechoslovakia and the industrial base fairly strong, the Communist government had been "hard line" since the "Prague Spring" of 1968 and at first seemed impervious to the changes taking place to her north and south. In the fall of 1989, however, the West German embassy was besieged by East German "tourists" and thousands more East Germans tried to board "mercy" trains evacuating these refugees to West Germany. Czechoslovakia was no longer immune. On October 12 a reform-minded Communist, Ladislav Adamec, became prime minister. Within a month the government had eased restrictions on foreign travel.

Police brutality against demonstrators in Prague, far from suppressing dissent, spurred creation of an opposition coalition under the name of Civic Forum. This differed from Poland's largely workers' Solidarity in being essentially a movement of students, intellectuals and artists. On November 24 Karel Urbanek succeeded the hard-line Milos Jakes as leader of the Communist Party and on December 7 an even more "soft line" Marian Calfa took over from Ladislav Adamec at the head of government. The dominoes continued to fall on December 10 with the resignation of Gustav Husak from the presidency. Three days later Marian Calfa formed a predominantly non-Communist government: in Czechoslovakia as in Poland the opposition followed the coalition route.

Alexander Dubcek, hero of the "Prague Spring", made a triumphant return to power on December 28, 1989 when he was elected speaker of the federal Czechoslovak parliament. The very next day the same parliament elected the popular playwright Vaclav Havel to the presidency. Four months earlier he had been in prison, an ascension surpassing Mazowiecki's in Poland.

Spearheaded by workers, the Polish freedom movement elected an electrician to the presidency. In Czechoslovakia and Hungary intellectuals were the driving force for reform and both selected writers to symbolize their newly democratic states. If this sounds idealistic, it was. None would have an easy tenure; all three would rapidly learn the hard way that politics is the stuff of democracy.

The wild pace of change in Czechoslovakia and other East European countries slowed. Broad coalitions formed to oppose Communism divided not without pain into "normal" democratic groups. Such is the price of democracy. A not less important factor was the dearth of trained and experienced personnel which blocked replacement of Communists in senior official positions. There is an important role here for Western universities and professional organizations. Expert assistance is needed as much as financial aid. [3]

In October 1991 Vaclav Havel made his second presidential visit to the US, signing political and trade agreements with President Bush and seeking both more American investment and greater access to US markets. One of the agreements gave US investors assurances on currency convertibility and patriation of profits. New markets were needed to compensate for the shrinking of Eastern European and Czecho-Soviet trade exchanges. However, Havel looked for stronger security ties with Poland, Hungary and NATO. Despite ethnic unrest he also discounted a Czech-Slovak split. He brought back from Washington the accord signed in 1918 by Slovak leaders and Thomas G. Masaryk, the father of modern Czechoslovakia, which pledges national equality for Slovaks and Czechs. Havel could also not allow himself to forget that there are 600,000 ethnic Hungarians in Czechoslovakia. The nation's family feuds threatened economic recovery.

Empire of the people
Speaking at Lehigh University in Pennsylvania on October 26, Havel avoided immediate, contentious issues to share his moral and political philosophy with transatlantic friends. The new Europe, he declared, must be an empire of the people. In a plea for respect for human dignity, Havel evoked the layers in a human being's "home": sex, culture of origin, nationality, religion, family, political philosophy, Europe, humanity and, ultimately, the world itself. Self-identification and mutual respect he saw as vital to creation of a civic society of equals. "My language, too, is part of my home", he declared. For Havel no group may dominate another: political sovereignty must revere civic sovereignty and this, in turn, must entertain respect for human sovereignty. One layer of identification may not suppress another. It was ironic that Havel's speech was disrupted by the unfurling of a Slovak flag and by shouts for Slovak independence. Havel waited out the interruption with a tolerant smile.

The Slovak issue contined to haunt Havel on his return home. If Czechoslovakia could not remain united, he declared, it should separate in a civilized manner. Havel rejected a comparison with Yugoslavia's warring republics. Speaking in the Slovak capital, Bratislava, he admitted the Slovaks had lived in the shadow of the Czechs, relegated to a largely agricultural role. It was necessary to take action to equalize the two regions.

The Czech-Slovak issue came to a head on January 21 when Slovak parliamentarians in the federal parliament blocked President Havel's proposal for a national referendum on the future of the federation. The Czech deputies and some Slovaks voted in favor but could not muster the required majority. The Assembly also rejected a Havel proposal which would have permitted him to go directly to the people to secure adoption of the new Constitution before the next general election. In maneuvering to hold the country together, the play-wright-president was learning by experience the downside of democracy.

Lustrum without luster: the "purification" of Czechoslovak politics
In addition to the difficult task of holding together the Czech and Slovak Fed-erative Republic, federal authorities in Prague had for months been at grips with the intractable question of what to do about former communists holding public office. The opening of the files of the former secret police has given rise to a purification process often resembling a witch hunt. The question of whether democracy must tolerate intolerance is no mere philosophical exer-cize; it faces all societies which seek to be free and open (not least in the United States, where the Civil Liberties Union defends the right of the Ku Klux Klan to march). The present situation in Czechoslovakia is not an iso-lated one, as witnessed by the opening of the Stasi files in the former GDR.

In 1990 the Czechoslovak parliament voted a moratorium on the transfer of communist property, and then a law permitting both the state and private individuals to recover property confiscated by the communists since 1950. The operation was legitimate if barely profitable: many apparatchiks had not waited for the new law before laundering their questionable gains, taking advantage of denationalization to buy into the private sector. Indeed, who else had capital to spare? In fact, in order for privatisation to take off, the new authorities had to turn a blind eye to some questionable operations.

In October 1991, however, parliamentarians of the right-wing Civic Demo-cratic Party (ODS) went further by pushing through the law of *lustrace* which debarred former communist officials from holding public positions for five years. This measure was justified not only on moral grounds but also because, it was alleged, such bureaucrats were slowing up reforms. (Earlier, as we have seen, maintenance of such officials in influential positions had been justified by the lack of trained or experienced "democrats" to run the machinery of state). However, this sweeping measure tarred all former communists with the same brush. According to this law, Alexander Dubcek, who as a reformed communist became a national hero in the "Prague Spring" of 1968, could serve as the honored speaker of the federal assembly but would have been debarred from managing a post office! An equivalent law in Russia would apply to Yeltsin, to Gorbachev, to Marshall Shaposhnikov ... In the vigorous politics of contemporary Czechoslovakia it is easy to see how implementation of such a law could precipitate a witch hunt motivated by party political advantage. In December 1990, the Czech minister of justice, Leon Richter of the Civic Movement, was forced to resign. Nevertheless, one year later another text was adopted, banning the diffusion of communist ideas. Politicians of the right clearly have the parties of the left and, in particular, the Movement for a Democratic Slovakia, in their sights.

Struggling to hold the country together, President Havel expressed misgiv-ings at the way things were going. He signed the law banning former commu-nists from public office while at the same time calling for its amendment.

Treaty of unfriendship?
Yet another ethnic minority problem was cast up in the post-communist
Carpathian kaleidoscope. Adding to Havel's Czech and Slovak ethnic woes
was the problem of the Sudeten Germans. One of Hitler's "justifications" for
invading had been the reattachment of the German-speaking Czechoslovak
citizens of the Sudetenland to the Fatherland: *Heim ins Reich*. The disputed
territory had been ceded to Germany under the infamous Munich appeasement treaty of 1938, to which France and Britain (Chamberlain's "peace in our
time") were signatories. In the event, Hitler simply took over the whole
country, tearing up the Munich "piece of paper" as his goose-stepping storm
troops entered Prague.

Following defeat of Nazi Germany, in a moment of understandable but
inglorious fury, the Sudeten Germans were expelled from Czechoslovakia.
Under the communists most of their property ended up in state hands. Today
the Germans have returned, their pockets stuffed with D-Marks. Eighty per
cent of foreign investment in Czechoslovakia comes from the Federal Republic. Volkswagen has taken over the Skoda works. Both Czechs and Slovaks
want the investment but are in two minds about its origin. However, Sudeten
expulsion survivors and heirs demand the return of their property.

The friendship treaty signed by Chancellor Kohl and President Havel in
February 1992 skimmed over these issues. On his way to the presidential cas-
tle to sign the treaty (a signature already delayed by the powerful Sudeten
lobby back home), Kohl had to run the gauntlet of jeering cries of *Heim ins
Reich* — now with a "Bosch go home" connotation — orchestrated by an unholy
alliance of Havel's ex-communist and right-wing nationalist enemies, accusing
him of selling out to Prague's powerful western neighbor. Rarely it seems has
a friendship treaty brought forth so much unfriendliness. Yet Europe may not
be built by turning one's back on her history: Europeans may forgive; they
must not forget. Europe of shame, Europe of pride . . .

Eight million overnight capitalists
A gigantic wave of privatisation was organized between May 18 and June 8,
1992, by Vaclav Klaus, the federal minister of finance. An original "coupon
method" sought to denationalize most public enterprises in a single operation
after 46 years of public ownership under communism. This audacious venture
was closely watched by other nations of eastern Europe.

943 Czech and 467 Slovak firms were included in the operation. All citizens
over 18 years of age had a chance to buy a booklet of coupons for 1000 crowns
(about $40 or a week's wages). The average national investment was expected
to be about 35,000 crowns. Coupons could be invested in any of the firms but
shares would rise in cost when issues were oversubscribed. However, many
citizens preferred to entrust their investment to one of 400 mutual funds which
sprang up almost overnight.

The Czech and Slovak Federative Republic, as this fragile nation now called
itself, had come through an international *lustrum* review in gaining admission
to the "democratic club" of the Council of Europe, implying a solemn com-

mitment to human rights and, like Poland, Hungary and the Baltic states, negotiating an association agreement with the European Community. The Strasbourg organization has shown tolerance and understanding to the point of laxity for the situation of former communist countries by setting the bar relatively low, the only serious *de facto* condition being the holding of free elections. Central European countries critical of western neighbors will now have to look to the beam in their own eye and, without being held hostage to history, examine the purity of their purification process.

Condemned to separation?

As the results of the June general election became known it seemed as through Havel's efforts to hold the country together had failed. In the Czech republic to the west (Bohemia and Moravia) the artisan of Czechoslovakia's economic reform, Vaclav Klaus, leader of the Civic Democratic Party (ODS), won a clear mandate while the ex-communist separatist leader Vladimir Meciar and his Democratic Slovakia Movement (HZDS) came out ahead in Slovakia. Meciar's success increased tension between Slovaks and Slovakia's 600,000 Hungarian minority, already at odds over a vast Danubian barrage project in their region. After the Klaus-Meciar dialog faltered the Hungarian Slovaks were quick to serve notice that they would in turn claim autonomy. On the eastern border with Ukraine even the former communists did well.

After four long meetings the two leaders were unable to agree on a formula to save the republic. Klaus wanted a federation and rejected the loose confederation of independent states, with separate UN representation, which would have been acceptable to Meciar's Democratic Slovakia Movement (HZDS), as "a joke". The only solution seemed to be an agreed separation, avoiding a self-destructive conflict. Bratislava was not Sarajevo. The two leaders put in place a limited transitional government to liquidate the federation.

The last remnant of the post-Hapsburg disposition in Central Europe seemed to be crumbling but President Havel angrily refused to accept defeat. In his weekly radio address he said a national referendum was "the only moral way" for Czechs and Slovaks to decide their future. He intended to stand for re-election as federal president and would set out his vision of the country's future. Havel found support in Slovakia's Christian Democratic Movement, which attacked the HZDS policy as "dangerous for the long-term interests of Slovakia".

Politicians across Europe echoed their dismay. Czechoslovak membership of the CSCE and the Council of Europe would cause no lasting problems (the two states would doubtless be accepted as full, distinct members); but cooperation between Czechoslovakia, Poland and Hungary would be disturbed and entry into the EC seriously delayed. Moreover, the question would arise as to which new republic—Czech, Slovak or neither—would "inherit" the association agreement with Brussels.

Geography would doubtless also be a factor. Slovakia has a common border with Ukraine. The Slovaks risk being locked into slower-moving Central and Eastern Europe as the Czechs turn even more resolutely to the West.

But which West? The Czechs may find themselves more drawn to Berlin than to Brussels. Once more the predictable unpredictability of nationalism becomes a major factor on the winding road to Europe.

When the re-election of Vaclav Havel to the federal presidency was blocked by the Slovaks in the Federal Parliament on July 4, 1992, the Velvet Revolution came to a sudden end. Within three weeks the leading opponents, Klaus and Meciar, agreed on a peaceful division of the country, calling on the Federal Assembly to dissolve the federation by September 30, 1992, leaving nevertheless in place a customs union with free movement of goods, labor and capital.

74 years of misunderstandings

The Czech and Slovak languages — like English and American, Flemish and Dutch — are almost identical; but what else do the five million Slovaks and the ten million Czechs have in common? For a thousand years as "Upper Hungary" Slovakia had lain under Hungarian domination. When Tomas Masaryk, Edvard Benes and Milan Stefanik conceived the Czechoslovak state around 1916, the two nations had never lived together. The Czechs had a prestigious history as the heart of Bohemia but the Slovaks were essentially rural, over a quarter of them illiterate, compared with only 3% among the Czechs.

When the Republic of Czechoslovakia was born in 1918 on the ruins of the Austro-Hungarian empire, the Pittsburgh Agreements signed by Masaryk with the US and supported by Slovak emigrants guaranteed, on paper, a large measure of autonomy to the Slovaks. The new country became a parliamentary democracy until 1938. Yet Prague feared being obliged to grant autonomy to the even more numerous German-speaking Czechs; consequently, the Agreements (a copy of which Havel brought back with him to Bratislava in 1992 from his second US visit) were never implemented. Led by Monsignor Tiso and his People's Party, Slovakian nationalism became more insistent. In 1938, after Nazi Germany had annexed the German-speaking Sudetenland, Tiso proclaimed Slovakian autonomy. A fascist state was founded in 1939 under German protection. Tiso remains today a tainted hero. Even though the Slovaks rose against the fascist regime in 1944 and despite a federalisation law of 1968, they never regained true autonomy after the communist takeover. Four decades later, with the Velvet Revolution of November 1989, history gave the Slovaks another chance. Negotiations dragged on for two years but the two sides, according to Slovak negotiator Frantisek Miklosko, "were not speaking the same language". Economic interest should incite Slovakia to remain in the federation; the Hungarian minority will want its own autonomy: it seems the time is past for such arguments. Slovaks can taste the heady wine of independence and will empty the cup to the lees.

On July 17, 1992, the Slovak provincial parliament proclaimed its sovereignty. Less than an hour later the final federal thread unravelled: unable to exercize his office according to his principles, Havel resigned. He even telephoned the news personally to a Vladimir Meciar taken aback by the speed of events he had himself set in train. Dignified as ever, Vaclav Havel, philosopher, humanist, president, playwright, declared he would continue to play a role at the right time and in the right place. Like the last musician from Haydn's Farewell Symphony, he quietly left the presidential stage; and walked home.

Bulgaria

Bulgaria is one of the poorest and industrially least developed of East European states. For nearly half a century it hewed most faithfully to the Moscow line. Late to move, it was not immune to change, however. Rising pressure for reform to pre-empt opposition from outside Communist Party ranks finally forced the ouster of Todor I. Zhivkov on October 29, 1989, coinciding with major changes in Czechoslovakia. Petar T. Mladenov became leader of both the Bulgarian government and the Communist Party. Zhivkov had been leader since 1954 and president since 1971 but his fall was both rapid and complete: on December 13 he was expelled from the Communist Party. As though the nation were now rushing to catch up with the rest of Eastern Europe, the New Year brought no let up in the pace of change. In January 1990 the government entered into negotiations with the opposition and the Communist Party relinquished control of the army and police, an important step in separating the functions of party and government. Even though the monopoly of power was broken, however, the Union for Democratic Reform, grouping thirteen opposition parties, feared being tainted by power-sharing and declined to enter into a governmental coalition. The government was forced to resign and Mladenov, while remaining head of state, was replaced by Alexandar Lilor as party leader. On February 11, 1990, the Bulgarian Communist Party split in two and the Alternative Socialist Party was formed.

Two months later, on April 3, the parliament accepted the inevitable and adopted legislation providing for free elections. In anticipation of this event the Communist Party changed its name, as had been done in Poland, Hungary and Czechoslovakia, as though rejuvenation would be assured by a facelift. It renamed itself the Bulgarian Socialist Party. Petar Mladenov engineered his own survival and assumed the newly created post of president.

The first free elections to be held in Bulgaria in forty-five years took place in June. The former Communists managed to win but on July 6, 1990, Petar Mladenev's tight-rope act came to an end; accused of using force against demonstrators, he resigned the presidency after only three months in office. On August 1 Jelio Jelev was appointed Bulgaria's first non-Communist head of state in four decades. Democratic forces were now on the upswing and at the end of November demonstrations forced resignation of the "Socialist" government. Dimitar Popov, an independent, became premier of a new coalition government in January 1991 and immediately set about preparing a draconian plan to strengthen the economy. The plan was announced on January 23, 1991. In February Todor Zhivkov's fall became complete: the former supreme ruler of Bulgaria was put on trial for embezzlement. The government also moved to improve relations with Bulgaria's Turcic and Islamic minorities.

The political fever fell and Bulgaria settled into a long, slow, painful period of economic recovery.

Popov, a little-known judge from Sofia, was in many ways a non-political choice. He had risen to prominence as secretary of the Central Election Commission, which steered the nation through its first free elections. He immediately set about drafting a new constitution (before a new electoral law) and Bulgaria became the first eastern European country to take such a step. He was criticized by some opposition members for working with the former communists but was undeterred. He riposted that a new constitution and basic laws taking all tendancies and groups into account had to be adopted first: "How could we pass a new electoral law without a new constitution?" he asked. "We first needed to know what kind of parliament we would have." The Parliament adopted the new constitution on July 9, 1991. Replacing the communist law of 1971, it instituted the inviolability of private property and freedom of opinion.

Popov asserted that US links would not limit his country's relations with other nations and political groups. He held talks with the EC and prepared the ground for Bulgarian membership in the Council of Europe.

Under the new constitution, the elections took place for six and a half million voters on October 13, 1991, finally bringing a democratic majority to Bulgaria. The contest was a cliff-hanger. The opposition Union of Free Democratic Forces edged the former-communist Socialists by 34% to 33%. The party representing the Turkish-speaking minority came in third and holds the balance of power. It should be noted that sixty-one parties contested the election – the thirst for democracy and free speech overcoming, as in Poland a year earlier, the pragmatic need for stability.

The new era thus began in Bulgaria with the challenge of setting up a delicate coalition. With over one-third of the seats the Socialists retained the power to block further constitutional reform. The economy was also crippled by a 700% annual inflation rate. Yet in fostering democracy, Churchill's "least bad" of political systems, Dimitar Popov has emerged as the father of the new Bulgaria. His stewardship in the aftermath of left-wing totalitarianism may be compared with King Juan Carlos' achievements in bringing Spain out of right-wing Falangism.

His transitional role completed, Popov quietly retired from politics. January 1992 saw the first presidential election in the history of the country. Acting president Jelio Jelev, leader of the UDF, led strongly in the first round, with 44% against 30% for the candidate of the former communists, Velko Valkanov. He was deprived of outright victory by the "Tyminski effect" (named after the Polish-Canadian businessman who had opposed Lech Walesa) created by the fencing champion George Gantchev, who had made his money abroad and now represented the business bloc. Although the latter had achieved only 1% in the parliamentary elections, the "Bulgarian Tyminski" now drew 17% of the vote and refused to withdraw in favor of any candidate in the second round.

Jelev, a champion of resistance to totalitarianism and of peaceful progress to democracy, won an outright victory with 52.85% of the vote in the second round on January 19; a victory which merits comment if only because Bulgaria's road to democracy had been the least noticed among the former satellite countries and because Bulgaria has become an island of stability in the troubled Balkans.

The election was calm and orderly despite exploitation of nationalist themes and attacks on the Turkish-speaking minority, made scapegoats for centuries of Ottoman domination, by Jelev's opponent Velko Valkanov, who enjoyed the support of former communists. The closeness of the result should put the West on notice that Bulgaria needs help in combating rampant inflation, coping with half a million unemployed and restructuring state-controlled agricultural cooperatives. A writer-philosopher like his Czechoslovak and Hungarian counterparts, Jelev—the first freely re-elected head of state in eastern Europe—has undertaken to reform the Bulgarian market-place in five years. He cannot do it alone.

Commenting on the result in Sofia where she had observed the democratic nature of the proceedings, the Secretary General of the Council of Europe, Catherine Lalumière, declared that there was no longer any obstacle to Bulgaria's membership. By May 1992 the procedures were complete and Bulgaria had become the 27th member state of the Strasbourg organisation.

Nowadays Bulgarians listen to Bruce Springsteen and Voice of America, as they drive in their Russian Ladas to a fast food store, past enormous billboards advertising Johnnie Walker whisky. For long reputed the most russophile of the European satellites, Bulgaria is making up for lost time and enjoying the forbidden fruit offered by the West. US Vice-president Quayle enjoyed a delirious reception in Sofia in June 1991 and might have wished he were running for election in that country.

The US may perceive some strategic value (both commercial and military) in the location of Bulgaria at the cross-roads of Ukraine, the Balkans, the Middle East and the Mediterranean. To some, American motives are suspect. Philip Bokov, shadow foreign minister in the Bulgarian opposition Socialist Party, suggested to the newspaper *Douma* in January, 1992, that whereas the Europeans were building the "Common European home" dear to Mikhail Gorbachev's heart from the Atlantic to the Urals, the United States was undermining it with the perfidious Vancouver to Vladivostok concept. [4]

Be that as it may, Americans seem to be beating Europeans to the punch in Bulgaria. Westinghouse won the contract to treat nuclear waste; the national airline bought Boeings in preference to Airbus. Bulgarians are flying to (relative) prosperity on the coattails of Uncle Sam: Walesa's accusation that Europeans were not risking enough venture capital in Poland may be true of Bulgaria also.

Bulgaria's geographical location may appear valuable to the West but it puts the country at the heart of an explosive area. As Bulgaria makes amends to her Turkish and Muslim minorities, civil war rages in neighboring

Yugoslavia and resentment at having been "tricked" by former communists smolders in Romania. Deferring to Greek sensibilities at the expense of Bulgarian ones, the West hesitates to recognize Macedonian independence. Finding herself isolated Macedonia may turn to Bulgaria (which has a significant Macedonian minority): not a recipe for peace in the region.

Bulgaria is moving steadily forward in her efforts to make up for economic delays and political servitude to the Soviet Union. One example of recent initiatives is the setting up of a bank consolidation mechanism (not unlike the German *Treuhandanstalt*) to manage the privatization of some seventy state banks and to consolidate their number to about ten. In recent years branches of the Bulgarian National Bank have been converted to commercial banks. Now state shares will be pooled through the bank consolidation company, since most of the commercial banks are too small and regional to be viable. The consolidated banks must clear their debts, probably with assistance from the national budget, before being sold to the private sector. International financial institutions should support the process with more than words.

The election of October 1991 brought promise to Bulgaria that the pace of privatization and foreign investment would quicken. The Community's new European Bank for Reconstruction and Development is considering a plan to help design a new banking system and the EBRD is expected to act as a catalyst for increased private investment from the West. A team of foreign consultants are advising the Bulgarians, while the EC has promised twenty million ECU ($24.6m) to finance restructuring and privatizations.

The Bulgarian government has prepared privatization laws and opened a privatization agency in the capital, Sofia. Balkancar, which makes fork-lift trucks and the petrochemical complex Neftochim are among the privatizations already agreed. Industries being denationalized include road haulage and gas station chains. More significantly, firms such as British Petroleum, Shell and Texaco are bidding for oil exploration and development contracts in the Black Sea off the Bulgarian coast.

Balkan island of peaceful change
Like others in the region, Bulgarians need unstinting assistance in their crossing of the social and economic minefield to a free market system; understanding for the needs of their minorities (devoid of hypocrisy from western European nations which do not always treat their own minorities with the sensitivity they deserve); and most of all a guarantee that Brussels will not turn a deaf ear to their overtures when they finally complete the painful qualification steeplechase. Bulgaria needs hope as well as bread and computers. It must mean something that, squeezed between Yugoslavia and Romania, Bulgaria has demonstrated that it is possible to make a social and economic revolution peacefully in a region where conflict seems endemic.

Until these recent developments, Western aid to Bulgaria has been negligable. Unlike her larger neighbor, Romania, Bulgaria has not filled the television screens. There is probably no other East European country about which western countries know, or care less. (The wine is cheap . . . the language difficult . . . the common border with Turkey no longer of strategic importance). Bulgaria's recent entry into the Council of Europe will help; but to be more aware of her place in the European order we shall doubtless have to wait until western tourists, weary of the Mediterranean's expanding concrete jungle, discover the Black Sea resorts . . . unless, of course the oil derricks get there first.

Latin island in a Slavic sea

Romania, largest of the East European countries after Poland, is in many ways a case apart. Her name, Latin-based language and ethnic origins are more Mediterranean than Slavic. Without going as far as Tito's Yugoslavia by breaking away completely, the Bucharest regime adopted an independent stance in COMECON and the Warsaw Pact (Romania refused to participate in the crushing of the Prague Spring in 1968). She also maintained close diplomatic relations with Western Europe, particularly France, with which she felt a linguistic and cultural affinity. (Eugene Ionesco and his theater of the absurd provide a somewhat ironic connection). Such political independence in foreign relations could be misleading, however; it masked under Nicolae Ceaucescu one of the harshest Communist regimes in the world. Independence in foreign policy was intended to send a message not of softness but of non-interference, even by the Soviet Union, in internal affairs.

As Eastern Europe stirred and the grip of Communism was loosened in 1989 and 1990 the long-suppressed issue of ethnic minorities came to the fore, not least in the Soviet Union itself. This proved to be the tinder-spark in Romania. After the Second World War Romania lost Moldavia, which became a republic of the Soviet Union, but gained Transylvania, a Hungarian-speaking area in the north and west. On December 15, after the events of 1989 had seemed to pass Romania by, a crowd gathered in Timisoara, in Western Romania, to prevent the hated secret police from arresting a Hungarian-speaking priest, Father Tokes. The melee rapidly became a demonstration. The next day security forces fired on demonstrators. President Ceaucescu declared a state of emergency in Western Romania but the protests rapidly spread to the capital, Bucharest. When the President addressed the crowd he was for the first time shouted down. The next day Ceaucescu and his wife Elena fled Bucharest. Corneliu Manescu, a former Communist, announced on television the formation of the National Salvation Front. The new government was immediately recognized by the Soviet Union and the United States. Events in the other former Soviet satellites had been amazingly free of violence and bloodshed but Romania came close to civil war. The hated secret police hat nothing to lose: it was the army which turned the tide by first permitting, then joining the popular uprising.

On December 24, Ion Ionescu became president, Petre Roman prime minister. On Christmas Day, 1989, Nicolae and Elena Ceaucescu were intercepted, hastily tried in a secret location and summarily executed.

Following these violent events the situation remained unstable throughout January 1990. The National Salvation Front proved less reform-minded than many had hoped. Its leaders were called "Communists with masks" who had dispensed with a hated dictator only to grab power for themselves.   On January 26 Dumitru Mazilu, Vice-President of the Front, resigned, charging "Stalinist practices".   After a "true" opposition rally in the capital the Front proposed power-sharing until elections could be held.   Veteran Communist Silvia Brucan resigned from the leadership, followed by defense minister Nicolae Militaru, criticized for disrupting the revolution.   In February, the government claimed to have disbanded the secret police.   In May protesters asserted that the revolution had been "stolen" by former Communists, but the greatest shock of all came on May 20, 1990.   A traumatized electorate voted for stability rather than a swift move to a market economy.   The fragmented opposition — the Peasant Party, the National Liberal Party and the Hungarian Democratic Union — failed to dislodge the ex-Communist National Salvation Front which achieved 66% in parliamentary races, while Ion Ionescu scored an amazing 89% in the presidential election.   Three weeks later, prompted by the government, highly-paid miners were trucked into the capital and violently broke up an opposition rally.   True to form, the Romanian domino had fallen the other way.

Marauding miners waving clubs
In September 1991 the dreaded miners commandeered trains and swept once more into Bucharest and on to the streets of the capital, brandishing batons. After initial resistance the Roman government resigned.   In their earlier descent the miners had been supporting President Ion Iliescu but now the latter condemned them as unreconstructed communists.   Romanian leaders pledged to keep the country on the road to a market-style economy.   Theodor Stolojan, a former finance minister named premier, promised to make adjustments to quiet social unrest but vowed to continue Roman's reform policies. It was feared that repeated outbursts of civil unrest would deter western assistance.   In a symbolic incident, a member of the World Bank team in Bucarest to negotiate a $300 million loan, timed to cushion the impact of currency reform, was hurt in a clash between miners and security forces.   Yet the national Peasants' Party, previously attacked by the miners, gave their leaders a standing ovation at its party congress.   Even as they made communist-style demands and attacked private shops the miners now shouted "Down with communism".   In Romania the political landscape is still fraught with confusion.

Why did barely-reformed, thinly-veiled communism manage to hang on in Bulgaria and especially Romania when it was so rapidly swept away in the other eastern-block countries?   It may take years of analysis to provide a definitive answer to this question.   However, there are troubling pointers.   As the lid to the political pressure-cooker was partially unscrewed, old resentments and prejudices, long suppressed, bubbled up.   Former communists managed to give their movement a nationalist face which fomented prejudice against Jewish and other linguistic and cultural minorities.   The phenomenon has not been limited to Romania.   Xenophobic attacks on immigrants, blacks and muslims occured in the early nineties in a number of European countries, both east and west, but especially in eastern Germany. In Yugoslavia, of course, ethnic alienation degenerated into civil war. Europe's democrats must be on the watch against the rebirth of Fascism.

Minorities within minorities: a fragile mosaic

Some sixty-five percent of the four million inhabitants of the small former Soviet republic of Moldova (capital Khisinau, formerly Kishinev) between Ukraine and Romania are Romanian-speaking. Under the name of Bessarabia, Moldova was annexed from Romania in 1812 and again in 1940, with the Baltic states, under the treaty between the USSR and the Third Reich known as the Molotov-Ribbentrop pact. The question of reuniting the two Romanian-speaking states has gained momentum since the fall of the Ceaucescu regime and the demise of the Soviet Union. According to the *New York Times* (Jan. 2, 1992) a private opinion poll in Romania in November 1992 showed 44% in favor of union, 45% opposed and 11% undecided. Most of the opposition comes from the Russian-speaking (24% Russian, 25% Ukrainian) population in Bendery and north of the Dniestr river and has led to severe armed clashes. Known as Transdniestr, the region was transferred to Moldavia from the Ukraine in 1954 by Nikita Kruschev in order to provide the largely rural republic with an industrialized belt.[5] While economic problems in both states remain uppermost in people's minds, there is consensus that cross-border travel and trade should be eased. Broadcasting and publishing are already showing the way. As the economic situation improves and public opinion evolves, political union may not be far behind. Between a fragile CIS and uncertain democracy in Romania, the Moldovans have a difficult choice. Moldova is one of three CIS states which has refused to maintain the unity of the Red Army. This may leave it a little room for maneuver, but not if this former minority continues to repress its own minorities.

The severe reversal suffered by the Romanian government party, the National Salvation Front, in the local elections of February 1992 may weigh in the Moldovan decision. The main cities, Bucharest, Brasov and — a powerful symbol — Timisoara fell to the opposition in the first round. More disquieting was the success of the ultra-nationalist Romanian National Unity Party in Hungarian-speaking Transylvania. On the other hand, the Union of the Democratic Left was successful only in the steel town of Galat. Romania remains the only former Soviet satellite where ex-communists are still in power. Moreover, even as democracy emerges it opens the door to extremist and xenophobic sentiments of a most disquieting kind. In their disarray, eastern peoples are sometimes tempted to look to a nostalgic past. After twice being denied entry, ex-King Michael 1st of Hohenzollern, who abdicated in 1947, received a warm welcome in the streets of Bucharest from both monarchists and the idly curious when authorities allowed a three-day visit in April, 1992. There was even talk of a referendum on whether the monarchy should be restored. The visit was successful, because in July 1992 the National Liberal (PNL) opposition leader Radu Campeanu proposed ex-King Michael as presidential candidate. Romanians, like Romans before them, need circuses as well as bread.

Two Germanys or one?

Unrest in East Germany — the German Democratic Republic — began with street demonstrations in Leipzig. Throughout August 1989 West German missions in East European countries were swamped by would-be *Volksdeutsche* emigrants from the German-speaking diaspora seeking to get to the Federal Republic where, in accordance with the *Heimatsrecht* law and Article 3 of the constitution, they could acquire immediate citizenship and unemployment assistance. A number of special trains were arranged to relieve the pressure on the West German missions in Poland, Czechoslovakia and Hungary. On September 10 Hungary suspended her agreement to block the passage of East Germans to the West. The situation was serious for the GDR because those seeking to emigrate were usually the young and well educated. On October 3 and 4 some ten thousand East Germans tried to board trains already full with people who had taken refuge in the missions. Despite the wave of homeless refugees to accomodate in schools and city halls, for the most part West Germans gave the long-separated brethren a euphoric welcome.

Meanwhile a peaceful opposition was organizing itself in the GDR. New Forum issued a manifesto on September 12, but in early October protest marches in East Berlin, Dresden and Leipzig were violently broken up by security forces. Following a visit to the GDR by Mikhail Gorbachev, in which he was well received in the streets and seemed to distance himself from the authorities, Communist Party leader Erich Honecker was replaced by Egon Krenz. Like his counterparts in other "satellite" countries, he endeavored to retain power for communism by making limited concessions. Only in Romania would this strategy prove successful for a time.

Wall of shame

On November 9, 1989, a jubilant crowd breaches the infamous Berlin Wall before which President Kennedy declared *"Ich bin ein Berliner!"*. East Berliners flood into the Kurfürstendam — Berlin's Champs Elysées — amazed at the wealth of merchandise available but also stunned by high prices. East German border guards who for years had been under orders to fire on fugitives stood by bemused or even framed smiling faces in gaps in the wall.

East German Finance Minister Ernst Hofner resigned, declaring a budget deficit of 130 billion marks, seventy billion dollars at the official exchange rate. A week later moderate Hans Modrow became head of government. Within days the elite living conditions enjoyed by Erich Honecker and other former GDR leaders were exposed to a shocked and deprived citizenry.

Stepping up his campaign for reunification, Federal German Chancellor Helmut Kohl· proposed a confederative structure for the two Germanys; GDR response was cool.

The exodus continued, with thousands crossing the north-western tip of Czechoslovakia to reach the Federal Republic. On December 9 Gregor Gysi replaced Egon Krenz as Communist Party leader.

A *New York Times* poll revealed that the US public favored German reunification by 67% to 16%. On December 12 Secretary of State Baker visited Berlin and a wall which was rapidly disintegrating under the hammers of souvenir hunters. Proposing a "new architecture for a new era", Baker put forward a four-point plan for German reunification: free votes in both Germanys; continuing EC and NATO membership for a reunited Germany; acceptance of present borders in East and West; a step-by-step process of reunion. An eventful year closed out with a visit to the GDR by West German President Richard von Weizsäcker, where he had discussions not only with Premier Modrow but also with Church leaders, and a formal reopening of the Brandenburg Gate before world-wide radio and television.

In a now familiar evolution, the East German Communist Party purged its former leaders, including Egon Krenz, on January 23, 1990. A week later Mikhail Gorbachev conceded a major policy shift during a meeting in Moscow with Hans Modrow, agreeing to German reunification. The East German Premier then made public his plan for a reunited Germany, with Berlin as its capital. Initial reaction in the Federal Republic was positive. However, West Germany declared unacceptable the principle that the new Germany should be neutral and that all foreign troops be withdrawn on both sides, insisting that a reunited Germany remain in NATO. The next day, in what looked like a somewhat desparate rearguard action, Soviet foreign minister Schevardnadze proposed an international referendum on German unity.

Political leaders on both sides of what was beginning to appear an increasingly irrelevant border were being swept forward on an irrepressible tide of public opinion. On February 7 the two Germanys set up a committee to plan a single currency. There was serious haggling over the exchange rate but the principle of fusion was never in doubt. The four occupation powers agreed to hold unification talks. Bonn approved major aid to East Germany. An eversensitive Poland demanded border guarantees and a seat at the table before reunification was consummated. On March 14 the "2+4" conference (two Germanys, four occupation powers) opened in Bonn.

Thanks to active campaigning by Chancellor Kohl in the GDR's first free elections for sixty years the conservatives under former violist Lothar de Maizière – whose name betrays his Huguenot French origins – won a sweeping victory and reunification mandate on March 18 (Christian Democrats 41%, Social Democrats 22%, former communist Democratic Socialists 16%). One more Eastern European country had achieved democracy. However, the citizens of the GDR held an avantage over Poland, Hungary and Czechoslovakia: they had counterparts in the West – cousins, brothers, sisters – waiting to absorb them into a unified German state and the western economic system. Rostock, Potsdam, Weimar and Leipzig would move in a matter of months from COMECON to the European Community.

Even more astonishingly, East Germans were to switch military protectors. Three weeks after this unequivocal election result the Soviet Union gave ground, declaring it would accept a united Germany as a member of both defensive military blocs, NATO and the Warsaw Pact, for a period of five to seven years, leading to formation of an all-European security system. The United States reacted negatively, perceiving in this gesture a veiled move to make Germany neutral and confident it could achieve more.

A new half-member for the EC

On April 12 de Maizière formed a coalition government, the first non-communist administration in the German Democratic Republic, with a policy of achieving early reunification under Article 3 of the Federal German constitution. This article, crafted with great prescience, obviated the necessity of a constituent assembly of the two Germanys by making it possible for the *Länder* comprising East Germany to be assimilated directly into the Federal Republic, thereby ensuring the predominance and continuity of the West German democratic institutions. Shaking off all suzerainty from the Soviet Union or the WTO, de Maizière asserted his independence in negotiating union with the Federal Republic. However, he pointed out that since the latter would bring automatic membership of the European Community, protection for the Eastern German economy would be needed for a transitional period just as in the case of other "new members" even though Germany would now be a single country.[6]

April 1990 was marked by particularly rapid progress towards unification. On April 25 German leaders set July 2 as the unification date for a single currency. Four days later Lothar de Maizière rejected the Soviet concept of neutrality for the new Germany, calling instead for changes in NATO's structure and strategy. De Maizière considered that a buffer zone would emphasize rather than diminish the existence of opposing blocs. The details of monetary union were agreed on May 2, with the West German currency (*D-Mark*) replacing that of the GDR.

A meeting commonly known as the last superpower summit opened in Washington on June 3 between Presidents Bush and Gorbachev. President Bush put forward a nine-point plan for German reunification but this too would be overtaken by events. Upon returning home Gorbachev made a speech to the Supreme Soviet easing his opposition to membership of "Eastern Germany" in NATO. Instead, it was suggested, NATO troops would not cross the former GDR boundary and Soviet troops would only gradually be phased out of their positions in Eastern Germany.

Reunification and the German diaspora

One of the most delicate issues of German reunification and one on which Helmut Kohl dragged his feet until the last moment in order to retain the support of the right wing of his Christian Democratic party, was that of the "new" Germany's eastern borders. The Poles feared that once reunited Germany would seek to recuperate other former German territories — Upper Silesia,

West and even East Prussia – now deep inside Poland and even, in part, within the Soviet Union. (Kaliningrad on the Baltic, now part of the Russian Federation, is the former Königsberg, capital of East Prussia). A great step forward was achieved on June 21, 1990, when both German parliaments recognized the current border along the Oder and Neisse rivers as the definitive frontier with Poland and renounced all claim to territories further east. They did however seek measures to protect the culture of the remaining German-speaking minority within Poland.

July 2, 1990, marked economic, social and financial union, with inauguration of the West German *D-Mark* in East Germany. The final rush to unification was on. On September 11 France, the United Kingdom, the USSR and the United States signed a treaty terminating occupation status – a measure of great symbolic importance but which had practical effect only in Berlin. The four powers subsequently suspended their occupation rights pending ratification of the treaty so that Germany might achieve full sovereignty at the moment of reunion.

On August 18 the East German Socialist Party withdrew from the GDR government in disagreement over the proposed date of union and election procedures; but Helmut Kohl the master tactician had once more been underestimated: the movement was unstoppable.

Endlich, die Wiedervereinigung!

On October 2, 1990, at midnight the German Democratic Republic ceased to exist and its five federated states were absorbed into the Federal Republic of Germany, with Berlin as the new capital, in name if not yet in fact. An objective judiciously yet single-mindedly pursued for forty-five years had been achieved with astonishing suddenness. With little regard for alcoholic or economic hangovers, Germans everywhere, but especially in Berlin, danced and sang the night away. The very next day the parliaments held an emotional and symbolic joint session in the former burned-out Reichstag, refurbished for the occasion. On November 9, one year to the day since the Berlin Wall had been breached, Germany and the Soviet Union signed a treaty of cooperation.

For Chancellor Helmut Kohl, the underrated "great bear" of German politics, reunification was a personal and political triumph. On December 2 the Christian Democrats swept to victory in the first all-German federal elections. Social Democratic leader Oskar Lafontaine not only acknowledged defeat but also resigned the leadership and returned home to the Saar.

It would be a full year before certain chickens came home to roost. Kohl had promised the West German electorate that taxes would not be raised to pay for rehabilitation of the new eastern *Länder*. Yet a few months later moves were made to raise taxes to pay for German unity. (Moreover, Germany had to indulge in checkbook diplomacy to cover its inability to send troops to the Persian Gulf because of post World War II constitutional restrictions). In April 1991 a crushing defeat in his home state, Rhineland-Palatinate, gave not only regional government but also control of the Federal upper house, the *Bundesrat* or Council of the Federated States, to the Social

Democrats. Fall in value of the prestigious *D-Mark* and rising unemployment in 1991 provided further evidence that the transition of eastern Germany to a flourishing market economy would probably take longer and cost more than originally envisioned. In April 1991 the name of Wolfgang Schäuble was circulating as a possible successor to Helmut Kohl after eight years at the helm ... Such is the tug and haul of democracy.

Kurt Biedenkopf, a western German who became the Christian Democrat premier of Saxony, eastern Germany's largest state, has warned that the eastern Germans cannot be humiliated or their accomplishments besmirched if reunification is to succeed. Biedenkopf arrived at Dresden University as a visiting professor in 1990 and ended up leading the Christian Democrats to electoral victory. Pointing to the continued trek west of young eastern German talent, Biedenkopf warned against the creation of a "German *Mezzogiorno*": "A hundred years after Italian reunification southern Italy remains a region of high unemployment and migration ... National unity does not necessarily lead to economic unity". Biedenkopf added that he would not dare to judge those who had worked through the party system in the GDR. "The non-economic factors are extremely important for the process here ... In this part of Germany you have no one of working age who has lived under conditions other than a command society or a dictatorship. This is a big difference with 1948 and West Germany".

Unscrambling the ownership omelette
As we have seen in discussing land reform in Hungary, one of the major stumbling blocks to privatisation and development of a market economy in the former communist bloc is the ownership of enterprises taken over by the state. In many cases claims go back to the Nazi era when Jews were expropriated and the new "owners" subsequently themselves expropriated by the Communist regime which took over in 1945. "Our action is not political; it is about justice", declares Geza Hambruch, President of the Federation of Hungarian Germans (yet another minority!) which collected twenty thousand signatures to protest against a Hungarian law which in the Federation's view does not reach back far enough. Many see 1949 – the Hungarian limit – as individious, discriminating between terror victims of the right and the left.

It is also necessary to distinguish between compensation and possession. In a move to unblock eastern Germany's progress to a free-market economy, where foreign investment was stalled by ownership disputes, Germany's supreme court ruled that landowners and industrialists whose East German property was seized by the Soviet Union during its occupation from 1945 to 1949 are entitled to compensation but not to return of the property. Had the court ruled for restitution about a third of eastern Germany's land area would have been subject to challenge from previous owners or their heirs. For example, construction of the Coca-Cola bottling plant in Dresden, which occupies the site of a former brewery, was slowed by an ownership claim from the heirs of the brewery's pre-Communist era owners, two elderly sisters residing in California!

The German *Treuhand* or Public Trustee office, a state holding organization which sells off state-owned industries to the private sector, asserts that the ownership question is not the only issue impeding privatization.   Lack of locally available capital and the poor state of the general economy in eastern Germany makes operations more difficult. By June 1990 only one thousand out of nine thousand undertakings had been sold. Things got worse still: on March 29, 1991, the *Treuhand* office in Bonn was firebombed. Two days later the Public Trustee himself, Detlev Rohwedder, was assassinated. Responsibility was claimed by the extreme left-wing organization Red Army Faction. Clearly such events do nothing to promote private investment in eastern Germany's state-owned industries.

Under authoritarian regimes it was not difficult for the state to break eggs or make omelettes; unscrambling in a free society is another matter.

One Germany, two capitals?
Berlin's re-emergence as a national and international capital was consecrated on June 20, 1991. On that day, as the CSCE Council deliberated in the refurbished Reichstag, the lower house of the Federal German parliament voted by 337 to 320 to transfer its seat to Berlin. The decision was confirmed by the upper house on July 5. The Bundestag moves to Berlin over a four-year period, whereas the Bundesrat remains in Bonn. Berlin also becomes, over ten to twelve years, the principal seat of the government.

The closeness of the lower house vote resulted from a strange coalition of material and political interests against the move. In Bonn, the sleepy old-world city on the banks of the Rhine, overshadowed by Cologne, government had become over a hectic half-century an important growth industry. Not only parliamentarians and federal employees, but generations of delegations to the Federal Republic, keen to observe its economic miracle, had been accommodated there. This was an important lobby. The other group consisted of those who felt that Berlin carried dark memories of national socialist and communist dictatorships. However, with some compromise, national pride in cultural history and the new Germany won the day. Was it also a recognition that Europe's political center of gravity had shifted east? Germany's pin-striped diplomats were far too suave to utter such a thought.

Anniversary hangover
On October 3, 1991, the first anniversary of German reunification, there was no ceremony at the Brandenburg Gate, no dancing in the streets at midnight. Chancellor Kohl maintained a low profile. He had been forced to rescind a prediction that growth would take care of East German economic rehabilitation without new taxes. Unemployment, reaching 45% in some areas, was unacceptably high; a new xenophobia against foreigners had brought skinheads into conflict with immigrants and ethnic minorities; four former East German border guards were on trial under West German law for shooting compatriots fleeing over the Berlin wall . . . Even newly arrived ethnic Germans found themselves being settled in communities seething with frustration.

Germany's pivotal role

It is important however to keep a sense of perspective in these matters. Let us remember the Federal Republic's post-war reconstruction, the *Wirtschafts-wunder*, the economic miracle, fostered by Adenauer, Erhard, Brandt and Schmidt ... The new Germany of eighty million inhabitants occupies the pivotal middle ground — geographically, economically, culturally, politically — in Europe. Not only is Germany well positioned for trade and development in eastern Europe but she also can call on the vast resources of the European Community's development program to bring balance to her economy, a goal which should be fully achieved by the end of the century and possibly within five years.

Political alliances within the Community will depend on how the new Germany's role is assessed. Since its inception with the ECSC, one of the principal tenets of the Community has been to anchor the Federal Republic in the West — a friendly version of containment — and to make conflict between European powers impossible. German reunification and the entry of East Germany into NATO and the EC as part of the "new" Germany appeared to most observers as a resounding vindication of policy. Such was certainly the reassuring note sounded by German politicians. One of the strongest arguments in favor of the Maastricht Treaty of European Union was to anchor the "new Germany" more firmly to the European Community.

The self-congratulation is not unanimous. A minority of convinced Europeans of the left fear that the success of the market economy (what the French call *libéralisme*, with a right wing connotation closer to American republicanism then to the British liberalism of the center), and the discreditation of the checks, balances and safety-nets of socialism, may open the door to the hegemony of "Greater Germany" at Community level. In the colorful phrase of Maurice Duverger, the "liberal" hare is outrunning the European tortoise. [7]

Post Scriptum: from Nazi to Stasi

On November 14, 1991 the German parliament approved a law allowing citizens access to former East German secret police archives documenting both their political activities (real or alleged) and their private lives. All major parties supported the law. Many legislators and government officials have been forced to resign following disclosure of their secret police connections.

A Cologne University study estimates that some 50,000 citizens are still suffering the after effects of *Staatsicherheitsdienst* (Stasi) abuse. Some 85,000 former full-time agents and half a million part-time informants may now be looking over their own shoulders or even following each other.

Secret service activities in the West German portion of the Federal Republic are not covered by the law. *Natürlich.*

Albania and the stability of denial

With less than two million people, Albania, a former Italian colony, is the smallest of the Balkan republics in both population and land area. To the extent that religion has been tolerated at all under a fierce communist regime, its culture is Islamic and Turcic. The language, as with Basque in the west, is unlike other European tongues and of mysterious origin. The country's borders with Greece and Yugoslavia are mountainous. Until recent years, few foreigners penetrated to Albania's capital, Tirana, and emigration was prohibited.

Even more than Romania, therefore, Albania under Enver Hoxha succeeded in remaining a hermetically enclosed and tightly controlled dictatorship, spurning eastern and western defense and economic organizations alike. She left the Warsaw Pact in September 1968 and did not join the CSCE. Albania had no private ownership, no cars on the streets of its capital. Her sole ally was far-away China, in an association based largely on a common rejection of reform in the Soviet Union.

This stability of denial was shaken finally by the death of Enver Hoxha in 1989. Vice-president Ramiz Alia stepped into the presidency and effected cosmetic reforms. Maintaining a you-mind-your-business-and-I'll-mind-mine posture, Albania laid no claim to the 90% Albanian-speaking republic of Kosovo in neighboring Yugoslavia.

It eventually became apparent, however, that the ostrich could not keep its head in the sand forever. On April 19, 1990, Albania moved to strengthen her ties with both the United States and the Soviet Union. The following month curbs on religious freedom and even travel were eased. Spontaneous demonstrations for greater freedom broke out in July and, as had happened elsewhere in eastern Europe, citizens took refuge in foreign embassies. The poet Ismail Kadare, a national figure, sought refuge in France. Faced with student demonstrations which he was unwilling to put down with force, President Alia agreed in December to the formation of opposition parties. The founding rally of the Albanian Democratic Party took place in Tirana on December 12. Reformist Communist Fatos Nano was appointed general secretary of the Albanian government. Elections were hastily scheduled for February 10, 1991, denying the opposition time to organize its campaign. Demands for a postponement were at first firmly rejected; however, the poll was subsequently postponed.

Street clashes grew, with five people killed on February 25. Refugees, especially members of the Greek-speaking minority, were now straggling across Albania's southern border, often under fire. On March 6 a mass exodus across the Adriatic Sea to Italy began with the population commandeering boats in the Albanian harbors. On April 2 the army fired on the crowd: three persons died.

Such was the climate of fear and disorder in which the elections were finally held on April 10. Despite opposition victories in the cities, including defeat of President Alia himself, the Labor (formerly Communist Party) machine retained firm control in the countryside, winning 168 of 250 seats. Despite his parliamentary defeat, Alia retained the presidency.

On April 10 the government proposed a new constitution, with separation of party and state. With only 82 parliamentary seats, less than one-third, the opposition could do little to influence the outcome. As in Romania and at first in Bulgaria, Albania's old regime had survived the electoral process.

The reprieve was of short duration. It rapidly became apparent that the election results, engineered through communist control of the country areas, did not mirror Albanian aspirations. Forced by strikes, demonstrations and divisions within the ranks of the Communist Party itself, the Albanian government resigned on June 4, 1991. Democratic Party leader Sali Berisha agreed to join a government of national union. Albania finally came out of its self-imposed diplomatic exile by joining CSCE on June 17.

Uncle Sam enters forbidden city
Following Albania's entry into CSCE, US Foreign Secretary James Baker visited the capital, Tirana, on June 23. It was the first visit by a senior US official after Albanians had been isolated from the outside world for four decades. Showered with flower petals, Baker declared: "On behalf of President Bush and the American people I come here today to say to you: Freedom works". The 6 million dollars in powdered milk, medical equipment and medicine was the first US aid Albania ever received.

Secure once more in the comity of nations, Albania followed with increasing concern the unrest on its northern and eastern borders, particularly regarding the Albanian-speaking majority in Serbian controlled Kosovo.

The comity of nations seemed less assured in mid-August, 1991, when the breakdown in production and distribution of food in the drastic transition from collective to free market production provoked a new wave of emigration across the Adriatic to Bari and Brindisi. In pursuit of a policy of immediate repatriation the Italian authorities deliberately withheld adequate sanitary and sleeping facilities. President Cossiga made a brief visit to Tirana to promise President Alia material assistance but Giorgio La Malfa, secretary general of the Republican Party, criticized both his own government and the European Community: "Without a Community initiative we will not be able to contain the pressures from people in the East". In a less publicized development two shiploads of Albanians reached St Paul's Bay in Malta. Unlike their counterparts who reached Italy, they were given food, medical supplies and hospitable treatment but also firmly repatriated. The last crumbling bastions of European communism have not finished sending shockwaves west. The major institutions have yet to face up to the potential dimensions of European migrations, whether "economic" or "political" and to devise a plan to address the issue at its roots, in the countries of origin. The Community can no longer afford to turn a deaf ear to the German proposal, made at the Luxembourg summit in June 1991, for the EC to define and adopt a common immigration policy.

There was hope for substantial assistance from another quarter in the fall of 1991 when on October 15 Albania became the 156th member of the International Monetary Fund and the International Bank for Reconstruction and Development, known as the World Bank. In the final analysis only development at home will stem the exodus of refugees.

In December 1991 Dr Sali Berisha withdrew his opposition Democratic Party from the government coalition. The Democrats, who had seven of the twenty-one cabinet seats, charged that the ex-communist Socialist Party was blocking changes after half a century of Stalinism, particularly with respect to land distribution to poor farmers; and that former leaders should face trial for corruption.

Getting through to the needy

The New Year brought little consolation to Eastern Europe's smallest nation and most backward economy. The attempt to reform the system created the same grave shortages as had been seen elsewhere. Seventeen policemen were wounded in February, 1992, while trying to prevent the pillaging of a warehouse of foodstuffs at Kavaje. The rampaging citizens complained that emergency supplies sent by Italy were distributed both inequitably and too slowly. At Rogjine, in the south, thirty tons of goods from Britain were stolen. Peter Brindle of Britain's Feed the Children said similar events were happening elsewhere. One of the major problems of emergency aid is making sure it gets through to those who need it most rather than being diverted for the enrichment of black market operators.

Second general election

Despite the victory of the "Socialists" in the first free election and the short-lived coalition government, the country remained in a parlous state. Some estimates set unemployment as high as eighty per cent. Assaults on stored food awaiting distribution continued unabated. Another general election, the second within a year, was called for March 22, 1992.

More than 500 candidates from eleven parties stood for 140 seats. Berisha's Democratic Party was certain to take the cities but the unknown factor remained the conservative rural areas, with 70% of the population. In fact the opposition forces gained a 72% majority. On April 3, president Ramiz Alia drew the logical conclusion from the outcome and resigned. Thus did eastern Europe's last Stalinist head of state, who for decades had stood shoulder to shoulder with the dictator Enver Hoxha, slide quietly into "retirement". A devastated nation, Albania has finally made a clean break with the past. Dr. Sali Berisha has the daunting task of giving a new Albania both political freedom and food on the table. He also has to bring his country out of institutional isolation: a start was made when Albania became a founder member of the eleven-nation Black Sea Economic Cooperation organization at Istanbul in June 1992.

Yugoslavia after Josip Broz

Developments in Yugoslavia call for detailed analysis both as the first European war since the Greek conflict in 1946 and as a testing ground for EC foreign policy towards eastern Europe.

Like Albania, Yugoslavia under Josip Broz, who retained his wartime partisan alias of Tito, steered a course independent of both blocs after World War

II. Unlike Albania's brand of virulent Marxism, however "Titoism" was a milder form of communism which generated contacts in both camps. For many years Yugoslavia welcomed western tourists and enjoyed associate status in OECD. Now in the post-communist era Yugoslavia has again lived up to its reputation as the tinder-box of Europe: the map of the Balkans patched together at Versailles has come apart at the seams.[8]

For thirty-five years after 1945 Tito, himself half Croat, half Slovenian, held this disparate nation together by means of an authoritarian regime and force of personality. He brooked little opposition and nurtured no heir apparent. When he died, on May 4, 1980, he left a political testament whereby a presidential council of the leaders of the eight provinces and autonomous republics was set up under an annually rotating presidency.

What works for Switzerland has not worked well for Yugoslavia. Regional and ethnic rivalries soon bubbled up. The collective presidency staggered forward as long as the leaders were all communists. However, when the Eastern European domino chain reached Yugoslavia and several provinces ousted the Communist Party in free elections, nationalist sentiment was used by both anti-communists and communists to seize or retain power. Slovenia and Croatia asserted the right to secede and joined with Macedonia in opposing Serbia and Montenegro which had maintained communist rule.

At the federal congress of the Communist Party in January 1990, the party's renunciation of a monopoly of power failed to dissuade the Slovenian delegation from walking out. The same month an explosive situation developed in Kosovo when the ethnic Albanians sought greater freedom from Serbia. The conservative Croatian Democratic Union won the provincial election in May and called for a Yugoslav federation of sovereign states. In June Slovenia drafted an independence constitution, to be approved by referendum in December. A non-communist majority came to power in Bosnia-Herzogovina in November. A month later Croatia followed Slovenia in drafting a constitution providing for secession. On the other hand, on December 23 the "former" (renamed) communists under Milosevic won a decisive victory in Serbia, skillfully imitating the Romanians in passing off ideology under the guise of nationalism.

Europe was now facing the first major war on its territory since 1945.

Clashes developed between provincial and federal forces, especially in Croatia, where Serbians dominate in some areas (in particular Krajina and Slavonia). Things came to a head on January 24, 1991, when Croatia refused to disband her paramilitary police, fearing the Serbian sympathies of the federal army and declaring that Serbia was no longer to be trusted. Raising the stakes, the Croatian parliament gave itself veto power over federal laws and adopted the Slovenian model for secession, to be triggered as necessary.

Despite protests by anti-communists inside his own province, Milosevic went on the offensive, renouncing recognition of the federal collective presidency in March, while Croatian Serbs declared the Krajina region a part of Serbia. With the country on the brink of civil war, presidents Milosevic of Serbia and Franjo Tudjman of Croatia met to discuss their differences

(Milosevic being strongly opposed to break-up of the federation) but were unable to head off a number of deadly communal clashes in Borova Selo and Krajina.

Tension increased further when Serbia, Montenegro and the Serbian-controlled "autonomous" regions of Vojvodina and Kosovo blocked the "rotating" elevation of the Croatian representative to the federal presidency (May 15). The same day the Croatian electorate approved by 96% a new constitution permitting secession from Yugoslavia. In June, brushing aside warnings of non-recognition from the EC and the US, Slovenia and Croatia declared independence a day earlier than expected.

Civil war effectively broke out on June 28 when federal troops in Slovenia left their camps to assert control over the frontier posts with Austria, Italy and Hungary.

European cross-currents

This conflict on her own territory put Europe to the test. Croatians and Slovenians had hoped, perhaps naively, that their resistance to and separation from the communist regime in Serbia would generate sympathy in the West and bring rapid recognition. In the event, European governments in both EC and CSCE clung to old concepts of political stability and respect for national frontiers. Behind Slovenia and Croatia, as earlier behind the Baltic States, loomed the unnamed specters of Irish, Basque, Catalonian, Corsican, Slovak, Baltic, Moldavian and Georgian separatism. The guns of Lubljana were heard in Derry, Balboa and Calvi. A Yugoslavian break-up could trigger unrest across the whole continent: national frontiers had to remain sacrosanct. On the other hand, those same governments could not countenance military repression of freely-elected governments, especially since the principle of non-intervention in "internal" affairs had recently been undermined in the case of the Kurds of Iraq. As Europe is integrated and sovereignty increasingly shared, the notion of what constitutes "internal" affairs must of necessity come under review.

EC's ministerial *troïkas*

A quirk of the political calendar brought the heads of EC governments together in the European Council in Luxembourg just as the shooting started in Slovenia. It took only two hours of discussion on June 29, 1991, to dispatch a troïka of foreign ministers to Belgrade. (The *troïka* is a representative team composed of past, present and impending representatives of the EC's rotating presidency). When the delegation returned to Luxembourg it was heralded as the architect of a cease-fire, a return of troops to barracks, a three-month cooling-off period, the unblocking of Stipe Mesic's election to the federal presidency — and of the first international success of European foreign policy ... The exultation proved premature. True, the Serbian bloc relented on the presidency, thereby supposedly providing a constitutional tether for the loose cannons of the army, agog to erase the memory of an unexpected setback at the hands of a Slovene militia who knew what it was fighting for; but when the

Slovenes refused to abandon control of their frontier posts (they sensed that Austria's "neutrality" was sympathetically tilted), the agreement unravelled and new clashes occurred, this time in Croatia as well as Slovenia. A new EC mission to Belgrade was required. Another meeting of EC foreign ministers, now under Dutch chairmanship, showed a veiled shift, urged on by Denmark and Germany, to the Slovenian-Croat position. Not only was aid to the central government suspended, but Yugoslavia was also warned that if force were again employed against the dissident republics, the EC attitude might "change" – a clear reference to recognition. Thus did the EC seek to reconcile its adherence to the conflicting principles of the peaceful resolution of disputes, respect for the integrity of states and the right of peoples to self-determination. As a balancing act, it could not endure.

Meanwhile the CSCE, meeting in emergency session, was also trying out on the hapless Yugoslavs its new mechanism for conflict resolution. The "recommendation" it issued to Yugoslavia, in effect at Belgrade's own request, looked for maintenance of an integrated Yugoslavia on the basis of a negotiated solution.

The second troika of foreign ministers, representing CSCE as well as the European Community, met with the conflicting parties on the island of Brioni on July 7 and hammered out a second agreement, leading Slovenia to claim a measure of international recognition. The agreement included dispatch of an EC observer mission of 30 to 50 members, a derisory figure. Slovenian president Milan Kucan insisted on submitting the agreement to the Slovenian parliament for ratification.

In an exclusive interview with *The European* of July 12, 1991, Yugoslavia's Croatian federal president, Stipe Mesic, supported the Brioni breathing space but warned that Slovenia and Croatia would not renounce an independence ratified by the people. A peaceful dissolution had to be negotiated. In unusually frank terms for a federal president, Mesic warned that the federal army was dominated by Serbia and that Serbian president Slobodan Milosevic "has a huge appetite for territory... He is using protection of Serbs living in Croatia and other parts of Yugoslavia as an excuse to gain land". Mesic accused Milosevic of behaving like Hitler and Mussolini in the build-up to World War II.

EC sponsors a peace conference

On August 21, the Yugoslav presidium declared a new ceasefire, with each republic entitled to autonomy. It lasted one day. Under Dutch foreign minister, Hans van den Broek, the EC produced a more far-reaching plan: a peace conference to be attended by all Yugoslav parties and all EC countries. The Serbians were the last to agree; they also demanded representation for Serbian minority areas within Croatia but desisted when denied.

The conference, chaired by Lord Carrington of Britain, former Secretary General of NATO and successful mediator of independence for Zimbabwe, sought to set up an arbitration procedure to settle issues inflaming Yugoslavia.

The conference created a panel of five judges, three from the EC and two from Yugoslavia, but battlefield thunder drowned out the voices of peace.

Southern discomfort: the Macedonian domino
The situation became even more tense with the September 1991 independence referendum in the southern republic of Macedonia. The citizens did not have an easy choice. They resented the overwhelming influence of Serbia in the federation and feared that the Croatian-Serbian confrontation might spill over into Macedonia. On the other hand, Macedonia has its own minorities: Albanian, Greek, Bulgarian. Bulgaria and Greece — the latter an EC member governing its own Macedonian region and with power to influence Community attitudes towards the southern Balkans — gave notice that they would not recognize an independent Macedonia. Bulgaria has since done so but Greece has vowed not to recognize a state with such a name, fearing claims upon its own territory. By the spring of 1992 Greece was isolated in the EC on this issue although Brussels was reluctant to demonstrate once more its political disarray by according Macedonia recognition over Greek protests.

EC flunks policy test on Yugoslavia
In October, as ceasefires came and went, Slovenia and Croatia reconfirmed their declarations of independence, following a three-month moratorium, and were joined by Bosnia-Herzegovina. Former US Secretary of State Cyrus Vance was appointed special representative of the UN Secretary-General Perez de Cuellar to assist Lord Carrington and the EC mediators — an implied admission that the Community was not up to the task, with consequences not only for the combatants but also for maneuvers towards a European foreign policy.

Why were the Community's results so meager? In the Yugoslavian conflict each combatant was somebody's friend. Pushing for early recognition of Slovenia and Croatia, Germany aroused memories of the Ustashe-Nazi alliance of the Second World War and was suspected of seeking a sphere of influence to the south based on the historical Hapsburg outlet to the sea. The French on the other hand, whose close ties to the Federal Republic set up by Adenauer and De Gaulle have somewhat cooled since a power shift eastwards following reunification has become possible, have closer links with Serbia than Croatia. The United Kingdom counselled a hands-off policy, opposing the insertion of armed peacekeepers between combatants in a conflict where the front lines are by no means clear: "There has to be a peace to keep". Solicited by the EC conference under Lord Carrington, Western European Union recoiled from sending in armed troops.

Meanwhile, in September 1991 the UN Security Council tried to bolster EC action by ordering an arms embargo on Yugoslavia, a move interpreted by some as favoring the federal army, allied to the Serbian cause, since, without access to arms depots, the Croats had been scrambling to purchase weapons on the international market.

US: an uncomfortable bystander

The US had as yet played no direct role in the Yugoslav imbroglio, although, recalling her own civil war, she clearly preferred federal union to fragmentation. With few vital interests at stake, Washington was only too happy to leave this mess to the Europeans. However, US military thinking did not remain unaffected. Chief of Staff Colin Powell reminded the West that the Soviet Union was still capable of destroying western civilization in half an hour. He also cautioned that the bombs falling on Zagreb pointed to the need for NATO to develop a strategy of mobile intervention even as US forces "stepped down the nuclear ladder" and halved their troop numbers in Europe.

Sovereignty redefined

The recent history of Eastern Europe and the Persian Gulf has contorted the definition of sovereignty. States which lay claim to political independence, old or new, are unable to attain full economic autonomy. Moreover, respect for political sovereignty upon which the United Nations Organization was founded was undermined by the Gulf War and its aftermath (protection of the Kurds, enforcement of disarmament measures).

When civil war broke out in Yugoslavia the Community, like the US, would have preferred not to become involved in this so-called "internal" affair of a non-member country, yet if a common European foreign policy had any hope of achievement, there really was no choice. As Josef Joffe wrote in the *Süddeutsche Zeitung* on August 9, 1991, history came back to haunt the new Europe. When Mussolini invaded Abyssinia in 1935, Emperor Haile Selassie invoked Article 16 of the League of Nations Charter, yet Italy annexed Abyssinia and the League headed for demise. For Joffe a similar fate threatened the Community as a political power and, even more acutely, the Conference on Security and Cooperation in Europe, if Europe's greatest armed conflict since 1945 could not be halted. It remains to be seen whether governments will continue to put narrow national interests ahead of broader political and moral considerations. Borders are still sacrosanct, even within the Community, yet these days the seeds of conflict are more often intranational than truly international. Ethnic groups and regional cultures need to be able to retain their identity without bringing down the whole structure. In 1991 Eastern Europe seemed poised between the nineteenth and the twenty-first centuries. As Vukovar and Dubrovnik went up in flames, Europe had no choice but to abandon the paralysing pretense that Yugoslavia still existed. On the other hand recognition could also precipitate violence, as subsequently happened in Bosnia-Herzegovina. 1991 alone offered several precedents for intervention: the Security Council sanctioned a return to northern Iraq to defend the Kurds against their own government; the OAU allowed a multinational military force from West African nations to intervene in the Liberian civil war; the OAS intervened diplomatically in Haiti following the overthrow of President Bertrand Aristide; UN Secretary-General Perez de Cuellar personally brokered the ceasefire in the Salvadoran civil war minutes before his mandate expired.

The Serbian attack on Dubrovnik caused particular outrage. "There are no Serbs in Dubrovnik", declared Carrington; "It has never been part of Serbia; it's always been in Croatia; and the attack is absolutely unwarranted". This stone-walled Adriatic port city thrived for centuries as a city republic and trading post. It became the cradle of South Slav literature and is listed on the UN Heritage List of monuments of "universal value" whose safekeeping, like Venice, is "the responsibility of mankind". The world took note of this vandalism: destruction of historic monuments sometimes seems to ignite more outrage than destruction of lives.

After twelve ceasefires and spread of the war to Zagreb, capital of Croatia, and even Istria, less than a hundred kilometers from Italy, Community foreign ministers met in Rome on November 8, 1991, to review Lord Carrington's mediation effort. The ministers agreed to impose trade sanctions on Serbia and its satellite Montenegro as the only hold-out republics, hinting also that Slovenia and Croatia might soon be recognized. The sanctions included suspension of the Community's 1980 trade agreement with Yugoslavia, limitation of textile imports, elimination of trade benefits under the General System of Preferences and suspension of Yugoslavia from the EC's recovery plan for eastern Europe. The EC also agreed to compensate Greece for losses in applying the sanctions, since 40% of Greek trade passes through Yugoslavia.

Ministers called upon the US to support the economic blockade and urged the UN to impose an oil embargo, because Serbia's main suppliers, the Soviet Union and Libya, are not EC members. The US response was immediate: during a visit to The Hague, President Bush pledged full support for the EC move. In a separate statement, NATO leaders condemned the use of force to achieve political goals. In Dubrovnik shellfire drowned out the message.

By December, after fourteen broken ceasefires – used more to regroup and resupply than to seek peace – with television spreading gruesome pictures across the globe, the time was ripe for a new initiative. Germany, long tagged as an economic giant and political dwarf, stepped firmly forward, announcing her intention of recognizing the independence of Croatia and Slovenia. Only one week after the fragile Maastricht summit such independent foreign policy action by the EC's most powerful member seemed intolerable. Germany did have a case, however: the Helsinki (CSCE) accords of 1975 guaranteed Europe's borders, including major internal administrative borders. Hesitancy and appeasement would send a message that force would pay off. The German action was purely political, since the Federal Republic was precluded by its constitution from sending troops to the region, but she did not wish her perceived impotence in the Gulf conflict to be repeated here. Defying the combined opinions of the EC, the UN and the US, Germany won the day. Rather than expose political disarray to the world once more, EC foreign ministers agreed to recognize the breakaway republics (subject to certain conditions involving human rights and minorities) on January 15, 1992. Rumblings in London and The Hague about Austro-Hungarian conflicts with Serbia and German occupation of the Balkans and alignment with Croatians in World War II were given short shrift: the German cabinet met on December

19 to declare its intention of upgrading its consulates in Maribor and Zagreb to embassies on January 15.

The world had abruptly been reminded of two new political facts: the German political dwarf had undergone a growing spurt to match its economic gianthood; and whereas West Germany had been counted among the Atlantic nations, reunited Germany was unquestionably a central European power.

The New Year brought muted new hope. On his fifth peace mission to Yugoslavia, Vance obtained agreement by Croatia, Serbia and the federal army to withdrawal of Yugoslav army and Croatian national guard units from those crisis regions where Serbs were in the majority, designated as UN-protected areas. If the ceasefire held UN peacekeepers (infantry, police and support personnel) would be able to move in. However, Serbian leaders stressed they were not abrogating their claim to about one-third of Croatia as an independent Serbian republic. Conversely, the Croats averred that they would not renounce one centimeter of Croatian territory.

Community recognition of two republics
On January 15 EC representatives met in Brussels to consider the cases of the Yugoslav republics applying for recognition under the terms set out at the Brussels conference. Four files had been studied by the commission chaired by Robert Badinter, former French justice minister: those of Slovenia, Croatia, Bosnia-Herzegovina and Macedonia. The commission had recommended in favor of independence for Slovenia and Macedonia, expressing reservations with respect to Croatia and Bosnia-Herzegovina. (Serbia and Montenegro maintained their claim to Yugoslav institutions and legal continuity, as Russia had done with respect to the USSR. In fact, on April 27, abandoning any attempt to keep the former Yugoslavia together, the two republics formally proclaimed their union in the new Federal Republic of Yugoslavia).

If there was a positive consensus of the Twelve on Slovenia, a unanimous decision in favor of Croatia was not easily achieved, since a large segment of that republic's population, some 600,000 Serbs, still opposed separation, as noted by the Badinter commission. It took a special letter from President Tudjman, produced under prodding from Italian Foreign Minister Gianni Michelis, and promising prompt action to strengthen legislation protecting ethnic minorities, to pursuade France and the United Kingdom to follow the Federal Republic's leaders in overriding the Badinter commission's reservations. The Twelve considered that in the case of Bosnia-Herzegovina early recognition would provoke a new outbreak of hostilities; and they followed Greece's lead in refusing recognition to Macedonia. Since Macedonia and Bosnia had declared their independence from Yugoslavia, the ultimate status of these republics remained undetermined. In summary, the Badinter recommendations were followed in only two cases (Slovenia and Bosnia-Herzegovina), demonstrating that politics took precedence over legal niceties, as the Community found unity behind the original German initiative. It also did not go unnoticed that the insignia of the German embassy in Zagreb were erected on January 15 before the final outcome in Brussels was known ... As for the political impact of recognition, there is room for cynicism: prompt recognition of Croatia and late recognition of Bosnia produced the same result: war.

In mid-January 1992 US newspapers reported that a team of foreign observers had in the waning months of 1991 documented Serbian atrocities designed to incite non-Serbs dwelling in Serbian majority areas inside Croatia to flee their homes. Later similar, albeit more limited, acts by Croats were reported. "Ethnic cleansing" had begun. Yugoslavia is a signatory to the Second Protocol of the Fourth Geneva Convention, concerning "armed conflict not of an international character".

UN peacekeepers in Croatia
In mid-February the Security Council agreed with Boutros-Ghali that it was better to send in UN peacekeeping troops to Croatia, risking failure through lack of cooperation, than to court breakdown of the ceasefire because of further delay. Although the UN brief concerned Croatia it was decided to establish UN headquarters in the Bosnian capital, Sarajevo. UN intervention with 14,000 FORPRONU troops from some thirty countries had been achieved only at the cost of an unresolved ambiguity: whether it would favor the expunging of advantages which Serbia had wrested from Croatia by military force; or, on the contrary, establish *de facto* new frontiers, thereby strengthening Serbian claims to autonomy in the disputed areas. A compromise might be found by means of "ink blot" formations at sensitive spots. Intervention by the world body was clearly a prerequisite to but no substitute for negotiations.

Bosnia-Herzegovina: a precarious equilibrium
First Slovenia, then Croatia: the tragedy's third act promised to be the bloodiest of all. Surrounded to the west and north by Croatia, to the east by Serbia and to the south by Serbia's ally, Montenegro, Bosnia-Herzegovina contends with a delicate geographical location mirrored by diverse ethnicity. The west is home to the highest concentration of Croats (99%) in Yugoslavia. Bosnian Krajina abuts on Croatian Krajina in the north-west and is largely Serbian. There are also Serbs to the south-west (behind Dubrovnik) and even a predominantly Albanian group near Sarajevo. As for the Muslims, designated by religion rather than by ethnicity, they are both the largest and the most widely distributed group, with no solid "base" in a neighboring republic; Bosnia is their only home.

After the republic declared its autonomy from Belgrade, the Bosnian Serbs declared independence from Bosnia-Herzegovina (as Krajina had done in Croatia).

The UN ceasefire, following fourteen EC-monitored attempts, delayed explosion of this powder keg but failed to prevent it. On January 17, 1992, President Alija Izetbegovic proposed a referendum on total sovereignty. The Sarajevo parliament set the referendum for February 29 over Serbian protest. The Serbs met the next day to demand a confederation of three nation-states, urging their compatriots to boycott the referendum. Fearing Serbian and

Croatian link-ups with neighboring "bases" leaving many of them as isolated minorities, the Muslius favored an independent but undivided republic.

Third shoe falls

In late February the conflict reached Bosnia-Herzegovina. The referendum had been rendered largely meaningless by the boycott of the Serbian faction. Having long supported maintenance of their republic within Yugoslavia, the Bosnian Serbs now called for break-up into three ethnic republics, claiming 65% of the territory for themselves. Nevertheless, PROFORNU commander Satish Nambiar of India made it clear that the UN Blue Helmets would not be deterred from establishing their peace headquarters in Sarajevo. By the time they did so, they found themselves sitting in the middle of a war zone. The conflict had spread to Bosnia as each group tried to consolidate its zones of influence before the ethnic boundary commission coaxed into being by Lord Carrington's conference (still dragging on in Brussels) issued its recommendations.

As is usually the case with compromise solutions, interpretations differed. The Serbian leader Radovan Karadzic felt confident that there would in future be "three Bosnias", whereas the Muslims' Alija Izetbegovic considered that reattachment of a portion of Bosnia-Herzegovina to "greater Serbia" was now out of the question.

The conflict had moved south. By June 1992 tranquillity if not official peace had returned to Slovenia and a relative calm to Croatia. In Bosnia-Herzegovina the battle increased in intensity. Mostar in the south-west fell to the Serbs and was retaken by the Croats; but the capital Sarajevo took the heaviest pounding with civilians of all ethnic groups brought together in death. Bosnia-Herzegovina officially declared war on Serbia to permit general mobilization and made a direct appeal to the UN ... The UN tried to reopen the airport ... Lord Carrington tried to restart the EC "peace" conference, in Strasbourg ... US Secretary of State Baker hinted at recourse to other means ...

Serbia was not without problems at home. On May 24 Kosovo, an Autonomous Region of Serbia, organized clandestine elections and voted massively for independence. Serbia turned a blind eye but on June 23 prevented the new "parliament" from meeting. Even in the streets of Belgrade there were massive demonstrations against the Milosevic administration ...

UN troops under Canadian command were moved into war-torn Sarajevo but it took a courageous and spectacular visit by French President Mitterrand on June 28 – anniversary of the assassination of Archduke Ferdinand which started World War I – to open up the airport to humanitarian supplies.

Events took an even more bizarre turn when in mid-July a US millionaire, Serbian expatriate Milan Panic, was appointed prime minister of the "new" federal Yugoslavia (Serbia, including Vojvodina and Kosovo, and Montenegro). He deplored the violence but would not be drawn into criticizing Milosevic. It was unclear whether Panic would be his ally, pawn or opponent. Milosevic, meanwhile, was assuring the world's press that he had no control over Serbs fighting outside Serbia . . . The Security Council remained unconvinced. Lord Carrington enlarged his plodding international conference to include the UN and CSCE. Boutros-Ghali lost patience, referred cynically to "a war of the rich"; and finally got some action on behalf of famished tribal conflict victims in Somalia. "Rich" or "poor", children were dying in both.

Painful lessons for Europe
Yugoslavia's painful dismemberment has demonstrated that the Maastricht (European Union) measures for foreign policy coordination, so "dangerous" to those sensitive to loss of sovereignty, really represent a minimum requirement. In this sector it is the European Council, not the Commission, which shares the power of initiative and decision-making, without coercive powers. It is highly questionable whether consensus politics will suffice to decide:

— What is an "internal" matter and when is "intervention" justified?
— How is a balance to be struck between regional or national identity and economic and social integration? At what point does the autonomy of micro-cultures become counterproductive?
— How is the Community to prepare continental solutions to continental problems?

If sovereignty is the power to act effectively and independently, no nation has demonstrated sovereignty on Yugoslavia; except, of course, to watch the fires burn and hope they won't spread.

The Community's failures have been highlighted in the Yugoslav issue. However, the entire world accepted not only the EC mediation effort but also considered Community recognition of the Baltic States, Slovenia, Croatia, Bosnia and ultimately Macedonia as the touchstone of these republics' existence as independent nations. Community foreign policy may not be strong but it can no longer be denied. It is already recognized in its weakness if not in its strength.

Above legal issues of sovereignty and political issues of foreign policy, there is one overriding consideration. If creation of a Greater Serbia is permitted in the name of a single race, a single religion, a single cultural group, through the violation of frontiers and the eviction of those who do not "belong", then it is not Yugoslavia alone but ultimately the whole of Europe which will pay the price.

Disarmament and world affairs
Meanwhile, progress had been made in East-West relations. In January 1989 the CSCE conference in Vienna mandated new arms reduction negotiations for conventional forces in Europe (CFE). These opened in Vienna on March 16. START talks between the US and the USSR resumed in Geneva the same day. In July a WEU Assembly delegation to Moscow initiated an annual parliamentary exchange with the Supreme Soviet.

In January 1990 Bush proposed and a few weeks later Gorbachev accepted mutual reduction of conventional land forces to 195,000 troops. This would require a greater reduction on the Soviet side. Subsequently the agreement ran into a roadblock when the USSR transferred certain units to the coast guard and navy: hence, not to be counted. The US found this unacceptable and signature of the CFE treaty was delayed into 1991.

The Soviet Union was active on other fronts, adapting foreign policy both to create a climate of cooperation with the West and to reduce cost burdens. Withdrawal from Afghanistan had been completed on February 15, 1989, with the commanding officer General Alexandr Rutzkoi, later to become Yeltsin's deputy as vice-president of Russia, the last to walk across the bridge into the Soviet Union. In May a Sino-Soviet summit normalized relations in the Far East (and probably led to false hopes in China which culminated in the Tiananmen Square crackdown). On October 25, in Helsinki, President Gorbachev pronounced the demise of the Brezhnev doctrine mandating the leading role of the Communist Party in Eastern Europe.

Eastern Europe received the signal; although Gorbachev doubtless did not intend it for the Soviet Union's own republics. On December 20, 1989 the Lithuanian Communist Party asserted its independence from Moscow, triggering a whole series of more or less daring gestures from Estonia, Latvia, Azerbaijan, Georgia, Moldavia and the Ukraine. There were even opposition demonstrations in Mongolia. In some cases manifestations resulted in violence. However, Lithuania continued to lead the way. Multi-party elections on February 24, 1990 resulted in the first anti-communist majority in the Soviet Union. On March 11 the new parliament immediately voted independence from the USSR, declared "illegitimate" by Moscow two days later. Local elections in Russia and the Ukraine gave opposition majorities in Moscow, Leningrad and Kiev.

Amid this widespread unrest Namibia became Africa's last independent nation on March 21. On April 22, 1990, the world celebrated Earth Day. As they peer through our smog and gunsmoke at clear-cut forests and flattened towns, little green men from outer space may be forgiven for wondering why.

CSCE Council: from Vancouver to Vladivostock via Berlin
The first meeting of the CSCE Council of Ministers, under the machinery set up in Paris in November 1990, took place in Berlin — symbolically convened in the renovated *Reichstag* — on June 19 and 20, 1991. The concert of European nations became virtually complete with the admission of Albania, a significant step in that country's political reintegration, so much so that British Foreign Secretary Douglas Hurd described the CSCE as "acting as a Congress of Europe from Vancouver to Vladivostock". The occasion of this purple passage from the normally low-key minister was a joint declaration on Yugoslavia stressing the need for "democratic development, unity and territorial integrity" in that divided nation.

The Berlin meeting also made significant progress in the creation of machinery to mediate situations threatening peace, security or stability. For the first time since its creation in 1975, CSCE went beyond the unanimity rule by allowing 12 of the 35 members to convene an emergency meeting over the objections of the member state or states concerned. This represented a significant concession on the part of the Soviet Union and Turkey, which feared being called to account over the Baltic republics and Cyprus, respectively.

The Council also agreed to develop the exchange of information, to oppose proliferation of arms of mass destruction and to hold talks on conventional disarmament in Europe (linked to but distinct from CFE) in preparation for the CSCE summit meeting in 1992.

B — Soviet disunion

It must be obvious (one hopes, not too obvious) that in progressing from history to contemporary events, we are taking aim at a moving target. In no case is this more true than in writing about the Soviet Union; or do we mean Russia; or the Commonwealth of Independent States? We crave indulgence if not all present tenses have been transposed to the past! In any case, we make no claim to write the full history of the break-up of the Soviet Union but rather to show consequences for Europe — its integration, its future, its very definition.

We take up the story in the summer of 1991. Mikhail Gorbachev has been in power for six years. The transformation of the economy is slow, uneven, painful but speech is free. As their society disintegrates and breadlines lengthen, Soviet citizens keep themselves going with humor. In Muscovite bathhouses political jokes abound: "Who invented perestroika, politicans or scientists?" — "It must have been the politicans, because the scientists would have tried it out on the dogs first".

Albeit long expected the August 19 *putsch* came, like death, as a surprise. President Gorbachev, as Kruschev before him, was on vacation. So too was George Bush: Mikhail had headed south to the Crimea; George had flown north to Maine. Like Kruschev, too, Gorbachev was reported "too ill" to govern. The leaders of the coup were Gennadi Yanaev, vice-president (elected only on a second vote at Gorbachev's urging after having first been rejected by the Supreme Soviet!), Marshal Yazov, minister of defense, and Vladimir Krioutchkov, head of the KGB. Yanaev took over as president in the self-appointed State Committee for the State of Emergency. However, the Committee had severely under-estimated the depth of change in the Soviet Union during six years of *glasnost*. Short of bread and with *perestroika* disastrously incomplete, the people nevertheless clung to their new freedoms and rallied massively behind Boris Yeltsin, the elected president of Russia, who with Eduard Shevardnadze risked his life in a public appeal to the citizens from the top of a tank and from the balcony of the White House of the Russian Federation. The Soviet Communist Party declined to ratify the coup. Following one brief skirmish the army refused to follow the junta. The tide turned. After two days the plotters fled and were arrested in Central Asia. The steadfastness of the Soviet people, Boris Yeltsin, Mikhail Gorbachev (who for three days resisted pressure to resign) and refusal by the West to recognize the new régime paid off. The fiasco had cost six lives but actually accelerated political and economic restructuring. It was rapidly demonstrated that the "gang of eight" lacked not only legitimacy but also credibility and authority. It had now become obvious that, in the USSR as earlier in Eastern Europe, communism could not be reformed from within. A new system called for new men. In this sense, on August 21, 1991, at the very moment of Gorbachev's return to Moscow, the Soviet Union was entering upon the post-Gorbachev era. Betrayed by those whom he had called to power, Gorbachev had been saved by his adversaries. His return to Moscow from house arrest in the Crimea was necessary not to govern a rapidly disintegrating Union but to re-establish legitimacy. In the week that followed failure of the coup the centrifugal movement of the Baltic states, the Ukraine, Moldavia and others accelerated, while the top communists were replaced in the Union government and Gorbachev himself finally resigned as General Secretary of the party. Overtaken by the amazing events he had set in train, he suffered the irony of being seen to do too little, too late. The basic difference between Gorbachev and Yeltsin was that the former wanted reform to save the system, the latter to discard it. Gorbachev the *apparatchik* relied on the party machine and lost; Yeltsin the so-called populist, whom Gorbachev had expelled from the Central Committee, relied on the people, and won.

Gorbachev struggled, with limited success, to re-establish his authority. Numerous government changes were made, including replacement of Alexandr Bessmertnykh at the Foreign Office by Boris Pankin. Yet, there was a cascade of autonomy declarations. The new Treaty of Union, which was to have been signed on August 19 and had precipitated the coup, was now seen as inadequate even by the nine republics which had intended to sign it. The Ukraine, a founding state of the Union, declared her independence on August 24, as did Moldavia (renaming itself in Romanian as Moldova three days later). The following day Russia and the Ukraine signed a treaty of political and economic cooperation without the participation of the Union authorities, thereby creating a parallel structure of free association. [9]

For the Baltics total independence seemed finally at hand. Iceland, Denmark and Finland sent ambassadors. On August 27, 1991 the twelve EC members unanimously agreed to recognize the Baltic states as sovereign nations.

The people of Brussels were forcefully reminded that they were not managing the "Community of Western Europe" but the nucleus of a future European Community in the widest sense of the term. As the republics of the USSR, beginning with the Baltic states (recognized by President Bush on September 2), achieved independence, the issues of economic assistance, association and ultimate accession to the Community would have to be reconsidered. An immediate consequence was a renewed and more pressing endeavor to complete the EC-EFTA negotiations to create the 19-nation European Economic Area.

Dismantling of the Communist Party apparatus, settlement of relations between the Union and the republics and other political restructuring, while essential, does not solve the economic issues facing the USSR. Over seventy years the economies of the republics of the USSR have become tightly interdependent: Russia, for instance, needs the breadbasket of the Ukraine whereas Russian oil and gas are in wide demand.

Paradoxically, one might claim that the Soviet Union already had the economic integration the European Community is seeking. Like the Community, it was looking for a better balance between political freedom and economic solidarity, but approaching that balance from the other end of the spectrum. It would be ironic if the two great ships were to pass in the night on the ocean of European integration.

Rise of a rebel

The tumultuous special session of the Congress of Soviet Deputies convened in the wake of the failed coup accepted after vigorous debate a proposal put forward by Gorbachev and Yeltsin (still trying to find common ground) and the leaders of ten of the republics (the three Baltics and Moldova did not participate and Georgia did not sign) to create a free association of independent nations linked by economic union, joint defense (with nuclear weapons controlled from the center) and a common foreign policy. Human rights would be protected, including in particular the interests of ethnic minorities, but with existing borders guaranteed. President Yeltsin assured the Congress that there would be no hegemony from Russia:

> Russia will build relations with all sovereign states on the basis of equality, good neighborliness, mutual benefit and non-interference in the internal affairs of others. The Russian state, having selected democracy and freedom, will never become an empire, nor an elder or a younger brother. It will be equal with all others.

Like Gorbachev and Shevardnadze, Boris Yeltsin, a man of humble origins and simple life-style, was a product of the party system but he soon ran foul of Gorbachev, accusing him of lacking the courage to implement radical reform. He had been expelled from the Moscow city Politburo in November 1987 but the definitive break came with his elimination from the Soviet Politburo on February 18, 1992, for attacking privilege and inefficiency among soviet leaders. Yeltsin retained enough of his old party reflexes "humbly" to request rehabilitation in July but, fortunately for him, was rejected. From that point on he gave his total allegiance to Russia, being elected president of the parliament on May 29, 1990 and the first popularly elected president of Russia on June 12, 1991, with a 57.3% majority. Yeltsin's disgrace in party and Union circles had become his ticket to success in the dominant republic. Decried as a populist he used his crowd appeal to undertake a decisive program of institutional and economic reform. Two months later he decreed suspension of the Communist Party in Russia (August 23, made final on November 7), one week before the Supreme Soviet banished it from the entire Soviet Union and declared its own dissolution. On December 1, 1991, the Russian parliament granted Yeltsin special powers to carry out his reforms.

September 5, 1991, was one of the most important dates in Russian history since the liberation from the Mongols at the end of the fourteenth century. A vote rammed through the Congress of People's Deputies by a reinvigorated Gorbachev gave massive support, under threat of national disintegration, to an immediate reform of the country's institutions. While much power was ceded by the center to the republics, the transfer was devised so that fears of renewed Russian dominance would be assuaged. At the same time, certain essential attributes were retained at federal level: foreign and military policy, law enforcement, security and management of an integrated economy.

Pending approval of a new constitution, the Congress set up transitional institutions, including a State Council, an Interrepublican Economic Committee and a bicameral Supreme Soviet or parliament. The proposed constitution would never be approved: the Supreme Soviet voted not only itself but the Soviet Union out of existence three months later).

It was further decided that all republics could apply for UN membership. Thus, the new Soviet Union presented some of the characteristics of the European Community: legal sovereignty for participating republics, with maintenance of joint action and economic integration. [10]

Baltic independence . . . and aftershocks . . .

At its first meeting on September 6 the interim State Council recognized the total independence of Estonia, Latvia and Lithuania, abruptly terminating fifty-one years of occupation.

After two months of negotiation eight of the remaining twelve republics agreed to a pact of economic cooperation considered essential to the conversion of the Soviet economy to the market system, signed in Moscow on October 18, 1991.[11] The Soviet President put the best face on this considerable yet still partial success. The most important absentee was the Ukraine, which refused to compromise its new-found autonomy. "History has given us a chance to become an independent nation and we do not wish to continue to be a colony", asserted Ivan Pliusch, first deputy chairman of the Ukrainian parliament. Russian Vice-President Alexandr Rutskoi was in defiant mood. "I do not know if the Ukraine will survive without Russia", he declared; "but I definitely know Russia will survive without the Ukraine".

The Ukraine proclaimed its independence after the 1917 Bolshevik Revolution and saw fierce fighting in the civil war. After seventy-four years of communism Ukrainian nationalists were determined to assert their sovereignty, even to the point of creating their own currency and army. There was also major concern about how the Union debt would be apportioned among the republics. This strong stand was influenced by the Ukrainian presidential election set for December 1. Armenian President Levon Ter-Petrosian, recognized that the treaty gave more autonomy to the participants: "For the first time in seventy-four years", he declared, "economic relations have broken free of ideology"; but he refused to attend the first meeting of the new Supreme Soviet. By early November ten of the twelve republics remaining after Baltic independence had accepted the treaty. Only Georgia and Armenia held out. The change of heart in Moldova and the Ukraine came only after considerable hesitation and misgivings.

On November 7, after seventy-four years of Communist Party domination, Boris Yeltsin issued a decree dissolving the party throughout the vast lands of the Russian Republic. Blasé, the West barely blinked.

Biter bit: Russian autonomists defy Boris Yeltsin

Yeltsin got a taste of his own medicine in November when the Muslim region of Chechen-Ingush in the Russian Caucasus declared independence from the Russian Republic.

Russia, which includes 70% of the Soviet land mass and 51% of the population, encompasses thirty-one autonomous republics, several districts and over a thousand ethnic groups. The Chechen move was led by General Djokhar Dudayev, who had gained the presidency on October 27 with over 85% of the vote. Yeltsin decreed emergency rule, ordered Dudayev's arrest and sent troops to enforce his decision. Dudayev swore he would resist "provocative acts of state terrorism". When the Soviet troops arrived they were surrouded and contained at Grozny airport. Support was quickly forthcoming from President Gamsakhurdia of Georgia, which borders on Chechen-Ingush, fanning the flames of nationalist fervor throughout a region already beset by the Armenian-Azeri conflict.

Yeltsin suffered a major rebuff for his policy of force following an appeal by Chechen members, when the Russian Parliament in Moscow reversed his decree by an overwhelning margin: 177 to 4. Yet his dilemma is not hard to understand. As the chief apostle of sovereignty for the Soviet republics Yeltsin was bound at some point unwittingly to fire ambition within the borders of his own far-flung, diverse domain. Had he not acted in the Chechen case, made more sensitive because the enclave is Islamic, unrest would rapidly have spread to other areas. Yet in doing so he not only risked being accused of inconsistency (... sauce for the gander) but also, as Gamsakhurdia's reaction underlined, of arousing fresh fears of Russian hegemony over the other Soviet republics. A chastened Yeltsin now found himself on the same side of the issue as Mikhail Gorbachev, trying to hold his domain together by standing in the way of self-determination.

History added an ironic "footnote to the footnote" when a few months later Gamsakhurdia was himself overthrown for being too dictatorial...

German diaspora

Standing in need of German support but also wishing to show sensitivity to ethnic concerns after the Chechen *gaffe*, Yeltsin responded positively to Chancellor Kohl's concerns for the welfare of ethnic Germans in the Russian Republic. The Volga Germans had clung to their culture despite Stalin's destruction of their homeland and their deportation to Siberia in 1941. In November, as the two countries signed a joint declaration on cooperation, Yeltsin promised Kohl that the Volga Republic would be re-established. Although it could not be restored over all the original 30,000 square kilometers because others now lived there, some 6,000 sq.km. of the former territory near Volgograd and Saratov had been set aside. Kohl congratulated Yeltsin and called on western partners to share the burden of humanitarian aid. Doubtless he was also seeking to stem the flow of *Volksdeutsche* to a Federal Republic already hard pressed to absorb a constant influx of immigrants.

For the Soviet people a timely warning came from an unexpected source. Russian Orthodox Patriarch Aleksy II, leading a church emerging from seven decades of atheism, said his greatest disappointment was the "growing separatist tendencies" in the church as in the state:

> Freedom is a great gift of God but it must be used for good. Regrettably, our society has not been able to handle that great measure of responsibility which fell on its shoulders with the achievement of freedom. The yearning for independence, freedom, turned in practice to confrontation, greediness, intolerance, hostility and even open hatred.

Alexsy feared not only friction between Catholics and Orthodox in the Ukraine but also schism within the Orthodox church itself.

Yeltsin had to face brush fires from another quarter in December when his own vice-president, Alexandr Rutskoi, came out against reforms which were starving the military-industrial complex of resources.

Soviet centrifuge: a stillborn Union of Sovereign States
Mikhail Gorbachev, who had escaped removal from office in the coup only to see, in effect, his office removed from him as federal powers were cut away by assertive republics, did not give up easily. On November 14 he notched up a limited victory in persuading the interim State Council and seven republics — but not Ukraine, Moldova or Georgia — to adhere to a new treaty of political cooperation (not to be confused with the treaty of economic union signed four weeks previously), replacing the Soviet constitution and renaming the once-proud Soviet nation the Union of Sovereign States. The "center" was to retain jurisdiction over a much-reduced range of sectors: foreign affairs, aspects of finance and the currency, nuclear weapons. The agreement was designed to complement the treaty of economic cooperation, previously signed by ten republics, creating a free market area replacing the former centrally-directed economy.

Eleven months after his sudden resignation with a dramatic warning of impending dictatorship and three months after the August coup in which he was proved right, Eduard Shevardnadze returned as Soviet foreign minister. This followed the republics' decision to retain a central Ministry of External Affairs merged with External Trade. The man who had joined Yeltsin at the Moscow barricades said he saw a marked change in Gorbachev and told *Izvestia* he could not remain a passive onlooker as the Soviet Union disintegrated. He also warned that the danger of a return to totalitarian dictatorship was still strong. Significantly, his first visits were not to foreign countries but to the Union's own breakaway republics. After only three months in office, a demoted Boris Pankin packed his bags for the embassy in London.

Bankruptcy looms

Still concerned about the dispersal of nuclear weapons as well as default on their debts, the G7 powers supported this last-ditch effort by signing with eight republics in Moscow on November 21 a financial agreement rescheduling part of the USSR's external debt. The center nevertheless continued inexorably to decay. On November 29 the USSR brushed with bankruptcy as the Russian Republic refused to authorize further deficit spending. The Soviet Central Bank stopped disbursements. Denied authorization to print more money by the Soviet lower house the bank ran out of cash to pay salaries and meet other financial committments. Without the Russian deputies the Soviet parliament, now including only seven other republics, could not function. On November 30, in a move which apparently came to the rescue of the Union but in fact confirmed its decline, Yeltsin assumed the Soviet debt on behalf of the Russian republics. Naturally, this went over very well among western creditors. Yeltsin was laying the groundwork for massive aid, after the demise of the USSR, to Russia.

Ukraine: a disputed borderland goes its own way

Sauce for the goose... If Boris Yeltsin resented the Union's centralizing power, the Ukraine had never accepted Russian hegemony. On December 1, 1991, the electorate of the Soviet Union's second most powerful and populous republic turned out to ratify by over eighty per cent its parliament's independence declaration. At the same time Leonid Kravchuk, a former CP *apparatchik* who underwent sudden and suspect conversion to Ukrainian nationalism only after failure of the August coup, defeated six other contenders to sweep the presidency in the first round of voting. In vain did his opponent Ycheslav Chernovil protest that he had struggled for Ukrainian independence for three decades. "Change is natural", declared the disingenuous victor.

Hub to rim: a major US policy shift

Undercutting one of the last bases of Gorbachev's authority, that of privileged spokesman with the West, President Bush did not await the outcome of the Ukrainian vote to announce that the US would recognize Ukrainian independence. Clearly, a new policy was emerging. Only three months earlier, in a speech in Kiev, Bush had warned against "suicidal nationalism"! Now Washington was preparing to by-pass Soviet Moscow and deal directly with the republics. (Canada, with its large population of Ukrainian origin and its own "Ukraine" in Quebec, took a more cautious line).

Ukraine was seeking to shake off centuries of Russian hegemony. Its capital, Kiev, on the Dnieper river, has a thousand years of history as a center of European culture. With over 50 million inhabitants, Ukraine takes its place as one of the largest nations in Europe. Yet for all their differences the Ukrainains and Russians trace their ancestry to the common roots of Kievan Rus, a 9th century Slavic kingdom stretching from the Baltic to the Black Sea, which fell to the Mongols in the mid-13th century. Until that time they even spoke a common language. Today this borderland, split between the Catholic and Orthodox versions of Christianity, enfolds a large Russian minority, to the north and in the Crimea (The latter was transferred to the Ukraine from Russia by Kruschev only in 1954).

First to recognize the new state was Boris Yeltsin of Russia, followed by Poland and Hungary. The US at first fine-tuned its stance by announcing that it would send an "envoy" to Kiev to discuss "issues", but soon followed suit.

Crisis of statehood

Gorbachev's calls for a halt to national disintegration sounded increasingly desperate after the Ukrainian vote:

> "The collapse of the state is the collapse of society, of social ties, of cooperation and links among republics, peoples, collectives," he said. "It shows in our cultural ties, which were a source of special pride. It is evident in our entire life. This disintegration must be stopped by our common effort, without delay."

Yeltsin turned a deaf ear. He called for cooperation within an equal association of sovereign states. Gorbachev's lament was a voice crying in the wilderness of the Russian steppe. Hungry Muscovites scoured empty shelves for scarce high-priced food which had "fallen off the truck" on the way to the state stores.

On December 8 the three most populous and powerful republics, Byelo-Russia (renamed Belarus), Russia and Ukraine agreed to form a Commonwealth of Independent States (CIS), with headquarters in Minsk, not Moscow, and open to other members. Gorbachev's Union of Sovereign States was aborted and the Soviet leader had lost credibility: "Nobody", said a Russian commentator, "could have been more effective in breaking up the Soviet Union than he who sought to preserve it". The Soviet system had used its new-found freedom to terminate its own existence.

Miffed at not being involved from the start, the five Muslim republics flirted briefly with the beguiling notion of an Islamic union with Iran or Turkey; reason prevailed. For Gorbachev the game was finally over: the Minsk agreement, while attractive to him in some respects, destroyed the unitary state.

Yeltsin insisted that without the CIS treaty borders would have been closed. Only a new commonwealth was capable of preserving the political, legal and economic space that had been formed over centuries, he told the Russian Parliament. Now a single currency would be preserved and economic policy coordinated. Prices would be freed on January 2, 1992. Human rights would be respected, discrimination outlawed. This was the only possible formula for the cooperation of members of the former USSR. The plea prevailed. The Russian Parliament approved the treaty on December 12 by 188 votes to 6. The two rivals' aims sounded uncannily similar, but Gorbachev was a man clinging to an outdated institution, inextricably linked to communism, while Yeltsin was fashioning new institutions to meet the needs of men.

On December 13 US Secretary of State Baker convened a conference to organize aid to the former USSR, to distribute food and to dismantle nuclear weapons. The Europeans were unenthusiastic: Europe was already doing more than the US. When the 54 planes flew off from a US forces airbase in Germany in the New Year, the happening was denounced as a giant photo-opportunity for election-conscious America.

Big fish, no pond

Gorbachev was looking increasingly like the monarch in *The Little Prince*, a king without subjects. "The main task of my life is over", he declared wistfully. On December 20 all the former Soviet republics except Georgia and, of course, the Baltics, met in Alma Ata, capital of Kazakhstan, to review and expand the Commonwealth set up in Minsk. It was agreed to rework the text to include all eleven republics as founder members. (Civil strife in Georgia prevented that republic's participation).

The Declaration of Alma Ata covered military and economic cooperation as well as UN representation. Russia was supported as the USSR's "continuation state" for the Security Council seat and veto power. The vagueness of the text (of which further details are given in Part III, Chapter 9) covered over differences but sufficed to bury the Soviet Union. On December 23 EC foreign ministers recognized Russian independence. A day later a minority rump of the Soviet Parliament met to dissolve both itself and the Union (Gorbachev did not attend). Finally, on December 25, 1991, Gorbachev went on "national" television to dissipate the last shred of Union legitimacy by himself resigning as the first and last president of the Soviet Union. On Christmas Day Charlemagne was crowned; on Christmas Day Gorbachev resigned. Brought down from the Kremlin masthead, the hammer and sickle were consigned to the Russian archives and replaced by the red, white and blue horizontal bands of the Russian Federation. There may be a lesson for the US, the last superpower, that it was ultimately domestic issues which failed the Soviets more than outside pressure. The Soviet Union did not explode; it imploded. Saluted across the globe as the world statesman who had ended the Cold War and changed the course of history, Gorbachev received few fond farewells from his own people, too preoccupied with finding something to eat at a price they could afford. When ex-President Gorbachev returned to his office after his broadcast, a gentleman named Boris was sitting in his chair and using his telephone . . .

Mikhail Gorbachev has not confessed the error of his ways nor humbly begged rehabilitation. A retired statesman, he awaits with dignity, like de Gaulle, the judgment of history . . . but, who knows? De Gaulle was recalled . . .

Armies without countries; countries without armies

On December 28 the eleven CIS defense ministers met in Moscow to prepare a summit designed to flesh out the Declaration of Alma Ata. Although a CIS defense council was set up, Ukraine, Moldova and Azerbaijan made it clear they planned their own armed forces. At the Minsk summit two days later the Commonwealth Defense Council was set up but Russia and Ukraine started a long tussle over ownership of the Black Sea fleet. In the economic sphere

Yeltsin refused further postponement of price liberalization, so that Belarus and Ukraine were forced to follow suit, lest scarce consumer goods be drawn from their republics into the Russian Federation. It was also noted that price rises in raw materials would being a quick bonanza to the largest CIS member.

Was it worth all the pain? Poland had already slowed the pace of her reform and Yeltsin had parted company with his more conservative vice-president, Alexandr Rutskoi. Like a kindly dentist Yeltsin assured his people that the worst would be over by the fall of 1992. Anticipating unrest, Moscow police chief Arkady Murashov put a thousand extra officers on the beat. Yeltsin assumed the post of prime minister in order personally to absorb the backlash and staked his political capital on the reforms. He did, however, maintain some controls, notably on food and fuel, and moved to protect the poor through soup kitchens and special discount stores.

On January 2, 1992, former Soviet republics entered the free market; prices went through the roof...

Western debate
In the bleak mid-winter the beleaguered Russian president could find some comfort from Britain's John Major, who told the press that when the UK assumed the EC presidency, Community enlargement would be a priority. "The Community should not be a rich man's club and should be open to Russian membership", declared Major. He did not say when.

The Prime Minister's comments were part of a broader debate in the West on how to react to cascading events on Europe's eastern confines. There were three streams to this discussion: assessment of Gorbachev's achievements and of the potential of his successor (the latter ranging from playboy to hero); concern about the nuclear inheritance from a fractured command structure (unheard-of lands being discovered to have a finger on the button); vigorous debate on providing economic assistance. Speaking on National Public Radio, Congresswoman Pat Schroeder (Democrat of Colorado) called for "a new Marshall Plan" while the US enjoyed "the moral high ground". Such authority had enabled the West to steer Germany and Japan to democracy after World War II. If the US failed to act, she persisted, it would face "a Yugoslavia with nuclear weapons and possibly millions of refugees trekking west". Republican Senator Richard Lugar of Indiana was more sanguine. Reminding listeners of recession and deficit in the US, he advocated private investment rather than taxpayer funds. President Bush made a speech which sounded like a funeral oration for Gorbachev; then the apostle of the free market flew with his captains of industry to Japan to seek a better managed deal for US exporters. He seemed to prefer the dubious moral high ground afforded by a Lee Iacocca to the quicksands offered by the decline of a Gorbachev, the rise of a Yeltsin or the change of heart of a Kravchuk.

Ferment on the Black Sea
In Soviet Georgia, meanwhile, events continued to demonstrate that a change of men is not enough to guarantee democracy in the absence of systemic

renewal. After being holed up in the parliament for two weeks, President Gamsakhurdia, elected by a landslide in May 1991 but now turned autocrat, fled to Armenia. After seizing power the "freedom-loving" opposition fired on a pro-Gamsakhurdia rally in Tbilisi. CIS leaders were doubtless relieved that Georgia remained outside the Commonwealth. The Black Sea republic was indeed too deeply troubled to have hope of benefitting from the G7 lifeline organized in Washington. Following Gamsakhurdia's clandestine return from his brief exile, the republic erupted in civil war, while the Abkhaze and South Ossetian regions stepped up efforts to achieve their own autonomy. Meanwhile in Moscow Russian parliamentarians threatened to claim back the largely Russian-speaking Crimea if Ukraine did not relinquish its claim to the Black Sea fleet. With or without airlifted aid, the chain-reaction in fragmentation of the Soviet Union may be far from over.

Russia on the brink

After the Chechens the Tatars: the independence virus which had caused the Soviet Union to explode in a matter of weeks continued to undermine the Russian Republic, itself a federation including some twenty "autonomous" regions. In March the inhabitants of Tatarstan, north of the Caspian, although completely surrounded by Russia, voted massively for independence. Boris Yeltsin, now in the role of a Gorbachev, seemed caught in a race against time to head off the break-up of Russia. He appeared to have achieved his goal on the last day of March, 1992, when eighteen of Russia's twenty autonomous republics put their signatures to a Treaty of Federation; only Chechen-Ingush and Tatarstan stayed away.

The treaty contains eight articles. It charges the Russian federal authorities with preparing a new constitution, fixing the limits of Russian territory (a point of interest to Japan, which claims the Southern Kuriles, and China); deciding foreign and defense policy; issuing currency and directing the finances of the Federation. The treaty grants the regions greater control over their economic policies and the right "to participate independently" in international relations, a decidedly ambiguous concession.

It remains to be seen whether this treaty and the new Russian constitution will be ratified by all parties. Still the largest state in the world in land area, Russia is poised between fragmentation and great power status. It would be a gloomy outlook for the world if Russia itself were balkanized. One wonders whether the industrialized nations, preoccupied as they are with self-reappraisal in the Cold War aftermath, are fully aware of what is at stake and of what is required of them.

Walzin' with Yeltsin

In February, 1992, Boris Yeltsin made a number of visits to western capitals — London, Paris (where he was received in great pomp to efface the memory of an ungracious reception a year earlier), Washington. At the Security Council summit in New York he proposed nuclear power cooperation on a joint SDI defense, an idea which appeared seductive to George Bush. Yeltsin had now "replaced" Gorbachev as a world statesman as he had already supplanted him in domestic leadership. Russia's place was now secure in the *valse diploma-tique*.

The same could not be said of the Commonwealth of Independent States, with tension and sometimes outright conflict in several republics and fifty-four American Starlifters ferrying western aid out of Frankfurt, evoking the potent memory of the anti-Soviet Berlin blocade... There was a glimmer of hope in April 1992 when it seemed Russia was about to be admitted to the IMF and the G7 were poised to set up a ruble stabilization fund. It will indeed take more than a photo-opportunity airlift.

When the Winter Olympics opened in Albertville, France, on February 8, the penniless, flagless team of the CIS, its training camps abruptly and pre-maturely closed, filed past in the image of the sundered superpower, brought to penury and disarray but still dominated by Russia (118 members against 8 for Ukraine, 8 for Kazakhstan, 3 for Belarus, 2 for Uzbekistan), only twelve years after the Moscow games. By July, for the Summer Olympics in Barcelona, the ephemeral *Equipe unifiée* took its share of medals and gave a superb display of gymnastics before ceasing to exist. Meanwhile, the rickety CIS continued to hold nuclear weapons and its rag-tag team to pick-off medals of gold, silver and bronze... If sport is above politics, why do we train national teams and harvest medals by countries?

Yard sale for the Red Army?
St. Valentine didn't seem to be present at Minsk on February 14 when CIS summitteers held their fourth meeting. Although they signed a number of agreements the top prize eluded them. The future of the Red Army was seri-ously compromised when the political leaders failed to agree on maintenance of unified conventional forces, although agreement on a unified command for strategic (nuclear) forces was confirmed. The Kirghiz and Tadjik presidents did not attend the summit, but it was Ukraine, Moldova and Azerbaijan which insisted on creating their own national armed forces. Although the Ukrainian presidency minimised the importance of this decision ("The future of CIS must not be tied to the armed forces issue... CIS is mainly about economic and political issues"), Boris Yeltsin slipped away without attending the final press conference. Given Ukrainian intransigeance, Russia might actually pre-fer an agreement limited to eight republics. For Mikhail Gorbachev it must have been *déjà vu* ... The climate of discussion was characterized by the com-plaint of the Moldovan delegation that "233 tanks, 345 armed vehicles and 60 artillery pieces have been spirited out of our territory... We expect nothing good out of the CIS as long as people continue to remove from the small republics what is rightly theirs". The Baltic fleet, Soviet possessions abroad ... the agendas remains substantial.

Stemming the brain drain
In the winter of 1992 there were several scandals and more scares of impover-ished former Soviet high-ranking military officers selling military hardware

and fissionable material, with the fear that they would fall into the hands of unscrupulous regimes, threatening the stability of the post-Cold War world. The fact that Iraq continued to throw up roadblocks to UN-ordered dismantling of heavy weapons added to sensibility on the subject.

An even more critical aspect of the issue came to light when it transpired that ex-Soviet specialists in weapons of mass destruction were offering their own expertise to the highest bidder. This threatened world security not only directly but also indirectly by creating a drain of brainpower needed for peaceful reconstruction of CIS economies.

Meeting in Brussels on March 11 in response to a Community initiative, EC, US, Japanese and Russian officials, including US Secretary of State Baker and Russian Foreign Minister Andrei Kozyrev, decided to set up an international center for science and technology (ICS) in Russia. The center will hire and provide retraining and research facilities for nuclear, chemical, ballistic and biological experts. German Foreign Minister Hans Dietrich Genscher circulated lists of potential recruits, which could number as many as 5000. The center will be located at Troitsk, near Moscow, but may have dependent agencies in other CIS states. A parallel meeting was taking place the same day in Paris, where OECD experts agreed to help Russia and other eastern European countries fight the brain-drain and maintain their scientific potential. The French Minister of Research Hubert Curien, who chaired the 28-nation meeting, pointed out that the concern here was even broader, covering civil as well as military technology. While the West might gain short-term advantage from the brain-drain, he declared, in the long term world peace depended on balance of human and technological resources. The meeting proposed setting up a special fund or agency to help scientists by subsidizing research. The meeting was attended by Czech, Hungarian, Polish and Russian observers.

Also on the same day, China announced her intention to recruit former Soviet scientists . . .

CSCE peace plan for Caucasian hot spot
Conflict in Ngorno-Karabakh intensified during February, with the Armenians supplying the "freedom fighters" of the Azerbaijanian enclave by helicopter until they captured the airport of Stepanakert, capital of the ethnically Armenian region inside Muslim Azerbaijan.

On February 28 two events took place which were of more than local importance, symbolically at least. The ex-Soviet army, which had entered the area in an attempt to restore order after Yeltsin's mediation attempt, decided to withdraw completely. Marshall Shaposhnikov ordered Regiment 366 to pull out from all positions after several soldiers had been killed and CIS arms stolen.

The same day the CSCE, which had recently admitted both republics and now numbered 48 countries, met in Prague at the level of senior officials and adopted a peace plan. Although in this instance the chances of success may be slim, the CSCE is now responding to its new vocation of European policeman or regional "security council". The CSCE plan included the following measures:

— Immediate ceasefire
— CSCE delegation to visit the region
— Armaments embargo
— Opening of humanitarian supply corridors
— Hostage exchange and restitution of bodies.

The despatch of UN "Blue helmets" to Yugoslavia a few days earlier was doubtless not foreign to the CSCE decision: Europe had to settle its own problems and, politically if not entirely geographically, the CIS states were part of Europe.

A new generation will fill the void caused by the Soviet Union's collapse, although it will take time for people to rise to the top who never had ties to communism. The new world economic order dictates that the republics come together again in a free association, even through they are currently seeking political disengagement. Should this giant process go seriously awry the travail in Yugoslavia will seem like a Sunday picnic.

Addressing a conference on Europe and her regions, President Mitterrand chose this moment to renew his call, first launched with President Havel in Prague, for a confederation of all the states of Europe, completing a Europe of concentric circles (with the Community at its center) which he saw as the only bulwork against numerous interethnic conflicts. Mitterrand did not explain, however, how transnational entities such as Basques, Celts, Kurds or ethnic Serbs, Hungarians and Armenians living outside their "mother country" would be represented in such an assembly, much less how its decisions would be taken and implemented. Nobody wants a replay of the League of Nations and the Spanish Civil War. One thing is clear: if a European Confederation, a Europe of concentric circles is to have any chance of success, it must be held together by a strong and accessible center. The European Community must not only be open to enlargement but strengthen its structures to survive the shocks that such enlargement will inevitably engender.

Turkish delight
For the Central Asian republics formerly members of the Soviet Union, the road to Europe passes through Ankara and Istanbul. The break-up of the USSR has given Turkey a new role of regional leadership which could not have been imagined a few years ago. The fact that these republics are also predominantly Muslim, at a time when fundamentalism is strong not only in Iran but also in Algeria, Sudan, Pakistan and elsewhere, charges Turkey with the delicate task of demonstrating that it is possible to be economically westernized, democratic and Muslim all at once. Despite doubts which may be entertained about Turkey's own democratic record, no country is better placed to play out, on behalf of Europe as a whole, at the crossroads of Europe, Asia, the Balkans and the Middle East, the politics of its geography.

On February 3, 1992, in a related development under Turkish leadership, President Turgut Ozal opened a nine-nation conference convened in Istanbul to create a new regional body crossing, like the Danube basin initiative before it, former Cold War lines, Black Sea Economic Cooperation (BSEC). Although not present at Istanbul, Greece was invited to join.

Greece accepted the invitation and on June 25, 1992, leaders of eleven nations returned to an ornate Ottoman palace overlooking the Bosphorus in Istanbul to sign the Black Sea economic pact (BSEC), pledging to end regional conflicts. "We are dealing not just with economic but also with political cooperation and our common will to end bloodshed in this basin", declared President Yeltsin.

Calls by President Shevardnadze of Georgia for a more elaborate secretariat in Istanbul were dismissed as "bureaucratic" by Yeltsin and termed "premature" by Premier Suleyman Demirel of Turkey.

The treaty covers a market of 400 million people. It seeks cooperation in energy, transportation, communications, information and environmental conservation. A joint investment bank will also be founded. The ultimate goal is free movement of people, goods and services in a market economy broadly covering the Black Sea region, although not all member countries enjoy direct access to the Black Sea.

The BSEC founding members are Albania, Armenia, Azerbaijan, Bulgaria, Georgia, Greece, Moldova, Romania, Russia, Turkey and Ukraine. An invitation to Yugoslavia was suspended because of UN sanctions.

Despite the upbeat mood of the signing ceremony, speechmakers recognized that regional disputes would constitute an obstacle to rapid progress. Shevardnadze called for a "committee" to resolve conflicts and guarantee borders. On leaving the conference with its air of peace and optimism, some of the orators hastened home to resume fighting each other. Turkey's rival in the region, Iran, dismissed the BSEC as "ink on paper": Greece and Turkey lacked the strength to revitalize nine former communist nations.

According to its founders, BSEC is complementary to the EC and, recognizing economic interdependence, seeks integration into the world and European economies. Nevertheless, since the new treaty provides for the free circulation of goods and services, as a BSEC leader Turkey's loyalties will be seriously tested when Brussels takes up its application for EC membership and asks it to move inside the Common External Tariff. It may be necessary for the EC to consider setting up an "Eastern EEA" before admitting BSEC countries to full EC membership. Although already sitting pretty as a member of both groups, Greece too will have to address the CET problem as soon as BSEC starts lowering tariffs among its members.

Azerbaijan from A to Z

Turkey finds it natural to develop cooperation with a region of shared language, culture, history and, for the most part, religion. (However, it is a surprise for many Europeans to discover how many countries and regions speak dialects of Turkish). Although Greece remains cautious, most Western governments welcome the Turkish role. For an Azerbaijan which recently decided to switch to the Roman alphabet, an airlift of typewriters can only serve to improve communication with the West ... Turkey has offered to channel western aid to the Central Asian republics in order to avoid routing it through Moscow (which would enhance Russian leverage and potential hegemony over the region).

If there were any doubt about Turkey's pivotal role in the region, it should be dispelled by another "first", this time in Teheran. A little-noticed organization with a "generic" name, the Economic Cooperation Organisation (ECO) was founded in 1985 by Turkey, Iran and Pakistan, held its first summit in the Iranian capital on February 16 and 17 admitting Azerbaijan, Uzbekistan and Turkmenistan as new members. Three other applicants, Kazakhstan, Kyrgyzstan and Tajikistan, were represented by observers. Despite protestations of friendship, it was apparent that Turkey and Iran were locked in a struggle to establish their spheres of influence. The *Teheran Times* accused Turkey of being a US pawn bent on imposing a western model of society on the region at the expense of its Islamic identity. The three founding nations nevertheless signed an agreement reducing certain tariffs. The Iranian foreign minister, Ali Akbar Velayati, announced that Armenia and even Romania had expressed interest in becoming ECO members.

Turkey has long used her strategic importance to the West to counterbalance serious doubts about her human rights record. Her assumption of the chairmanship of the Council of Europe's Committee of Ministers in May 1992 brought these misgivings to the fore once again. In 1986 the Turkish chairmanship was postponed as part of a "friendly settlement" of a human rights challenge brought by Norway, Sweden and the Netherlands. Another human rights report denouncing "political violence, torture and summary executions", presented by Dutch and Luxembourg parliamentarians, was due to be debated in the Assembly in February 1992 but the delegation from Ankara managed to obtain a postponement. Disingenuous claims of differences of "culture" and "perception" were put forward. However, the existence of the Turkish Kurds is now recognized and Turkey is a signatory of the European Convention against Torture ... Strasbourg's parliamentarians prefer for the time being to place the emphasis on "reason to hope". It was doubtless in this spirit that Catherine Lalumière visited Georgia and the Turkic former USSR republics in July 1992 in the company of Turkish Foreign Minister Hikmet Cetin. True, Mr Cetin was also Chairman of the Strasbourg agency's Committee of Ministers at the time. Perhaps the two travelers were not working to the same agenda ...

C — Southeast Asia eyes free trade

The eyes of the world are on Brussels. The emerging shape of the Western world since the collapse of the Soviet Union is of great concern to the member countries of the Association of Southeast Asian Nations (ASEAN).[12] For the past decade the countries of ASEAN have experienced remarkable growth and prosperity. The engine powering this development has been international trade. With the future of GATT uncertain and the trend toward economic regionalism, which could develop into regional protectionism, ASEAN feels threatened and is cautiously preparing for the worst.

The advent of an integrated European common market, along with the prospects for a three-nation North American Free Trade Area (NAFTA), has government and business leaders throughout Asia watching carefully for walls which might arise and impede access to valuable export markets. The concern in Asia is not just over potential lost trade, but also for continued investment.

ASEAN's exports to the EC accounted for roughly 15% of its total exports in 1989. Among EC countries, the top three recipients of ASEAN exports, the UK, Germany and the Netherlands (the latter having historical links to Indonesia), clearly dominate, accounting for approximately 70% of ASEAN's exports to the EC. This trade will not dry up overnight. Concern in ASEAN is not so much over impending tariffs from EC92, but for miscellaneous regulations designed to protect specific industries (e.g. textiles, clothing and footwear) and developing companies. While the EC does not account for as large a percentage of ASEAN's exports as Japan or the U.S., it is clearly an important market as well as a valuable source of potential investment.

330 million people
Confronted with the economic consolidation of the EC and NAFTA, ASEAN had to consider following suit. From its inception in 1967, ASEAN has sought to further economic cooperation, yet few concrete steps have been taken. Only recently have the six member nations been able to move convincingly towards economic cooperation and integration. The 1992 Singapore summit of the ASEAN heads of state has been deemed by some as a watershed summit for ASEAN, due to the signing of an agreement to create an ASEAN Free Trade Area (AFTA) within 15 years.[13] With the realization of AFTA, ASEAN will have created a combined market of approximately 330 million people, and a gross national product of $310 billion. (EC92 and NAFTA represent some 350 and 360 million people and GNPs of $4.37 trillion and $6 trillion, respectively). With 8% annual growth ASEAN offers an example of successful Third World development.

The new Asian Free Trade Area presents the European Community with an import test of its intentions. At the Singapore summit, leaders cited the development of large regional markets in Europe as the impetus to proceed with AFTA. They fear that without the guarantee of a large regional market in Asia, ASEAN would be less attractive as a trading partner and investment site, especially if Western markets penalize or exclude Asian exports. Given ASEAN's sketchy track record for economic cooperation, the initiation of AFTA is a very significant step; even though it is not as big a development as the European Market.

The goal of AFTA is to lower intra-ASEAN tariffs on manufactured goods towards a common effective external tariff (CEET) of no more than 5% by the year 2008, thus integrating ASEAN's domestic markets. This is an important measure, since intra-ASEAN exchanges currently do not exceed 20% of members' trade, but AFTA's actual effectiveness remains to be seen. Initially, only 15 categories of manufactured goods will be eligible for tariff cuts; and loopholes have been left open permitting individual member countries to exclude specific goods. This leniency is intended to accommodate countries which feel the need to protect developing industries as they grow more competitive and to guarantee the participation of all the ASEAN countries, but it could prove to be AFTA's undoing. How successful AFTA becomes will depend partly on how rapidly it is expanded to include more products.

Towards an East Asian Economic Group
While AFTA is intended to advance intra-ASEAN economic cooperation, the proposal for an East Asian Economic Group (EAEG) goes further toward creating a trading bloc to compete with EC92 and NAFTA. Initially proposed and expounded by Malaysia's Prime Minister Mahathir in late 1990, just after the GATT talks in Brussels broke down, the EAEG would include East Asia's largest players — Taiwan, South Korea, and Japan — and would exclude the US. That ASEAN and the other countries of East Asia are even considering forming a group such as the EAEG indicates their desire for some insurance against unsuccessful conclusion of the GATT talks and any protectionist tendencies which might develop in Europe or North America.

Japan has witheld its endorsement of the EAEG concept, primarily because of strong opposition from the United States to the formation of an East Asian trade grouping which excludes them. As the US is Japan's largest trading partner, and the second largest recipient of ASEAN exports, Japan and some of the ASEAN members are hesitant to pursue the EAEG at this time. Washington's response to the EAEG carries much more weight than reaction from the EC. The US alone is a larger recipient for East Asian exports than all of the EC. Roughly 30% of East Asian exports went to the US in 1989, compared with 15% for the EC.

However, if EC92 or NAFTA limit Asian access to their markets sufficiently, Japan might be persuaded to support or possibly share in the leadership of EAEG. Within ASEAN, support for the EAEG concept is mixed. Most outspoken in opposition is Indonesia's President Suharto, who is concerned that the EAEG would divide Asia from its trade partners elsewhere. Rather, President Suharto favors the regional organization Asia Pacific Economic Cooperation (APEC) as a vehicle to provide a counterweight should protectionist tendencies arise in EC92 or NAFTA. [14]

Concern in Asia is not just over trade; direct investment is also an issue. At the 1992 Summit, concern was expressed that investment would flow away from ASEAN into EC92 and NAFTA unless ASEAN could present itself as an equally attractive base for multinational investment. It is also possible that the newly freed economies of East Europe and the former Soviet Union could deflect EC aid and investment away from ASEAN. However, investment usually depends on the business outlook and anticipation of profit: in ASEAN these are very promising.

Do ASEAN and East Asia need their own trade bloc? If regions with economic blocs, such as EC92 and NAFTA, discriminate against those not involved in an economic grouping, then Asia should at least explore common strategies for preserving an open system. The economies of ASEAN and East Asia are currently too reliant on the rest of the world to be able to maintain current economic levels without access to US and European markets. For ASEAN to be truly effective as a competing economic bloc the six member countries would need to combine with Japan, South Korea, and Taiwan. However, the time is not ripe for such a formal regional grouping.

The next few years will better determine if such a grouping is warranted. If the trend toward economic regionalism in Europe and North America turns into regional protectionism, then ASEAN should be prepared to follow suit. This would require joining with East Asia, not to create a retaliatory bloc against EC92 or NAFTA, but one which could work with them to keep open the channels of world trade.

There is also an important political dimension to the strengthening of ASEAN through trade. China is primarily a military power, Japan an economic giant. The drawing down of Russian and US forces in the region could generate the instability of a power vacuum. This is yet another reason for Brussels to link up with AFTA.

The European Community has vast experience in assisting developing countries which are not seen as competitors. It will be instructive to observe how Brussels reacts to ASEAN's modest but dynamic presence. Did those Europeans really mean what they said about development?

Notes

1 Holed up in the Chilean embassy in Moscow, in 1992 Erich Honecker was still wanted for trial in Germany on that "shoot to kill" policy.

2 *Forum*, Council of Europe, December 1990.

3 In June, 1992, a Council of Europe conference proposed creation of an international corps of experts.

4 Apart from its alliterative attraction, the "Vancouver to Vladivostok" concept of Europe arises from the fact that Canada and the US are members of CSCE; and that Russia is territorially more Asian than European. See Part III, Chapter 8.

5 As fighting continued in June 1992, President Yeltsin threatened to reverse Russia's non-intervention policy (set out in a solemn declaration to the Congress of Soviet Deputies after the August coup of 1991) and come to the aid of the Russian-speaking minority in Moldova or the South Ossetians in Georgia. Moldova has also repressed the autonomy aspirations of its Islamic Turcic minority.

6 It should be noted that trade between the two Germanys had for long enjoyed special privileges under a derogation to the Community's CET.

7 See Duverger, Maurice, *Le Lièvre libéral et la tortue européenne*, Albin Michel, Paris, 1990. As an antidote to this threat, Duverger proposes creation "from the Atlantic to the Danube" of a European *Internationale* of democratic socialist parties. Presumably today Duverger would extend his notion to the Volga or the Urals.

8 Yugoslavia was created after World War I from remnants of the Austro-Hungarian and Ottoman empires. It was more ethnically diverse than any other country in the region. There are two official languages (Serbian which has the Cyrillic alphabet and Croatian, with the Roman alphabet), three main religions (Catholicism, Greek Orthodoxy and Islam) and, until recently, six provinces (Slovenia in the north, the most westernized, ethnically united, economically developed and 95% Catholic; Croatia, the second-largest republic, incorporating most of the Adriatic crastline; Serbia, Bosnia-Herzegovina, Montenegro and Macedonia in the south. Serbia also exercizes considerable powers in the so-called autonomous region of Vojvodina in the north-east — with a substantial Hungarian minority — and Kosovo in the south-west, 90% Albanian-speaking. Serbians form the predominant ethnic group not only in Serbia itself but also in large enclaves within the other entities, especially Croatia and Bosnia. There are several smaller ethnic groups, including Hungarians, Romanians, Greeks and Turks. Slovenia is the most homogeneous region. Croatia, Serbia and Bosnia all include significant minorities from each other's ethnic groups, but Bosnia's largest group consists of the Muslims, Slavs of Islamic religion which Tito established as a distinct ethnic entity.

The republics of the north feel a natural affinity for western Europe. Although Croatia and Serbia are linguistically close, they are divided by a thousand years of life along one of the "fault lines" of history and religion (Hapsburg and Ottoman empires, Catholic and Orthodox) and, more recently, of political confrontation between fascism and communism. Croatia was divided from Serbia when the Roman empire was split in AD 395, being "reunited" only when the Austro-Hungarian empire was dismantled after World War I. During the Second World War, the German occupiers set up Greater Croatia as a puppet state. When the Yugoslav partisans were not fighting the Germans they frequently fought each other. For Croatian Serbs those years have left lasting bitterness.

The officer corps of the federal army is predominantly Serbian. There have been large-scale desertions by other ethnic groups, with the result that the federal forces have been accused of fighting for Serbia against Slovenia, Croatia and Bosnia. The independence of these three republics has been recognized: they are now members of the UN and CSCE. Recognition of Macedonia's independence has been held up by Greek objections to its name.

9   The Ukrainian Republic was formed on Dec. 25, 1917, and assimilated into the USSR on Dec. 30, 1922. Western Ukraine was annexed from Poland in 1939. Romanian territory was added in 1940 and parts of Russia in 1945 and 1954. There are thus territorial claims on an independent Ukraine. Ukraine and Byelo-Russia are full members of the UN (a "deal" negotiated by Stalin to give the USSR three votes in partial compensation for France and the UK being permanent Security Council members). Population 52 m. (18% of USSR). The Ukraine produces 22.3% of Soviet agricultural output, especially wheat and potatoes, 18.2% of consumer goods. The Republic also has extensive coal, natural gas and oil deposits. Capital Kiev, principal seaport Odessa. With Chernobyl on its territory, Ukraine is very sensitive to nuclear issues and has agreed to relinquish its nuclear weapons to Russia for destruction. Difficult bilateral relations were further strengthened on June 23, 1992, when Yeltsin and Kravchuk signed a second treaty of cooperation including sharing the Black Sea fleet, although both nations still claim the Crimea.

10   Five of the republics adopted new English-language versions of their names: Byelorussia-Belarus; Kirghizia-Kyrgystan; Moldavia-Moldova; Tadzhikistan-Tajikistan; Turkmenia-Turkmenistan. The Ukraine becomes simply Ukraine. In 1991 European map-makers worked overtime.

11   The recalcitrants were Azerbaijan, Georgia, Moldova and Ukraine. Later, Armenia refused to attend the new Supreme Soviet.

12   This ASEAN section was written by Jason Lewis of Pacific Forum CSIS and the University of Hawaii, to whom we express our appreciation. The member states of ASEAN are Brunei, Indonesia, Malaysia, Philippines, Thailand and Singapore.

13   The heads of government met in Singapore on January 27 and 28. In addition to launching AFTA they renewed ASEAN's overall objectives following dissipation of the Cold War and resolution of the conflictual relationship with Cambodia, Laos and Vietnam. The summit agreed to negotiate membership with Laos and Vietnam. It also discussed Singapore's acceptance of the US fleet following its withdrawal from the Philippines.

14   On July 17, 1992, sensitive to alleged acts of oppression in its former colony of East Timor, Portugal threatened to hold up an EC-ASEAN free trade accord unless Indonesia improved its human rights record.

9

Western Horizons (1989-1992)

As turmoil prevailed in Eastern Europe, all was certainly not quiet on the western front. Once the EC had accommodated itself to the 1986 accession of Portugal and Spain, both events in the east and a number of internal issues forced deep reflection on the next stage of unification. The major issues before Community leaders, apart from the pace of enlargement ("widening" versus "deepening") included monetary union, European security (the pursuit of a common defense policy somewhat independent of the US but "disguised" as "strengthening the European pillar of the Atlantic Alliance"), development of a European foreign policy ("speaking with one voice on world affairs"); and a range of social issues, particularly crime control, consequent upon removal of frontier restrictions. These in turn provoked debate about the institutions required to manage the Europe of the twenty-first century. Britain once again, particularly in the person of Margaret Thatcher and her "Bruges group" (named after an anti-federal graduation address made by the Rt. Honourable lady at the College of Europe), was determined to hasten slowly.

In default of legislative power, the European Parliament pursued its role of Community conscience by stirring the institutional pot on January 18, 1989. On that date the MEP's decided to transfer some of their activities to Brussels (the Belgian members of course being never so European as when serving their own interests), but remained incapable of taking a definitive decision on their ambulatory seat. The intractability of the issue was demonstrated on June 28, 1991, when Italian premier Giulio Andreotti abandoned a mission to find a solution to the issue of EC institutional seats. European elections were held on June 15 and 18. On that occasion Maurice Duverger, a French professor and author, made history by being elected as an independent on the electoral list of the Italian Communist Party. He thereby became the first truly European deputy, representing not his country but a constituency of the Community.

Council of Europe: fortieth anniversary

On May 5, 1989, the Council of Europe celebrated, in delighted surprise at its own continuing vigor and new-found role as eastern Europe's gateway to the west, forty years of activity. Following up her entry into EFTA on January 1, 1986, Finland became the twenty-fourth member of the Council of Europe on May 5, 1989, the fortieth anniversary of that most venerable of European intergovernmental organizations. On that occasion also Lech Walesa received the 1989 Council of Europe Human Rights prize. However, after the award questions were raised about Poland's compliance with provisions of the European Convention on Human Rights, particularly as regards women's rights (abortion) and state links to the Catholic Church (freedom of religion).

Council of Europe parliamentarians welcome CSCE counterparts

For nearly half a century the Parliamentary Assembly of "greater Europe" has kept the flame alive for countries under regimes of the left and right excluded from the Council of Europe for lack of democracy, not only in communist Eastern Europe but also in corporatist Portugal, falangist Spain and, for a few years, reactionary Greece. The recent admission of Hungary, Czechoslovakia and Poland has given triple satisfaction: it was a first step in bringing together the two "halves" of Europe; it was a triumph for the moral values enshrined in Council of Europe statutes and practice; it gave the Strasbourg agency a new vocation at a time when impending further EC enlargement and creation of the 19-nation EEA were threatening the Strasbourg agency with a measure of duplication and hence irrelevancy. However, the Assembly went further in the fall of 1990 by entering the debate on the institutionalisation of the CSCE. With an eye to the Paris summit, elected representatives from all 34 countries which had signed the Helsinki Final Act, brought together on the initiative of the President of the Assembly, Anders Björck (but following a proposal by President Bush), declared that the Council of Europe should be involved in the CSCE process both at intergovernmental level and through a parliamentary dimension, to be set up in cooperation with Canada and the US. The Council of Europe had experience to offer the CSCE in many spheres: human rights, with the affirmation of standards which should become a benchmark for all CSCE countries; the functioning of democratic institutions; legal cooperation; culture; health; the environment . . . Many of its conventions, some 150 in number, are open to signature by non-member countries. To avoid duplication, the Council of Europe Assembly could act as the core of a CSCE assembly. Secretary General Catherine Lalumière declared that the Council of Europe did not intend to take over the possible parliamentary dimension of CSCE, but to provide support for it. Her words were doubtless sincere. On the other hand, while such an initiative shows the value of the Council of Europe in the short term, creation of a CSCE assembly could prove threatening to it in the long run.

An American journalist who observed the joint meeting, Tom Mashberg, deplored the fact that no delegation was present from the US Congress, whose members were engaged in an electoral campaign at the time. Beyond this, however, they were probably displeased with the Bush Administration for recommending a CSCE parliamentary body, based on the Council of Europe Assembly, without consulting Congress. Mashberg also conceded, however, that Americans have little understanding of European institutions, frequently confusing the Council of Europe and the Community, much less seizing on the former's potential for bringing together all the countries of Europe on any issue except defense.

Conservative schizophrenia in Britain: the European headache

In the United Kingdom the Conservative Party has long been of two minds about linking the island nation to "the Continent". In October British Chancellor of the Exchequer (finance minister) Nigel Lawson opened up the British malaise – and a latent split in the Conservative party – over the Community's plans for union by resigning in protest at Prime Minister Thatcher's refusal to allow the UK to enter the European monetary system. He was replaced by John Major, the "wonder boy" Londoner without a college degree, who eventually persuaded Thatcher to reverse herself. In fact, the Conservative split was papered over by Major's own move next door, at Thatcher's expense, from the Chancellor's residence at 12 Downing Street to the Prime Minister's, at number 10. *Tant pis pour la Dame de Fer* if, six months after his elevation, she found her young *protégé* gray not only of hair but also of character.

In November WEU set up an institute for security studies in Paris, a small enough event in itself, but one which clearly showed that Europe's parliamentarians, whether responding to or leading public opinion, no longer accepted unquestioningly the gospel according to St. Nato.

EBRD: jump-starting the free market in the East

Concerned that the European Community had not adopted a common position on the breakneck pace of reform in eastern Europe and the problems to which this was giving rise, President Mitterrand took advantage of his prerogative as president of the European Council to call a working dinner in Paris on November 18, 1989. The EC leaders endorsed the changes taking place and asked the past, present and future EC chairmen (Gonzales of Spain, Mitterrand and Haughey of Ireland) to examine the feasibility of a European development bank, modelled on the existing European Investment Bank, but designed specifically to channel aid to reform projects in eastern Europe. The three leaders were also asked to look into creation of a foundation to train eastern European managers.

Economic assistance was made conditional on progress to democracy. "We are ready to cooperate", declared Mitterrand, "by all available means toward the creation of healthier economies, in exchange for ... a verified return to democracy, respect for human rights and the calling of free and secret elections". It was further agreed, that Poland and Hungary could not wait even until creation of the new bank. The Commission was charged with coordinating aid from the 24 most developed countries and the International Monetary Fund was asked to conclude an economic framework program for the two countries.

It rapidly became apparent that a piece-meal or band-aid approach to the problem would not suffice. On May 29, 1990, the European Bank for Reconstruction and Development (EBRD) was established. In a piece of side-line horse-trading, Mitterrand accepted London as the headquarters of the bank (the first siting of a major European institution in the UK) in exchange for the appointment of a Frenchman, Jacques Attali, as its first director.

Fostering success or subsidizing failure? US concerns over EBRD

Creation of the new bank did not pass unchallenged. The US was asked to become a member and to put up a major portion of the capital. Two months previously, on March 7, 1990, Senator Robert W. Kasten, Jr. of Wisconsin had vigorously attacked the proposal on the floor of the US Senate. As reported in the Congressional record, he thought it would be "an inappropriate use of Western funds" to lend money to the Soviet Union:

> It is the crisis of communist economics that made Soviet liberalization possible — and the West should not be subsidizing that failed system.

Since the Soviets had no experience in promoting private sector growth, nor hard currency, Senator Kasten felt massive western lending would only produce further delays. However, Senator Kasten went further — and lost some credibility — by also attacking Western European governments "indifferent — if not hostile — to free market economics, not disciples of American-style capitalism", singling out the French for favoring central planning over free markets. His conclusion was that "a European-led development bank will tend to promote this brand of socialist economics". Senator Kasten further suggested that in Eastern Europe itself there was a common fear, as reported by former senator Bill Brock, that large international loans would only be used to sustain inefficient and non-competitive state-owned enterprises. (Americans, even senators, often fail to distinguish between quasi-communist "socialism" and social democracy. Perhaps they should look north to Canada).

Senator Kasten concluded that all loans should be conditioned on market-oriented economic reforms. He failed to report, however, that such a condition had been enunciated at the very first meeting by President Mitterrand and Prime Minister Margaret Thatcher. The latter at least could scarcely be accused of being soft on socialism. The Senator also said most of the lending should be limited to the private sector and to easing the transition by providing for basic human needs like health care, food and shelter "until the restored economies can take up the shock". The US could also provide tax incentives for American businesses investing in Europe. The Bush Administration kept its distance from such hawkish views. In a written response to Senator Kasten, released under the Freedom of Information Act, Janet G. Mullins, Assistant Secretary for Legislative Affairs, ignored the remarks about Western European governments, but agreed:

> There are serious questions that must be addressed before the US can join the EBRD, in particular the role of the USSR in the EBRD. We believe the EBRD can best support the economic and political transformation of the countries of Central and Eastern Europe by fostering the development of market-based economics and pluralistic societies. Other governments, including the reforming Central and East Europeans, agree on the importance of fostering the private sector.

Today Senator Kasten's concerns are largely met, inasmuch as the USSR is no more[1] and the whole of Eastern Europe (except Serbia) has abjured communism. Is the senator as concerned about rising nationalism as he was about moribund communism?

Whose head on the banknote?

At the end of the Irish chairmanship of the EC, the European Council met in Dublin. On June 26, 1990, it agreed to convene conferences on economic and monetary union and on political union in Rome in December. The UK delegation expressed serious misgivings (John Major had already proposed circulation of a Community ECU alongside rather that instead of national currencies). However, since the present issue was a process and no final decisions had been taken, majority opinion prevailed. The conferences were given a year to report back at the Maastricht summit with new draft treaties. Malta applied for EC membership on July 16, 1990, followed by Sweden on July 1, 1991. The future of EFTA would be seriously called into question.

Meeting in Rome in November, the EC's European Council decided over British objections (majority vote) to create a central banking system by January 1994. This set a deadline for creation of a single European currency without necessarily obliging all member states to join the system at the same time. European-minded Tories in the UK such as Michael Heseltine and Edward Heath rejoiced. Right-wing Conservatives sensed that Britain was being drawn in, her sovereignty destroyed. They denounced the "F-word".[2] However, the failure to agree on farm subsidy cuts was of more immediate significance, on account of current GATT negotiations in the Uruguay Round.

Human rights forty years on

On November 5, 1990, the Council of Europe marked in Rome the 40th anniversary of the European Convention on Human Rights. The agency has never surpassed this achievement, which continues to characterize the institution as a whole (one recalls the expulsion of first Greece, then Turkey, during somber periods of those countries political fortunes; and the long wait for admission imposed on Portugal and Spain). Newly-formed European democracies are required to meet the same high standards. Offering to coordinate human rights issues for the CSCE, the Council of Europe invited Canada, the United States and the Soviet Union to join some of its functions. In a public address, the US Assistant Secretary of State for human rights declared that his country wished to work with the Council of Europe to assist emerging democracies. Hungary was admitted as the 24th member country and first former communist member, with seven assembly seats, in November.

In Brussels the EC finally reached agreement on tariff and subsidy reductions in agriculture to be proposed to GATT nations at Uruguay Round talks in Geneva: 15% in price supports, 30% in tariffs over five years. The US reacted negatively, considering the proposals insufficient.

The US decision to transfer over half the 200,000 troops stationed in Europe to the Persian Gulf to confront Iraq, which had ignored repeated UN calls to withdraw from Kuwait, while understandable in the circumstances, nevertheless highlighted the shift in priorities in the first "post Cold War" regional crisis, where the US and USSR were working together. After the Gulf War many of those troops did not return to their European postings.

Crackdown on dirty money

On November 8, 1990, the Council of Europe approved a convention of interest to the US and Canada as well as Europe, and open to signature by those countries, on the laundering, search, seizure and confiscation of the proceeds from crime. It was immediately signed by 16 member countries. While liberalization of financial services and the free movement of capital are advantageous to the European economy it must not benefit organized crime. The Council of Europe's crackdown on dirty money reaches beyond the banks, covering all the "instrumentalities" (means or property) used for arms trafficking, terrorism, fraud and drugs. The US, Canada and Australia were closely involved in preparing the text.

The convention proscribes measures to be taken at both national and international levels. In urgent cases diplomatic channels and those of national authorities may be bypassed to secure rapid action. Moreover, a state may not invoke banking secrecy for refusing cooperation. Even the decease of a targeted individual does not stand in the way of cooperation. The Council of Europe convention facilitates action by both courts and banks by allowing them to exploit the criminal's window of vulnerability between acquisition of cash and its deposit in a bank, thus rendering it anonymous.

A G7 task force has estimated drug sales at 122 billion annually, of which up to 70% is available for laundering and investment. This convention hits the drug barons in their secret pockets, making it harder for them to wash their sins away.

Britain and Europe: a leadership issue

Meanwhile, the strains of further steps toward the European union of the Twelve continued their ripple effect across the Channel. On November 14 Michael Heseltine decided to challenge Margaret Thatcher for the Conservative Party leadership over European policy and other issues, such as the community charge (regional taxation), derisively known as the poll tax. After failing by four votes to reach a decisive majority among Conservative MP's on the first ballot, Thatcher resigned. Chancellor of the Exchequer John Major entered the fray in the second round and defeated Heseltine and Douglas Hurd to become prime minister on November 28. At its Rome meeting on December 14 the European Council welcomed the less abrasive "tone" of the UK delegation under Major.

In a perceptive review of two recent books on Europe by British authors, Peter Pulzer suggests that the change of heart in Britain is actually a change of head, and none the worse for that.

Pulzer asks whether Britain's leaders are lagging behind public opinion:

> That two Conservative public figures should, within a space of three weeks, publish books urging Britain in almost identical terms to go the whole European hog, is surely remarkable. More than anything else, it indicates the post-Thatcher agenda: Europe was certainly the occasion of Mrs Thatcher's going, even if not its principal cause. It was also the cause of her two most damaging Cabinet crises, the Westland affair and the resignation of Nigel Lawson; of her most ridiculous embarrassement, the Ridley affair; and of her one national electoral defeat, in the European elections of 1989. Perhaps if she had not insisted on inventing the poll tax, she might still be in Number Ten. But if so, she would be severely and increasingly constrained, more by European questions than by any other. [3]

With notable exceptions like Edward Heath, Roy Jenkins and Michael Heseltine, Britons are rarely passionate about Europe. John Major has declared himself "intellectually" rather than "emotionally" in favor of European unification; but, again, Europe does not have many Spaaks, de Gasperis or Monnets these days. The handing over of Europe to the technocrats is a mark of its success even as it constitutes a danger. Europe is now a part of daily life. John Major could be the man for the times.

It should also be noted in this context that while until the mid-eighties the British Labour Party was committed to withdrawal from the EC, on July 8, 1991, the Labour opposition produced its strongest statement ever in support of European unification. Party leader Neil Kinnock declared economic and political union to be inevitable, asserting that UK economic policy should be geared towards convergence with the EC.

1991

On February 21, 1991, Czechoslovakia became the twenty-fifth member and the second Central European member of the Council of Europe, with eight assembly seats.

In another Council of Europe development, the UK transferred decisions on the early release of offenders from the Home Secretary (minister of the interior) to the Parole Board. The action was taken following a finding by the European Court of Human Rights that the previous British procedure made the government both judge and party in such cases.

The Council of Europe took a firm stand in June when the Committee of Ministers refused renewal of the European Diploma for Nature Conservation for the first time in a quarter century. Renewal was denied for the French National Pyrenees Park for failure to protect wild animals, especially brown bears (of which only about a dozen remain) and to control illegal building within the park boundary.

Fast track

Urged on by the new US Secretary of Agriculture, Edward Madigan, who had succeeded Clayton Yeutter in January, Congress voted "fast track" authority on May 23 and 24 for the Bush administration to negotiate tariff quota and subsidy reductions in North American Free Trade Area (NAFTA) and Uruguay Round negotiations. "Fast track" limits the Congress to an "up or down" vote on a trade package without separate votes on each item, thereby facilitating a positive outcome by making government positions at the negotiating table more credible. By creating a market even larger than that of the EC, NAFTA itself will strengthen the North American position in dealings with the Community. NAFTA negotiations between Canada, Mexico and the US opened in Toronto on June 13.

Reshaping North Atlantic defense

Following dissolution of the WTO military alliance in February, the Supreme Soviet ratified the treaty on German sovereignty a month later, definitively changing the defense map of Europe. The search continued in the West for a definition of NATO's new role. In March the last cruise missiles left Britain's Greenham Common (scene of anti-nuclear demonstrations in earlier times) for destruction under the INF Treaty. On May 28 defense ministers planned a 50% force reduction in Europe and creation of a rapid intervention group under British command. At its June meeting in Copenhagen, the NATO Council gave formal support to European efforts to forge a security policy, while at the same time, in an obvious attempt to maintain balance, stressing the need for "complementarity" between a renewed Atlantic Alliance and European defense.[4] Thus an institutional split is avoided even as the principle of a European security agency is strengthened. Of course a "security agency" such as WEU is a far cry from a joint military force. WEU is a political and administrative coordinating body and possesses no equivalent of the NATO military command. Moreover, the role of the former "neutrals" in the European Community if WEU is absorbed by the EC is not yet clear. The problem is a real one, since it is generally accepted that a European foreign policy will not be credible without a corresponding security component. Of course the neutrals do have armed forces and one could argue that in the absence of confrontation everyone becomes neutral.

Towards a "European confederation"?

On June 15 Presidents Havel and Mitterrand took the initiative of convening a "private" international conference in Prague on the future shape of a European confederation. If the two presidents agreed on the concept they were not yet at one on the content. Mitterrand saw the need for some sort of institutional capstone to coordinate three levels of European cooperation, as represented by CSCE, the Council of Europe and the European Community. Havel, on the other had, was reticent about a developed confederation secretariat, the existence of which might delay Central European entry into the EC. It remains to be seen whether this gathering was no more than an occasion for politico-philosophical musings or a new "Hague Congress", destined to chart the future of a Europe whole and free.

Sweden jumps ship

Both the European security issue and the future of EFTA were brought to a head by the Swedish government's resolve to seek EC membership. In a decision described by many speakers as its most important since World War II, the *Folketing* or parliament of the traditionally non-aligned nation had voted on December 12, 1991 by 198 to 105, with 26 abstentions, to authorize the application. In making formal application in Madrid to the new Community presidency, the Netherlands, on July 1, 1991, Swedish premier Carlsson, a Social Democrat who succeeded the mysteriously assassinated Olof Palme in 1986, expressed the hope that his country would enter the Community by 1995. Only Sweden's small leftist and environmentalist parties remain implacably opposed to EC membership.

Sweden is a sparsely populated country of Northern Europe. The fourth largest country in Europe (173,731 sq. miles, 449,964 sq. km.), it is nearly twice the size of Britain, a little larger than California but with only 53 inhabitants per square mile (20 per sq. km.). Until a hundred years ago Sweden was mainly a nation of peasant farmers. However, according to the 1980 census, 83% of its population of just over eight million people lives in urban areas. The largest cities are Stockholm (1.4 m.); Gothenburg (700,000) and Malmö (450,000). Over a million Swedes emigrated to the US in the 19th century.

Traditional minorities include Lapps (about 15,000) and Finns in the northernmost regions but postwar immigration has brought other Scandinavians, Yugoslavs, Greeks, Turks and Latin-Americans, mostly in search of jobs but some of them political refugees. Nordic collaboration among Scandinavian countries (Denmark, Finland, Iceland, Norway, Sweden) provides a common labor market.

Sweden has vast resources of timber and important deposits of iron, copper, zinc and gold ores. Rivers are extensively exploited for hydro-electric power. The business sector has gone through major changes since the fifties. Today only 4% of the labor force is employed in agriculture, which is nevertheless subject to government regulation and price guarantees. Most people work in the industrial or service sectors. The traditional basic industries — iron, steel and forest products — have met severe foreign competition in recent years. The engineering industry is now very strong, with 42% of industrial value-added and 12% of Sweden's employment. Nearly 70% of its production is exported. High living standards, a cold climate and industrial structures generate high energy consumption.

Social welfare protection is highly developed and taxation correspondingly heavy. Sweden is a middle-class country with an even distribution of living standards. Education standards are high. A single, coherent system of post-secondary education was developed in 1977. The country has a long tradition of adult education.

Sweden is a traditional and popular monarchy. Regardless of sex, the oldest child of the royal couple, currently King Carl XVI Gustaf and Queen Silvia, is heir to the trone. Since World War II, the same five parties — Moderates (formerly Conservatives), Center Party, Liberals, Social Democrats, Left Party Communists—have dominated politics. The Social Democratic Party has been dominant in government. A characteristic feature of the public service is a separation between ministries which serve governments and central administrative agencies which administer the country at large. Justice is based on written laws.

Defending the Swedish paradox

Sweden's foreign policy has been dominated by neutrality since the 19th century. This has not impeded active participation in peaceful bodies such as OECD, the Council of Europe and EFTA. Now that political and military confrontation in Europe has waned, the concept is interpreted even more liberally, as also in the case of other European neutrals, to permit application for membership of the European Community, although the new European Union's assimilation of WEU will doubtless give rise to a careful delimitation of multilateral commitments with respect to defense and security. Swedes now feel that with a voice in the EC rather than EFTA Sweden can better protect the political, commercial and cultural interests of this paradoxical nation of a large public sector, high taxes, powerful trade unions—but also large and vigorous companies and low unemployment.

Hot debates in a cold climate

Within a few months, however, the relative consensus on EC-entry had broken down. On September 15, 1991, a center right coalition ousted Carlsson and the Social Democrats. Consequently the impending referendum of 1994 which was to ratify Swedish entry became embroiled in national politics. The Social Democrats announced that they would not join forces with the Conservatives to campaign for a yes-vote. The Social Democrats have softened their position: national salvation does not depend on EC-entry. A splinter group even formed an "EC alternative" campaign. More radical still is the "No to the EC" group, composed of greens and former communists who voted against in the parliamentary debate, which does not even accept Sweden in the EEA. Used to governing, the Social Democrats seem to be suffering from withdrawal symptoms. Now that they are out of power, they are insisting that "the most important issue to be put to the people since the Second World War" be organized before the next general election. Will Sweden "do a Norway" and vote no? It is too early to predict, but even before negotiations have begun, much less terms of entry established, battle lines are being drawn.

Sweden's accession to the Community will not provide a marked numerical expansion. However, there are other strengths. Sweden has a long democratic tradition and one of the highest living standards in Europe. Sweden will almost certainly be a net contributor to the EC budget. Her economy is fundamentally sound and on the cutting edge of technology, with special strength in steel and automobiles. After East Germany, Sweden will further strengthen the protestant presence in the Community, somewhat diluted in recent years by the Iberian accessions. Finally, with her privileged contacts in both East and West, Sweden can help bring balance and cohesion to the new Europe.

Meanwhile the EC-EFTA negotiations on creation of a European Economic Area for tariff-free trade after 1992 had become somewhat bogged down on account of the harsh terms set by the EC. However Community negotiators were now motivated to reach agreement in order to head off a rush of applications to join the EC from both Western and Central Europe. Success was finally achieved with the birth of the 19-nation European Economic Area in October 1991. However, this did not deter Finland and Switzerland from following Sweden in applying for EC membership. Furthermore, Norway's Prime Minister Gro Harlem Brundtland has said she does not rule out another Norwegian bid to join, even though the last one was defeated in a national referendum. Since Central European countries have negotiated bilateral association agreements directly with the Community, EFTA's days seem numbered: trade between Iceland and Liechtenstein is hardly voluminous.

G7 + G: a new horizon for the USSR

In 1975 President Valéry Giscard d'Estaing of France took the initiative of convening the six major economic powers (G6) at Rambouillet for an informal review of the world economy. Over the years the meetings of the six, become seven with the addition of Canada,[5] have become increasingly formal and important, although France has always maintained that the group should not become an institution or world economic directoire.

In his first presiding role as Prime Minister, chairman John Major characterized the 1991 meeting on July 16 and 17 in London as historic. The seven were for the first time joined by the Soviet Union in the person of President Gorbachev. In addition to agreeing action in eight major fields,[6] G7 received a detailed report on problems in the Soviet Union and agreed six points of cooperation with President Gorbachev:

1. The Soviet Union would become an associate member of the International Monetary Fund and the World Bank, with access not to loans but to expertise;
2. Permanent cooperation between USSR and the four major multilateral institutions: IMF, World Bank, OECD and EBRD, would help the USSR to become integrated with the world economy;
3. Intensification of technical assistance to USSR and her European neighbors;
4. Increased trade;
5. Follow-up to G7 resolutions by means of close contact with the chairman (John Major, UK, in 1991; Helmut Kohl, FRG, in 1992);
6. Visit of G7 finance ministers and ministers responsible for small business to the USSR.

Gorbachev had now achieved a partial opening to the economic institutions of the West. He had no intention, however, of giving up the game and embracing the capitalist system. He neither saw the western economies as monolithic, nor accepted that the Soviet experience had little of value to offer. He had explained his views on complementarity when addressing Italian business and financial circles during an official visit to Italy on December 1, 1989:

> As for differences between the socialist (Gorbachev's use of the word "socialist" should not of course be confused with socialism or social democracy as understood in Canada and Western Europe) and capitalist economies, they really do exist. It is wrong, however, to say that these systems are fundamentally incompatible in an integrated mechanism of the world economy. The leading historical trend consists in the growing rapprochement rather than divergence of the different economic structures. Take the question of the market, for example. There is no "pure" market economy in any capitalist country any longer. In one way or another, it is combined everywhere with state regulation, and the structure of ownership and the extent of government interference in the economy even in the countries belonging to the European Economic Community are by no means the same.
>
> As regards the socialist countries, most of them and, of course, the Soviet Union are working on developing market relations and competition, and on utilizing all the diverse forms of ownership. We have realized the harm monopolism can do in any sphere, including foreign economic ties, and are resolutely giving up this practice, although this is not at all easy.
>
> Interdependence enables all of us to overcome the disunity of the world. The world economy needs the kind of balance it has never known before.

Gorbachev's formula is tempting and, as regards his description of the West's mixed economies at both national and international level, not to be denied. Nevertheless one senses here the hesitation — or self-delusion — which eventually led to his downfall from internal rather than external pressures. The Soviet president fails to understand or to concede (as does also the West) that Marxism-Leninism has lost its ideological fire among the party faithful; there is a failure of political will sapping the state from within. For Gorbachev perestroika was to reform the Soviet system, not to replace it. Boris Yeltsin was already showing himself to be far more forthright. Recognized as the "continuation state" succeeding the USSR, Russia now receives western support to participate in the international agencies listed in the G7 London summit agreement.

Moscow summit

Not the least historic part of the London Summit occurred in the wings, when Bush and Gorbachev announced that they had cleared away the final obstacles to a START agreement in Geneva[7] and to their own fourth summit. The latter took place in Moscow on July 29 and 30. The START treaty was duly signed, following nine years of negotiations in Geneva, although its very completion brought to the fore a related issue: Moscow's reluctance to discount the nuclear strike forces of France and the United Kingdom, not subject to bilateral US-Soviet START commitments.[8] It was perhaps a sign of the times, both military and economic, that on July 30, while President Bush was in

Moscow, the US announced the closing of 79 bases in Europe and the House of Representatives approved closing of 34 more in the US. On the other hand, skeptics pointed out that the treaty left the US with 9000 missiles and the USSR with 7000 — approximately the same number as when negotiations began — and permitted development of new delivery systems.

Even as the two presidents were signing the treaty, the Baltic states, pushed from the headlines by events in Yugoslavia, returned to the front pages and demonstrated the delicacy of Gorbachev's tight-rope act. Six Lithuanians were killed in a Soviet police assault on a Lithuanian "frontier post" and presidents Landsbergis of Lithuania and Yeltsin of the Russian Republic signed a cooperation agreement wherein Russia recognized Lithuanian independence, bypassing the central Soviet authorities.

Spain's rising star

Another summit was taking place in Guadalajara, Mexico, and drawing far less attention. It is conceivable, however, that the meeting of heads of state and government from Latin-American countries and Spain (the latter playing to the full its role of EC link to Latin America) might prove of even greater long-term significance than the London G7 gathering. At the very least it offered Fidel Castro an opportunity to come out of isolation without loss of face. Spain played a leadership role in this first meeting of the "Hispanic Commonwealth". The Spanish delegation was led by King Juan Carlos himself — a daring initiative by a consitutional monarch which brought him both praise and criticism.

Spain also played a major role in another conference, this time in Madrid. While in 1492 Arabs and Jews were driven from Spain, in 1991 the Moncloa Palace was selected by all parties as the host site for the first Middle East peace talks in forty-five years. Over the last two decades, under providential moral leadership from Juan Carlos and with the dynamic drive of Socialist Prime Minister Felipe Gonzalez, Spain has provided the world with a role model of how to effect a peaceful transition from dictatorship to democracy and peaceful development.

Before the center of gravity of the Community moved east with the reunification of Germany, it had moved south with the enlargement embracing first Greece, then Portugal and Spain. 1992 was to be the year of consecration and consolidation of Spain's European dowry. Five centuries after Christopher Columbus landed in the New World, through the Universal Exhibition on Cartuja Island, rich in links to the voyage of 1492, Seville sought to regain the central role which it once played in Southern Europe. The past comes together with the future. "Our time has come", declared Alfredo Jimenez, the Seville exhibition's cultural director; "In the neglected south of Southern Europe we are moving directly from a pre-industrial to a post-industrial region". New highways and high-speed train links are being carved across the country. In 1992 Madrid was Europe's cultural capital, Barcelona hosted the Olympic Games, Seville the world exhibition. Spain renewed her destiny as the crossroads of Europe, North Africa, the Mediterranean world and Latin-America.

It is hardly surprising that today the hot spot for foreign investment in Europe — in cash, joint ventures and production — lies south of the Pyrenees. In November 1991, for instance, Pepsico sought to counter sluggish sales at home in the US by announcing a one-billion dollar investment in Spain to build soft-drink plants, open fast-food restaurants and set up a computerized system to track snack-food sales. Pepsi's business overseas has been growing twice as fast as in the USA. Pepsico plans to derive 25% of its sales and profits from foreign markets by 1996. Spain is a gateway to Europe.

Within the European Community the Big Four have almost become the Big Five. This was demonstrated at the Maastricht summit in December when Spain successfully spearheaded a drive by the Community's "poor four" (Spain, Portugal, Greece, Ireland) for increased economic assistance from the EC).

EC and EFTA fumble fish, finance and freightliners

Meanwhile, in Brussels, after months of tough bargaining, the EC-EFTA negotiations for creation of the "European Economic Space" finally foundered and were suspended on July 30. Although both sides urgently sought the agreement (especially after Sweden had joined Austria in applying for EC membership), three delicate issues defied solution: free EFTA access to EC fish markets, EFTA financial aid to underdeveloped EC regions and transit conditions through Austria and Switzerland for EC freightliners. It would take three more months of table pounding before these obstacles were eliminated.

Skirting Austrian neutrality

However, Austria's case was progressing on another front: on July 31, 1991, the EC Commission issued its official opinion on Austria's application for membership. Viewed as a model of democracy, the Alpine republic was never in serious danger of refusal.[9] Given the hesitations of certain existing members on political union, however, the Commission nevertheless forcefully made the point that Austria's constitutionally enshrined neutrality must not be allowed to pose additional obstacles to political union nor to a joint security policy for the Community.[10] Thus, negotiations were planned for 1993, by which time the new treaty of political union and joint foreign and security policies should form part of the *acquis communautaire* and must be accepted by new members. The same of course applies to Malta, Cyprus and Sweden. The Community will seek assurances from the Austrian authorities on their legal capacity to undertake the commitments relevant to the future foreign and security policies of the Community.

After seven centuries: Switzerland in search of a role

A day later, on August 1, 1991, Switzerland celebrated seven hundred years of confederation. Tradition has it that at the beginning of August 1291 the representatives of three cantons bordering on Lake Lucerne came together in Gruetli field to join forces against Austrian overlords. The legend of William Tell, reputed fearlessly to have split the apple on his son's head with an arrow when commanded to do so by the tyrant Gessler, was born at the same time. In July 1940, when Switzerland was surrounded by Axis forces, General Henri Guisan affirmed from the same spot the Swiss will to resist. [11]

The President of the Confederation, Flavio Cotti, exhorted his compatriots to overcome their doubts and to have confidence in the future. The right of co-decision must accompany any renunciation of sovereignty. However, René Felber, the Swiss "foreign minister" (government is collegial in Switzerland) was more forthright. "Switzerland is not an island", he declared. "The time is past when we could expect special treatment from the international community". Within months, having succeeded Cotti in the presidential chair, Felber would lead his colleagues in putting aside lingering hesitancy. Whether the conservative electorate will follow the lead remains to be seen. Switzerland's direct democracy is notoriously unpredictable.

Turkey's pivotal role

In Turkey's national elections on October 18, former prime minister Demirel's right wing True Path party ousted President Turgut Ozal's Motherland Party, in power for eight years. However True Path failed to gain an overall majority and was faced with the choice of forming a coalition with either the outgoing Motherland Party or the Islamic Fundamentalist Welfare Party. This was a stark choice. Turkey is a candidate for EC membership and western aid, both of which are blocked by lack of a settlement in Cyprus and Turkey's dismal human rights record, especially towards its Kurdish minority. In October 1991 Turkey actually bombed Kurds in northern Iraq, accused of terrorist acts across the border, while officially cooperating in the protection of the Kurdish region from Saddam Hussein. The presence of fundamentalists in power in a NATO and Council of Europe country would be unsettling to the west. On the other hand, many Turks were looking east to cooperation with Central Asian republics emerging from the break-up of the Soviet Union. Turkey has tried to keep politics and religion apart since Attaturk's creation of a modern secular state in the twenties. Her importance as a bridge between Europe and Asia has changed but not diminished since the end of the Cold War. The break-up of Yugoslavia, with its own Moslem minority, to the west and the Azeri-Armenian confrontation on the other side of Mount Ararat makes Turkey's role as important and as delicate as ever.

If Turkey is to remain anchored in Europe and to provide regional stability, settlement of the age-old Greek-Turkish dispute is of interest well beyond Athens, Ankara and the UN peace-keeping Green Line which snakes through Nicosia.[12]

Elusive force: the European Army again

On October 16, 1991, — thirty-seven years after the rejection of the European Defence Community — France and Germany called for creation of a corps-strength Western European army designed to give the Community an independent defense capability. The two governments announced that they would expand their 5,000-member brigade to 30,000 troops and invited other member countries of Western European Union to join them. WEU's weakness, as we have seen, has always been that while possessing an international secretariat and even a parliamentary assembly, it lacked the most fundamental resource of a military organization, its own armed forces.

The Franco-German initiative was at once challenged by Britain (which had also scuttled the EDC) as a potential threat to NATO. Foreign Secretary Douglas Hurd castigated as "useless and dangerous" any duplication of what NATO is doing. One may well suspect, however, that the United Kingdom's true concern, as in 1954, was still to put the brakes on a move to create a federal Europe or to create a European foreign policy not based on consensus. Following the failure of a Dutch "political Europe" proposal and the return to the less far-reaching position paper from Luxembourg, the Franco-German initiatives and the swift British response were part of the thrust-and-parry forming the run up to the December summit in Maastricht.

Nevertheless, opposition was not confined to the British response. Writing in *Die Zeit* on September 26, Hans Ruhle attacked the idea from inside Germany itself even before it was officially announced. Against the background of the European political fiasco in the Yugoslav conflict, Ruhle asks where any European rapid intervention is to come from: which organization is to be in charge; what is the task force's position to be in relation to the security structure in Europe; and where its manpower is to come from. He seemed to be anticipating the Franco-German proposal to give muscle to WEU's paper tiger when he declared:

> The outsize American stake in NATO ... rules out any hope that the North Atlantic pact as it stands might function simultaneously both with and without the United States ...
>
> Most people specifically affected, and even some politicians, now seem to have realised that any European rapid reaction force that is to be answerable to the WEU will need its own political bodies, separate military command structures and, in particular, a wide range of military capabilities.
>
> In NATO these capabilities — reconnaissance, communications, logistics, strategic means of transport and specific strategic operation facilities, such as aircraft carriers and tactical anti-missile capacity — are wholly or mainly provided by the United States ...
>
> The desire felt by many Western Europeans to Europeanise security policy and to arrive at a short-term *fait accompli* is here again seen to be due more to a generally felt need for greater detachment form the Americans that to any clear assessment of the international situation or of true progress toward European integration.

A European rapid reaction force, says Ruhle, must await the creation of a common foreign and security policy. It cannot bring such a policy, much less a full political union, into being. "Mountains aren't, after all, scaled from the peak downward".

Wary Washington

Expansion of the brigade met a cautious response in Washington, not dissimilar to the British reaction. Deficit pressures and dissolution of the Soviet threat having brought about a fifty-percent reduction in US troop strength in Europe, the US wants to see Europe take greater responsibility for her own defense. On the other hand, if NATO is bypassed US influence in Europe will be much diminished. "We have an interest in seeing that as the European security identity is developed it be complementary to NATO and not detract from NATO's missions", declared a State Department spokesman. However, now the Cold War is over, US interests in Europe no longer have to be chan- nelled through NATO. A Franco-German force can bring a German military contribution to regional peace-keeping, notably absent from the Gulf conflict. The favorable view was forcefully argued by the *New York Times*:

> Americans who are overly preoccupied with the economic challenge posed by the Euro- pean Community tend to forget how advantageous it was to the U.S. for Europeans to overcome past hostility and form such a community. From that perspective, French-Ger- man willingness to set up a joint force, roughly 30,000 strong, should be reassuring to Americans. By weaving them together into another set of military ties besides NATO, it could ease worries, especially in France, about Germany's newfound capacity for indepen- dent action.[13]

European Economic Area

1991 had been a year of Community foreign policy failures: Yugoslav peace- keeping intervention and withdrawal of Dutch political community plans. In the early hours of October 22, the EC-EFTA negotiations, which had been going on for eighteen months, maintained nailbiting Community marathon traditions by going down to the wire. When officials finally emerged a 19- nation economic community of 380 million people — by far the world's largest — had been conceived as the European Economic Area (EEA), stretching from the Artic to the shores of Africa and from the Caribbean to the Aegean.

While not creating a total common market, since there is no common external tariff, the EEA goes much further than the EFTA free trade area. EFTA governments accepted EC trading, financial and labor regulations and Community legislation on consumer protection, company law, environmental protection, competition and social policy. In exchange, EFTA goods, workers, services and capital are granted broad access to the Community. Politically more significant is the creation of common institutions such as a joint council of ministers.

Compromises were found in three key holdout areas of dispute: fishing rights, trucking rights and special support payments for poorer EC members.[14]

Not surprisingly, integration in the sensitive area of farm products was postponed.

A jurisdictional hitch

The original treaty also provided for a court, modelled after the European Court of Justice (ECJ) in Luxembourg, to settle disputes arising among EEA members. However, the new court was subsequently held by the ECJ to be incompatible with its own functions and supremacy and, as such, incompatible with the EC, ECSC and EURATOM treaties. Both sides accepted this judgment and returned early in 1992 to the negotiating table. In February a compromise settlement was agreed by the Nineteen which respected the powers of the ECJ.

The compromise sets up an EEA committee on competition policy to which proposed mergers may be referred if a substantial portion of the firm involved does business in EFTA countries. However, the EC may insist on the matter being referred to the ECJ if the merger has important repercussions in the Community. In all matters other than competition policy an arbitration procedure is established. Thus in a "safeguard" dispute whereby a country imposes a temporary halt to imports of a product, the dispute may first be referred to a joint committee and, if necessary, to a panel of three members (EC, EFTA and neutral) with binding powers. The European Parliament asked that this arrangement also be reviewed by the ECJ, which subsequently accepted it.

Doing the numbers in NATO: not exactly a Roman holiday

On November 7 and 8, 1991, the NATO Council met in Rome at the level of heads of state and government. The sixteen leaders conducted a far-reaching review of the role of the Atlantic Alliance in a post-Cold War and post-Gulf War Europe. They de-emphasized the nuclear option but failed to reach a conclusion on Franco-German proposals for a measure of European defense autonomy, an issue on which the Europeans themselves remained divided in the run-up to the Maastricht summit.

Criticized at home for spending too much time abroad on foreign policy, President Bush was particularly sensitive on the issue of the costly US military presence in Europe. Irritated by the French go-it-almost-alone tight-rope walk, a testy Mr. Bush told his colleagues:

> Our premise is that the American role in the defense and the affairs of Europe will not be made superfluous by European union. If our premise is wrong, if, my friends, your ultimate aim is to provide independently for your own defense, the time to tell us is today.

The French response was not long in coming, hinting that Bush's real troubles lay in Washington:

> We all support the presence of US forces in Europe; it is not we Europeans who are pushing the US out of Europe.

In urging the Europeans to assume greater responsibility for their defense without causing the elimination of their own influence in Europe, US officials managed to square the circle by speaking of "complementarity" for the respective Atlantic and European institutions.

It remained for the Europeans to decide whether WEU would be subsumed into the Community institutions. The traditional neutrality of countries such as Austria, Ireland and Sweden was no longer a major obstacle: with the Cold War over the whole notion of neutrality had become somewhat anachronistic. (Austria, Finland, Sweden and even Switzerland, have now applied for EC membership). At the Rome summit President Mitterrand said there was "never a question" of a European Army (built up from the Franco-German brigade) seeking to challenge NATO. In its final document, the summit glossed over the distinctions, welcoming the proposal for a new force under WEU "both as the defense component of the process of European unification and as a means of strengthening the European pillar of the Alliance". Is this shadow boxing? One is constrained to muse on the improbability of WEU going to war without the other NATO allies.

North Atlantic Cooperation Council

One important institutional change was made at the Rome meeting. NATO leaders urged creation of a new 25-nation body, the North Atlantic Cooperation Council (NACC), enabling former Warsaw Pact (WTO) countries, including the USSR and newly independent Estonia, Lativia and Lithuania, to enjoy consultative status with NATO.

The November NATO summit also discussed a new policy statement, entitled "The Alliance's new strategic concept", representing a break with the 1967 doctrine of flexible response. With this change diplomatic measures to dissipate a threat and flexible conventional responses gained stature at the expense of the nuclear deterrent option. However, the issue of deploying Alliance forces outside the NATO area, made current by the Gulf War, had long been divisive and continued to prove intractable in Rome.

The Alliance ended its summit with a warning to the Soviet Union and its republics to bring their nuclear arsenals under control. In this respect the Soviet dis-Union was seen to be almost less trustworthy than the former communist-dominated Soviet Union. Concern for what Chancellor Kohl described as an "explosive situation" was directed above all at the Ukraine, which not only had nuclear weapons on its territory but was also considering creation of a national army. The NATO summons called on the Soviet Union and the republics "to ensure that all international agreements signed by the USSR are respected, ratified and implemented".

President François Mitterrrand refused to suscribe to such "preaching" but Prime Minister John Major of Britain hinted that European food aid could be imperilled by military build-ups in the republics which "made no sense economically and no sense politically".

Britain and Europe, again

In the run-up to the Maastricht summit, due to consider two major treaties, all the principal players began staking out positions designed to preserve a margin of negotiation. On November 20, 1991, the House of Commons held a debate which, while somewhat flabby in its conclusions, nevertheless was remarkable for the fact that all three major parties favored Britain's EC membership, albeit not at any price. Liberal Democrat support was a foregone conclusion but Labour demonstrated a warmth which may have had more to do with splitting the Conservative right-wing from its mainstream than with enthusiasm for a federal Europe. John Major managed to obtain solid support while keeping his Dutch poker cards close to his chest: Britain should be at the center of Europe but not at any price. Margaret Thatcher managed to oppose the substance of the government's moderate position while voting in favor of the resolution (*élection oblige*). (Her daughter was late in paying her poll tax but Margaret can read the polls). Perhaps the best comment came from that French left-wing Thatcher with a ready tongue and a taste for *risqué* remarks, Prime Minister Edith Cresson: "You British should understand that the European Community is a marriage of convenience and not of love."

The accuracy of this comment was brought home a week later when the Council of Europe's Court of Human Rights ruled that the UK government had violated press freedom by blocking publication of extracts from *Spycatcher*, by the former intelligence officer Peter Wright. The European Court ordered the government to pay legal costs of $360,000 to the *Guardian, Observer* and *Sunday Times*. Margaret Thatcher's firm line had been disavowed but, more importantly, freedom of expression had been upheld at the highest European level.

From the Middle Ages to 2001: Andorra's constitutional leap

On January 30, 1992, resignation of all members of the Andorran parliament blocked sovereignty negotiations with the Spanish and French co-princes.

Since Spain's entry into the European Community in 1986 it had become manifest that Andorra would have to update her constitution and economic situation. This Pyrenean micro-state of 60,000 inhabitants, only 12,000 of whom are of Andorran nationality, could not afford to see a tariff wall erected around her 468 square kilometers of territory by two EC member countries, creating a small island of third country territory inside the Community. Negotiations were begun in 1986 and completed in 1989.

The EC-Andorra agreement which entered into force on July 1, 1991 was the first of its kind between the Community and a micro state. (It later served as a model for the agreement with San Marino). The Principality of Andorra is integrated into the Community's customs union for industrial products but is treated as a third country for agricultural produce. In this way the Principality can count on the continued supply of a considerable quota of agricultural products, such as milk and sugar, in oversupply within the EC, at low cost. Meanwhile, the European market is opened up to Andorran products.

Apart from its economic importance the EC agreement was of considerable political significance to Andorra, which had for centuries been under Franco-Spanish tutelage. In ratifying the agreement the European Parliament in effect recognized Andorra as a state. There are also financial changes. Since customs duties on industrial goods are eliminated and Andorra has never raised revenue by means of direct taxation, an indirect tax of 7% has been instituted on all goods entering the Principality. However, the tradition of taxing neither capital nor income is maintained.

Traditionally governed by co-princes, the French President (succeeding the Counts of Foix and the kings of France) and the Spanish Bishop of Urgel, Andorrans are now under pressure to adopt a new constitution.

The Council of Europe, in particular, is insisting on guarantees for basic rights and freedoms in a country which has permitted neither political parties nor trade unions. In April 1991 a tripartite commission of representatives of the co-princes and Andorran parliamentarians set about drafting a constitution. Vassals would become citizens. However, good intentions were frustrated on January 30, 1992, when the General Council (parliament) dissolved itself by unanimous vote, following the blocking of measures submitted by the chief executive, Mr Oscar Ribas. Government of the Principality was paralysed. At the heart of the dispute figured the drafting of the constitutional provision concerning human rights, in particular the right to strike and the right to life, abortion being illegal in Andorra. Religion was also at issue, since one of the co-princes is a Catholic bishop. The bishop's delegates wanted catholicism to be declared the state religion, to which Andorrans and French were opposed. Also at issue was whether direct taxation should be introduced. Voting procedures caused problems, since at present the four small parishes have equal representation with the three large ones, namely four representatives per parish. Finally, the question of international relations runs up against the system of co-principality. It is not yet clear how Andorra will be able to negotiate treaties independently of France and Spain.

Tourism the key

The future clearly lies with tourism. Andorra's economy has evolved considerably during the XXth century. For centuries after her creation by virtue of agreements or *paréages* drawn up between the Bishop of Urgel and the Comte de Foix in 1278 and 1288, Andorra remained largely agricultural. A hydro-electric network brought electricity and roads to the Principality in 1929. The Spanish Civil War and World War II brought trade with the belligerent nations, an influx of refugees and smuggling. In 1939 there were 115 commercial enterprises for 5,000 inhabitants; today the figures are 3,200 and 60,000. Tourism was developed in the fifties, growing from 300,000 visitors in 1955 to over ten million in 1990. The figure today is closer to twelve million but new recreational and cultural infrastructures are needed. Many tourists spend less than two days in the Principality, drawn by tax-free products on sale along the main highway. Andorra's 30,000 hotel beds are frequently under-occupied although at New Year, carnival time and Easter they are inadequate. Meeting-rooms, congress halls and auditoria are being built to encourage visitors to stay longer. Major projects include ski resorts, the Escalades-Engordany spa and a tourist center, under the direction of architects such as Robert Ruols and Ricardo Bofill.

Andorra is on the road to sovereignty and to Europe, but it is unclear when she will arrive. The question is of interest to both individuals and commercial undertakings which have brought capital to Andorra and in turn enjoyed the advantages offered by a Pyrenean tax haven. There seems little doubt; however, that Andorra will shortly cast off her feudal bondage; and that a Catalan-speaking micro-state will take her place alongside Liechtenstein, Malta, Monaco, San Marino and the Vatican, with Council of Europe membership to follow.

Finland enters her bid

On February 27, 1992, Finland announced her decision to apply for Community membership. Since the Swedish application the move had become inevitable. With several neutral nations (Austria, Cyprus, Malta, Sweden) already in line neutrality, despite a certain amount of lip-service from premier Esko Aho about "maintaining the essentials of neutrality" in a post-bloc Europe, was no longer a major issue. If Finland remained outside the EC she would risk geographic and economic isolation, especially after the collapse of Finno-Russian trade following the Soviet upheaval. Two-thirds of Finland's exports go to Western European markets.

Finland would be valuable to the EC in strengthening links with the newly-independent Baltic countries (a Finno-Estonian trade fair was held in Tallinn in February) and with northern Russia. Finland has "transferred" her friendship treaty with the Soviet Union to Russia and has a special interest in cultural and economic ties with Russian Karelia, where there are some 200,000 Finnish speakers in annexed territory which before 1940 represented 13% of Finland. The accession of Finland and Sweden to the EC would restore a measure of unity to the Baltic region. A latter-day Hanseatic League could not only promote trade and cultural exchanges but also fight the serious pollution common to all Baltic shores. Finland also has a vital contribution to make on the Arctic environment.

Finland's accession should prove all the more acceptable inasmuch as she has a trade agreement with the EC since 1973 and is a member of EFTA, EEA, GATT and the Council of Europe.

There seems little doubt that despite her modest population (about five million) and her eccentric position, Finland will figure among the elect. She will bring to the Community vital links to both north and east, an ancient culture and an attachment to democracy and freedom so fierce that during World War II she did not flinch from confronting both nazis to the north and communists to the south.

The independence of Finland, writes Max Jakobson in an analysis which may be more generally applied, measured by her capacity to safeguard and promote the interests of her citizens, surely now is far greater than it was at the time the country was poor and backward and dependent on the export of forest products. Within a larger economic unit Finland can maximize the benefits of integration and minimize its negative effects. Although, like other nations, Finland is being "Europeanized", national extinction is not the inevitable outcome of economic integration.

More controversial, perhaps, is the notion that protectionism is as self-defeating in the cultural sphere as it is in economics. Jakobson is tolerant, if not tender, for "the inane TV programs which satellites beam around the globe ... If deprived of Dallas and Dynasty, would Finns devote their evenings to reading Finnish classics or listening to Sibelius?".[15] He is confident that both nation states and their diverse ways of life will survive both economic integration and the relative homogenization of Western culture.

According to popular myth, the Finnish nation lived on the razor's edge, in the shadow of Soviet power, for most of the 20th century and certainly since the Winter War, a conflict in which, caught on the "wrong" side, the Finns fought Soviet power alone while the West looked on. In reality, Finland's progress from the ordeal of World War II to present-day affluence is a success story almost without parallel, even if Finland's neutrality, at first at least, was a political balancing act rather than an expression of philosophical conviction. Estonia's independence, with that of Latvia and Lithuania, brought comfort to her northern cousins across the Gulf of Finland. Finland's move to join the European Community is a logical further step towards reunion of the entire European family. The CSCE, born in Finland, and the "spirit of Helsinki" have foreshadowed the ultimate goal.

At the European Council meeting in Lisbon in June 1992, heads of state and government agreed to open negotiations with EFTA applicants. The Community must now urgently address the implications of a much-expanded organization for the Community's structure and operations. Such aspects as official languages, weighted voting, the unanimity rule (where applicable), the size of the Commission, the Parliament and its committees will all be affected qualitatively and politically. For this reason the Community might favor grouped entry over one-by-one expansion.

Notes

1 The first meeting of the North Atlantic Cooperation Council, held in Brussels on December 20, 1991 produced a bombshell. The Soviet delegate received new instructions during the meeting, requesting all reference to "the Soviet Union" to be deleted from the final press release. The USSR was dissolving before the eyes of Europe's and North America's defense ministers. The meeting itself resolved little. To what extent the Council might duplicate the peace-making efforts of the CSCE remains to be determined. The call of Poland, Czechoslovakia and Hungary to become full members of NATO was considered premature by western delegations.

2 "F-word": federalism, based on George Bush's "L-word": liberalism.

3 Pulzer, Peter, "Head over heart for Europe" in London Review of Books, March 21, 1991, pages 9, 10. The books reviewed are Thomas, Hugh, "Ever closer Union: Britain's Destiny in Europe", Hutchinson, London, 1991, 96 pp. and Heseltine, Michael, "The Challenge of Europe: Can Britain win?", Pan, London, 1991, 226 pp.

4 Creation of the integrated rapid intervention force within NATO was clearly not entirely pleasing to France, which does not participate in the military activities of NATO. In its editorial of July 16, 1991, Le Monde criticizes the hasty character of the US initiative, taken "with British complicity" before the EC negotiations on security policy are complete. Le Monde sees in this action a US reminder that the European "pillar" is concerned only with the integration of NATO forces. France reacted by proposing joint action within WEU to stengthen Europe's strategic intelligence gathering, shown by the Gulf War to be overly dependent on American spy satellites. Such action would strengthen the role of the EC and WEU. It seems that the notion of "complementarity" still papers over a number of cracks; and the question whether the creation of European security policy will reshape that of NATO, or the reverse.

5 The seven are in fact eight: Canada, France, Germany, Italy, Japan, United Kingdom, United States and the European Community.

6 Strengthening of the UN; control of arms sales; action to strengthen economic recovery; commitment to complete Uruguay Round by December 1991; support for the countries of central and eastern Europe; debt relief for the world's poorest nations; environmental protection; war on drugs and, in particular, money laundering.

7 START and CFE differ in several important respects. CFE talks deal with reductions in troops and directly concern all European countries. START talks concern the two superpowers (and later the CIS states Russia, Belarus, Ukraine and Kazakhstan) and deal with limits on long-range (intercontinental) missiles. INF of course concerns intermediate-range nuclear missiles, especially in the European theater.

8 The UK nuclear strike force was never placed under NATO command and France, of course, does not participate in NATO's military activities. President Mitterrand had set out the following conditions for French participation in nuclear disarmament measures:

a. Considerable reduction in the differential between superpower and French levels of nuclear armament;
b. Improved "balance" in conventional armament levels in Europe through CFE:
c. Elimination of chemical weapons;

d. Cessation of the international armaments race with respect to anti-missile, anti-satellite and anti-submarine defenses.

These conditions were largely reiterated in Mitterrand's press conference on July 14, 1992.

In the name of their own military autonomy and political sovereignty, France and the United Kingdom reject Soviet attempts to treat the three western nuclear deterrants as a single entity. Consequently they resisted the siren call of observer status at the US-Soviet bilateral negotiating table. Such reluctance suits US purposes, although the US is careful not to say so.

9 "This opinion is essentially positive. Austria is a country which, with respect to its democratic traditions, economic structure and social behavior, belongs to the European family".

10 Writing in *Le Monde* on August 28, 1991, Mr Peter Jankowitsch, former Austrian minister of European affairs, offered a clear statement of the relationship between his country's neutrality and its commitment to security responsibilities within the European Community. The strength of public opinion in favor of Austrian membership in the Community had been demonstrated when 175 members of the national Assembly out of 183 had voted for EC application. Jankowitsch recalled that Austria had made certain facilities available to the allied forces in the Gulf War. Austria understood her neutrality to be a contribution to European stability and a guarantee of the independence and territorial integrity of Austria. It had never been a philosophy based on equidistance between ideological poles. Since Austria had always considered herself an integral part of the western world, her neutrality would in no way constitute an obstacle to defending European stability and public order against any external threat.

11 With about five million inhabitants Switzerland is one of the smaller countries of Europe. It is also a model of cultural harmony, with four official languages: German (70%), French (18%), Italian (11%), Romantsch (1%).

12 Ever since the civil strife and the Turkish invasion of northern Cyrus in 1974, which caused Turkish-Cypriot minorities to flee north and Greek-Cypriot minorities to flee south, the little town of Pyla, population 1000, has been the only officially bicultural community in Cyprus. The ceasefire line splits here, some 25 miles south-east of Nicosia, to bypass the town to north and south. There are two administrations—two mayors—and two "ethnic" cafes on the central square. An Austrian UN contingent keeps the peace and arbitrates disputes.

Pyla has seen invaders come and go since the Bronze Age—Cretans, Crusaders, Venetians, British. By its very uniqueness Pyla illustrates the Cyprus problem; optimists claim it also provides a laboratory where hostile communities prove they can co-exist in relative harmony. According to the *NYT* (Oct. 23, '91) Giovanni Guareschi's *Don Camillo*, which tells how the Catholic priest and communist mayor of an Italian hill village maintained a fragile peace, is required reading for UN peacekeepers.

13 *NYT*, Oct. 21, 1991. Although it now only numbers 5,000 men, the symbolic significance of the Franco-German brigade is not to be underestimated. It is a declaration of faith in Franco-German solidarity as the cornerstone of European cooperation and a challenge to British attachment to American apron strings. The provinces of Alsace and Lorraine have changed hands four times since the Franco-Prussian war of 1870 and many Frenchmen are mindful of the Strasbourg memorial with a mother grieving over two dying sons—one for each side—and Hitler's Charlemagne division which enlisted right-wing Frenchmen to fight for Europe's New Order.

14 The fishing dispute stemmed from the refusal of Iceland to open its fishing grounds to community members, because of the overriding importance of fishing to the Icelandic economy. It was finally resolved when Norway allowed Spanish fishermen a larger quota of fish from Norwegian waters in exchange for gaining greater access of its own fishing products in the larger market.

Poor Community members had been demanding a larger contribution from EFTA countries, which all enjoy high living standards, to a special regional development fund. The Seven finally agreed to provide $1.8 billion in low-interests credits and $600 million in grants.

The final dispute involved Austria's and Switzerland's environmental opposition to heavy traffic from Community members. Under the compromise, Greece was offered a special quota, and the EC agreed to reduce truck emissions by 60 percent over 12 years in Austria and to make greater use of railroads in Switzerland.

15 Jakobson, Max, *op. cit.*, p. 154 *et seq.*

10

Maastricht and the Promised Land
(1991-1993)

"Typical" is a dangerous word to use in Europe, where diversity is a precondition of unity. It would nevertheless be difficult to find a more characteristic town, a more fitting forum than Maastricht—history, charm and everyday businesslike air—for what both supporters and opponents called the most important European conference since the signing of the Rome Treaties en 1958.

Maastricht, the capital of the southern Dutch panhandle province of Limburg, is both peripheral to the Netherlands and central to western Europe. Almost an enclave within an enclave, it actually protrudes into Belgian Limburg on the western side of the Maas (in French, Meuse) river. In Maastricht, as in the Community itself, opportunities come in several languages: it is at the center of an important Euro-region covering parts of Belgium, the Netherlands and Germany and only a stone's throw from Luxembourg. In Maastricht you can speak Dutch, its close cousin Flemish, German, French (Liège is next door) and (of course! the Dutch are excellent linguists) English. The people of Maastricht, who have been around since before the Romans threw a bridge across the Meuse (*trajectum ad Mosam*) from which the city is named, hold themselves a part of a cultural community numbering some five million people artificially divided by nationality. Charlemagne headed a European empire in the Ninth century: he lies in the cathedral of Aachen (Aix-la-Chapelle) just across the German border.

It was against this backdrop that the twelve heads of state and government were welcomed by Queen Beatrix of the Netherlands (herself largely of German blood) to a state banquet. In the streets of the city a festival of European food, poetry and music held sway. The twelve states settled to their historic conference in the new regional council hall on December 7, 1991. Scheduled over two days, it was to prove, in true Community tradition, to be a marathon. After much compromise—too much, said the *purs et durs*—they emerged in the small hours of December 11 with a series of agreements designed to bring closer political, economic and social unity in 1993 and common foreign and defense policies and a single currency by the end of the decade. None of the previous 45 sessions of the European Council had been more meticulously prepared than this one. The Dublin meeting of June 1990 had agreed to convene parallel standing conferences on political and on economic and monetary union, which first met in Rome in December of the same year. It will be recalled that there were many setbacks along the way, including outright rejection of a Dutch draft treaty by the United Kingdom. It was a draft offered by the smallest member country, Luxembourg, which was finally selected as a basis for agreement.

The agreed procedure had provided for consultation of the European Parliament. The summit opened with a presentation by the Parliament's president, Enrique Baron Crespo, of his assembly's views on the proposals for political, economic and monetary union, since formal ratification would take place at national level . . . or would it?

As agreed by the European Council, the two drafts were consolidated into a single text bearing the title "Treaty on European Union". In deference to strong objection from the United Kingdom delegation, the word "federal" was deleted from the text (whereas for many federalism suggests decentralisation the British have given it a connotation of centralized power, loss of sovereignty and another layer of bureaucracy).[1]

Social policy: skirting a stumbling block

Again on British insistence, and to avoid an outright veto, a third text, known as the Social Charter (not to be confused with the Council of Europe convention and protocols on the same subject) was dropped entirely from the Treaty on European Union. However, the elements of social policy enshrined in existing texts were confirmed by all delegations as an *acquis communautaire*.

To understand the British position it must be recalled that successive Conservative governments had spent a decade taming the power of the British trade unions (particularly the miners' union led by Arthur Scargill), which in the eyes of many had become the "British disease" standing in the way of competitiveness and prosperity. Downing Street was not prepared, for instance, to commit itself to 14 weeks of paid maternity leave. In the conservative view such matters should be left to direct employer-employee negotiation. Critics, of course, and in particular the opposition Labor Party girding for an election in 1992, took sardonic pleasure in asserting that John Major was presenting as a triumph of diplomacy the isolation of Britain and the institutionalization of a lower standard of social protection than that enjoyed by her EC partners. Her Majesty's Government was not unhappy to accept a "two-speed Europe" in this sector, partly in the name of sovereignty and partly, if more discreetly, to gain a competitive edge. Yet the Eleven were as adamant on going forward as the UK was on holding back:

> The European Council notes that eleven Member States desire to continue on the path laid down by the Social Charter in 1989. To this end it has been agreed to annex to the Treaty a Protocol concerning social policy which will commit the Institutions of the Community to take and implement the necessary decisions while adapting the decision-making procedures for application by eleven Member States.

Thus it was agreed that while the institutions of the EC would be used, adapted as necessary, to implement the Social Charter, the United Kingdom would neither participate in this activity nor be bound by its outcome.[2] It remains to be seen whether non-accession to the Social Charter provides UK firms with a trading advantage. While first appearances suggest that this will be the case, be it also noted that UK firms working on the territory of the Eleven will have to conform to the legislation and standards of the Eleven, so that employers may have to manage dual standards within the same organization. Conversely, employees of the Eleven may insist on "Eleven" standards wherever they are more favorable when working in the UK. It seems a safe bet that a Labor government in Westminster and even a future Conservative administration will sign and implement the Charter.

A single currency before the year 2000

The landmark achievement of the summit was the decision to create a single European currency and European Central Bank by 1999. Here again, the UK insisted on deferring a decision in its own case but did not oppose the plan. In fact, membership will be far from automatic. To join, a country must have an inflation rate no more than 1.5% above the rate of the three least inflationary members and a budget deficit below 3% of GDP. Overall government debt and long-term interest rates must also fall within strict norms. Once locked into the system member countries would lose the ability to control such factors on a national basis.

Reduction of deficits and inflation will be painful in the short-term but eventually European business will benefit from increased capital investment and elimination of currency conversions within the Common Market.

In a separate protocol, the UK was granted the right to make a decision at a later date.

Treaty on Political Union

From a legal and technical point of view, the new treaty carries forward the existing Paris and Rome treaties and the SEA. It therefore incorporates both amendments to the existing texts and new provisions. The Union, "founded on the European Communities", "marks a new stage in the process creating an ever closer Union among the peoples of Europe, where decisions are taken as closely as possible to the citizens". It sets itself the following objectives:

- to promote economic and social progress which is balanced and sustainable, in particular through the creation of an area without internal frontiers, through the strengthening of economic and social cohesion and the establishment of economic and monetary union ultimately including a single currency in accordance with the provisions of the present Treaty;
- to assert its identity on the international scene, in particular through the implementation of a common foreign and security policy which shall include the eventual framing of a common defence policy;
- to strengthen the protection of the rights and interests of the nationals of its Member States through the introduction of a citizenship of the Union;
- to develop close co-operation on justice and home affairs;
- to maintain in full the "acquis communautaire" and build on it with a view to considering to what extent the policies and forms of co-operation introduced by this Treaty

may need to be revised with the aim of ensuring the effectiveness of the mechanisms and the Institutions of the Community.

The objectives of the Union shall be achieved as provided in this Treaty and in accordance with the conditions and the timetable set out therein while respecting the principle of subsidiarity as defined in Article 3b of the Treaty establishing the European Community.

Citizens

The Treaty establishes a legal identity known as "citizenship of the Union" open to all nationals of member countries as defined by the national law of the member state concerned. Every citizen has the right to petition the European Parliament and to apply to an Ombudsman against alleged injustice on the part of the administrative bodies of the Union. These provisions update those of the EEC Treaty.[3]

Governments agreed to establish common foreign and security policies with a view to increasing their international influence by safeguarding common values, strengthening security and preserving peace,[4] promoting international cooperation, consolidating democracy and respecting human rights. These objectives will be pursued through policy cooperation and joint action. Signatory states undertake to uphold "common positions", defined by the European Council, in international organizations and conferences.

Defense issues: WEU's enhanced role

For issues having defense implications "the Union shall request the Western European Union, which is an integral part of the development of the European Union, to elaborate and implement decisions and actions of the Union". Policy must further respect the obligations of certain member states under the North Atlantic Treaty.

It follows from the foregoing that WEU is given a new impetus as the coordinating agent for the security policy of the European Union.

Since the European Council must act by unanimous agreement on matters of foreign and security policy, except for "detailed arrangements" and "procedural questions", Maastricht does not endow the Community with a binding, single foreign policy, defense policy or European army. However it does take an important step in that direction, since "common positions", once defined and agreed, must be upheld. Moreover the Treaty institutionalizes the existing practice of allowing the Presidency to "represent the Union for matters coming within the common foreign and security policy".[5]

The Treaty further provides for diplomatic and consular missions of member states and Commission delegations in third countries to cooperate; and for the European Parliament to be consulted on the main aspects of the common foreign and security policy.

In order to further the development of WEU as the "defense component" of the European Community, the seat of the WEU Council and Secretariat will be transferred to Brussels.[6] It should of course be noted that at the time of the Maastricht summit Greece, Ireland and Denmark were not members of WEU, although Greece had applied. In a final declaration WEU members invited European Union states to join WEU, "or to become observers if they so wish". Other European members of NATO were offered associate membership of WEU: this would apply to Iceland and Norway. Since WEU is specifically a European agency this attempted extension of WEU's reach obviously did not directly affect the US and Canada.

The Union and the Parliament

The European Parliament was given limited new powers to influence Community legislation and to monitor the budget (it already was empowered to reject the budget as a whole). The Parliament failed in its bid to initiate legislation and to share the veto rights of member governments.

Single currency, central bank

The section of the treaty on economic and monetary affairs sets out the following activities:

- The irrevocable fixing of exchange rates, leading to introduction of a single currency;
- The definition and conduct of a single monetary policy and exchange rate policy, to maintain price stability;
- The support of general EC policies, in accordance with the principle of an open market economy with free competition.

These activities entail compliance with the guiding principles of stable prices, sound public finances and a sustainable balance of payments.

With respect to the EMU, on a recommendation from the Commission the EC Council, acting by a qualified majority, formulates a draft for the broad guidelines of the economic policies of the Member States and of the Community. It subsequently adopts a recommendation setting out these guidelines. Recommendations may be made to any Member State found not in conformity with the guidelines.

The Treaty also provides for a European System of Central Banks (ESCB) and a European Central Bank (ECB) to be set up. ECSB's major objective is price stability. It defines and implements monetary policy, conducts foreign exchange operations, holds and manages foreign reserves and promotes smooth operation of payment systems.

Three stages to monetary union

The first stage toward monetary union began on July 1, 1990, when EC governments undertook to coordinate their monetary policies. The second stage commences on January 1, 1994, by which time EC governments must abolish restrictions on the movement of capital and adopt programs for price stability and sound public finances. In the second stage Member States "shall endeavor to avoid excessive government deficits". The second stage will also see tighter control of exchange-rate fluctuations.

A European Monetary Institute (EMI) will be set up, eventually to become the European Central Bank. It will help central banks to coordinate their policies.

The starting date of the third stage was not set, since it depends on a simple majority of countries (seven, at present) meeting the required conditions. From 1996 onwards, EC governments decide which national economies have met "convergence" criteria, evaluated according to inflation, interest rates, budget deficits and currency stability. At this point the Community may decide by a two-thirds majority to form a single currency, the ECU and central bank, effective January 1, 1997. If those conditions are not met, the currency will in any case be established on January 1, 1999. There is nothing in the Treaty to prevent issuance of national designs and language versions of the currency, locked together at par, as already exists between Belgium and the Grand Duchy and between the Channel Islands and the United Kingdom.

The UK delegation declined to commit itself to move to the third stage of economic and monetary union (the single currency) without a separate decision to do so by its government and parliament.

The new Community institutions are further described in Part III, Chapter 5 and Part IV, Chapter 3.

Social policy: the Eleven set standards

The separate treaty on social policy agreed by the Eleven, with the UK as lone dissenter, authorizes recourse to the institutions, procedures and mechanisms of the EC. The Eleven commit themselves to

> the promotion of employment, improved living and working conditions, proper social protection, dialogue between management and labour, the development of human resources with a view to lasting high employment and the combatting of exclusion.

Action will be taken, by qualified majority to "support and complement" governments' activities in the following fields:

— improvement in the working environment to protect workers' health and safety;
— working conditions;
— the information and consultation of workers;
— equality between men and women with regard to labour market opportunities and treatment at work;
— the integration of persons excluded from the Labour market.

However, directives on these issues

> shall avoid imposing administrative, financial and legal constraints in a way which would hold back the creation and development of small and medium-sized undertakings.

Unanimity among the Eleven is required for

- social security and social protection of workers;
- protection of workers where their employment contract is terminated;
- representation and collective defence of the interests of workers and employers, including co-determination, subject to paragraph 6;
- conditions of employment for third-country nationals legally residing in Community territory;
- financial contributions for promotion of employment and job-creation, without prejudice to the provisions relating to the Social Fund.

Justice and home affairs

The Treaty of European Union creates a major extension of Community action to justice and home affairs with most decisions taken unanimously, some by weighted majority of at least 54 votes (calculated according to EC rules) and eight countries. Policies are coordinated on asylum, immigration and third country nationals (very important for a Community of open borders), including conditions of entry and residence and the combatting of unauthorized entry, residence and work; fighting drug addiction and fraud; civil and criminal judicial cooperation; customs; and police cooperation against terrorism, drug trafficking and other crimes.

To this end machinery for exchanging information was set up within a newly-created European Police Office (EUROPOL) similar to the INTER-POL office in Lyon.

These matters are to be dealt with in compliance with the European Convention for the Protection of Human Rights and Fundamental Freedoms and the Convention relating to the Status of Refugees.

The European Council ordered that the EC ministerial Council adopt provisions to guarantee the secrecy of discussion on foreign and security policy and on justice and home affairs.

A Coordinating Committee of senior officials was set up to facilitate action, issue opinions and prepare the EC Council's discussions on matters of justice and home affairs. It will not be long before "home affairs" becomes a misnomer; indeed with the opening of borders this has already occurred.

Other matters

The heads of state and government of the European Council took advantage of their meeting to address other issues of world concern. They reasserted that any European state "whose systems of government are founded on the principle of democracy" may apply to become a member of the Union.[7] The Council reiterated its "firm commitment" to a "substantial, balanced and global package of results by the end of the year" (a deadline not met); stressed its determination to fight illegal drugs, urging rapid establishment of EUROPOL;[8] issued statements on the food supply situation in Moscow and St. Petersburg (envisaging further aid or credit guarantees); on the release of hostages; on the Middle East peace process; on developments in the Soviet Union (calling on republics to respect CSCE and disarmament commitments); on "steadily growing" racism and xenophobia in Europe.

European business reacted promptly and positively to the Maastricht outcome despite the short-term pains it would engender. The plan to unify the currency was particularly welcomed.[9] The United States applauded the pact, although President Bush immediately warned against limits on American exports, alluding to trans-Atlantic disputes in the Uruguay Round. Americans also feared that the new currency might undermine the dominant role of the dollar if central banks around the world abandoned dollar assets in favor of the ecu, as the new currency has now been officially baptized. American business generally welcomed the pact, especially those corporations which already have subsidiaries in Community countries. Expansion of WEU's role was hailed in the US as being in accordance with the long-standing American desire for Western Europe to play a larger role in her own defense, especially since the European Council specifically eschewed any interest in undermining the Atlantic Alliance.

Dissenting voice

Not all reactions were positive, however. The painter and writer Guy Leclerc-Gayran discerned selfishness and lack of judgment in the Maastricht outcome. Far from creating Europe from the Atlantic to the Urals, he declared,[10] considering Boris Yeltsin's recent approach to NATO, a Europe from the Urals to the Atlantic was possibly to be feared. The only remaining blocs in the world were those of the rich and the poor; but Maastricht had not sufficiently taken into account that Europe was now divided into three or four segments with divergent interests:

> Western Europe (which continues to put out standards for quince concentrate); Central Europe; East Europe ... not to speak of Mediterranean Europe ... whence demographic pressures will soon give rise to legitimate claims.

EFTA ministers sign Joint Declarations with eastern Europe countries

With all the klieglights turned on Maastricht, another interministerial meeting on trade went almost unnoticed in Geneva on December 10 and 11, when EFTA ministers held their half-yearly Council meeting, with the Finnish Minister for Foreign Trade, Mr Pertti Salolainen, in the chair. They looked to early resolution of the legal issue (competence of the proposed court of justice) which was holding up signature of the EEA agreement with the Community, stressing the need for EEA to begin on January 1, 1993. Ministers noted the substantial progress achieved in negotiations on free trade agreements with Czechoslovakia, Hungary and Poland, which, together with the agreements signed with the EC, would represent a significant contribution to the further transformation of these countries into market economies and facilitate their integration into a wider European free trade system. Five Joint Declarations were signed on cooperation between EFTA countries and Bulgaria, Estonia, Latvia, Lithuania and Romania. The unification of Europe requires small steps as well as large; different parts of the puzzle are pieced together at the same time.

Budget: squaring the circle with Delors - 2

The Treaty of European Union was signed at Maastricht on February 7, 1992. On February 12 the European Commission had an important rendez-vous with the European Parliament: presentation of the EC budget for 1993. In fact, following the success of the first "five-year pact" implementing the Single European Act, the Commission requested a second agreement, to run from 1993 to 1997, to implement the Maastricht decisions. During this period the EC budget would rise from 67 billion ECU ($85b) to 87 billion ($112b) with the ceiling of resources rising from 1.2% of GNP to 1.37%.

"Delors 2", as the five-year bill for the Maastricht party was dubbed, paid special attention to an equitable distribution of cost-benefit ratio among member countries, while creating a solidarity fund to help the poorer peripherals (Greece, Ireland, Portugal, Spain) meet their commitments, particularly as regards monetary union. At the same time, the Commission could not afford to alienate the "net payers", France, Germany, Netherlands, the UK, especially since even the rich members of the Community had their own pockets of underdevelopment in need of structural reform. Thus the Commission was caught between the Scylla of increasing revenue and the Charybdis of economic recession, which made governments reluctant to increase Community expenditure faster than the increase in national budgets.

Behind the preparation of this budget, as of any other, there lay a debate of political and economic philosophy. Indeed, such discussions may be more tense at European level, where no single "party" is in power on the basis of a stable "majority" but where all currents must achieve a relative consensus.

Behind agreement on the need for increased competitiveness, for instance, to be achieved in part by developing transport and telecommunications infrastructures, rages a debate between those who oppose adoption of an industrial policy as interventionist and those who consider that the Community is called upon to facilitate industrial change, especially where such change is generated by its own actions. The budget debate is one of the most important of the Parliament's activities, since this is one area where it has the power to say no.

In fact, initial reaction in the Parliament to the Commission's proposals was largely positive. Negative noises came essentially from those countries which would be called upon to pay the lion's share of the increase. Mr. Delors blunted somewhat the German reaction by proposing inclusion of the former GDR-provinces in the group of peripherals eligible for the special solidarity fund. The loudest squeals came from London. When Margaret Thatcher thumped the table and cried "I want my money back!", she not only got a rebate but won the next election. It was not surprising, therefore, that, facing a difficult spring rendez-vous with the voters, John Major exclained that the 30% increase called for by the Delors package was "out of the question". This was partly electoral theater, of course, since everybody knew that "Maastricht" would cost more money. Major was also doubtless mindful that the special rebate scheme negotiated by Margaret Thatcher would expire in the fall of 1992...

"Delors 2" included greater emphasis on research. High technology goods represent 31% of US exports, 27% of Japanese exports and only 17% for the Community. Research funding in the EC equals 2.1% of GNP against 2.8% in the US and 3.5% in Japan. Delors also saw a need to increase funding for "external action", namely financial assistance to central and eastern Europe and to Mediterranean countries.

A good man with figures (he is a former finance minister of France), Delors also has to be an astute politician. He not only suggested the UK might postpone payment of her dues until after the British general election, but also that a special meeting of the European Council might be convened at that time to address the whole politico-financial question of paying for the fruits of the Treaty of European Union. One shrewd trial balloon (sent up by French Finance Minister Bérégovoy), suggested a direct European income tax: would this prove too "federal" for the "Brits" or, on the contrary, let them off the hook? As one of the beneficiaries of the 14 million dollars reserved for the less-developed EC members, EC chair Portugal had a difficult job preventing a rift between Europe's rich and poor.

Database piracy

Meanwhile, the Commission did not wait around until "Maastricht" had been rectified to continue to reach into every sector of Europe's business life.

Database creators and operators need a harmonized, secure and stable legal environment. At present copyright protection exists in some member countries but is uncertain in others. In February 1992, the Commission proposed a directive harmonizing EC copyright laws to insure they cover databases. The directive would also prohibit unfair database copying for ten years. Producers could take legal action against pirate competitors. Third-country database producers would receive EC rights as long as their governments provided similar protection to EC databases.

EC energy deregulation plan

The same month the Commission issued plans to create a single market in energy. The three-stage approach plan would save consumers "billions of ecus" annually and make EC industry more competitive in the world market. Said Energy Commissioner Antonio Cardoso e Cunha: "Our aim is to transform the energy market in Europe—which is fundamentally national and based on administrative focusing of prices—and replace it with a European unit in which cross-border trade could be significant and prices would react according to negotiations between buyer and seller".

Implementation of existing directives on electricity and gas transit and price transparency constitutes stage one. Stage two, the crux of the Commission's proposal, would start on January 1, 1993, and include abolition of exclusive rights for electricity generation and the building of electricity and gas lines; institution of more transparent accounting procedures in vertically integrated energy companies; introduction of a system of third-party access (TPA), whereby transmission and distribution companies would have to offer large industrial users and distribution companies access to their networks at reasonable rates. Slated for January 1, 1996, stage three would entail extension of the TPA system to less energy-intensive users.

As many as 500 large industrial consumers whose annual consumption exceeds 100 GWh of electricity or 25m cubic meters of natural gas would be eligible for TPA. These heavy consumers would come mainly from the aluminium, steel, chemicals, construction materials and glass sectors. Distributors of 3% of the electricity or 1% of the natural gas consumed in a member state would also qualify for TPA. Smaller distributors could join forces to reach or exceed the TPA threshold.

Member states would retain pricing-powers over all end-users not qualifying for TPA and could still impose requirements relating to energy policy, environmental protection and land-use planning.

Lithuania and the Community

In the field of external relations, the Commission completed an association agreement with Lithuania. The agreement is similar to those with other central and eastern European countries but includes new features such as removal of import quotas. Lithuania is thus assured most-favored-nation treatment in trade, economic cooperation and establishment of a joint committee to oversee EC-Lithuanian relations.

Switzerland too?

On March 17, 1992, *Le Monde* published a rare and important interview with the president (for a year) of the Swiss Confederation, the Socialist René Felber. (The Swiss Federal Council is a collective form of government, not a coalition and not based on a commonly agreed or binding program of government). Felber made it clear that Swiss acceptance of the EEA was a step towards an EC membership application, although both EEA and ultimate EC membership would require ratification by national referenda.

Justifying this important change of objectives, Felber declared that it would be intolerable after Maastricht for Switzerland to remain outside the decision-making process; and that neutrality in the post-Cold War period was no substitute for solidarity and responsibility. As for Swiss identity within the Community, it would be protected above all by Switzerland's particular form of political culture, with its federalism and people's rights (which include a people's army involving annual military service and frequent referenda and town fora).

Felber made it clear that he was speaking in the name of the Federal Council. Since it is inconceivable that a Swiss application would be rejected by the EC, EFTA's days appear numbered. Norway and Iceland will have to reconsider their options. Maybe Liechtenstein should despatch delegations to Andorra, Monaco and San Marino . . .

The Swiss decision finally fell on May 18 when the Federal Council voted 4: 3 to apply for Community membership. Although it came as no surprise, the Confederation's application acquired immense symbolic significance. One day after Margaret Thatcher's renewed attack in a speech in The Hague on the Commission's alleged "centralized superstate" ambitions, from its Alpine enclave Berne confirmed that the Brussels siren-song was irresistible to the nation which invented neutrality. As a sardonic cartoon in *Le Monde* expressed it, Switzerland, of all countries, wanted to open a bank account in Brussels.

The long road to ratification

It took the European Parliament four months after the Maastricht meeting of the European Council to ratify the Treaty of European Union, on April 7, 1992, by 226 votes to 62, with 31 abstentions. (The French Communists, the Greens and the far Right voted against). The Rapporteur was the British Labour MEP David Martin. Concerns expressed in Strasbourg included objections to the special provisions made for the UK, the failure to increase the German parliamentary delegation (to reflect reunification) and, above all, the "democratic deficit" arising from the limited nature of the European Parliament's own powers. The EP also regretted its inability to monitor military matters, since these remain vested in WEU.

While not sufficient to threaten ratification in the European assembly, these issues surface again at national level. Ratification is by no means a foregone conclusion. In France the opposition parties (UPR and UDF) were divided on the issue and opposition was particularly strong in Denmark. In these countries and others there was reluctance to cede further sovereignty to "an unelected body" (the Commission).

Two or three views of Maastricht: UK ratification debate

On May 21, in a free vote, the British House of Commons approved the Treaty of Union on second reading.[12] While the aye vote included representatives of all parties and the noes both Labour and die-hard Thatcherite votes, the official Labour position favored abstention as a protest against the government's opting out from Maastricht's social provisions. The Labour abstention was somewhat disingenuous in as much as it would never have been advocated had defeat been threatened.

An outside observer could have been forgiven for thinking that two vastly different texts were under discussion. Prime Minister John Major faced the task of assuring pro-Europeans that the Community is essential to Britain's interests while responding to right-wing scepticism in the Tory ranks. (He was buoyed in this task by the Conservative Party's fourth consecutive electoral victory and his first as leader. Major was now "his own man", which in the circumstances meant not Thatcher's).

Interestingly Major made a case for "Maastricht" being less "federal" than its predecessors:

> For the first time in a single treaty, agreements between governments are given equal standing with action under Community law. In foreign and security policy, in justice and interior matters, the member states will work together when it is in their common interest to do so . . . It means we cannot be forced into policies we do not approve of . . .

Meanwhile Mrs, soon to be Lady, Margaret Thatcher was writing in *The European* that "the Maastricht treaty passes colossal powers from parliamentary governments to a central bureaucracy". She did not go out of her way to state that the Maastricht treaty was in many respects "son of SEA", a follow-up to the Single European Act which she had signed.

Major claimed that the principle of subsidiarity and the Luxembourg Compromise (the delaying veto for matters of vital national interest) allowed states more than one approach to a problem: to act through the Treaty of Union, through intergovernmental cooperation or on their own. He also asserted — on a day when France and Germany were setting up their European brigade at the La Rochelle summit — that Maastricht provided no diminution of the role of NATO. Moreover, the impending enlargement of the Community to Sweden, Austria and Finland and, before the end of the century, to eastern Europe made it even more important to have a flexible framework. Major was clearly developing a "variable speed" policy for the EC. He claimed that belief that action at Community level was always the answer was diminishing among member states.

If Major is right there are opposing motivations for "Maastricht before enlargement" — those who think the Treaty of Union will bind the states more closely and those who think precisely the opposite.

In one of his last major speeches before he stepped down as Labour's leader, Neil Kinnock attacked the government's opting out from social provisions. Since the UK would not be associated with decisions in this sector, he declared, far from asserting sovereignty it was resigning sovereignty. He went on to detail Britain's shortcomings in the social sector, such as the EC's longest working hours, no statutory paid annual leave and poor conditions for sickness and maternity leave. Despite Labour's recent electoral defeat, Kinnock was in fine fettle. Britain's prolonged recession, he claimed, demonstrated that inferior working conditions didn't translate into superior economic performance.

Human rights and the human body: challenge of a bioethics convention

In March 1992 an important conference took place in Madrid which illustrates the complementarity of the European Community and the Council of Europe in their present form even if the relationship between the two institutions will have to be reviewed as EC membership increases. This complementarity does not stem from membership (the "little" and "big" Europe's), structures and powers alone. When all is said and done, despite the diversification of its mandate afforded by the new Treaty of Union, the EC remains essentially an economic body. The Council of Europe, on the other hand, continues to symbolize the moral Europe, the Europe of human rights and fundamental principles, the Europe of the spirit.

In 1989 the Community issued a directive which allows human plasma to be traded for profit. (The vote was unanimous, under French chairmanship). In 1992, on the other hand, the Council of Europe convened in Madrid the first conference of national ethics or bioethics committees, at the very moment when the French government was preparing national legislation on the same subject.

The Madrid conference was convened as a forerunner to a standing conference of bioethics committees (which would be provided with a secretariat by the Council of Europe) and a European Convention on Bioethics, to be opened for signature in 1993. Catherine Lalumière, Secretary General of the Council of Europe, declared before the national committees in Madrid that it was urgent to give serious consideration to the relationship between bioethics and the economy.

The Convention will set out basic principles, to be given concrete expression in a series of protocols. The convention, to be drafted in a manner compatible with and parallel to the European Convention on Human Rights, will establish that elements of the human body may not be used for commercial transactions (an approach diametrically opposed to the EC directive); fix the responsibility of society and its representatives, obliging public authorities to issue regulations and set limits; and establish the principle of non-discrimination of nationality, race or religious belief. Signatory states would also undertake to incorporate the provisions of the convention into national law following ratification of the Convention.

It is rare to find such a direct conflict of "philosophy" between the institutions although one can imagine that others will arise, in the environmental sphere for instance. The debate promises to be lively.

The additional protocols will successively cover such questions as experimentation on the human body (Dr Mengele is not forgotten), organ transplants, human genetics, medically assisted procreation.

There is always a danger, of course, that undesirable or reprehensible practices banned in developed countries get pushed out to the developing world. The risk is not new: it has already occurred with infant-feeding products and vaccines. Nevertheless, as with the human rights convention, the Council of Europe has an important opportunity here to hold up a model for the world. In this spirit the European Convention on Bioethics will be open for signature by non-member countries; always assuming that the member-countries ratify it in the first place.

Controversial territory

It requires a certain moral courage for the Council of Europe to attempt to draft, sign and ratify a convention of this type, for it is very easy to slip into highly contraversial territory: definition of life and death and the related issues of the right to life, abortion and euthanasia. The recent case in which an Irish woman was denied permission to go to England for an abortion after she had been raped demonstrated (even through the Irish supreme court overturned the decision) that European legislation and jurisprudence cannot avoid such issues.

If further confirmation were needed, it is provided by two judgments of the European Court of Human Rights in March 1992. By a 15 to 8 majority, the Court condemned the French Government for denying official recognition of a sex change. A week later, France lost another case before the Court, being condemned for not acting "within a reasonable period" on an appeal for help from a haemophiliac dying of Aids as a result of tainted transfusions. Mr X was not alive to hear the verdict. If "common values" are vaunted as one of the principal foundations of the European idea, after the economic, social and cultural dimensions the ethical dimension inevitably follows.

Ray of hope in Ulster

An early summer sun broke through the clouds of a cold, damp spring to light the honeystone face of Stormont, the graceful Northern Irish parliament building. It had stood empty for two decades, ever since direct rule had been imposed on this impoverished corner of Her Majesty's realm, torn by civil strife. For the first time in seventy years Northern Ireland's protestant leaders were meeting with representatives of the Irish government. An ecstatic UK Secretary of State for Northern Ireland, Sir Patrick Mayhew, and Irish Foreign Minister David Andrews claimed a breakthrough in the struggle which opposes terrorist extremists from among both the catholic minority and the two-thirds protestant majority. The last face-to-face was in 1921 over the partition of Ireland, when all but the six north-eastern countries from Belfast to Londonderry were granted independence.

The Dublin delegation agreed to discuss removal of a claim to Ulster from the Republic's constitution if the Northern "loyalists" would discuss the possibility of pooling sovereignty in the province.

Even the protestants are divided. The Democratic Unionists under Ian Paisley favor devolution (provincial government), whereas James Molyneaux's Ulster Unionists seek greater integration into the "United" Kingdom. However, power-sharing between Westminster, Belfast and Dublin and between protestants and catholics in the province seems the only political principle which might conceivably lead to a solution. Other groups participating in the meeting included the catholic Social Democratic and Labor Party, led by John Hume, and John Alderdice's non-confessional Alliance Party. Sinn Fein, the

IRA's political arm, was excluded for not having renounced violence, although behind-the-scenes contacts are growing.

It is high time for a settlement in this anachronistic and murderous conflict, the only blood feud, apart from the Basque independence movement, involving, albeit indirectly, two member states of the European Community.

Danish mouse roars; European elephant hunkers down

On June 2, 1992, a mouse roared in Denmark.

Forty-six thousand Danes, the wafer-thin majority of negative notes in the national referendum on the Maastricht treaty (50.7% to 49.3%), struck a nerve throughout the Community. Many Danes had dared to express what others had suppressed, a desire for more citizen input, less bureaucracy, less centralism. Even though, according to some, European union was being held to ransom by a population the size of a small town, it was immediately clear that in all twelve countries there was a groundswell of discontent that the public had not been sufficiently informed or consulted in the preparation of the treaty. Irritating regulations emanating from Brussels, setting European standards seeming to be at best the product of zeal rather than necessity and at worst a homogenizing threat to valued cultural diversity, certainly did not help. The Danes had spoken for those unwilling to trust Europe's future to politicians and bureaucrats.

Initially stunned even though a close vote had been predicted, the other eleven members of the Community and the Danish government itself moved rapidly into damage control. There could be no question of renegotiation; ratifications would proceed, declared the foreign ministers after an emergency meeting in Oslo.[11] The only other nation which had announced a referendum, Ireland,[12] would go ahead as planned on June 18. President Mitterrand of France immediately announced a referendum on the issue for the fall (not unhappy to throw the two wings of the RPR-UDF opposition into bickering disarray, even through he insisted that European and domestic politics were not to be confused). However, Mitterrand joined Kohl and the EC President Premier Anibal Cavaco Silva of Portugal in confirming that the treaty could not be renegotiated: ratifications would go forward and, after legal adjustment for fewer signatories, the treaty would be implemented as planned in January 1993. A chorus of opposition voices immediately clamored that the treaty was null and void.[13]

As to the reasons for the setback, there seems little doubt that the principal concern was that "Brussels" is seen as remote, insensitive and undemocratic. However, the cry for more democracy, namely a stronger public voice, found expression in different, even contradictory ways. It was unclear, for instance, whether greater parliamentary control should be vested in national assemblies or in the European Parliament. The treaty does in fact strengthen EP powers.

Another motivation among the Danes seems to have been a fear that small countries would be marginalized by developments in Brussels. This was a new view of the Community, since countries such as Luxembourg and Belgium undoubtedly have acquired additional influence through European institutions.

Writing in *Le Monde* of June 2, before the result was known, Niels I. Meyer, a Danish professor of physics and no-vote organizer, gave further reasons for his compatriots' opposition. A community which gave priority to economic growth was based on an "obsolete model". Economic and social justice required that barriers against eastern Europe and the developing world be broken down. Indeed, the world no longer needed superpowers . . .

It soon became apparent that the Danish protest was not directed at European unification as such, but against a certain kind of Europe. After initial jubilation that such a small country could produce so profound an effect, many Danes started to show hangover symptoms, stressing that they did not wish for their country to withdraw from the Community. Some Danes may even have allowed themselves the "luxury" of a protest vote against Maastricht precisely because it had little bearing on Denmark's existing membership of the Community.

John Major of Britain, who assumed the Community's presidency on July 1, appeared in the unexpected role of champion of the treaty. He pointed out that Maastricht sets brakes on the powers of the Commission's unelected "mandarins" and proscribed majority voting by governments in new areas of cooperation such as defense, foreign policy, education and the environment.[14] Major now found himself more than ever at odds with Margaret Thatcher, who had hailed the Danish vote as a triumph for democracy over bureaucracy.

Major suggested drafting a declaration or protocol to the Maastricht text defining how the treaty would operate and underlining its decentralizing characteristics. This would fall short of full renegotiation and might persuade Danish voters they had been wrong to reject the treaty. He found few takers.

Legal conundrums

After the initial stand-pat damage control reactions of the European enthusiasts certain doubts crept in. The legal spin doctors were having a ball. Ardent Europeans from Paris to Palermo insisted that the Eleven—with Denmark not Britain now the odd man out—could implement the Union without a nod from Copenhagen. Yet doubts were expressed whether the Irish abortion issue and an impending general election in France would snarl the referenda in national politics. It took the resounding success in Ireland—an over two-thirds majority in favor of the treaty—and the constitutional change in France (permitting ratification) to lift the gloom. Nevertheless, outright opponents, led by nationalistic and anti-immigration movements on the extreme right and ex-communists on the left, together with Euro-sceptics in all parties continued to claim that the treaty would have to be abandoned or, at best, "untied" and renegotiated.

It certainly seems likely that this issue will end up in the European Court. Even if the Eleven go ahead, in effect confirming the existence of a "multispeed" Europe not only between EC members and non-members but even within the Community itself (a trend initiated by the opt-out clauses granted to the UK in social and monetary affairs), the fact remains that the Maastricht Treaty of Union modifies the treaties of Paris and Rome; and that such modifications require consent of all twelve member countries. Some jurists even claimed that by going ahead the Eleven would in effect themselves become "opters out" while Denmark remained legally clean *vis-à-vis* the ECSC, EEC, EURATOM and SEA treaties. It would be the Eleven and not Copenhagen's little mermaid who had no clothes . . .

At the very least, if Denmark effects its own damage control and continues to play a full role under the treaties it has ratified, Danish delegates should abstain from debates held and decisions made under Maastricht provisions. While this might not be hard to organize in the governmental bodies (it will in any case be done for Britain on social and possibly on currency questions), it would be virtually impossible in the European Parliament.

Pro-Europe groups were quick to point out, however, that the very disruption engendered across the continent by the defiant swish of the mermaid's tail ironically demonstrated the extent to which the nations of Europe are already interdependent. Applicant nations from EFTA (Sweden, Austria, Switzerland) promptly confirmed their desire to join the Community. Promising to champion eastern Europe's cause for membership during his EC presidency, John Major went ahead with visits to Poland, Czechoslovakia and Hungary. To put it bluntly, there was no lack of applicants to take Denmark's place.

We are so used to complicated treaties being ratified that the occasional setback assumes undue proportions. Europe will not be denied. After the EDC failure came WEU and the EEC negotiations; after two vetoes the United Kingdom finally joined the common market; after Norway's no-vote Greece, Portugal and Spain acceded and Austria, Sweden, Switzerland and Finland applied . . . not to mention Cyprus, Malta, Turkey . . . The road to Europe winds on. The Danish majority has said no to a treaty; the European majority will continue to say yes to unification.

Kohl: saving the terrible century

Perhaps the most extremely pro-European view of the Danish vote was taken by Chancellor Helmut Kohl. He went so far as to suggest that events in Germany's northern neighbor could actually speed up the process of unification by acting as another kind of warning. Withdrawal into old nationalist states would be a denial of history, he declared in a radio interview, especially for Germany:

> It became clear to me during the German unification process that scarcely anyone in Europe really wanted German reunification. Now Germany is united and there are fears in Europe. If we do not link German unification with European unity, if what we undertook in Maastricht fails and we do not achieve European union in the last decade of this terrible century, then we will revert to nationalist disputes in Europe next century.

Most people would concede that those disputes are already upon us. It may be a race against time for western Europe to "spread" its integration to the east before eastern Europe spreads its violent nationalistic disintegration to the west, where cracks are already appearing. There is clearly a need for greater citizen participation in the European process and firmer reassurance that national and regional identities will be protected before they express themselves in virulent form. Although the Maastricht text does speak of subsidiarity and of taking decisions as close to the people as possible — Major is right about that — the Danish reminder was timely. Kohl may have been indulging in scare tactics in his radio interview; but given his words and the ghastly "ethnic cleansing" we have witnessed in Yugoslavia, nobody can say we haven't been warned.

The consensus seems to be that the Danish referendum delivered a painful but salutary lesson; but that the political will exists to overcome the legal obstacles which have arisen. The door will remain open to Denmark and no undue concessions will be granted; however some accommodations may be found which meet the concerns of all partners. Maastricht treaty ratification is not subject to a deadline and the single, obstacle-free market will in any case be created as planned at midnight on December 31, 1992.

The prickly Danes may have done the rest of Europe more of a favor than they did to themselves. Now there's Europeanism!

Hopes and fears: exorcising Maastricht

Walter Hallstein, the redoubtable German who as first president of the European Commission faced up to General de Gaulle, had a dictum which the reluctant and unlikely duo, Major and Delors, could take to heart. "Our business is not business", he said, "it's politics".[15] Before, but most certainly after the Danish referendum, the Maastricht treaty brought out all the hopes and all the fears of European unification: not only relinquishment of that emotionally-charged abstraction, political sovereignty, but threats to age-old identity, bureaucratic hyper-activity, weaning from America, the reunification not only of Germany but of Europe, the rise of the new Asia . . .

It is evident to many people that most of the great problems of our age defy even continental solutions, let alone those of national governments clinging to outdated illusions of their autonomy: environmental pollution and resource dilapidation, disintegration of rural society, the global mafia of drugs and extortion, economic interdependence, the homogenization of society . . . These are world-wide phenomena.

It is small wonder that, in the face of these overwhelming and life-threatening forces, the citizens of Europe should be sceptical about the dawning of a "new world order" based only on the decline of Cold War tensions . . . Small wonder that people should turn inwards to what they know best, to their ethnic, religious and cultural roots.

Those who would inform and educate the citizens of Europe about the historic movement of unification in which they are involved have the daunting task of demonstrating that a united Europe offers peace; a social and economic solidarity which does not threaten "who we are" and "feel ourselves to be"; and an opening to the world, a chance to share in solutions to global problems.

Europe's citizens have a "right to know". They should read the treaty; but they should also be reassured that the dense thickets of small print, far from threatening to provide "eurotechnobureaucrats" with a victory, clearly demonstrate that there is no machiavellian master-plan: Europe is being made up as we go along. Those who participate get a chance to stir the brew.

Europe would survive a Maastricht rejection, but would be set back several years, possibly a decade as the tentacles of the new nationalisms invaded the body politic. Legally, it is an untidy document; politically, it offers a vital dynamic. The devil will always be in the details: let those who read it read it whole.

47th European Council summit at Lisbon

A strange atmosphere pervaded the Lisbon summit. The European Council met, for the forty-seventh time, in a political no-man's-land (to quote the French foreign minister, Roland Dumas): after the Maastricht signature but also after the Danish rejection, after the Irish acceptance and before the French referendum ... It was a time when John Major spoke of slaying bureaucratic monsters and Helmut Kohl hoped the train would pick up speed, with twelve, not eleven, carriages. Surrounded by 500 journalists, in the glare of television lights, ministers made a somewhat ludicrous attempt to keep a low profile. "Now is the time for politicians to keep quiet"; said Tristan Garel-Jones, Britain's minister of state for Europe, "but that is something they find difficult to do".

The few decisions taken (and not taken) caused little surprise. Major's reference to the voracious appetite of the Commission was shown to be largely a television bite of his own (for home consumption) when he voted with his eleven colleagues to extend the Delors tenure as Commission head for another two years. Agreement was quickly reached to prepare for negotiations with EFTA applicants, to begin as soon as "Maastricht" had been ratified by the Eleven (fingers crossed for the French referendum). Now Norway would have to decide ... and maybe acceptance of the *acquis communautaire* (including Maastricht, including common security policy ...) by so many new countries would give Denmark pause to reflect. For the others, Turkey, Cyprus, Malta ... Poland, Hungary, Czechs and Slovaks (together or separately), the wait would continue. For them the antechamber could be decorated, in the form of a consultative council ... John Major kept his promise of speaking up on behalf of Central Europe but it didn't make much difference.

Placing political solidarity above individual preferences, the Council supported Greece in refusing to recognize the independence of Macedonia without a change of name.

In all of these debates the Eleven went out of their way not to pressure the Danes. The TEU would not be renegotiated but there was no more loose talk of punishment. Foreign Minister Uffe Elleman-Jensen enjoyed grudging respect: he was, after all, wearing the scarf of his country's victorious European Cup football team. With the Queen's 25th wedding anniversary, too, it was quite a year for Denmark.

There was serious discussion about money, however, even if no figures were mentioned. Delors was prepared to stretch out his budget proposals over seven years instead of five; the UK and Germany were unwilling to raise the budget above the current 1.2% of GNP; the poorer states refused to have their equalization fund sacrificed and gently hinted at a veto of any enlargement until they received solid guarantees. Major was glad to gain time so that these issues might be handled under the UK chairmanship, starting July 1, 1992, and culminating in the December summit, in Edinburgh.

The summit raised the stakes on Serbia, hinting that the Community would back a UN military operation to relieve Sarajevo. The "low-profile" summit dispersed without surprises; until, instead of going home, the 75-year-old French president, François Mitterrand, caught the world unawares and forced admiration by turning up at Sarajevo airport, closed for months, touring the war-torn streets and comforting the wounded. It was June 28, 78th anniversary of the assassination of Archduke Ferdinand in Sarajevo, which started World War I . . .

Two weeks later another ceasefire came; and failed. Life — and death — went on. The Belgian and Greek parliaments voted massively in favor of the Maastricht treaty; but everyone was looking to France and the referendum of September 20 . . .

The U.K.'s EC chairmanship, from July to December 1992, had been fraught with problems: Danish denial, agricultural wranglings, monetary crisis, the French referendum cliffhanger, Yugoslavia. As the Edinburgh summit approached John Major himself called the agenda a Rubik's cube of interconnected problems.

The outcome proved better than anyone had expected, demonstrating once more the resilience of the European idea. The contentious farm issue was barely mentioned. Denmark was granted opt-outs on defense (WEU), the single currency, European citizenship and judicial cooperation, with a view to a new referendum in May 1993. The deal was made with no renegotiation of the treaty. The European Council set a seven-year budget with a ceiling on spending (1.2% of GNP, rising to 1.21%), and a 15bn. ECU Cohesion Fund to help the poor four. Negotiations with Austria, Finland and Sweden were set for January 1993, with Norway and possibly Switzerland to follow. An investment fund was created to promote economic growth. Subsidiarity was duly revered, if not espoused. The European Parliament was also strengthened: Germany received her 18 extra MEP's, with smaller increases to other states, raising the EP total from 518 to 567. It will grow further with each accession. Even the vexed question of the site of institutions was settled with recognition of the status quo. Public relations will be improved, with more open meetings.

On December 31, 1992, the night sky of Europe was aglow with beacon fires saluting the advent of the great single market. Only in Yugoslavia were the fires of a more grisly nature; and even here realism was setting in. . .

Notes

1 The original version, removed at UK insistence, read as follows: "This Treaty marks a new stage in the process leading gradually to a Union with a federal goal". Removal of the reference to federalism is more political than substantial, since it has no effect on subsequent provisions.

2 It is open to challenge in the ECJ whether the Eleven may legally have recourse to the institutions of the Twelve in this manner. With UK consent written into the treaty it seems probable that they may.

3 Admendments to the existing treaties are too numerous to present here in detail. Detailed texts may be obtained from the EC information office in Luxembourg and the EC Delegation in Washington, 2100 M Street, NW, 7th Floor, Washington DC 20037, to which we are indebted for extensive documentary assistance.

4 "... in accordance with the principles of the UN Charter as well as the principles of the Helsinki Act and the objectives of the Paris Charter" (both CSCE).

5 "Presidency" refers of course to the member country in the chair of the European Council according to the half-yearly rotation. The Presidency may be assisted by the previous and next Member State to hold the Presidency. This *troika* practice had already been followed in certain dealings with Iraq and Yugoslavia.

6 Ireland appended a declaration to the Treaty, expressing reservations about the closer association of WEU and NATO with the European Union. Ireland considers that such provisions should be continued in a declaration by Member States which are also members of the WEU and NATO. The joint WEU/EC members did in fact issue an extensive declaration (including the provision for moving the seat of WEU to Brussels). This declaration is discussed in Part III, Chapter 4, The politics of Armies: the Western European Union.

Another Irish protocol to the Treaty seeking to preserve Ireland's constitutional prohibition of abortion (ratified by public referendum in this Catholic country in 1983) was rapidly overtaken by events when in February 1992 a 14-year-old Irish girl was denied the right to have a rape-induced pregnancy terminated in England. Amid street demonstrations by both sides and suggestions that the Irish provision was contrary to both Community law and to the European Convention on Human Rights, the Irish Supreme Court surprised most people by reversing the decision. Could the Irish constitution be ... unconstitutional ?

7 Following ratification of the new Treaty on European Union, the name "Union" may replace that of "Community". In this publication, to avoid confusion, we continue to refer to the "EC Council" to distinguish the Council of Ministers established by the Paris and Rome treaties from the European Council of heads of state (France) and government institutionalized by the Single European Act.

8 The European Council also decided to draw up a list of countries whose citizens require visas to cross the Community's external borders, effective January 1, 1993.

9 In 1992 the ECU was composed as follows: D-Mark 30.36%, FF 19.32%, UK 12.60%, IL 9.49%, BF 7.78%, SP 5.15%, DK 2.52%, Irish punt 1.11%, PE O.78%, Grk.drachma 0.70%, LF 0.31%.

10 *Le Monde*, January 22, 1992.

11   With the exception of the Irish, the ministers were in Oslo for a NATO meeting.

12   Passage of laws in the House of Commons is subject to three readings (not to mention approval in the House of Lords, which may amend but cannot ultimately block legislation). Substantive debate and vote usually takes place on second reading. However, after the negative Danish referendum result there was a backbench revolt by "Eurosceptics" in the Tory ranks. The British Government therefore delayed the third reading in the Commons in order to pick the most favorable moment for passage.

13   It should be noted that completion of the single economic market on December 31, 1992, was set in place by the Single European Act of 1986 and does not depend on the Maastricht Treaty of Union. Moreover, Maastricht has little impact on farm policy. However, there is a danger that these issues may be confused in the mind of the electorate.

14   In the prevailing political atmosphere no one dared suggest that a governmental veto power at European level might be *un*democratic.

15   In the difficult period following the Danish rejection Major and Delors depend on each other. As Major advocates subsidiarity he must also define it, recognizing that there can be no subsidiary level of decision-making without higher, wider levels. In other words, subsidiarity (a concept popularized by none other than Jacques Delors himself, in his 1989 Bruges speech), is an essential aspect of the very federalism Major abjurcs. There is everything to play for in negotiating which issues should be decided at the highest level. Writing in *The Independent* on the day the UK assumed the EC presidency, Tim Jackson expressed the EC-UK interdependency in stark, even overstated terms: "The stakes are high. If the British presidency fails, the Maastricht treaty will lie in tatters, and Europe's aspirations to world influence will be dashed. Even the EC's achievements before Maastricht, most notably the creation of a single market, will be left in doubt. If it succeeds, on the other hand, Britain will have set the EC back on track. By demonstrating an ability to get things done and to get on with its partners, Britain will have secured its own position in the Community".

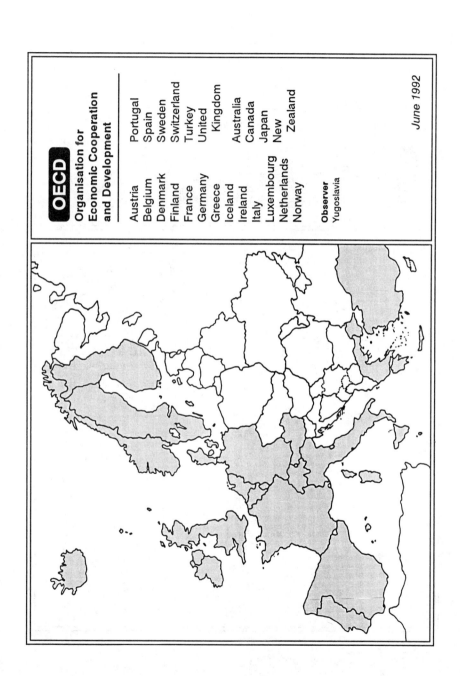

OECD

Organisation for Economic Cooperation and Development

Austria
Belgium
Denmark
Finland
France
Germany
Greece
Iceland
Ireland
Italy
Luxembourg
Netherlands
Norway

Portugal
Spain
Sweden
Switzerland
Turkey
United Kingdom
Australia
Canada
Japan
New Zealand

Observer
Yugoslavia

June 1992

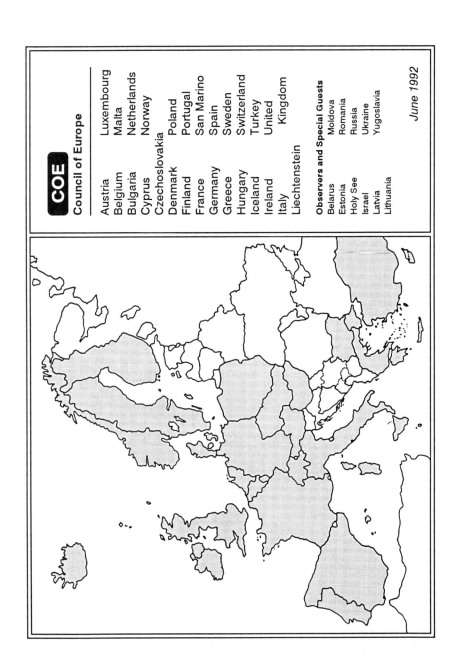

COE

Council of Europe

Austria	Luxembourg
Belgium	Malta
Bulgaria	Netherlands
Cyprus	Norway
Czechoslovakia	
Denmark	Poland
Finland	Portugal
France	San Marino
Germany	Spain
Greece	Sweden
Hungary	Switzerland
Iceland	Turkey
Ireland	United
Italy	Kingdom
Liechtenstein	

Observers and Special Guests

Belarus	Moldova
Estonia	Romania
Holy See	Russia
Israel	Ukraine
Latvia	Yugoslavia
Lithuania	

June 1992

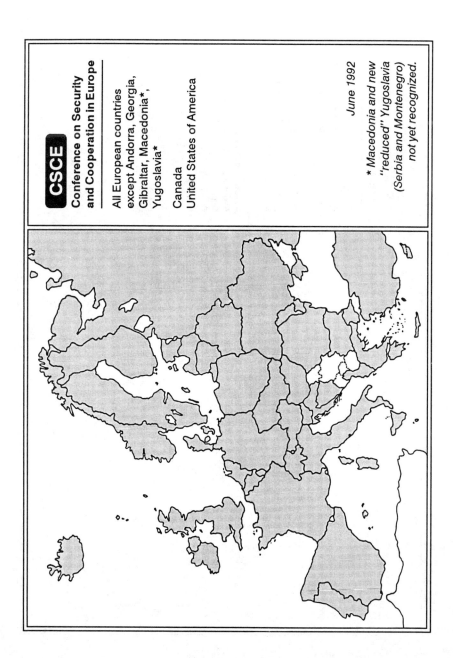

CSCE

Conference on Security
and Cooperation in Europe

All European countries
except Andorra, Georgia,
Gibraltar, Macedonia*,
Yugoslavia*

Canada
United States of America

June 1992

* Macedonia and new
"reduced" Yugoslavia
(Serbia and Montenegro)
not yet recognized.

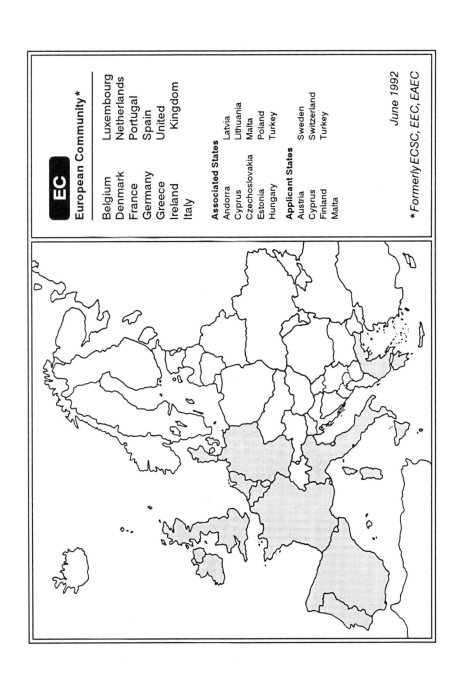

EC
European Community*

Belgium	Luxembourg
Denmark	Netherlands
France	Portugal
Germany	Spain
Greece	United
Ireland	Kingdom
Italy	

Associated States

Andorra	Latvia
Cyprus	Lithuania
Czechoslovakia	Malta
Estonia	Poland
Hungary	Turkey

Applicant States

Austria	Sweden
Cyprus	Switzerland
Finland	Turkey
Malta	

June 1992

*Formerly ECSC, EEC, EAEC

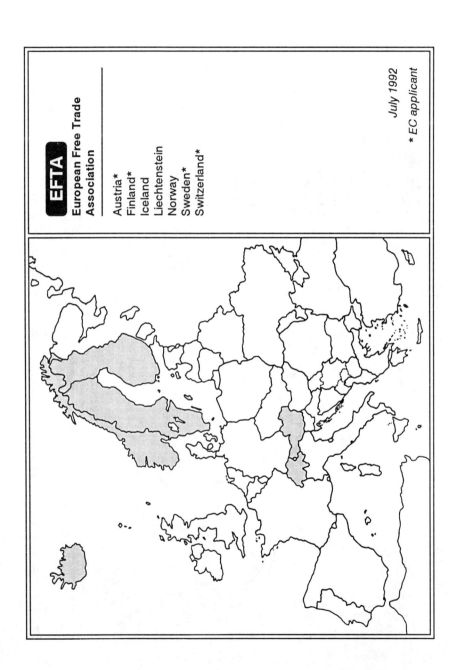

EFTA
European Free Trade
Association

Austria*
Finland*
Iceland
Liechtenstein
Norway
Sweden*
Switzerland*

July 1992

* EC applicant

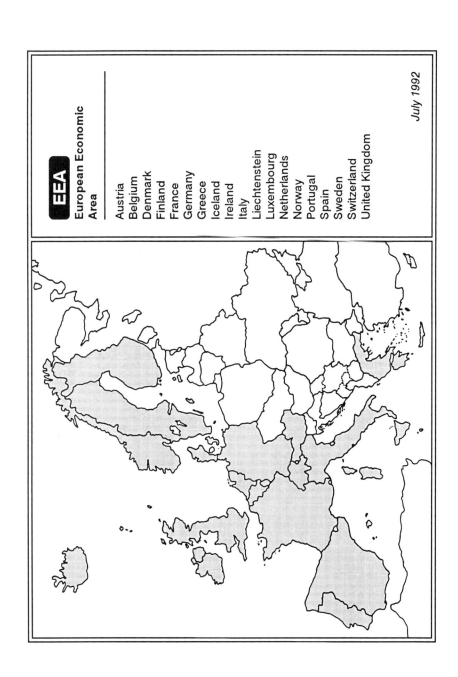

EEA

European Economic
Area

Austria
Belgium
Denmark
Finland
France
Germany
Greece
Iceland
Ireland
Italy
Liechtenstein
Luxembourg
Netherlands
Norway
Portugal
Spain
Sweden
Switzerland
United Kingdom

July 1992

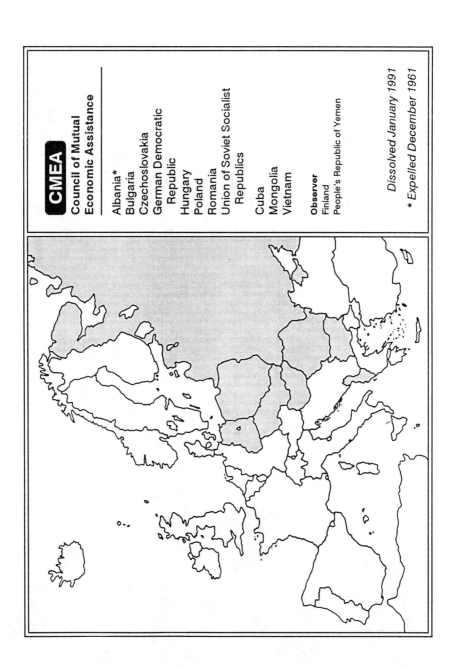

CMEA

Council of Mutual Economic Assistance

Albania*
Bulgaria
Czechoslovakia
German Democratic
    Republic
Hungary
Poland
Romania
Union of Soviet Socialist
    Republics

Cuba
Mongolia
Vietnam

Observer
Finland
People's Republic of Yemen

Dissolved January 1991

* *Expelled December 1961*

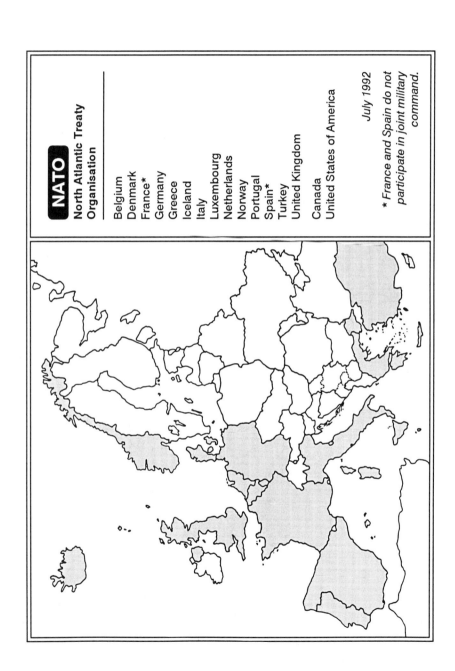

NATO

North Atlantic Treaty Organisation

Belgium
Denmark
France*
Germany
Greece
Iceland
Italy
Luxembourg
Netherlands
Norway
Portugal
Spain*
Turkey
United Kingdom

Canada
United States of America

July 1992

* France and Spain do not participate in joint military command.

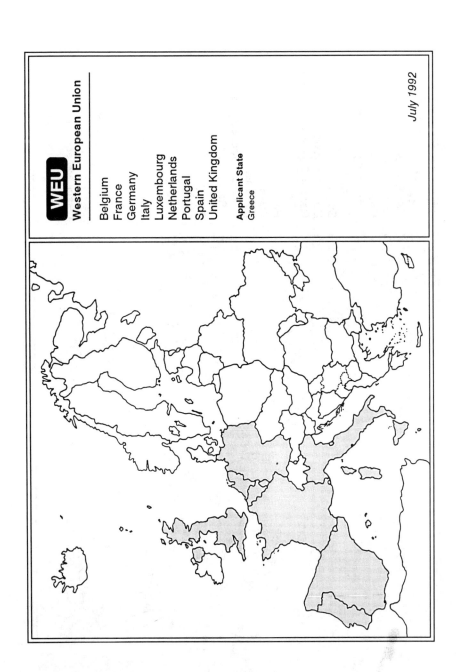

WEU
Western European Union

Belgium
France
Germany
Italy
Luxembourg
Netherlands
Portugal
Spain
United Kingdom

Applicant State
Greece

July 1992

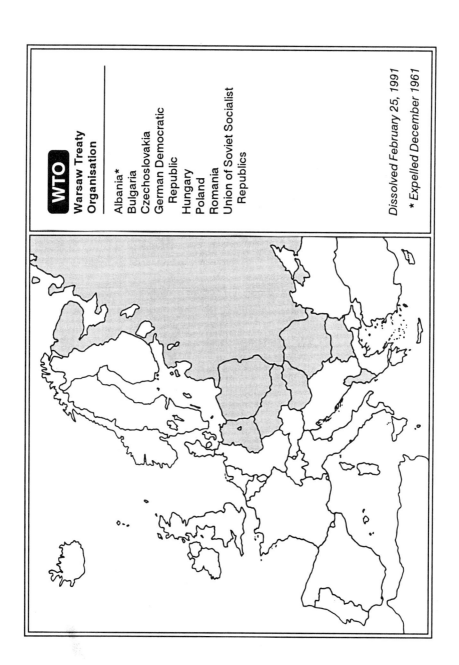

WTO

Warsaw Treaty Organisation

Albania*
Bulgaria
Czechoslovakia
German Democratic
    Republic
Hungary
Poland
Romania
Union of Soviet Socialist
    Republics

Dissolved February 25, 1991

* Expelled December 1961

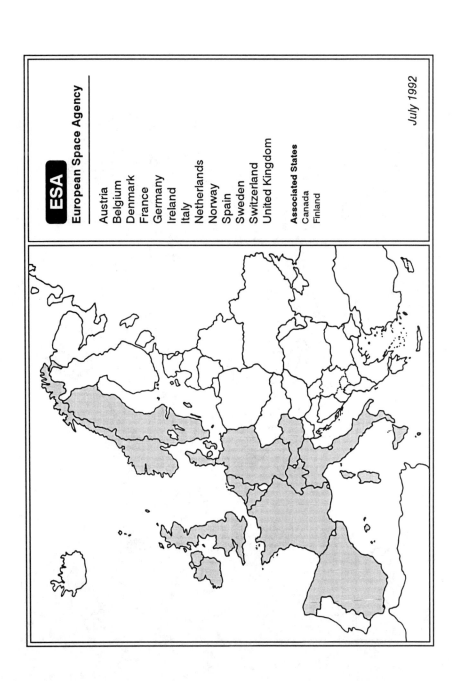

ESA

European Space Agency

Austria
Belgium
Denmark
France
Germany
Ireland
Italy
Netherlands
Norway
Spain
Sweden
Switzerland
United Kingdom

Associated States
Canada
Finland

July 1992

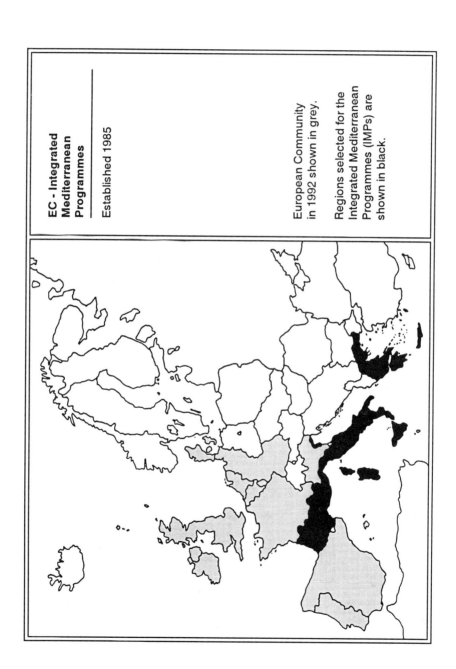

EC - Integrated Mediterranean Programmes

Established 1985

European Community in 1992 shown in grey.

Regions selected for the Integrated Mediterranean Programmes (IMPs) are shown in black.

	OECD	COE	CSCE	EC	EFTA	EEA	CMEA	NATO	WEU	WTO	ESA
Albania			CSCE				CMEA			WTO	
Andorra				EC							
Austria	OECD	COE	CSCE	EC	EFTA	EEA					ESA
Belgium	OECD	COE	CSCE	EC		EEA		NATO	WEU		ESA
Bosnia-Herzegovina			CSCE								
Bulgaria		COE	CSCE				CMEA			WTO	
Croatia			CSCE								
Cyprus		COE	CSCE	EC							
Czechoslovakia	OECD	COE	CSCE	EC		EEA	CMEA			WTO	
Denmark	OECD	COE	CSCE	EC		EEA		NATO			ESA
Estonia			CSCE	EC							
Finland	OECD	COE	CSCE	EC	EFTA	EEA	CMEA				ESA
France	OECD	COE	CSCE	EC		EEA		NATO	WEU		ESA
FRG/Germany	OECD	COE	CSCE	EC		EEA		NATO	WEU		ESA
[GDR]			CSCE				CMEA				
Greece	OECD	COE	CSCE	EC		EEA		NATO	(WEU)	WTO	

Member: **ABC**
Associate or Observer: ABC
Applicant: (ABC)

Notes: All countries, including CIS republics, are UN members except Andorra, Monaco, Georgia, Holy See and Switzerland. GDR and FRG signify before reunification; Germany signifies after reunification. Albania expelled from CMEA and WTO in 1961. Cyprus both Associate and Applicant with EC.

Situation in May 1992, except CMEA/WTO/GDR (dissolved).

	OECD	COE	CSCE	EC	EFTA	EEA	CMEA	NATO	WEU	WTO	ESA
Holy See		COE	CSCE								
Hungary	OECD	COE	CSCE	EC			CMEA	NATO		WTO	
Iceland	OECD	COE	CSCE		EFTA	EEA		NATO			
Ireland	OECD	COE	CSCE	EC		EEA					ESA
Italy	OECD	COE	CSCE	EC		EEA		NATO	WEU		ESA
Kosovo											
Latvia			CSCE	EC							
Liechtenstein		COE	CSCE		EFTA	EEA					
Lithuania			CSCE	EC							
Luxembourg	OECD	COE	CSCE	EC		EEA		NATO	WEU		
Macedonia											
Malta		COE	CSCE	EC							
Monaco			CSCE								
Netherlands	OECD	COE	CSCE	EC		EEA		NATO	WEU		ESA
Norway	OECD	COE	CSCE		EFTA	EEA		NATO			ESA

Member: **ABC**
Associate or Observer: ABC
Applicant: ABC

Situation in May 1992, except CMEA/WTO (dissolved).

Notes: *Kosovo, a province of Serbia, voted for independence in clandestine referendum May 23, 1992. Macedonian independence not generally recognized. Malta both Associate and Applicant with EC.*

	OECD	COE	CSCE	EC	EFTA	EEA	CMEA	NATO	WEU	WTO	ESA
Poland		COE	CSCE	EC (assoc)			CMEA			WTO	
Portugal	OECD	COE	CSCE	EC		EEA		NATO	WEU		
Romania		COE (assoc)	CSCE				CMEA			WTO	
San Marino		COE	CSCE								
Slovenia			CSCE								
Spain	OECD	COE	CSCE	EC		EEA		NATO	WEU		ESA
Sweden	OECD	COE	CSCE	EC (appl)	EFTA	EEA					ESA
Switzerland	OECD	COE	CSCE	EC (appl)	EFTA	EEA					ESA
Turkey	OECD	COE	CSCE	EC (appl)				NATO			
[USSR]/ CIS			CSCE				CMEA			WTO	
United Kingdom	OECD	COE	CSCE	EC		EEA		NATO	WEU		ESA
[Yugoslavia]	OECD (assoc)	COE	CSCE	EC (appl)							
Canada	OECD		CSCE					NATO			ESA (assoc)
USA	OECD		CSCE					NATO			

Member: **ABC**
Associate or Observer: ABC (gray)
Applicant: ABC (outline)

Situation in May 1992, except CMEA/WTO/USSR/Yugoslavia (dissolved).

Notes: USSR succeeded by CIS, composed of 11 of the 15 former Soviet republics; Estonia, Georgia, Latvia and Lithuania not CIS states. All 11 CIS states are members of CSCE. Yugoslavia applied for EC membership before break-up. Serbia Montenegro claim to Yugoslavia succession not recognized. Turkey both Associate and Applicant with EC.

III

THE INSTITUTIONAL FRAMEWORK: ORGANIZATIONS AND FUNCTIONS

1

Rebuilding a Continent: Organization for Economic Cooperation and Development

The Organization for Economic Cooperation and Development (OECD) was set up in 1960, following the 1959 "western summit" meeting in Paris, on the basis of the Organisation for European Economic Cooperation (OEEC) established in 1948 to administer the Marshall Plan.[1] Albeit enlarged to include Canada and the United States, OECD retained the characteristics of its predecessor, being essentially an economic rather than a political organization. This is reflected in the participation as full members of neutral countries such as Austria, Finland, Ireland, Sweden and Switzerland. Yugoslavia had observer status.

The technical character of the OECD is further highlighted by the absence of "supranational" components and of a parliamentary assembly. Its structure is simple: a Council of Ministers, an Executive Committee, committees of experts, national delegations and the secretariat.

The Council of Ministers consists of representatives of all the member governments, meeting either at full ministerial level (usually twice a year) or at the level of permanent representatives. This structure is similiar to the ministerial organ of the Council of Europe; however, whereas the latter specifies foreign ministers as the governmental representatives, in OECD ministers are nominated from economic departments.

The Executive Committee consists of fourteen members, seven permanent (Canada, France, Germany, Italy, Japan, United States, United Kingdom) and seven elected annually. It prepares the agenda of the Council of Ministers and coordinates the work of the other OECD bodies. The Committee holds special sessions to initiate study of economic questions.

The OECD committees, more than twenty in number, bring together representatives of member countries and an associated country, Yugoslavia (the question of Yugoslavia's "succession" having not yet been settled). They prepare annual work programs and, where necessary, set up working parties of specialists to assist them on particular points.

Under the leadership of its Secretary General, the secretariat's international public servants, who are nationals of member countries, prepare the work of the Council of Ministers and other OECD bodies and implement the Council's directives. There are over 1700 permanent staff members and 530 professionals appointed for two or three years. This staff is supplemented by consultants drawn from universities, businesses, banks and governments. The secretariat is located at the Château de la Muette in Paris.

National delegations are in a sense "economic embassies" accredited to the organization. They facilitate international cooperation, promote adoption of new policies and represent their respective countries in committees and working parties.

A number of special agencies have been set up over the years. These are designed to meet the needs of certain member countries and to respond to particular economic situations. The most well-known of these is the International Energy Agency, established following the oil crisis of the seventies.

OECD encourages the cross-fertilization of work and ideas. Chairpersons and experts from one committee may sit in on the proceedings of other committees or contribute to their work. This policy has helped OECD to understand the growing links among economic activities and to anticipate social and technological developments, too often treated as separate or even unrelated issues.

Development, growth and stability

The three basic aims of OECD, defined in Article 1 of the Founding Convention are:

— to achieve the highest sustainable economic growth and employment and a rising standard of living in Member countries, while maintaining financial stability, and thus contribute to the development of the world economy;
— to contribute to sound economic expansion in Member as well as non-Member countries in the process of economic development;
— to contribute to the expansion of world trade on a multilateral, non-discriminatory basis in accordance with international obligations.

OECD inherited from OEEC a legacy of proven working methods, such as basing the organization's work on economic data from each member country which are not only comprehensive and reliable but also statistically comparable. Obvious as this may seem, prior to the existence of OEEC such data had been rare and their intergovernmental exchange even rarer. OEEC has helped to create a common mode of thought about international economic issues.

There are vast disparities among the member nations of OECD. The United States, with a population of some 250 million people, has one thousand inhabitants for every Icelander. Not surprisingly, it relies on export of goods and services for only ten percent of its national income, whereas the figure for Belgium and Luxembourg is sixty percent. Some thirty Greeks in every hundred are employed in agriculture: the corresponding figure for the United Kingdom is three.

Nevertheless, in their commitment to the market economy, to democracy and to third world development, these countries think alike and enjoy a close community of interest. Moreover, as the twelve-nation European Community sought to complete its trading union in 1992, OECD provided an essential forum for the broader economic community of the developed world to maintain its economic cohesion and outward-looking stance in trade. The EC could doubtless exist without OECD but the latter is of great importance to the other member countries in their dealings with the EC's "Common Market".

Intellectual persuasion

In the words of Jean-Claude Paye, its Secretary-General, OECD is not a supranational organization but a place where policy makers can meet and discuss their problems, where governments can compare their points of view and experiences. The secretariat helps to find and point a way to go, and acts as a catalyst. Its role is more than merely academic but OECD does not have the authority to impose its ideas. Its power lies in its capacity for intellectual persuasion. This is why sensitively neutral countries such as Switzerland had no problem participating from the beginning. [2]

Through quantitative and qualitative studies, the OECD secretariat clarifies economic and social problems facing member countries. It pools experience by exchanging information and analyzes the effectiveness of economic and social policies in the various countries. Through discussion, the secretariat makes member nations aware of the impact of their actions on others, thereby fostering solidarity, common approaches and strategies and, ideally, common solutions.

In rare instances, the ministerial council takes binding decisions. It did so, for instance, in 1961 to facilitate movements of capital; and again in 1984 to control the movement of hazardous waste across frontiers. (This action was followed up in 1984 by the Basel convention on the international shipment of hazardous waste). Americans and Canadians are well placed to understand this problem which besets their own administrations. The "not in my backyard" attitude to the transport and dumping of waste across state or provincial lines necessitates a binding policy.

Most of the time, however, decisions and opinions of the Council take the form of recommendations to member governments. The statement issued at the end of each ministerial meeting sets forth agreements and offers the principal channel for bringing them to the attention of the public. Naturally, also, numerous studies are published and offered for sale.

Macroeconomics

Stop-go economic policies, roller coaster trade cycles and stagflation are demons to be exorcized. Reduction of unemployment without re-igniting inflationary expectations is a central objective for OECD. Unemployment is increasingly seen as structural rather than cyclical, brought on by inflexible labor, underdeveloped capital markets and excessively large public sectors which discourage private initiatives. (OECD does not take sides between employers and labor and usually finds enough blame for all to share!). Such structural rigidity makes it hard to respond to new technology and to the growth of dynamic exporters in the developing world, such as those of the "Pacific rim" — Korea, Taiwan, Hong Kong, Singapore.

OECD's macro-economic policy has been shaped to sustain expansion without inflation and to promote more stable exchange rates by attaining a better balance among countries. It is not clear that national monetary and fiscal policies "add up" across countries either negatively, as domestic objectives are frustrated by international conditions, or positively, improving performance everywhere. OECD's economic policy committee seeks the assistance of solid data and sophisticated forecasting techniques to grapple with these issues. Originally provided on paper, such information is increasingly received and disseminated "on line" through a computer network. OECD also acts as a clearing house for non-quantitative information. This includes measures to reduce unemployment, new trade regulations and obstacles to foreign investment.

OECD plays a pre-eminent role in economic forecasting. Its Economic Outlook is published twice a year. The Organization also prepares an annual Economic Survey of each member country.

Structural adaptation to new economic challenges

Economic decline can be of two basic types-cyclical and structural. The former is due to fluctuations in the trade cycle — supply and demand — on account of changes in a given sector or across the economy as a whole. National economies are today so intertwined that no industry — indeed no national economy — can be managed in isolation. Both negative and positive measures produce a ripple effect.

Structural decline needs more radical action than cyclical downturn, leading to lasting if not permanent change in working conditions. High interest rates for instance, are a cyclical phenomenon. They will adversely affect demand for automobiles or refrigerators, which in turn will depress the market in steel. Such trends are reversible: as borrowing declines, banks lower their interest rates, demand rises and the cycle begins again. On the other hand, as plastic and fiberglass replace steel in the manufacturing process, there is a lasting and not merely cyclical change in the structure of the market. To meet this situation, steel producers will have to reduce production or diversify their product, producing cheaper steel or even plastics and fiberglass. This will involve capital investment, displacement or retraining of labor and many other repercussions. In an atmosphere of free trade, where tariff walls are coming down, exchanging short-term protection for long-term efficiency and market expansion, economic restructuring acquires even greater urgency.

This long-term structural adaptation, known as positive adjustment policy, is central to the work of the OECD. The international trading community must help member countries to adapt to change. This is achieved by moving economic resources out of declining industries, occupations and areas into new, expanding ones so as to remain productive and competitive. At the same time, governments must be careful not to hurt low-income groups, dislocate labor unduly, or harm trading partners. Positive adjustment policies are important to both industry and agriculture. Examples of this focus are the provision of venture capital and the reining-in of public spending. (The latter has grown from 14 to 25% in OECD countries since 1960, due in large measure to improved social services which, while excellent in themselves, weigh heavily on production costs). The committee for manpower and social affairs addresses the labor market aspect. It facilitates job and career changes; discusses the effect of government subsidies; gives attention to especially sensitive sectors, such as steel and shipbuilding.

A basic requirement: free trade

The boom years of the 1960s saw a staggering 70% increase in the gross national product (GNP) of OECD countries. This gave way in the seventies to inflationary pressures, especially following the oil crisis of 1973. The combination of rising costs and sharp recession posed a range of new problems. Shocks to the monetary and trading systems threatened to undermine capitalism's traditional commitment to free trade. When hard times hit, it is not easy for an individual member of parliament or congress, expected to defend economic enterprise "back home" in the constituency, to advocate acceptance of present pain in exchange for future advantage. In 1974 OECD governments undertook not to try and solve their own balance-of-payments problems by means of import controls or subsidies. This commitment was followed in 1980 by a Declaration on Trade Policy pledging governments to improve the trading system and to strengthen the role of the General Agreement on Tariffs and Trade (GATT). OECD often examines trade issues before they move on to GATT for negotiations.

Monitoring of new trade measures has in recent years included the problems of trade in high technology products. The use of export credits has also been closely watched.

The activities of multinational corporations—whose GNP can sometimes exceed those of whole countries—are naturally of interest to OECD. A cooperative approach was adopted in 1976 in order to "improve the foreign investment climate, encourage the positive contribution multinational enterprises can make to economic and social progress and minimise and resolve difficulties which may arise from their various operations". It was agreed to grant foreign investors the same treatment as national firms. One may fantasize that by 2050 it may be more significant to belong to—work for or invest in—a multinational cooperation than to hold any particular national passport.

Energy

With respect to energy, OECD has addressed oil import ceilings, energy saving and research on alternative energy sources, information on international workers, relations between producing and consuming countries and the equitable distribution of resources in emergencies.

In 1974, the International Energy Agency (IEA) was set up within OECD. It included all members of OECD except Finland, France and Iceland. IEA governments have agreed to share oil supplies in the event of a major disruption. Energy planning is also coordinated. From 1974 to 1984 the share of oil in OECD energy consumption fell from 52 to 43 percent. This indicates considerable success in energy diversification. However, oil supplies are expected to contract again in the 1990s: as demand soars we could be facing a new crisis.

The Nuclear Energy Agency (not to be confused with the EC's EURATOM or the UN agency in Vienna) was set up within OEEC as early as 1957. It addresses all segments of the nuclear fuel cycle from production to waste disposal as well as safety matters. Two conventions for compensating accident victims were opened for signature in 1960 and 1963. Nuclear energy accounts for 18 percent of OECD's electricity production.

Agriculture

The agricultural economy is undergoing rapid structural change in all member countries. OECD follows and promotes policy changes to counter worker imbalances (excess of supply over demand), rising costs and trade tensions. (Who does not remember the US/European "chicken war" a few years back?). Discussions take place in the context of wider economic, social and trade policies. Special attention is paid to Mediterranean issues and "North-South" problems. Production and consumption forecasts provide valuable working tools.

The extension of exclusive economic zones to 200 miles in the eighties has had a major impact on fishing. The Fisheries Committee has studied the problems of overfishing and trade liberalization.

Aiding the developing world

OEEC was restructured into OECD not only to bring Canada and the United States into the Organisation but also to place increased emphasis on cooperation with developing countries. However, the developing world is economically much less homogeneous than it was when OECD and its Development Assistance Committee (DAC) were formed in 1960. A "second wave" of builders and exporters of high-technology manufactured goods has grown up, particularly on the Pacific rim. Through ASEAN South-east Asia is following suit. Oil-producing developing countries have seen boom-and-bust cycles as OPEC has struggled without complete success to control production quotas and prices. Many developing countries have run into excessive debt. Yet access to international capital alone will not boost the trade of developing countries: they also need skilled workers. OECD countries must therefore at the same time maintain their own growth, resist protectionist measures, and provide training programs. These interrelated issues are examined in OECD's committees on economic policy and on international investment and multinational enterprises.

There are other countries, however, typified by those in sub-Saharan Africa, which cannot yet aspire to full partnership within the industrialized world. Devoid of resources, threatened by ecological imbalance and climatic extremes of drought and heat, the world's poorest countries need outright grants or long-term loans at low interest: aid as well as trade. OECD has created the Club du Sahel to foster such policies, providing food aid alongside self-help measures to improve agriculture and rural facilities. DAC member countries have set an aid target of 0.7 percent of GNP which, although modest enough, has not yet been met by most member countries. Can we not spare seven-tenths of a cent in the dollar?

Special issues which have received attention in recent years include promotion and monitoring of multilateral (as opposed to bilateral) aid projects, the contribution to development of non-governmental organisations, primary health care, environmental issues and the role of women in development.

In the press release following its meeting in May 1988, the ministerial council saw strong and sustainable global growth as essential to long-term development. OECD countries undertook to promote both open markets for the exports of developing countries and increased assistance. They committed themselves to industrial and technical cooperation and direct investment. At the same time, however, "developing countries have important responsibilities in improving their own performance and policies, strengthening their creditworthiness, creating a more attractive climate for investment and ensuring open markets".[3]

OECD has made a significant contribution to combatting inflation and to addressing the problems of unemployment, structural disequilibrium, protectionism, financial imbalances, world hunger and environmental hazards. Completion of the common market and renewal of the economies of Eastern European countries will complicate these issues and create new ones. Doubtless the Organization itself will be restructured and open its doors to new members. The intergovernmental, non-supranational character of OECD provides a flexible, non-threatening instrument for strengthening and broadening the "European Economic Area" and ensuring continuing cooperation with North America, the Pacific and, indeed, the rest of the world economy. Since the gap between rich and poor nations continues to grow, OECD's task is far from complete.

Notes

1 The original member countries of OECD (December 14, 1960) are Austria, Belgium, Canada, Denmark, France, the Federal Republic of Germany, Greece, Iceland, Ireland, Italy, Luxembourg, the Netherlands, Norway, Portugal, Spain, Sweden, Switzerland, Turkey, the United Kingdom and the United States. The following countries joined subsequently: Japan (April 28, 1964), Finland (January 28, 1969), Australia (June 7, 1971) and New Zealand (May 29, 1973). The Socialist Federal Republic of Yugoslavia took part in some of the work of OECD (agreement signed October 28, 1961).

2 Switzerland's role is in fact more important than its population of five million would suggest. It is a host country to the UN and other international bodies, both governmental and non-governmental, offers a model of cultural integration and is a financial "giant".

3 Secretary-General of OECD, *Activities of OECD in 1988*, OECD, Paris, 1989, pp. 95-96.

2

Free Trade:
The GATT and the New World Order

The General Agreement on Tariffs and Trade, universally known as GATT, has a curious history. How can an international organization be called an agreement? In October 1947 twenty-three countries were engaged in drawing up the charter for an international trade organization, planned as a specialized agency of the United Nations. The General Agreement was based on sections of the proposed ITO charter relating to trade policies. Agreed upon separately as an interim measure to get trade liberalization under way quickly, it was provided with minimum institutional arrangements, since it was expected that the ITO would soon be in place. The ITO never saw the light of day but the GATT, which came into force on January 1, 1948, flourishes nearly fifty years later and is now adhered to by over a hundred countries, with some thirty further countries applying GATT rules on a *de facto* basis. The Agreement's headquarters are in Geneva. Its scope is, of course, global rather than specifically European. However, GATT has been instrumental in setting the ground rules for free trade and the creation of trade groups. Member countries fund it in a very realistic way: each state contribution is calculated not on the basis of population, like most other international organizations, much less on surface area but on its share of world trade. In other words, states pay to the extent that the General Agreement works for them. The GATT is a world body rather than a European one, but the principles it enshrines are essential to European economic cooperation and to Europe's business dealings with the rest of the world. The Agreement is complex but includes three basic principles essential to the organization of trade relations. The first principle, in Article 1, addresses "most-favored nation treatment":

> With respect to customs duties and charges of any kind imposed on or in connection with importation or exportation or imposed on the international transfer of payments for imports or exports, and with respect to the method of levying such duties and charges, and with respect to all rules and formalities in connection with importation and exportation ... any advantage, favour, privilege or immunity granted by any contracting party to any product originating in or destined for any other country shall be accorded immediately and unconditionally to the like product originating in or destined for the territories of all other contracting parties.

Simply stated, GATT signatories agree to give each other equal treatment in the matter of trade advantages. Such commercial purity is rarely exercized completely; strong nations frequently exact a political price for the granting of most-favored-nation treatment, which is in any case conditional upon reciprocity. Moreover, there are exceptions to the general principle. Since it is not possible for the global trading community to move at once from restricted to free trade, trading associations of groups of countries are permitted under specific conditions. These exceptions are allowed according to the theory that such groups of nations, while they may appear restrictive in the short term, raise the level of world commerce in the longer term and act as free-trade "amplifiers". A perfect illustration of the latter is the growth of the European Economic Community from the original membership of six to twelve and the dramatic rise not only in its exports but also in its imports. Since one country's purchase is another country's sale, existence of the Community has benefited world trade as a whole.

Common markets and free trade areas

Following "most-favoured nation" treatment as described in Article 1 of the General Agreement, then, the second principle which it is important to understand is that of the "free trade area" (Article XXIV. 8.b.):

> A free trade area shall be understood to mean a group of two or more customs territories in which the duties and other restrictive regulations of commerce ... are eliminated on substantially all the trade between the constituent territories in products originating in such territories.

The European Free Trade Association is an example of such a free trade area. The important concept here is the notion of a free trading zone for all products (with certain exceptions permitted). If the free trade were too selective with respect to the economic sectors covered, it would be considered an infringement of the "most favoured nation" principle as far as the other GATT countries were concerned.

The third basic principle is that of the customs union, popularly known as a "common market" (Article XXIV.8.a):

> A customs union shall be understood to mean the substitution of a single customs territory for two or more customs territories, so that
> (i) duties and other restrictive regulations of commerce ... are eliminated with respect to substantially all the trade between the constituent territories of the union or at least with respect to all the trade in products originating in such territories, and,
> (ii) ... substantially the same duties and other regulations of commerce are applied by each of the members of the union to the trade of territories not included in the union.

This latter concept is usually referred to as the common external tariff or, more popularly, the common tariff wall. It constitutes the principal commercial difference between a common market and a free trade area. [1]

Since the member countries of a free trade area do not have equal external tariffs they have to set up a system of certificates of origin for trade amongst themselves. Countries outside the area will tend to seek the country of entry with the lowest "wall" or external tariff on a given product; and then to move their products across the tariff-free internal border into another member country thereby circumventing that other country's external tariff wall. For such cases the country of final destination must charge a compensating tariff where origination of all or part of the product from outside the free trade area is proven.

In both a customs union and a free trade area, duties or other regulations affecting the trade of members of the group with non-members must be no more restrictive than those applied before the group was set up. In other words, while members of the group may grant each other favored treatment, the net effect of their action may not result in greater protectionism against other GATT members, thereby increasing obstacles to world trade. Walls may be lowered or averaged but may not be raised overall.

The GATT provides that where protection is given to domestic industry, it should be afforded essentially through a customs tariff—a financial charge or import "tax"—and not through other commercial measures such as quantitative restrictions ("quotas").

Fair competition is naturally a major concern of the GATT. It allows governments to respond to the "dumping" of products in their domestic markets.[2] Similarly, where a government is alleged to have promoted its exports by means of export subsidies, "countervailing duties" may be imposed to negate the effects of the subsidy. As we have seen, quantitative restrictions, or quotas, are generally prohibited. However, exceptions are permitted when a country experiences balance-of-payment difficulties or, in the case of developing countries, an excessive drain on foreign exchange reserves caused by the demand for imports generated by development, or because they are establishing or extending domestic production.

Settling disputes

Naturally, disputes and differences of interpretation frequently arise. Consultation, conciliation and the settlement of disputes is an essential aspect of the GATT's activities. If bilateral consultations fail, a panel of experts is set up. The panel's conclusions are based in interpretation of the Agreement and upon the precedent provided by previous cases. The panel's report is submitted to the GATT Council. If the panel's findings are approved violating parties must implement the recommendations. Failure to do so may result in retaliation measures being authorized. GATT panels handle about a dozen disputes each year.

How the General Agreement works

The senior body of the GATT is the Session of Contracting Parties, usually held once a year. Between sessions the Council of Representatives meets about nine times a year.

The GATT also has a number of standing committees: trade and development; trade restrictions to protect balance of payments; textiles and clothing; tariff concessions; dumping; customs valuation; government procurement;

subsidies and countervailing measures; import licensing; technical barriers to trade; trade in meat; trade in dairy products; trade in civil aircraft; and budget, financial and administrative questions. Special working parties are set-up for current questions, especially applications for GATT membership.

Most GATT decisions are taken by consensus. On the rare occasions when voting takes place, each member country (known as a contracting party) has one vote. Major decisions are taken by simple majority.

The International Trade Centre, operated jointly with the UN, promotes the exports of developing countries. More important to these nations, however, would be an end to the short-sighted and selfish wrangling of America and Europe, so that their own international trade, more fragile and more critical to the health of their economies than some of the issues which have dominated the Tokyo and Uruguay Rounds, might receive the attention they deserve.

The current director general of GATT is Arthur Dunkel, a Swiss national. The Secretariat employs some four hundred international officials. It is located in Geneva, Switzerland, the European "capital" of the United Nations.

Multilateral negotiations

The Agreement is not simply a static document, a collection of rules combined with an arbitration system. It is also a forum where governments conduct an on-going discussion on international trade, a negotiating machine designed to liberalize commercial exchanges and to adapt the Agreement's own rules, subscribed to by the Contracting Parties, to the evolving pattern of trade.

Since its inception there have been eight cycles of multilateral negotiation, each longer and more complete than its predecessor:

1947 - Geneva	1960-62 - Dillon Round
1949 - Annecy	1964-67 - Kennedy Round
1950 - Torquay	1973-79 - Tokyo Round
1956 - Geneva	1986- - Uruguay Round

Since the Kennedy Round negotiations have been dominated by US/EC rivalry, in particular over the Community's common agricultural policy. Nevertheless agreements have been reached on other topics. Thus the Tokyo Round, in which ninety-nine countries participated, resulted in nine "codes" on such topics as subsidies, dumping (selling abroad below cost to maintain production and "export" unemployment), state purchases and trade in aircraft. Agreements were even reached for dairy products and beef although these are now under review.

The Uruguay Round was launched on an American initiative at Punta-del-Este in September, 1986. Once again, the CAP is at the center of discussion. The US objective is to rectify what Washington considers to be market distortion: the Community, and France in particular, should produce less, export less and import more. The EC considers this approach to be harmful and unbalanced and looks for compensatory concessions. The European negotiators are interested in freeing up trade in textiles, strengthening protection of intellectual property (trade-marks, warranties of origin, authors' rights) and the extension of GATT rules and discipline to services, the so-called "invisible exports", such as banking and insurance (worth $800 billion in 1990 as compared to some $3,500 billion of goods).

Reform in Eastern Europe

At the 45th Session of the Contracting Parties, in December, 1989, there was consensus that changes in the economic policies of Eastern European countries would be aided by the involvement of these countries in the GATT multilateral trading system. (Czechoslovakia, Hungary, Poland, and Romania were already members. A working party had been set up to examine a membership request from Bulgaria).

During the session the United States stated that it would support the granting of observer status to the Soviet Union. Poland requested renegotiation of its terms of accession to take account of recent liberalization and opening of its economy. Czechoslovakia, noting it had embarked on fundamental economic reform, asked for early termination of the suspension of GATT obligations between itself and the United States; and speeding up of elimination of quantitative restrictions applied to its exports by the European Economic Community.[3]

Transnational corporations

The traditional pattern of one country trading with another is rapidly being overcome by new concepts. The "global village" engendered by instant electronic communication, where even newspaper production can be remote-controlled by satellite, is creating a world market in which transnational suppliers compete to meet frontier-leaping global demand.

Frontiers pertain to nations, to cultural and trading units controlled and administered by governments. Yet international, albeit mainly American corporations like IBM, Exxon, Citycorp, MacDonalds, – but also "Canadian" Seagrams, "Anglo-Dutch" Unilever, "German" Siemens, "French" Peugeot, "Japanese" Nissan and Mitsubishi in fact enjoy international networks and produce gross "national" (actually international) products (GNP's) far greater than those of many governments. Ownership is increasingly diffused. Just as shipping companies fly flags of convenience so too do faceless, invisible holding companies translate slick slogans into fifty languages and manipulate their millions behind their logos.

New forms of trade outflank the shipment of goods. The "invisible trade" of services – always important to countries such as the United Kingdom – is now of increasing significance. Another important form of frontier hopping is the acquisition of major real estate. During the oil crisis of the seventies, Arab "petro-dollars" bought up venerable London hotels.

Tariffs and production quotas are avoided through "colonisation" — the creation of new firms or the purchase of existing firms abroad. Allentown's Bulldog trucks are built in Normandy through a joint venture between Mack and majority shareolder Renault — associating a nominally private firm with a French state corporation. Canadian whisky profits are invested in Seagrams' own vineyards in Bordeaux. While United States and Japanese representatives haggle over trade barriers and "voluntary" quotas, American and Japanese cars roll alternately off the same Japanese-managed production line in Tennesee... and the "Japanese" version outsells the virtually identical "American" model in the United States market!

The Uruguay Round

On the occasion of its historic meeting in Maastricht on December 9-11, 1991, the European Council issued the following statement on the slow-moving negotiations of the Uruguay Round:

> The European Council reiterates its firm commitment to a substantial, balanced and global package of results of the Uruguay Round by the end of the year. This package should cover GATT rules and disciplines, market access, agriculture, textiles, services, TRIPs and the institutional reinforcement of the GATT system, excluding any recourse to unilateral action by any partner. It urges other partners in the Uruguay Round to join in its efforts to finalize the negotiations on this basis.
>
> The European Council invites the Commission to elaborate a good negotiated outcome of the Round encompassing substantial and credible results in all major areas, consistent with the objectives of the European Communities...

Negotiations proved intractable indeed; we now know that the end of year deadline was not met. As 1992 dawned George Bush took his special pleading (increased imports for US cars) to Tokyo in search of "jobs, jobs, jobs" and, of course, electoral votes. The quotas Bush sought, even if voluntary, were clearly contrary to GATT principles and did not improve the mind-set of European negotiators. The world still hung in the balance between free trade, special preference and increased protectionism.

Negotiations dragged on through the winter of 1992 without a breakthrough. Artificial deadlines were ignored, although everybody knew that eventually a trade-off among the major negotiating partners was inevitable. To many free trade at any price was unacceptable, especially if it led to a homogenisation of cultures. Behind the negotiation there also lay the great debate on the role of government intervention in the market, perceived by some as a legitimate instrument of industrial policy, by others as an unlevelling of the playing field.

The European role was complicated by the fact that the Community's interests were represented by the Commission, requiring that a common position be reached on all major issues among the Twelve before they could be negotiated in the Round. Yet even among themselves the European governments failed to lay out their vital, non-negotiable interests.

The posturing and the statements of principle did not hide the evidence that the confrontation between Europe and the United States remained central to the conflict. To the US objection to European export subsidies for agricultural products, Europeans retort that the US also subsidize their exports, albeit in a less visible manner, and that anyway their share of the world cereals market is three times that of the Community. Moreover, if European states were bound by a Brussels signature, the states of the Union ("sub-federal entities") should be equally committed by undertakings made by Washington.

It is difficult to respect deadlines when each side is waiting for the other to move first. Many Europeans (and doubtless quite a few Americans) shared the view of the French Secretary of State for foreign trade, Jean-Noël Jeanneney, that it was better to wait until the lobbies which paralysed constructive bargaining had loosened their grip. Moreover, having made their gesture with CAP reform in May 1992, taking the heat from their farmers, European governments felt the ball was now clearly in the American court. With Pat Buchanan, Ross Perot and "America first!", it promised to be a slow summer for GATT, awaiting November 4 and the outcome of a presidential election in which George Bush, after all, appeared more committed to free trade than his opponents on either the right or the left. The key to the Uruguay log-jam is an understanding between France and the US on agriculture. EC and US finally struck a deal in November. Caught between the French farmer's rock and the Community's hard place, Mitterrand chose Europe. It is doubtful that French electors share his vision.

Tightrope to the future

In general the GATT organization can be well pleased with the growth of world trade. Yet protectionism and nationalism still lurk and vast problems remain. In Asia, Africa, Latin America, the poor grow poorer, even hungrier, as the rich munch into obesity—and jog out of it. Single-product economies, lacking education, infrastructure, health services and price stability struggle to diversify. New rules must be devised to control new patterns of trade while we continue to combat recalcitrant, endemic problems.

The problem facing the Agreement is not so much its own survival (it could well win the Oscar for the world's most necessary international organization) as the nature of its role. The Agreement is in many ways the victim of its own success. It lays down strict rules for free trade and then allows controlled discrimination to flourish under the guise of regional associations—free trade areas—because these are seen as stepping stones to world-wide liberalization.

The most stunningly successful of these bodies is obviously the European Community. It has not only doubled in membership and vastly increased its trade in the last forty years, with seven or eight applicants lining up at the door, but has also given rise to "Olympic rings" of emulants on several continents. First there came CMEA, EFTA and EEA in Europe; then the US-Canada deal in North America (currently giving even Quebec separatists pause for thought), followed by NAFTA, bringing in Mexico. These were followed by new projects in Central and South America and a proposal from President Bush for an Enterprise for the Americas initiative from Alaska to Tierra del Fuego. More recently ASEAN gave birth to AFTA in South-East Asia, with an even broader economic grouping (including Japan and excluding the US!) on the horizon. Turkey is fostering economic rapprochement round the Black Sea and among the new Turcic-speaking nations of Central Asia.

Only Africa, it seems, lags behind (as usual, alas); but even here one may expect that Azania, the newly enfranchized multi-racial South Africa, after casting off the last shackles of apartheid, will furnish the motor for a Sub-Saharan trade grouping; provided, of course, that enlightened statesmen arise to find a way between the ethnic borders of tribalism and the political borders inherited from the colonial age. (Through its ACP agreements the Community is facing up to its responsibilities in what used to be known as the Dark Continent but the need will increase even without conflict and desertification).

So what should GATT officials be thinking as they contemplate their post-World War II handiwork? The economic map of the world has been profoundly changed. The threat now is that, having broken through national boundaries, the new regional groupings may be content to become economic superpowers facing off indefinitely behind trade defenses originally intended to be temporary and transitional: not merely Fortress Europe but Fortress America, Fortress Asia ... forgetting that in the Olympic ideal the rings are interlinked. GATT's new challenge is to walk a tightrope to the future, a fine line between a closed regional protectionism and an open economic regionalism. Uruguay Round negotiators play for high stakes. At least the GATT is not a bloated bureaucracy: but neither is it about to waste away on the genteel shores of Lake Geneva.

Notes

1 There are of course many non-commercial aspects such as decision-making by majority, judicial institutions, right of establishment for citizens, etc., involved in a common market which are consciously avoided under a free trade arrangement.

2 Dumping occurs when a country sells a product abroad below cost in order to maintain employment at home or to use up excess production unsaleable at home. The net result is unfair price competition abroad and "export" of unemployment.

3 *Focus*, GATT newsletter, Nr 67, December 1989, p. 1. On a bilateral basis, the US and the USSR opened negotiations in Washington on February 12, 1990, to end half a century of US discrimination against Soviet imports and certain Soviet actions against US products, under measures in force since the thirties, culminating in the Jackson-Vanik amendment of 1974 denying the Soviet Union most-favored-nation treatment until it relaxed emigration laws.

3

A Fresh Vision:
The Council of Europe

The OEEC had specific and fairly narrow objectives: to promote and coordinate the economic rebirth of a war-torn continent. The Council of Europe enjoys the distinction of being the first and today the largest of the purely European political organizations. Its broad statute provides an umbrella for European parliamentary democracy, a meeting point for countries respecting human rights and fundamental freedoms. Thus, although not specifically designed as a "western" body, for forty years it restricted its membership to western Europe. Indeed, Spain and Portugal and, at one stage, Greece were excluded from membership as long as their regimes were undemocratic.

It appeared at one time that the growing membership of the European Community, with the greater institutional powers vested in the European Commission, would overshadow and even render superfluous its mother institution, the Council of Europe. There was a temptation among Community bureaucrats to "re-invent the wheel" with respect to the social, legal and environmental achievements of the Council of Europe. Ultimately, however, it became clear that the somewhat ponderous yet less threatening methods of the latter were well-suited to the vision and needs of certain countries which for economic or political reasons could not aspire to EEC membership in the foreseeable future. In certain areas, moreover, particularly human rights and cultural cooperation, the Council of Europe's leadership remains strong and unique. In 1989, as the Council of Europe celebrated the fortieth anniversary of its creation and dominoes fell in the East, its mission appeared triumphantly confirmed: it provided a gateway for the renascent democracies of Czechoslovakia, Hungary and other European nations to join a new and broader Europe. President Gorbachev selected the Parliamentary Assembly of the Council of Europe to present his concept of a "common European home" to the western alliance. He could not have done so in NATO, or in WEU, a politico-military body, nor yet in the EEC, with its supranational decision-making machinery and its emphasis on economic issues. The Council of Europe was the natural choice:

> Europeans can meet the challenges of the century only by pooling their efforts. We are convinced that they need one Europe-peaceful and democratic, a Europe which preserves all of its diverse features and which abides by common, humane ideals, a prospering Europe which extends a hand to the rest of the world and which confidently marches into the future. We see our own future in such a Europe. Perestroika with its goal of fundamentally renewing Soviet society also predetermines our policy aimed at the development

of Europe exactly in this direction. Perestroika is altering our country, leading it to new frontiers. This process will continue, becoming deeper and changing Soviet society in all respects — economically, socially, politically and culturally, in all internal affairs and in human relations.[1]

Today, although the Soviet Union is no more, Czechoslovakia, Hungary, Poland and Bulgaria are full members; they will soon be joined by the Baltic States and Slovenia. CIS states, including those of Russia, attend the Parliamentary Assembly with "special guest" status.

Functionalists and federalists

When on May 5, 1949, the ten charter members signed in London the convention establishing the Council of Europe, they fashioned a compromise between two divergent if not opposing concepts of European cooperation. Visionaries such as Jean Monnet — who came to be known as the Father of Europe — and Alcide de Gasperi inspired France, Italy and the Low Countries (Belgium, Luxembourg, Netherlands) to seek the political union evoked in Winston Churchill's Zurich speech of September 19, 1946 — "a kind of United States of Europe". This "federalist" tendency was characterized by the creation of a parliamentary assembly. Although composed of delegations from national parliaments (rather than directly elected members) and denied decision-making power, the Consultative Assembly (now called the Parliamentary Assembly) was nevertheless the first international "parliament". In this it differed from the assemblies of the League of Nations, between the two world wars, and the United Nations, since 1948, which were set up with delegations nominated by governments. The distinction is much more than symbolic. The parliamentary process speaks for all tendencies and exercizes control over government. The shift from diplomatic concertation to supranational union is inconceivable without the parliamentary arm.

The "functionalist" tendency, a more conservative concept led by Britain and neutral countries such as Sweden, fought to further European cooperation along traditional diplomatic lines rather than to create a truly supranational organism. Then, as still today, the issue was sovereignty. (It is now more readily conceded, however, that sovereignty is not absolute and may be shared or sub-divided; and that shared decision-making may give access to greater power than sovereignty exercized in ineffective isolation). However, the functionalist viewpoint of the time finds its expression in the Council of Europe statutes not only in the limitations set upon the authority of the Assembly but, above all, in the creation of a Committee of Ministers (with parallel ambassadorial deputies) whose major decisions require unanimous consent.

Did a diplomatic conference atop an unelected parliament amount to more than a hill of beans? Paradoxically, the Council of Europe's lack of strong decision-making authority has proved a strength as well as a weakness. Despite, but also because of its limited powers, the Council of Europe has a remarkable list of achievements to its credit. By the end of 1991 it had negotiated 142 international agreements in a vast range of social, cultural and legal fields. Moreover, its membership had grown from ten to twenty-seven countries.[2]

Committee of Ministers

The members of the Committee of Ministers are the foreign ministers of the member states of the Council of Europe. The Committee provides an instrument for the multilateral discussion of subjects of European interest. Through proposals to member governments it responds to the recommendations of the Parliamentary Assembly and numerous committees of experts.

Ministers meet twice yearly, usually in Strasbourg, to assess their program of European cooperation and to issue directives for the Council's work. Chairmanship of the Council rotates every six months. Between sessions at full ministerial level the work of the Committee is carried forward by the Ministers' Deputies who, as in the case of the OECD, are permanent representatives accredited like ambassadors to the organization. The Deputies meet monthly for two or three days. The Deputies are not the only diplomats in Strasbourg. Like other international organizations the Council of Europe enjoys extra-territorial status for its buildings and consular or diplomatic status for its staff of some nine hundred employees. The Council even issues its own postage stamps. There are several consulates in Strasbourg. In addition to serving US citizens, the US Consul closely follows Council of Europe activities.

Within the Committee of Ministers political decisions require unanimous consent. However the power of veto is almost never used since countries which do not wish to participate in an activity are not constrained to do so. Budgetary decisions require a two-thirds majority and procedural matters a simple majority. Unlike the EEC, where there is a system of weighted voting based roughly on population, each member government of the Council of Europe has one vote.

In addition to the institutional meetings of the foreign ministers and their deputies, conferences of ministers in various specialized fields are held at regular intervals under Council of Europe auspices. These include education, justice, social security, family matters, culture, the environment and sport.

Parliamentary Assembly

As we have seen, the members of the Parliamentary Assembly are nominated by national parliaments. As such they represent all political tendencies and not government policies alone. The Assembly thereby lays claim to being the "European conscience".

Although devoid of legislative powers, the Assembly provides the main impetus for Council of Europe actions. Its recommendations have launched numerous programs to strengthen European unity, including human rights and the harmonization of laws, education and culture, public health, youth and sport, social matters, municipal and regional issues and environmental protection. Moreover, with the assistance of its extremely able secretariat the Assembly keeps a careful watch on how national governments and parliaments implement Council of Europe recommendations. Assembly members are their own best lobbyists "back home"!

The number of each country's representatives in the Assembly varies in relation to population. Thus Liechtenstein has two seats whereas the four largest countries, France, Italy, the Federal Republic of Germany and the United Kingdom, have eighteen each.

The representatives to the Parliamentary Assembly, nearly two hundred in number, have formed six political groups based on political convictions rather than country of origin. The Assembly meets in plenary sessions lasting a week or ten days three times a year. Its debates are prepared by a number of specialized committees drawn from its members. Members unable to attend a session or committee meeting may be represented by official substitutes. In addition to adopting recommendations to the Committee of Ministers, the Assembly issues an opinion on the intergovernmental program of work before its final adoption. The Assembly also elects the judges of the European Court of Human Rights.

In September 1990 the Assembly hosted a meeting of parliamentarians from CSCE countries as a possible forerunner to creating a parliamentary organ for that intergovernmental body.

Activities of the Council of Europe

Each year the Committee of Ministers adopts a Program of Work to be implemented by its committees of experts. Despite their impressive, even astonishing diversity, the intergovernmental activities of the organization may be summarized in nine broad fields:

- Human rights and fundamental freedoms
- Legislation and the harmonization of laws
- Protecting the natural and architectural heritage of Europe
- Education, culture and sport
- Youth activities
- Public health
- Social security and crime prevention
- Local and regional governments
- Media in a democratic society

Assembly deliberations and ministerial discussions are naturally not limited to these topics. The regular parliamentary debates on political and economic issues enable Assembly members to consider relations between "greater Europe" and the European Economic Community, North America and the third world.

Furthermore, the Council of Europe was founded as the Cold War developed; in the four decades since that time the situation in Eastern Europe has never been overlooked. Today the Council of Europe is acquiring special significance in this regard. Not every country can join or be accepted into the European Economic Community. The Council of Europe's wide membership, the breadth of its activities and its consensual decision-making procedures provide a flexibility which is of major political significance in Europe today. The House of Europe in Strasbourg furnishes the roof for a common democratic European home. Indeed, the Council of Europe is affirming cultural identity in an increasingly technological world. Its democratic ideals are reaching beyond continental borders to serve as a focal point for democracies across the globe.

The Committee of Ministers and the Parliamentary Assembly are assisted by a secretariat of some 900 international officials, sworn to serve the organization and not their countries of origin. The current Secretary General is Catherine Lalumière (France), the Deputy Secretary General Gaetano Adinolfi (Italy) and the Clerk of the Assembly Heinrich Klebes (Austria).

Human rights and fundamental freedoms

Nowhere is this claim of setting a standard for international behavior more justified than with respect to human rights. Not by accident was the European Convention on Human Rights the first international instrument proposed by the Assembly at its inaugural session in 1949 and adopted by member governments. (It has since been expanded by nine additions, known as protocols). Not by chance did the Convention provide for a Commission and a Court to make individual rights effective against abuse of power by the governments themselves. This is the one area where the Council of Europe does enjoy the power to bind governments.

No government, no constitution, however democratic, is immune from "blind spots". Thus, in May 1991, the UK was constrained to transfer decisions on the early release of offenders from the Home Secretary (minister of justice) to the Parole Board, the European Court of Human Rights having ruled that decisions relating to punishment must be taken by a judicial body and not by the government. "The Council of Europe", declared the eminent French jurist, René Cassin, who was the first judge to preside over the European Court of Human Rights, "sets the standards for the whole world where the protection of human rights is concerned; it is the ideal organization for cooperation in this field".

The basic rights and freedoms covered by the convention, which have been further defined and extended on a number of occasions,[3] are protected by a carefully calibrated mechanism which gives full consideration to laws and legal procedures on the national level. Any individual—not necessarily a citizen— under the jurisdiction of a member government may lodge an appeal with the Council of Europe. Appeals are first considered by the European Commission of Human Rights, which sets up a sub-commission to consider whether the appeal is covered by one of the rights or freedoms included in the convention and its protocols; whether the appellant has exhausted all the remedies—

appeals procedures—available at national level; and whether there is a *prima facie* basis for the complaint.

If the Commission concurs with a positive finding by its sub-commission it organizes a hearing of the parties. The Commission must then decide whether to reject the application or to seek a friendly settlement.

If the application is not rejected and no friendly settlement achieved, the Commission brings a case before the European Court of Human Rights. States which accept the jurisdiction of the Court bind themselves to implement its findings. In this limited but significant respect, therefore, the Council of Europe is indeed vested with supranational authority. There have been over 13,000 individual petitions since 1950. A number of friendly settlements have been reached and the European Court has rendered over fifty judgments.

In 1991 the Commission received 1,648 individual petitions from citizens claiming to have exhausted national remedies. The rising number of applications does not imply that human rights are less respected in member countries but rather that the right of individual petition is becoming better known. (France led the way in 1991, with 400 petitions, due in part to the strict application of laws limiting political asylum).

The Council of Europe's record may be considered less glorious with respect to cases brought by one government against another; or when a member government's entire policy, rather than the application of law in a particular case, is under scrutiny. A blind eye was turned on the massive repatriation of Albanians by Italy and on Turkish operations against Anatolian Kurds. The Commission's report on Cyprus has been awaiting action since 1979.

Of course, this does not prevent the Council of Europe from laying down severe human rights requirements for potential new members. Extension of membership will depend in large measure on how Latvia treats its 48% of minorities; on whether regional governors will continue to be able to oust elected mayors in Romania... Will it suffice that such countries hold free elections? Before becoming a member Bulgaria provided legal guarantees for its Turcic and Islamic minorities. No less may be expected of former Yugoslav states. The Assembly at least, if not the Committee of Ministers, is watching carefully, as shown by the delay imposed on Polish entry in 1990.

The Council of Europe continues to extend its human rights activities. In addition to imposing its own and national procedures for safeguarding human rights it is exploring areas of potential abuse arising from contemporary society, such as conscientious objection, sexual exploitation and scientific and technical progress in medicine and biology. The protective mechanism is in place and has proved its worth; the rights covered evolve with society itself.

The human rights achievements of the Council of Europe, and in particular the judgments of the Court, have changed national legislation and contributed to the harmonization of laws in Europe. The current president of the Commission is Carl Aage Nrgaard of Denmark. The president of the Court is Rolv Ryssdal of Norway.

It is easy to dismiss human rights matters as concerning only a few; and as being far removed from the "real stuff" of politics. Yet the few who do have recourse to the procedure protect the rights and freedoms of those who find no need to do so. Without human rights there can be no democracy. Without the right to life and liberty, without freedom of expression and assembly, without majorities and minorities conjoined in a free society, the real stuff of politics, economics and the social contract would find no space to move or grow. Human rights and fundamental freedoms are the oxygen of democracy and even of economic development. As the Soviet Union discovered too late, where there is no free voice there is no glasnost; without glasnost there can be no perestroika. Freedom finds its own justification in the human spirit; but it is also good for business!

Legislation for Europe's future

The European Committee on Legal Cooperation supervises the program for international, civil, administrative and commercial law. The program seeks to harmonize the legislations of member countries and to bring them up to date, to make judicial procedures more simple and efficient and to seek common solutions to legal and ethical problems arising out of scientific and technical progress.

The conventions and agreements drawn up by the Council of Europe and ratified by member states represent an important body of "European laws" and a major contribution to unification. In recent years the Council of Europe has negotiated conventions to fight crime, to compensate its victims and to define territorial asylum. Such measures are essential as barriers to the free movement of people, goods, services and capital are reduced. A concerted approach to modernizing national law has been adopted with respect to family laws and the dual nationality of married couples and their children.

In addition, legal gaps have been filled where no regulations existed because national legislation had failed to keep pace with developments in society. Among the most important of these is computer technology. In 1981, for example, the Convention for the Protection of Individuals with regard to the automatic processing of personal data was opened for signature. This was followed in 1989 by a Convention on insider trading. There have been a number of agreements on television programming, culminating in the European Convention on transfrontier television, completed in 1989.

Other areas of cooperation include foreign liabilities, information on foreign law, consular functions, bearer securities, state immunity, motorists' liability, adoption nationality, animal protection, child custody, bankruptcy and the legal status of non-governmental organizations. Thus, although the Council of Europe has no power to make European law, a European jurisprudence is in fact emerging from the relentless harmonization of national laws, completed by international conventions. [4]

The European environment

Long before the environment became a political issue or "ecology" had left the dictionary for dinner-table discussion, the Council of Europe was already drawing attention to the fact that nature and its conservation know no frontiers. Similarly, the architectural treasures of Europe were regarded as a common heritage demanding joint action. To save the Camargue and its flamingos in the Rhone delta from the twin threats of urban blight and rice-field desalination or the city of Venice from sinking beneath its lagoon is to exercise a European, indeed a world responsibility.

Both the Parliamentary Assembly and the governmental experts in the steering Committee for the Conservation and Management of the Environment and Natural Habitats have worked to protect fauna, flora and landscape and, in conjunction with the International Union for the Conservation of Nature and the World Wildlife Fund, to extend protective measures beyond Europe. The Convention on the conservation of European wildlife and natural habitats protects rare and endangered animal and plant species, thereby safeguarding the genetic heritage of countries concerned.[5] Inventories have been made of natural habitats. Since 1982 this convention has protected over two hundred species. The European Diploma is awarded for areas both well-managed and of particular importance for the international natural heritage. The Committee also supervises a network of biogenetic reserves. It has promoted action to fight soil, water and air pollution. The European Information Centre for Nature Conservation (NATUROPA) fosters public awareness of the issues. A more detailed analysis of the Council of Europe's conservation program is made in Part IV, Chapter 2.

The Council of Europe has also sought to conserve the continent's architectural heritage and to safeguard the sources of collective memory. 1975 was declared European Architectural Heritage Year. The Steering Committee for Integrated Conservation of the Historic Heritage maintains contact between authorities in charge of historic buildings and encourages public interest. A third conference of ministers responsible for conservation of the architectural heritage was held in 1990/91. A Convention for the Conservation of the Architectural Heritage of Europe entered into force in 1987. In 1987-1988 a Campaign for the Countryside sought to reconcile development with conservation. A particularly original venture is the European Centre for Training Craftsmen, which runs specialized courses. A European network of heritage trades (stonecutters, carpenters, plasterers, etc.) has been set up to coordinate the activities of training centers designed to preserve traditional skills.

Education and culture

The promoters of European unification realised in the earliest days that a sense of common cultural identity must underlie political and economic initiatives. This does not imply pursuit of a stultifying homogeneity but, on the contrary, the realisation that Europe's rich cultural diversity must be preserved through common values and joint responsibility. It is not surprising therefore that the Council of Europe's cultural program is broad and dynamic.

Opened for signature in 1954, the European Cultural Convention provides the basis for cooperation in education, culture, youth programs and sport.

This convention may be adhered to by non-member states who then become full partners in the cultural cooperation program. The cultural convention has provided a "stepping stone" to countries such as Finland, Portugal and Spain, until such time as they were willing or able to become full members of the Council of Europe. Early in the process of political transformation in Eastern Europe, Poland and Hungary adhered to the convention. The Holy See and Yugoslavia also signed the convention. The Council for Cultural Cooperation (CDCC formerly the CCC), set up in 1962, is the instrument for implementing the convention. It enjoys a certain autonomy from direct governmental control in allocating financial resources from the Cultural Fund.

The CDCC has sought to strengthen awareness in the European public of its common heritage through art exhibitions, perhaps the most widely acclaimed of which was on the Romantic movement. Recent exhibitions have included "The Portuguese discoveries and Renaissance Europe" and, coinciding with the 1989 bicentennial, "The French Revolution and Europe". A sense of cultural identity is fostered through study of cultural routes such as medieval pilgrimages, the silk routes and the baroque routes. Cultural research networks and data banks have been set up. Equally important, however, are the steps taken to preserve cultural diversity through cultural exchanges, interlibrary cooperation, action to promote reading, poetry and translation and the preservation of minority languages.

In its work for schools the CDCC has promoted exchange of research findings and documentation on teacher-training methods. It has also developed human rights education, media education and intercultural education. Perhaps its most significant contribution has been made in the development of tiered objectives, known as threshold levels, in modern language instruction. This system is available in twelve languages and has greatly influenced the reform of national curricula.

Action with respect to adult education has featured steps to combat illiteracy and unemployment and to make the most of leisure time, such as early retirement.

In higher education the CDCC has facilitated the free movement of academic staff and research workers and the international recognition of qualifications for university admission and of diplomas and doctorates. In science, important work has been done on the prevention of national and technological disasters.

The Council of Europe's youth program is designed to prepare young people to be active citizens in their own country and at the international level. The European Youth Centre in Strasbourg is a forum for meetings and courses. Some 14000 youth leaders pass through the Centre each year. Major themes of the Youth Centre's work include unemployment, women's rights, peace and disarmament and protection of the environment. The European Youth Foundation provides organizations with funds for international programming. The projects sponsored have involved some 90,000 young people from over forty countries. Other activities include the European Schools Day essay competition and the European Documentation and Information System in Education (EUDISED). The CDCC secretariat also services the biennial standing conference of European ministers of education and the triennial conference of ministers responsible for cultural affairs.   There is close cooperation with the EC and UNESCO on education and culture.

A sport for every European

The task of the Council of Europe is fundamental yet frequently unspectacular.   In catering to the needs of nearly thirty governments and millions of Europeans it is easy to be shallow and impractical. The Council relies heavily not only on governments but also on private bodies for implementation of its findings and recommendations. Nowhere is this more true than in sports. The Council does not seek to displace sports federations, much less the Olympic movement. Leaving champions and championships to more specialized agencies, the CDCC has sought to improve opportunities for sports activities for the ordinary European citizen, to safeguard sporting values and to address the problems of wider participation. The CDCC has had a sports program since its inception; in 1977 this "came of age" with creation of the Committee for the Development of Sport. The "Sport for All" charter (1975) drew attention to the need for regular exercise. Meetings of sports administrators and architects have addressed the practical issue of providing low cost facilities, such as swimming pools. The role of sport in society has been addressed in its medical, political, ethical, educational and (excessive) commercial aspects.

The Committee prepares the conference of European ministers responsible for sport. In 1984 the conference adopted an Anti-Doping Charter for Sport (which led to a European convention in 1989) and in 1985 a convention was approved to prevent violence at sports events, such as the Brussels football stadium tragedy in 1985. A set of physical fitness tests has been devised for children and adolescents. The CCC's earliest publications included a handbook on sports administrations and *Training the Trainer*, a one-hundred hour program for youth leaders to develop skills in teaching physical fitness and sport.

The CDCC would do well to review some of its early publications, many of which have not lost their relevance for new member countries, with a view to reissuing or reprinting them.

Public health

In public health, the Council of Europe has sought to harmonize national health policies and to promote disease prevention and education. For many years it has worked patiently, product by product, on a European Pharmacopoeia, setting standards of quality and safety for medicines. Many countries have adopted these standards in their national legislation.

Blood transfusion centers in various countries are grouped in a European network. A frozen blood bank has been set up in Amsterdam for rare blood groups. In the organ transplant field techniques for tissue-typing are being harmonized.

Other areas of cooperation include drug and drug trafficking (the Pompidou Group of nineteen states),[6] the fight against AIDS, the rehabilitation of disabled persons.

There is also extensive cooperation in the administrative area. This includes introduction of standard health regulations, common standards for medical care, control of hospital expenditure, use of pesticides and prevention of the contamination of foodstuffs, food additives and cosmetics.

Social action

In the social field the Council of Europe has achieved equal treatment for nationals of member states and of host countries. This is of great importance in promoting the free movement of citizens in a unified European society.

The most important instrument for this cooperation is the European Social Charter of 1961. In an action parallel to that on human rights, it safeguards social prerogatives such as the right to work, the right to a decent wage, to social security, vocational training, collective bargaining and to strike. The rights of migrant workers are also guaranteed. A recent protocol covers equality of the sexes in the workplace and protection for old people.

An October 21 1991 ministers of labor and social affairs met in Turin to mark the 30th anniversary of the signing of the Social Charter and to adapt it to the needs of eastern Europe's emerging democracies. A new protocol was signed giving employers, unions and non-governmental organizations a greater role in developing social laws. Hungary and Czechoslovakia signed the charter a few days later and Poland followed in November.

The European Code of Social Security sets minimum benefit levels for maternity, sickness, invalidity and unemployment, whereas the European convention on social security ensures equal treatment for nationals of all contracting parties and guarantees transfer of benefits and maintenance of accrued welfare rights. The convention on the legal status of migrant workers and refugees, which entered into force in 1989, ensures for legally resident nationals of other member states the same living and working conditions as those enjoyed by citizens of the host country. The convention also upholds the principle of the right to family reunion, which means that close relatives must be admitted to join a legally established individual. A social development fund finances projects for the social and economic reintegration of jobless and homeless people and those who lack work skills. Loans for social centers, housing and projects in public health and education exceed ten million dollars. With respect to professional development and research, the Council operates a fellowship program for social service personnel and promotes comparative studies in social welfare and labor issues.

These extensive and practical projects, which have a direct impact on the lives of many European citizens, are coordinated by special conferences of ministers of social affairs.

Population

The European Population Committee, an intergovernmental body of scientists and government officials engaged in demography, monitors and analyses population trends in member states and informs governments and the public of developments that may require political action. It compiles an annual review of demographic developments and publishes the results of studies of particular aspects of population. These include the implications of declining fertility, the changing age structure of European populations, parental responsibilities, and the demographic consequences for Europe of the increase in world population. Seminars and conferences are held; a Population Conference took place in 1992.

Municipalities and regions

It is a common misconception that European unity necessarily implies centralisation and an overbearing "curocracy". In many ways, however, by respecting minorities and regional differences and fostering appreciation of cultural diversity, unification fosters decentralization and thereby enhances democracy. One of the Council of Europe's most successful initiatives in this regard is the Standing Conference of Local and Regional Authorities. This assembly of mayors and regional representatives meets every year to discuss the working of democracy at municipal and regional levels.

The Council of Europe did not await the Maastricht Treaty of Union to give subsidiarity a place in European cooperation. Just as in the United States governors and mayors may agree about the problems of dealing with federal authorities, so in Europe locally elected officials from various countries may find themselves of like mind with regard to their relations with national governments. The European Charter of local self-government (1985) lays down the constitutional principles and legal basis for government below the national level and suggests administrative procedures. For convinced "Europeans" it is no paradox that local officials unite to protect their autonomy.

The Europe Prize honors municipalities for exceptional service to European understanding. Council of Europe action has enhanced the role of local authorities and reduced imbalances between regions. Further, it has facilitated the integration of immigrant communities. A convention on transfrontier cooperation facilitates contacts between frontier municipalities and regions. In recent years, transfrontier cooperation among local and regional authorities has produced results in the environmental field, such as the treatment of waste, and in joint rescue operations in response to catastrophes.

The media in a democratic society

In the European democracies, as in all democratic countries, the activities of governments, parliamentarians and public servants depend ultimately on citizen approval. The national mindset dies hard: international cooperation implies compromise as well as material advantage and, in some cases, the sacrifice of short-term benefit for long-term gains. The free exchange of information and culture is therefore not merely a fundamental right but an essential ingredient of success in European cooperation.

In 1982 the Committee of Ministers adopted a Declaration of freedom of expression and information which forms the basis for the Council of Europe's mass media activities. The agency's action seeks to safeguard freedom of expression and to broaden its scope; to adapt the legal system to technical progress; and to promote the cultural content of programs. Activities are developed and coordinated by the Steering Committee on the Mass Media (SCMM).

While a number of agreements have already been completed, such as the convention on transfrontier television (1989), this is a rapidly evolving sector. Work is in progress, in both the public and private sectors of broadcasting, on violence in the media, use of satellites, cable networks, technical standards for recording and the training of technicians.

Legal aspects of European media cooperation include the right to privacy and copyright. A convention to combat unauthorized private broadcasting from outside national territories (ships at sea) was completed in 1965.

The Council of Europe's press and information service publishes a quarterly review, *Forum*, in English, French, German and Italian.

More than ever, a common European home

The unification process in Europe is not always rapid, much less dramatic. Celebrating its fortieth anniversary in 1989, the Council of Europe was nevertheless still attracting new members. Between OECD, EEC and EFTA, this mother of European intergovernmental organizations was once in danger of being overtaken by events. Today, it is recognized for its essential contribution to the warp and woof of European integration, a record of practical achievement which draws newly democratized nations to the House of Europe. This process is by no means complete. In July, 1992, Catherine Lalumière spent a week "prospecting" in Georgia and the Turcic-speaking former Soviet republics. Relations already exist with the Ukraine and Russia. By the end of the millennium the Council of Europe will doubtless have stretched her embrace beyond the eastern confines of Europe itself. In the Council of Europe Gorbachev's "common European home" already exists. It remains open, subject only to the "entrance fee" of a free society, to countries seeking to add new rooms to the mansion.[7]

Notes

1 Address to Parliamentary Assembly, July 6, 1989.

2 The 27 Council of Europe member states: Austria, Belgium, Bulgaria, Czechoslovakia, Cyprus, Denmark, Finland, France, Federal Republic of Germany, Greece, Hungary, Iceland, Ireland, Italy, Liechtenstein, Luxembourg, Malta, Netherlands, Norway, Poland, Portugal, San Marino, Sweden, Switzerland, Turkey, United Kingdom. The Holy See, Russia and Yugoslavia participate fully in the Council for Cultural Cooperation. Israel has observer status, European CIS states and Yugoslavia "special guest" status in the Parliamentary Assembly. Listing as of July 1992.

3 See, for instance, the Protocol of 1963.

4 Unlike the European Community, the Council of Europe does not issue directives (except for the judgments of the ECHR) or establish "Council law". Prompted by two "consciences", the Assembly and the Secretariat, the Committee of Ministers does however exercize a limited judicial oversight in following the implementation of its recommendations and conventions on the national level and seeking explanations of non-compliance. Moreover, Assembly members ask probing questions in their own parliaments. Although not coercive, these procedures have produced significant results.

5 While naturalists have long deplored the extinction of species, of which the lamented dodo is offered as the archetype, only in recent years have scientists awakened to the dangers of narrowing the earth's genetic pool in terms of ecological balance, the weakening of bloodstock and the loss of source material for medical remedies.

6 A pilot project to prevent young people from taking drugs is being carried out in eleven European schools. The scheme is run jointly with the World Health Organization and the EEC. See also Assembly Recommendation 1116 on AIDS and human rights (September 29, 1989).

7 It should be noted that some countries like Malta and San Marino and soon possibly Andorra are not represented in any group other than the Council of Europe and CSCE. Liechtenstein is represented in EFTA by Switzerland but the Council of Europe is the only organization in which it has direct membership. The Council of Europe's "umbrella function" is one of its most important attributes. For further information about the Council of Europe write to BP 431, R6 - 67006 Strasbourg Cedex, France; or telephone (88) 61.49.61; telex 870943; fax (88) 36.70.57.

4

The Politics of Armies:
Western European Union

We saw in Part II that Western European Union (WEU) was established in 1955 as a result of the failure of the European Defence Community (EDC). It is no surprise, therefore, that its structures and powers, like those of the Council of Europe (which in some respects served as a model), are the result of a compromise.

> France was forced to agree to WEU by fear of isolation, Germany impelled to it by the promise of sovereignty. WEU was the expedient whereby the Federal Republic at length regained its sovereignty on the one hand and accepted limitations on its rearmament on the other.[1]

When WEU was created, many considered that its main virtue was that the United Kingdom was a full member, since she had declined to joint the EDC and thereby contributed to the latter's defeat in the French parliament. At that time the United Kingdom was certainly not prepared to contemplate joining an organization with supranational powers. Today, of course, with the United Kingdom a full member of the European Community, the situation is different; the Maastricht Treaty of Union provides for WEU's assimilation into the Community.[2]

Like the Council of Europe, WEU has two main organs, a Council of Ministers and a parliamentary assembly. In order to provide continuity of insight and to avoid unnecessary duplication, the members of the parliamentary assembly are drawn from the respective national delegations to the Parliamentary Assembly of the Council of Europe.

Council of Ministers

The treaty provides that the WEU Council of Ministers "shall be organized as to be able to exercise its functions continuously". This is only natural for a defense agency. It implies both that governments may be represented at the level and in the manner they wish and, on the other hand, that the Council may meet at the level of permanent representatives. In this way it is possible to provide both for day-to-day continuity and for high-level, ministerial meetings when necessary.

For some thirty years the ministerial-level meetings were composed of foreign ministers, usually convened twice a year. As part of the reactivation proposals of 1984, and in response to the frequent urgings of the Parliamentary Assembly, the Council now brings together both foreign ministers and ministers of defense. This means that military coordination is given equal consideration with political cooperation.

It is important to understand why some member countries were reluctant to nominate defense ministers to Council meetings. It is normal for foreign ministers to represent their governments in international affairs: such is their function. Defense, however, may be seen as the ultimate and most sensitive repository of national sovereignty.

Notwithstanding the continuing existence of NATO and the unfaltering commitment of both its North American and European members, political changes in Europe have led Western European countries to acquire an increased sense of responsibility for organizing and funding their own defense.[3] Far from encountering the hostility of the United States, this position was actively fostered by the Reagan administration, on account of the thawing of relations with the Soviet Union and with an eye to the cost of European defense to the American taxpayer.

The presidency of the Council is exercized by each member state in turn, for a period of one year. In principle, meetings are held in the country holding the presidency.

Permanent Council

Like the committee of Ministers' Deputies of the Council of Europe, the Permanent Council meets at the seat of the organization, in this case Grosvenor Place, in London (moved to Brussels by a decision taken at the Maastricht summit in December 1991). As its name implies, the Permanent Council is a standing substitute for the Council of Ministers itself. Chaired by the Secretary General of WEU, it is composed not of special representatives but of ambassadors of member countries to the United Kingdom or, as the official style goes, the Court of St. James. The United Kingdom representative is a senior official of the Foreign Office. These arrangements will of course be updated with the move to Brussels. When necessary, and in particular, to prepare ministerial meetings, the Permanent Council is expanded to include the political directors of foreign ministers and their defense ministry counterparts. This body is called the Enlarged Permanent Council. Since it reviews the work of the organization, finalizes reports and prepares ministerial agendas, the Permanent Council fulfills the requirement of the modified Brussels Treaty that the Council of Ministers must be able to exercize its functions continuously.

In addition to these regular meetings of the Council at ministerial and deputy level, the treaty provides in Article VIII that any member government may require immediate convening of the Council in order to permit governments "to consult with regard to any situation which may constitute a threat to peace or a danger to economic stability". This was done for the first time in August 1987 in the Persian Gulf crisis (Iraq-Iran war), inasmuch as the treaty does not limit events to Europe but provides for action "in whatever area this threat should arise". On the occasion in question, the Council organized a joint minesweeping force. In July 1992, during the CSCE summit in Helsinki, the Council met to coordinate its role in the marine blockade of Yugoslavia and protection of humanitarian supplies to Bosnia-Herzegovina.

Working groups

The Permanent Council is assisted by several working groups.

The Special Working Group, consisting of representatives of foreign affairs and defense ministries, undertakes political studies on European security interests. The group's work has included the follow-up to the Conference on Security and Cooperation in Europe, disarmament negotiations and verification, the defense implications of the European single market after 1992. The group follows events in other parts of the world which may affect European security interests. A standing sub-group studies Mediterranean issues.

The second major advisory body of the Permanent Council is the Defence Representatives Group, also composed of members drawn from both foreign and defense ministries. Its primary task is to follow the military aspects of European security.

Subsidiary organs of the Council

On November 13, 1989, the WEU Council of Ministers set up an institute for advanced security studies in order to promote a European security identity. Its main tasks are to carry out research; to help institutes in member countries to promote greater awareness of security issues; to organize meetings with institutes in non-member countries, particularly those in (now former) Warsaw Pact countries – a ground-breaking development at the time; to establish and maintain a data bank on national defense efforts and European security; finally, to contribute to academic work on these topics. The WEU parliamentary assembly may also assign work to the institute. The institute, which has a director and five permanent experts, has been operational since July 1, 1990 and is provisionally located in Paris. [4]

The Agency for the Control of Armaments (ACA) was set up to provide the Council with a guarantee that member states respect their commitments in conventional, atomic, biological and chemical arms. As such it was the first arms control agency freely accepted among states with equal rights. Commitments assumed by member countries are of several kinds. For the forces assigned to NATO, the seven countries committed themselves not to exceed the peacetime levels established by the EDC treaty of May 27, 1952 and four divisions and a tactical air force for the United Kingdom. The seven countries also accepted limits on weapons production. The Federal Republic of Germany undertook not to manufacture atomic, biological and chemical weapons and certain other armaments. The limits imposed on the Federal Republic were abolished by the ministers in June, 1984. In October, the Council decided to terminate limitation and control of conventional armaments with effect from January 1, 1986. The ACA was reorganized and its staff reduced, although is still had to verify levels of non-conventional weapons. For the latter the Agency was to continue to inspect establishments believed to be capable of producing non-conventional, i.e. atomic, biological and chemical (A/B/C) weapons.

Dismal record

In practice, this power of inspection for ABC weapons proved more theoretical than real. On December 14, 1957, the member states signed a convention designed to protect private interests which might be harmed during an inspection. This convention, which provided for a procedure of appeal to an international tribunal, was never ratified by France. Consequently, verifications became the subject of agreement rather than due process of international law. Morcover, in regard to A and B weapons the Agency was unable to conduct controls, although for biological weapons a list of weapons subject to control was drawn up. In the case of chemical weapons, production in member countries has never gone beyond the experimental stage. Hence the Council has not had to fix the level of stocks member countries are authorized to hold. If the US and CIS countries agree both to ban and to destroy chemical weapons altogether it is highly probable that WEU countries will follow suit.

The Agency reports yearly to the Council. It must also report immediately any manufacture of armaments contrary to the commitments of a member government. In 1988 the ACA also followed the work of the Geneva conference on disarmament. The ACA's dismal record serves to bring home the point that even among close allies, governments are most reluctant to renounce any significant measure of sovereignty with respect to security matters.

The WEU Assembly

As we have seen in Part II, the failure of the European Defence Community was linked to its supranational character. It was normal therefore, that WEU should be an intergovernmental body, in which member states retain sovereignty.

Nevertheless, the "progressive" Europeans, advocates of what was called at the time the "European idea" as a prelude to political, even federal union, wished to have the same type of democratic representative institutions as in the national framework. They were strongly of the opinion that, in accordance with the principles of parliamentary democracy, European organizations with political responsibilities should include a representative parliamentary body to provide balance and monitor action by the governmental arm. Hence, a parliamentary assembly was set up under the modified Brussels Treaty of 1954. To satisfy the traditionalists, led by Britain, however, direct election of assembly members by universal suffrage remained out of the question. The signatory countries therefore agreed that the assembly would be formed of members of their national parliaments. To avoid complications, and duplications, they further agreed that their national delegations to the Council of Europe assembly should also serve in the WEU assembly.[5] The WEU Assembly meets twice yearly in plenary sessions in the chambers of the French Economic and Social Council in Paris. It has also held sessions in Bonn, Brussels, London and Rome. The Assembly's permanent seat and secretariat is at 43, avenue du President Wilson, Paris, XVIe. Thus, WEU's headquarters remain divided between France and the United Kingdom until such time as Ministerial Council and Secretariat are transferred to Brussels under the Maastricht agreements.

Parliamentary delegations are represented as follows:

Belgium	7	Luxembourg	3
France	18	Netherlands	7
Federal Republic		Portugal	7
of Germany	18	Spain	12
Italy	18	United Kingdom	18

The Assembly is composed of 108 representatives and a like number of substitues who sit, speak and vote when representatives are absent. Appointees must be drawn from national parliaments and include representatives of both government and opposition parties.

The Assembly, which defines its own powers, states in Article I of its charter that it may deliberate on any matter arising out of the modified Brussels Treaty. As the only official international parliamentary assembly with competence for defense questions, it pays special attention to matters of security but also addresses political issues. On occasion, the Assembly has extended its debates to both civil and military aspects of technological and scientific cooperation. The ministerial Council responds to its recommendations and may, where appropriate, transmit them to the North Atlantic Council, the ministerial arm of NATO.

In his speech to the Assembly at its first session on July 5, 1955, Chairman-in-Office Paul-Henri Spaak of Belgium stressed that the Assembly was intended to enjoy considerable freedom. The ministerial Council "relied upon the experience and wisdom" of the Assembly, which was to be independent of all other assemblies. In response to this invitation the Assembly drew up its own Charter and organizational structure.[6]

Assembly committees

The Assembly set up two steering bodies, the Bureau and the Presidential Committee and a number of specialized committees.

The Bureau is composed of the President and eight elected vice-presidents, one for each of the nine member countries. The Presidential Committee consists of the President, vice-presidents, chairpersons of committees and former presidents who are still members of the Assembly. The chairpersons of political groups are usually also invited to meetings of the Presidential Committee.

The Presidential Committee organizes the Assembly's business, acts on behalf of the Assembly between sessions and drafts the budget in cooperation with the Committee on Budgetary Affairs and Administration.

The Assembly appoints the members of six permanent committees at the beginning of each session. It may also set up special committees. The thirty-four member Defence Committee meets eight to ten times a year. It visits NATO and national military headquarters and installations. It also meets with chairpersons of national parliamentary defense committees. The committee studies the state of European security, joint armaments production, control and limitation of armaments and disarmament. The Political Committee (34 members) meets with the same frequency and also holds joint meetings with the Ministerial Council. It reports to the Assembly on the political organization of western Europe and major world problems. In March 1989 the Committee held a symposium entitled "The Future of European Security" in Florence.

The other committees each have 26 members. The Technological and Aerospace Committee reports to the Assembly on research, space technology, aeronautics, computers and oceanography. It sought creation of a "European NASA" or space administration prior to creation of the ESA, aeronautical cooperation in European industry and a European approach to advanced technology. The Committee also advocates creation of a European research agency for advanced defense.

The Committee on Budgetary Affairs and Administration drafts the Assembly's budget in consultation with the Presidential Committee and issues opinions on administrative matters. The Committee on Rules of Procedure and Privileges meets as necessary to revise or interpret the Assembly's rules. The Committee for Parliamentary and Public Relations selects significant texts adopted by the Assembly for debate in national parliaments and conducts public relations on Assembly affairs with parliaments and the general public. Four political groups exist in the Assembly: Communists, Christian and European democrats, the Liberal group and the Socialist group. Speeches in the Assembly and its committees may be made in the official languages of the member states, with the assistance of simultaneous interpretation. Documents are published in English and French.

Institutional overlap:
the Assembly's place in European and Atlantic cooperation

It is apparent that in the early post-war years there was no broadly accepted over-arching concept of European unification. The organization with the broadest membership, OEEC, had a relatively narrow mandate, more technical than political. It was, moreover, a "classical" intergovernmental body with no parliamentary arm. Although more limited in membership, the Council of

Europe had a parliamentary assembly and broader terms of reference, which nevertheless excluded defense on account of the neutral members' susceptibilities. Narrower still in membership and role, WEU nevertheless also had a parliamentary assembly. Meanwhile, more "federalist" endeavors, such as the European Defence Community and the European Coal and Steel Community, drew the allegiance of only six states and met varying degrees of success.

Topsy or turvy?

It would be untrue that Europe grew "like Topsy". Each institution reflected the political and economic circumstances of its time. Nevertheless, in the sixties certain "Europeans", like Fernand Dehousse, Belgian Socialist president of the Council of Europe's Consultative Assembly (as it was then called), were conscious that the institutional trees, taken together, created more of a jungle than a well-cultivated European plantation.

This caused some frustration, since nobody could offer a satisfactory solution. On one occasion, when the Consultative Assembly in Strasbourg was discussing its competence for economic matters and comparing it to that of the OEEC in Paris, Monsieur Dehousse wryly observed that there was little prospect of merging the two at the midway point, in Bar-le-Duc!

Albeit jealous of its own prerogatives, each institution was nevertheless constrained to avoid unnecessary duplication and, worse yet, divergent policy-making by the same governments wearing different hats. This was particularly sensitive for WEU, which drew characteristics from both the North Atlantic Treaty Organization and the Council of Europe and was even "shadowed" by an unofficial body of "NATO parliamentarians", the North Atlantic Assembly.

Today these issues are less acute as roles have become more clearly defined.[7] OEEC evolved into OECD, ECSC expanded to EEC/EURATOM, then the three merged again to a single community (EC). As the latter's membership grew, so also did the Council of Europe's membership reach out to the Iberian peninsula, to smaller countries like Malta, Liechtenstein and San Marino and now to Eastern Europe. WEU itself comes back into focus as the military relationship between North America and Europe evolves under the pressure of events in Eastern Europe and the Soviet Union. Perhaps WEU's ambiguous relationship to NATO and even the EC will be finally resolved. The possibility of duplication still exists, however: thus, the Council of Europe has recently moved to rationalize its relationship with the Conference on Security and Cooperation in Europe.

Coordinating Assembly action

The WEU Assembly, then, has been careful to coordinate its action with that of the other European parliamentary assemblies. Such coordination goes beyond the mere selection of dates and places for meetings. Coordination with the Council of Europe Assembly has been relatively easy. The EEC's European Parliament has posed more intractable problems, having spread its activities to areas covered by the WEU Assembly, particularly since its election by direct universal suffrage. In recent years an exchange of observers and documents has been developed between the Defence Committee of the WEU Assembly and the Sub-committee on Security and Disarmament of the European Parliament. However, there is no denying a certain duplication here, for which the European Community must accept the larger share of blame. One senses a certain arrogance and desperation on the part of the European Parliament as its endeavors to extend the relatively limited powers and influence conferred upon it by the EC treaties at the expense of an assembly whose authority is even less well defined. The lack of reaction from countries like Ireland, an EC member, to these machinations demonstrates that in the glasnost era neutrality is no longer the burning issue it once was.

NATO . . .

Similarly, the WEU Assembly has followed the work of NATO's unofficial North Atlantic Assembly, despite the absence of official links. There are a few dual mandates and the subjects discussed are often identical. Despite the North Atlantic Assembly's lack of official status (it is not in the NATO statute and not based on an international treaty) there is a strong case for improving coordination. The defense committees of the two bodies already meet from time to time.

. . . and even the USSR

In recent years all European countries of NATO not represented in WEU have been invited to send two parliamentary observers to Assembly sessions. The WEU Assembly attaches particular importance, moreover, to maintaining regular contacts with the Canadian Parliament and the Congress of the United States. Even more striking was the development of relations with the Soviet Union. In 1986 a WEU Assembly delegation visited Moscow. In return, a delegation from the Supreme Soviet went to Paris in July 1989 for meetings with WEU Assembly committees. It was agreed at that time that parliamentary delegations would meet once a year, alternatively in Moscow and Paris. As the USSR's internationally-recognized successor state, Russia assumes this relationship.

Enhancing WEU's political profile

Western European Union offered no substitute for the European Defense Community in terms of the political integration of Europe; indeed, it was designed not to do so. The ECD failed essentially because in the absence of Britain France was not prepared to integrate its military forces with those of a renascent Federal German defense arm; and in 1954 and 1955 Britain was clearly not prepared to choose "the Continent" over the "open sea" (i.e. the remnants of empire and the so-called special relationship with the United

States). The fault was not entirely that of the United Kingdom, however. In the French parliament too there was a hesitancy to commit the nation to "fast track" political union. EDC would have established European union even more tightly than ECSC had done.

Nevertheless, WEU did achieve the more limited goal of anchoring the new Federal German armed forces in the west. Thereafter, it tended to languish, triply overshadowed by the broader membership and greater military powers of NATO; the economic strength and supranational institutions of the EEC; and the wider mandate and membership of the Council of Europe. As for dealings with the East, the United States negotiated directly with the Soviet Union and broader exchanges took place in the Helsinki Conference on Security and Cooperation in Europe.

Since the adoption of the Hague platform on European security interests on October 26, 1987, the importance of WEU as an instrument for harmonizing European security policies and as an aspect of the European integration process has been growing. Glasnost, the United States budget deficit and the crumbling of the Warsaw Pact (the Communist NATO) to a point where Poland, Czechoslovakia and other East European countries, the former "satellites", negotiated withdrawal of Soviet forces from their territory: all these accelerated the political rehabilitation of WEU. The Bush administration declared its support for development of a European security identity. In July 1989, the President of the United States specifically endorsed WEU's revival. He did so, however, on the assumption that by strengthening the European "pillar" of NATO, WEU would reinforce the alliance while at the same time leading Europe to assume greater financial and logistic responsibility for her own defense. Bush endorsed the security component of the Maastricht treaty on the same premise.

Nevertheless, even the European Community has defense concerns, since it is not possible to develop a common foreign policy without a common basis for security. Even if, after the Danish rejection, the Maastricht Treaty of European Union were not to be implemented in its present form, the logic would remain, particularly after the Community's poor showing in the Yugoslav civil war.

The Maastricht proposals

WEU's long walk in the wilderness, as an institution suspended between NATO, the European Community and (by its parliamentarians) the Council of Europe, finally seemed to come to an end at the European summit in Maastricht in December 1991, when the agency was built into the new European Union as the latter's defense and security component, with an invitation to the remaining EC countries, Denmark, Greece and Ireland, to join. (Greece later made admission to WEU a condition of TEU ratification).

The TEU text specifically describes WEU as "an integral part of the development of the European Union"; and requests WEU "to elaborate and implement decisions and actions of the Union which have defence implications".

In accordance with this decision the nine member states of WEU issued an important policy statement at the Maastricht summit, agreeing on "the need to develop a genuine European and security and defence identity and a greater European responsibility in defence matters". The statement went on:

> This identity will be pursued through a gradual process involving successive phases. WEU will form an integral part of the process of the development of the European Union and will enhance its contribution to solidarity within the Atlantic Alliance. WEU Member States agree to strengthen the role of WEU, in the longer term perspective of a common defence policy within the European Union which might in time lead to a common defence, compatible with that of the Atlantic Alliance.
>
> WEU will be developed as the defence component of the European Union and as the means to strengthen the European pillar of the Atlantic Alliance. To this end, it will formulate common European defence policy and carry forward its concrete implementation through the further development of its own operational role . . .

After quoting the relevant section of the Treaty of European Union, the WEU statement addresses relations with the European Union (i.e. the Community):

> The objective is to build up WEU in stages as the defence component of the European Union. To this end, WEU is prepared, at the request of the European Union, to elaborate and implement decisions and actions of the Union which have defence implications.

WEU will synchronize dates and venues of meetings, harmonize working methods, establish close cooperation between the councils and their secretariats, exchange information, consult as appropriate and encourage close cooperation between the WEU Parliamentary Assembly and the European Parliament.

This is harmonization, not yet a merger, but it does seem as though Fernand Dehousse's old wish to see the rationalization of European institutions is coming closer three decades later.

Squaring the NATO circle: distinct but not separate

The statement then addresses the thorny issue of WEU's relationship to NATO. As always, the objective is to be distinct but not separate. Faced with the daunting task of squaring the circle, WEU slides into jargon:

> The objective is to develop WEU as a means to strengthen the European pillar of the Atlantic Alliance. Accordingly WEU is prepared to develop further the close working links between WEU and the Alliance and to strengthen the role, responsibilities and contributions of WEU Member States in the Alliance. This will be undertaken on the basis of the necessary transparency and complementarity between the emerging European security and defence identity and the Alliance. WEU will act in conformity with the positions adopted in the Atlantic Alliance.

WEU declares its intention of strengthening its operational role (an attainable goal, since so far that role has been negligeable). There will be closer cooperation in planning, logistics, transport, training and strategic surveillance and even in military units answerable to WEU. Longer-term objectives include a European armaments agency and development of the WEU Institute into a European Security and Defence Academy (ESDA).

Finally, WEU announces its intention to renew administrative arrangements. The seat of the WEU Ministerial Council and the Secretariat are transferred from London to Brussels. A "double-hatting" formula whereby the same diplomatic representatives would represent their government in the Atlantic Alliance and the European Union is envisaged. In any case, WEU undertakes to review the present provisions in 1996: they are clearly perceived as transitional.

This is progress of a kind; on the other hand, "closer cooperation ... in military units answerable to WEU" is a far cry from what might have been, had EDC passed muster way back in 1954!

Franco-German *fuite en avant*

Is there a crumb of further comfort — or a seed of discord — in the fact that the Maastricht summit specifically admitted closer bilateral cooperation in military matters, an obvious reference to the Franco-German military brigade? Here again attitudes are ambiguous, according to whether the brigade is looked upon as separating France and to a lesser extent Germany from NATO or, on the contrary, drawing France closer to European and hence NATO military cooperation.[8]

Ever since its creation in 1955, WEU has suffered from a lack of political space, always appearing hedged in by NATO, the European Community, the Council of Europe, even the CSCE. In some ways its political role was over almost as soon as it began: once the reintegration of the Federal Republic into western military command had been achieved. Will it have a more clearly defined role under TEU auspices? A small step was taken in this direction on June 18, 1992, when the Council voted to use WEU for the setting up of a European emergency intervention force.

According to the WEU statement, units attached to WEU would be employed in humanitarian missions or the evacuation of nationals; peace-keeping missions; combat force missions for crisis management and missions to restore peace. Whether the political will existed to use that force to improve a settlement in Yugoslavia remained to be seen. "I don't think that there is a country here of a mind to send troops into battle", declared the Secretary of the Foreign Office, Douglas Hurd. It seemed as though the wording had been carefully crafted to do everything but just that ... (The agency only inched forward a month later at Helsinki, still sounding more like a scout pack than a military force). Certainly WEU seemed to be hastening slowly by deciding to set up a planning unit three months later, on October 1. With any luck, by that time the Serbs, Croats, Bosnians, Muslims *et al.* would have annihilated each other; then WEU could plan its emergency intervention in peace; for next time.

A sobering reminder that essential decisions are still reserved to the US and to the USSR's successor-state, Russia, was delivered to the western European powers (and to the "lesser" CIS members) by George Bush in his annual State of the Union message to congress on January 28, 1992. If the nuclear CIS states agreed to eliminate all their land-based multiple warheads (MIRV's), the US were ready to reduce by a third their 5000 submarine-based warheads, to eliminate their Peacekeeper missiles entirely and to convert many of their strategic bombers to conventional armaments. Within 24 hours – and only two days before the Security Council summit in New York – Boris Yeltsin laid claim to Gorbachev's mantle of international statemanship, a force to be reckoned with, by accepting the American proposal and, trumping Bush's ace, proposing the dismantling of SDI. Such were, broadly speaking, the terms agreed, at the Bush-Yeltsin summit in Washington on June 16, 1992. The two leaders undertook to cut their strategic nuclear arsenals to less than half the total stipulated in the unratified START treaty.[9] By 2003 both countries will have 3,000 - 3,500 warheads apiece; todays combined total is close to 21,000. The two leaders also invited other "interested countries" to join them in preparing a global protection system against limited ballistic missile attack.

Western Europe is certainly "interested"; but it was not a party to the discussions; Bush and Yeltsin signed START II in January, 1993.

In explaining a veto on British entry into the EEC, De Gaulle criticized Harold Macmillan for buying American nuclear Polaris missiles for an illusory UK military and hence political "independence". Today the European Community, the world's premier economic power, is still asking itself whether a veiled American hegemony through NATO (albeit a hegemony Americans themselves no longer want to pay for) is consistent with a need for greater European unity and a stronger European voice in the political sphere. It seems doubtful whether WEU, even assimilated into the Community structure, is strong enough to be the vehicle of such a profound change.

Forty years on, the *corps de ballet* of European institutions, with WEU in the lead, is still today dancing around the recumbent figure of the European Defence Community.

Meanwhile the search is also on for a single, over-arching, all-European security agency embracing "east" and "west". Before defense and security can be redefined, rationalized and restructured everyone, it seems, must address some tantalizing questions: can the US be a "European power" without dominating European policy; conversely can the Community be a "world power" without renouncing the American military umbrella; how "European" is Russia; what happened to neutrality; are the nuclear stockpiles still usable; whose fingers are on what triggers; and who, for heaven's sake, is the enemy?

Let's hope the politicians and generals will prove as smart as their bombs.

Notes

1 McLachlan, Donald H. in Chatham House Study Group, *Britain in Western Europe: WEU and the Atlantic Alliance*, London and New York, Royal Institute of International Affairs, 1956, p. 86.

2 The founding membership of WEU is Belgium, France, the Federal Republic of Germany, Italy, Luxembourg, the Netherlands and the United Kingdom. Portugal and Spain signed a treaty of accession on November 14, 1988. They were of course already full members of the North Atlantic Treaty Organization (NATO) and the European Community, a fact recognized by member governments in inviting them to join WEU. When the TEU was negotiated in Maastricht in 1991, WEU invited non-member countries among the EC Twelve to join. Greece did so on November 20, 1992.

3 France and the United Kingdom represent a case apart in this regard. There is a "legacy of empire" which leaves them with world-wide responsibilities. Thus, France is responsible for its overseas departments and territories (DOM/TOM); the United Kingdom for Gibraltar, Ascension, Saint Helena, Tristan da Cunha, the Falklands, Bermuda, some small territories in the West Indies and Pacific Ocean and, until 1997, Hong Kong. Both countries have special defense associations with certain countries in Africa and, as regards the United Kingdom, the Arabian peninsula and SEATO. Both are also permanent members of the UN Security Council.

4 The Agencies for Security Questions and the Standing Armaments Committee (SAC) were abolished when the Institute for Advanced Security Studies was created. The SAC had been in existence for thirty-four years and made a significant contribution to the coordination of armaments design and production.

5 There is an irony in this arrangement, since the Council of Europe is forbidden by its statute to discuss defense, while many of its assembly members (admittedly, the non-neutrals) proceed to Paris or London to debate those very issues in another forum.

6 It is a measure of the Assembly's independence that even when, under President de Gaulle, France left its seat in the Council vacant (February 14, 1969 to June 15, 1970), the French Delegation continued to sit in the Assembly.

7 Rationalization is still a hot topic within the European Community, particularly as regards the peregrinations of the European Parliament between Brussels, Luxembourg and Strasbourg. To understand the political dynamics involved, the American reader need only consider the military base-closing issue in the United States Congress: support in principle, "but no cutbacks in my district . . ."

8 The question is posed as to whether the first loyalty of its German component lies with the brigade or with NATO, since French forces are not NATO integrated. France is thus having it both ways: integration into a symbolic European brigade but no integration into Atlantic Alliance forces. Could the brigade also form an operational nucleus for WEU? An invitation to other WEU member states to join the brigade has found no takers (Aug. 1992). The UK is openly suspicious that the brigade could drive a wedge between WEU and NATO. These musings sound familiar. Four decades after the EDC, Britain is still not ready for a truly integrated European Army; but is anyone else?

9   The 1991 START treaty was not ratified because of the break-up of one of its signatories, the USSR. Accesssion by the 4 CIS nuclear successor states would be required; but START is in effect overtaken by the new agreement announced in Washington, since Belarus, Ukraine and Kazakhstan are committed to destruction of their "share" of the Soviet nuclear arsenal.

5

New Structures for
New Communities

The integrated European Community was created from the merger in 1967 of the European Coal and Steel Community of 1952 with the European Economic Community (Common Market) and the European Atomic Energy Community, both established by the Rome treaties of 1958. The unified Community has four main institutions. These are the ministerial Council, the Commission, the Assembly (which calls itself the European Parliament) and the Court of Justice. [1]

A fifth body, the European Council, for political cooperation, grew out of the meetings of heads of government and is not enshrined in the original treaties. However the Single European Act makes provisions, in its Title III, for European cooperation in the sphere of foreign policy. The European Council meets twice a year under rotating chairmanship and is now established as a regular Community mechanism.

The European Commission

Compared with traditional diplomatic cooperation the most original body established by the Community treaties is the European Commission. With the European Court, which issues binding judgments, it embodies truly supranational powers but also enshrines new methods of international cooperation. Too often, ill-informed observers have spoken of an embryonic "United States of Europe". President Mitterrand, Chancellor Kohl, Prime Minister Major (and *a fortiori* his predecessor Margaret Thatcher) are not interested in dissolving their national identities; nor are they called upon to do so. European union is finding a "third way".

The seventeen members of the European Commission, which includes at least one but no more than two nationals of each member state,[2] are assigned a quadruple role. The Commission is the guardian of the treaties; it serves as the executive arm of the Community (or Communities, if one considers the three treaties); it defends the Community interest in the ministerial Council (where national interests are foremost) and, perhaps most importantly, it initiates Community policy.

As the guardian of the treaties the Commission investigates an infringment alleged either on its own initiative or as a result of petitions from governments, firms and even private individuals. If an infringement is established the member state in question is usually allowed two months to respond, although in serious cases disrupting the market the time-limit may be shorter. If the practice continues and the Commission remains unsatisfied, the latter issues a reasoned opinion, with a deadline for compliance. If necessary the Commission may refer the matter to the Court of Justice, in Luxembourg, whose judgment is binding.

In 1987 the Commission instituted proceedings in no less than 572 cases, issued 197 opinions and referred 61 cases to the Court. About 70% of the cases involve the inadequate incorporation of Community directives into national laws. However, the matter is usually one of interpretation rather than a deliberate attempt to evade the treaty in question. However, most Community law is directly applicable in national courts.

The Commission as policy initiator

The merger of the ECSC, EURATOM and EEC Commissions in 1967 facilitated the drawing up of common policies for industry, energy, research, agriculture and technology. Progress in these areas became more rapid, particularly since the EEC Commission, established later than the ECSC High Authority, had always regarded the launching of common policies as one of its principal functions.

It should also be noted that the ECSC and EURATOM treaties are narrower, more technical and therefore more rigid than the EEC treaty. With EEC the Commission, Council and Parliament have more flexibility. Thus it may be said that true "Community law" is being built up. A prime example is the agricultural policy developed since 1962 without recourse to new treaties (which would have required parliamentary ratification by all member states). Indeed, meeting as the European Council, heads of state and government have opened up new fields of cooperation not actually covered by the treaties, such as monetary policy and environmental protection. Such sectors have now been institutionalized under the Single European Act and would be further entrenched by TEU implementation.

The Commission usually meets weekly and acts by consensus or, if necessary, by majority vote. It puts forward policy proposals to the Council but in certain areas it can make regulations, issue directives and take decisions binding on member countries. Each Commissioner has an assigned area or areas of responsibility, in which he or she is assisted by a chef de cabinet. Secretariat activities are allocated to twenty-two directorates-general. The EC public service numbers some 10,400 employees.

The Commission as executive body

The Commission's wide executive powers are conferred by the treaties or by decision of the Council. This authority is further strengthened by the Single European Act. The Commission's executive power falls into three broad categories:

— Decisions and regulations implementing treaty provisions or Council acts;
— Application of treaty rules to specific cases;
— Administration of safeguard clauses in the treaties.

The Commission is also responsible for the administration of Community funds.

All the treaties give the Commission legislative powers. The coal and steel text is particularly specific in this regard but the Commission's powers have been greatly extended by the implementing of economic common policies under the common market treaty, particularly as regards agriculture.

Application of treaty rules in individual cases is vast. It covers such matters as restrictive practices, state subsidies, taxation, worker redundancy and covers a wide range of economic sectors from fisheries to coal, as well as trade policy and the environment. Under the EURATOM treaty the various aspects of the peaceful use of nuclear energy are covered: fissile materials, inspections, information and protection from radiation.

Although treaty provisions and Commission directives are usually precise and strict, in exceptional circumstances member governments may invoke waiver provisions which require monitoring by the Commission. The latter's responsibility in this regard is weighty indeed, since abuse of waiver provisions undermines the treaties. To make sure that states do not simply act as they please, only the Commission may authorize such "derogations", as they are called. The Commission seeks to help the country concerned without interfering unduly with the functioning of the market.

Derogations may be permitted in many ways: during the transitional period they often involved tariffs and quotas but these are no longer permissible except in the case of new members which are granted a transitional period.[3] Certain special measures may be allowed when a country has serious balance of payments difficulties.

Administering Community funds

The Community has raised funds through ECSC levies since 1952. Apart from running the secretariat, such funds are returned to the coal and steel industries for research, interest subsidies on investment and capital expenditure, retraining of workers and other restructuring measures. Similar activities, with emphasis on research centers in Italy, Germany, Belgium, the Netherlands, and the United Kingdom, are funded in nuclear energy. In recent years community research has been extended to new technologies such as computers and telecommunications.

Four major Economic Community funds have been set up. The largest of these, the European Agricultural Guidance and Guarantee Fund (FEOGA) came to account for two-thirds of the Community expenditure (a fact to which the United Kingdom, in particular, took great exception). The Fund finances organization and support of the agricultural market and implements the only instance where an entire sector of the economy is covered by a common policy.

The recently implemented reform of the Common Agricultural Policy (CAP2) is gradually stabilizing the size of the Fund, which reached 24 billion ECU in 1987.

The European Social Fund (ESF), for which provision was made in the Treaty, promotes vocational training and facilitates vocational mobility, the latter being an inevitable product of free trade and competition. In 1983 it was revised to cope more directly with unemployment. The Fund reached 3,100 million ECU in 1987.

The Commission also manages the European Regional Development Fund (ERDF), established in 1975 to correct regional imbalances such as those occurring in southern Italy and northern Britain.

The ERDF is not to be confused with the European Development Fund, which provides assistance to African, Caribbean and Pacific countries formerly linked to Europe by colonial ties. The Fund operates on the basis of agreements concluded with the countries concerned, in particular the Yaoundé conventions associated with the Community of Six and, after the first enlargement, the Lomé conventions. Sixty-six ACP states were party to Lome III, signed on December 8, 1984. The Commission also provides development assistance and food aid to non-ACP countries.

The other Communities, ECSC and EURATOM, also manage important funds. In fact, since the ECSC treaty provided for the Community to levy its own funds, it was able as early as 1952 to finance operations in the coal and steel industries. The principal activities include research, interest subsidies on investment and conversion loans, retraining grants and other social measures related to restructuring the steel industry.

EURATOM funds Community nuclear research, in particular the activities of the Joint Research Centre, with its four research establishments at Ispra (Italy), Karlsruhe (Germany), Geel (Belgium) and Petten (Netherlands). The research activities of member states are also coordinated by the Community. The Single European Act placed great emphasis on research, particularly in new technologies. The multi-annual program also covers energy, the environment and raw materials.

The Commission is anxious to exercise its extensive powers in close consultation with member governments. To this end it has set up a number of advisory committees.

Initiating policy = defending Community interests

The ECSC High Authority and the EURATOM Commission had wide powers in limited fields. Their function was therefore largely supervisory. The EEC Treaty is less specific and relies upon the institutions of the Community to "fill in the blanks". The EEC Commission therefore emphasized policy development from the outset. Since the merger of the three authorities the unified Commission, even though it acts under the legal treaty "hat" of the sector under discussion, has been able to follow suit, developing policies in sectors of much broader scope (industry, energy, research, technology), previously hampered by the existence of three distinct executives. In the economic area, in particular, an important European jurisprudence has developed. The areas covered are not necessarily included in the treaties themselves: regional development, the environment, consumer protection and, above all, the European Monetary System. Many of these have since been confirmed or validated in the Single European Act and Treaty of European Union.

The Council of Ministers

Unlike the European Commission, the members of the Council of Ministers cannot be individually named or even numbered. Although the Council consists of the twelve foreign ministers when the most important decisions are taken, it may equally well consist of ministers of agriculture or finance or even scientific research. In some cases, depending on the distribution of responsibilities within a given member government, a country may be represented by more than one minister.[4]

When the ministers themselves are not present, the more routine work of the Community is carried forward by the Committee of Permanent Representatives who are the national ambassadors to the European Community. Each Permanent Representative is assisted by a staff of national public servants, stationed in Brussels.

The presidency of the Council rotates at six-month intervals in the alphabetical order of the countries' official names in their own language. The six-month period has proved sufficient for each presiding country to make its mark without danger of undue domination.

There is an ongoing dynamic dialog between the Commission, which is formally charged by the treaties with the task of defending, strengthening and developing European union and, implicitly at least, the institutions of the Community, on the one hand, and the Ministerial Council and the European Council, on the other, whose task it is to represent national problems and viewpoints, albeit in a spirit of cooperation and common interest. Once a political compromise has merged and blended the separate policies of the member governments, it is up to the institutions of the community to formulate and implement the Community policy that is to replace them.

The co-existence of the three treaties in a single community gives rise to minor differences in the decision-making procedure. Under the ECSC treaty, the commission (replacing the High Authority) actually takes the decisions, with the Council's assent. Under EEC and EURATOM procedures, the Council takes the final decision, on a proposal from the Commission.

Voting in the Council of Ministers

Voting is carefully weighted under the treaties in order to give each member state voting power in rough proportion to its population. Steps were nevertheless taken to effect some political levelling out. Each of the four "large" countries has the same number of votes. (This principle has not been called in question even though German reunification has added 16 million people to what was already the largest EEC country. Germany accepted this sacrifice in order not to be accused of exercizing unacceptable influence). Conversely, the smallest countries have a voting power somewhat larger than their population might warrant. If assayed strictly on population, for instance, the Grand Duchy of Luxembourg would not qualify for a single vote!

The Single European Act, adopted in Luxembourg on December 2, 1985, under United Kingdom chairmanship (a detail which may surprise "anti-Thatcherites") confirmed the following voting distribution, taking account of the new members, Portugal and Spain, due to enter in 1986:

Belgium	5	Ireland	3
Denmark	3	Italy	10
Germany	10	Luxembourg	2
Greece	5	Netherlands	5
Spain	8	Portugal	5
France	10	United Kingdom	10

A second problem with respect to Council voting concerns the delegation of sovereignty – the power of European institutions to impose a policy or a decision on a member government. A qualified voting system avoids both the paralysis of veto by a minority and the imposition of major decisions by a bare majority. It also ensures that decisions are not dominated by any one group, whether of large or small countries.[5]

A Commission proposal is adopted with 54 favorable votes. Proposals not emanating from the Commission require both 54 votes and support from at least 8 countries. This voting ratio will of course change as other states join the Community.

Naturally, certain purely procedural issues can be settled by simple majority and, conversely, in a very few cases (such as the declaration of a "manifest crisis" in the steel industry) unanimity is required.

Only in rare cases can the Council proceed without a proposal from the Commission. It is therefore incumbent upon the latter to initiate action. In 1987 the Commission placed 699 proposals and 192 reports and memoranda before the Council. Under the EEC and Euratom treaties the Council cannot amend a Commission proposal unless it is unanimous in doing so. A qualified majority of the Council can only accept or reject the Commission's proposal in its entirety. The debate takes place on terms of the Commission's choosing, a fact which gives the Commission some leverage against the formidable combined power of the governments. Significantly, this leverage allows the Commission, in drawing up its proposals, to give due weight and protection to the governments finding themselves in the minority on an issue. In practice, then, majority/minority dynamics frequently evolve into policies of consensus. At the same time, an impartial Commission, enjoying a fixed term of office, can act as the guardian of coherence and continuity through evolving governmental positions and even changes of government in member states.[6]

The European Council

Strictly speaking, the European Council, composed of heads of government (for France, because the presidency has executive powers, both the President and the Prime Minister) was not at first an institution of the Community, not being provided for in the treaties. However, it has now become so. Since March 1975 the European Council has met twice a year with foreign ministers and the President and one of the vice-presidents of the Commission. The existence of the European Council was formally enshrined in the Single European Act in 1986.

The European Council has given great impetus to Community affairs in several domains, such as agriculture, direct elections to the European Parliament, accession of new members and institution of the European Monetary System. Discussion of Community matters has also been combined, in an atmosphere free of institutional formalities, with political affairs ranging beyond the Community domain *stricto sensu*. As Community governments have confronted and sometimes aligned their positions on world affairs such as relations with Eastern Europe and with South Africa, an informal if not a formal European foreign policy has been seen to emerge. The deliberations of the European Council have also served to enhance the role not only of the Council presidency, rotating on a six-monthly basis in step with the other governmental bodies of the Community, but also of the President of the Commission, who participates in all these European "summit" meetings.

At its Dublin meeting under Irish presidency in June 1990, the Council agreed to convene special committees to strengthen both political and economic cooperation. The precise nature of Europe's future union may still remain uncertain; however the momentum, even after the Danish TEU rejection, has become inexorable.

European Bank for Reconstruction and Development

This newest of EC institutions was created on May 29, 1990, with headquarters in London, to channel aid to eastern European countries to assist their programs of economic and institutional reform following the collapse of communism.

The bank brings together both European and North American countries supplying capital (including, interestingly, Mexico, which is engaged on its own market-economy and free trade conversion).

The EBRD's first director is Jacques Attali, of France.

The European Parliament

The parliamentary body of the European Community, officially named in the treaties as the Assembly, but calling itself the European Parliament, was originally composed, like the assemblies of the Council of Europe and WEU, of delegations from national parliaments. However in June 1979 the Parliament became an elected body with a five-year mandate. Each state uses its national electoral system.[7]

An important feature of the European character of the Parliament – always in the vanguard of integration – is that there are no national sections. As in Europe's other parliamentary assemblies, political groups of the left, center and right cross national boundaries. The Commission is answerable to the Parliament which in return watches over the Commission's independence. In practice, the two bodies together form a "progressive" alliance (in terms of integration) *vis-à-vis* the more "conservative" national interests of the member states of the ministerial Council.

When the parliamentarians, known as MEP's, were first elected to the Parliament the latter was enlarged considerably to 518 members. Moreover only a very few now "cumulate" national and European representation. These changes, while not increasing the powers of the Parliament, have made it more effective.

Vexed question: the seat of the European Parliament

The question of the seat of the institutions is one of the most intractable issues of European integration. As in the case of the official languages, efficiency, politics and psychology do not necessarily point in the same direction.

Those who plead in favor of a single seat for the principal EC institutions (Council of Ministers, Commission, Secretariat, Parliament) have a strong case. The argument really centers on the parliament, since no one has suggested moving the Commission out of Brussels (even though Brussels is the *de facto* not *de jure* location) or, for that matter, the Court, which can find judicial detachment in a certain remoteness, out of Luxembourg. There seems little doubt that the parliamentarians could act more efficiently and at less cost (currently 14% of the budget) if they were closer to the Commission and Council whose activities they monitor. "Efficiency" in this case means more effective democratic control. How else, with their already limited powers, will they be taken seriously?

This is certainly the view of the European Parliament itself except, perhaps, for some of the French members.

The Parliament's regular sessions consist of one week each month except August. The secretariat is in Luxembourg and the 18 permanent ("standing") Parliamentary committees meet in the Grand Duchy or in Brussels to prepare the Parliamentary sessions. The latter are usually held in Strasbourg in an impressive modern assembly hall, fully equipped with interpretation facilities, shared with the Council of Europe. This shuffling back and forth has frequently been deplored but is bolstered by entrenched political interests. It is the price to be paid for the more-or-less equitable distribution of institutional rights and privileges. On June 28, 1991, Giulio Andreotti, former premier and foreign minister of Italy, abandoned in frustration a mission to solve the vexed issue of the seat of European institutions. Later the same year, in one of his final acts as EP President, Enrique Baron Crespo (Spanish Soc.) signed an 18-

year lease on an assembly hall in Brussels, newly-built with Belgian assistance, of course.

When President Mitterrand made a state visit to the Grand Duchy of Luxembourg in January 1992, the two governments (both interested parties) reaffirmed their attachment to the polycentric *status quo*. Turning a blind eye to administrative inefficiency, they saw no reason for the Community to have a single seat, in Brussels. In a joint declaration they castigated the *fait accompli* whereby the European Parliament had not only held a session in Brussels but even transferred certain secretariat services to that city. "If an issue is raised for one seat, declared Mitterrand, "it will be raised for all three".

Another who was quick to respond was Catherine Trautmann, the chic, vivacious and highly effective mayor of Strasbourg. While her vested interest is obvious, she presents a viewpoint not without validity: "We consider Strasbourg as the parliamentary capital of Europe". Trautmann pointed not only to the EC Parliament but also to the Consultative Assembly of the Council of Europe (conveniently omitting the WEU Assembly, which meets in Paris). Trautmann averred that something would actually be lost if all the major institutions were in the same city: the sense of a distant bureaucracy remote from the people (already a factor in the UK) would be exacerbated. Trautmann's argument may be reinforced — or undermined — by the rapid growth in the Council of Europe's membership as it moves from representing "greater Europe" into a new "all-European" role. A new "seat" issue looming on the horizon is the location of the European Bank. Ultimately, one suspects, parliamentary sessions, secretariat and committees will come together in a single location; but in all probability neither logic, nor democracy but political horse-trading will settle the issue.

2942 questions

An important method of parliamentary control of the institutions of the Community is provided by written questions from the MEP's. In 1987, for instance, 2591 questions were addressed to the Commission, 201 to the Council and, in the field of political cooperation, 150 to the foreign ministers. There is also a question time at each session of the Parliament.

Debates are usually based on Commission "communications" which are discussed in committee before their consideration in plenary session. However, this protracted procedure can be bypassed in special cases for urgent discussion of current issues.

The Parliament enjoys important budgetary powers, increased by treaty in 1970 and 1975 over the original provisions.[8] Parliament now has the last word on all non-compulsory expenditure, including administrative costs and the various special funds, representing over a quarter of the total Community budget. (Most of the rest is committed for agricultural price supports). Modifications proposed by the European Parliament in the "compulsory" sector, which cannot exceed the total amount of proposed expenditure, are considered approved unless the Council rejects them by a qualified majority.

The European Parliament
Seats by country

	Current	Future
Germany	81	99
France	81	87
Italy	81	87
United Kingdom	81	87
Spain	60	64
Netherlands	25	31
Belgium	24	25
Greece	24	25
Portugal	24	25
Denmark	16	16
Ireland	15	15
Luxembourg	6	6
	518	567

Following reunification Germany sought additional seats. The number of seats for all member countries was revised at Edinburgh (December 1992).

Distribution by political groups, January 1992

Left Unity	13
European United Left	29
Greens	27
Rainbow Group	15
Socialists	180
Non-attached	12
European People's Party (Chr. Dems)	128
European Democratic Alliance	21
Liberal Democrats and Reformists	45
European Democratic Group	34
Technical Group of the European Right	14

The Parliament also has the right to reject the budget as a whole, an extreme measure resorted to in 1979, 1980, 1982 (supplementary budget) and 1985. One final parliamentary "weapon" is the prerogative enjoyed by the president of the European Parliament to declare when all necessary procedures have been followed for budget approval. [9]

The European Parliament has been concerned for some time, and especially since its election by direct universal suffrage, to enhance its limited legislative powers. The treaties limit its function to an essentially consultative role, since governments were unwilling to have the European Assembly supercede the powers of national parliaments. The Community's critics are caught between a desire to protect national sovereignty and a perceived "democratic deficit" in the limits set on EP control of the Council and Commission. However, the Parliament's authority over the budget does give it a certain leverage and the SEA and TEU treaties go some way to meeting the Parliament's claim to greater democratic control. Thus, accessions and cooperation agreements now require parliamentary assent, a power which associates the Parliament with negotiations leading up to such accession and to association agreements. Furthermore, a complicated but balanced procedure has been worked out to associate the Parliament with the decision-making of the Commission and the Council. A parliamentary rejection of a Council decision can only be overriden by unanimous vote of the Council. If the Parliament has proposed amendments, the Council votes by qualified majority in cases where the Commission has endorsed them and unanimously if Commission endorsement has not been granted.

Finally, it should be noted that the European Parliament has the authority to dismiss the entire Commission, although this power has never been exercized.

Economic and Social Committee

This appointive body has functions similiar to those of the Parliament, albeit with lesser and narrower powers. One third of its members represent employers, one third trade unions and the remainder various professions and consumers. It plays a significant advisory role in the formulation of Community policies.

Court of Auditors

The EC budget has become so huge (50 billion ECU's in 1990) that the Court of Auditors has become an important if politically unspectacular body. Each government proposes one member to the Council of Ministers. Each auditor is assigned special responsibility for a part of the Community budget. From its seat in Luxembourg the Court of Auditors also issues collective opinions on the financial implications of proposed regulations. Relations with Brussels are not always easy. In May 1990, for instance, the Court severely criticized the Commission's management of export subsidies for agriculture.

European Court of Justice

Inasmuch as its decisions are binding upon states and supercede national law, the European Court in Luxembourg is possibly more significant as a supranational institution than the Commission and majority voting in the Council.

The Court may be approached in a number of ways, by the Commission or by a member state, against another member state or a firm. It also settles disputes between the various Community institutions, or between institutions and their staff. A judge in a member state may also approach the Court for an advisory opinion, known as a "preliminary ruling".

The Court consists of twelve judges, one for each member state. The seat of the Court is in the Grand Duchy of Luxembourg. The European Court is an essential guardian of the integrity of the treaties and of Community law and procedures. Between 1952, when the ECSC Treaty came into force, and the end of 1987, 3606 cases were brought before the court. An immense body of European case law has been built up to guide the work of the Community.

Under the TEU a European Court of First Instance is created by modification of the ECSC, EURATOM and EEC treaties to relieve the Court of some of its immense roster of cases. Establishment of such a court will enhance the prestige of the European Court, limiting its roster to major cases and appeals.

In December 1991 the Court rejected as incompatible with its own supreme authority as provided by the treaties, and hence unconstitutional, a provision in the European Economic Area (EC-EFTA) Agreement for an EEA court of justice. The agreement was renegotiated, replacing the EEA court by an alternative appeals mechanism.

Single European Act

The major changes effected by the Single European Act, which entered into force on July 1, 1987, are summarized in note 16 to Part II, Chapter 6. It was the SEA which set December 31, 1992, for the final elimination of some 250 technical obstacles to the single market. This goal was in large measure achieved.

European Union: the Maastricht expansion

The Treaty on European Union approved at the summit of December 9-11, 1991 and signed in Maastricht on February 7, 1992, instituted a number of important changes in both the field of activity and the institutions of the European Community. Since these have been discussed at some length in a preceding chapter, we summarize them here mainly for purposes of completeness.

Major treaties
The Treaty on European Union modifies and updates existing treaties and introduces new elements. The following are the main texts concerned:

1 Treaty establishing the European Coal and Steel Community, Paris, April 18, 1951;
2 Treaty establishing the European Atomic Energy Community, Rome, March 25, 1957;
3 Treaty establishing the European Economic Community, Rome, March 25, 1957;

4 The Single European Act, agreed Luxembourg, December 2, 1985; signed February 17 and 28, 1986; unified market completed December 31, 1992;

5 Treaty establishing the European Economic Area, agreed October 22, 1991; signed Lisbon, April, 1992; entry into force January 1, 1993;

6 Treaty on European Union, approved Maastricht, December 11, 1991; signed Maastricht February 7, 1992; awaits Danish, UK ratification.

Major program developments
Common monetary policy, leading to single currency
Common foreign and security policy; consular cooperation
Justice and home affairs
Social Charter
Environment
Trans-European networks
Development cooperation
Education
Regional cooperation.

Major institutional changes
Citizenship of the Union
Commission reduced to one member per member state (currently 12), with term office extended, effective January 1995, to 5 years
Extended powers for the European Parliament, including approval of European Commission; committees of enquiry to investigate maladministration; scrutiny of Community finances; amendment and veto of certain acts of the Council of Ministers
European System of Central Banks; European Monetary Institute, leading to European Central Bank
Committee of the Regions[10]
Western European Union becomes the defense and security arm of the Union, with its secretariat moved to Brussels; the Defence Institute becomes the European Security and Defence Academy.
Ombudsman.[11] Court of First Instance set up.

It is not yet certain, following the negative result in the Danish referendum of June 1992, whether these provisions will be implemented by the other eleven EC member states or "reworked" in a manner acceptable to Denmark. There is a strong consensus that the substance of the treaty should be implemented. The issue which has raised the strongest objections in several countries is the right to vote in local elections in another member state. More generally, there is concern that "eurocracy" and excessive centralisation should not diminish the voice of the people (especially in the smaller countries) nor blur the unique character of each nation, region and culture. There are in fact several elements in the Treaty designed precisely to this end.

Notes

1 The European Parliament and the Court of Justice have been common to the three communities since 1958, whereas each treaty provided for distinct Councils and separate Commissions ("High Authority" in the ECSC) until the merger treaty of 1967. The original intent, not yet implemented, was to replace the original treaties of Paris or Rome by a single treaty. However, Community action was further coordinated and expanded by the Single European Act in 1986.

2 Commissioners are nominated by their government and appointed by common accord of all the member governments for renewable four-year periods. According to the terms of the TEU, the term of office of Commission members would be extended to five years in 1994 but their number reduced to nine: expanding the Commission with each enlargement would be counter-productive. Commissioners must by nationals of an EEC country. Each Commission member is assisted by a chief of staff, normally of his own nationality, and by a personal staff. Unlike other EC officials they are appointed by the commissioner and leave with him or her. This is a system of "political appointees" well known to Americans but which in EC countries is essentially limited to France.

3 For Portugal and Spain the transitional period ends at the end of 1992 or, in some sensitive sectors, 1995.

4 Naturally, multiple representation has no effect on the votes assigned by the treaties to each member country.

5 Speaking in an interview with *Le Monde*, published on June 26, 1990, the foreign minister of the Netherlands, Hans van den Broek, expressed concern that the larger EC countries might eventually dominate the small ones. He said that in a future "federal-type European system" there should be a European senate with equal representation from each member country and a commission limited to a single national from any member country.

6 The crisis of 1965-1966, in which France threatened rupture and practiced a boycott, resulted in the "Luxembourg Compromise" whereby a government could demand unanimity — in other words exercise a veto — when its "very important interests" were at stake. This slowed progress towards European union until majority voting was restored in almost all cases by ratification of the Single European Act. The Gaullian veto is no more.

7 Single-ballot majority voting by constituency is used in Great Britain (a fact which explains why the UK's smaller but most pro-European party, the Liberal Democrats, is not represented in Strasbourg). In Northern Ireland and the other EC countries various forms of proportional representation are employed.

8 As has been noted, the ECSC treaty provided for direct funding through levies. Financial resources are also provided from import duties on goods imported from outside the Community. When the Council gave the Community financial resources of its own, the Member States agreed, on April 22, 1970 and July 22, 1975 to increase the Parliament's power. The latter decision also established the Court of Auditors.

9 In 1986 the European Court of Justice defined the extent of this prerogative in accepting an appeal from the Council.

10 The Committee of the Regions established by the Treaty on European Union has the following members:

Belgium	12	Ireland	9
Denmark	9	Italy	24
Germany	24	Luxembourg	6
Greece	12	Netherlands	12
Spain	21	Portugal	12
France	24	United Kingdom	24

The members of the Committee and an equal number of alternate members are appointed by the Council, acting unanimously on proposals from the respective Member States, for four years. Their term of office is renewable. Chairman and officers are elected from among the members for two-year terms. The members of the Committee may not be bound by any mandatory instructions. They are completely independent in the performance of their duties, in the general interest of the Community. The Committee of the Regions corresponds in some sense to the highly successful Standing Conference of Local and Regional Authorities of Europe (SCLARAE, formerly ECLA) of the Council of Europe.

11 The European Parliament shall appoint an Ombudsman empowered to receive complaints from any citizen of the Union or any natural or legal person residing or having its registered office in a Member State concerning instances of maladministration in the activities of the Community institutions or bodies, with the exception of the Court of Justice and the Court of First Instance acting in their judicial role.

The Ombudsman conducts enquiries for which he finds grounds, either on his own initiative or on the basis of complaints submitted to him directly or through a member of the European Parliament except where the alleged facts are or have been the subject of legal proceedings. Where the Ombudsman establishes an instance of maladministration, he refers the matter to the institution concerned, which has a period of three months in which to inform him of its views. The Ombudsman then forwards a report to the European Parliament and to the institution concerned. The person lodging the complaint is informed of the outcome of such enquiries. The Ombudsman reports annually to the European Parliament.

The Ombudsman, who enjoys complete independence in the performance of his duties, is appointed after each election of the European Parliament for the duration of its term of office and is eligible for reappointment. At the request of the European Parliament the Ombudsman may be dismissed for cause by the Court of Justice.

6

Trying to Have it Both Ways:
The European Free Trade Association

The Stockholm Convention establishing the European Free Trade Association (EFTA) was signed in Stockholm, Sweden, on January 4, 1960. The original signatory countries were Austria, Denmark, Norway, Portugal, Sweden, Switzerland and the United Kingdom. [1]

The EFTA convention, which entered into force on May 3, 1960, was drawn up in response to the Rome Treaty establishing the European Economic Community. Following application of this treaty on January 1, 1958, negotiations took place in OEEC to establish a free trade area among the seventeen OEEC countries. It soon became clear, however, that the two different concepts of European integration which had come to the surface in the Council of Europe statutes and the ECSC negotiations were still present. The United Kingdom did not want to give up its Commonwealth rights and obligations, nor its "special relationship" with the United States; nor did it seek the political union of Europe. Other countries, such as Austria, Sweden and Switzerland were concerned to preserve their neutral status. For Finland, indeed, an immediate neighbor of the Soviet Union, this was such a delicate matter that instead of joining EFTA, it signed an agreement of association and did not become a full member until January 1, 1986. Iceland acceded to the Convention on March 1, 1970.

However, since membership of EFTA and EEC are incompatible, the two groupings being based on the free trade area and the customs union, respectively, the latter enshrining certain supranational principles and mechanisms, certain member countries withdrew from EFTA after negotiating entry to EEC. Thus, Denmark and the United Kingdom withdrew from the Convention on January 1, 1973 and Portugal on January 1, 1986. (Greece, Ireland and Spain joined the European Community without first being members of EFTA).

There are currently six member countries of EFTA, namely Austria, Iceland, Finland, Norway, Sweden and Switzerland, the latter also representing Liechtenstein.

EFTA's principal achievements

Over the last thirty EFTA has achieved its objective of establishing a free-trade area in industrial products (the Convention does not cover agriculture) for "substantially all the trade" as required by Article XXIV of the GATT rules. All tariffs were eliminated three years ahead of schedule by 1966. (One year later abolition of tariffs between EFTA countries and Finland was also completed).

A major threat loomed however when certain EFTA countries withdrew from the Convention and adhered to the EEC Treaty in 1986. Since the latter requires a common external tariff, there was a danger that tariff barriers between Denmark and the United Kingdom and other EFTA countries would have to be re-erected. The free trade agreements between EFTA countries and the European Community, concluded in 1973, were therefore of paramount importance. The goal of building a bridge between the two economic groupings was achieved.

A successful venture of a different kind was the setting up in 1976 of the EFTA Industrial Development Fund for Portugal. This fund remained in place even after Portugal left EFTA to join the European Community on January 1, 1986. Designed to assist small and medium-sized firms, the fund has helped to create thousands of new jobs in Portugal and secured many existing ones. It has thus made a major contribution to Portugal's economic development.

An important event in European economic integration was the first meeting, in Luxembourg in April 1984, of ministers from all EFTA and EC countries. The Luxembourg Declaration published on this occasion declared a common objective of creating a dynamic "economic space" in Europe. In May 1984, meeting in Visby, Denmark, EFTA heads of government decided to accelerate removal of technical barriers to trade, to simplify rules of origin (required for a free trade area because it has no common external tariffs) and customs documentation and to facilitate border controls.[2] It was also decided to increase cooperation with respect to research and protection of the environment.

How EFTA functions

EFTA's principal task is to operate a free trade area, mainly for industrial goods, but also having regard to agriculture and fisheries where these are important to member countries. Negotiations are constantly in progress to adopt economic and social structures to new realities.

For this purpose the Stockholm Convention provides a framework which was deliberately kept simple, so much so that the convention formally establishes only one institution, the Council of governmental representatives. The Council set up committees and working parties. The daily running of the Association at Geneva headquarters is based on the interaction between permanent delegations, institutions and the secretariat.

The Council

The Council is the governing body of the Association, a forum where the government representatives consult, negotiate and take joint decisions. Each member state has one vote, exercised at the level of ministers or their permanent representatives. The Council meets twice a month in Geneva at the level of the officials, twice yearly at full ministerial level. The agenda is prepared at deputy level. Chairmanship of the Council is rotated every six months.

According to Article 32 of the convention, it shall be the responsibility of the Council:

(a) to exercise such powers and functions as are conferred upon it by this Convention,

(b) to supervise the application of this Convention and keep it under review,

(c) to consider whether further action should be taken by member states in order to promote the attainment of the objectives of the Association and to facilitate the establishment of closer links with other States, unions of States or international organisations.

Procedures are provided for amending the convention. Council "decisions" are binding on all member countries. However, there is no dilution of sovereignty since decisions are made by unanimous vote, except for procedural matters. "Recommendations" or less formal invitations to members to conform to majority opinion are issued in connection with disputes between countries.

Settlement of disputes

A participating country considering that benefits conferred by the convention or objectives of the Association are not being achieved may bring a formal complaint before the Council if the member states concerned are unable to reach a settlement among themselves. Article 31 of the convention provides that the Council "shall promptly, by majority vote, make arrangements for examining the matter". The Council may use the permanent EFTA institutions or set up a special Examining Committee (as set out in Article 33).

The Council studies the ensuing report and issues a Recommendation. If it subsequently finds that an obligation under the convention has not been met, the Council may, by majority vote, authorize other countries to suspend applications of specified obligations under the convention.

However, this formal complaint procedure has not been used since 1967. Many disputes have been handled in a more informal manner, with both commercial and legal aspects being taken into account in the discussion and the countries involved defending their position before the EFTA Council. The pressure on member countries fully to observe the letter and spirit of the rules and to permit examination has helped to keep recourse to formal complaints to a minimum.

Standing Committees

EFTA has created a number of permanent committees to advise the Council. From time to time it sets up *ad hoc* groups to advise on a specific problem.

The Committee of Trade Experts meets about four times a year to make proposals to the Council on questions related to the operation of the trade provisions of Articles 3 through 12 of the convention. This committee also considers relations with the European Community.

A permanent committee on technical barriers to trade was set up in 1984. It deals with the harmonization of technical regulations and standards and reciprocal recognition of tests, inspections and certification. The committee periodically holds joint meetings with the EC Commission.

The Committee on Origin and Customs Exports advises the Council on product origin and other customs issues. It meets about ten times a year.

Regular reviews of the economic situation in member countries are conducted by the Economic Committee. This body also holds twice-yearly exchanges of views on the economic and financial policies of member governments. It meets annually with Community experts.

Other EFTA advisory bodies include the Committee on Agriculture and Fisheries, the Economic Development Committee and the Budget Committee.

The Consultative Committee is a little different. It is composed not of official government delegates but of representatives from economic bodies in member countries: industry, commerce, trade unions. Five members from each country sit in a personal capacity. The committee thus provides the Council with views from outside governmental circles. It is roughly equivalent to the Economic and Social Committee in the European Community. Conversely, it helps to create a body of informed opinion in member countries about EFTA aims and activities. The Consultative Committee's deliberations are wide-ranging, touching on such matters as unemployment and economic restructuring. The Committee meets twice yearly with a European Community delegation. Its Economic and Social Sub-Committee advises on economic and social problems engendered by the process of European integration.

Finally, mention should be made of the Committee of Members of Parliament of the EFTA Countries, set up in 1977 by the Council. The Committee held its first meetings in Strasbourg but is now convened in Geneva. It is composed of parliamentarians from the Parliamentary Assembly of the Council of Europe. Thus, although EFTA has no formal parliamentary organ it does receive parliamentary "input" on its activities.

The Secretariat

The small EFTA secretariat consists of a secretary-general, assisted by a deputy secretary-general and six departments. The latter deal with trade policy affairs, legal affairs, economic affairs, press and information services. They also include a Council secretariat and an administrative section.

When Denmark, Portugal and the United Kingdom withdrew from EFTA, the Council magnanimously retained in their employment members of the secretariat who are nationals of those countries.

Free trade rules and the problem of origin

A free trade area is defined in Article XXIV of the General Agreement on Tariffs and Trade (GATT) as a group of customs territories in which the duties and other restrictive regulations of commerce are eliminated in substantially all the trade between the constituent territories in products originating in such territories. The General Agreement thus provides the international legal basis for EFTA's Stockholm Convention and for the free trade agreements concluded between EFTA countries and the European Community.

As discussed in the chapter on GATT, a free trade area involves departure from the principle that all GATT countries should treat each other equally, without preference or discrimination, in trade matters. This exception to the most-favored-nation clause is permitted because GATT recognizes that formal regional agreements, while discriminating in the short term, should ultimately promote freer trade world-wide.

Since EFTA exists on the premise that its member countries seek to retain greater independence than that permitted by European Community membership, its organization and activities are pervaded by a minimalist philosophy. EFTA countries balance gains from integration against losses in autonomy. Consequently, its rules were designed to interfere as little as possible with the fiscal policies of participating governments. They can raise revenue in any way they see fit provided they do not interfere with the agreed elimination of protective barriers to trade.

Article Six of the Convention provides for elimination of duties, taxes and other charges which contain an "effective protective element". This is understood as a charge which protects domestic products, exceeds the cost of services rendered or restricts imports. Border charges are therefore monitored by the Committee of Trade Experts. [4]

Rules of origin

The essential difference, as defined by GATT rules, between a customs union, such as the European Community of "The Twelve", and a free trade area is the absence in the latter case of a unified level of charges or "common external tariff" on imports from non-member countries. It follows that, in the absence of a control mechanism, a third country could avoid a high tariff on its product by shipping that product to a free trade area country with a lower tariff and then moving the product across the tariff-free borders within the free trade area. To take a hypothetical example, let us suppose that Iceland charges 10% on widgets and Sweden 15%. A widget-exporting country, say Canada, could avoid 5% of duty on its product by selling to Sweden via Iceland.

To make things even more complicated, it must be noted that a product — say Canadian widgets — may be added to or transformed inside the free trade area prior to their ultimate sale. Perhaps they will by assembled (including locally-produced handles) and boxed in Sweden, for instance. It must then be decided whether the product is essentially Canadian or Swedish.

We are now confronted with three classes of product: those wholly produced inside the free trade area, those produced inside the area from imported goods or a mixture of indigenous materials and imported goods; and those which have been produced entirely outside the area.

It follows that the tracking of goods in a customs union is simpler than in a free trade area. For the latter a foolproof system of certificates of origin, establishing "what comes from where" is of supreme importance. For commodities not wholly produced within the area, it was necessary to set a minimum to the value added within the area or a processing criterion, in order to determine whether or how much duty should be charged on such products.

All three criteria ("wholly-produced", "value added" and "processing") were used in the original EFTA regulations. However, the problem became more complex when EFTA and the European Community negotiated free trade in most industrial products between their two groups in 1971-72, with all tariffs to be eliminated by mid-1977. Based on its experience with former colonies (the Yaoundé Convention), the Community proposed a system with two criteria, the "wholly-produced" (internals) and "processing" (partially external) criteria.[5] The EFTA countries accepted this system not only for trade with the Community but also among themselves. The rules were imposed and simplified in the light of experience (allowing, in particular, for "cumulative origin", or successive stages of manufacture in more than one country). The improved system was adopted by EFTA countries in 1973.

The Convention also provides several other defenses against unfair or unequal trading practices within the group, such as provoking increase of imports into another member country. The Convention also forbids repayment or remission of duties to exporters on imported materials used in making their products. Known as "drawback", this practice would have the effect of putting one EFTA country at an advantage when exporting to another EFTA country, since competing producers in the latter may also have had to pay duty to import manufacturing materials from outside the free trade area. Finally, there is a range of regulations controlling and restricting government subsidies to home industries. A home industry, already favored by its home location, would enjoy an unfair double advantage in competition with a similar imported product if the home product were subsidized. (This of course is at the base of farm product disputes between the EC and the US).

Taken together, EFTA regulations create what Americans like to call a level playing field — equal conditions of trade among all the partners of the free trade association. Naturally, some of these rules apply to all GATT members and, to an even greater extent, to members of a common market. Countries which join together to form a trade group where, as American Express would say, membership has its privileges, must not only be loyal to each other but also as fair as possible to GATT countries outside the group. Those who seek free and fair trade for themselves must grant it to their trading partners.[6]

Reducing technical barriers to trade

A problem besetting all trading partners, whether in GATT, EFTA or EC, is that of technical barriers to trade (TBT's). This is a generic term embracing obstacles to trade stemming from differing national product requirements or standards of a technical nature. These can affect not only the product itself but also its transport from one country to another.

For example, everyone accepts the need for health and safety regulations and for environmental protection. However if such regulations are used to impede imports rather than to promote reasonable safeguards they clearly constitute an unfair trading practice. By increasing production costs in the exporting industry, TBT's have an effect comparable to quotas or customs duties. Europe-wide and indeed global efforts have been under way for several years to create universally accepted technical standards. [7]

Agriculture and Fisheries

The countries which came together in the Stockholm Convention were not seeking to institute a common agricultural policy. They all support their agricultural sector in various ways and intend to continue doing so. A centrally managed EFTA "CAP" similar to the Community's would have impinged too greatly on the sovereign rights of member states. Consequently, the Convention does not provide for elimination of price supports and tariff and quota restrictions on agricultural products. Nevertheless, the countries did agree to promote mutual trade in such commodities, including trade in fish and other marine products. (It should be noted that while overall trade in agriculture among EFTA countries is small compared to industrial exchanges, some EFTA countries are among the most important fishing nations of the world. Export of fish and fish products is for Iceland by far the most important component of the national economy). An opening up of the fisheries market was therefore an essential condition of continued Icelandic membership, not to mention that of Norway. At its meeting in Kristiansand, Norway, in June 1989, the EFTA Ministerial Council welcomed the report of its working group on the liberalization of trade in fish and decided to amend the Convention accordingly.

Benevolent incrementalism: EFTA and the European Community

Paul Krugman, Professor of Economics at the Massachusetts Institute of Technology, pointed out in a recent study that as an association of advanced European economies which for political and historical reasons chose not to join the EEC, EFTA was in its original incarnation "in a mild way a rival or at least an alternative commercial bloc to the EEC", and that "with the entrance (*sic*) of the United Kingdom into the EC this ceased to be true in any practical sense".[8]

EFTA's current membership is composed of countries which are very large traders on a *per capita* basis because of both their high income and open economies, while at the same time consisting of small, geographically, dispersed populations.

As Professor Krugman states, EFTA does not therefore in any real sense form a trading region. It was hence not surprising that EFTA and the Community should move closer together to form a trading partnership, at least in industrial goods. Thus, the creation of what was at first called the European Economic Space (EES) goes far to demonstrate the validity of the original GATT premise that trade groups, while discriminating against non-member countries in the short term, would promote freer world trade in the long term.

Abolition of tariffs among EFTA countries was achieved on December 31, 1966. Meanwhile, the United Kingdom was making repeated attempts to join the EEC. A treaty on the accession of Denmark, Norway, the United Kingdom and Ireland was finally signed on January 22, 1972, although Norway's membership was rejected in a national referendum the following September. On July 22, 1972, free trade agreements with the EC were signed by Austria, Iceland, Portugal, Sweden and Switzerland and initiated by Finland. Upon ratification, the agreements gave impetus to European economic integration by creating free trade for industrial goods among over 350 million people.

A summit meeting of prime ministers and other ministers of EFTA countries was convened in Vienna on May 13, 1977. The meeting agreed not only on the need for intensive cooperation within EFTA but also on the desirability of further development of trade and economic relations with the Community. It took seven years for this wish to receive political fulfillment. On April 9, 1984, the smallest EC country, Luxembourg—a psychologically judicious choice—hosted the first meeting of ministers from all EFTA and EC countries, a "benchmark" event for wider European economic relations. Since that date progress has been gradual but the mood increasingly positive: "benevolent incrementalism sets the tone of the dialogue". [9]

At the conclusion of this meeting a joint statement was issued. The Luxembourg Declaration, as it came to be known, addressed four principal issues.

To contain protectionist pressures and improve free circulation of industrial products, the ministers called for cooperation on harmonization of standards, elimination of technical barriers, simplification of border formalities and rules of origin and elimination of unfair trading practices, including government procurement. [10]

The second general commitment involved EFTA/EC cooperation beyond trade, particularly as regards research (telecommunications, information systems and audio-visual media); transport; agriculture; fisheries; energy. Social, cultural, environmental and legal issues were to be addressed, while taking into account the work in progress in the Council of Europe and other international bodies. (Duplication is an ever-present danger as each institution acquires its own dynamics. Secretariats are probably as guilty as any in discounting the activities of other bodies).

The third area of cooperation concerned measures to sustain economic recovery and contain unemployment.

Finally, ministers agreed to coordinate their relations with other parts of the world, as regards economic development and international trade, both bilaterally and in international bodies such as OECD, GATT, the International Monetary Fund and the World Bank.[11]

To define the goal of closer cooperation between the nineteen countries in the European free trade system, the Luxembourg Declaration coined the term "European Economic Space". Fifteen years later, when this notion was finally enshrined in a treaty, the terminology was changed to European Economic Area.

EFTA and Eastern Europe

In the late eighties events and aspirations in central and eastern Europe gave the term an even wider connotation. As former COMECON countries turned to the market economy and sought to make their currencies convertible (not enjoying the immediate absorption into the Community and the economic union with the west which was available to the former German Democratic Republic), they increasingly felt the need to become part of the European Economic Space.

The meeting of the EFTA Council at ministerial level, on December 11 and 12, 1989, addressed this issue. In a special statement ministers welcomed the economic changes in Eastern Europe, as well as the establishment of political pluralism and democratic freedoms. They looked forward to contacts between such countries and EFTA, noting that the Hungarian Government had already presented a draft common declaration on EFTA-Hungarian cooperation. They entrusted the Council at official level to enter into discussions with individual countries in Eastern Europe and to work out forms of cooperation. They also declared themselves ready to join with the European Community in a "constructive discussion" of proposals for financial support. [12]

Settlement of disputes in EEA

As we have seen in a previous chapter, EFTA and the EEA suffered a setback in late 1981 when the proposed machinery for settling EEA disputes, the EFTA Surveillance Authority (ESA) was found by the European Court of Justice in Luxembourg to be in conflict with its own supreme jurisdictional powers for the interpretation of EC treaties. According to the ECJ, its freedom to rule in an EC case could have been curtailed if a similar case had already been decided by the joint EEA tribunal.

On renegotiation an alternative arrangement was arrived at which leaves the ECJ's powers intact. On competition policy most matters are settled by a conciliation committee but the EC retains the right to refer certain matters to the Court if its vital interests are involved. On matters other than competition policy the procedure involves first a joint committee then, if necessary, binding arbitration by a panel of three personalities, one of whom must be selected from outside the EC and EFTA.

Perhaps the most surprising thing about EFTA is that over thirty years after its creation it still exists and may even be enjoying a limited fresh flowering under the newly-emphasized notion of "multi-speed Europe". This term should be used with caution, however, since whereas EFTA was originally conceived as an alternative to the European Community, "multi-speed" carries a connotation of all states ending up in the same organization even if they arrive there at different times and in dispersed formation.

EFTA is inured to the hot-and-cold showers of the *douche écossaise*. It seemed as though its days were numbered each time the UK, Denmark and Norway applied to the EC but salvation twice came from an unlikely source — the Gaullian Elysée. When under Goeroges Pompidou they succeeded on the third attempt Norway promptly voted no in a national referendum; and stayed in EFTA. Then as Portugal left it it met Finland on the way in.

The prospect of closer integration of the Community economies which follows removal of all obstacles to internal trade on January 1, 1993, combined with the "downgrading" of neutrality resulting from the end of the Cold War has created among EFTA governments what we may call the "trailer effect". Neutrality is no longer seen as an obstacle to EC membership. After Ireland (never an EFTA member) has shown that its conception of neutrality can survive in Brussels, Austria, Sweden and Switzerland, half the EFTA membership, have all despite the EEA applied to join the other, stronger club. Even after another "hot shower" for EFTA — the Danish rejection of Maastricht — they were quick to confirm their applications and may soon be followed by Norway.

Will EFTA last another thirty years? Can it become a sort of economic CSCE or Council of Europe for all countries not members, for the time being at least, of the Brussels inner circle? This seems unlikely. Eastern European states are showing a preference for association agreements with the EC over full membership of EFTA. There has been no new entry into the Association since Finland's accession "replaced" Portugal's departure in January, 1986.

It is hard to imagine EFTA reduced to a free trade area between Iceland and Liechtenstein! Its days do seem to be numbered. This should not be a cause for regret. EFTA's beginnings were antagonistic, despite protestations to the contrary, but its career has been honorable, finally contributing to avoidance of a major economic split in western Europe; now times have changed, as such powerful bodies as CMEA and WTO recently discovered. It will take a few years for the EC enlargement to be consummated but even today management of the EEA could be absorbed into Brussels.

But the Free Trade Association is perfectly capable of demonstrating, like Mark Twain, that news of its demise is premature. . . .[13]

Notes

1　At the same time a protocol extended the Convention to the Principality of Liechtenstein, which has a customs union with Switzerland. Switzerland was appointed to represent Liechtenstein on matters pertaining to the Convention, although the Principality usually attends Council meetings at FM or PM level.

2　Since January 1, 1988, all EFTA and EC countries have implemented the Single Administrative Document, replacing numerous national customs documents, and common procedures for the transit of goods through a participating country.

3　A unanimous vote is defined as one in which no negative vote is cast. Abstentions therefore carry no weight, since they do not block a decision.

4　It should be noted that export duties which protect home industries against loss of key indigenous materials are also disallowed (Article 8).

5　In this system, the processing criterion requires products to be transformed sufficiently to be classified in a tariff classification different from that of the materials used.

6　It is beyond the scope of this study to review all the countervailing (retaliatory) mechanisms provided by national laws and international agreements to allege, prove and combat unfair trading practices. The ultimate sanction employed by the United States is that of countervailing duties (CVD's). During the period 1980-1985, the United States initiated 252 cases against other countries and the European Community. During the same period, only one countervailing duty was initiated against the US. It should be noted however that many countries prefer court action to imposition of countervailing mechanisms. See Hufbauer, Gary, Procedures for Monitoring and Disciplining Government Aids, EFTA Economic Affairs Department, Occasional Paper Nr 30, Geneva, 1989, pp. 20 and 21.

7　Organizations cooperating in this effort include GATT, OECD, EC, EFTA, the Economic Commission for Europe (ECE) of the United Nations, the International Standardization Organization (ISO), the International Electrotechnical Commission (IEC), the European Committee for Standardization (CEN) and the European Committee for Electrotechnical Standardization (CENELEC). It is the setting of a date — December 31, 1992 — for completion of these standards and hence removal of final obstacles to the free flow of trade within the EC which has captured American imagination as the ominous and almost mythical challenge of "1992".

8　Krugman, Paul, EFTA and 1992, EFTA Economic Affairs Department, Occasional Paper Nr 23, Geneva 1988, p. 1.

9　Wallace, Helen and Wessels, Wolfgang, Towards a new Partnership: the EC and EFTA in the wider Western Europe, EFTA Economic Affairs Department, Geneva, 1989, p. 22.

10　Governments traditionally favor their own national industries when issuing calls for tender to fulfill government contracts. While such preferences are sometimes justified on security grounds they can also constitute significant unfair trading practices, since the government itself is frequently the largest customer in a national economy.

11　Only six weeks later, meeting in Visby, Sweden, an EFTA "summit" gave precise instructions to its advisory committees to follow up on the Luxembourg Declaration. The speed with which this action was taken highlights the importance of the Luxembourg meeting to EFTA governments.

12 As noted in the preceding chapter, on May 18, 1990, the EC set up the European Bank for Reconstruction and Development (EBRD/BERD), with headquarters in London, to assist Eastern European countries with economic reconstruction. Participation is not limited to Community and recipient countries.

13 For further information contact the EFTA secretariat at 9-11, rue de Varembé, CH 1211 Geneva 20, Switzerland; telephone (4122) 749.11.11. A Brussels office (118, rue d'Arlon, B 1040 Brussels, Belgium; telephone (322) 231.17.87) specializes in EFTA/EC relations and supervision of the EEA.

7

More Equal than Others:
The CMEA and Trade Cooperation in
Eastern Europe

Although the Council for Mutual Economic Assistance (CMEA) was founded as early as January 1948, by Albania, Bulgaria, Czechoslovakia, Hungary, Poland, Romania and the Soviet Union as a counterpoint to the Marshall Plan, the organs of the Council were not fully developed until 1962.[1] According to its Charter, signed in Sofia, Bulgaria, on December 14, 1959 and amended in 1962 and 1974, CMEA, otherwise known as COMECON, seeks

> ... to contribute to the further intensification and improvement of cooperation and the development of socialist economic integration, the planned development of the national economic integration, the planned development of the national economies, the acceleration of economic and technical progress, the raising of the level of industrialization in the less-industrialized countries, the steady increase in the productivity of labor, the approximation and gradual equalization of levels of economic development and the constant improvement in the welfare of the peoples of the member countries.

> ... Economic, scientific and technical cooperation ... is carried out in accordance with the principle of international socialism, with respect for state sovereignty, independence and national interests, non-interference in internal affairs, full equality of rights, mutual advantage and mutual fraternal assistance.

COMECON's principal organs are the Assembly (a supreme ministerial council, not a parliamentary body), the Executive Committee (created in 1962), the International Organization Committees, twenty or more standing Sectoral Commissions and ten permanent conferences and scientific institutes. The Secretariat, with headquarters in Moscow, was set up in 1954. By agreement of its remaining members, the organization was dissolved in January 1991, with the intention of replacing it by a newly-structured Organization for International Economic Cooperation (OIEC). For historical purposes, however, let us consider that CMEA is still operational ...

De jure, "sovereign equality," de facto ...

Convened at least once a year, the CMEA ministerial Assembly meeting has authority to take advice on matters within its competence and to adopt recommendations and decisions on a basis of sovereign equality. National delegations are headed by the Prime Minister or his deputy. The Assembly meets annually in turn in the capital of each member country, with the host country in the chair. Extraordinary sessions may be held at the request of one-third of the member countries.

Article III of the CMEA Charter sets out the organization's functions and powers. The Council is directed to organize economic, scientific and technical cooperation to make the most rational use of natural resources, to accelerate production and to contribute to socialist economic integration. CMEA fosters improvement of the "international socialist division of labor" through coordinated planning. It studies economic, scientific and technical problems and assists member countries in joint measures for industry, agriculture, transport, investment, construction, trade and the exchange of expertise. This action may include agreements with member countries, third countries and international organizations.

Formed in 1962, the Executive Committee meets quarterly to implement and monitor the Council's policies. The Committee is convened at the level of deputy heads of government. The Committee's well-defined and wide-ranging powers reflect its function as the principal executive organ of the Council. It not only directs the CMEA's work and approves its budget but may set up control bodies. In 1971, for instance, the Committee on Cooperation in Planning Activities and the Committee on Scientific and Technical Cooperation were formed in this way. The Committee on Cooperation in Material and Technical Supply followed shortly thereafter.

Some twenty Standing Commissions promote economic, scientific and technical cooperation in specific sectors. Each has its seat in a country with a special interest in the activity, such as coal-mining in Poland, tool-making in Czechoslovakia. However, the Soviet Union exercizes a *de facto* hegemony; key commissions, such as those for foreign trade, currency and finance, are located in Moscow.[2] Other economic sectors covered by the Standing Commissions include the chemical industry, ferrous metallurgy, oil and gas, coal, electric power, food, agriculture, transport, public health and posts and telecommunications.

Permanent conferences cutting across economic sectors cover legal affairs, pricing (we are not dealing here with a free-market economy), water management, internal trade, freight and shipping and state labor bodies.

The CMEA has coordinated a number of research, production and trade organizations such as the Institute for Nuclear Research (Dubna, USSR); the Ball Bearing Coordination Center (Warsaw) and Intermetall (Budapest). There is extensive coordination of railroad operations, including a pooling of rolling stock, one of the Council's more successful ventures. In October, 1963, COMECON created the International Bank for Economic Cooperation. It did not function well owing to currency conversion, credit and capital investment problems.

Bartering in the bazaar

From its structure and activities one may infer that CMEA achieved far-reaching integration, especially in the heavy industrial sectors, without loss of national sovereignty. However, appearances do not reflect achievements. The International Bank for Economic Cooperation did not succeed in creating a true multilateral payments system. The "transfer rouble", used as a joint unit of account, was not a freely traded currency. (In the West the ECU has known similar limitations, but at least it is composed of a "basket" of all participating currencies). Consequently, bilateral trade between COMECON countries always had to be balanced. To make things worse, the very creation of the organization replaced existing trade flow between Eastern and Western Europe. Finally and most importantly, Marxist-Leninist principles of state control and centralized planning did not lend themselves to true international cooperation in the economic sector. The sovereignty issue, already so troubling in the unfolding of Western European cooperation, is vastly more sensitive among authoritarian regimes. The principles of "mutual assistance" and "socialist division of labor" resulted in practice in the Soviet Union exporting low-cost raw materials and energy to the fraternal socialist countries while the latter manufactured industrial goods which they could sell to no country other than (who else?) the Soviet Union . . . with colossal environmental pollution as a significant by-product. All this looks more like bartering in the bizarre (a misprint for "bazar" but apt enough to retain!) than true multilateral trade. Nevertheless, as the countries of Eastern Europe developed their appetite for hard currency, their limited output of high quality items was wherever possible shipped to western countries so that they could in turn purchase products from the West.

The political shake-up of 1989 and 1990 in Eastern European spelled death to the organization. The German Democratic Republic left CMEA when it joined the Federal Republic and with it the European Community. The former state-owned industries of the GDR found themselves unable to export goods to the Soviet Union. Their erstwhile trading partners were either unable to pay or preferred to devote their limited foreign exchange to acquisition of the best available truly western products.

Why did COMECON fail? We have seen that the international Socialist principles of "mutual assistance" reflected in COMECON's name implied reciprocal duties as well as rights. These principles provided an institutional basis for interference in internal affairs in the name of the higher interests of the socialist camp. When the CMEA charter was amended in 1974, explicit mention was made of the principle of socialist internationalism.[3] In practice, however, the interests of the member states were diverse. Romania early adopted an independent stance. The smaller countries were forced into a tributary role *vis-à-vis* the Soviet Union. Cuba, Vietnam and Mongolia, geographically diverse and far from Europe, had nothing in common other than their status as poor developing countries. They remained heavily dependent on foreign aid. In Bulgaria and Romania the old guard retained power. On the other hand, Czechoslovakia, Hungary and Poland made overtures to the West, commencing with the Council of Europe. They have since dismantled the state economy and become associate members of the European Community.

OIEC: a singed phoenix

The domino defections from socialist theory and practice by Eastern Europe in 1989 and 1990 proved too much for COMECON. On January 5, 1991, the Council's Executive Committee voted to dissolve the organization and to replace itself with a more market-oriented body, the Organization for International Economic Cooperation (OIEC). Nikolaus Piper wrote that there was no real justification for the successor organization to COMECON. "It seems sure", he declared, "to be shortlived".[4] Even this proved an understatement: OIEC never lived at all. Less than a year later the USSR had ceased to exist.

Threshold of pain

The mixed economies of Western Europe have evolved in a careful balance between private and public sectors. In moving a totally state-owned system over to the free market, East Europeans did not know where to begin. The state cannot sell off what its salaried employees cannot afford to buy. Individual enterprise is not free while wholesale distribution channels remain under state control. Where small businesses do arise, they frequently set up a parallel economy, or black market, paying no taxes to government, which is then further strapped in effecting reforms. Inertia is all the greater where Communist managers prove irreplaceable because the new, reform-minded generation has not yet been trained to an adequate technical level.

On achieving political emancipation many citizens expected the good life to follow in its wake. In fact, speed of reform and pain threshold are in direct correlation. So far, in choosing to move fast only Poland among the ex-CMEA states outside the former Soviet Union has accepted a high level of pain and even here there are clear signs of public weakening.[5] In such a climate national minorities become increasingly restive. Boris Yeltsin and the Russian Federation, while courageously addressing reform are beset by centrifugal forces not only at the ex-Soviet CIS level but even within Russia itself. At their Washington summit in June 1992 President Bush called Yeltsin's reform effort "the most important foreign policy issue of our time" (foreign to Bush, domestic to Yeltsin) but so far it is Germany which has given the most money.

With such monumental problems on the national level, the discipline essential to international cooperation (which also implies competition) seems almost like a luxury.

Unfortunate timing: restructuring in a depression

With the western market economies in depression there could scarely have been a worse time for Central Europe to embark on massive economic restructuring. The recession which made its mark in 1990 deepened in 1991 as the former COMECON countries reduced their intra-bloc trade. The former USSR, which had been the dominant partner in the organization, reduced its imports by over 50% — not surprising in view of the fact that the USSR itself was breaking up.

Over two years, industrial production in Hungary fell 20% (although that country had been instituting reforms for over a decade). For Czechoslovakia the figure was also 20%; 30% in Poland; 40% for Bulgaria and Romania.[6] During this period, these nations freed prices, put an end to the state monopoly in external trade and made their currencies convertible albeit subject to some exchange controls. In many cases, however, salary increases were pegged to control inflation. As real income declined, internal demand plummeted. Intra-"COMECON" trade was hindered by the replacement of a barter system (with the rouble as unit of account) by payment in foreign exchange at world prices. Balance of payments deteriorated; external debt rose; but the most troublesome indicator was the rise in unemployment, virtually unknown under the command economy of the communist system. With weak internal demand, the prospects for private western investment are not attractive, which in turn slows down the whole process of selling off state monopolies. After forty years of paying the price of totalitarian domination, an aspect of the Cold War from which the West was spared, the economies of Central Europe need and deserve the steadying influence of a long-term reconstruction plan in partnership with Western Europe, even if, as Germany is now discovering, western economies must accept part of the load and settle for a slower recovery for themselves. The choice may well be one of partnership or mass immigration. Is the West to say no to vegetables from Poland or Czechoslovakia when what is really needed is a new Marshall Plan? . . . Or, at the very least, as an angry Walesa declared in Strasbourg in February, 1992, to risk some serious investment rather than just looking to make a fast buck?

EC Association agreements with Eastern Europe

In December 1991 a breakthrough was achieved for the non-Balkan countries of Central Europe, Poland, Czechoslovakia and Hungary. The European Commission initialed association or "Europe Agreements" just a year after negotiations began. The agreements are designed to quicken the reform process in the three countries, paving the way for eventual Community membership. In some respects therefore they fit into the 19-nation EEA agreement between the EC and EFTA, also concluded in the fall of 1991. They actually represent a second step, building upon the trade and cooperation agreements already in place since June 1990.

The structure of all three pacts is identical, but they vary in content according to the needs of the individual countries. For example, the agreements reflect the fact that Poland and Hungary are more dependent on agricultural exports than Czechoslovakia. In term of goods, the ten-year agreements are preferential and aim to create eventual free trade. They contain trade concessions to the three countries and special protocols on textiles, customs cooperation and rules of origin. Agriculture and fisheries trade will be based on mutual concessions: some EC countries are nervous about having to compete with cheap foodstuffs from Poland and Hungary, even through everyone knows that more trade means less aid in the long run.

Right of establishment for businesses and professionals is based on national treatment; the EC extended this immediately to the three countries, while they enjoy a transition period before EC entities gain reciprocal rights. The three countries are adapting their laws to Community legislation, particularly to competition rules, to promote integration with the EC economies. "We are exporting our legislation", commented the Community's chief Negotiater, Pablo Benavides. In addition, the free movement of capital is written into each accord (i.e. EC investors will be able to repatriate profits and vice versa). These countries continue to receive financial assistance through PHARE (the program of Western economic aid for the reconstruction of Central and Eastern Europe, which is coordinated by the Commission) until the end of 1992. Further, they receive EC assistance in areas of common interest: compilation of reliable statistics, EC product and safety standards, education and training, regional development, prevention of money laundering and drug trafficking, environmental protection and clean up, transportation and telecommunications.

Poland, Czechoslovakia and Hungary have made a clear choice, preferring to link up with the dynamic western economic machine rather than recreate an eastern economic bloc. The other countries of Eastern Europe have little option but to seek to do the same.

These three agreements were followed in the Spring of 1992 by similar accords with Estonia, Latvia and Lithuania.

Notes

1 Mongolia joined the CMEA on June 7, 1962, and Cuba on July 12, 1972. A cooperation agreement with Finland was ratified on June 8, 1973. Yugoslavia participated in some activities. Albania was expelled in 1961. Vietnam became a member on June 29, 1978. The People's Republic of Yemen was granted observer status on June 28, 1979.

2 In accusing the Soviet Union of "hegemony" one must consider whether the United States can be tarred with the same brush in the West. The answer is negative, for several reasons:

1. The US does not have contiguous boundaries with its European partners.
2. The population ratio between the US and Western Europe is more balanced than that in the East (70:30 in favor of the Soviet Union).
3. Far from seeking "war reparations" as was the case in the East the Marshall Plan provided aid.
4. Democratic political systems gave voice to a greater diversity of opinion and policy in the West.
5. US military presence was subject to free acceptance (with the exception of the FRG immediately following WWII) as demonstrated by de Gaulle's ejection of NATO forces from French territory.

3 Article I, Paragraph 2. For the text of the Charter and a useful analysis of CMEA's structure, see Schiavone, Giuseppe, *The Institutions of COMECON*, Holmers and Meier Publishers, Inc., New York, 1981.

4 *Die Zeit*, Hamburg, January 11, 1991. A letter addressed by the author to CMEA for information about OIEC remained unanswered.

5 The problem also exists inside the CIS. In July 1992 Ukraine dismissed its reform-minded premier and appointed an ex-communist committed to a slower pace of change.

6 Figures from *Le Monde - L'Economie*, February 18, 1992.

8

Lifting the Curtain:
The Conference on Security and
Cooperation in Europe

The Conference on Security and Cooperation in Europe (CSCE) was officially created by the Final Act signed in Helsinki on August 1, 1975, by thirty-five countries. The countries of Western Europe, NATO, the Warsaw Treaty Organization, the three ex-Yugoslav states, the neutrals — all except Andorra and unrecognized segments of Yugoslavia are represented in this organization, the first specifically European body to span the Iron Curtain and, as such, the single most important European forum for promoting security and cooperation and the non-violent resolution of conflicts throughout the continent.

The CSCE is remarkable not only for the breadth of its membership and its overriding purpose, but also for its method of operation. From 1975 to 1990 the Conference had no secretariat and no headquarters at all. Its decisions are taken by consensus and all states — from the US and Russia to Monaco, Liechtenstein and San Marino — have an equal voice. The CSCE is Europe from . . . Vancouver to Vladivostok.

Such a body, if indeed "body" is the right term for so ephemeral yet durable an entity as a conference alternately convened and adjourned, called into plenary session and scattered in a diaspora of self-sustaining committees of experts and working parties, — such a body may appear at first sight to have little chance of survival in the stressful climate of four decades of East-West confrontation. Compared to the CSCE the Council of Europe is a tower of strength. Yet just as some nations can more readily accept the consultative machinery of the Council of Europe than the political and economic constraints of the European Community, so also did the CSCE prove a well-adapted instrument, like a giant amoeba of infinite plasticty, to bridge the chasm of suspicion between East and West; or a balloon, unweighed-down by infrastructure, which could rise above and float across the minefields and guard-towers of Europe's entrenched divisions.

Even the years which the CSCE needed to reach any significant level of achievement were an asset. It threatened no one. Confidence-building requires nurturing; commitment is a fruit which cannot be hastened to maturity.

Basket cases

CSCE activities are divided into three areas called "baskets". The first addresses confidence-building measures, political *détente*, security and the peaceful settlement of disputes. Basket 2 includes the economy, science, technology and the environment. Basket 3 covers international contacts, including travel and emigration; free movement of information; East-West cultural cooperation; human rights; and educational projects (exchanges, research, foreign language teaching).

We have noted that from 1975 to 1991 the CSCE had no secretariat: Committee services and facilities were provided by host countries. At the Paris CSCE summit in November 1990 — fifteen years after CSCE's creation — it was nevertheless agreed to establish a small, deliberately modest secretariat in Prague. The choice of this central location was clearly political as well as geographic, avoiding both superpowers and Western Europe, which hosts many international bodies, and offering a role in the institutional constellation to the emergent democracies of Central Europe.

The decision to set up a limited administration established CSCE as a permanent body without allowing it to become dominated by an independent-minded bureaucracy. It plays the "EFTA" of security to NATO's "Common Market". Progress in East-West cooperation has been spectacular in recent years. At the same time relations between East and West and among former East bloc members remain delicate. The absence of a strong secretariat leaves maximum control in the hands of member governments not only collectively but also individually, since in virtually all cases decisions are taken by unanimous consent.

CSCE pursues its objectives through specialized conferences and working parties held in wide-ranging locations. Examples include the expert conference on peaceful resolution of conflicts (Montreux 1978); cooperation in the Mediterranean (Valletta 1979); science forum (Hamburg 1980); human rights (Ottawa 1985); a very important meeting on conventional force-reductions (CFE) (Vienna 1989); environmental conference (Sofia 1989); Europe's cultural heritage (Cracow 1991). The fourth plenary follow-up conference opened in Helsinki on March 24, 1992, ending with a summit in July.

CSCE employs negotiating procedures linking various "issue-areas". A process of bargaining, even bartering, pairs and trades principles of interest to different groups — not necessarily solidly "East" versus "West". Perhaps the most notable of these was acceptance at the founding conference of the geopolitical status quo in Eastern Europe in exchange for greater freedom of movement (notably emigration of Jews) and individual rights.

The delicate issue of human rights provides an illuminating example of this dual conciliation procedure. The definition of human rights in the concluding document of the Vienna conference of 1989 brings together two previously conflicting definitions. The western concept of human rights, as manifested in the UN Declaration and the Council of Europe's convention, enshrines fundamental individual freedoms. The Marxist tradition focuses on collective economic, social and cultural rights. The unemployment and homelessness permitted in the capitalist-democratic system were virtually unknown under communism, as is evidenced by the current difficulties of adjustment in eastern Germany (the former GDR), Poland and the East European countries.

Role of personal contacts and public opinion in *détente*

The Peace Research Institute in Frankfurt, Germany, has undertaken a comprehensive review of the CSCE. A report issued in 1985 to mark the Conference's tenth anniversary pointed out the symbiotic relationship between public opinion and transnational personal contacts on the one hand and *détente* on the other:

> Without the pressure exerted by the groups of people affected by the easing in human contacts, without the mobilizing forces of mass tourism, without the universalist tendencies of the mass media, of culture, science and education, and without the economic incentives to supranational cooperation, the incentives to make the "Iron Curtain" more permeable would probably have been much weaker. [1]

CSCE has made a major contribution toward integrating East and West in a mesh of political, economic, environmental and humanitarian initiatives essential to the common security concept. Today the line of confrontation between East and West has all but melted away: Bush and Yeltsin propose to cooperate on SDI! Let historians decide, with the perspective of time, whether Mikhail Gorbachev succeeded or failed; what is certain is that for him as for Boris Yeltsin the genie is out of the bottle.

Despite its panoply of baskets and varied agendas, CSCE could state its purpose in a single word: peace. When the Ministerial Council first met under the new permanent structures in Berlin on June 19 and 20, 1991, it set up machinery for the settlement of disputes threatening "peace, security or stability" in Europe. In a departure from the consensus rule, it agreed that a quorum of twelve countries (one third of the membership) might convene an emergency meeting at the level of senior officials. The consent of the country or countries directly concerned is not required: unlike the UN Security Council procedure, no veto power is provided. However, in order to obtain this concession from the Soviet Union (and also Turkey) it was necessary to include in the text a reference to the primordial importance of CSCE principles and, in particular, to the principle of non-intervention in the internal affairs of a member country. A statement issued by the Council favoring the "democratic development, unity and territorial integrity" of Yugoslavia could scarely serve as a precedent in this regard, since the Yugoslav government had itself requested the statement in an attempt to head off the breakaway of Croatia and Slovenia. It therefore remains to be seen whether CSCE intervention will be limited to the international aspects of a crisis; and, if so, how meaningful this will be. [2]

The members of the body responsible for the peaceful settlement of disputes are appointed by the Center for the prevention of conflict already set up by CSCE in Vienna.

President Bush's suggestion of providing the CSCE with a parliamentary arm has not been taken up. We have noted that in September 1990 the Parliamentary Assembly of the Council of Europe hosted a meeting open to parliamentarians from all CSCE countries.

Building a structure, defining a role

After failing to exercize any lasting impact on the Yugoslav situation CSCE faded somewhat from the international scene in the Fall of 1991, concentrating on the organization of its secretariat in Prague. Nonetheless a conference was held in Moscow in September on the theme of human rights – a Conference preoccupation since the earliest days in Helsinki – at which time Albania, Estonia, Latvia and Lithuania were admitted to membership.

The Conference was convened at full ministerial level in January 1992. At that time the membership reached 48 with the admission, not without hesitation, of all ten CIS members. Reservations were expressed over the conflict in Azerbaijan but the Azeris declared themselves ready to receive an observer mission. Croatia and Slovenia were admitted to observer status. Yugoslavia, still a legal entity even if profoundly modified politically, opposed their admission as full members.

These difficulties over Yugoslavia and Azerbaijan gave pertinence to the CSCE's reconsideration of its procedures. The unanimity rule which had served it so well in the fragile political atmosphere of perestroika now threatened to block action on serious issues, such as the prevention or elimination of conflict. On January 30, 1992, spelling out its June 1991 limitation of the unanimity rule, the Conference unanimously adopted the "Prague document", a fourteen-page declaration on the further development of CSCE structures. Henceforth, in order to increase CSCE's ability to guarantee human rights and democracy by peaceful means, appropriate measures may be taken, if necessary without the consent of the state concerned, in cases of flagrant, serious and persistent violation of CSCE commitments.

However, the measures which may be taken are singularly limited: "political declarations" or "other measures of a political nature" to be applied outside the territory of the state concerned. This excludes economic embargoes or the dispatch of missions of inquiry. It remains that the unanimity rule has been breached.

President Havel of Czechoslovakia, supported by the German delegation, would have liked to see a European peacekeeping force set up, but the US, British and French delegations were unenthusiastic. "For the third time in a century", declared Havel, "Europe must create within herself a balance eliminating further wars, whether hot or cold". The German foreign minister agreed that the CSCE should be able to set up its own "blue helmet" force. Not surprisingly, he found support in the person of Raffi Hovanissian, the Armenian foreign minister, since his own country was confronting Azerbaijan over the Ngorno Karabakh enclave. (Seven weeks after Maastricht, major EC members failed to achieve consensus on an important issue of foreign policy). The item was tabled when the CSCE noted that peacekeeping would be addressed at a later meeting. As a sop, at the suggestion of France and Germany, the CSCE undertook to study creation of a European center for conciliation and arbitration (ECCA).

The Conference expressed concern at the accumulation of conventional armaments and the danger of their transfer to areas of tension. All members declared their support for the register of international arms transfers created by the UN in September 1991. They undertook to supply the UN secretariat with pertinent information. However, *business oblige*: such worthy sentiments did not prevent President Mitterrand from visiting Oman at the same moment, where one of his avowed intentions was to challenge the British monopoly in arms supply and military training... Oman, of course, is not in Europe; indeed it commands the Straits of Hormuz...

The Conference took another step forward in its watchdog role in early March, 1992, when the 48 member states reached a successful outcome in Vienna to three years of negotiations designed to add new confidence-building and security measures to those already approved. The aim was to improve "transparency" (that is, to avoid the reality, appearance or presumption of a threatening military build-up) by means of annual exchanges of military information (troops, budgets, armaments systems), voluntary checks on military activities and compulsory ceilings on tanks and men participating in military manoeuvers. Unlimited manoeuvers may henceforth be held only once every two years. These new measures, effective May 1, 1992, naturally apply to the five Central Asian republics of the former USSR which joined CSCE in January 1992.

Given the present conflicts in ex-Yugoslavia and Azerbaijan, these regulations appear unrealistic if not ridiculous. They seem to hover between the unnecessary (in peacetime) and the ineffectual (in time of war). The Conference may have sensed this when, on opening their fourth plenary session in Helsinki on March 24, 1992, 51 governments (Croatia and Slovenia having been promoted to full membership) decided to convene an international conference on Ngorno-Karabakh. This will put the new peacemaking machinery seriously to the test. Robert Badinter of France went so far as to propose an Arbitration Court.

Despite its name, the Conference was rapidly acquiring an organizational structure and seemed even to be taking on the attributes of a regional UN: [3]

* Council of Foreign Ministers;
* Committee of High-ranking Officials (ministers' deputies);
* European Center for Conciliation and Arbitration (Vienna);
* Bureau for Democracy and Civil Rights (Warsaw);
* Secretariat (Prague).

With the weakening of the unanimity rule, the Council of Foreign Ministers was now able to function as a kind of European Security Council, but one in which no state has a veto and all are permanent members.

Meanwhile, the German commentator Wolf J. Bell suggests that the CSCE should do more in the way of technical assistance. He proposes a clearing house for the transfer of management skills. [4]

The "summit segment" of the Conference which closed in Helsinki on July 10, 1992, showed slower progress in organizing the protection of European security. Some concrete steps were taken and others deferred for further study. Behind-the-scenes manoeuvering, with France and the US at opposite ends of the spectrum, concerned NATO's relationship to CSCE and, indirectly, the American role in Europe. The American delegation saw in such linkage a possible new *raison d'être* for NATO in the Europe of the nineties.

On a Dutch proposal the Conference created a position of High Commissioner for National Minorities to provide an early-warning system for conflict. The Conference confirmed its peace-keeping role in providing for recourse to assistance from the EC, NATO, WEU or CIS but without "coercive" action ... On the peaceful settlement of disputes, it was decided to study further the French proposal for an arbitration court (ECCA) and the US counter-proposal of a conciliation procedure. A report was requested by December 14, 1992 (ministerial meeting in Stockholm). The conference decided to continue with military confidence building measures (29 countries declared troop ceilings) which in future will apply to neutral countries. Finally, CSCE declared itself officially to be a UN regional body.

When the CSCE first appeared on the international scene it represented a break-through: through the Iron Curtain. With the end of East-West confrontation, to which it so largely contributed, it has in effect rewritten its own ticket. Can it now become a military police force if not for the United States of Europe at least for the united countries of Europe? Can it channel resurgent nationalisms into less destructive or even creative paths? The inventive vulcanologists of Mount Etna managed in 1992 to turn aside a lava flow and save a village. It remains to be seen whether CSCE can perform a like miracle in the Balkan and Caucasian crucibles.

At present energies may be too widely dispersed: some rationalization of institutions appears desirable, at least in theory. The secretary general of NATO, Manfred Wörner has NATO's own survival to worry about in post-Cold-and-newly-Hot-Regional-War Europe, seeming only too happy to leave the thorny issues of Central and Eastern Europe to his CSCE colleagues. He nevertheless floated the vague notion of an interlocking institutional network between NATO, CSCE, the EC and WEU. It was doubtless this which developed into the suggestion from the NATO Council in June 1992 that NATO provide a military force for policing duties under CSCE auspices ... a surreal proposal which was bound to trouble the relative consensual serenity of the Conference. Are we to witness the UN, the CSCE, NATO, the EC and WEU trying to undertake (or not to undertake) the same tasks? The suggestion that such intervention should not be coercive emasculated the proposal.

NATO has avoided any real extension of its constitutional treaty responsibilities to Eastern Europe by creating its consultative Cooperation Council (NACC). One can see why. In the first place, NATO was not yet prepared to open up its military secrets and strategy or to extend its nuclear umbrella to erstwhile opponents such as Russia, other CIS states or even to Central European countries, especially where democracy still appeared fragile. But there is another reason: having "managed" friction between Greece and Turkey for four decades, thereby succeeding in avoiding open hostility between two NATO members on NATO's southern flank where the communist world meets the Middle East, NATO was highly reluctant to assume responsibility for defusing conflicts such as those in Ngorno-Karabakh, Georgia, Moldova or Bosnia-Herzegovina. As newly "domestic" disputes they could at best under-mine the solidarity of an extended Alliance and, at worst, trigger its solidarity mechanism (an attack upon one is an attack upon all). On the other hand, neglect in these cases is unlikely to prove benign . . .

The purpose of this digression is to demonstrate that not only the CSCE but the whole security situation in Europe is in mutation. Resurgent nationalism is its ferment. Gone are the days of the common enemy, clearly defined. After the Cold War the Hot Peace has to be won, but there is as yet no master plan. If the Bush suggestion of endowing CSCE with a parliamentary arm is taken up; or if Europe's relative paralysis in the face of regional conflicts per-sists the matter will have to be seriously addressed.[5]

Like one of those fuel economy record-breaking aircraft we admired on television, CSCE has circled the globe, well-served by its ultra-light structure. It is difficult, however, to predict a future for the organization. In the security sphere much depends not only on how NATO and, to a lesser extent, WEU evolve but also on how local tensions and conflicts (Moldova, Azerbaijan, Georgia, Slovenia and, above all, Yugoslavia) evolve. In other areas, however, Baskets 2 and 3, organizations with stronger executives may be required to achieve substantive progress. The entry of Czechoslovakia (now Czech Republic and Slovakia), Hungary, Poland and Bulgaria into the Council of Europe — essentially the same countries which tried to join the Marshall Plan in 1948 — and the creation of NATO's all-European Consultative Council sug-gest a risk of duplication. The Franco-German brigade, a WEU contingent and a NATO standing group have all been mooted for rapid intervention duties. There will have to be an institutional shake-out and more realistic peace-keeping machinery at some point. At the present delicate evolutionary stage the advice must be: if CSCE works better than anyone dared hope, don't fix it. Unfortunately, the answer to that question may echo in the guns of Sarajevo rather than on the peaceful waterfront of Helsinki.

Notes

1 Mathias Jopp, Berthold Meyer, Norbert Rospers and Peter Schlotter, *Ten Years of the CSCE Process: Appraisal of, and Prospects for, All-European Détente and Co-operation*, PRIF Research Report, Peace Research Institute Frankfurt, Frankfurt, 1985, p. 71.

2 The Yugoslav conflict has demonstrated that a definition of "state", and therefore the distinction between a civil war and an external agression, depends on who recognizes whom; and that so-called internal affairs can be as deadly as a fire in a row-house. Diplomacy has to catch up with reality: in today's Europe no major problem can be ignored as internal — unless we want to add an ostrich to the twelve — star emblem.

3 A status actually authorized by Article 8 of the UN Charter.

4 *General-Anzeiger*, Bonn, January 31, 1992.

5 NATO has the troops but is Atlantic. WEU is Western European and cannot afford to get out of step with NATO. The EC is Western European, essentially economic and about to increase its "neutral" membership. The Council of Europe, while Western European in origin is expanding to Central Europe but has no mandate or experience in security matters. (We have already noted that the Council of Europe is monitoring CSCE's development in a spirit of cooperation). The CSCE is all-European but also Atlantic and Asian; while addressing "security" it is not a military organization. WTO is defunct but ex-Soviet troops remain in several newly-independent states . . .

9

Commonwealth of
Independent States

When Mikhail Gorbachev assumed power on March 11, 1985, the day after Constantin Chernenko's death, he knew that the nation was in a parlous economic state. He also knew, however, that the reality of the situation and hence the need for reform would not be brought home to and receive the support of the people unless the strongarm methods which had suppressed the truth were relaxed. People had to feel free to speak their mind. There could be no economic reform without awareness: glasnost went hand in hand with perestroika. Historians may argue, however, that Gorbachev went about things in the wrong order: by first opening up the political system he in large measure deprived himself of the very levers of power which he needed to effect economic restructuring.

However an even greater trap was waiting down the road. Under the communist system Russia, with 148 million people and over sixty per cent of GNP (not to mention its vast land area) enjoyed a natural hegemony over the other components of the Union. After the disintegration of the external empire (Central Europe, Afghanistan) the internal empire in turn began to unravel. Gorbachev had correctly diagnosed the Soviet Union's economic ills but had underestimated the volcanic power of the long-suppressed nationality crisis. When Gorbachev was finally forced from power on December 25, 1991, it was not his presidency which was abolished but the nation under him, over which he presided like a leader enthroned on a melting iceberg. The melting process continues today and has now attained a third stage, reaching inside the republics themselves. After Poland, the Soviet Union; after the Soviet Union, Russia; after Russia, Tatarstan . . .

It is astonishing therefore that there was no hiatus between the end of the Soviet Union and the beginning of the Commonwealth of Independent States. Indeed, it was the creation of the CIS at Brest-Litovsk, in Belarus (formerly Byelorussia) on December 8, 1991, by the three Slavic republics which, despite the 76.4% referendum majority only nine months earlier for a renewed "union of sovereign republics",[1] constituted the coup — at once *coup d'état* and *coup de grâce* — which put an end to the Soviet Union.

Actually, the Slavic move was a political error, rectified at Alma Ata two weeks later when the CIS was "re-founded" so that eight other republics from the even less-developed south and east might join as equal founder members.

How did such a paradox come about? Firstly, while denying hegemony over the old system or the new, Boris Yeltsin's Russian Federation shrewdly abstained from declaring independence from the USSR in order to lay claim to historical continuity. The ploy worked and the world—in particular the UN, the EC and the United States—recognized Russia as the successor state, complete with Security Council seat and veto. Secondly, even as the newly-independent republics claimed international recognition, complete with flags and national anthems, they knew that they could not aspire to total economic autonomy. With the possible exception of the Ukraine, second only to Russia in population and resources and geographically close to the rest of Europe, they could not legislate away seventy-three years and more of economic interdependence.[2]

Despite suspicions of Russia's motives, therefore, all the republics of the former USSR acceded to the new Commonwealth in Alma Ata except for the three Baltic states and Georgia.[3] The fact that so many leaders gathered in Alma Ata and so rapidly overcame, on paper at least, weighty issues of defense, economic cooperation, protection of minorities and foreign representation, shows that they realized that total economic if not political independence was an illusion. After three-quarters of a century of central control and facing the mighty Community of nations and EEA in the western half of the European continent, the "Eleven" still needed each other.

Nevertheless, the Commonwealth in no way approximates the EC in its structure and powers. The latter has institutions half a century in the making; the former was hastily concocted as a response to Gorbachev's last-ditch effort to preserve the USSR as a Union of Sovereign States. (The EC, for instance, is moving towards a single currency as CIS members threaten to break free from the ruble).

Five declarations were signed by the leaders of all ten republics and Russia.[4] A sixth declaration, on nuclear arms, was signed by the four members holding nuclear weapons on their territory.

An introductory protocol

The first text is a diplomatic protocol providing that the agreement on creation of the Commonwealth (CIS) is established "on equal basis". Thus did the three Slavic members meet the demands of the eight other republics, and especially Kazakhstan, that the text be reworked to treat all eleven as equal founding parties. The protocol also provides that the agreement creating the Commonwealth comes into force for each high contracting party from the moment of ratification. The fact that no minimum membership or date of entry into force was prescribed highlights the felt need for continuity with the ex-USSR. The hasty "framework" character of the texts was nonetheless acknowledged by the statement that documents regulating cooperation in the Commonwealth would be worked out "taking into consideration reservations made during its ratification". Finally, the protocol provides that all eleven language versions are equally valid and that the original will be kept in the archive of the Republic of Belarus.

The Alma-Ata Declarations

The first declaration establishes the CIS on the basis of equality and mutual recognition, acknowledges the "deep historic roots" of the states' association and their responsibility "for the preservation of civil peace and inter-ethnic accord". (We have since seen how traditional adversaries such as Armenians and Azeris, or Romanian-, Turcic-, Russian- and Ukrainian-speaking Moldovans in the Commonwealth's tiniest republic have failed to live up to this commitment). The declaration further asserts that the CIS "is neither a state nor a super-state structure", the latter an obvious refusal to be equated with the EC or the former USSR. It nevertheless commits members to "allied" command of military forces and "single control" of nuclear weapons. (Yeltsin of Russia assumed that control from Gorbachev a few days later). "Non-nuclear" or "neutral" status is specifically recognized. The CIS remains open to new accessions, assumes the international obligations (including foreign debt) of the former USSR, which "ceases to exist". It commits itself to "cooperation in the formation and development of the common economic space, and all-European and Eurasian markets". By referring specifically to "all European" bodies, the CIS signalled that it was not setting itself up in opposition to western European bodies such as the EC and the European Economic Area. Obviously, however, it remains to be seen whether the "all-European" and "Eurasian" (former Soviet) markets will eventually come together. There could in fact be interim steps in this process, such as expansion of OECD and GATT or an enhanced role for CSCE.[5] Such arrangements would of course have to conform to GATT principles for free trade areas.

The Declarations then outline military and institutional cooperation:

> Proceeding from the provision, sealed in the agreement on the establishment of a Commonwealth of Independent States and in the Alma-Ata declaration, for keeping the common military-strategic space under a joint command and for keeping a single control over nuclear weapons, the high contracting parties agreed on the following:
> The command of the armed forces shall be entrusted to Marshal Yevgeny I. Shaposhnikov, pending a solution to the question of reforming the armed forces . . .

Councils of heads of state and government

Two governing bodies were proposed:

> A supreme body of the commonwealth — a "Council of the Heads of State" — as well as a "Council of the Heads of Government" shall be set up with a view to tackling matters connected with coordinating the activities of the states of the new commonwealth in the spere of common interests.
> The plenipotentiary representatives of the states of the new commonwealth shall be instructed to submit proposals concerning the abolition of the structures of the former

Soviet Union, as well as the coordinating institutions of the Commonwealth for the consideration of the Council of the Heads of State.

It is evident from the reference to "coordinating institutions" that the CIS recognizes the need for a joint bureaucracy to implement agreements but seeks to keep it to a minimum. It is also obvious from the declaratory form and use of the future tense ("shall be set up") that the Alma-Ata text does not in itself constitute a treaty.

CIS member states declared their intention of joining the United Nations (Byelorussia and Ukraine being already members) and of supporting Russia as the successor-state to the USSR as a permanent member of the Security Council with power of veto.

All CIS states have since been admitted to UN membership. The West moved rapidly to support this policy, not entirely for altruistic reasons. The United States, Britain and France were all concerned to ensure continuity of responsibility for implementing arms reduction agreements. (As though to drive home the point, President Bush signed the CFE treaty on December 26, following its ratification by the Senate). In addition, the United Kingdom and France wanted to forestall any request for review of permanent seats on the Security Council.[6]

Four republics, Russia, Ukraine, Belarus and Kazakhstan signed an additional agreement on the delicate issue of nuclear weapons. Pending destruction of all nuclear armaments, the existing weapons would insure the collective security of CIS members, which committed themselves against first use. Decisions on the need to use them are vested in the President of Russia "by agreement with the heads of the member states". Belarus and Ukraine undertook to join the 1968 non-proliferation treaty and "to conclude with the International Atomic Energy Agency the appropriate guarantees". They will thus become the first countries officially to go non-nuclear after having been nuclear powers. The text also provides that there shall be no transfer of weapons to another state (meaning, in fact, Russia), except for the purpose of destroying them. The agreement requires ratification by all member states.

It is one of the ironies of European history that, while in Western Europe the question of establishing a European army has for four decades been a touchstone of political integration and as such is still not settled, on the territory of the new Commonwealth of Independant States the prior existence of integrated armed forces and nuclear armaments is an equally delicate political issue.

When one week later CIS leaders met in their new "administrative seat" of Minsk (Belarus) (pointedly not called a capital city and not located in Russia) to fill in crucial details of their framework agreement, it became clear that the broad wording of the Alma-Ata texts, while sufficing to deliver the *coup de grâce* to the moribund Soviet Union, masked substantial differences of intent in both economic and military matters. Ukraine was already issuing its own "coupons" or embryonic banknotes—the *sine qua non* of a separate currency. The three smaller nuclear powers were resisting the ambiguous four-hands-one-Russian-finger dispensation for control of nuclear firings.

From USSR to CIS
The fifteen republics

Republic	Population (millions)	Capital	% Soviet PNB	Independence declaration
Russia	148.0	Moscow	61.6	Dec. 8, 1991 •
Estonia +	1.6	Tallin	0.6	Aug. 21, 1991
Latvia +	2.7	Riga	1.1	Aug. 21, 1991
Lithuania +	3.7	Vilnius	1.2	March 11, 1991
Belarus	10.2	Minsk	4.2	Aug. 25, 1991
Ukraine	51.8	Kiev	16.2	Aug. 24, 1991
Moldova	4.3	Kichinau	1.2	Aug. 27, 1991
Georgia +	5.4	Tbilissi	1.6	April 9, 1991
Armenia	3.3	Erevan	0.9	Sept. 23, 1991
Azerbaijan	7.1	Baku	1.7	Aug. 30, 1991
Uzbekistan	20.3	Tashkent	3.3	Aug. 31, 1991
Turkmenistan	3.6	Ashkabad	0.8	Oct. 27, 1991
Tajikistan	5.2	Dushanbe	0.8	Dec. 21, 1991 *
Kyrgystan	4.3	Bishkek	0.8	Aug. 31, 1991
Kazakhstan	16.7	Alma-Ata	4.3	Dec. 16, 1991

• Brest-Litovsk declaration (CIS founded)   * Alma-Ata declaration
+ Has not joined CIS   (CIS expanded)

Was Gorbachev to be proven correct in his warning that comity of the former Soviet nations could not be established without a true union? Would not Yeltsin, already the dominant leader, or his successor, not inevitably be drawn into a mediatory, and hence central role, even as he protested (perhaps too much) that Russian hegemony need not be feared? Some of the other leaders might have been forgiven for musing that it was precisely the central Soviet power which had kept Russian dominance in check. [7]

Meeting in Minsk on December 30, 1991, the CIS leaders officially set up three coordinating bodies for the new Commonwealth: the Council of Heads of State, the supreme policy-making body; the Council of Heads of Government; and the Defense Council, composed of representatives of defense ministries. The powers of the latter are not clear, since it was also confirmed that member countries could create their own armed forces.

Tension between CIS member states

The heads of state continued to meet monthly through the winter without resolving any major issue. The tense relationship between Ukraine and Russia and the open warfare in Ngorno-Karabakh raised doubts about survival of the

Commonwealth. In Kiev in March, after the Ukraine had halted moving her nuclear warheads to Russia for destruction, as previously agreed, the CIS failed to resolve the dispute over the future of the Red Army and the Black Sea naval forces. Agreement on a CIS intervention force, proposed by Kazakhstan ("Red Helmets" modelled on the UN "Blue Helmets"), intended in particular for the Azeri-Armenian conflict (an agreement never enacted) did not prevent Leonid Kravchuk, president of Ukraine, from condemning the CIS as a failed dream . . .[8]

Russia not immune

Meanwhile, the tidal wave of decolonisation rolled on inside Russia itself. First came the Chechen-Ingush incident, in which the Russian Parliament reversed a Yeltsin decree annulling the independence declaration of the small Russian republic. Then on March 22 the 3,600,000 inhabitants of Tatarstan, 48% of them Turcic-speaking muslims, voted for independence. Russia may soon need her own CIS inside the Commonwealth . . . As Mikhail Gorbachev tours Germany in triumph and pens his memoirs, Boris Yeltsin is feeling the pain and, increasingly, adopting the tone of the biter bit . . . And Eduard Shevardnadze, who has taken over the destinies of Georgia after the Gamsakhurdia *débacle*, is biding his time before deciding whether to join the Commonwealth of Independent States. On July 14, 1992, the first CIS "peace force" arrived in South Ossetia, in Georgian territory!

Ultimately, Russia can get along without the CIS. It is still an open question whether the other members of the Commonwealth can find a way to live close, but not too close, to Big Mother in a new uniform. Necessity may well prove the . . . mother . . . of invention; or maybe they could ask Finland to draw upon its vast experience for advice.

Notes

1 Eight republics recoiled from signing this hastily-negotiated treaty on November 20, 1991.

2 Upon declaring independence on August 24, 1991, Ukraine did away with its article ("The" Ukraine) as though to shake off a long-resented regional connotation.

3 In Tbilissi President Gamsakhurdia was resisting insurgency from the basement of his presidential palace.

4 Russia is itself a federation of some twenty autonomous republics, not a unitary state.

5 In its draft position paper on EC enlargement, submitted to EC FM's on June 20, 1992, the Commission recommended creation of an institutional structure within the "European architecture" for dialog and partnership with countries not yet ready to assume the obligations of membership. Whether such a linkage would apply to CIS states, together or severally, is unclear.

6 The UK and France obtained their permanent seats and veto power in the aftermath of World War II. Today Germany, Japan, India, Brazil or Nigeria might make a reasonable claim to a permanent seat.

7 On June 20 President Yeltsin and Vice-President Rutskoï warned Georgia and Moldova that Russia would not "stand idly by" as Russians were killed in local conflicts such as those of South Ossetia and Transdniestr.

8 Although Kravchuk later moderated his language, tensions persisted between Russia and Ukraine over both the Black Sea fleet and the status of the Crimea, a largely Russian-speaking territory transferred from Russia to the Ukraine by Nikita Kruschev in 1954, at the same time that the Transdniestr region was attached to Moldavia . . . which, incidentally, explains Ukraine's reluctance to become involved in the Moldovan conflict: if Ukraine claimed Transdniestr it would undermine its case for retaining the Crimea. The CIS is going to have to live with the "lesser evil" of its policy of respecting existing borders.

10

Europe's Stars in the Sky:
The European Space Agency

1992, the year when the international market was scheduled for completion, was also designated as International Space Year. It marked 28 years of cooperation in one of Europe's least known yet most successful intergovernmental organizations, the European Space Agency (ESA).

The ESA was created in 1973 by unifying the European Space Research Organisation (ESRO) and the European Launcher Development Organisation (ELDO), developed in the sixties. There are thirteen member countries and two associate members. Cooperation agreements are in force with the US (NASA) and the USSR (succeeded by Russia). Not the least of ESA's special characteristics as an intergovernmental body is that it earns money by launching satellites under contract as well as spending it.[1] ESA headquarters are in Paris. The technical and research center (ESTEC) is in Noordwijk, Netherlands. Orbiting satellites are monitored by an operations center in Darmstadt, in the Federal Republic, with smaller relay points at Redu, Belgium, Villafranca, Spain, and Salmijärvi, Sweden. A computerized documentation center has been set up in Frascati, near Rome. In preparation for a move to manned operations by means of the European shuttle, Hermes, an astronaut training center is being built near Cologne. ESA staff strength levelled off in 1990 at 1748 employees.

Europe first got off the ground when the European Space probe, Skylark, was orbited from Sardinia in 1964. ESA research rockets and satellites are now launched from the northern coast of South America at Kourou in French Guyana. As an overseas department (DOM) of France, French Guyana is part of France and of the European Community. Its location near the equator is favorable to the achievement of geocentric orbits.

At almost two billion dollars the Agency's budget is some six times smaller than that of NASA. This obliges ESA to select projects with care and to pool resources with other organizations. Cooperation between the two agencies is extensive in research, engineering and launching. ESA's launch pad came into its own after the US Challenger shuttle disaster. It now has over fifty launches to its credit, only five of which have been unsuccessful.

While NASA has in recent years concentrated its launching efforts on reusable shuttles, ESA has relied on five generations of its Ariane rocket. The launcher is named after Ariadne who, according to Greek legend, led Theseus out of the Cretan labyrinth. The latest model can put 18-tonne payloads into low orbit or eight tonnes into geosynchronous (stationary) orbit.

ESA's basic activities may be divided into four categories: scientific research, technological research and development (mechanical and electrical systems, automation and informatics, product assurance and safety, in-orbit technology demonstration), data handling and archiving and technical infrastructure facilities. Installations are of several types: computer systems, ground facilities for space systems, mission support, satellite operations, administrative units and the European Astronauts Centre.

The Agency's development program covers seven distinct types of activity: the scientific program, the earth observation program, the telecommunications program, space transportation systems, space stations, the microgravity program and the astronauts corps.

Manned space flight

ESA is also developing Hermes, a smaller version of the US shuttle. The small size saves costs; however it is also the Agency's policy to use automated missions wherever possible. An even smaller research station, the Man-Tended Free Flyer (MTFF) will permit human visits for research data collection without requiring permanent human presence on board.

ESA has so far concentrated on unmanned space flight but is training astronauts in cooperation with both the United States and Russia. In July 1992 a French astronaut flew in a Russian crew and Swiss and Italian astronauts flew in the NASA shuttle Atlantis. Speaking with President Mitterrand after entering the permanent Russian space station Mir, the French astronaut Michel Tognini entered a plea for the ESA shuttle Hermes, threatened with cutbacks. Mitterrand asserted that France had no such thoughts: "Conquest of space is the key to mastery of the future. The success of these flights represents a step forward for humanity so significant that nothing must stand in their way".

The Hubble space telescope was launched on April 24, 1990. The orbital verification of the telescope initially ran into a number of minor problems, all of which were resolved. Two months later telescope focus adjustment failed to achieve the required performance. Analysis showed that the optical telescope assembly was suffering from spherical aberration. An assembly error had been made in building a reference null lens, which had been used as an optical reference in the polishing process of the primary mirror. Consideration is being given to recuperating the telescope by shuttle for re-assembly on Earth.

The Ulysses spacecraft was launched by NASA shuttle Discovery on October 6, 1990, with a five-year mission to explore Jupiter and the inner heliosphere. It conducted a first Jupiter fly-by on February 8, 1992 at an altitude of 376,000 km. The small, 370-kilo unit is travelling at 98,000 miles an hour and telemetric instructions take forty minutes to reach it, so that the accuracy of commands and trajectory represent a major technical achievement. Until now spacecraft have flown orbits in a single plane, the so-called ecliptic orbit common to most planets of the solar system. Ulysses creates a scientific first by studying the sun's magnetic field in polar orbit, overflying the Sun's south pole in June 1994 and the north pole in 1995.

Spacecraft Giotto, launched on July 2, 1985, has a multiple mission. It first encountered Halley's comet on March 14, 1986, 144 million miles from Earth, then flew past the planets, moving past Earth at a distance of 22,731 kms on July 2, 1990. It thus became the first man-made satellite to approach Earth from deep space and on a high-inclination orbit. Giotto met up with Grigg-Skellerup's comet on July 10, 1992.

Wanted: stellar sweepers

The problem of waste disposal is not limited to man's terrestrial environment. It is estimated that 7,000 objects litter the skies around our planet; only six per cent of them are functioning satellites, the rest consisting of booster rockets and expired probes and satellites.

Most of these objects are in near-circular orbits below 2000 km altitude. They represent a danger to manned space flight and even to the population on Earth. Monitoring of space débris is one of the unglamorous tasks assigned to ESA's mission support team, which also deals with mission analysis, flight dynamics, satellite simulation and software engineering.

The Agency's future projects include the first return of an undisturbed sample of a cometary nucleus to Earth. Rosetta is the planetary cornerstone of ESA's Horizon 2000 program. A joint ESA/NASA project, the mission is scheduled for launch in 2002 to rendez-vous with comet Schwassmann-Wachmann-2. The sample will be returned to Earth some eight years later. The unit consists of a cruiser, an aerocapsule and a lander. ESA will provide the sample acquisition system and the Earth return capsule.

Long-term projects include international cooperation for the study of the Martian surface, using a network of landers and an orbiting planetary telescope proposed by the German Space Agency (DARA).

Earth observation

In addition to probing space ESA has an extensive program for observation of Earth: weather, oceans, land (with potential for environmental protection, agriculture, mapping, archeology and the Columbus Polar Platform for Earth observation missions in polar orbit).

Columbus itself will be ESA's principal manned space station. It will take the form of a unit to be attached to a NASA space station under construction by Boeing and McDonnell Douglas.

ESA's Microgravity Program is designed to promote fundamental and applied research in materials, fluid and life sciences in space. Experiments cover such areas as solidification physics, physical chemistry, fluid sciences in space, biology and human and animal physiology. The essential features to be found in the microgravity environment include elimination of gravity-driven convection, lack of sedimentation and buoyancy and absence of fluid static pressure. The Agency selects space-relevant experiments according to scientific merit, provides flight opportunities for these experiments and develops multi-user experiment facilities.

Notes

1 ESA members, with percentage share of budget contribution (1990) are as follows:

Austria	0,7%	Spain	3,0%
Belgium	3,3%	Sweden	1,7%
Denmark	0,7%	Switzerland	1,7%
France	21,5%	United Kingdom	4,9%
Germany	17,2%		
Ireland	0,2%	Associates members	
Italy	11,3%		
Netherlands	2,0%	Canada	0,6%
Norway	0,6%	Finland	0,3%

Member countries do not participate equally in all projects. Payments are based on projects commissioned and direct benefits received, not on population or GNP, as is the case in other GO's. Income from other sources, mainly telecommunications satellites, contributed 30,3% to the 1990 budget. Customers include the People's Republic of China and the Arab League.

Source: ESA Annual Report, 8, rue Mario-Nikis, 75738 Paris Cedex 15, France.

IV

LOOKING AHEAD SPECIAL ISSUES AND THE CHALLENGE OF 2000

1

Agriculture

Economists and sociologists usually divide economic activity into three sectors. The primary sector is involved with production of raw materials, such as wood, iron ore, oil and coal. The secondary sector processes raw materials, transforming them into articles of daily use, contributing the "added value" of mixing and processing (face cream, furniture, cars, ships . . .). The tertiary sector, most highly developed in advanced economies, covers products of a more elusive character, such as intellectual as opposed to physical property (inventions, design, the creativity of artists) and services (banking, insurance, transport, real estate . . .). However, these categories are somewhat theoretical and abstract: most work and productivity involves a combination of categories. Production and marketing of books and newspapers, for example, involves all three categories.Agriculture, and hence the agricultural policy of governments, have always held a special place in this hierarchy. For instance, modern farming methods involving heavy machinery, intensive production of poultry and cattle and genetic manipulation have blurred the border-line between "farming" and "industry," spawning hybrid terminology such as "agro-business" and "bio-technology." However, a nation's emotional, almost instinctive attachment to its farms and farmers goes much deeper. Farming answers a basic human need without which life could not continue: food. Only hunting, fishing and foraging (the gathering of wild fruits and plants) have more primitive origins than subsistence farming and certainly could not sustain today's population.

Agriculture transformed nomadic peoples to sedentary populations, thereby laying the foundations of distinct societies, cultures and property ownership. Being involved with extensive land areas in relation to population density, agriculture has an enormous impact on the character and quality of a nation's life. It is in no small measure the shaper and the guardian of the landscape — a service for which no renumeration is provided, but which is essential to the aesthetic quality of life, to good health and to the preservation of natural resources. The homogenization of modern society — people, buildings, transport — affects cities more than the countryside. In other words, a nation's agriculture is essential to its national identity; even though the political constituency of the farmer is small and growing smaller.

To these historical, social and cultural factors leading governments to protect their agriculture and, by the same token, their rural way of life, must be added a number of distinct economic characteristics:

Agricultural commodities are homogeneous products. Where cars, clothes and cakes are produced in infinite variety, wheat of the same type and grade, whether it be cultivated in Kansas, Canada, Cantal or Canton, is used to make flour. Consequently, manufacturers regard price as the main determinant of their wheat purchases.

Commodities are produced in greater dispersal than industrial goods, on a large number of farms, each accounting for a small part of total output (a factor multiplied ten-fold when we compare small, traditional European farms with North American producers). In many western economies, the productive capacity of agriculture exceeds the demands of domestic and foreign markets by a wide margin. Unlike most other economic activity agriculture is directly and forcefully influenced by climate and by short-term weather variations.[1]

Because food is such a basic, essential commodity, a relatively steady demand must be met whatever the fluctuations of production conditions. Farmers cannot respond as freely to market conditions as industrialists. Moreover, strategic considerations require that trade with the rest of the world be kept in balance and not lead to dangerous dependence on other countries. Stability of price and supply, even where artificially engendered, is in the interest of producers, consumers and government alike. A massive exodus from the land to the cities, for instance, is harmful to the landscape and to society.

It is very hard for farmers to influence market forces in any lasting fashion. Prices swing rapidly and are highly dependent on the level of output: one year's gain in "productivity" can be wiped out the following season. On the other hand, higher production usually translates into lower prices. At such times, the income of most farmers is bolstered by commodity programs (in Europe, less coyly named price supports) designed to even out large price fluctuations.

In the US, federal involvement in farm commodity programs began during the Great Depression, with the Agricultural Adjustment Act of 1933 (AAA). This was supplemented in the eighties, during a period of over-production, by the Food Security Act of 1985. Trends were similar in the European Community, although the strength of the dollar in the eighties exacerbated the problem for the United States by making excess produce harder to sell. While parts of the world, particularly sub-Saharan Africa, starved, the barns of western industrial democracies were gorged with surpluses purchased by governments with taxpayers' contributions to maintain price stability. So much for markets common and free: agriculture is indeed a special case.[2]

Between the two world wars, in response to the Depression, Western Europe was equally energetic in turning her back on the free flow of market forces for agriculture but in a manner both uncoordinated and essentially opposed to that of the United States. Agricultural output plummeted during the thirties as commodity prices collapsed. Most governments imposed import quotas, although Britain did so selectively through Imperial Preference, favoring her dominions and colonies (Canada, West Indies, Australia, New Zealand, the Rhodesias). However, import quotas proved insufficient to raise output and governments began to intervene more directly, increasing production through subsidies and price supports. Thus as the US sought to curtail production, European countries such as France and Germany were seeking to expand it.

Negotiating the birth of Green Europe

Because of its special place in the economy and its specific role in each country, agriculture long remained a reserved sector – you might call it a *chasse privée* – excluded from intergovernmental cooperation. It was not covered at all, other than in general studies and debates of limited consequence, in the Council of Europe and OEEC and certainly not in the first treaty of the Six, restricted to coal and steel. Progress in GATT was far more limited for agricultural products than for industrial goods.

It was the Spaak negotiations for the EEC Treaty which first brought agriculture to the fore. Certain economic sectors and countries, led by France, saw a treaty limited to industrial goods favoring economies dominated by the industrial sector, such as that of the Federal Republic of Germany. Even after it had been agreed to extend the treaties to "Green Europe," national infrastructures, institutions and policies were so diverse that the treaty did little more than set out basic principles for agriculture (although, as seen in Part III, putting flesh on the bones helped the Commission and the Court to assert Community powers). The main objectives outlined in the EEC Treaty of March 1957 are defined in a single article (Art. 39), namely to increase agricultural productivity, to ensure a fair standard of living for the agricultural community, to stabilize markets and to ensure that supplies are available to consumers at "reasonable" (significantly, not "the lowest possible") prices. Where these objectives were in conflict compromises would have to be thrashed out and priorities set.

A few figures will illustrate the delicacy of negotiating a Common Agricultural Policy. In the mid-fifties the farming population in the Six consisted of some 17.5 million people, representing 33% of the working population in Italy, 25% in France, 10% in Belgium and about 5% in the FRG. Yet it was in Italy that holdings were of smallest average size (85% under 5ha compared with 55% in Germany and 35% in France). Agriculture accounted for 36% of all the goods produced in Italy, 30% in France, 15% in Germany. A Belgian farmer earned triple his Italian counterpart. Moreover, Northern Europe specialized in raising livestock, whilst in the south crop production was more common. The patchwork fields of Europe reflected the diverse reality of her rural economy.

Nevertheless, the political bargain had been struck. The countries with a large farming sector had to reap the benefits in the same way as those with a more industrial economy. At the same time, the essential and unique contribution of these quite small economic sectors to each national way of life and to the enduring heritage of Western Europe's essentially man-made landscape had to be preserved, even enhanced.

In July 1958, six months after the EEC treaty came into force, a historic conference of the Six at Stresa, in Italy, laid down the guidelines of the CAP. Agricultural prices were to be brought closer together ("approximated"), necessarily in many cases at a level above the world market level: "Green Europe" would provide a common market but not a free one. Moreover, to enhance the competitive position of the Community, European agricultural structures were to be "improved" (a euphemism which did not exclude some rationalization without in principle putting the family farm at risk.)

Environmental concerns

The problems facing the Stresa conference were complex enough. Nevertheless, since those heady pioneering days Europe's rural economy has evolved greatly (thanks largely to the CAP itself) and society has been beset by new concerns. One of these is increased awareness of environmental dangers (the rise of "green" parties has seated "ecolos" in the European Parliament itself and even won them a vice-presidency). Agriculture is now perceived not only as protective of the environment but also, in some respects, as harmful to it, through impoverishment of soils, excessive use of fertilizers and pesticides, pollution of surface and groundwater (exacerbated by intensive livestock farming), deforestation ... Thus, yet another constraint is placed upon producers as consumers and taxpayers complain of the high cost of market intervention.[3]

A legion of former ministers of agriculture, caught between grower and consumer, not to say bank and ballot-box, government and GATT, now banished to early retirement and cultivation of their own garden, will testify that the CAP squeezes policy makers in a no-win situation. Clearly, however, there was no way but forward in the fifties: governments were condemned to breaking new ground.

The policy which finally resulted from long and tortuous negotiations, much brinkmanship and many marathon sessions presented a double paradox. In a six-nation union ostensibly devoted to promotion of a free and open market agriculture was and remains today the most contrived, artificial and rulebound sector of the economy; and it is this most sensitive and jealously guarded of national preserves which is most subject to supranational control and intervention. The future of Galway, Rioja and Pulia depends more on decisions taken in Brussels than those arrived at in Dublin, Madrid or Rome.

Agriculture is indeed a case apart; Europe's fields are criss-crossed by many hedgerows.

Price, production and structures

In December 1960 the EEC Council of Ministers adopted the principles of the new policy. As with the Common Market in industrial goods, it provided for uniform management of the internal market and the application of common rules towards third countries. Here however the resemblance ended: production and prices were to be severely controlled. The market would be common but it would not be free. There now began a process of organizing the market sector by sector. Cereals were among the first. In the early stages just over half the market of the Six was covered. By 1970 the figure had reached 87%; by 1986 it had risen to 91%.

It soon became apparent, however, that price and production controls would not suffice to effect long-term improvements in Europe's agriculture. Restructuring was unavoidable and a policy to this end had to be formulated. Directives were adopted by the Council in 1972. The twin pillars of the CAP were now in place.

Three principles

Albeit in its application the most complicated of EC policies, the CAP may be expressed in three clear principles: a single market, Community preference and financial solidarity.

In order to achieve the free movement of agricultural products through all member states, the CAP not only forbids customs duties and national subsidies but also insists on approximation of public health, veterinary and environmental regulations (which, in addition to their intrinsic importance affect both production costs and the movement of products across borders), common rules on competition and stable exchange rates. To achieve this the market must be managed centrally and uniform rules applied at external frontiers. Community preference gives priority to the sale of EC produce by protecting the internal market from cheap imports and excessive fluctuations in world prices. Such protection may take the form of external levies[4] or internal subsidy payments. Financial solidarity is provided by the European Agricultural Guidance and Guarantee Fund (EAGGF, usually known by the more manageable French acronym of FEOGA). The fund is financed largely from external levy payments collected by member countries. It follows that national agricultural policies, including subsidy payments to farmers, have in most sectors been taken over by the Community. However, direct taxation and social security for farmers remain national responsibilities.[5]

Since market conditions vary from one sector to another, a single system would not produce the desired result. We may distinguish four main types: external protection with intervention; external protection without intervention; aid to complement prices; flat-rate aids.

Over 70% of EC agriculture enjoys both external protection by means of levies and intervention arrangements on the internal market which buy up and store surplus production. In this way EC prices are stabilized. When the market is once again in balance the produce brought in is released for sale to EC or non-Community countries. (Sales to third countries must be effected at prices competitive with world rates. This means that the third-country "housewife" may sometimes buy EC products more cheaply than *die Hausfrau* or *la ménagère*. In 1973 200,000 tonnes of cheap butter were sold to the USSR in this way.) At first the intervention price was fixed annually for each product, such as cereals, butter, milk powder, sugar and beef. Recently, invitations to tender, which reflect more closely the market situation, have been issued. This is not yet a free-market situation, since the Community is still seeking artificially to raise EC price levels to farmers and does not "need" the products it calls for. Such internal market support would of course be pointless unless accompanied by external protection against imports offered at lower world prices. This is one of the points at issue in GATT negotiations.

Products which are not staple foods or do not depend directly on the soil (eggs, poultry, quality wines, flowers and certain fruits and vegetables) receive external protection without internal price support.

Import duties on products already covered by GATT must be kept at a constant level to respect commitments made under GATT rules. In these cases (rapeseed, cottonseed, peas and beans), where import levies may not be imposed, processing industries receive a subsidy if they use products grown inside the Community. Naturally, third countries question this practice.

In a small number of special cases, such as flax, hemp, hops, silkworms and seeds, flat-rate subsidies, calculated by land area or by quantity produced, are paid directly to the growers.

Blood on the barn floor: CAP price reviews

Naturally, the CAP annual price review is a highly sensitive economic and political undertaking. Many factors have to be taken into consideration, including the standard of living of farmers, prices to consumers, market equilibrium, market organization, world trade relations and agreements and, not least, the Community's agricultural budget. Compromise is essential to the balancing of interests.

One might expect that guaranteed prices to the producer would result in unacceptably high prices for the consumer. Generally, this has not been the case. In May 1988 the US Department of Agriculture issued the following prices in US dollars for a basket of 15 items:

EC cities		Other cities	
Bonn	53	Pretoria	33
London	56	Ottawa	49
Rome	57	Washington	50
Madrid	59	Stockholm	98
Paris	59	Tokyo	139

The EC prices are well within the world range. From 1977 to 1987 the index of EC farmgate prices rose from 100 to 163, an annual average growth of 5.1%. Over the same period consumer food prices rose from 100 to 202 (7.3% p.a.) whereas the general consumer index moved from 100 to 205 (7.5%). Yet more significant is the fact that the net disposable income for inhabitants rose 8.5% annually, from 100 to 225. Considered as a direct relationship, disregarding the indirect benefits mentioned earlier, a system which offers protection to the producer cannot be ideal for the consumer. Clearly, however, the burden is not intolerable.

Correcting currency fluctuations

All CAP prices are now quoted in ECU's, then converted into national currencies. Since the CAP depends on stable prices, however, the European Monetary System does not suffice to cushion the policy against currency fluctuations. A complex system of compensatory payments was therefore set up in 1969. However, since products from outside the Community must be paid for at the new official rate for the currency concerned, the unequal treatment of internal (EC) products (paid for at "green" rates) and external (non-EC) products (paid for at official rates) can lead to serious market distortions. Monetary compensatory amounts are therefore destined to be phased out. Governments will have to accept the full consequences of currency devaluations and revaluations. However, the problem will diminish as EC exchange rates are progressively pegged closer together and disappear entirely when a single European currency is achieved.

Structural policy

Market organization and price policies alone cannot achieve greater efficiency, productivity and market balance. Europe's ten million farm holdings vary immensely in size, specialization, climate and soil quality, as do the social conditions in which they must operate and the level of education and training of the farmers themselves. These disparities increased as the Community grew from 6 to 12 members. They will resurface when further enlargement negotiations begin. As we have seen in other industries, such as steel, improvements in agricultural structures were required. However, the very differences in national conditions led to diverse expectations and made it difficult for member governments to agree on a structural policy for agriculture.

Not surprisingly, therefore, the beginnings were modest. During the sixties they were limited to coordination of national measures and response to individual projects. This was clearly insufficient, however, especially in less developed regions. Even where there was improved productivity this was not always reflected in a better standard of living for farmers.

The first comprehensive "socio-structural directives" were issued in April 1972. The main problems were insufficient land (European farms being far smaller than North America's) for optimum use of modern methods and equipment, shortage of investment capital, inadequate training and lack of alternative employment.

The first coordinated package of measures facilitated early retirement for farmers able and willing to augment other holdings by transferring their land, while also making such expanded holdings more productive. To qualify for a modernization grant, farmers had to show that the planned investment would increase their holding. Training grants promoted entrepreneurial thinking.

Toward the end of the seventies economic recession made these schemes harder to implement: with high interest rates, inflation and general unemployment ("stagflation") modernization receded and the mobility of farmers and land was circumscribed. Farm incomes came under renewed pressure. The Community responded to changed circumstances by lowering qualification limits for assistance.

Meanwhile, price guarantees resulted in increased surpluses which had to be bought in, stocked and, in most cases sold at a loss.

Marketeer's nightmare: guaranteed outlets at guaranteed prices

With mounting surpluses, galloping expenditure, increasing economic and diplomatic strains in world markets and declining farm incomes CAP reform had become inevitable by the mid eighties. Gone were the days when production increases were needed to secure supplies. Consumer choice, stable food prices and agricultural evolution from traditional exploitation to agro-business were undoubted achievements but could not mask the huge problems faced by "Green Europe" and the Community budget.

As supply outstripped demand, pushed further by social factors such as lower birthrates, butter mountains and wine lakes grew apace.[6] Because of guaranteed farmgate prices these surpluses brought no budget relief to the family food basket. On the contrary, the European taxpayer was simultaneously subsidizing excess production, storage and sell-offs at knockdown prices to non-EC countries. Naturally, such practices also brought accusations of dumping, prohibited by GATT rules. Visitors from eastern Europe might be forgiven for imagining they had ended up in the superstate-controlled economy they had just left!

With such a heavy burden on the Community budget, enter Maggie Thatcher. Of course she had a national interest: Britain was paying huge levies into EC coffers because of her reduced but still significant patterns of trade with Commonwealth partners, while her small but relatively efficient farm population was drawing fewer benefits than most other countries. The raucous cry of "I want my money back!" hit home, however, because the Iron Lady forced the Community to face up to more general truths.

Policymakers recognized the need for CAP change, on the one hand because the EC economy had itself changed through

**Percentages of Agricultural Price Support Guarantees
Received and Production**

Official order of countries	Price support(*)	Market share (**)
Belgium	4.60	3.1 (***)
Denmark	3.86	3.4
Germany	15.93	14.5
Greece	7.04	3.9
Spain	10.51	12.6
France	20.17	22.8
Ireland	5.22	2.2
Italy	16.53	18.4
Luxembourg	0.01	3.1 (***)
Netherlands	7.84	7.7
Portugal	1.01	1.7
United Kingdom	7.27	9.7

(*) Source: FEOGA, 1991
(**) Source: French Gov't., 1988
(***) Belgium and Luxembourg combined

enlargements, new technology and economic growth, and on the other hand because goals had not been met due to the nature of the policy itself. With two-thirds of its income going to agriculture (today it is down to one half), the EC was on the verge of bankruptcy. Between 1975 and 1988, FEOGA guarantee spending increased six-fold, far outstripping expenditure on long-term structural solutions. Even within guarantee spending there was imbalance, with 40% going on export refunds and 15% on storage (in the latter case reaching 49% for beef). The inevitable outcome was that the farmers themselves were not benefitting as much as they should from the burdens borne by taxpayers and consumers. Simply stated, the CAP had become too expensive.

Under the pressure of EC surpluses world prices dropped and relations were chilled with countries such as Australia, New Zealand and Canada but above all the United States. The reaction could have been anticipated: an export promotion program adopted by Congress in 1985 sparked a subsidy war with the Community. Today, farm policies continue to provide the major stumbling block to agreement in GATT's Uruguay Round free-trade negotiations.

Red light for Green Europe

In July 1985 the Commission set out its proposed reforms in a Green Paper. The program adopted after much debate, while retaining the principles of market unity, Community preference and financial solidarity, sought to reduce surpluses and their concomitant budget burdens by scaling down price supports, limiting intervention guarantees, raising quality standards and, generally, emphasizing the co-responsibility of the producer. Nevertheless, as world prices rose, so also did agricultural guarantee expenditure. In February 1988, therefore, further budget stabilizers were accepted, the most notable of which was a "set-aside" fund to pay farmers to let arable land lie fallow. This was the ultimate irony: from guaranteed prices for production to guaranteed payments for non-production the CAP had extended its intervention to a full 180 degrees! At least, however, farmers would now produce for the market rather than for intervention: the wine lake evaporated, the butter mountain melted.[7] The revised CAP also included a monitoring system to keep farm spending within budget limits.

It should be noted here that, with the notable exception of a volume restriction on milk hurriedly introduced in 1984 when dairy support reached 30% of all guarantee expenditure, the Community has generally eschewed the introduction of internal quotas. (As for external quotas, Americans will recall the squabble over beef hormones, presented in the States as an import restriction and in Europe as a public health issue. Quotas are often disguised in other forms.)

New structural measures

The revised pricing and marketing policy was accompanied by new structural measures, especially for small farmers. The US objected through the GATT to direct social welfare payments on the grounds that they subsidized inefficient farmers. In 1989 such assistance was made transitional (to 1993) and decoupled from prices and markets. Where member governments have introduced such non-binding schemes the Community paid part of the cost.

Farming and feeding the globe

By virtue of the Lomé Convention ACP countries receive highly favorable treatment and even, in some cases, guaranteed prices for their agricultural exports to the Community. The fact remains that the First World— composed largely of former colonial powers—continues to control the agricultural outlets of the Third World. As for former East-bloc countries, voices are already being raised in the Community against their "cheap labor" exports; selfish and short-sighted voices indeed, if one considers that to move to a self-sufficient market economy they have to sell their products. For the foreseable future, however, the EC's principal competitor in farming remains the United States. As we have seen, the US has frequently criticized and reacted to European protectionism in this sector. However, successive American governments have also protected their agriculture; the farm lobby is powerful on "the hill". In the early eighties each American farmer cost the US Treasury an average of $20,000 p.a. or 38% of his income, compared with $8,000 (27% of income) for his European counterpart.

Even though the Community's principal opponent in the GATT negotiations is a US administration in the throes of agonizing reappraisal of its own agricultural policy, Brussels cannot ignore what is happening in the rest of the world:

> Even though deeply rooted in each mentality and each national history, with each passing day agriculture becomes more universal. To feed Russians with Canadian grain; or to decorate one's Parisian salon with flowers from Columbia which have transited via Amsterdam airport; or again to sample an Aosta ham cured in Auvergne from pigs fattened on Brazilian soybean transported to Ghent by Polish cargo ships . . . this too is agriculture. [8]

It is a world where traditions die hard. While protectionist winds forever blow in Japan and the US, in Australia subsidies are a dirty word. First in diversity, first in technology after thirty years of protection, European farmers feel the wind turning. Meanwhile, much of the Third World is undernourished and the agricultural economy of the former Communist bloc must be reconstructed (literally) from the ground up.

European-American trade relations of the last thirty years are littered with agricultural "wars": the chicken war, the meat war, the hormone spat, pig trough wrestling (cereal substitution products) . . . More than an ocean separates the European farmer from his American counterpart; in way of life, production methods and socio-economic influence they belong to different worlds. There are ten million of them in Europe, 2.2 million in the United States. Until the eighties, however, they also had this in common: both were so protected that they had little notion of world economic realities, a luxury which even the world's richest nations could no longer afford. From then on, it became clear from the prairies to Pont l'Evêque that while agriculture policy might continue to hold prices steady it could no longer guarantee incomes.

Despite the US/EC trade "wars", United States actually has a greater interest in free competition on the world market. In the late eighties US agricultural exports to the EC were double the value of those in the other direction, whereas the positions were reversed for total world-wide sales, in a market some fifteen times larger than US-EC exchanges.

Round and Round

To avoid debilitating dissensions between allies, it was agreed to address the issues globally in GATT's Uruguay Round, named after the country in which the first session was held (Punta del Este, September 1986. Previous negotiations were called Tokyo Round, Kennedy Round, Dillon Round.) This was the first significant extension of GATT discussions to agricultural products. Corn, cereals, soybeans and cotton are the exports most affected on the American side; conversely, US protection is strongest for sugar, dairy products and meat. It has also been US policy to guarantee farmgate prices in ways similar to CAP measures. In the thirties American farm problems were diagnosed as relating to overproduction. While providing price supports, the Agricultural Adjustment Act of 1933 actually sought to limit exports. Quotas were imposed and cultivation areas reduced for wheat, corn, cotton, peanuts, rice and tobacco.

The European CAP, especially in its initial form, was seen by American agricultural economists as boosting production and pushing European products in world markets. As US policy evolved in the late sixties and early seventies towards greater overseas sales (both to boost US farm income and to counteract a rising trade deficit), intense transatlantic competition on the world market became inevitable, especially since this rivalry was added to the protection each side afforded its own internal market. Dollar depreciation helped the US side and by 1980 over a third of the USA's cropland was producing for export. However, global recession, the debt crisis, dollar decline and grain embargos (European governments do not use food as a political weapon) hit the American farmer so severely that farm foreclosings had a spin-off effect on the US banking industry.

The 1985 US Farm Bill, equivalent to the annual EC agricultural price-setting "marathons," was intended to reduce subsidies, including set-aside (crop reduction) schemes. In the spirit of "reaganomics" market forces were reintroduced on the land, while export subsidies were inaugurated to win back world markets lost to Brussels. However, pressure from a Democratic (and somewhat more protectionist) Congress subsequently led President Bush to modify this stance. The same year the EC produced a Green Paper on CAP prospects.

US-EC face-off

While pointing out the basic differences between the American and the European farm, the Community has in principle been willing to negotiate on agriculture in the Uruguay Round. However, Brussels has insisted on a quid pro quo in the form of negotiations on services (telecommunications, insurance, banking, shipping, etc.), largely excluded in post-war trade negotiations.

While each of the Twelve is represented in GATT negotiations, they cannot in fact negotiate separately because of their treaty commitments to each other. Before the Commission can represent the EC in trade talks, the Twelve must first reach an agreed negotiating position amongst themselves. While this two-tier procedure has on occasion caused disgruntlement on the part of one or another member government, there is really no alternative. After laborious discussions the Twelve managed to reach a compromise acceptable to themselves and put forward proposals to the GATT conference in 1988. With respect to agriculture, the package contained significant structural changes, including early retirement incentives to farmers and assistance to employees sidelined by such retirement.

Ultimately, however, the 1988 measures satisfied nobody. Costs continued to rise and the food mountains returned. 1990 went by in recriminations and numerous unheeded appeals for reform.

Speaking before the US Senate Committee on Agriculture, Nutrition and Forestry on February 7, 1990, Secretary of Agriculture Clayton Yeutter made it clear that exports were henceforth a keystone of American agricultural policy:

> Our policy must be one that commits US agriculture to compete, because without greater access to foreign markets US agriculture will stagnate ... We have a unique challenge in 1990. U.S. farm policy will be written while our government concurrently engages in the most significant multilateral trade discussions ever. However, it would be incorrect to state that farm legislation will be unaffected by the GATT negotiations or that the GATT will not be affected by actions taken in Washington. Clearly there is a relationship between these two important initiatives. As the world's major agricultural exporter, changes in agricultural trading rules will obviously affect the United States- and we intend to do everything in our power to make sure these changes are for the better. They can only get better. [9]

The final comment succinctly records the tensions existing among agricultural trading nations. Those relations did not improve. In the summer of 1990 the Uruguay Round deadlocked in Brussels. The US accused the EC of offering too little on agriculture; the EC accused the US of expecting too much and of refusing a quid pro quo on other GATT issues, such as services. Arthur Dunkel, GATT's Swiss-born director, was charged with further consultations.

MacSharry on a tightrope

Such was the agro-political atmosphere in which EC Commissioner Ray Mac-Sharry, from Ireland, found himself caught between too little for the farmers and too little for the Community's trading partners. Reporting to the European Parliament on December 13, 1990, Commissioner MacSharry stressed the need for a positive review rather than mutual recriminations. Nevertheless he made no new proposals at that time and criticized the US for not meeting the EC halfway.

By the summer of 1991 the situation in the Community had reached crisis proportions. There were 24 million tonnes of grain in storage. 750,000 tonnes of beef had been bought in at $1,900 a tonne above the world price. Butter was being purchased at $2,250 in excess of the world level. In July the Community sold 40,000 tonnes of beef to Brazil at a knock-down price and then bought in a further 34,000 tonnes ...

After another half-year of behind-the-scenes Community negotiations, public debate and pressure from the London G7, the Commission adopted yet another reform proposal (five-year plan) on July 9, 1991. MacSharry claimed that this would put the EC in a stronger negotiating position in the Uruguay Round, halt the slide in farm incomes and slow down budget increases. The new proposals included agro-environmental action, reafforestation of agricultural land and improved early retirement conditions. Productivity and farm-gate price guarantees would continue to fall. Cereal prices would drop 35%, beef 15%, milk 10%. These proposals would be counterbalanced by direct income assistance, less objectionable to the Americans than price supports.

The balancing act proved unsuccessful: EC agriculture ministers refused to approve the cuts. The United States, on the other hand, insisted that the EC must cut export subsidies as well as payments to farmers. The MacSharry plan made no reference to export subsidies at all. Evidently, however, one does not embark upon a negotiation by revealing fall-back positions or ultimate concessions. Nevertheless, Secretary Yeutter's 1990 statement to the Senate Committee had made it clear that the US was prepared to meet the EC head on by threatening further use of the export subsidies introduced by President Reagan:

> We propose reauthorization of the Export Enhancement Program (EEP) without mandated program levels or programming requirements. The EEP has proven an important part of our trade policy strategy to achieve a successful Uruguay Round. We want our competitors, especially the European Community, to know that we stand ready to use this program to the maximum extent. We want them to phase out their export subsidy practices which have severely distorted world markets for many years. Those subsidies have cost American farmers billions of dollars in exports and in income.

In December 1991 negotiations in the Uruguay Round came to a halt once more.

Agricultural policy or political agriculture?

As 1991 melted into 1992 the EC's agricultural policy had still not been reformulated by the Council of Ministers, let alone merged into a final settlement of the Uruguay Round. Yet the Commission did not give up the fight. In the closing speech to a colloquium at Châteauroux (L'Espace rural, une chance pour la France et pour l'Europe), Commission President Jacques Delors both castigated the GATT proposals formulated by Arthur Dunkel and defended those of his Commissioner for Agriculture, Ray MacSharry:

> The present proposal, serving as a basis for GATT negotiations, is scandalously unfavorable to Europe, which is why we have rejected it . . .

Delors raised once more the countervailing issues of industry and services upon which the US was much more reticent. However, he went on to state that the MacSharry reform would be advantageous to Europe and to France, being contrary to the vested interests only of the largest landowners, who would have to "make an effort." As for the subsidy war with the US, it took place on the backs of the poor countries.

In his comprehensive study on the economics of European integration, Willem Molle has neatly encapsulated the political nature of the problem. The intense regulation of the agricultural sector sets it apart from the main purpose of the European Economic Community. Heavy pressure has been brought to bear by those directly interested, the farmers, to create mechanisms for the transfer of resources from both consumers and taxpayers to themselves. Rome Treaty rules set economic needs at loggerheads with political realities. The CAP restructuring commenced in 1986 through limits on agricultural price increases (and thereby on production surpluses) was the beginning of a long and necessary process.

How, asks Molle, did a policy for a major sector of the economy with considerable negative effects come to be elaborated in the first place? And how could a system so evidently incapable of correction be maintained for so long? ... The answer to both questions is largely contained in the workings of the EC institutions in general and the specialized Council of Agricultural Ministers in particular. Special interest groups (supported by their power in elections) have been able to force decisions, and many observers are now conviced that to understand the CAP, its political rationale should be primarily considered, its economic rationale being at best of secondary importance. [10]

Since these thoughts appeared in 1990, change has been glacially slow. The power of the farm lobby in Europe is rivalled only by that of the gun lobby in the United States!

The Community's agriculture retains an essential role in feeding 330 million citizens, in safeguarding the environment and in maintaining the economic, social and human fabric of many regions which have problems of development to overcome. Nevertheless, the budgetary, economic, social and political constraints upon the policy are enormous. The final chapter is more likely to be written in the world arena of GATT than within the European Community alone.

One is reminded of those hollow Russian dolls: inside GATT we come upon the Uruguay Round. Open the Round and find the EC US twins. Open the US twin and find a Kansas banker festooned with failed mortgages (the real estate crisis is part of the problem) ... Open the EC twin and find CAP. Inside the CAP look for a French (or German) farmer ... In late 1991 and early 1992, through a long winter of discontent, the "sherpas" of CAP reform [11] struggled with interest groups and vote-counting politicians to effect some progress. France proved particularly allergic to changing policy because French agriculture includes every category of producer from the smallest family holding to immense agro-business undertakings. Meeting in Brussels in January and again in March the farm ministers failed once more to achieve consensus on CAP reform, although they did decide (small comfort) not to await progress in GATT (Uruguay Round) before moving on agriculture. This was important because of the vicious circle of EC waiting on GATT and GATT waiting on EC ... French Minister Louis Mermaz declared that CAP discussions were not merely a "by product" of GATT negotiation. In fact, as a major exporter of subsidized farm products, France remained an implacable opponent of the Dunkel proposals. The French grain lobby is considered one of the most powerful in the Community. Sensing that the sherpas could go no higher, the Portuguese minister, Arlindo Cunha, who as chairman held the responsibility of keeping things moving, suggested that it was time to move to political negotiations. EC Agriculture Commissioner MacSharry said much the same thing when he told ministers it was "time to bite the bullet". Commission President Delors even turned on his countrymen: "The farmers for whom you show so much care are not the only ones in the world". He could have added that France is the world's fourth largest exporter and needs open markets in Europe and beyond.

Bush in a box

On March 10, 1992, US Secretary of State James Baker carried a personal letter from President Bush to Commission President Delors in Brussels. Bush tried to move the six-year-old Uruguay Round forward, suggesting a new "deadline" (ignored of course) of April 15. At the same time, Bush made a "gesture" by suggesting enlargement of the Green Box of payments to farmers not deemed critical to production levels and thereore not subject to phasing out. However Bush did not move on two other EC demands, namely that the US limit the volume of its agricultural exports and not be permitted to impose duties on imports of CSP's. The Bush move, while looking like a concession, shrewdly wrong-footed the French who, seeking to control cereal production through pressure on prices, do not favor too large a Green Box. Let us hope the "boxing" match doesn't go fifteen "rounds" . . . [12] The political fact is that many of the leading players — France, Britain, Germany, Italy, not to mention the US, — were facing regional or national elections in 1992. We will have to see how the new tenant in the White House treats the matter in 1993 and beyond.

$200 for bread and potatoes

In 1990 the CAP cost $36 billion and, according to Rory Watson of The European, could soon hit $55 billion or $200 for every man, woman and child in the EC. Some Eurocrats might even have been regretting the Thatcher demise. Moreover, stocks of unsold, unconsumed products bought in by EC guaranteed price policy have again reached record levels. Many voices have been raised in protest at the cost of the "Delors II" five-year EC budget submitted after Maastricht. As agricultural surpluses are sold off at a loss, the tight budgetary controls now exercized in the Community may enforce cutbacks in payments to farmers.

Despite the technicalities and complexities of the agricultural sector, the public was not unaware that the CAP had failed to find a balance between special interests and those of the citizens as a whole. They were helped on by some hard hitting editorials, like this gem abridged from *The European* of February 20, 1992:

> The EC Budget is dominated by one huge scandal, the Common Agricultural Policy. Well over half the current spending goes on propping up Community farming through a dazzling array of schemes to buy, burn, bury or "buffer-stock" food that should have never been produced in the first place.
>
> This is not just the fault of the Commission. Farm ministers from all Community countries are doing their best to protect their own farmers from plans to bring in limited CAP reforms.
>
> But the measures which are being discussed so painfully slowly are not really aimed at helping European consumers and taxpayers; they are designed to head off criticism from the rest of the world.

So instead of paying to dump food on the rest of the world, the Commission now wants to pay farmers just for being farmers with no pretence at all that they are running a system related to Europe's food needs . . .

While this goes on, eastern European countries are desperate for money to buy goods from the West because farm produce, the one area where they have an advantage, is kept out by protectionism. If the EC needs to find money to pay "the price of Maastricht", it ought to find it by good housekeeping and cutting out the waste in what it spends down on the farm.

Cash, crops and corruption

The editorialist could have added another string to his bow. Ever since creation of the European Communities "fraud artists" have found ways to turn regulations to their own advantage. There was the celebrated case of the canal barge which collected various benefits as it crossed watery borders without ever unloading its cargo. Illicit profiteering can take a thousand forms. Who is going to check whether you are cultivating fifteen olive trees or ten? By definition, fraud is not quantifiable, but the European Parliament has set it between 2 and 6 billion (*milliard*) francs. Excessive bureaucracy facilitates cheating. Community auditors have pointed out that there are over 1200 categories for export subsidies (more for cereals to China than to Bangladesh; more for beef hindquarters than forequarters, for males rather than females) . . . British criticism of Brussels bureaucracy is more than just politics . . . When this mess is cleaned up (assuming it can be), there could be a ten percent saving in the CAP budget.

In a public declaration in March, 1992, the Portuguese prime minister and chairman-in-office of the EC Council, Cavaco Silva, declared that the Community had to show internal courage by facing up to realities:

Today's agricultural policy is not rational; nor is it viable in the long term. It guarantees balance neither in the market, in the budget nor in the regions . . . Of course, it would be much easier to sit by, watching how GATT evolves, and only thereafter discuss this reform. That would be a mistake. The two issues must be treated in tandem . . . Of course Portugal too has its problems . . . but at European level four fifths of the subsidies go to one fifth of the farmers and there is immense regional imbalance.

Everyone knows that there must be a conclusion. World trade and global protectionism cannot be permitted to hang indefinitely in the balance while the French and Americans exchange green boxes and invisible exports. The final chapter will most likely be written in GATT's world arena. At that point, with an imposed political solution, Europe's farmers might come to regret not accepting the MacSharry proposals with the safeguards they contained.

Maybe GATT pressure is doing the Community a favor. One day, by dint of overproduction, the CAP cow may run out of milk . . .

CAP reform at last

On May 21, 1992, EC ministers of agriculture reached a long sought agreement to make fundamental changes in the CAP. When the final vote was taken at dawn after a five-day marathon and an all-night session, only Italy offered token dissent (dissatisfied with her failure to achieve a milk quota increase).

The historic agreement was partly the result of pressures in the Uruguay Round from the US and third-world nations against EC export subsidies; but it came above all from the need to control both excessive production and excessive costs. The system of price guarantees in place for thirty years had proved counterproductive in a number of ways:

— It encouraged excessive production;
— Excess production had to be stored;
— Attempts to cut back production by lowering price guarantees reduced the standard of living of farmers;
— High guaranteed prices necessitated export subsidies, disturbing patterns of world trade and blocking GATT free trade agreements;
— Guaranteed price payments to farmers, storage costs and export subsidies made excessive demands on the Community budget;
— Annual price-settings gave rise to protracted and debilitating political haggling;
— Anomalies arose like paying farmers both to produce (guaranteed prices) and not to produce (compensation for land left fallow);
— Europeans paid too much not once but twice for food, as both taxpayers and consumers (through high shelf prices).

In theory at least the new policy—let us call it CAP2—addresses all these issues. It avoids the "Malthusian" trap of reinforcing quotas, leaving the farmer free to produce but transferring financial support from production to acreage. Overnight, quality becomes more important than quantity.

The main points of CAP2, the most sweeping reform in Community farm-policy history, are as follows:

— A 29 percent reduction in subsidized grain prices over a three-year period, ending with the 1995-96 marketing year;
— A 15 percent reduction in subsidized beef prices over the same period, and a substantial cut in the total tonnage of beef eligible for EC subsidies;
— A 5 percent reduction in subsidized butter prices over the three-year period; milk quotas, introduced in 1984, are maintained;
— Direct payments to farmers to compensate for the subsidy reductions, provided that the farmers take 15 percent of their land out of production;
— Social restructuring through early retirement schemes and other measures encouraging young farmers to stay on the land.

"We want a GATT agreement," declared EC agriculture commissioner Ray McSharry as he left the negotiation chamber at the end of the marathon; "We've made our contribution to world trade. Now let the Americans make their contribution." Six months after Maastricht and in the middle of the ratification procedure for the Treaty of European Union, when cities were claiming that new doubts were creeping in, the Community had once again demonstrated its capacity for bouncing back. (CAP2 is unaffected by the subsequent Danish "no" to Maastricht).

In 1993 farmers will have to leave 15% of their land uncultivated in order to qualify for the acreage payments designed to replace price supports. This percentage will be reviewed annually according to market conditions. With respect to meat production a maximum of two "large bovine units" (an LBU is one cow or ox per hectare) is the maximum permitted under the acreage payments system. Withdrawal of price supports will result in lower grain and feed prices and should help Community farmers to regain part of the market in animal feed currently lost to third countries, in particular the US.

To set CAP2 in proper perspective, it is important to remember, firstly, that, like its precessor, the new policy is a framework agreement subject to annual adjustments; secondly that large sectors, such as pork, poultry, wine, cheese, vegetables and fruit are covered only partly or not at all; and that, in the final analysis, farmers will be dealing with their own government rather than with Brussels.

CAP2 does not seek to reduce overall expenditure on agriculture so much as to make a better use of the monies available. Funds devoted to storage costs and export subsidies should now end up in the pocket of the farmer. Nevertheless, first reactions from farmers were largely hostile, especially in France. The paysans were not convinced that governments would maintain the level of their direct aid to farmers through periods of economic downturn and budgetary stress.

The new policy is still far from creating a free market, but it takes a major step towards that goal by treating maintenance of rural structures as a societal and environmental issue. Jacques Delors declared that the reform would make it possible to keep farmers on the land in sufficient numbers to maintain rural development, under conditions similar to those provided under the price guarantee system. However farmers' organizations accused EC governments of giving in to US pressure. US Trade Representative Carla Hills gave the agreement a cautious welcome. Even though there was no official linkage between CAP2 and GATT, the challenge is clearly before GATT's 108 members, led by the US, to respond. [13]

Maybe then finally world trade will be substantially freer; and agriculture will achieve a new level of quality and more rational distribution of resources, production and outlets among consumers, animal feed, industrial applications and the needs of the Third World.

Notes

1   Adapted from *National Food Review*, US Dept. of Agriculture, Vol. 13, January 1990, page 1.

2   American policymakers diagnosed their problem as one of overproduction rather than of international barriers to trade. The AAA limited exports and provided price supports, reduced areas of cultivation, offered loans to farmers, established marketing quotas, guaranteed prices, provided foreign aid to distribute surplus production and instituted protectionism in some sectors. See Hopkins, Raymond, *Global Food Interdependence: Challenge to American Foreign Policy*, New York, Columbia University Press, 1980 and Paarlberg, Don, *Farm and Food Policy: Issues of the 1980's*, Lincoln, University of Nebraska Press, 1980.

3   Farmers have traditionally lived and worked in harmony with nature, shaping, maintaining and protecting their land from damaging ecological consequences. In the past forty years, however, technological revolution has led to widespread mechanization, the growing use of agrochemicals and vastly improved cultivation techniques. Such intensification has produced higher yields and greater wealth but has also left its mark on a bruised countryside. The resultant environmental problems include deterioration of animal habitats and extinction of species due to disturbance, pollution and wetland drainage; low water quality arising from the misuse or overuse of chemicals, animal manures and other organic material; soil degradation or erosion, caused both by the abandonment of farming in uneconomic mountainous regions and by the direct application of intensive farming techniques; and declining air quality due to ammonia evaporation from fertilizers and manure.

Recent reviews of the common agricultural policy have led the EC to affirm the importance of taking environmental considerations into account. It has adopted agricultural measures directly or indirectly aimed at promoting environmental objectives and reducing the impact of modern farming, including the payment of aids to farmers who comply with certain practices in environmentally sensitive zones, subsidies to help maintain farming in less-favoured areas, the prohibition of harmful pesticides, incentives for less intensive farming, the setting aside of surplus arable land and early retirement. (See also, in Part IV, Chapter 2.)

4   A tariff is set at a fixed rate, such as 10 or 20% of price, whereas a levy counteracts an external/internal price differential and varies in accordance with market conditions.

5   The EC has never become involved in income tax and social security payments.

6   By December 1986 EC cold stores were bulging with 1.3 m. tonnes of butter, 15 m.t. of skim milk powder, 600,000 t. of beef and 280,000 t. of olive oil.

7   Set-aside funding has its limits. To remove all surpluses about one-tenth of EC arable land would have to be taken out of production. This figure would grow as productivity rose. The environmental impact of modifying an ancient landscape shaped by farming must also be considered. However, the CAP reform of May 1992 sets the figure at 15%.

8   Gill, Stephen, ed., *Atlantic Relations beyond the Reagan Era*, Harvester Wheatsheaf- St. Martin's Press, New York, 1989, p. 123.

9   Text supplied by US Department of Agriculture.

10 Molle, Willem, *The Economics of European Integration*, Dartmouth, 1990, p. 269.

11   On the Indo-Tibetan border sherpa carriers open the way for mountain climbers by carrying supplies and setting up base camps. In Europe the expression is picturesquely used to denote senior officials who prepare ministerial or summit meetings.

12   The shadow boxing over GATT continued in another ring in mid-March (1992) when GATT itself warned the US that its plans for a free trade area from Alaska to the Antartic (Enterprise for the Americas) held "potentially devastating consequences" for world trade. GATT principles were being eroded by regionalism and "managed" trade. The US will no doubt consider that what is sauce for the European goose is sauce for the American gander.

13   Without the CAP many of today's protesters would not have been in business to protest. CAP does not contravene the letter of GATT (the spirit is another matter) because the Agreement was not designed to include farming. However, "Uruguay" sought to extend coverage to new areas, including both farming and sectors of US protection which Europe wanted opened up (insurance, shipping, etc.) at state and federal levels. The US and EC finally reached a settlement on agriculture, in particular the production and export subsidies on oil seed crops, on November 22, 1992. French farmers exploded; however, it was inconceivable that France would ultimately block so universal a liberation of trade. The settlement includes the 15% set-aside for oilseed, a 29% price reduction and a 21% quantitative reduction of exports over six years, starting 1994. It was quietly ratified at the Edinburgh Summit, freeing the path for GATT negotiators.

2

Nature Knows No Frontiers: Saving the Planet from Ourselves

When *homo sapiens* evolved some million years ago, like every other species he was born into a hostile environment. He not only managed to survive, but thanks to the evolution of hand and brain came to dominate other species and to exploit the land on which he lived. An initially defensive struggle developed into systematic conquest. With or without World War III, this evolution is now moving into a phase of environmental dilapidation which could make our planet unhabitable.

> It became second nature to man to destroy more than necessary. Only recently has the toll of destruction and irresponsible exploitation of natural resources been seen to be disturbingly serious. Vast numbers of animals have been destroyed; huge tracts of forest have been razed, leaving soils a prey to erosion; plant life has been decimated; mineral resources are running out ... the downhill slide has been very steep in the last two hundred years as the urban revolution brought with it transport, storage and trade, making man more independent of the vagaries of production. The cities were born. Human populations began to grow. . . .[1]

Man's reaction to his own destructiveness has been rather slow. Environmental protection is considered a recent phenomenon. In fact, however, several nineteenth-century figures were sensitive to the ravages of the industrial revolution and scientific "progress". The Forest of Fontainebleau was declared a nature reserve in 1853. In the US, Yellowstone National Park dates from 1872. The economist Malthus was conscious of the threat of overpopulation. Generally speaking, however, it took time before the threat to certain species was linked to the question of their habitats. After World War I, the international character of conservation was recognized in a series of conferences held in Switzerland and Paris. However, the International Union for Nature Protection did not come into being until 1948.

Evolution of the names of official bodies corresponds to changing definitions of what is involved: from "protection" to "conservation" to "management", from "natural habitats" to "nature" to "the environment". There has for many years been a certain tension between "protectors" and "developers", with "managers" holding an uneasy balance between the two. Even the relatively short history of the Council of Europe's work in this area reflects the progression. When first established in 1962, the committee of experts, the first intergovernmental body of its kind, was called the "Committee of Experts for the Conservation of Nature and Landscape". This was subsequently changed to "European Committee for the Conservation of Nature and Natural Resources", with terms of reference which did not include air pollution, much less ozone layers . . .

1. the conservation of nature and natural resources;
2. the preservation of landscape and natural habitats and especially sites or areas of special scientific interest or outstanding natural beauty;
3. the establishment of new nature reserves and national and intra-European parks.

Complementary programs

Today the Committee is called the Steering Committee for the Conservation and Management of the Environment and Natural Habitats (CDPE). With more extensive legal powers and financial resources than the Council of Europe, the European Community has also entered the field. Concern has been expressed that the work of the two bodies on environmental issues overlaps (the Twelve also being Council of Europe members); in fact the two organizations tend to reflect differing and complementary approaches. The Council of Europe emphasies conservation of species, habitat, landscape and natural resources such as water and forests: one might summarize it as conservation of the environmental capital, what the French call *le patrimoine*. The Community on the other hand concentrates on pollution control, on land and in the air, in fresh and salt water, on waste management, and generally on factors which are linked to the state of the economy.

Against the background of relative prosperity and stability of the seventies, EC governments felt that economic expansion should result in improvements in the quality of life, including better environmental protection. To this end they decided to set up an environmental action program. This first program was largely remedial. It took over a decade for the Community's thinking to evolve towards a more preventive stance. Thus environmental resources were seen not only as the basis of but also, as setting limits to further social and economic advances. The obligation to take into account environmental considerations when formulating national and Community policies is enshrined in the Treaty of Rome by virtue of the amendments of the Single European Act and further strengthened by the Treaty of European Union.

The Community's environmental impact assessment directive, which came into force on July 3, 1988, has given force to this important principle. It integrates ecological awareness into the planning and decision-making process in all major sectors, notably agriculture, the oil industry, energy, transport, tourism and regional development. Projects such as crude oil refineries, thermal power stations, chemical installations and motorway constructions must be subjected to an impact assessment. The assessment must identify the effects of a project on human beings, fauna and flora; soil, water, air , climate and landscape; and material assets and the cultural heritage. The public must be consulted and can propose alternatives. Under the directive the competent planning authority must take into account information and opinions received in the environmental study before taking its decision.

Another principle of Community policy is the conviction that strict standards of protection are an economic as well as an environmental necessity. Nowadays, customers read labels before buying. Given the "greening" of consumers and the growing demand for environmentally friendly goods, EC industry will not be successful unless it gears up to confront the challenge of an increasingly polluted society. High environmental standards should no longer be seen as imposing red tape and unnecessary costs on industry, transport and agriculture. Strict norms can and should be associated with economic growth and job creation.

Furthermore, in recent years, as the Community directive has begun to "bite", the strict application of EC policy by all commercial partners has been seen as an essential ingredient of fair trade. Taking care of the environment such as "scrubbing" smoke, purifying waste water and relandscaping mines, slag-heaps and quarries or meeting common standards limiting noise[2] represent significant overhead factors in production costs. Those who neglect such practices may gain competitive advantage, at least in the short term. Polluters must pay, not profit.

Other differences between Council of Europe and EC action in the environmental field become apparent here. The Council of Europe is more concerned with governmental action and general principles, the EC with the private sector and specific cases; the Council of Europe with the protection of wildlife, natural resources and landscape, the Community with the protection of people in their private and professional activity. Again, however, the difference in emphasis may be seen as complementary rather than conflictual.

Regardless of the institutions involved, many of the problems such as acid deposition or water pollution arise because of the transfer of pollution from one part of the environment to another. Action to limit the damage is more effective when taken at source rather than in each sector separately. Ultimately, then, environmental policy must be coordinated at local, regional, national, international and, ultimately, world level. If acid rain is a problem of continental proportions, the greenhouse effect and depletion of the protective ozone layer around the earth are issues of global proportions of which mankind was barely conscious when European environmental cooperation began.

The Council of Europe program

Given the diversity of issues facing governments the new committee set few criteria as parameters for action. It concentrated on subjects which were, firstly, limited in number; secondly, ones where European co-operation was of undoubted value in solving national problems; thirdly, where results would be practical and tangible; and fourthly, not duplicating work already done or in progress in other organizations. To implement its projects it used the classical methods of intergovernmental bodies: working parties, consultants, cooperation with NGO's such as IUCN and other NGO's.

Wildlife and natural habitats

The committee recognized very early that it was not sufficient to catalog threatened species and environmental changes. It was necessary not only to analyze the effects of human activity but also to redress the balance. In addition to protection of flora, fauna and their habitats, there were the problems of deforestation, overgrazing, overuse of pesticides, and fresh-water, marine and air pollution to be tackled. At the same time it was impossible to ignore the technical and economic repercussions on natural habitats of industrialisation, major public construction projects, urban development, agricultural and forestry projects, misuse of land, and speculation of all kinds. The natural heritage must be managed rationally.

Not all the committee's endeavors were successful. A survey of national environmental legislation ran into insurmountable problems of translating a huge body of diverse and rapidly evolving legislation. Nevertheless, the aborted project did show up significant strengths and lacunae, with the result that national authorities drafted supplementary texts in some cases.

Air pollution

In 1962 the parliamentarians asked the Committee of Ministers to convene a European Conference on Air Pollution. The 1964 meeting was the first of its kind, confronting the diverse viewpoints of doctors, biologists, toxicologists, meteorologists, urban planners, economists, lawyers and (of course!) politicians. A committee was set up and European and national policies implemented. In 1979 a European Convention on long-range transboundary air pollution was opened for signature. With smoke from Britain's industrial heartland killing off Norwegian trees and the Black Forest under acid rain from Lorraine, it did not come too soon. Now European environmentalists face an even greater challenge in Poland.

The Water Charter

Three projects of the early years were particularly successful in reaching a broad public not yet educated to environmental issues. (There were no "green parties" in those days). These were the European Water Charter, the European Diploma, and the broader European Conservation Year 1970.

In 1963, the Consultative Assembly approved a study on controlling freshwater pollution and asked member governments to take action in the matter by drafting and solemnly promulgating a European Water Charter. By early 1964, the text of the Water Charter had been drawn up. The European Committee for the Conservation of Nature and Natural Resources also devized a comprehensive action programme for the official promulgation of the Charter and an accompanying water conservation campaign. There was agreement on the need to arouse public concern for preservation of water quality and quantity. The Charter was promulgated in 1968.[3]

The European Diploma

Early in its deliberations, the Committee proposed creation of an award or seal of approval for national parks and nature reserves of European interest to encourage effective protection. The Committee of Ministers instituted a procedure for the award of this distinction, known as the European Diploma of the Council of Europe. The diploma is awarded for a period of five years, which may be renewed on a proposal from the Committee after the area has been inspected. An annual report must be submitted, stating whether conservation standards have been maintained or improved, what effects the Diploma award has had on management, what improvements have been carried out, and whether the site is threatened in any way. The Committee's task in this matter is not easy. Selection criteria are extremely rigorous, inspection absolutely impartial, and all pressures of a political nature must be vigorously resisted. Sometimes the Committee might have to step in to help the park authorities, and this has to be handled very carefully, especially in extreme cases where there is no choice but to withdraw the Diploma. Such was the case in 1991, when it was felt that the bears of the Pyrenees National Park in France were inadequately protected. In such severity lies the whole value of the award.

The first awards included the Rhone delta wetlands of the Camargue (France), the Peak District National Park (UK) and the high moorlands of the Hautes Fagnes in Belgium. Recent additions to an impressive list covering many unique areas include the Teide National Park in Spain and the Wurzacher Ried Nature Reserve in Germany. As always, the recommendation proposing award of the Diploma is accompagnied by specific recommendations designed to improve and protect the habitats concerned. The award is made subject to acceptance of these conditions by the national and local authorities.[4]

European Conservation Year (1970)

In 1965 the Committee of Ministers decided to plan a European Conservation Year, to be held at national and European levels. During the preparation period governments and public came to appreciate the extent of nature conservation problems. They saw them from a wider viewpoint: on the one hand there was the seriously threatened natural and urban environment to be protected, and on the other a way of life which they wanted to improve at all costs. The European Conference on Air Pollution, the promulgation of the Water Charter, the sessions of the Conference of Local and Regional Authorities devoted to regional planning and nature and landscape conservation (1964) and to the role of local authorities in the conservation of nature and natural resources (1970), made an important contribution to creating this new state of mind.

Prepared down to the last detail, not only by the Council of Europe in Strasbourg but also by the national committees in each member country. European Conservation year was successful; all the resources of the mass media were mobilised; education as well as the full range of private nature protection bodies played an active part. National and regional activities were many and varied. The most important event at European level was the Conference on environmental planning in tomorrow's Europe. Royalty, ministers, parliamentarians officially representing their countries, mingled with some three hundred participants from seventeen members countries, ten non-member countries, nine international governmental organisations and forty-three international non-governmental organisations. The Conference culminated in a Declaration on the management of the natural environment of Europe, calling on governments to commit themselves to an environmental policy. Not only did the conference stir public opinion, but it also succeeded in giving a boost to national policies and encouraging the creation of bodies to deal with these problems. In many countries it spurred the creation of governmental ministries responsible for nature protection and the environment. It called for regular meetings of ministers responsible for the environment in the member countries. Such conferences at ministerial level are now a regular aspect of the Council of Europe's program of work. A filiation could be claimed from the 1970 Council of Europe conference to the Rio Earth Summit of 1992.

In 1987 the European Community organized a similar if less extensive event, the European Year of the Environment (EYE) in the twelve member states. EYE helped stimulate Community citizens to give serious new thought to the problems of the environment and increased awareness of the importance of integrating environmental thinking into all elements of policymaking. The Commission also organized a pilot project encouraging the teaching of environmental studies in primary and secondary schools as part of the curriculum. Brochures were produced to assist teachers in this task. Training schemes have been held for professionals, such as university staff, engineers and scientists, while conferences, seminars and scholarships on all aspects of environmental protection are organized regularly.

To return to the Council of Europe, the European Committee has also undertaken a number of less spectacular but more specific initiatives. These include studies of the harm caused to wildlife by pesticides, the ecological consequences of intensive cultivation of conifers in deciduous zones, birds requiring special protection, protection of coastal areas, conservation of mountain soils, a European vegetation map, a European network of biogenetic reserves, ecological impacts of gene technology, natural balance in the countryside and environmental education in agriculture.

Education, training and information

Ecological conservation is a relatively young science which has gained immeasurably in importance since the industrial revolution of the nineteenth century and the nuclear and other technological developments of our own age. It is rarely taught in normal school curricula. Moreover, in practical situations involving construction or agricultural exploitation its immediate costs are more apparent than its long term benefits. The Council of Europe has for many years accordingly paid great attention to education, training and information of specialists and the general public in the conservation of natural resources. NATUROPA is the name given to information activities on nature and the environment.

A European Campaign for the Countryside (1987-88) attempted to reconcile development with conservation.

Naturopa Centre

The Naturopa Centre, based in Strasbourg, exists to create awareness among the people of Europe about their natural environment, the threats to it and the need for its conservation. The Centre stimulates, guides and co-ordinates European action. Its network of Agencies covers the 27 member states of the Council of Europe; the Centre also has correspondents in other countries, including the USA and Israel. The network links secretariat, agencies, organizations and individuals. At national level the links extend across the nature conservation spectrum from voluntary bodies to central government. The network is used to give and to receive information, to share experience and to conduct a dialog. The closeness and informality of its links allow communication that is frank, speedy and authoritative. The Centre is a clearing-house for information about Europe's natural environment and its conservation.

The Naturopa Centre has sponsored information campaigns at European and regional levels on soil, freshwater, wetlands, European wildlife and natural habitats, the water's edge, the relationship between farming and wildlife, Mediterranean coasts and Europe's freshwater fish species. A thematic illustrated magazine, *Naturopa*, is published three times a year in English, French, German, Italian, Spanish and Portuguese. A monthly newsletter appears in ten languages. Both publications may be obtained from the National Agencies. The Centre holds some 5,000 books, 400 journals and a range of other publications on Europe's natural environment for consultation by experts and the general public. General and specialised bibliographies are available as part of the Centre's documentation and information service.

Professional development

The European Committee has held a number of courses for the training of officials responsible for the planning and management of natural areas. In particular, managers of areas awarded the European Diploma are afforded opportunities to exchange information and experience. Furthermore, a large number of IGO's and NGO's follow the Strasbourg conservation program. Cooperation has been particularly close with the EC and IUCN.

Financial realities: the Community's incentive program

There is no doubt that it requires money to maintain a clean environment. Quite apart from "quality of life" factors, it usually costs more to maintain a dirty one. However in the first case the costs are apparent whereas in the latter, unfortunately, they may long remain hidden. Consequently there is rarely an immediate financial incentive to protect natural resources and the landscape.

It was therefore decided among the Twelve to provide incentives by meeting a share of the costs, an action which would be out of the question for the Council of Europe's far more modest budget. The EC's prime financial instruments for funding better environmental protection are its structural Funds: the European Social Fund, the non-price support section of the European Agricultural Fund and, notably, the European Regional Development Fund. These have been fine-tuned as part of the overall effort to reduce economic disparities within the Community and to promote the least-favored regions. Thus in June, 1988, it was agreed to concentrate on five priorities: promoting the restructuring of the most economically backward areas of the Community; transforming areas affected by industrial decline; combating long-term unemployment; easing access to the jobs market for young people; and improving agricultural structures and developing rural communities in the light of the reforms of the common agricultural policy. Although at first sight these objectives appear remote from environmental concerns a damaged environment is often a feature of disadvantaged regions. Initiatives in this field are likely to be of long-term economic benefit as well as fitting in with the Community's broader environmental objectives. The European Regional Development Fund, for instance, has contributed to many projects, including the laying of sewers, waste-water treatment and the incineration and recycling of waste. As we have seen, the Maastricht Treaty of Union confirms environmental conservation as an official EC activity in its own right which should therefore benefit from more direct and specific funding.

Some 1.2 billion ECU have been earmarked for environmental projects for the period 1989-93 in the less developed regions. Measures to be financed include schemes to combat air pollution, to conserve the countryside, to promote clean technologies, and to fight soil erosion and desertification.

Conscious that more specific initiatives are needed, the Commission, in late 1989, agreed to set up a special program (ENVIREG) to tackle pollution in the most depressed coastal areas of the Community, notably in the Mediterranean. A complementary program (MEDSPA) was approved to cover coastal regions of the Mediterranean not eligible for structural fund resources, as well as for non—EC countries in the Mediterranean basin.

The aim of ENVIREG and MEDSPA is not just to improve the quality of life for people living in the regions concerned, but to enhance their tourist appeal and thus boost their prospects of longer-term economic expansion. Of course pollution control schemes must provide for the increased pressure on the environment which a rise in tourism will itself generate.

ENVIREG funds help install purification systems and equipment to combat pollution from tourists and industrial plants, and improve inadequate sewage facilities. It has been calculated that 250 coastal towns with populations of between 10 000 and 100 000 inhabitants in regions eligible for ENVIREG support either have no infrastructure for disposing of or treating sewage, or are deficient in some way. In Italy 48% of the existing 1580 sewage treatment works no longer function—a figure which rises to 66% in the south of that country. In Spain 80% of municipalities are without treatment plants and some existing ones do not work. It is a key objective of these programs to improve member states' record of compliance with EC legislation on health and safety standards. Funding has assisted compliance with directives covering sea pollution caused by dangerous substances, bathing water quality, toxic and hazardous wastes, the disposal of waste oils and the protection of wild birds.

Less eye-catching than the 500 million ECU allocated to ENVIREG in the period 1990-93, but potentially just as important, is the ACE program (actions by the Community relating to the environment) established for the first time in 1987 to fund demonstration projects. Encouraging the development of clean or low-polluting technologies, new techniques for reusing waste and new methods for measuring and monitoring the quality of the environment are among the priorities here, with the Community's contribution covering between 30 and 50% of the costs. Projects providing an incentive to protect or to reclaim land threatened by fire, erosion and desertification, or contributing to the maintenance or re-establishment of seriously threatened habitats of endangered species, are also eligible for support under ACE. The European Investment Bank tends to concentrate its medium and long-term lending on the more depressed regions of the Community, but since 1984 has extended its criteria to include projects for environmental protection. The EIB now assesses all projects on the basis of their environmental impact, while EIB project managers encourage customers to make investments which involve minimal pollution.

The legal aspect

Since Council of Europe action, while effective, is based on consensual action, legal instruments at European level are not of primordial importance, although conventions have played a significant role. The situation is not the same for Community action, which usually requires a legal infrastructure for its implementation and monitoring. Where specific environmental provisions were lacking recourse was sometimes had to regulations under public health or fair trade.

Prior to the Single European Act taking effect in 1987 there was no explicit legal provision for Community environmental actions. In spite of this history more than a hundred instruments, mainly directives, were adopted in the fifteen years after the EC heads of state or government took the first tentative steps towards developing a policy at the Paris summit in 1972.

An important impetus came from Article 30 of the Treaty of Rome guaranteeing free exchange of goods and services between member states, to which certain exceptions, including measures capable of justification on environmental grounds, are now accepted. As a result, environmental initiatives were pursued either under Article 100 of the Treaty of Rome—the principal basis for harmonizing laws which directly affect the establishment or functioning of the common market—or under the more wide-ranging Article 235, which allows the Community to take appropriate measures to attain one of the objectives not expressly provided by Treaty powers. The EC's directive on the conservation of wild birds is an example of this latter approach. In practice, therefore, Community environment policy has often been driven by the collective desire to remove trade distorsions—measures as much to ensure consistency of practice between the member states as to secure an improvement in environmental standards.

The Treaty of European Union negotiated at Maastricht specifically includes environmental protection and the conservation of natural resources in the expanded range of Community cooperation.

Nevertheless, the European Court of Justice did not await the Treaty of Union to create jurisprudence in this field. Take the Danish bottle case, for example, published in the ECJ ruling of, September 20, 1988. The Commission argued that the Danish system for requiring returnable containers for beer and soft drinks, and for licensing new types of container, represented a barrier to trade and should therefore be outlawed as contrary to the principles of the free market. The Court accepted that the Danish action did indeed constitue a constraint on trade. However, in what has been widely seen as a landmark judgment, the Court said that the Danish measure could be justified on grounds of environmental protection.

The Court specified that it was up to a member state to respect the principle of proportionality: the means should not be so drastic as to be disproportionate to the final objective; and that efforts should be made to minimize the adverse effect on freedom of exchange. On the substance of the arguments, however, the Court upheld the Danish position.

The principal legal instrument for environmental protection developed by the Council of Europe is the "Berne Convention" on the conservation of wildlife and natural habitat, which entered into force in 1982 and gives total protection to 119 species of plants, 55 mammals, 294 birds, 34 reptiles, 17 amphibians, 115 freshwater fishes, 81 invertebrates and their habitats.

Community enforcement procedures

In implementing environmental policy, the EC's main legislative weapon is the directive. Although legally binding, the directive leaves the method of application to member states. Each state must pass appropriate national legislation, apply it and then enforce it in the field. In some cases the original objectives of the directive become distorted or diminished. The Commission has been giving this matter attention with respect to environmental policy, identifying deviations and omissions in national law and starting infringement proceedings where necessary to bring offenders into line. Legal actions often arise from failure to transpose EC directives into national legislation, or refusal to provide details to the Commission, as well as from failure to enforce agreed standards.

When the Commission is not satisfied with a member state's compliance it may take the case to the European Court. Thus, in 1989, the Commission challenged the United Kingdom over the quality of drinking water. The case created intense public interest because of the UK government's plans to privatize the water industry. The UK which, as it turned out, was only following in the footsteps of Belgium and France, has since been joined by Germany and Luxembourg, and will almost certainly be joined by other countries in due course. Drinking water quality is basic to public health and even to human survival.

Public's watching role

Public pressure plays an important role in improving compliance records. The Commission receives an increasing number of complaints about the situation in member countries from non-government organizations, local authorities, MEP's, local pressure groups and private individuals. In 1984 there were about ten complaints of inadequate implementation of EC directives; by the end of the decade the annual figure was close to 450. The new Environmental Agency established by the Treaty of European Union will provide data to help the Commission in its policing role. In the absence of a full-time EC inspectorate, however, the information gathered by the public is vital to achievement of the Community's environmental goals.

A survey of public opinion on twelve European issues placed the environment second only to unemployment. · Speaking in Sofia on October 16, 1989, Carlo Ripa di Meana, the member of the European Commission responsible for the environment, affirmed that the public's voice had been heard:

> Pressure from the population and from special-interest groups has been of great importance for the acceleration of environmental policy within the Community. The latest elections for the European Parliament, in June of this year (1989), which resulted in a more than 100% increase of Green Members, have clearly shown how much the European population is concerned about the condition of the environment. It is quite easy to see why. The quality of the environment is closely linked to the quality of life in general. If people become ill because of the deterioration of the environment, if people read in the newspapers that life expectancy is lower in environmentally deteriorated areas, it is quite understandable that the population becomes concerned. If we follow this line of thinking one may even say that the deterioration of the environment can be a source of political instability.

An indication that information and education programs have sensitized public opinion to the importance of joint action on environmental issues is provided by a poll conducted in 1989 by the European Commission. The poll produced the following responses:

**Poll as to whether Member States should act together or separately
to protect the environment (%)**

	Together	Separately	Don't know
Belgium	61.0	8.6	30.5
Denmark	70.4	12.0	17.6
Germany (FRG)	83.2	5.7	11.1
Greece	69.0	18.4	12.6
Spain	60.5	19.0	20.5
France	80.6	15.9	3.5
Ireland	64.4	29.1	6.5
Italy	83.3	7.7	9.0
Luxembourg	83.7	11.6	4.7
Netherlands	91.0	7.2	1.8
Portugal	62.3	10.2	27.5
United Kingdom	76.0	16.5	7.5
Average	77.1	12.2	10.6

Environmental questions have now become a standard issue in national, regional and local elections throughout Europe.

A Conservation Strategy for greater Europe

The most recent conference of ministers responsible for the environment, the sixth of its kind, took place in Brussels under Council of Europe auspices in October, 1990. Ministers approved a European conservation strategy designed to meet the following objectives:

  i. To promote a culture which respects nature for what it is and not only for what monetary value can be placed on it; such a culture would make room for nature in our way of life and would lead to co-existence with nature rather than a desire to subjugate it to our immediate needs;
 ii. To meet the legitimate needs and aspirations of all Europeans by seeking to base economic, social and cultural development on a rational and sustainable use of natural resources and the maintenance of a healthy environment;
iii. To secure the co-operation of all Europeans in the further development and implementation of the Strategy by making them aware of environmental and conservation issues and involving them;
 iv. To suggest how sustainable development and conservation can be integrated and achieved.

Ministers further declared that in order to meet these objectives, the European Conservation Strategy should be based on the following principles;

  i. Safeguarding of species, ecosystems and essential natural processes as an obligation on all people;

ii. Acceptance by all European states of the principle of sustainable development, helping to meet the needs of the present without compromising the abilities of future generations to meet theirs;

iii. A commitment by all European states to carry out their economic and social development within a healthy environment, free from the degrading effects of pollution, human health hazards produced by wastes and chemicals, and the loss of values and opportunities associated with a broad and stable natural resource base;

iv. Share responsibility in all sections of society, in all institutions and at every level of authority for the conservation of the environment.

In setting out their strategy, the Ministers first addressed general elements, in particular the role of governments, and stressed the need for a holistic or non-sectoral approach:

> The ability to anticipate and prevent environmental damage requires that the ecological dimensions of policy be considered at the same time as the economic, trade, energy, agricultural and other dimensions. They should be considered on the same agenda and in the same national and international institutions.

This last sentence implies that discrete and distinct conservation programs should be considered as transitional, pending full integration of the conservation ethos into every phase of social and economic life.

Ministers called for flexible and anticipatory conservation policies, spatial planning and the implementation of effective regulatory mechanisms. There should be public awareness and participation in defining not only material requirements but also the cultural, aesthetic and spiritual needs in the context of a healthy and attractive natural environment.

The conference then turned to sectoral aspects, setting out the specific needs for air (quality, pollution control, ozone layer destruction), inland waters, lakes and rivers, seas, soil, wildlife, landscape, biotechnology (protecting ecosystems from manufactured species; broadening the genetic base of seeds threatened by excessive use of clonal material), agriculture, forestry, recreation and tourism, urban and industrial areas, rural areas, waste and dangerous substances, energy and transport. [5]

Waste management

One issue which everyone understands, and which grows clearly worse as living standards rise, is the problem of waste management. We live in a throw-away society. The New York borough of Staten Island is looking to secede from the city largely because, as it alleges, it has been turned into the world's largest refuse dump over which the gulls never cease to wheel and cry. The problem of how to deal with waste — above all dangerous or toxic wastes — poses a growing challenge for industrialized and developing worlds alike. Responding to it has become a major priority for Community environment policy. In the mid-1970s, against a background of worsening oil and energy crises, policy-makers sought ways to preserve and recycle precious raw material supplies. Waste as a valuable secondary resource remains today an important feature of the Community's approach but the threat it poses in terms of uncontrolled pollution is now an equally pressing concern. Some two thousand million tonnes of waste are generated in the Community each year. It may come as a surprise that "only" 150 million tonnes arise from industrial sources, with 20 to 30 million tonnes classified as hazardous. Thus while the most dangerous waste is of industrial origin, by far the largest quantity is generated by households. Economic growth will add to these quantities.

The Community's response is inspired in part by the unacceptable cost of environmental damage caused by waste. With roughly 60% of household waste dumped, 33% incinerated, and 7% composted there is already a clear shortage of disposal facilities and landfill sites in densely populated areas, notwithstanding the size of the waste treatment sector (at least 2 million employees and sales somewhere in the range of 100 to 200 billion ECU in 1990). As frontier restrictions are relaxed, Community citizens are alarmed by the specter of large quantities of hazardous waste moving freely across Europe in search of the cheapest and least regulated outlets.

The Community's waste management policy has developed three key strands: waste prevention, waste recycling and safe disposal, with growing emphasis on the potential contribution of clean technologies and clean products. Preventing waste is clearly the number-one priority and the support provided to demonstration projects is of key significance. The Commission believes more resources should be made available, while it has also put forward proposals for a green-labelling scheme to inform consumers accurately about the ecological character of the products they are buying and the packaging they are wrapped in. As for reuse, the Community has adopted rules for the recycling of waste oils, waste paper, and drink containers. Proposals for used batteries and plastic waste are under study, while the ban on metal packaging in some countries has highlighted the need for a common Community approach in this field. With disposal still the only option for vast quantities of waste, harmonization of dumping standards is also an urgent Community priority. Dumping should be a last resort and every alternative treatment should be examined and encouraged, but dumping will remain the final destination for residues from other processes.

The ENVIREG fund is drawn upon to improve incineration and storage facilities for toxic and other dangerous industrial wastes in coastal areas. To promote recycling wherever possible, such support is limited to non-recyclable waste.

The pattern of regulation in the Member States is uneven, with growing differences of site selection, site development, site operation, pre-treatment and supervision. The Commission has presented proposals for approximating dumping standards and has drawn up a list of wastes which should either not be dumped at all or should be covered by special conditions.

Economic and social disparities will inspire a shift in investment behaviour, thereby putting pressure on some regions and leaving others underequipped. Measures should be taken to encourage the disposal of waste as close as possible to the place where it is generated. The EC and its member countries have adhered to the 1989 Basle convention on the international shipment of hazardous waste .[6]

Planetary pathology

This chapter has brought together two complementary approaches to environmental issues. The Council of Europe concentrates on landscape and wildlife protection and broader moral and aesthetic issues; the European Community highlights economic factors and pollution control. However, if proof were ever needed that the whole planet is in bad health; and that a holistic approach is required, it is dramatically provided by a recent report from the World Health Organization (WHO) in Geneva. Published in March, 1992, the report shows that illnesses linked to the environment and way of life are responsible for 75% of the forty-nine million deaths registered world-wide each year. Dr Hiroschi Nakajima, WHO Director-General, and Simone Veil of France, chairperson of the Commission on health and the environment which authored the report, warned that an intolerable crisis is at hand. Against the sobering background of critical planetary pathology, the problem of the traditional clash between the interests of economic development and those of environmental conservation appears less pressing than the need for concerted global action. Millions of premature deaths are caused by biological and chemical agents in water, air and soil. Hundreds of millions of people are exposed to avoidable risk at home, in the work place and in society.

The WHO report does not separate artificially such diverse afflictions as disease, smoking, pollution, environmental poisoning and traffic accidents: all affect health, all are considered in the broad sense to be environmental. All, too, are aggravated by population explosion (8 trillion in 2020). Not merely individuals, not countries, nor even Europe alone but the world as a whole must act to develop a global management strategy for the environment shared by all living things.

In June 1992 the UN Earth Summit was held in Rio de Janeiro on the theme of sustainable development. The developing nations accused the advanced economies of producing most of the pollution while expecting the developing nations to sacrifice development potential to environmental protection. The EC Commissioner responsible for the environment, Carlo Ripa di Meana at first refused to attend, esteeming that the conference had received inadequate preparation and lacked firm commitment from the leading economic powers. Ultimately, the European Community was represented by Jacques Delors himself. This was important not only because Europe is home to developed nations which must learn to live more frugally, to reduce pollution and to contribute more to Third World development but also because that same Europe leads the world in international environmental cooperation.[7]

Has anybody noticed that the Third World War has begun?

Notes

1   Tendron, Georges, *Man and his environment*, in Naturopa, Nr 41, 1982, periodical of the Council of Europe Information Centre for Nature Conservation. Mr Tendron, of the Paris Muséum National d'Histoire Naturelle, represented France for many years in the European Committee for the Conservation of Nature and Natural Resources.

2   Community measures to limit noise were first thought of in the context of removing technical barriers to trade. The problem of free circulation, for example, was a major issue in countries like France and Italy, where companies traditionally manufactured noisy products, and in Member States like Denmark and the Netherlands where national noise standards tend to be very strict.
     Measures adopted have been concerned with the setting of maximum noise emissions from products, notably motor vehicles, motor cycles, aircraft, tractors, plant and equipment, lawnmowers and household appliances. The rules of the directives require companies to provide details of noise levels—generally conforming with norms already established by international standards bodies—and to make it easy for official inspections to be carried out. In 1986, in the framework of the Community's social action programme, the Council adopted a directive on the protection of workers form noise.

3   The text of the European Water Charter is available from the NATUROPA Centre, Council of Europe, BP 431 R 6, F-67006 Strasbourg Cedex.

4   Here, for example, are the conditions and recommendations concerning the Wurzacher Ried:

    Conditions:
    1.   That no more peat is removed from the nature reserve as such by the town of Bad Wurzach, after 1995 when the present permit expires;
    2.   That there is no intensive farming inside the nature reserve;

    Recommendations:
    1.   The policy of land purchase should be continued, and even stepped up, partly so that intensively worked fields may be given over to extensive farming, to encourage the nesting of rare bird species and combat eutrophication of the waters;
    2.   The use of chemical fertilisers in the reserve and its periphery should be discontinued;
    3.   Motoring on the road from Bad Wurzach to Unterschwärzach should be banned; only bicycles should be permitted;
    4.   A nature trail should be created in the Dietmannser Ried;
    5.   A programme of systematic zoological and botanical research should be drawn up;
    6.   The edges of the fen area should be trimmed by scything, and the water level should be regulated by discontinuing drainage and bringing water into the former streams;
    7.   Particular attention should be given to the schedule of field sports.

5   The full text of the European Conservation Strategy is available from the Naturopa Centre. In recent years the Center's review, NATUROPA, has produced detailed studies of such diverse topics as the European coastline, protection and management of freshwater fish, European soil quality (including a European Soil Charter), farming and wildlife, information and education (including the impact of in-schools programs).

For a comprehensive bibliography on EC policy and action, see *Environmental Policy in the European Community*, Office for Official Publications in the EC, Luxembourg, 1990, pp. 57-60.

6   As we saw in Part III, Ch. 1, in 1984 the OECD took steps to control the movement of hazardous waste across frontiers and, in a rare move, went further by making its resolution binding on member states.

7   The UN Conference on Environment and Development developed the Rio Declaration and Agenda 21, an action plan for the twenty-first century, covering The Prospering World (sustainable growth); the Just World (poverty, consumption patterns, demographic dynamics, health); the Habitable World; the Fertile World; the Shared World (global resources); the Clean World; the People's World (education, training and public awareness). A major convention on climate change (global warning) was watered down on US insistence. The US signed the convention but under pressure from industrialists (in an election year) President Bush declined to append his signature to the "biodiversity" convention, designed to reinforce protection for plants and animals threatened with extinction. However, the Conference made it clear that the issue is not environment or development but environment *and* development. Only viable economies can afford pollution control and resource management. However, on both sides of the development divide it must now be clear that preserving the environment is a matter of both national self-interest and international solidarity.

Monetary Union in the European Community

Tanya M. Atwood

Since the creation of the European Economic Community (EEC) in 1957, the idea of economic and monetary union has always been a prominent issue. Nevertheless, adoption of a single currency has never been an all-or-nothing question. A single currency does not guarantee the success of the EEC, nor does its absence necessarily mean failure. However, at the Maastricht conference in December, 1991, the European Community agreed to create such a currency by the year 1999. This landmark decision will have a tremendous impact on the economic policies of the European Community.

Steps taken in the past, such as the creation of the European Monetary System (EMS) and the European Currency Unit (ECU), more or less naturally led the EC in the direction of economic and monetary union. Now that the decision to have a single currency has finally been made, the EC members must prepare themselves for the steps ahead.

In establishing the EEC, the Six founding members were declaring their commitment to the free movement of goods, services, capital and persons throughout the Community.

Although large economic and political differences still existed among the member states, the Werner Report of 1970 confirmed that the Community was in favor of economic and monetary union (EMU). With the creation of the European Monetary Cooperation Fund (EMCF) in 1973, interbank operations became more frequent. At the same time, the ECU became the major reserve currency of the Community. EC countries' gold and US dollars were deposited in the EMCF and ECUs were drawn out in return. The central banks of participating nations then used the ECUs to intervene in currency markets. As central bank interventions became more numerous, the EMCF was replaced in 1979 by the European Monetary System to maintain monetary stability within the EC.

European Monetary System

The EMS is a joint float system with the ECU as its central currency. The ECU consists of fixed amounts of European currencies, and the quantity of each country's currency in the ECU reflects that country's relative economic strength in the EC. (The *Deutsche Mark* currently has the largest weight). In order for the EMS to work, a mutually agreed central exchange rate is determined for each member country's currency, and each rate is denominated in currency units per ECU. Participating countries are required to keep their currency within a 2.25% margin of central cross exchange rates (Italy has a 6% margin). The cross exchange rates are found by creating a grid of central rates. For example the following rates were in effect on March 1, 1992:

42.02	Belgian francs
7.91	Danish kroners
2.04	Deutsche Marks
2.30	Dutch guilders
6.95	French francs
0.76	Irish pounds
1.536.00	Italian lira
0.71	Pound sterling
128.00	Spanish peseta
234.00	Greek drachma
176.00	Portuguese escudo[1]

The central cross exchange rate for the DM and the FF would be determined in the following manner:

2.04 DM / 1 ECU * 1 ECU / 6.95 FF = 0.294 DM / FF or 3.407 FF / 1 DM

These rates are allowed to fluctuate within the 2.25% margin. If the upper or lower limit is reached, then the central banks of the respective countries intervene. If this intervention is unsuccessful, a realignment of rates occurs. By early 1988, EMS currencies had been realigned eleven times despite central bank intervention. Obviously the EMS is not without its faults, but it has created more stability within the Community's economic environment.

The European Currency Unit

Since the decision was made at Maastricht to have a single European currency, much speculation has surfaced surrounding the future of the ECU. Since its first important function in the EMS beginning in 1979, the role of the ECU has grown tremendously. The ECU was originally designed with three main functions in mind: a unit of account; a means of settlement between monetary authorities in the Community; and a reserve asset for the participants in the EMS. Because of the success of the ECU and its official EC backing, the ECU has already to some extent become a common currency of Europe.

In addition to playing the central role in the EMS, the ECU is becoming a bigger player in the International Monetary System (IMS). There has been an increase in the use of the ECU in international transactions, as well as financial portfolio shifts in favor of ECU-denominated assets as a result of success in commercial markets. Bank treasuries now offer a full range of financial instruments denominated in ECUs, and much bank lending of ECUs takes place. The wholesale banking market offers spot exchanges against all European and most other currencies, forward exchange swaps up to 1 year, lending and deposits from 2 days to 5 years and forward rate agreements. The retail banking market offers transfers, drafts, letters of credit and traveler's checks, all denominated in ECU. The ECU is also popular in the bond market and other financial markets. For example, the New York Stock Exchange and the International Money Market in Chicago offer ECU/$ futures. Swaps and options are also available in ECU denominations.

Flexibility, innovation

There are several reasons for the success of the ECU in numerous commercial markets. As a Eurocurrency, the ECU is free from national controls because it does not have a single national base. As a result, the ECU market may be more flexible and innovative in developing new financial instruments. For capital market participants, the ECU is likely to provide a better risk/return tradeoff than individual European currencies. This is because the ECU benefits from the fact that it is a composite currency. In other words, the exchange rate and interest yield of the ECU will be less volatile than the most volatile European currency.

Part of the success of the ECU is due to the official support it receives from EC institutions. The Community has adopted the ECU as the unit of account for budgetary purposes and even issued ECU-denominated securities. The European Investment Bank has on many occasions borrowed in the bond market in ECUs; and the European Commission has made payments in ECUs. In addition, payments for EC projects are usually quoted in ECU terms. [2]

With all of the ECU's success, it seems that the ECU would be a shoo-in for the role of the single European currency. After all, it is highly improbable that one of the existing national currencies would become the single currency of Europe, and the creation of a new thirteenth currency requires much time and management. Yet it is no easy decision: even though the ECU has displayed many advantages, it has its disadvantages as well.

Although the ECU benefits from having no national base, this also presents handicaps. The ECU does not have the support of a large national market to develop further its international commercial use. In addition, the ECU is more expensive to use than a national currency. Both importers and exporters would have to bear the costs of converting their respective currencies. This disadvantage is rectifiable only if national authorities start to incorporate the ECU into their own national base.

Another obstacle concerns payment systems. The current ECU clearing system fits the international financial uses of the ECU. However, regional ECU clearing systems need to be developed by linking payments with the various national payment clearing systems. In addition, retail clearing systems (credit cards and checks) need to be adapted so that residents of all EC countries are able to make ECU payments quickly and at a low cost in their own country, throughout Europe and beyond.[3]

Another obstacle for the ECU is the fact that it is still largely ignored by many business firms, even in Europe. Although the ECU is well known in the world's financial markets, some banks are still reluctant to promote its commercial use. To correct this ignorance widespread communication of the advantages of the ECU is needed, especially to the smaller enterprises which could benefit greatly from its use. The future of the ECU is unknown, but until the final decision is made, it will continue to play an important role and be further developed during Europe's transition to economic and monetary union.

Concerns regarding monetary union

The decision to create a single currency was not easily arrived at during the two day summit at Maastricht. Details remain to be worked out, but political and emotional concerns, rather than financial and economic considerations, are at issue.

The loss of sovereignty is perhaps the single greatest fear confronting European nations, with France and the United Kingdom feeling they have the most to lose. With Germany physically at the center of the Community and German speakers outnumbering the French almost 2 to 1, France is worried that Europe could be dominated by German ideas. This is contrary to what the French had intended when they became the driving force behind creation of the EC. They pictured more of a bureaucracy dominated by French ideas, and now they are seeing a free-market economy led by liberal doctrines. France is confronting inner turmoil, and the French may have to accept a role in the EC that is no longer dominant.

Economically speaking, the centralized state of France is not the European free-market model, thus giving France a serious disadvantage when it comes to EMU. French brokerage firms have been finding themselves with insuperable financial problems, and many are being acquired by foreign investors and banks. In addition, many French companies are undercapitalized. These problems will hurt France when European economic integration is completed. The old ways are no longer the best ways where French economic centralization is concerned.

In addition to the foregoing tangible problems, many French people are uncomfortable and anxious. They want to remain loyal to France but realize that loyalty to Europe is necessary in the future. France's weight in Europe is not what it used to be, and the thought of Germany taking over the lead role is not a pleasant one. Of course, there is also a strong current of thought which holds that loyalty to France and Europe are not in conflict; and that it is preferable for the new Germany to be anchored in Europe. Laurent Fabius, Secretary General of the Socialist Party and a former prime minister, has summarized the arguments in favor of the Maastricht treaty as "peace, economic weight and social progress".

The French may nevertheless have an easier time adapting to the new Europe than the British, as the Maastricht meeting itself showed. The summit might have ended unsuccessfully due to Britain's refusal to become part of any social policies, especially one that gives more power to the labor unions. In order to appease Britain's extreme concern about loss of sovereignty, the social provisions were extracted from the Treaty of the Union and included in a separate treaty signed by the other eleven countries.

Britain also refused to commit itself to a single currency and Central Bank of Europe, and Prime Minister John Major was granted his wish of being allowed to "opt out" of an irrevocable commitment so that the House of Commons could take a decision on this specific issue at a later date. The other EC countries are hoping that Britain will change its mind and follow the rest of the Community into the Monetary Union. If Britain does decide to "opt out", the repercussions could be detrimental. London's standing as an international financial center could be harmed, thus reducing the Bank of England's influence.

Britain's choice to "opt out" at present conflicts with its desire to have a prominent share of the action in the new European economy. Along with Frankfurt, Lyon, Milan and Barcelona, London is vying to host the European Central Bank (ECB).[4] Although the ECB will most likely adopt the Bundesbank's anti-inflation philosophy, the Bundesbank is not guaranteed the lead role. As a result, Britain should be looking into a credible anti-inflation policy in order to strengthen her chance of becoming the host for the ECB. Britain also wants to play a vital role in European market operations, similar to the Federal Reserve Bank of New York. With this goal in mind, it seems foolish for the British to want to opt out of monetary union. The British government seeks a strong position in the new Europe, and, at the same time, the option to remain independent. This is not a viable position in the long term. The rest of Europe will be moving towards economic and monetary union, a decision that cannot be reversed. By "opting out" of such a commitment, Britain will only face a less significant role in Europe as well as the likelihood of a weaker economy. It remains to be seen whether John Major's hesitations reflected profoundly held views or a maneuver to avoid a party split before a national election. Initial signs since the Conservative's fourth consecutive success at the hustings, in April 1992, are of closer ties and even British leadership in Europe. John Major has made it clear that he wants Britain to be "at the heart of Europe"; and that by endorsing subsidiarity the TEU actually halts the slide towards a federal Europe.

Britain and France are not the only countries apprehensive about Germany's influence in the EC, but the Germans feel these fears to be unfounded. German Chancellor Helmut Kohl insists that German and European unity go hand in hand. He firmly believes that despite political and economic strains, Germany and France will continue to drive European affairs together.[5]

The Germans also have their own concerns. If the plan for monetary union is not carefully worked out, Germany may lose its strong *Deutsche Mark* for a weaker currency. With the recent reunification of Germany, another concern has appeared, not just for Germany, but for the EC as a whole. Many worry that the poor state of the former East German economy will draw Germany's attention and resources away from the EC, thereby stalling economic integration. In 1992 Germany showed a clear preference for fighting inflation by keeping interest rates high over kick-starting the depressed European (and North American) economy. In addition, there is a concern that the former East Germans will not be enthusiastic EC participants, having been away from "Europe" for so long.[6]

These anxieties are understandable, but probably excessive. Eastern Germany will most likely show significant increases in productivity in the near future. Meanwhile, French industry has already felt the benefit of reconstruction needs in eastern Germany. Lack of "European consciousness" among former East Germans is also nothing to worry about. They are now integrated into the strongest driving forces of the EC — the Federal Republic itself.

With the unification of Germany, incredible opportunities are now available to the EC. Germany will be stronger than ever economically and emotionally. If anything, the other EC countries should welcome the unification of Germany with open arms. The new "European Germany" has no intention of upsetting the framework of the EC for it would hurt the Federal Republic as much as any other EC country.

There still remains some pessimism about the future success of economic and monetary union. In addition to fearing a single European currency weaker than the *Deutsche Mark*, some Germans feel that EMU will not succeed without political union first. This fear is heightened by differences in political programs in EC countries. EMU carries with it significant political ramifications, specifically that political unity is a must if EMU is to succeed.

As a halfway-house to currency union, EMS has not been entirely successful. This demonstrates the need for both EMU and political union. For instance, between 1979 and 1988, the French franc was devalued relative to the *Deutsche Mark* by more than 50%. The cross exchange rates between the FF and the DM were in constant turmoil, yet nothing was done due to political priorities taking precedence over monetary stability. Germany's economic policy makers were very concerned with inflation; therefore, they commanded price stability above all else. French economic policy makers, on the other hand, were faced with high domestic unemployment, and thus pursued a more expansive economic policy. It must be recognized, however, that the French have tamed inflation.

Neither France nor Germany was willing to permit exchange rate intervention that would affect or override political priorities. As a result, by 1983, the lack of stability was obvious. An investor could have bought DM 1 million for about FF 2.83 one day and sold the same DM 1 million for about FF 3.07 the very next day. This was a return of 8% in one day, which translates to an annualized return of 2.920%.[7] Such discrepancies cause many people to feel wary about monetary union without strong commitment to political unity.

One of the biggest advocates of European Political Union is Bundesbank president Helmut Schlesinger. Mr Schlesinger's recent criticism of the EMU should not be construed as an attack on current EMU plans but rather as concern over the political implications that accompany monetary union. With the anxiety and criticism surrounding the recent decision to create economic and monetary union, the benefits of a single currency are often overshadowed.

Benefits of Economic and Monetary Union (EMU)

There are many important benefits to economic and monetary union in Europe that helped the EC members decide to create a single currency. The overall impact on the economy of the Community will include efficiency and growth, stability and equity. A single market of 340 million people needs a single currency to run efficiently and at its maximum potential. In addition to a more efficient allocation of resources, a single currency will reduce information and transaction costs. The gap between private and public rates of return will also be narrowed. More important, perhaps, is the fact that a composite currency will have a better chance of withstanding destabilizing economic shocks due to its aggregate macroeconomic diversity.

One of the primary driving forces behind EMU is the price stability afforded by such a system. With a single currency, resource allocations become more efficient and price stability is easier to maintain. This will aid in the Community's efforts to keep inflation at low levels. Another advantage is equity. With economic and monetary union, no one region will enjoy a relative advantage. EMU will be a positive sum game, meaning that the single currency will be more productive for the community than the individual currencies together. In other words, synergy will be the end result.

Public finance will also benefit from economic and monetary union. National budgeting policies will be more conducive to macroeconomic stability. In addition, valuable gains will be made through the reduction in interest rates as inflation and exchange rate premiums are eliminated. EMU will also favor economic growth in the Community, thus increasing employment.

As banks and companies conduct more of their international business in their own currency, cost savings will result. Monetary authorities will also be able to economize in external reserves with a single European currency.[8] Overall, Europe will secure its place in the international market, just as the United States and Japan have done with the dollar and yen, respectively.

Monetary union will provide further benefits of a non-financial type. Economic and monetary union will be symbolic in Europe as it will represent the culmination of the EC's effort to create a "United Europe". Monetary union represents a point of no return, and there will most likely be a change in the behavior of the EC's inhabitants (specifically, pride in Europe) that will further enhance the economic well-being of the Community.

Qualifying to join

Now that the EC has decided to create a single currency, progress can be made in the next two stages presented by the Delors Report and approved at Maastricht. Stage I was set for July 1, 1990, and called for the preparation of changes to the Treaty of Rome necessary for carrying out Stages II and III. During Stage I, the role of the ECU was further promoted while reinforcing monetary policy coordination.

Stage II is set to begin on January 1, 1994. This stage calls for intensive preparation by each member government. Excessive budget deficits are to be avoided, and each government shall start the process leading to the independence of its central bank. EC governments must abolish remaining restrictions on movement of capital and adopt programs for price stability and sound public finances. The second stage will also see tighter control of exchange rate fluctuations. A European System of Central Banks (ESCB) will be established which will feed into a European Monetary Institute (EMI). The EMI will be directed in part by Governors of the existing 12 central banks and will in effect be the embryo of the European Central Bank.

By December 1996, the EC Commission and EMI will report to the Council of Ministers on the status of member states' policies and possible membership in EMU. They will also report on price stability, government finances, fluctuations in the EMS, and long-term interest rates. If enough member states (a minimum of seven) satisfy the criteria for EMU set forth at Maastricht, Stage III, the final stage will begin, whereby exchange rates become fixed and the ECB replaces the EMI. By December 1998, if EMU criteria were not met in 1996, member states must now move to the final stage, as a single currency will be in place by January 1, 1999.

Strict guidelines were set at Maastricht regarding which countries will be eligible to participate in the economic and monetary union of the Community. To enter prior to 1999, a country must have inflation and long-term interest rates within 1.5% and 2%, respectively, of the three best performing EC member countries. The country must also have an exchange rate that has been stable within the exchange rate grid of the EMS for two years before entry. Another major requirement is that the country have no excessive budget deficits. An excessive budget deficit is defined as an actual or planned budget deficit below 3% of gross domestic product (GDP) and a ratio of public debt to GDP not exceeding 60%.

Currently only three countries would be eligible for EMU — France, Denmark and Luxembourg. (It is an amusing irony that if Stage III were upon us, neither an enthusiastic Germany nor a foot-dragging United Kingdom would actually face a decision at this time!) The Maastricht guidelines were set to ensure that the single currency of Europe will be a solid one. With the *Deutsche Mark* being the strongest European currency, it was appropriate that Germany's Helmut Kohl officially presented the EMU eligibility rules at the summit. Another important decision reached at Maastricht concerning monetary union was that no country can halt the move to EMU. This means that the EC countries who are experiencing poor economic conditions are under a great deal of pressure to catch up with other EC countries. Unfortunately, many bankers, economists and businessmen believe that very few countries will likely pass the EMU test before 1999. After this date, the test is no longer relevant and introduction of the currency becomes mandatory (for all member states except the United Kingdom which maintains the right to "opt out"). If this were the case, then the currency would really be the *Deutsche Mark* with a different name.

With everyone criticizing and worrying about the strict EMU guidelines, the strong efforts being made by some countries are going unnoticed. For example, French Finance Minister (now Prime Minister) Pierre Bérégovoy announced at Maastricht that the Bank of France would henceforth act independently of the Government. And France is not the only EC member taking EMU very seriously. Italy is finally confronting the fact that it must tame its uncontrollable inflation, high labor costs and overinflating budget deficit.

Britain's response to monetary union was expected of Prime Minister John Major. He is forced to confront a Conservative Party divided on the issue back home in England. However, it is important to stress that Major did not attempt to veto the whole concept any more than he sought to block the Social Charter. Chancellor Helmut Kohl expects that Britain could decide to join EMU as early as 1996.

By September of 1992, the EMS found itself engulfed in crisis surrounded by political turmoil. Skepticism about a united Europe, reinforced by Denmark's rejection of the Maastricht Treaty in June, was further heightened by the Bundesbank's lowering of a key interest rate and France's narrow approval of the Maastricht Treaty on monetary and political union. Britain and Spain were forced to back out of the exchange mechanism with little hope of a speedy return. Italy devalued 7% but remained in the system.

A revised vision of monetary union is in the works due to the currency crisis in Europe. A two tiered economy is part of the new plan, with the first tier including the economically stronger countries — Germany, Belgium, the Netherlands, Luxembourg and France. This economic union might include a system of fixed exchange rates or a common currency based on the *Deutsche Mark*. The economically weaker countries — Britain, Ireland, Italy, Spain and others, would form the second tier and have looser economic links to the core. The two tiered economy of Europe would not be as competitive as a single economy due to varying growth rates, currency fluctuations and investment patterns.

The European Community has taken a huge step in agreeing to move towards economic and monetary union. New responsibilities have been assumed by the Community; and once EMU is achieved, the EC will become a leader in international finance. However, the road to EMU will not be an easy one. The largest obstacle will be attaining a higher degree of political unity. Until this is done, further criticism of one another's economic decisions will be heard. EC countries will have to work hard to get their economies in line with the EMU guidelines.

Most countries feel they have something to lose: Germany its strong currency, Britain its sovereignty or France its leadership in the EC. However, by agreeing to economic and monetary union, these countries have taken a major step towards creating an instrument worthy of, indeed necessary to, the largest international market in the world — a market that will be extremely profitable for all involved.

Notes

1 The central rates as of September 28, 1992 were the following: 40.198 Belgian francs, 7.548 kroners, 1.955 marks, 2.199 guilders, 6.616 French francs, .745 Irish pounds, 1637.209 lira, .770 Pound sterling, 137.823 peseta, 249.038 drachma, and 174.468 escudo. On April 6, 1992, the EC allowed entry of the escudo into the EMS exchange rate mechanism. The opening central rate was set at 178.735 escudo per ECU and the margin at 6%. The Greek drachma does not yet participate in the exchange rate mechanism. On July 29, 1992, the dollar value of the ECU was $1.385. A six-month deposit in ECUs paid $10^{7/8}$ - 11%, against $3^{1/2}$ - $3^{5/8}$ for dollars and $9^{3/4}$ - $9^{7/8}$ for DMs.

2 In 1992 *The European* became the first newspaper to quote value equivalents in ECUs rather than dollars.

3 Louis, André, "The ECU and its Role in the Process towards Monetary Union", in *European Economy*, Nr 48, Commission of the European Community, September 1991, p. 140.

4 The main functions of the ECB would include the formulation and implementation of a single monetary policy and responsibility for issuing ECUs. The ECB would also participate in international monetary functions and in the coordination of banking policies. In addition, the ECB would guarantee the proper functioning of capital markets and the payments system.

5 House, Karen and Philip Revzin, "Germany's Kohl Shapes Its New Policies", *The Wall Street Journal*, February 7, 1992, p. A10.

6 Hughes, Rachel, "A European Germany", *Europe*, Nr 304, p. 19.

7 Shapiro, Alan C., *Multinational Financial Management*, Allyn and Bacon, Boston, p. 82.

8 Commission of the European Communities, *Economic and Monetary Union*, Luxembourg, 1990, p. 13.

4

Cultural Diversity and European Unity

A. Immigrants and national minorities

Signing the Charter of Paris at the Conference on Security and Cooperation in Europe marking the demise of communism and the end of the division of Europe in November, 1990, western leaders could afford, it seemed, to rest on their laurels. Participants from East and West had agreed on common values and objectives, in essence those of the West, including respect for the ethnic, cultural, linguistic and religious identity of national minorities everywhere. Yet, having anathematized the division of Europe for some fifty years, they finally faced the prospect (even before the atrocious "ethnic cleansing" in Yugoslavia) of a wave of immigrants fleeing west from the former Soviet bloc to greener pastures. Already coping with significant "unassimilated" minorities from East and South and their national born offspring, western governments did not restore the Wall or the Curtain, but they did start blocking loopholes in immigration legislation.

The floodgates did not open yet economic recession in Western Europe proved double-edged in its effects. While on the one hand the high rate of joblessness may have proved a deterrent to immigration, it also caused a wave of xenophobia against those who did come and those already established in the West. The media have played up racism and extremist rhetoric in the Federal Republic but the phenomenon is more widespread. Western Governments have become more hard-nosed about their "values", enunciating through legislation or the courts increasingly restrictive interpretations of "refugee status".

The problem became more acute following relaxation of border formalities with implementation of the Single European Act in January 1993. As far as frontier controls are concerned the borders of France or Belgium have moved from the Rhine to the Oder, from Menton to Trieste. EUROPOL was envisioned in the Maastricht Treaty to counter the threat of increased criminal movement but has proved difficult to implement.

Europe is faced with mass migration from a potential 700 million people in Eastern Europe, the former Soviet Union and western Asia.[1] There are several contributing and interrelated factors: the opening up of borders; the collapse of state structures, such as those in the USSR and Yugoslavia; a nationalist resurgence; world-wide recession; and the change to free-market economies in the former communist world.

The latter, while holding out the promise of better times, causes increased unemployment and a collapse in *per capita* income in the short term. In April 1991 the Council of Europe parliamentarians held a major debate on the issue. Since then the Yugoslav conflagration has made things worse. Given the increased facility of movement within the European Community it seems probable that the poorer member countries, with their low proportion of non-EC residents (Greece and Portugal, 0.5%, up to Italy, 2.5%), will become springboards for migration wherever over one in twenty members of the population are already of non-community origin. Without massive western assistance to persuade potential refugees to stay home, the pressure to move west from Eastern Europe and North Africa could prove irresistible.

A rash of racial incidents struck eastern Germany in 1991 and 1992, where unemployment was high. In the former GDR clubs, trade unions and the family had lost much of their building power. After almost sixty years of dictatorship a collapsed socialist system had created a vacuum. Foreign workers and immigrants taking advantage of Germany's lenient laws became scapegoats of eastern German discontent: united political Germany remained economically divided. In 1991 1,219 aggressions by militants of the extreme right were tallied in reunited Germany; the figure for 1990 was 270. 92% of these attacks were made on foreign nationals.[2] In 1992 as "skinheads" and "neo-Nazis" torched immigrant hostels and the homes of Turkish—Germans born in the Federal Republic, the government financed the return of gypsies to an uncertain future in Romania and moved to restrict immigration rules.

Asylum and border controls: the shortcomings of Schengen
In 1990, in Schengen, a small town in Luxembourg, five Community countries (France, Germany and Benelux) agreed to reduce border controls between their countries and to remove them altogether at the beginning of 1993. The "Schengen states" took an early option on the Treaty of European Union and regarded themselves as a spearhead group within the EC. Portugal, Spain, Italy and Greece later joined the Agreement. The Schengen states subsequently agreed that the country which first handles an application for asylum remains responsible for that refugee. This means that a refugee may be sent back from one EC state to another. Moreover, an asylum decision by one country is binding on the other parties.

The system is pernicious in that it encourages states to reject asylum applications in order to avoid disputes with another member. There is no provision for supranational supervision or arbitration of disputes. The Netherlands has had second thoughts. It now claims that the Schengen Agreement violates both the Geneva Convention on Refugees and the European Convention on Human Rights. In fact, France is the only country to have ratified the Schengen Agreement.

One may be forgiven for wondering whether the "Schengen" reference to asylum is a euphemism for a consensus on barring the door: keeping people out rather than letting them in. Throughout Europe right-wing parties, such as the National Front in France, without actually coming to power, are having a deterrent effect. This was a factor in "Maastricht's" slender majority in the French referendum. At the same time one must recognize that governments are facing a real problem. While not having the strength to absorb unlimited numbers of refugees (whether "economic" or "political") their economies and social structures are strong enough to exercise considerable attraction to those set adrift by world upheavals.

Until the Community has settled this issue in an equitable manner — equitable to the host countries and equitable to the individuals involved — refugees will continue to be political pawns in relation both to the political "color" of their country of origin and to the politics of the host country. Moreover, the opening of internal Community borders, at least as far as judicial controls are concerned, will remain less than complete. The United Kingdom, in particular, is resisting total removal of border controls for arrivals from EC member countries. While emphasis is laid on "security", immigration is also a major concern. In Heribert Prantl's sardonic phrase (*Süddeutsche Zeitung*, Feb. 3, 1992), refugees are unlikely to conform like apples and tomatoes to some future ideal bureaucratic norm.

Rise of the regions
There is a related and possibly even more pressing issue. Reintegration of Europe's own minorities into one continental mosaic may be the greatest challenge facing our "social engineers" over the next quarter century. No nation, no state, no government, no region, no people can escape this issue. As Vaclav Havel pointed out in his address at Lehigh University, our culture is integral to our sense of self, to our spiritual home. The values we share help us to identify with our group — be it race, gender, language, religion, region or state — but also and by the same token distinguish us from others. It is not unnatural then that, in times of stress, changes occur: in clinging to one element we mark our distance from another. In doing so to excess, we may generate prejudice in ourselves or in others. [3]

As the twentieth century draws to a close the nation state in its governmental configuration is proving an inadequate authority to monitor and process human interaction. It finds itself assailed on two sides. Sovereignty is drawn off to conglomerates of continental proportions, as being the only units large and powerful enough to confront global issues. The process is far advanced in Europe but it is happening elsewhere: in the Organization of American States, the Organization of African Unity, The Association of South-East Asian Nations, The North-American Free Trade Area. Even as it broke apart the Soviet Union felt the compelling need to come together again in the Commonwealth of Independent States ... At the same time, and indeed partly in reaction to this confederation movement, national regions become more assertive and draw power down to themselves. [4] The process is frequently accelerated by the weakness of political borders which, as the fruit of conquest and defeat, took little account when created of regional, cultural or tribal realities and now lose their power of containment. Hungarians, Moldavians, Slovaks, Turks, Croats, Serbs, Armenians, Kurds, Macedonians, in the

East, but also Irish, Welsh, Scottish, Flemish, Finns, Alsatians, Germans, Corsicans, Basques, Catalonians and Bretons in central and western areas of the continent see opportunities in Europe's new political flux. The Celtic bow along Europe's western fringe is becoming a cultural entity in its own right.

Just as there are various categories of immigrants, there are several types of minorities. Even when tensions degenerate into violence, as in Northern Ireland, the Basque Country, Corsica and Cyprus, the gunmen rarely represent mainstream opinion within their own community. A major success story is offered by Belgium, which managed, despite high tension and without significant loss of central government cohesion or national identity, to devolve significant authority to Dutch-speaking Flanders and francophone Wallonia. In France, assisted by a tardy softening of attitudes from the central government (which with the possible exception of Corsica has never officially recognized minority groups), Bretons and Alsatians at opposite ends of the country have seen their cultural roots acknowledged and strengthened, notably through recognition of their languages for secondary school instruction and *Baccalauréat* examination. Italy has a mixed record, successful in the north-west, where the French-speaking citizens of Aosta valley appear content with a status which recognizes their language, less so in the north-east where German speakers of the Alto Adige (they call it South Tyrol) seek stronger ties to Austria. In Scandinavia the Lapps of the far north are split between Norway, Sweden and Finland but in these climes frontiers have little meaning. There are few Finnish speakers in Northern Sweden, while the 8% of Finns who speak Swedish enjoy full equality of language and culture. To the south, Spain, where regional disparities are greater and living standards lower, has contained the Catalonian issue but fights outright terrorism in Euskadi, the Basque provinces. Switzerland, of course, with its four cultures and languages, has been a model of the genre, although even here the immigrant worker problem is growing. Cultural and immigration concerns loomed large in Switzerland's rejection of EEA membership in December 1992.

In addition to internal minorities, frontier groups and those who have immigrated from afar, there are those who have no national motherland or "home state" such as the Kurds and the Basques. Border minorities occur whenever a political frontier disregards a cultural boundary. The problem is particularly prevalent in Yugoslavia (Serbs, Croats, Albanians, Macedonians . . .) but occurs in all regions of Europe: Russians in Estonia and Latvia, for instance, Germans in Poland, Romanians in Moldova, Hungarians in Slovakia, Serbia and Romania . . . However, when there is no national motherland neighboring national governments may find a common interest in containing the ethnic group concerned. Kurd has even been turned against Kurd across the Turco-Iraqi border.

Acute economic and social problems arise in the case of refugees and economic migrants who arrive from a distant land. These issues are particular prevalent in France, the Netherlands and the United Kingdom, where colonial links once facilitated such migrations.

The distinguishing characteristics of minorities include ethnicity and race, language, customs, arts and religion.[5] Friction with the majority group is more prevalent when several elements combine, and in particular language and religion, to set the minority apart. Thus Arabs with their Arabic language and Islamic religion are less easily accepted in France than black West Indians who speak French and identify with catholicism. In the United Kingdom, for similar reason, Pakistanis are less easily assimilated than English-speaking protestant West Indians. Jews stand out in all cultures for their customs, religion and sometimes language (Yiddish, Ladino).

Central Europe
Ethnic explosion in Central and Eastern Europe is not hard to explain. For decades the heavy flat stone of communism imposed national and international conformism and uniformity. Dissent took refuge in a repressed nationalism. As the totalitarian system broke down, however, free speech and cultural diversity returned before the checks and balances of institutional democracy were firmly in place. Long-repressed resentments bubbled up among minorities and majorities alike. In some areas anti-semitism flourished anew but ethnic prejudice was more widespread than hostility to Jews alone. The flames were fanned by former communist leaders quick to move with the tide of popular opinion, by embracing virulent nationalism, and thereby clinging to power and privilege: Kravchuk, Meciar, Milosevic. The heady wine of new-found freedom of expression split democratic forces asunder with devastating consequences in the ballot-box. Resentment was magnified by economic distress as stumbling, piecemeal conversion to a market system induced price rises, hoarding and shortages. Scapegoats were found in minorities, considered less worthy to share in the meager resources available.

These trends were more extreme in the Balkans than in the north. The Slovak independence movement and especially the Yugoslav conflict made it painfully clear that the redrawing of frontiers after the break-up of the Austro-Hungarian empire in 1919 did not satisfy many ethnic aspirations; and that dark memories of fratricidal conflict in World War II poisoned relations further. Given her tardy and half-hearted intervention, Europe has yet to demonstrate that her institutions have the resilience to tackle a threat of continental proportions. As ethnic cleansing succeeds the protestations of "Never again!" which followed the holocaust ring increasingly hollow.

How many is too many
Requests for political asylum climbed steeply in EC countries from 200,000 in 1986 to 600,000 in 1990; yet those who thought they might have left prejudice and abuse behind them were surely disappointed. In a recent EC Eurobarometer, over half of those polled in Belgium, France, Germany, Italy and the UK felt there were too many foreigners living in their country, over 40% in Denmark and the Netherlands. In Switzerland the number of people seeking political asylum rose 16% in 1991. Of course not all foreign residents are political refugees. Many of those now singled out for abuse were welcomed

when economic boom times required their labor, like Turks in Germany. Attacks by skinheads and neo-Nazis on immigrant hostels in Berlin and other cities awakened historic memories and fears (in Israel denunciation was particularly strong); but elsewhere in Western Europe extreme right-wing parties are making electoral gains. While not yet significant in absolute terms (except for LePen's National Front in some regions of France), these ballot-box successes give racism a veneer of respectability.

Moderate governments are getting the message. While the Maastricht summiteers expressed "revulsion against racist sentiments and manifestations ... including expressions of prejudice and violence against foreign immigrants and exploitation of them", most of the governments they headed were making new efforts to control immigration, both legal and illegal. Although all twelve countries signed a convention on political asylum in 1990, only Denmark has ratified it. The UK government introduced stricter rules in 1991. Between 1988 and 1991 asylum seekers in the UK grew tenfold from 5,000 to 50,000 annually. The British move followed similar steps by France and by Germany. France too had experienced a surge, of some 50,000 immigrants. In January 1992 even the liberal Netherlands followed suit reviewing immigration procedures.

Russians stay home

Apart from the special case of Jewish emigration to Israel, welcomed by the Israeli authorities, the flood gates have not opened on the western borders of the former Soviet Union. Soviet Interior Minister Viktor Barannikov brought out cold sweats in his audience when he told a Berlin conference in October 1991 that some twelve million Soviet citizens were expected to take advantage of relaxed travel rules in 1992; and that up to five million of them might decide not to return. The Soviet minister called upon the West for massive aid to forestall not just a wave but a Spring equinox of illegal immigration. Japanese aid is still blocked by the Kurile dispute. President Clinton and the Europeans will have to give serious attention to this issue.

While it seems clear that the swamptide of refugees from central Europe will not now occur (Italy's prompt and coercive repatriation of Albanians — questionable but effective — proved powerfully dissuasive), the issue remains uncertain with respect to the Commonwealth of former Soviet republics. Conflict in the Caucasus, traditional hostility between Ukrainians and Russians and chronic shortages of jobs and food in the cities may yet unleash mass movements westward.

In the long term the problem of immigration into Europe (a phenomenon in large measure balanced, numerically if not ethnically, by emigration, about which less is written) may solve itself. Population experts estimate that a decade into the twenty-first century Western Europe's economy will be hard hit by falling birthrates, resulting in a diminishing workforce, and an aging population. At that time business will be crying out for young immigrant labor and governments will scramble to review their policies. As Larochefoucauld pointed out in the seventeenth century, even humanistic action is rarely untinged with self-interest.

B. Some peculiarly British problems

In considering some minority questions in the countries of the European Community, the Council of Europe and other European countries, there has been a tendency to look east and south. In fact no country faces a more complete range of ethnic issues than the United Kingdom—one is tempted to write dis-united Kingdom. In addition to the racial legacy of empire—Indians, Pakistanis, West Indians, Africans of diverse origin—recently highlighted by the Salmon Rushdie affair and even such apparent trivialities as to whether London Transport bus fare collectors may wear turbans, Britain faces unique issues of devolution in Scotland, Wales, Northern Ireland and Gibraltar.

For many Scots the high road now leads through Brussels
When John Major objected to use of the epithet "federal" in the preamble to the Treaty of European Union agreed at the Maastricht summit, he obtained a ponderous substitute evoking "a new stage in the process creating an ever closer union among the peoples of Europe, where decisions are taken as closely as possible to the citizens." If the issues had not become so emotionally and politically charged, one might be tempted to declare that this was nothing less than a passable definition of federalism. Be that as it may, back in what is for some an excessively "united" kingdom Major's words may be turned against him. For many Scots London and its Scottish Office are a bureaucratic Brussels where decisions are taken as far as possible from the citizens directly concerned.

Scotland, it is true, has its own system of laws but this simply fuels the argument that the Scots are well able to govern themselves. With over five million people and a long and proud history (it was a Scottish king, James 1st, who united the two thrones in 1603), Scotland may lay claim to a place in the Community's hierarchy comparable to that of ... Denmark! The situation was made more sensitive because the governing party in London for over a decade, the Conservatives, had by the Spring of 1992 seen its Scottish representation dwindle to a mere seven seats out of a total of 72. Although the separatist Scottish National Party only held five seats, it set the tone and pace of debate through a shrewd policy of independence for Scotland "in Europe" rather than "from England."

Michael Maclay, leader of the Scottish National Party (SNP) appears more federalist than nationalist—provided "federalism" means European federalism, not the (for him) unsatisfactory halfway house of devolution from Westminster. SNP consider that limitation of Westminster's power is something to be welcomed rather than feared. They believe that federalism within the United Kingdom is unlikely to work because English MP's are not interested in making it work. For Maclay an independent Scotland would be more "pro-Europe" than the United Kingdom and would probably have voted for a single currency at Maastricht. Putting his head in the (Scottish) lion's mouth, John Major admitted to a Glasgow audience that no nation could be held to a union against its will. In a passionate plea for the *status quo* he said that the Labor policy of devolution would inevitably lead to an independence which would diminish both communities. Suddenly the language of Maastricht — "subsidiarity" and "taking decisions as close as possible to the people" — had disappeared from the PM's lexicon. If Major was right, however, that devolution would only be a staging post to independence, that is a prospect the Labour Party could scarcely relish: it needs Scottish seats to achieve a majority in the House of Commons. All parties now agree that some constitutional change is inevitable.[6] The issue is no longer whether to grant autonomy but when and how much. Britain's Tory government may justly claim that following the Conservative Party's fourth successive victory, in May 1992, the devolution issue has lost some of its immediacy. It has not gone away: how long can London invoke subsidiarity in Brussels and deny it to its own regions?

An aspect of the issue which must be on Foreign Office minds is that with separate Scottish representation in Brussels and Strasbourg (European Parliament and Parliamentary Assembly) the disunited Kingdom's weighted voting rights and parliamentary representation would be adjusted downwards below that of France, Italy, and Germany. One final point: the teams of Ireland, Scotland and Wales have long been accepted as representing fully-fledged nations, alongside England and France, in international sports.

Tragic anachronism: the Northern Ireland imbroglio
It is impossible here to do justice (if that is the right word) to the tragic situation in Ulster, the only one among Ireland's four provinces which in 1922 was retained in the United Kingdom because of its two-thirds protestant majority (mostly immigrated from Scotland 150 years earlier) when the rest of the island achieved independence from Britain. The British colonial heritage has given rise to several painful partitions (India, Palestine, Cyprus); in no case did they obviate conflict.

In Northern Ireland extremist forces on both sides are given over to violence, neither representative of the sentiments of the moderate majority in their community. There is irony, however, in the protestant majority vaunting its "unionist" sentiments. They call themselves Empire Loyalists long after the sun has set on the British Empire. There is further irony that Northern Ireland did enjoy devolution through its regional parliament, Stormont, gerrymandering constituency boundaries (the term was created there) to minimize Catholic (and usually separatist) representation. Catholics were so under-represented in all sectors of public life that with the rising conflict the Westminster parliament had to reimpose direct rule. The third irony, of course, is that Ireland and the UK are partners in the European Community, where frontiers are being effaced.

The British government, with its military patrols, curfews, internment practices and other measures of "law and order", falls easy prey to accusations of colonialism and excessive force. There certainly have been excesses but the fact remains that a substantial majority of the population has no desire to join the Irish Republic. Moreover, successive Dublin governments, while favoring reunification, have abjured terrorism, which would not necessarily fade away with reunification. With its violence and structural economic depression, a reunited Ulster would bring lower living standards to the Republic. Although it cannot say so, Dublin does not need such a *cadeau empoisonné* at this time.

Breaking the log-jam

Few "solutions" other than reunification and the *status quo* have been put forward. Perhaps the only viable one is to set a date, perhaps a decade ahead, for British military withdrawal, to be followed by a referendum, offering a choice between full independence and Irish reunification. In this manner the issue would lose its colonial connotation. The first step could be restoration of devolution to Stormont at the same time as it is offered to Scotland and Wales. (Scotland sought a parliament which it did not get, whereas a parliament Loyalists and Republicans alike did not want was imposed on Northern Ireland.) There is no guarantee, however, that the guns would then fall silent . . .

Following the May 1992 election in Britain a fresh start was made under a new Secretary of State for Northern Ireland, Sir Christopher Mayhew. All of the parties involved (except Sinn Fein, which has not renounced violence) sat down for talks. For the first time since Irish independence, representatives of the Dublin government and Empire Loyalists faced each other over a negotiating table . . . The second round of the talks was held in Dublin, with Ulster Unionists members agreeing for the first time to meet south of the border. Discussion lurched on until November but no breakthrough was achieved. London's Christmas shoppers again braved IRA bombs in garbage cans . . .

Gibraltar appeals to the European Court

The case of Gibraltar is unique in a number of respects. Under British administration since the Treaty of Utrecht in 1723, this tiny peninsular, a towering rock two and a half miles long, is home to some 27,000 people of diverse racial origin but united in their fierce political independence of Spain and, increasingly, of Britain. In January 1992 the Socialist Labor Party was re-elected to office on a platform of resistance to Spanish intervention: an eloquent majority of 73% left no doubt about the citizens' attachment to their way of life. As a territory for which an EC member has foreign policy responsibility, (we don't call them colonies any more) like Dutch and other British territories in the Caribbean and elsewhere, Gibraltar is covered by the EEC treaty.[7] However, it is the only such territory on the mainland of Europe and the only one claimed by another member state. (The Spanish authorities refuse any comparison to their own enclaves of Ceuta and Mellila on the African shore, claimed by Morocco, which are juridically part of Spain and, as such, part of the European Community. Gibraltar is not part of the United Kingdom).

Apart from foreign affairs and defense, Gibraltar is largely self-governing. The government and its 15-member parliament point out that even though 99% of their activities are domestic in nature and subject to Community Law, they have little say on EC issues in London and no voice at all in Brussels. Joe Bossano, the "Rock's" premier, considers that Gibraltar's relations with Spain should not be treated as foreign policy issues. Yet as an "overseas" territory Gibraltar has been specifically excluded from measures to open up Europe's air traffic. Air passengers from Europe, even Spain, to Gibraltar must first pass through London, the only European city with direct flights to the Rock.

Gibraltarians object to being denied EC benefits while subject to Community law. They also assert the principle that Community texts should not exclude one specific geographical area which wants to be included. Gibraltar has taken her case to the European Court of Justice in Luxembourg, pointing out that her population includes nationals of all twelve EC countries who should enjoy in Gibraltar the rights they would have in their country of origin. In other words, Gibraltar-born citizens feel themselves to be discriminated against in their own country. This argument is further strengthened by the Treaty of European Union, where European citizenship is anchored in Community law. Moreover, under the *status quo* the Gibraltar frontier with La Linea in Spain is the only one not fully opened up in January 1993 by the SEA and TEU, with Gibraltar continuing to be treated as a foreign country for purposes of tariffs, VAT and CAP.

The Gibraltar government considers it time to review the 1969 constitution to bring it into the modern world. Its strategy is to deal with issues as European rather than British citizens. Pursuing this policy, Gibraltar was the first territory to mint an ECU coin. One may add that the Rock's diverse population, melding British, Spanish, Jewish, North African, Maltese and other cultures, is quite distinct and a model of racial tolerance.

Monkey business
Britain and Spain must put Gibraltar's future before their national pride. With the evolution of modern warfare the Rock and its harbor, so vital in World War II, have lost their strategic significance. Gibraltarians are proud to be British but, like many Scots, increasingly consider themselves first as Europeans: the future does not lie in continued colonial status, even less in forced assimilation by Spain. Surely Europe can find a third way, giving Gibraltarians the benefit of membership, including an open border, a seat in the European Parliament and a limited voice in the Commission and Council of Ministers, through a treaty of association? Not least among the beneficiaries would be the economies of southern Spain and of Ceuta and Melilla, Spain's enclaves in Morocco. The judgement of the European Court can point the way.

If all else fails, one might consult the monkeys, Gibraltar's "apes", which roam free on the rockface and whose presence, according to tradition, keeps the Union Jack flying. Would they settle for twelve gold stars, a symbol of perfect union against a background as blue as the Mediterranean?

C. Languages

No discussion of cultural, ethnic and minority issues would be complete without consideration of the language question. Languages are cultural doors. We may ponder the fact that the European Community has more official languages than the United Nations; and that the Community provides interpretation at four times as many meetings as the world body. Nowhere in the world are more words translated and interpreted than in Brussels.

The Community already has nine official languages, ten if we include Irish Gaelic. The prospect of the Community adding more members evokes a linguistic nightmare. Why do it? The answer lies in the protection of national identities and cultural diversity. Additions create exponential, not linear increase. More staff, higher costs, greater logistical problems and slower decision-making is the price Europeans accept to pay for their cultural diversity.[8] When we refuse or are unable to address people in their own language we assault their cultural identity or, in Vaclav Havel's words, their spiritual home.

In most Community meetings interpretation is limited to French, German, English (six permutations) but delegates may express themselves in their own languages if they wish and make arrangements in advance. Thus there might be interpretation from Danish or Portuguese but not into those languages. Translators bear the burden of rendering official legislation and court judgements into all national languages. The Commission prefers to do this work rather than leave it to national capitals, since all versions must be both linguistically and legally equivalent. There is no primary language: all versions are considered "authentic" and are used as a basis for incorporating Community legislation and jurisprudence into national law.

International organizations usually restrict the number of languages in which they work. Even the UN, a world-wide body, limits itself to five (Chinese, English, French, Russian, Spanish). The Council of Europe, OECD and WEU function officially in English and French, although other languages may be used for one-way interpretations in the parliamentary assembles.

Regional languages

A more urgent issue is the threat to Europe's less used languages. Europe has about fifty languages, as distinct from the far more numerous dialects. (A language usually has a codified grammar, a written form, a literature). Experts of the European Bureau for the Lesser Used Languages (located in Dublin, where the official language of Ireland, Irish Gaelic, is barely spoken), have estimated that some fifteen to twenty of Europe's forty-one regional languages are threatened with extinction. If languages like Arumanian, spoken in central Greece, Friulian (north-east Italy) or Galician (north-west Spain) disappear (some, like Cornish have gone already), the ethnic groups and their culture will probably fade with them. Irish Gaelic and Maltese are protected by official status but still under pressure from English; Switzerland's fourth language, Rheto-Romantsch, spoken by 50,000 people in the canton of Graubunden, is surrounded by German.

Official status usually guarantees the four conditions which the Dublin bureau considers necessary for survival: education, administration, information and trial available in the language. Schools, services, media and systems of justice for minorities cannot be made available without government consent and subsidy.

A Council of Europe Minority Language Charter

The Council of Europe recently moved to protect regional languages. In 1988 the Standing Conference of Local and Regional Authorities of Europe (SCLRAE), which meets under Council of Europe auspices, drafted a charter on Regional or Minority languages in Europe. The Charter sets out objectives and principles to apply to both territorial and non-territorial languages (Yiddish would be an example of the latter). It goes on to guarantee use of or at least study of minority languages in education, public services, the media, economics and social life and transfrontier exchanges. However, while drawing public attention to the issue, this text is no more than a recommendation to governments.[9]

The Council of Europe has long recognized the importance of language learning for European citizenship. It's first major project carried the general title of *Learning and teaching modern languages for communication*. This was followed in 1989 by a new phase, *Language learning for European citizenship,* destined to last until 1995. It is intended to help member states take effective measures to enable all citizens to learn to use languages with a view to improved mutual understanding, personal mobility and access to information in a multilingual and multi-cultural Europe.

In helping to implement reforms and to promote innovation in language learning and teacher training, this major project concentrates on development of methods for language teaching and learning; and on the elaboration of models and methods for the training of teachers. An important first step was taken in November, 1989, with a symposium held at Sintra, Portugal, on *Language learning and teaching methodology for citizenship in a multi-cultural Europe*. The symposium launched a new series of international workshops.

The Community's LINGUA program also promotes the foreign language competence of EC citizens. It encourages in-service training of foreign language teachers and their trainers. In 1990 MERCATOR, a network of information and documentation centers in EC countries on regional languages and cultures, was established.

Recent advances in computer and satellite technology as applied to language learning will doubtless soon give rise to a third generation of instructional methodology.

D. On feeling European

In considering the interrelationship between the parts and the whole at national and European levels, we must address the issue of identity. For fifty years we have attempted to build Europe by defining what it is not rather than what it is. In opting to proceed by sectors, Jean Monnet and Robert Schuman set us on the road of the ECSC and economic unity. This was justified in a partially negative way: to prevent war. The concept was providential at the time, since it gave a vital fillip to integration. Today, however, the relationship between regional and national identity, emphasizing differences and distinctiveness over what we hold in common, poses the much more challenging question of "What kind of Europe?" or, more simply "What is Europe?".

Invasive banality

We have regional cultures and we have nations; we may compare them and attempt to reconcile them. Do we, like Pascal's fallen angel, aspire to something pre-existent, to a mythical "earlier Europe", harking back to the world of Charlemagne? Yet we know in our hearts that with the constant tension between regional identity and continental union, the Golden Age of a Europe united never really was; and if it had been, it would not be relevant to the Europe we seek, not of yesterday but of tomorrow.

When Charles Péguy went to war in 1914 he declared: "I leave as a soldier of the Republic for the war to end wars and for general disarmament." No contradiction between his national self-identification and his universal objective was apparent. In fact we have not sufficiently pondered the question of whether the new Europe will efface national identity or perpetuate it. A Europe of no national identities would be a Europe of banality. Europeans fear Coca Cola and McDonald's and American English, even as they consume them, not so much for their "Americanness" as for the deadening uniformity with which they threaten European diversity. Not unnaturally, some Europeans fear that integration may create its own monochrome banality.

The British and the French

A ceremony took place in a tunnel underneath the Dover Straits in December 1992. The British and French marked their first land border with commemorative plaques. There was sweet irony in the fact that this frontier was being established less than a month before EC borders were to be eliminated. A difference of perception on these unarticulated issues may be at the heart of British misunderstandings with other European countries. There is a British way of life, a method of doing things which, (like Britain's unwritten constitution) goes without saying. (The harmless arrogance of not printing the country of origin on her postage stamps is one example.) Since everybody knows what it means to be British (or so the British think, for how could one live otherwise?), the British feel they can afford to be sufficient unto themselves. They don't ask others to be British; how could they? The contrast with the cultural imperialism of Péguy and the micro-managed logic of the French could not be greater. Yet the two attitudes are equally illusory. The British long deluded themselves that they did not need Europe; the French that Europe would somehow be French.

This question of the relationship of cultural diversity and national identity with European integration was eloquently addressed by the eminent French administrator René Lenoir in *Le Monde*:

> It is good for humanity that men should eat, dress, build, pray to God, express themselves through dance and music in different ways. I like to see Senegalese women in their *boubous*, and Indian women in saris and not in jeans. All over the world there is a resurgence of self-awareness. Such claims are legitimate ... After all, human rights must include a sense of cultural, religious or national attachment. Yet there is a downside, too: there is a risk of oppression of minorities or of intolerant religious absolutism. If the only model we put forward is that of a market which standardizes habits and behaviors, we will rapidly lose our appeal and will find ourselves building a Europe depressing in its uniformity ... I don't believe in downgrading the nations of Europe. I don't see Great Britain or France becoming the equivalent of Virginia or Arizona. And in France at least the nation has always identified with the State. [10]

National identity: the experience of the small countries
Little Denmark's "no" to Maastricht served these truths. In Europe's smaller countries such questions of identity, while certainly present, rarely arise in such an overwhelming manner. Better than their larger neighbors, they have learned to absorb cultural shock and to divert its energy to national ends. They speak many tongues and have always been frontier people.

Is it possible to reconcile cultural regionalism and economic integration? Finland's respected internationalist, Max Jakobson, believes that it is:

> The Basques, the Scots, the Welsh wish to run their own lives and their cause cannot fail to receive sympathy from the Finns, who firmly believe that they would never have achieved their present wealth and freedom had they remained under the rule of Stockholm or St. Petersburg. [11]

Writing in 1988, Jakobson would probably see little reason to amend these lines now Finland has applied for community membership. Like Jacques Delors, speaking on French television on February 26, 1992, he makes a distinction between cultural and economic sovereignty. Both are confident that cultural identity can withstand the assaults of homogenization from the United States or any other source. Cultural identity cannot be cultivated artificially, within the walls of an ethnic reservation. It must be able to survive and grow in the open ... Material success is not in itself a victory of peas-in-a-pod consumerism or materialistic "values".

When Vaclav Havel received the Charlemagne Prize in Aachen in May 1991, he reflected on the tragic dimension of the four decades central and eastern Europe had spent under totalitarianism of the right and left. It should be humbling to western Europeans, who so often think of Europe in terms of selling more or buying cheaper, that Havel spoke of Czechoslovakia's "return to Europe", seeing the devastation of value concepts as one of the worst legacies of totalitarianism.

Future generations may feel themselves to be "born European" as an enrichment, not as a substitution – as naturally as we are born not only Lapplander or Alsatian or Sicilian but also Swedish or French or Italian; Manitoban and Canadian; Pennsylvanian and American. There is a tide in the affairs of men . . . Europe today is ripe for change. In the West as in the East old orders have proved themselves inadequate. Europe could still founder on the rocky islets of regional particularisms which should be jewels in the silver sea of union. Together Europeans can protect and celebrate their diversity. The opportunity must be taken at the flood.

Notes

1 UNHCR, IOM, ECE, Council of Europe. See article by Erich Reyl, *Düsseldorfer Handelsblatt*, April 12, 1991.

2 Official counter-espionage report cited by *Bild am Sonntag*, Jan 26, 1991.

3 The issue of minorities concerns everybody not merely as a threat to peace and security but also because from a European perspective, every culture will be in a minority and cultural identity an issue of universal concern.

4 The phenomenon was recognized (the time will tell how profoundly) by the framers of the Treaty of European Union when they provided for a Committee of the Regions. For how long will regional representatives be content to be nominated by national governments and to exercise only a consultative voice in the European integration process?

5 Frontier groups may also include economic minorities — those who commute across a national frontier to their place of work.

6 The Liberal Democrats, the smallest of the three main parties, have long championed devolution (as well as European integration) and retain a significant foothold in Scotland. The 1992 general election saw Conservative representation rise to 11 seats, still less than one in six.

7 Macao, Madeira and the Azores are part of Portugal, the Canaries part of Spain. The Dutch have 4 islands in the Antilles. French overseas possessions fall into 3 categories: four overseas departments, overseas territories, territorial collectivities. The Channel Islands and the Isle of Man are British self-governing Crown dependencies which have opted out of the EC.

8 The EC languages are Danish, Dutch, English, French, German, Greek, Italian, Portuguese, Spanish and for some texts, Irish. (Although limited in range, being concentrated like Celtic languages on the western fringe, Gaelic is an official language of Ireland and of considerable cultural and political significance). Permutation of nine languages gives 72 possible translations, 10-90, 15-210, 20-380! The commission employs 400 interpreters and 1000 translators. When negotiation for Finnish and Swedish accession commence in 1993, the question of official languages will again be on the table.

9 The languages Charter was adopted by the SCLRAE on March 16, 1988, on the basis of a report by the Committee on Cultural and Social Affairs. It was subsequently approved by the Parliamentary Assembly. Objectives and principles of the charter are as follows:

Objectives and Principles

1. The parties undertake, in respect of regional or minority languages spoken within their territories, to base their policies, legislation and practice on the following.
   a. the recognition of existence of regional or minority languages as a community attribute;
   b. the respect of the geographical area of each regional or minority language in order to ensure that the existing or new administrative divisions do not constitute an obstacle to the promotion of the regional or minority language in question;
   c. the need for resolute action to promote regional or minority languages in order to safeguard them;

    d. the elimination of all forms of discrimination concerning the use of regional or minority languages, together with any practice having such discriminatory effects, according to the spirit of the convention for the Protection of Human rights and Fundamental Freedoms;

    e. the promotion of the use of regional or minority languages, in speech and writing, in public, social and economical life;

    f. the right of each community employing a regional or minority language to maintain and develop relations with other similar communities in the state;

    g. the teaching and study of regional and minority languages at all appropriate stages;

    h. the provision of facilities enabling non-speakers of regional or minority languages living in the areas where it is spoken to learn it if they so desire.

    i. the promotion of study and research on regional or minority languages at universities or equivalent institutions;

    j. inclusion of respect, understanding and tolerance in relation to regional or minority languages among the objectives of education and training provided within their territories and encouragement of the mass media to pursue objectives;

    k. study of the possibility of applying appropriate types of transnational exchange to regional or minority languages used in identical or similar form in two or more contracting areas.

2. The Parties undertake to apply these principles *mutatis mutandis*, to non-territorial languages.

3. The Parties are encouraged to establish bodies for the purpose of advising the authorities on all matters pertaining to regional or minority languages.

10   February 11, 1992.

11   Jakobson *op.cit.*, p. 157.

V

CONCLUSION

Shuffling Blueprints

Most books have a conclusion: the road to Europe, over a thousand years long, has no apparent end. Where does political power reside and what is its purpose in 2001? It is not helpful, although hard to avoid, to use the vocabulary of the past to describe the institutional Europe we seek to create. There will be political parties; but they must change. There will be nations; but they must change. There will be a diversity of cultures; not seeping like toxic dumps the poison of conflict but preserved and valued as a common heritage. New scourges, most of them of our own making, will assail our selfishness; new opportunities, many of them undeserved, will challenge our versatility and our generosity. Europeans need to draw up a set of moral blueprints rather than precise institutional norms, not only because it is right but because an immoral or amoral society, engendering conflict within itself, will ultimately break down. If the end is worthy the means will fall into place.

What do we mean by a moral blueprint for Europe? Openness and generosity. We may not replace the nationalism of states by a European nationalism: we should be patriots, Europeans and internationalists. If "my country, right or wrong" is a recipe for conflict the same is true at European level. If being the first military power imposes responsibilities on the United States, being the first economic power imposes responsibilities on Europe. We cannot establish a moral blueprint for only part of Europe, be it wealthy, or western or both. We cannot establish a moral blueprint on economic criteria alone. We cannot establish a moral blueprint for Europe at the expense of national, regional, cultural, sexual or religious identities. Europe may not curtail basic rights and freedoms or flout democratic principles.

When we speak of the nation state, of confederations and federations, or even of "the United States of Europe", we circumscribe imagination and hamper debate, however unwittingly. Our institutional vocabulary may serve as scaffolding to an edifice under construction but must not impinge on the creativity of the new generation of builders. Institutions must evolve or die. The Europe of the next century will need political and institutional concepts as yet undevized. "The Community", Cavaco Silva has declared, "is an original and open model whose final political architecture we do not know".

This is not a recipe for paralysis: quite the contrary. Life is movement. Europe is more a direction than a goal.

> *Wer immer strebend sich bemüht,*
> *Den können wir erlösen.*

Consequently ignorance of the final outcome is no justification for immutability. This principle applies not only to political concepts but also to the institutions which express and implement them. Europe has recourse to diverse institutions to meet diverse needs. The history of the last few years has demonstrated that as those needs change Europe's institutions must evolve. They will doubtless retain different "personalities" and serve complementary functions, with some unavoidable duplication as long as they have different fields of competence and diverse membership. Ultimately one can imagine them coalescing around three main poles of attraction:

— human rights, education and culture (model: Council of Europe)
— economic, environmental and social affairs (model: EC)
— security (models: WEU or CSCE).

However, this clarification cannot take place until the membership in each institution is roughly equal and representative of Europe as a whole.

As part of this clarification process it will be important to strengthen democracy at European level by reinforcing the powers of the European parliamentary assemblies and, probably, eventually merging them into one, just as the institutions of the Rome and Paris treaties were merged in 1961.

No man is an island

An urgent task before Europe today is rebuttal of the politics of exclusion at personal, national and international level. The European citizenship outlined in the TEU is of both limited practical impact and great political significance. (It is strange that those who oppose voting rights in local elections for EC nationals are also vocal in criticizing the Community's "democracy deficit" [1]).

To exist, associations and states must have their borders. All societies combine the responsibilities but also the privileges of membership. Borders are not bad in themselves: they should express cohesion, not exclusion. Members must demonstrate the former in order to claim the latter. If Europeans come together to make peace, live better and exert influence they must also exercize their responsibilities towards the rest of the world. The lighthouse and the beacon are preferable as metaphors to the drawbridge and the fortress. No man, said John Donne, is an island. Families, schools, churches, hamlets, cities, regions, continents, we all cleave to the great tectonic crust. If at five billion souls in 1993 we cannot share and husband our resources, how shall we cohabit at eight billion in 2020? Europe will share in the special responsibility of the developed world for having sought to grow out of its deficits and for having dilapidated natural resources under that ironic heading of "growth": atmospheric pollution, ozone depletion, destruction of forests, global warming and the creeping garbage dumps of earth and space. Particularly sensitive will be those regions for which there is no sovereignty to claim: polar regions, the oceans and space, but in a broader sense the entire biosphere, since nature knows no frontiers. Development must be for all and sustainable by all. A coherent, effective environmental policy is one of the great moral imperatives of Europe's blueprint.

There is no paradox in regions and cultures pursuing their interests in a European context. The return of the nations is a process in full flood at the very time when old ideologies are called into question. People need to feel their roots or, as Vaclav Havel puts it, their levels of "home". The nation state is not called upon to disappear but rather to be reconfirmed as one level of human endeavor amongst others and, in many cases, the decisive one. The paradox of "Europe" and the "regions" is more apparent than real, especially since cultural entities and regions will be less and less inhibited by national frontiers. In most cases the threat to peace and stability arises not from cultures but from "minorities" on the "wrong" side of impermeable borders. The notion of frontiers must give way to that of interchange zones, so that language, geography, culture and religion can be celebrated in their diversity. Ethno-centric regionalism and globalizing forces are squeezing the old order of the nation state from above and below: an explosive phenomenon which we mismanage at our peril.[2]

Given these pressures from above and below, it is not surprising that, of all the political vocabulary which has changed its context or content, none is so besieged as the concept of the nation state. The quarrel between federalists and intergovernmentalists which animated the debate when the Council of Europe and the ECSC were founded has less significance today (notwithstanding John Major's objection to the term "federal" in the Maastricht treaty). It is a measure of the evolution of political thinking that in 1950 the United Kingdom was unwilling to sign the Coal and Steel Treaty whereas today "neutrals" such as Sweden and Switzerland are ready to accept the *acquis communautaire* of ECSC, EEC, EURATOM, SEA and TEU... We are in effect all neutrals now and, as such, can the more easily share our sovereignty. Conversely, splendid isolation from the center of real power may confer sovereignty in name only.

Today, most people accept that federalism implies taking decisions at the lowest level reasonably possible. Premier Major quotes carbonic gas emission controls as being the type of issue which must be decided on an international basis, although even there he expresses a preference for allowing member states some leeway as to how European directives are implemented. Major may have betrayed a *querelle de mots* when he rejected "federalism" and embraced "subsidiarity" and "taking decisions as close to the people as possible".[3] Refusal by a central authority to distinguish between aspects of sovereignty may lead cultural or ethnic groups to seek greater autonomy than originally envisaged or economically desirable.[4] In the United Kingdom the component nations, Welsh, Irish, Scottish *and English* are entering upon a phase not completely dissimilar to the Canadian experience.

European union — the TEU in particular — provides the regions of the continent with an outer framework which permits the free expression of diverse cultural sovereignties. John Major seemed isolated at Maastricht but the Danish referendum found Community-wide echoes just as he assumed the EC chairmanship, determined to save the union by promoting all at once enlargement, subsidiarity and institutional reform. To general surprise Socialist

Commission President Jacques Delors (confirmed in his job) and Conservative UK Prime Minister John Major found themselves joined in an unexpected alliance.

Commenting in the London *Daily Mail* on June 17, 1992, on the referendum debates in Denmark and Ireland, Brian James observes that the forces for "Yes" are likely to succeed: they are the big battalions. Nevertheless, the discussion may already have served a wider purpose:

> to ram home to politicians that everywhere, from Aberdeen to Athens, a suspicion grows that in the tramp towards the great giant state of Europe, what might disappear underfoot would be not great abstract concepts like sovereignty so much as tiny fragments of habit and tradition, of diet and custom that let a plain man know who, what and where he is.
> Maastricht cannot survive unless everywhere this gnawing unease is addressed.

James is right, of course; except for his rabble-rousing choice of words: nobody wants a "great giant state". The Danish vote was indeed a salutary shock. However, in explaining their vote the Danes made it clear that they were protesting certain aberrations, *excès de zèle* which do not invalidate the process as a whole. Europe must hearken to the voices from Jutland and Copenhagen but also be on her guard against the hi-jacking of the Danish ballot-box for purely negative purposes by a xenophobe minority playing on negative nationalist sentiment.

Ultimately the choice may lie between a union of Europe and not nation states but a mosaic of cultural and ethnic entities. The Soviet and Russian experiences may carry lessons for Europe despite the differences in social systems. After all, the Baltic States were the first new nations to be recognized in Europe since World War II. They were rapidly followed by others. If two million Slovenians or Macedonians, why not five million Scots? If Liechtenstein and San Marino, why not Corsica? Basques? Frisians? Wends? Is the Milosevic method of linking up with the diaspora and ghastly "ethnic cleansing" a model for "peace in our time"? Cultural rather than political borders will, indeed must continue to exist in the organization of any society. The break-up of Czechoslovakia and Yugoslavia, arbitrary Great Power creations of the Versailles Treaty, does not invalidate the case for voluntary federation. There is no stronger argument for a freely-consented overarching union than Europe's rediscovery of its diverse cultural roots.

Yet these trends will not diminish the need for a single currency, a common market, a European environmental policy or for joining together to build Airbus or to explore space.

Europe's established political parties have not yet come to terms with the situation since the Cold War melted away. President Bush's "new world order" remains to be defined. The political vacuum left by half a century of East-West confrontation is in danger of being filled by xenophobic movements of the extreme right: the National Front in France, the Lombard League in Italy and the Republicans in an allegedly "united" Germany. The traditional parties have yet to rearticulate their commitments and priorities.

One of the issues to be addressed concerns the creation of European parties.[5] Although we have cross-national groupings in the European parliamentary assemblies, we are still a long way from truly European parties. The center of focus is still national, with Europe as an added dimension. This may be a reasonable price to pay for preserving national cultures from bureaucratic homogenization.

Yet the immediate agenda will not go away: eradicating deficits, stabilizing currencies, fighting terrorism, drugs and international crime without border controls, coping with refugees and immigrants, developing a European security policy, countering regional conflicts, re-evaluating neutralism, moving from the "Europe of democracy" to the "Europe of geography", rethinking Community structures to cope with expanding membership: none of those problems can be solved on a national basis alone.

Hundred years' war

We have spoken of a moral agenda for Europe. Jean-Marie Lustiger, Cardinal Archbishop of Paris, has written eloquently of Europe's spiritual vocation. To grasp issues in perspective and to react appropriately to the opportunities afforded by the last decade of the twentieth century, says Lustiger, Europeans must see their continent as emerging from a Hundred Years' War.[6] Neither the end of the Cold War, symbolized by the fall of the Berlin Wall, nor the fifty years since Hitler's panzers unfurled across Europe suffice, says Lustiger, to give us the proper basis to show what brought these forces into play. Only the perspective of a century of war, from the late XIXth to the late XXth, wherein spiritual choices give rise to major economic and political consequences, enables us to understand the "enormous spasm" of Europe's history which dragged the whole world into its vortex.

If Lustiger is right, we need to look back a century to understand the present; yet in planning the future we rarely look beyond the next election . . .

Europe east and west: two halves of a spiritual entity

Lustiger's longer perspective enables us to distill the determining factors-ideologies of the left and right, global economies, the death of empire, the new dominance of science and technology. It also leads us to realize that since 1939 the eastern and western wings of Europe have lived through the same fundamental history, even if they have confronted each other for the last half century.

Western Europe must not lose sight of the fact that, with the temporary exception of Romania, no force was used to prevent the collapse of communism in the satellite countries; and that even in Moscow the reactionary *putsch* of August 1991 found no popular base. When Gorbachev set the glasnost and perestroika balls rolling he was recognizing an *état de fait*. The ideological fervor of communism's early years had long since waned, to be replaced by a desperate will among most leaders to cling to power and privilege for their own sake. As both the product and the accelerator of communism's post-ideological decline, Gorbachev was too close to the center to perceive until it was too late for the USSR that the system could not be reformed and had to be replaced. The vast popular consciousness of the East was ready to come home to Europe.

There can therefore be no peace, no security, no ultimate durability for an institutional system centered only on the West and which excludes half of the common European homeland. What will happen if the cost of change proves too heavy to bear? "There is not a single country in the region (Central Europe) where people today are not worse off, in terms of living standards, than they used to be", Hungary's foreign minister, Gyula Horn, courageously told CSCE's summer summit in Helsinki.

The West needs patience. Eastern Europeans have no experience of democracy and constitutional government. Before freely joining Europe they must first re-establish national identities buried for decades under centralist structures. Those who feel themselves to be first British, French, Italian or Danish and, second, European, should expect no less of their brothers and sisters to the East.

Since East Germany has been integrated into West Germany and hence into the Common Market with all its Community aid resources, one might reasonably expect that the former GDR would be better placed than other Central and East European countries. Nevertheless, a new German extra-parliamentary opposition group was set up in 1992 to put pressure on the Bonn federal government on behalf of inhabitants of the five new *Länder*. The new movement cuts across party lines, with Peter-Michael Diestel of the Christian Democrats and ex-communist Gregor Gysi (PDS) as leading figures. The new "justice committees" reflect widespread anger at the mountain of social and economic problems heaped on the ruins of four decades of East German "socialism". It could be a decade before eastern Germans attain living standards comparable with their western German counterparts. History will judge the West severely if it allows Europe to remain divided, in Walther Stütztle's colorful but premonitory phrase, between "an increasingly affluent EC and an increasingly large number of poorhouses in flames". [7]

We may not replace the Iron Curtain of fences and minefields with an Economic Curtain of tariffs and quotas. To the chronological continuity of the century of conflict corresponds the geographical continuity of Europe itself. The West can claim no moral superiority for having suffered totalitarianism only of the right while the East endured dictatorships under both nazism and communism. The fact that eastern Europe remained stifled under the heavy flat stone of communism while western Europe enjoyed the opportunity to move towards a freely-consented unification does not endow the West with exclusive rights or privileges; but responsibilities, surely.

Better business bureau

When East Berliners streamed through the breached wall to discover the gaudy materialism of the West it became clear that the East had long represented the suppressed conscience of the West. Should not the West have achieved more with its opportunities? Exultation over "winning the Cold War" is out of place if we have not made the best of our stewardship of democracy and the free market. Are we satisfied with the human and social rights which we dispense? There can be no stable Europe without this moral dimension.

It might be construed as an act of providence, therefore, for western economic liberalism to have found itself in the throes of a recession just as the eastern state monopolies collapsed. We have not yet devized a foolproof economic method. Man was not created to form the consumer society. European union, it should be clear by now, must be more than a better business bureau. The educational reforms necessary to the "staffing" of the new Europe must emphasize technology and science but not to the detriment of basic human values. Europe has not yet cast off the shackles of Yalta. Joining the "two halves" of Europe will be a lengthy process. It will be facilitated by an early declaration of intent from the Community to admit all Europeans on a footing of equality.

This process will involve a difficult debate on the "frontiers" of Europe, involving not only Asia on the eastern fringe ("How European is Russia?") but North America on the western horizon ("What is the proper American role in Europe?"). In his book on the new European concert, Jacques Delors pays considerable attention to the Community's responsibilities to the east and to the south. He does not exclude *a priori* the mitterrandian notion of a European confederation or the eventual accession of Russia to the Community. [8]

Europe and the Third World

We have pointed out more than once that 1992 is "Spain's year" in Europe. In fact Spain is likely to continue to play a key role as keeper of the European conscience. The reasons are not far to seek. Spain came late to "Europe" — not just the Community but the Council of Europe — because it first had to break out from under its own version of totalitarism, the Falange.[9] Secondly, while an important European nation Spain is neither in population, in military pretentions nor yet in level of economic development on a par with the leading nations: smaller than the largest, larger than the smallest, it can the more easily speak for all. Thirdly, and more importantly, at once southern, Atlantic and Mediterranean, Spain has special links to Latin America[10] and Africa. Spain must not allow Europe to lose sight of her responsibilities in the Third World development. New preoccupations between East and West may not occlude the North-South relationship. Yet if Spain has a leadership opportunity here, the responsibility belongs to all. Seeing starving children on television we can all get famine fatigue.

Some notion of the modest limits of aid from industrialized nations to the developing world can be gleaned from the fact that while with eleven and a half billion dollars a year the US is the biggest donor, this represents only 0.2% of economic output. The most generous donors are the Norwegians, with 1.2 bn or 1.14%, followed by the Danes, with 1.2 bn also or 0.96%,

Sweden (2.1 bn or 0.92%) and the Netherlands (2.5 bn or 0.88%). Relatively speaking, small countries are more generous than large ones but no "have" other than little Norway has yet given the "have nots" a hundredth of its national wealth.[11] The great trek north has only just begun ... Here the Rio Grande, there the desert dunes: if these frontiers fall to desperate populations the boundaries of Europe will seem puny and irrelevant.

America and the new Europe

As these great transformations are under way in Europe, the United States is undergoing its own *examen de conscience*. Militarily, America is a lone super-power with nobody left to fight. At the same time the nation is rediscovering its problems back home. Public scepticism about "politics as usual", resulting in the Buchanan and Perot phenomena, is not far removed from what we have observed in Europe. Isolationism appears attractive once more not only to the right wing of the Republican Party but also to protectionists among the Democrats. "America first" has become an ambiguous slogan. Americans are weary of the deficit, health costs, military burdens, educational deficiencies and the drug war. (Panama and Kuweit were "just causes", Yugoslavia of lesser strategic significance . . .). On the other hand, they are reluctant to give up their zones of influence.

The question of NATO's purpose arose even before the demise of the Soviet Union (our memories are short, as event succeeds event in rapid succession). "It should not be beyond the wit of man", declares Martin Hillenbrand astonishingly, even before the demise of the Soviet Union, "to find things that NATO can do, at least in the short term, to substitute for the provision of essential security for the West against feared Soviet aggression". NATO has become a Linus-blanket. Hillenbrand goes on to laud Secretary of State Baker's "ingenuity" in finding new functions. The Secretary set out his proposals in a speech in Berlin in December 1990, concluding with "a fundamentally different approach to security" providing an appealing model of international relations involving cooperation and the reconciliation of ancient enemies.[12] It is strange how contrived this epoch-making speech already seems to us today.

It is no wonder, then, that NATO, a US-dominated institution, finds itself almost as irrelevant as its antithesis, neutrality, in the Europe of the nineties. In fact there is a narrowing of the spread. If the neutrals join the Community, itself linked through WEU to NATO, the latter is in a sense neutralized. Nor is it surprising that the new Europe, which the US did so much to nurture, now assumes the proportions of a cuckoo in the economic nest. As Europe emerges from American tutelage we seem to be facing a period of love-hate relations. Americans always had a dual view of the world: one man's guerilla is another man's freedom fighter; one person's peacekeeping is another's intervention; the fall of communism for one the triumph of capitalism for another.

As for Europe, one person's pillar of the Atlantic Community is another's Fortress Europe; one person's new economic superpower is another's hot-bed of resurgent nationalism and dissident cultures. US troops in Europe? ... Both deficit spending and influence buying. Attitudes in America and Europe have reached a high level of mutual ambiguity. Is this a symptom of the search for a new order? Americans and Europeans can only attain that order if they work together as equals, with a clarification of security relations high on the list of priorities. Both must acknowledge that responsibility not only accompanies but also defines leadership.

In the good-old-bad-old days USSR and USA were in a sense two gigantic mirrors in which the superpowers each saw their own reflection and defined themselves in each other. Dear enemy, I miss you. Henceforth status will be defined in economic and cultural rather than in military terms — a trick which Germany and Japan, handed far fewer military responsibilities by the World War II "victors", have long since learned. Europe and America must find a middle way between an indefinite American presence, which the US deficit alone suffices to preclude, and the total severance of Europe's security ties with her transatlantic partners.

A Europe from Vancouver to Vladivostok was a happy catch-phrase for Douglas Hurd but does not represent a viable concept in the long run. Europe must enjoy her own subsidiarity, her sense of self, her identity. The Maastricht treaty, whether ratified in its present form or not, sets an unavoidable agenda for the coming years: enlargement, institutional reform, Central and Eastern Europe, nationalism, security, education, the environment, world trade, population explosion, Third World relations. Yet Europe may not turn exclusively inward; she is called to global coordination. The trade blocks now forming in North and South America and Asia must be stepping stones to global commerce not protectionism. That will only happen in partnership with the Community. The problems of peace and social and economic progress do not stop at Europe's external borders. Sovereignty, says Jacques Cousteau, is already a thing of the past and the Maastricht treaty a small wave when you have your eyes fixed on the horizon.[13] Europe is no longer an ideal; it is a necessity, even though it may be more exalting to fight for an ideal than for a necessity.

In his speech to the students of the College of Europe Jacques Delors concluded with these words:

> I say to these young people, you can, if our Europe succeeds, test your resources to the utmost and find space for your personal development. For you are summoned to share in a unique endeavor, bringing peoples and nations together for better and not for worse. In this venture you will rediscover your philosophical and cultural roots, those which have always existed in Europe. But for that you must enter into a personal commitment and demand of those who govern a calculated daring, a fertile imagination, a forthright commitment to make of the Community a necessity for survival and an ideal for action. [14]

Cynics may sneer; but what is the alternative to keeping our eyes on the horizon of which Cousteau speaks; on that last frontier? If we remain focused on our own material concerns, ultimately the consumer society, defying biodiversity, will devour not only material resources but cultures, even people.

When that society has used up the world it won't be able to buy another. It will finally have consumed itself.

The age is long past when man's influence was neutral, his impact neglige-able. Was he not always the greatest predator? Modern technology is an ambivalent instrument. War, famine, disease, environmental depradation and ill-considered development have placed the planet under siege. If we cannot unite Europe in this cause we have no hope of uniting the world. The road beyond Europe leads to global solidarity. Is this not motivation enough? If we cannot bring the nations together for the common good, how shall we manage this tiny planet, hurtling through space in the twenty-first century?

Notes

1 The cross-currents engendered by the emergence of a European political philosophy are illustrated by two issues arising from the TEU. Many of those who criticize the treaty for not being sufficiently "democratic" and "close to the people" are at the same time opposed to EC citizens resident in another country from voting in European elections.

2 There is of course a danger of chain reaction whereby former minorities attain a degree of independence and then turn against smaller minorities within themselves. Europe's moral agenda must be mindful of this phenomenon which is already finding violent and tragic expression in Central and Eastern Europe. On the other hand the unmanageable and unrealistic fragmentation of administrative structures must also be avoided. There can be no general rule for such politically volatile situations other than condemnation of violence and coercion.

3 Major reminded *Le Monde* (June 26, 1992) that British PM's are answerable directly to parliament at question time twice a week. While some people see the British as "less European" the impression might fade if other European leaders had to face the same test. However two months after Maastricht subsidiarity took on a different hue for Major when, facing the Scottish National Party in a general election he leaped to the defense of the (British) "Union".

4 Canada and Quebec, for instance, the Czechs and the Slovaks are groping towards each other in search of a form of "sovereignty-association" acceptable to both parties, respecting distinct identities within a single national entity. By the time they find it, it may be too late.

5 For a clear exposition of the case for European parties, see Duverger, Maurice, *Vers des Partis Européens*, Le Monde, Jan. 25, 1992. We have noted that Duverger is a French MEP elected on an Italian list.

6 Lustiger, Jean-Marie, *Nous avons rendez-vous avec l'Europe*, Paris, Mame, 1991, p.113.

7 *Berliner Tageszeitung*, July 11, 1992.

8 Delors, Jacques, *Le nouveau Concert européen*, Paris, Editions Odile Jacob, 1992, p. 189 *et seq.*

9 Portugal has a similar if less prominent role, playing "Canada" to Spain's "America".

10 Madrid hosted the second Ibero-American summit, July 23-24, 1992.

11 Public aid from industrialized nations in 1991

Country	Billions of $	% of Economic output
USA	11.5	0.20
Japan	11.0	0.32
France	9.5	0.80
Germany	6.8	0.40
UK	3.2	0.32
Italy	2.9	0.25
Canada	2.6	0.45
Netherlands	2.5	0.88
Sweden	2.1	0.92

Country	Billions of $	% of Economic output
Denmark	1.2	0.96
Norway	1.2	1.14
Spain	1.2	1.23
Australia	1.1	0.38
Finland	0.9	0.76
Belgium	0.8	0.41
Switzerland	0.8	0.32
Austria	0.5	0.34
Portugal	0.2	0.28

Source: OECD

12 Hillenbrand, Martin J. "Afterword", in Jordan, Robert (ed.), *Europe and the Superpowers: Essays on European International Relations*, New York, St. Martin's Press, 1991. For Baker's speech, see "A new Europe, a new Atlanticism: architecture for a new era", in US Department of State, *Current Policy*, Nr 1233, December 1989.

13 France 3 Radio, June 29, 1992.

14 Speech at Bruges, October 17, 1989, *op.cit*, p.338.

APPENDICES

Appendix I

European Milestones

1492

	Moors driven from Spain.
March 30:	Jews expelled from Spain.
Oct. 12:	Columbus sets foot in the New World.

1914

June 28: Assassination of Archduke Ferdinand in Sarajevo sparks WWI.

1918

Nov. 11: European armistice.

1919

June 28: Treaty of Versailles.

1920

Jan. 10: Foundation of League of Nations at Geneva
(42 nations; US did not join).

1929

Great Depression begins.

1933

Oct. 14: Nazi Germany withdraws from LN.

1939

Sept. 3: France and UK declare war on Germany.

1941

Dec. 7: Pearl Harbor attacked by Japanese; US enters war.

1942

Jan. 20: Nazi Germany adopts "Final Solution" policy
(Holocaust for Jews, Gypsies, homosexuals).

1944

May 14:	Field Marshall Rommel's abortive peace plan envisages "United States of Europe".
June 6:	Normandy landings (Operation Overlord).
June 10:	Oradour massacre.
July 20:	Von Stauffenberg plot against Hitler fails.
Aug. 24:	Paris liberated.
Nov. 7:	Roosevelt re-elected US president.

1945

Jan. 17:	Disappearance of Raoul Wallenberg in Budapest.
May 8:	Victory in Europe.
June 26:	UN Charter signed by 51 nations.
Aug. 6:	Hiroshima.
Aug. 9:	Nagasaki.
Sept. 2:	Japanese surrender.

1946

March 16:	Churchill's "Iron Curtain" speech at Fulton, Missouri.
Sept. 19:	In Zurich speech, Winston Churchill proposes "United States of Europe" and creation of a "Council of Europe".

1947

Jan. 16:	United Europe Committee set up in London.
March 4:	France and UK defensive alliance.
March 12:	Truman doctrine pledges support for free peoples resisting subjugation by minorities or outside pressures.
June 5:	George Marshall, US, Secretary of State, proposes Program for European Recovery ("Marshall Plan").
July 17:	Reported death of Raoul Wallenberg in Lubyanka prison .
Aug. 15:	India, Pakistan independent.
Oct. 5:	Soviet bloc sets up Cominform for ideological unity, following rejection of Marshall AId.

1948

Jan. 1:	General Agreement on Tariffs and Trade enters into force. N, B, L create customs union ("Benelux").
Jan. 8:	CMEA set up in Moscow by ALB, BG, CS, H, PL, ROM and USSR
March 17:	Brussels Treaty between B, F, L, NL and UK.
April 1:	Berlin blockade begins, becoming fully effective June 24. Berlin airlift lasts 323 days.

April 16: OEEC established in Paris. US partner is European Co-operation Administration.

May 7-10: European Congress in The Hague proposes European Union and a College of Europe.

June 11: Vandenberg Resolution urges US Government to resist attack through individual or collective defense, paving way for North Atlantic Treaty.

Dec. 10: North Atlantic Treaty negotiations open in Washington.

1949

Jan. 8: Establishment of CMEA by seven East-bloc countries.

Jan. 28: The consultative council in Brussels decides to establish a Council of Europe.

Feb. 16: On a proposal from Ernest Bevin, UK foreign secretary, Strasbourg is selected as seat of the Council of Europe.

April 4: North Atlantic Treaty signed in Washington (10 countries)

May 5: Statutes of Council of Europe signed in London.

May 9: Berlin blockade lifted.

Aug. 9: Council of Europe inaugural session. Greece and Turkey invited to join.

Aug. 24: North Atlantic Treaty enters into force.

1950

May 9: French FM Robert Schuman proposes Franco-German pooling of coal and steel production. "Benelux" and Italy join.

June 2: UK refuses to join ECSC.

June 20: "Six" open ECSC negotiations in Paris.

June 25: North Korea attacks South Korea.

Aug. 11: Consultative Assembly adopts Churchill's suggestion of a European army.

Oct. 24: French premier René Pleven proposes European army.

Oct. 26: French Assembly adopts Pleven plan.

Oct. 27: In NATO France opposes German rearmament.

Nov. 4: European Convention on Human Rights (Council of Europe).

1951

March 15: Nordic Cultural Agreement (NCA) signed.

April 2: NATO's Allied Command Europe operational; Eisenhower Supreme Commander.

April 18: ECSC Treaty signed in Paris. (France signs for Saar).

July 28: European Convention relating to the Status of Refugees.

Sept. 14: US, UK and France seek inclusion of a democratic Germany, in a European and Atlantic Community.

1952

Feb. 18: Greece and Turkey join NATO.

March 4:	Nordic Council established.
May 27:	EDC treaty signed in Paris. Although not joining, the UK entered into a treaty with the Six providing for military aid in the event of an armed attack in Europe.
July 25:	ECSC Treaty enters into force.
Nov. 4:	General Eisenhower elected US President.

1953

Jan. 1:	First European tax: ECSC levy.
March 5:	Death of Stalin.
March 9:	Paul-Henri Spaak submits to Georges Bidault, president of ECSC Council, EDC draft treaty.
July 23:	Korean armistice signed at Panmunjon.
Nov. 28:	Six create intergovernmental committee to set up a European Political Community.
Dec. 11:	Council of Europe convention on equivalence of diplomas leading to admission to universities.

1954

July 21:	Geneva Armistice agreement on Indo-China.
Aug. 19:	Death of Alcide de Gasperi
Aug. 19-22:	Six reject EDC compromise put forward by French PM. Pierre Mendès-France.
Aug. 30:	French National Assembly defeats EDC treaty.
Sept. 28-: Oct. 3	London conference of Six plus US, UK, Canada recommends FRG be admitted to western alliance, with limits on arms production. Brussels Treaty extended to FRG and Italy. UK undertakes not to withdraw its troops from continental Europe.
Oct. 5:	Italy and Yugoslavia settle Trieste frontier dispute.
Oct. 22:	Modification to Brussels Treaty admits FRG and Italy and establishes WEU. Occupation of FRG terminated. Franco-German Agreement on European Statute for Saar.
Oct. 23:	NATO invites FRG to join; approves WEU military functions.
Nov. 10:	Protesting failure of EDC, Jean Monnet resigns from ECSC presidency. He is succeeded by René Mayer.
Dec. 12:	European Cultural Convention (Council of Europe).

1955

May 5:	Occupation regime in West Germany ends.
May 6:	WEU headquarters set up in London; FRG joins NATO.
May 7:	First meeting of WEU Council including FRG in Paris.
May 14:	USSR concludes Warsaw Treaty with ALB, BG, CS, GDR, H, PL and ROM.
May 15:	Austrian State Treaty ends four-power occupation.

June 1-2:	Messina conference of the Six decides to extend European integration to the whole economy and nuclear energy.
July 5:	First meeting of WEU parliamentary assembly.
July 16:	Volunteers Law in Bundestag, recreating German army. Bundesrat approves July 22.
Oct. 23:	Saar electorate rejects European Statute, joins FRG.

1956

May 29-30:	Six receive Spaak report and decide to negotiate European Economic Community (EEC) and an atomic energy community (EURATOM).
June 26:	EEC-EURATOM negotiations open in Brussels.
July 17:	OEEC study group for a free trade area (Maudling committee).
Oct. 31:	Suez intervention by France and UK; Hungarian uprising.
Dec. 15:	Council of Europe convention on equivalence of periods of university study.

1957

Feb. 20:	Six decide conditions for associating former colonies and protectorates with EEC.
March 25:	Six sign EEC and EURATOM treaties in Rome. The parliaments ratify treaties between July and November.
April 8:	Suez canal reopened.
Oct. 4:	Soviet Sputnik launched.
Oct. 7:	International Atomic Energy Agency set up in Vienna.

1958

Jan. 1:	Rome treaties enter into force. Commission presidents are Walter Hallstein and Louis Armand.
March 19-21:	First session, in Strasbourg, of European parliamentary Assembly of the Six; Schuman president.
May 13:	Insurrection in Algiers.
June 1:	De Gaulle invited to head French government.
July 2:	EEC provisions on social security for migrant workers.
July 3-11:	Stresa conference lays groundwork for a European market in agriculture.
Sept. 28:	French Vth Republic constitution approved; colonies (excepted Guinea) approve French Community.
Dec. 10:	Boris Pasternak Nobel Prize for literature.
Dec. 15:	Free trade area negotiations fail in OEEC.
Dec. 21:	Ch. De Gaulle succeeds René Coty as French president.

1959

Jan. 1:   First reduction of EEC customs tariffs and quota increase. Fidel Castro assumes power in Cuba.
Feb. 19:   Cyprus independant.
March 12:   Hawaii 50th US state.
June 8:   De Gaulle refuses NATO installations on French soil.
Aug. 19:   CENTO founded.
Sept. 15:   Kruschev visits US.
Oct. 4:   Soviet Lunik III photographs far side of moon.
Dec. 1:   Antarctic Treaty reserves polar continent for scientific research.
Dec. 14:   CMEA Charter adopted in Sofia. Council of Europe convention on the academic recognition of university qualifications.

1960

Jan. 4:   Stockholm Convention creates EFTA in Geneva.
Jan. 21:   John Kennedy US President.
May 11:   Six create European Social Fund.
May 12:   EEC Council speeds up integration.
July 1:   EFTA treaty enters into force.
Sept. 5:   De Gaulle proposes regular political summit meetings of Six and referendum on Europe of Nations.
Dec. 14:   OEEC becomes OECD, with Canada and US as members.

1961

Feb. 10-11:   First summit of the Six meets in Paris.
April 12:   USSR orbits first man in space.
April 14:   Bay of Pigs fiasco.
April 21:   Dirk Stikker NATO Secretary General.
July 9:   Signature of treaty of association of Greece with EEC.
July 18:   Second European summit, in Bad Godesberg, proposes a Union of European States.
July 31:   Ireland applies for EEC membership.
Aug. 9-10:   UK and Denmark apply for EEC membership.
Aug. 13:   Berlin wall erected.
Sept. 30:   OECD convention enters into force.
Oct. 18:   European Social Charter (Council of Europe).
Oct. 28:   Yugoslavia becomes associate member of OECD.
Nov. 2:   Draft treaty on an indissoluble union of European states (Foucher Plan) submitted by France.
Nov. 8:   UK/EEC negotiations commence.
Dec. 9:   USSR breaks diplomatic relations with Albania, which is expelled from CMEA and WTO.

Dec. 15:	CMEA adopts Basic Principles of the International Socialist Division of Labor. Austria, Sweden and Switzerland apply for EEC associate membership.

1962

Jan. 14:	"Marathon" negotiation "stops the clock". EEC council decides to institute second stage of common market, effective Jan. 1. CAP principles adopted, FEOGA set up.
Jan. 18:	New French proposal for political union rejected.
Jan. 30:	CAP enters into force.
Feb. 27:	Council of Europe launches nature conservation action.
March 7:	EEC/US tariff agreement signed.
March 14:	Geneva disarmament conference.
March 19:	Evian Agreements on an independant Algeria.
April 11:	Europe/Africa trade agreement signed in Brussels.
May 15:	De Gaulle rejects supranationality. Five MRP ministers resign.
May 18:	Portugal seeks negotiations with EEC.
June 7:	Mongolia joins CMEA.
June 26:	Six agree on aid to Africa. EEC standing committee on agricultural structures set up.
Dec. 8:	Movement of capital freed within Six.
Dec. 17:	Council of Europe convention on the liability of hotel-keepers.
Dec. 20:	EEC and Associated States sign cooperation convention.

1963

Jan. 14:	De Gaulle vetoes UK admission to EEC.
Jan. 22:	Franco-German Treaty of Friendship.
Jan. 27:	Brussels negotiations break down not only with UK but also with EFTA countries seeking associate status.
May 4:	EEC Council approves agreement with Associated States.
June:	European Convention on Human Rights extended.
July 20:	Yaoundé convention on EEC/African association is signed by 17 African countries and Madagascar.
Aug. 5:	UK, US and USSR sign nuclear test ban treaty in Moscow.
Oct. 17:	Ludwig Erhard FRG Chancellor.
Oct. 22:	CMEA sets up International Bank for Economic Cooperation.
Nov. 22:	President Kennedy assassinated; Lyndon Johnson US President.
Dec. 16-23:	Second agricultural "marathon" on milk, milk products, meat and rice.

1964

Jan. 1:	IBEC begins operations in CMEA countries.
April 28:	Japan's entry into OECD marks re-emergence as major industrial power.

June 3:   Protocol to European convention on university admission.
Aug. 1:   Manlio Brosio NATO Secretary General.
Oct. 16:   Communist China explodes atomic bomb.
Dec. 12-15: Third agricultural "marathon" approves Mansholt plan on cereal prices, effective July 1967.

1965

Jan. 19:   Albania refuses invitation to rejoin COMECON and WTO.
Jan. 27:   Death of Sir Winston Churchill.
March 31:   EEC Commission puts forward proposals for financing CAP, including supranational powers for Commission to raise levies.
May 25:   Meeting in Vienna, EFTA ministers call for closer ties between EFTA and EEC.
June 15:   France opposes EEC Commission's proposals for direct CAP funding from levies.
July 1:   France walks out on Hallstein CAP proposals; boycotts Council meetings.

1966

Jan. 29:   Luxembourg "compromise". France returns to table, subject to unanimity rule when a member state's "vital interests" are at stake.
May 11:   CAP rules agreed. Six decide to reach customs union by July 1, 1968.
Dec. 31:   EFTA completes abolition of tariffs on industrial goods.

1967

Jan. 31:   Romania agrees to exchange ambassadors with FRG.
Feb. 9:   First steps toward harmonization of turnover taxes, leading to EC VAT system in 1970.
May 10-11: Denmark and UK, joined by Ireland, again apply to EEC.
July 1:   New joint EC commission, with 14 members, instituted under presidency of Jean Rey (B): executives of ECSC, EEC and EURATOM merged.
July 21:   Norway applies for EEC membership.
Nov. 29:   De Gaulle's second press conference veto of EEC enlargement.
Dec. 19:   EC enlargement negotiations fail again in Brussels.

1968

Jan. 19:   US/USSR nuclear non-proliferation treaty.
May 6:   European Water Charter (Council of Europe).
July 1:   EC customs union (common external tariff) complete. NNP treaty signed in Moscow by UK, US and USSR, open to all countries.

July 26:   Cooperation agreement between EEC and Kenya, Uganda, Tanganyika.
July 29:   Free circulation of workers in EC countries.
Aug. 20:   "Prague Spring" ended by WTO invasion of Czechoslovakia (Romania refusing to participate).
Dec. 18:   Mansholt Plan to modernize agricultural structures in ten years.

1969

Jan. 21:   Richard Nixon US President.
Jan. 28:   Finland joins OECD.
April 28:   Following referendum failure De Gaulle resigns.
June 16:   Pompidou elected French President.
July 21:   Neil Armstrong first man on moon.
July 29:   New Yaoundé Convention of association between EEC and African and Malagasy states.
Aug. 10:   FF 11% devaluation, leading to monetary compensation system for trade in agricultural products.
Oct. 23:   Nixon announces Vietnam withdrawal.
December: At Hague summit French President Georges Pompidou lifts opposition to EEC enlargement. Six agree to move to final EEC phase with agricultural rules and direct levy.

1970

March 1:   Iceland joins EFTA.
March 5:   Entry into force of NPT.
March 26:   Talks between France, UK and US on status of and access to Berlin.
April 16:   Strategic arms limitations treaty (SALT) talks open in Vienna.
April 22:   Treaty signed in Luxembourg permits financing of the EC through its own resources (customs duties plus share of VAT) and extends oversight powers of European parliament.
May 6:   First case brought by Commission before Court of Justice against Council of Ministers (road transport).
May 27:   NATO proposes exploratory contacts for a European security conference and balanced force reductions.
June 30:   Negotiations open in Luxembourg with 4 EC applicants (DK, IRL, N, UK).
July 2:   EC Commission membership reduced form 14 to 9.
July 10:   CMEA sets up International Investment Bank (IIB).
Aug. 12:   FRG and USSR sign non-aggression treaty in Moscow.
Nov. 2:   Second SALT session, in Helsinki.
Nov. 10:   Negotiations in Brussels between EEC and other European countries on a free-trade agreement.
Dec. 4:   European Parliament rejects EURATOM budget- the first exercice of the Assembly's powers.

Dec. 7:   Warsaw Treaty normalizes FRG-Polish relations.

1971

March: Community-wide demonstrations against Mansholt Plan.
May 19:   First EEC agricultural price support compensatory payments (to FRG and NL) for the strength of their floating currencies.
June 7:   Australia joins OECD.
Aug. 20:   NATO Defence Planning Committee transfers NAVSOUTH from Malta to Naples.
Oct. 1:   Joseph Luns NATO Secretary General.
Oct. 28:   UK parliament approves EEC entry in principle, subject to satisfactory terms (356 for, 244 against, 22 abst.).
Dec. 21:   Signature in East Berlin of Treaty between FRG and GDR.

1972

Jan. 22:   Denmark, Ireland and UK sign EEC accession treaties.
Feb.21-29:   Nixon in Peking.
March 14:   Sicco Mansholt (NL) EC Commission President.
March 26:   US and USSR sign SALT and ABMT in Moscow.
April 23:   French referendum approves EEC enlargement (68% for).
April 24:   Monetary "snake in the tunnel" limits currency fluctuations to 2.25% in relation to the dollar.
May 31:   NATO agrees CSCE talks, proposes exploration of MBFR.
June 3:   Four Occupying Powers sign supplementary Quadripartite Agreement on Berlin.
July 12:   Cuba joins CMEA.
July 22:   Brussels tariff agreement with the Five EFTA countries not applicants for EEC membership.
Sept. 26:   Norwegian referendum rejects EEC accession.
Oct. 19:   First EC summit of the "Nine", in Paris.
Nov. 21:   SALT II opens in Geneva.
Nov. 22:   CSCE preparatory talks open in Helsinki.
Dec. 21:   Basic Treaty between FRG and GDR signed in East Berlin.

1973

Jan. 1:   EEC enlargement. Denmark and UK leave EFTA.
Jan. 5:   François-Xavier Ortoli (France) EC Commission President.
Jan. 15:   First EC Council meeting following enlargement.
March 19:   200,000 tons of butter sold to USSR below CAP intervention price.
March 28:   First Ministerial Conference of European Ministers of the Environment (Council of Europe, Vienna).
April 28-May 2: Longest CAP price-setting marathon.
May 29:   New Zealand joins OECD.

June 8:	CSCE preparatory talks successfully concluded. CMEA Cooperation Agreement with Finland.
July 3:	CSCE first phase in Helsinki. Foreign Ministers discuss three "baskets" of topics.
July 19:	EC adopts environmental action program.
Sept. 18:	CSCE second phase in Geneva.
Oct. 5:	Finnish free-trade agreement with EEC.
Oct. 6-24:	Yom Kippur war.
Oct. 30:	MBFR talks in Vienna.
Dec. 14-15:	Copenhagen summit of Nine agrees more frequent meetings.

1974

Jan. 22-24:	Agricultural "marathon" of the Nine.
Feb. 28:	Labour wins UK election; Harold Wilson again PM.
April 25:	Military coup in Portugal.
June 19:	NATO Declaration on Atlantic Relations in Ottawa.
June 21:	In Sofia, CMEA approves amendments to Charter and five-year integration plan.
July 23:	President Nixon resigns; Gerald Ford US President.
Oct. 30:	Political Prisoners' Day created in USSR.
Dec. 9-10:	Second EC summit of the Nine agrees to meet three times a year as the European Council; proposes election of Assembly members by direct suffrage; launches ERDF.

1975

Feb. 28:	Lomé IEEC/ACP convention signed.
April 21:	Community (except UK) replaces the $-standard by EUA, with fluctuating external value.
May 31:	ESRO and ELDO merge to form ESA, with 11 members.
June 5:	In referendum UK votes to remain in EC.
July 6:	Comoro Islands independent of France (except Mayotte).
Aug. 1:	CSCE Final Act, including human rights and confidence-building measures, signed in Helsinki by 35 states.
Nov. 22:	Death of Francisco Franco.
Dec. 10:	EC summit launches a program in education and sets 1979 for direct elections to European Parliament.

1976

April 1:	EEC/ACP convention in force.
April 7:	EFTA Industrial Development Fund for Portugal.
July 27:	EEC opens membership negotiations with Greece.
Sept. 26:	European Council signs instruments for the election of members of Parliament by direct universal suffrage.
Dec. 8:	NATO Defence Planning Committee expresses concern at WTO's growing military strength.

Dec. 10:   NATO rejects WTO proposal to renounce first use of nuclear weapons.

1977

Jan. 1:   200- mile fishing zone declared around EC coasts.
Jan. 6:   Roy Jenkins (UK) EC Commission president.
Jan. 18:   EC agreements with Egypt, Jordan, Syria.
Jan. 21:   Jimmy Carter US President.
March 28:   Portugal applies for EC membership.
June 15:   Community bond issues proposed by Commission.
July 1:   Customs union complete between Six and Three. EEC/EFTA free trade agreements in force.
July 28:   Spanish application for EC membership.
August 3:   Death of Mgr. Makarios of Cyprus.
Oct.4-Mar.9, 1978:   CSCE meeting in Belgrade.
Nov. 22:   Davignon plan for ECSC restructuring (steel crisis).
Nov. 24:   Council of Europe convention on legal status of migrant workers.
Dec. 31:   End of transitory period for aligning agricultural prices for 3 new EC members.

1978

March 9:   EEC announces active role in CSCE (enhancing EC political dimension).
June 29:   Vietnam joins CMEA.
July 7:   France and FRG propose EMS at Bremen summit.
Oct. 17:   Portuguese negotiations open.
Nov. 23:   Liechtenstein joins Council of Europe.
Dec. 5:   EMS agreed at Brussels summit.

1979

March 13:   EMS begins with ECU mechanism.
April 6:   CAP uses ECU.
May 8:   EC-Greek Treaty of Athens.
June 7-10:   First direct elections of 410 members of EC Assembly.
June 18:   Carter and Brezhnev sign SALT II in Vienna (never ratified).
June 26:   EFTA Agreement with Spain.
June 28:   Peoples Democratic Republic of Yemen ("South Yemen") granted observer status in CMEA.
July 17:   First elected Assembly meets. Simone Veil (F) elected President.
Oct. 19:   Council of Europe Convention on the Conservation of European wildlife and natural habitats.
Oct. 31:   Lomé II signed between EEC and 58 African, Caribbean and Pacific nations (ACP).
Nov. 4:   Hostage crisis begins in Teheran.

Nov. 29-30:   At Dublin summit Margaret Thatcher calls for reduction of UK contribution to EC budget.
Dec. 13:   Assembly rejects EC budget and calls for CAP revision.
Dec. 27:   USSR invades Afghanistan.

1980

April 28:   Luxembourg summit fails over agricultural budget and UK contribution to EC budget.
May 4:   Death of President Tito of Yugoslavia.
May 20:   Council of Europe convention on custody of children.
May 30:   Council of Ministers agrees on two-thirds reduction of UK contribution; raises agricultural prices 5%.
Aug. 31:   Gdansk Agreements recognize Polish trade union solidarity.
Sept. 22:   Iran-Iraq war.
Oct. 30:   "Manifest crisis" declared in steel industry. Quotas applied. (Renewed until end of 1984).
Nov. 11:   CSCE Follow-up Conference opens in Madrid.
Dec. 23:   EP adopts EC budget over French and German objections.

1981

Jan. 1:   Greece becomes tenth member of EEC.
Jan. 6:   Gaston Thorn (Luxembourg) EC Commission President.
Jan. 20:   Ronald Reagan US President.
May 10:   François Mitterrand French President.
May 13:   Attempted assassination of Pope John Paul II.
Oct. 6:   Assassination of Egyptian President Anwar Sadat.
Nov. 30:   INF negotiations between US and USSR open in Geneva.
Dec. 2:   Spain applies to join NATO.
Dec. 13:   Martial law in Poland.

1982

Jan. 19:   Piet Dankert (NL) succeeds Simone Veil (F) as EC Assembly President.
Feb. 23:   Greenland referendum: withdrawal from EEC.
April 2-May 14:   Falklands conflict.
May 18:   Agricultural prices set over UK opposition.
May 24:   Further reduction in UK contribution to EC budget.
May 30:   Spain joins NATO.
June 22:   Ten denounce US trade policy and protectionism.
June 29:   START talks open in Geneva, in succession to SALT.
Nov. 10:   Death of Leonid Brezhnev.
Dec. 2:   Felipe Gonzalez Spanish Prime Minister.

1983

Jan. 25:	EEC fisheries policy ("Blue Europe") achieved after six years of negotiation.
March 23:	SDI announced by President Reagan.
June 19:	Stuttgart Summit adopts Declaration on European Union.
Sept. 14:	EC Assembly adopts proposal for a European Union.
Oct. 25:	Grenada invasion.
Dec. 8:	Third EEC/ACP convention signed.
Dec. 13:	New civilian government and constitution in Turkey.

1984

Feb. 9:	Death of Yuri Andropov, succeeded by Konstantin Chernenko
Feb. 28:	EC adopts ESPRIT research program in information technology.
April 9:	EURATOM launches controlled thermonuclear fusion research project at Culham, UK (JET).
April 18:	US proposes treaty banning chemical weapons.
June 14 & 17:	European elections. Pierre Pflimlin (F) elected Assembly president on July 24.
June 25 & 26:	UK budget contribution to EC agreed. Lord Carrington (UK) NATO Secretary General.
June 27:	WEU abolishes limits imposed on FRG for conventional weapons.
Sept. 26:	UK-China agreement on Hong Kong transfer in 1997.
Oct. 26:	First WEU Council at which ministers of defense join FM's as part of WEU reactivation. Rome declaration on political aims and institutional reform.
Nov. 6:	President Reagan re-elected.
Dec. 8:	"Lomé III" (ACP) agreement signed in Togo.

1985

Jan. 1:	First European passports issued. Jacques Delors president of EC Commission.
Jan. 14:	Addressing EP, Delors proposes abolition of internal frontiers by Jan. 1, 1993.
Jan. 28:	Council of Europe convention on protection of individuals in automatic processing of personal data.
March 11:	Death of Konstantin Chernenko, succeeded by Mikhail Gorbachev.
March 19:	8th ECHR protocol signed in Vienna.
March 30:	European Council accepts IMP's and agreement on entry of Portugal and Spain.
April 17:	France proposes EUREKA technology program, open to non-member states.
June 14:	Commission White Paper on 1992 achievement of internal market.

June 28-29:	Milan Summit approves EUREKA. Political union proposed by majority vote (UK opposed).
July 2:	ESA spacecraft Giotto launched.
Aug. 19:	Council of Europe convention on spectator violence at sports events.
Oct. 3:	Council of Europe convention for the protection of the architectural heritage of Europe.
Nov. 6:	In Hannover 18 countries adopt EUREKA charter and 10 projects.
Nov. 21:	At Geneva summit Gorbachev and Reagan agree on 50% reduction of strategic forces.
Dec. 4:	SEA signature strengthens treaties, restores qualified majority voting, establishes political cooperation.

1986

Jan. 1:	Portugal and Spain join EEC. WEU agencies established for arms control and disarmament; security and defense; armaments. Finland full member of EFTA.
Jan. 20:	France and UK decide to build Channel Tunnel.
Feb. 16:	Mario Soares (Soc) elected president of Portugal.
Feb. 17:	Nine countries sign SEA.
Feb. 28:	Last three EC members sign SEA. Assassination of Swedish PM Olof Palme.
March 12:	Spanish referendum supports continued NATO membership.
March 14:	European spacecraft Giotto flies by Halley's comet.
March 16:	Swiss electorate rejects UN membership.
March 20:	Jacques Chirac (neo-Gaullist) French Prime Minister under Socialist President Mitterrand (*cohabitation*).
April 26:	Chernobyl.
May 21:	CD gains in Dutch elections.
June 8:	Kurt Waldheim (Con) elected Austrian president.
June 11:	Joint Declaration by EP, Council and Commission against racism and xenophobia.
June 16:	Franz Vranitzky Austrian PM.
June 22:	Socialists win Spanish elections.
Oct. 11-12:	Reykjavik Summit ends in disagreement.
Nov. 1:	Sandoz fire pollutes Rhine.
Nov. 4:	Third CSCE follow-up conference in Vienna.

1987

Jan. 20:	Sir Henry Plumb (UK) EC Assembly president.
Jan. 29:	EC and US agreement on US corn sales to Spain. MBFR talks resume in Vienna.
Feb. 17:	NATO-WTO talks in Vienna on conventional force reductions
March 18:	EC-COMECON talks, Geneva.

April 14:	Turkey applies for EC membership.
May 9:	Nationalists (CD) win Maltese elections.
June 11:	Conservatives win UK elections.
June 19:	Chancellor Kohl proposes Franco-German brigade. Visit to Budapest by Marcelino Oreja, Secretary General of the Council of Europe.
July 1:	Single European Act enters into force.
July 22:	Gorbachev declares Soviet readiness to eliminate intermediate-range nuclear weapons.
Aug. 20:	WEU considers joint minesweeping in the Gulf.
Oct. 26:	WEU Ministerial Council adopts The Hague "platform" on European security interests.
Nov. 10:	The 13 ESA members, except UK, agree long-term funding of Ariane-5, Hermes and Colombus projects.
Nov. 26:	Warsaw Pact approves proposed US-Soviet INF Treaty.
Dec. 8-10:	Reagan-Gorbachev summit in Washington. They sign INF treaty eliminating land-based intermediate-range nuclear missiles; agree measures to monitor nuclear explosions at test sites; pledge cuts in strategic arms in line with 1972 ABM Treaty.
Dec. 11:	NATO welcomes INF Treaty. FRG and UK sign bilateral agreements permitting on-site inspections of missile bases, in accordance with INF Treaty verifications.
Dec. 13:	CVP lose seats in Belgian elections.
Dec. 17:	Milos Jakes General Secretary of Czech Communist Party.

1988

Jan. 22:	Franco-German Brigade agreed.
Feb. 13:	Brussels summit agrees to revise EC financing, setting limits on agricultural expenditure.
April 14:	Geneva agreements on Afghanistan.
May 3:	Hungarian Foreign Secretary Gyala Horn visits Council of Europe.
May 5:	Additional protocol to the European Social Charter (Oct. 18, 1961).
May 12:	In Stockholm Delors proposes EC Charter of workers' rights.
June 13:	EC finance ministers agree plan to free movements of capital.
June 25:	Luxembourg Joint Declaration establishes official EC-CMEA relations.
Aug. 20:	Iran and Iraq ceasefire.
Sept. 20:	Thatcher's "Bruges Speech" at College of Europe, favoring a Europe of the nations over supranationalism.
Sept. 21-27:	UNESCO 4th conference of Ministers of Education (Europe Region), Paris.
Sept. 26:	EC signs trade and cooperation agreement with Hungary.
Nov. 7:	George Bush elected US President.
Nov. 14:	Portugal and Spain join WEU.

Nov. 16:	San Marino joins Council of Europe.
Dec. 7:	Gorbachev announces unilateral conventional force reductions to UN General Assembly.
Dec. 8:	Failure of GATT negotiations on agricultural products; US threatens higher tariffs.

1989

Jan. 11:	Hungary's parliament allows independent parties.
Jan. 18:	EP transfers some activities to Brussels; France protests.
Jan. 19:	CSCE Vienna mandates new conventional forces reduction (CFR) negotiations.
Jan. 21:	George Bush US President.
Feb. 6:	In Warsaw, round-table fails between Government, Solidarity and the Catholic Church.
Feb. 11:	Hungarian CP endorses multi-party system.
Feb. 14:	*Fatwa* on Salman Rushdie.
Feb. 15:	USSR completes Afghanistan withdrawal.
March 6:	New CSCE negotiations in Vienna on CFR. WEU seminar on public perceptions of European defense.
April 5:	Government and Solidarity agree to legalize union and hold open elections.
April 17:	Solidarity re-registered.
April 20:	Council of Europe convention on insider trading.
May 2:	Hungary dismantles barbed wire along Austrian Border.
May 5:	Finland becomes 24th member of Council of Europe. Council of Europe convention on transfrontier television.
May 8:	Hungarian leader Janos Kadar is ousted.
May 15-18:	Sino-Soviet Summit normalizes relations.
May 17:	Poland recognizes the Roman Catholic Church.
May 30:	Council of Europe Conference of European Ministers responsible for Sport, Reykjavik. Hungarian CP concedes former Premier Imre Nagy was illegally executed for 1956 uprising. NATO summit decides postponement of nuclear forces in Germany and CFE speed-up.
June 1:	Spain joins EMS.
June 4:	Solidarity victory in Polish parliamentary elections.
June 12-15:	Gorbachev visits FRG.
June 15-18:	European Parliament elections. Soc./Lab. largest group. FF gains seats in Irish elections.
June 16:	Imre Nagy reburied with full honors in Budapest.
June 19:	START talks resume in Geneva.
June 27:	European Council in Madrid decides to start first stage of EMU on July, 1990.
July:	WEU Assembly delegation to Moscow initiates annual exchange with Supreme Soviet.

July 4:   Gorbachev visit to France.
July 6:   Gorbachev addresses Council of Europe Assembly, calling for "common European home". Death of Janos Kadar; rehabilitation of Imre Nagy.
July 14:   Western economic Summit (G7) in Paris. French revolution bicentennial. EC to coordinate aid to Hungary and Poland.
July 16:   Peseta joins EMS.
July 17:   Austria applies for EC membership.
July 18:   General Wojciech Jaruzelski elected Polish President.
July 25:   Jaruzelski invites Solidarity to join coalition.
July 29:   Mieczyslaw Rakowski Head of Polish Communist Party, succeeding Jaruzelski.
August: West German diplomatic missions in East Berlin, Budapest and Prague swamped with East Germans seeking to emigrate.
Aug. 24:   Tadeusz Mazowiecki (Solidarity) elected first non-Communist Polish PM since WWII.
Sept. 10:   Hungary suspends agreement to block passage of East Germans to West, opens frontier with Austria.
Sept. 12:   Manifesto of New Forum, opposition group in GDR.
Sept. 19:   EC and Poland sign trade and cooperation treaty. Hungarian Government and opposition agree on free elections.
Sept. 26:   EEC Commission proposes $600m economic aid to Hungary and Poland.
October: British Chancellor (Finance Minister) Nigel Lawson resigns over Premier Thatcher's refusal to allow UK to join EMS.
Oct. 3-4:   Ten thousand East Germans try to board refugee trains on their way from Prague to FRG.
Oct. 7:   Hungarian CP under Karoly Gross reconstiues itself as Socialist Party.
Oct. 7-8:   Protest marches in East Berlin, Dresden and Leipzig broken up by security forces. Hungary's CP splits into liberal (Socialist) and orthodox (H. Soc. Workers') wings
Oct. 12:   Ladislav Adamec Czech Prime Minister. Answering Thatcher, Delors sets out his vision of Europe before College of Europe, Bruges.
Oct. 18:   Erich Honecker, GDR CP leader, replaced by Egon Krenz.
Oct. 23:   Hungary independent Republic under new constitution.
Oct. 25:   In Helsinki, Gorbachev pronounces demise of Brezhnev Doctrine guaranteeing leading role of communism in East Europe.
Oct. 29:   Petar T Mladenov becomes Bulgarian Government and Communist Party leader in succession to Todar I Zhivkov.
Nov. 7-11:   Council of Europe Sintra (Portugal) symposium on language learning and teaching methodology for citizenship in a multinational Europe.
Nov. 9:   Berlin Wall breached. ECF creates European Foundations Centre.

Nov. 10:   UNESCO General Conference calls for feasibility study of a University of the Peoples of Europe and strengthening of CEPES.
Nov. 13:   WEU Institute for security studies set up in Paris at seat of Assembly. Departing GDR Finance Minister Ernst Hofner reveals budget deficit of 130 billion marks.
Nov. 14:   Bulgarian CP offers reinstatement to eleven dissidents. Czech government eases restrictions on foreign travel.
Nov. 15:   Solidarity leader Lech Walesa addresses joint session of Congress, asks US help for Poland's economy.
Nov. 16:   Hungary and Poland adhere to European Cultural Convention and Council of Europe cultural cooperation. Hungary applies for Council of Europe membership. Protocol to convention on European pharmacopoeia.
Nov. 17:   P. Mladenov Bulgarian President.
Nov. 18:   Mitterrand calls EC "summit" in Paris to discuss Eastern Europe and creation of a European development bank.
Nov. 19:   Police brutality in Prague spurs creation of opposition group Civic Forum.
Nov. 20:   Hans Modrow GDR Prime Minister.
Nov. 24:   Karel Urbanek succeeds Milos Jakes as head of Czech CP.
Nov. 26:   Hungarian voters reject election timetable of socialists (former CP), forcing abandonment of plan to elect first President while Socialists control government.
Nov. 27:   Politburo elite living conditions arouse GDR anger. Russian Orthodox leader Juveneras of Kolumma meets John Paul II in Rome to discuss Ukrainian Catholic Church.
Nov. 28:   Helmut Kohl proposes "confederative structure" for the two Germanys. GDR reaction cool.
Nov. 29-Dec. 1: Gorbachev visit to Italy and Vatican.
Dec. 4-5:   Thousands of East Germans cross Czechoslovakia to FRG.
Dec. 7:   Marian Calfa Czechoslovak Prime Minister.
Dec. 9:   Gregor Gysi chairman of GDR CP.
Dec. 10:   Czech President Gustav Husak resigns. Opposition assumes majority role in new government.
Dec. 12:   In Berlin, US Secretary of State James Baker outlines 4-point plan for German reunification.
Dec. 13:   Calfa heads predominantly non-Communist government. In Bulgaria, Zhivkov is expelled from Communist party.
Dec. 15:   In Timisoara, western Romania, demonstrators prevent arrest of a Hungarian minority priest Tokes. Jugoslav CP proposes free elections. Opposition rally in Sofia. Czechoslovak Defense Minister proposes dismantling defenses on FRG border.
Dec. 16:   Bush meets Mitterrand, President of France and EEC Council, on St Martin to discuss Eastern Europe.
Dec. 16-17:   Security forces fire on demonstrators in Timisoara.

Dec. 17:	President Nicolae Ceaucescu declares state of emergency in western Romania. West German President Richard von Weisäcker visits GDR, meeting premier Hans Modrow and church leaders.
Dec. 19:	Helmut Kohl visits GDR.
Dec. 20:	Lithuanian CP declares independence from Moscow.
Dec. 21:	EEC ministers reach anti-trust agreement. In Romania revolt spreads to the capital Bucarest.
Dec. 22:	Ceaucescu flees Bucarest. Corneliu Manescu announces formation of Romanian National Salvation Front. Army joins uprising. US and USSR recognize new government. Brandenburg Gate is reopened through the Berlin Wall.
Dec. 24:	Ion Iliescu Romanian President, Petre Roman Prime Minister.
Dec. 25:	Trial and execution of Nicolae and Elena Ceaucescu.
Dec. 28:	Alexander Dubcek Czechoslovak Parliament Speaker.
Dec. 29:	Vaclav Havel elected Czechoslovak President.
Dec. 31:	Mitterrand proposes European Confederation.

1990

Jan. 16:	Bulgarian government negotiates with opposition.
Jan. 23:	Yugoslav CP gives up monopoly on power. Party Congress breaks up as Slovenia walks out. In Azerbaijan 3 Soviet soldiers killed: parliament threatens to secede from USSR. GDR CP purges former leaders, including Egon Krenz. Opposition demonstrations in Ulan Bator, Mongolia.
Jan. 24:	Public protest in Bucarest that leaders of NSF are "communists with masks".
Jan. 25:	Speaking in Warsaw, Czechoslovak President Vaclav Havel proposes union between Poland, Czechoslovakia and Hungary.
Jan. 26:	Dumitru Mazilu, vice-president of Romania's ruling Council of National Salvation Front (NSF), resigns, charging "Stalinist practices" persist in Romanian government. In Bulgaria, CP relinquishes control of army and police. Miklos Nemeth, Prime Minister of Hungary, addresses Council of Europe Assembly.
Jan. 28:	Ethnic Albanians in Kosovo, Jugoslavia, seek greater freedom from Serbia and free elections.
Jan. 29:	Polish CP votes to disband. Social Democratic Party (SDP) founded to replace it. A breakaway group, led by Tadeusz Fiszbach, founds Union of Social Democracy (USD). In Bucarest, Romanians rally against new rulers.
Jan. 30:	Bulgarian opposition declines powersharing.
Jan. 31:	Bush proposes mutual reductions of conventional Soviet and US forces in Europe. Gorbachev clears way for German reunification. Poland applies for Council of Europe membership.
Feb. 1:	GDR premier proposes neutral reunited Germany with Berlin as capital. FRG insists on continued NATO membership. Roma-

nia's Council of National Salvation agrees to give up power monopoly and join with 29 other political parties in coalition. EEC Commission proposes associate status for PL, H, GDR, BG, CS, ROM and YU, subject to commitment to human rights, multiparty system and movement to a market economy.

Feb. 2:   Bulgarian Government resigns. UDR (13 opposition parties) declines to join government. CP leader Mladenev is replaced by Alexandar Lilor but remains head of state. Soviet FM urges international referendum on German unity. Azerbaijainis and Armenians begin peace talks in Riga, Latvia, under Baltic mediation and without Moscow authorities. President F.W. de Klerk of SA lifts ban on African National Congress (ANC), promises prompt release of Nelson Mandela.

Feb. 4:   Silvia Brucan, veteran communist, resigns from Romanian leadership. 100,000 rally in Moscow streets for end to CP power monopoly.

Feb. 7:   FRG sets up committee for a common currency with GDR. Yugoslavia applies for Council of Europe membership. Baker's speech on New Europe, Prague.

Feb. 10:   Nelson Mandela freed in South Africa.

Feb. 11:   Split in Bulgarian CP gives rise to Alternative Socialist Party.

Feb. 13:   Soviet Union accepts US proposal to reduce troops in central Europe. The 4 occupying powers and 2 Germanys agree on German unification talks.

Feb. 14:   Poland demands a role in German unity talks. Polish foreign minister calls for reunited Germany to remain in NATO. Bonn approves major aid for GDR.

Feb. 15:   Government and CP leaders resign in Soviet Tadzhikstan. Latvian parliament votes to work for independence.

Feb. 16:   In USSR, ethnic violence spreads to Uzbekistan. US/USSR agreement on flights over Bering Strait. Romanian Defense Minister Nicolae Militaru resigns. Poland demands border guarantees before German reunification.

Feb. 21:   Czech President Vaclav Havel, addressing Congress, calls on US "paradoxically" to help USSR on road to democracy. Bucarest claims secret police disbanded.

Feb. 24:   Multi-party elections in Lithuania give first Soviet anti-Communist majority. Hungarian Foreign Minister suggests joining political arm of NATO.

Feb. 25:   Free election in Moldavia (USSR).

Feb. 27:   New Forum declares its GDR role eclipsed by Bonn's ascendency. Poland renews diplomatic ties with Israel.

March 4:   Direct elections for a new legislature of Ukraine.

March 11:   Lithuanian parliament declares independence. Patricio Aylwin replaces Gustavo Pinochet as President of Chile.

March 13:	Soviet parliament votes greater powers for presidency. Gorbachev calls Lithuania's independence declaration "illegitimate".
March 14:	German unity "2+4" talks in Bonn.
March 18:	Conservatives win GDR elections under Lothar de Maizière. First free elections since 1940 in Latvia and Estonia.
March 19:	Soviet local elections. Opposition majorities elected in Moscow, Leningrad, Kiev. Soviet pressure on Lithuania increases.
March 21:	Namibia independent.
March 25:	Free elections in Georgia, USSR. Free elections in Hungary won by UDF.
April 3:	Bulgaria adopts legislation for free elections. Mladenov elected to newly-created presidency. CP renamed Bulgarian Socialist Party (BSP).
April 8:	Conservatives win Hungarian elections.
April 10:	Soviet Union accepts a united Germany in both military blocks (NATO, Warsaw Pact) for 5 to 7 years, leading to a new European security system. Soviet government warns of presidential rule in Lithuania.
April 12:	De Maizière heads first non-communist government in GDR. Coalition seeks early reunification.
April 19:	Vatican restores ties with Czechoslovakia after 40 years. De Maizière asserts East Germany will need transitional protection in EC like other new members. Albanians seek stronger ties with US and USSR.
April 20:	Pope visits Czechoslovakia.
April 22:	Environmentalists celebrate Earth Day.
April 23:	Gdansk Solidarity convention criticises Polish government's "shock therapy". Finance minister Leszek Balcerowicz resists calls for slowing down.
April 24:	Hubble Space Telescope launched.
April 25:	ESA/USSR Cooperative Agreement signed in Paris. UK opposes acceleration of EC political integration sought by France and Germany by Jan. 1, 1993. Julieta Chamorro President of Nicaragua.
April 26:	Paris and Bonn ask Lithuania to suspend independence moves for a while to negotiate settlement with Moscow.
April 29:	De Maizière calls for changes in NATO structure and strategy, states German neutrality not a solution.
May 4:	Latvian parliament favors secession from USSR by 138-0. Bush reaffirms commitment to cut short-range nuclear missiles in Europe; asserts US remains a European power.
May 6:	EC considers revolving fund to help Eastern Europe.
May 7:	EC and Czechoslovakia sign trade and cooperation agreement. Arpad Goncz (Free Democrat) Hungarian premier.
May 8:	Conservatives win Croatian election. CDU calls for Jugoslav federation of sovereign states.

May 9:   Albania eases curbs on religious freedom and travel; seeks ties to US and USSR. Visit by UN Secretary-General.

May 13:   Romanian protesters assert revolution "stolen" by ex-communists.

May 16-18:   Council of Europe Conference in Budapest on Economic Reform in Central and Eastern Europe.

May 18:   FRG/GDR treaty on monetary union signed in Bonn.

May 19:   Schengen agreements on free circulation of people (B, F, L, NL, FRG).

May 20:   Free elections in Romania; Iliescu wins presidency with 89%. NSF (ex-communist) achieves 73% in parliament.

May 24:   Josef Antall (HDF) Hungarian Prime Minister. USSR agrees to withdraw troops from Hungary.

May 27:   Solidarity wins local elections in Poland.

May 29:   Gorbachev opponent Boris Yeltsin elected president of Russian Republic. EBRD established in London.

May 30:   First Free elections in Bulgaria in 45 years.

June 3:   Washington summit between presidents Bush and Gorbachev: "the last superpower summit". Bush proposes plan on German reunification.

June 4-8:   Conference of European Ministers of Justice, Istanbul, with Hungarian participation.

June 7:   WTO declares end of ideological conflict with West. Unrest in Soviet Kirghizia; 48 killed.

June 8:   Free elections in Czechoslovakia. Czech Civic Forum and Slovak Public Against Violence assume power.

June 10:   Socialists (former Communists) win Bulgarian elections.

June 12:   Gorbachev meets with leaders of Baltic states. Marian Calfa reappointed prime minister of Czechoslovakia. USSR eases opposition to united Germany as NATO member. Shamir forms right-wing government in Israel.

June 13:   Government miners break up opposition demonstration in Romania.

June 20:   UK Chancellor of the Exchequer (Finance Minister) John Major proposes circulation of ECU in EC alongside national currencies.

June 21:   FRG recognizes Polish/German frontier; adopts treaty of economic union.

June 22:   French parliament ratifies creation of EBRD. EC and European Investment Bank are full members. EC countries hold 51% of capital and majority of seats.

June 23:   Hurd puts forward 4 points for political union of EC countries. In Canada, unratified by Manitoba and Newfoundland, Meech Lake unity agreement with Quebec fails.

June 26:   European Council in Dublin agrees to convene conferences in Rome on economic and monetary union (Dec. 14) and political union (Dec. 15). Hungarian parliament votes withdrawal from Warsaw Pact. Dutch FM Hans van den Broek proposes European senate with equal representation from each state to defend interests of small countries. Slovenia drafts independence constitution.

June 29: Lithuanian parliament votes 100-day suspension of independence measures to negotiate with Moscow. FRG president Weizsäcker favors Berlin as capital of reunited Germany.

July 1: All capital transfers freed in EC countries.

July 2: FRG/GDR economic and financial union with single currency.

July 4: Cyprus applies for EC membership.

July 5: NATO Council invites Gorbachev to a NATO meeting; abandons "forward" strategy and graduated nuclear response: "cold war" confrontation dissipated. Havel re-elected Czech president. Unrest in Albania; many flee to foreign embassies. Bush conditions US aid to USSR on reduction of Soviet military expenditure and support for Communist regimes (Cuba, etc.).

July 6: Bulgarian President Mladenov resigns, accused of force against demonstrators.

July 16: Malta applies for membership of EC. Gorbachev accepts NP membership for reunified Germany. Gorbachev accepts NATO membership for reunited Germany.

July 25: UK reduces forces in FRG.

July 31: USSR and Albania restore diplomatic relations.

Aug. 1: Opposition leader Jeliou Jelev, elected by parliament, becomes Bulgaria's first non-communist president in four decades. Albania legalizes foreign investments.

Aug. 2: Iraq invades Kuwait.

Aug. 18: East German Socialist Party withdraws from Government.

Sept. 9: Bush and Gorbachev confer on first "post cold war" crisis: Helsinki declaration on Iraqi agression.

Sept. 11: Moscow four-power treaty ends German occupation statute.

Sept. 18: Lech Walesa candidate for Polish presidency: divisions in Solidarity premise new democratic party system.

Sept. 24: Gorbachev granted exceptional powers by Supreme Soviet to effect economic reforms.

Sept. 26: Soviet Union restores religious freedom. Joint CSCE/Council of Europe parliament session in Strasbourg.

Oct. 1: Four World War II allies suspend Berlin occupation rights pending ratification of treaty signed Sept. 11.

Oct. 2: At midnight GDR ceases to exist, is absorbed by FRG and becomes part of EC. Berlin capital of new state.

Oct. 3: First meeting of joint German parliament, symbolically convened in Berlin Reichstag for first time since 1933. US and USSR agree on conventional arms reduction. ESA launches Ulysses.

Oct. 8: In policy reversal, Britain joins 9 other currencies in EMS.

Oct. 12:   Council of Europe's 6th European Ministerial Conference on the Environment adopts European Conservation Strategy.

Oct. 13:   Czech Finance Minister Vaclav Klaus elected Chairman of Civic Forum, announces move to right.

Oct. 14:   Christian Democrats win 4 out of 5 states in former GDR local elections.

Oct. 15:   Nobel Peace Prize to Mikhail Gorbachev. US Defense Secretary Dick Cheney addresses Soviet Committee on State Security.

Oct. 17:   Ukrainian Parliament agrees to adopt new constitution to support declaration of sovereignty.

Oct. 19:   Supreme Soviet adopts Gorbachev's market economy reform plan.

Oct. 25:   Slovak parliament votes Slovak official language of Slovakian Republic, with language rights granted to Hungarian minority. Kazakhstan Parliament declares sovereignty, implying precedence over Soviet laws. Chuvash Republic (enclosed in Russian Republic) declares sovereignty over natural resources. Albanian writer and chair of Democratic Front Ismail Kadare seeks asylum in France.

Oct. 28:   European Council decides over British opposition to create a central banking system Jan. 1, 1994, but fails to agree farm subsidy cuts. Demands Iraq's unconditional withdrawal from Kuwait. EC also demands international peace conference on Arab-Israeli conflict. In Paris, France and USSR sign treaty of friendship.

Oct. 30:   Moscow dedicates monument to victims of Stalinism. Russian Republic parliament rejects rehabilitation of all political prisoners since 1917.

Oct. 31:   Ethnic confrontation in Romanian-speaking Moldavian Republic. Moldavians oppose autonomy for their own Turcic minority. Soviet troops guard frontiers with Romania.

Nov. 1:   British Deputy PM Sir Geoffrey Howe resigns to protest PM Margaret Thatcher's opposition to EMS.

Nov. 5:   Council of Europe marks 40th anniversary of European Convention on Human Rights in Rome. Offering to coordinate human rights issues for CSCE, the Council invites US, Canada and USSR to join some of its functions

Nov. 6:   Hungary becomes 24th and first East European member of Council of Europe, with 7 Assembly seats. Council of Europe convention on equivalence of periods of university study. European code of social security 9th protocol to European convention on human rights. World Climate Conference in Geneva; US refuses to set new goals to reduce carbon dioxide emissions and combat global warming. EC agrees tariff and subsidy reductions in agriculture to be proposed to GATT nations at Uruguay Round talks in Geneva.

Nov. 8:	US decision to transfer troops stationed in Europe to Persian Gulf highlights change in priorities in first "post cold war" regional crisis. Council of Europe convention on money laundering.
Nov. 9:	Germany and Soviet Union sign treaty of cooperation and non-aggression. Chandra Shekah Prime Minister of India. Nepal proclaims democratic constitution.
Nov. 14:	Michael Heseltine challenges Margaret Thatcher for Conservative leadership over European policy and other issues.
Nov. 18:	Elections in Yugoslavia's Bosnia-Herzegovina result in non-Communist majority for Serbian, Croat and Muslim nationalist parties. However, Serbs oppose break-up of Yugoslav federation.
Nov. 19:	CSCE in Paris signs CFE treaty, limiting conventional weapons from Atlantic to Urals.
Nov. 20:	EC-US Transatlantic Declaration establishes partnership principles and bi-annual consultations at level of presidents and FMs.
Nov. 21:	CSCE conference concludes with signature of Charter of Paris, ending "cold war" and setting up Secretariat in Prague, Center for Resolution of Conflict in Vienna and Warsaw.
Nov. 22:	After failing to defeat Michael Heseltine on first leadership ballot, Margaret Thatcher resigns.
Nov. 25:	Polish presidential elections. Walesa leads 1st round.
Nov. 26:	Polish Premier Tadeusz Mazowiecki resigns after running third in presidential election; cites voter backlash against necessary austerity measures. Rail strikes in E. Germany and communist successes in Czech local elections reflect similar resentment.
Nov. 28:	John Major UK Prime Minister.
Nov. 29:	Demonstrations force resignation of Socialist (ex-communist) government of Bulgaria.
Dec. 2:	CDU wins first all-German federal elections.
Dec. 3-7:	Farm subsidies dominate Uruguay Round in Brussels.
Dec. 8:	Large pro-democracy rallies in Albania.
Dec. 9:	Socialists (ex-CP) win Serbian elections.
Dec. 11:	Albanian President Ramiz Alia allows opposition parties.
Dec. 12:	WEU Council backs Kohl, Mitterrand call that EC assume defense responsibilities to promote political and economic integration; urges Iraq to withdraw from Kuwait. Sweden's parliament agrees to EC membership application. Albanian Democratic Party founded in Tirana rally. US food aid to USSR. Czech parliament approves federal system.
Dec. 14:	EC Rome summit welcomes new UK "tone" under John Major. CELAD set up to fight drugs.
Dec. 16:	Timisoara protests against new Romanian government, alleging failed promises.
Dec. 18:	Council of Europe conference on protection of forests.

Dec. 19:	Joint EC/EFTA ministerial meeting in Brussels urges acceleration of assistance to Central and Eastern Europe and of EEA negotiations. Soviet FM Shevardnadze resigns.
Dec. 21:	Croatia approves new constitution, allowing secession from Yugoslavia.
Dec. 22:	Polish President Jaruzelski leaves office amid "traitor/ hero" assessments. Walesa Polish President.
Dec. 23:	Slovenia approves constitution allowing secession. Ex-communists' massive victory in Serbian 2nd round. Reformist Fatos Nano Gen. Sec. of Albanian government.
Dec. 25:	Supreme Soviet adopts constitutional reform, grants President Gorbachev direct governmental control and sets up Federation Council of Soviet republics; rejects presidential police force.
Dec. 26:	Former King Michael visits Romania and is expelled. Russian Republic cuts share of Soviet budget.
Dec. 27:	Gennadi I. Zanayev Soviet Vice-President. Albanian government refuses opposition request to postpone elections.
Dec. 29:	Walesa nominates Jan Krzystof Bielecki Polish PM.

1991

Jan. 5:	CMEA decides dissolution, proposes OIEC. Germany and Yugoslavia invited to join new market-oriented body.
Jan. 7:	First legal Orthodox Christmas in USSR in 73 years. Soviet paratroops enter seven republics to enforce draft. US purchase of Soviet nuclear reactor as used in spy satellites marks turning-point in technology exchange.
Jan. 8:	Lithuanian Government resigns.
Jan. 9:	US and Iraqi FM's discuss Gulf crisis in Geneva.
Jan. 11:	Macau 101st GATT member.
Jan. 13:	Soviet military kills 14 in Lithuania. Mario Soares re-elected Portuguese President.
Jan. 14:	NATO condemns Baltic repression. UN peace mission to Baghdad.
Jan. 15:	UN Kuwait withdrawal deadline ignored by Iraq. Alexander Bessmertnykh, former ambassador to Washington, Soviet FM.
Jan. 16:	Massive air attacks by "coalition" on Iraq.
Jan. 17:	WEU decides to coordinate Gulf activities, its first such action in war. Helmut Kohl re-elected German Chancellor.
Jan. 18:	Death of King Olav of Norway. Soviet military intervention in Latvia.
Jan. 20:	King Harald of Norway takes oath of allegiance. In Moscow 100,000 march to protest Baltic crack down.
Jan. 22:	EC suspends food aid to USSR to protest Soviet Baltic intervention. Gorbachev denies shift from liberalization.

Jan. 23:   Bulgarian coalition premier Dimitar Popov announces economic plan.

Jan. 24:   Croatia refuses to disband paramilitary police, fearing national army dominated by Serbian officers.

Jan. 25:   Edward Madigan US Secretary of Agriculture, succeeding Clayton Yeutter.

Jan. 28:   Moscow US/Soviet summit postponed because of Gulf War; START treaty not ready; Baltic crackdown.

Feb. 4:   SA announcement apartheid laws to be scrapped prompts EC FM's to lift sanctions. Ministers also decide to strengthen common foreign and security policies.

Feb. 5:   Canada joins USA and Mexico in NAFTA talks. EC agriculture ministers reject Delors plan.

Feb. 7:   J-B Aristide President of Haiti.

Feb. 8:   Lithuanian referendum favors independence by 75%.

Feb. 14:   CFE talks resume in Vienna.

Feb. 15:   After Iceland, Czechoslovakia recognizes Lithuania as independent nation. CS, H and PL resign cooperation agreement to facilitate integration with W. Europe. UNESCO launches CORDEE education project.

Feb. 20:   Slovenian parliament votes for autonomy.

Feb. 21:   Czechoslovakia becomes 25th member of Council of Europe (8 assembly seats) and USSR accedes to European Cultural Convention. Croatian parliament assumes veto power over Yugoslav federal law and mechanisms for declaring independence. Street clashes in Albania.

Feb. 24:   Poland reaches 3-year agreement with IMF. Marian Krzaklewski replaces Lech Walesa as Solidarity leader.

Feb. 25:   WTO military alliance dissolved in Budapest by 6 remaining members, effective March 31, 1991. Todor Zhivkov tried for embezzlement. Political violence kills 5 in Albania.

Feb. 26:   GATT Trade Negotiations Committee (TNC) agrees to restart Uruguay Round trade talks without setting deadline. Czech law returns property confiscated by CP to former owners.

Feb. 27:   Gulf ceasefire.

Feb. 28:   Strikes in eastern Germany.

March 3:   Latvian and Estonian plebiscites approve independence even in Russian-majority areas.

March 5:   USSR ratifies friendship treaty with Germany.

March 6:   Last Cruise missiles leave Greenham Common (UK) for destruction under INF Treaty. Albanian refugees flee across Adriatic to Italy.

March 11:   US, Albania restore diplomatic ties after 52 years. Albania frees political prisoners.

March 13:   Protesting Serbs demand ouster of Serbian communist president Slobodan Milosevic.

March 14:	Japan invites US and Europe to join in developing 6th-generation supercomputers. Slovak separatists demonstrate for independence: Havel seeks referendum.
March 15:	Soviets transfer Erich Honecker to Moscow.
March 16:	Milosevic renounces recognition of Yugoslav federal presidency.
March 17:	9 of 15 Soviet republics conduct unity referendum. In Croatia, Serbian separatists declare Krajina region part of Serbia.
March 20:	Walesa in Washington, vows to fight anti-semitism. French draft law admitting EC citizens to French public service, following principle of free movement of workers.
March 29:	Public Trustee office in Bonn firebombed. (This office privatizes E. German state enterprises).
March 31:	Georgia (USSR) referendum favors independence. CP victory in free Albanian elections. Warsaw Pact lapses.
April 2:	Albanian army fires on demonstrators (3 killed).
April 3:	First major price increases in USSR in 30 years. Gulf ceasefire resolution adopted by Security Council.
April 4:	Russian parliament creates elected presidency.
April 6:	Iraq accepts UN terms. Ceasefire.
April 7:	Albanian elections give victory to Labor (former CP) with 168 of 250 seats.
April 9:	In USSR Georgia declares independence. Luxembourg EC summit accepts UK proposal for a protected Kurdish zone in N. Iraq.
April 10:	Albanian Labor proposes new constitution, separating party and state. UNESCO European Seminar on Education, Training and Employment opens in Poitiers.
April 16:	Gorbachev first Soviet leader to visit Japan. No agreement on S. Kurile islands or on level of Japanese technical assistance.
April 23:	Kohl favors Berlin as seat of German government. German Supreme Court rules former owners expropriated by Soviets entitled to compensation but not return of property.
April 24:	9 of 15 Soviet republics agree on power sharing. Gorbachev and Yeltsin make plea for unity.
April 30:	Taiwan ends 43 years of state of emergency.
May 1:	N. Ireland peace talks open. Angolan Government and UNITA sign peace agreement in Lisbon.
May 2:	Croatian, Serbian police clash in Borovo Selo.
May 6:	Kremlin transfers coal mine control to Russian Republic.
May 10:	Bessmertnykh visits Israel.
May 15:	Croatian election to "revolving" Yugoslav presidency blocked. 96% favor secession in Croatian constitutional referendum. Michel Rocard replaced by Edith Cresson, first French woman PM. Following ECHR judgement, UK transfers decisions on early-release of offenders from Home Secretary to Parole Board.

May 16:	State visit to US by Queen Elizabeth II. Soviet republics agree economic plan (except Estonia, Georgia).
May 20:	Walesa visits Israel. Soviet parliament votes to allow citizens to emigrate.
May 21:	Indian PM Rajiv Gandhi assassinated. Ethiopian President Mengistu Haile Mariam resigns and flees to Zimbabwe.
May 23:	US House votes "fast track" authority for Bush Admin for NAFTA and GATT-UR negotiations.
May 24:	Senate votes "fast track". Ethiopian Jews evacuated by Israel.
May 27:	Nationalist Zviad Gamsakhurdia wins Georgia's first presidential election. Assembly of National Fronts formed in Kishinev, Moldavia, by 6 separatist Soviet republics.
May 28:	Rebels take Addis Ababa. NATO defense ministers plan 50% force reduction in Europe, creation of rapid intervention group under British command.
May 31:	Peace agreement signed in Lisbon by Angola government and UNITA rebels, includes unified armed force, free elections in 1992.
June 3:	Pope denounces abortion on Polish visit. Bush asks waiver of Jackson-Vanik amendment as emigration rises from USSR, BG, CS, Mongolia.
June 4:	Democrat Robert Strauss named US envoy to USSR. Unrest forces Albanian government resignation: Democratic Party leader Sali Berisha agrees to join national union government. In Oslo Nobel Peace Prize speech, Gorbachev says aid to USSR in West's interest.
June 7:	NATO Council supports efforts for European security policy but stresses need for "complementarity".
June 11:	Tlli Bufi forms coalition in Albania.
June 12:	First presidential election in Russia gives Boris Yeltsin 57.3% victory. Moscow and Leningrad mayors Popov and Sobchak elected by over 60%. Leningrad votes (54%) to change name back to Sankt Petersburg.
June 13:	NAFTA negotiations open in Toronto.
June 15:	Prague conference on a European confederation, jointly sponsored by Presidents Havel and Mitterrand.
June 17:	FRG-Polish friendship treaty signed. Gorbachev and 9 Soviet republics agree on Union treaty. Iceland plans currency link to ECU.
June 20:	Bundestag decides by 337 votes to 320 to move to Berlin. First meeting of CSCE ministerial council, in Berlin, sets up crisis mechanism and admits Albania as 35th member.
June 23:	Secretary Baker makes first US visit to Albania.
June 24:	Last Soviet troops leave Czechoslovakia and Hungary. EC twelve agree on gradual VAT alignment (15% normal minimum, 5% reduced rate minimum).

June 25:   Slovenia and Croatia declare independence a day earlier than expected despite EC, US warnings of non-recognition. Yugoslav parliament calls on army to guarantee national integrity.

June 26:   Council of Europe refuses renewal of European Diploma for Nature Conservation for French Pyrenees National Park.

June 28:   Civil war in Yugoslavia. Luxembourg EC summit blocks aid, sends mediation mission, invokes CSCE dispute settlement procedure. Third tunnel link-up under Channel. Giulio Andreotti gives up mission to find a solution to issue of seat of European institutions.

June 29:   Final dissolution of CMEA. In apparent EC diplomacy success, 3 months truce agreed in Yugoslav conflict.

July 1:   Final dissolution of WTO (Political Consultative Committee). Election of Stipe Mesic (Croatia) to Yugoslav rotating presidency. Sweden applies for EC membership. EC/Andorra association agreement enters into force. 70th anniversary of Chinese CP.

July 2:   Democratic constitution approved by referendum in Burkina Faso.

July 3:   MacSharry CAP proposals. Renewed conflict in Yugoslavia. IBM cooperation agreements with Apple and Siemens. Failure of Northern-Ireland multi-party talks.

July 5:   BCCI banking scandal.

July 7:   2nd EC mission to Yugoslavia (Brioni Agreement).

July 8:   UK Labor Party leader Neil Kinnock declares "inevitable" economic and political union of Europe, a major policy change.

July 9:   Bulgarian parliament adopts new constitution.

July 12:   Democratic constitution approved by referendum in Mauretania.

July 16:   Ariane rocket orbits European environmental observation satellite.

July 17:   Prince Sihanouk elected president of Cambodia's Supreme National Council.

July 18:   19 Latin-American countries, Portugal and Spain hold first Ibero-American summit in Mexico. (Castro refuses democratic reform). Bush visit to Greece, seeking Cyprus solution. Yugoslavia agrees to withdraw federal troops from Slovenia (tacit independence recognition). EC-Japanese declaration on trade relations.

July 19:   EC Commission adopts MacSharry reform plan for CAP. Lukewarm reception from ministers, resisting subsidy cuts

July 20:   Yeltsin issues decree banning party politics in Russian workplace.

July 25:   Renouncing Marxism, Gorbachev proposes abandonment of "class struggle", seeks "human and democratic socialism".

July 29:   Russian Republic recognizes independence of Lithuania. EC-Japan auto-import agreement abolishes quotas by 2000.

July 31:	Moscow Bush-Gorbachev summit: START treaty signed; Bush agrees to MFN status for Soviet imports; call for Middle East peace conference. EC-EFTA "single European space" negotiations suspended. EC sets new measures for Yugoslav ceasefire. EC Commission favors Austrian admission.
Aug. 1:	700th anniversary of Swiss Confederation.
Aug. 2:	4th EC "troika" visit fails to bring peace to Yugoslavia.
Aug. 10:	PRC and Vietnam renew diplomatic relations.
Aug. 15:	Muslim republics in Soviet Central Asia sign cooperation agreement bypassing federal authorities. Denmark and Sweden agree to construct a tunnel between Copenhagen and Malmö. Kurdish unrest in Turkey.
Aug. 16:	First papal visit to Hungary.
Aug. 18:	Forced to resign from Soviet CP, Alexandr Yakovlev warns of a possible *coup d'état*.
Aug. 19:	*Coup* in Moscow; Gorbachev arrested; Yeltsin urges resistance. Western solidarity with Yeltsin and Gorbachev
Aug. 21:	Failure of *putsch*, leaders arrested. Gorbachev returns to Moscow.
Aug. 22:	Latvia and Estonia declare independence.
Aug. 24:	Ukrainian parliament declares independence, subject to referendum (Dec. 1). Soviet government replaced. Gorbachev resigns as CP general secretary. Violent clashes in Croatia.
Aug. 27:	Moldavia declares independence, renames itself Moldova. EC governments recognize total sovereignty of Estonia, Latvia and Lithuania.
Aug. 29:	Supreme Soviet votes to suspend CP nationwide and recommends its own dissolution to Congress of Deputies.
Sept. 2:	Soviet Congress of Deputies debates new constitution (political independence, economic integration) supported by all republics except Baltics, Moldova, Georgia. US recognizes Baltic independence. EC plan for Yugoslav peace. Bulgaria accedes to European Cultural Convention.
Sept. 7:	EC conference on Yugoslavia opens in The Hague.
Sept. 8:	Referendum in Macedonia approves independence from Yugoslavia. In USSR Tadzhikstan votes for independence.
Sept. 10:	CSCE human rights conference in Moscow admits 3 Baltic states. At Harvard defense conference Soviets announce 25% troop reductions. Renewed Yugoslav fighting.
Sept. 14:	Baker first US official to visit Baltics.
Sept. 15:	Conservative plurality in Swedish general election, ousting Social Democrats; Carl Bildt replaces Ingvar Carlsson as prime minister.
Sept. 17:	EC decides to consider membership application from Republic of Cyprus (which does not include Turkish controlled north). UN admits 3 Baltics, 2 Koreas, Marshall Islands, Micronesia,

	raising membership to 166. Canada cuts its military forces in Europe by 80%.
Sept. 24:	Armenia declares independence. Yeltsin mediates Azeri-Armenian dispute. Fourth Yugoslav ceasefire.
Sept. 26:	Lord Carrington reconvenes EC conference on Yugoslavia. EC majority rejects Dutch blueprint for political union. Salvadoran civil war settlement signed at UN.
Sept. 27:	Bush proposes sweeping unilateral cuts in tactical nuclear weapons.
Sept. 29:	Renewed fighting in Yugoslavia.
Sept. 30:	Haitian president Aristide deposed by military coup.
Oct. 1-2:	Soviet republics sign economic agreement. Theodore Stolojan succeeds Petre Roman as Romanian premier.
Oct. 4:	24 countries sign Antarctic protection pact in Madrid, banning mineral and oil exploration for 50 years.
Oct. 5:	Gorbachev announces sweeping arms cuts in response to US decisions. USSR granted associate IMF membership.
Oct. 6:	Social Democrats and premier Anibal Silva win Portuguese general elections.
Oct. 7:	Alexander Karadjordjevic, British-born pretender to Serbian throne, makes first visit to Yugoslavia.
Oct. 13:	Union of Democratic Forces defeats Socialists (former CP) in Bulgarian national elections.
Oct. 14:	Daw Aung San Suu Kyi of Burma wins Nobel Peace Prize.
Oct. 15:	Bosnia Herzogovina declares independence from Yugoslavia. Albania 156th member of IMF and World Bank; Baltic states also attend Bankok meeting.
Oct. 16:	Gorbachev attempts to mediate Yugoslav conflict. Responding to US and Soviet initiatives, NATO announces major cuts in nuclear arms. France and Germany propose expansion of joint brigade as nucleus for European army. Council of Europe conference of ministers of education.
Oct. 17:	NATO cuts atomic weapons 50%.
Oct. 18:	8 Soviet republics sign economic pact. Serbian chief rejects peace plan at Hague parley.
Oct. 22:	EC and EFTA agree 19-nation EEA. EC Parliament adopts code against sexual harassment. Ukrainian parliament creates army.
Oct. 27:	Polish national elections: indecisive multi-party result with small democratic majority over former CP.
Oct. 29:	WEU in Bonn discusses compromise between French-German and British-Italian plans on whether European defense should be anchored in NATO or EC.
Oct. 30:	Middle East peace conference opens in Madrid. EC threatens Serbia with sanctions. Kiichi Miyazawa Japanese premier.

Oct. 31:	Berlin conference on immigration sets cooperation to combat illegal immigration.
Nov. 1:	UK government proposes stricter immigration laws.
Nov. 5:	Serbia rejects EC plan for a loose confederation of independent republics: EC threatens sanctions. Death of Czech-born British federalist and founder of *The European*, Robert Maxwell.
Nov. 7:	NATO summit in Rome seeks new security relationship in Europe. Yeltsin abolishes CP in Russian Republic. "Leningrad" reverts to "St. Petersburg"; first visit by Grand Duke Vladimir Romanov. Moscow rations bread.
Nov. 8:	Walesa nominates Bronislaw Geremek as premier.
Nov. 9:	Chechen-Ingush Autonomous Republic inside Russia defies Yeltsin state of emergency banning independence.
Nov. 10:	14-nation research team (EC, Sweden, Switzerland) makes 200m-degree nuclear fission in Joint European Torus (JET) project in UK.
Nov. 11:	Russian parliament reverses Yeltsin decree banning Chechen autonomy.
Nov. 13:	EC Security Council members Belgium, France, UK propose UN peace force for Yugoslavia.
Nov. 14:	Eight Soviet republics agree to replace USSR by Union of Sovereign States (USS). In Yugoslavia, Carrington seeks 13th ceasefire to permit entry of UN peacekeepers. Prince Norodom Sihanouk returns to Cambodia after 13 years exile. Ivan Silayev confirmed by State Council as Soviet Premier. New German law gives citizens access to former GDR secret police (Stasi) files. Baker in China.
Nov. 19:	8 Soviet republics refuse to sign new treaty for Union of Sovereign States; agree to assume responsibility for foreign debt. Eduard Shevardnadze returns as FM, succeeding Boris Pankin.
Nov. 20:	Security Council nominates Egyptian Deputy Prime Minister Boutros Ghali as UN Secretary General in succession to Xavier Perez de Cuellar of Peru. Canadian Premier Mulroney warns Quebec separatists they cannot be "part-time Canadians", retaining economic advantages. House of Commons supports John Major on European policy.
Nov. 21:	EC signs Association agreements with PL, CS, H.
Nov. 22:	UN special envoy Cyrus Vance brokers 14th Yugoslav cease-fire.
Nov. 24:	Rightist and environmental parties gain in Belgian elections.
Nov. 25:	US transfers 500 mn from Pentagon budget to fund Soviet nuclear disarmament. UN envoy Vance favors peacekeepers at "flashpoints", skirting frontier dispute.
Nov. 26:	European Court of Human Rights condemns UK injunction against "Spycatcher" book by former agent Peter Wright.
Nov. 27:	Soviet State Council orders repeal of Azeri takeover of Nagorno-Karabakh enclave. Yugoslavia asks UN for peacekeepers. Serbs

relocated in abandoned Croat homes. Association for the Monetary Union of Europe proposes extending ECU to Eastern Europe.

Dec. 1:   Almost 90% majority for independance in Ukraine referendum. Leonid Kravchuk elected president.

Dec. 3:   Gorbachev warns of "crisis of statehood".

Dec. 4:   Democratic Party opposition withdraws from Albanian coalition.

Dec. 6:   In reluctant step backward, Walesa nominates market economy critic Jan Olszewski as Polish premier. In Russia Yeltsin's own vice-president, Aleksandr V Rutskoi, speaks out on behalf of military industrial complex.

Dec. 7:   On 50th anniversary, Japanese parliament declines to apologize for Pearl Harbor attack. Renewed fighting blocks start of UN peacekeeping in Yugoslavia.

Dec. 8:   Byelo-Russia, Russia and Ukraine declare demise of Soviet Union and form commonwealth of independent states with headquarters in Minsk. Albanians rally in Tirana to celebrate anniversary of pro-democracy protests.

Dec. 10:   Historic EC summit in Maastricht accepts new treaties on single currency, economic and political cooperation and agreement on strengthening defense cooperation through WEU. Eleven agree to harmonize social legislation without UK. EFTA signs joint declarations on cooperation with Bulgaria, Romania and the Baltic countries. Byelo-Russian and Ukrainian parliaments ratify commonwealth accord. Romanian electorate approves multi-party constitution.

Dec. 11:   Armenia and Kirghizia join commonwealth accord. Bush welcomes Maastricht agreements, looking for a greater European responsibility for world economy. 45 nations hold Islamic Conference summit in Senegal. Bulgarian Parliament approves takeover of former CP property.

Dec. 12:   Russian parliament ratifies new commonwealth, 174: 6. Erich Honecker seeks refuge in Chile's Moscow embassy. President Gorbachev says the main task of his life is over. 5 Islamic republics agree to join Commonwealth as "founder members". Baker convenes international conference on emergency aid to democratic Soviet republics. Jaruzelski defends Polish martial law of 1981 as "lesser evil", averting threat of Soviet invasion. Albanian rally demands Alia resignation.

Dec. 13:   Baker convenes January conference in Washington to organize emergency aid to "democratic" former republics of the USSR (apparently excluding Georgia and Azerbaijan). EC environment ministers agree to explore tax on oil to combat global warning.

Dec. 14:   European Court of Justice in Luxembourg rules proposed EEA court incompatible with Treaty of Rome, causing postponement of treaty signing. Central American summit gives priority to eliminating poverty. Bush and Salinas de Gortari reconfirm FTA intentions.

Dec. 15: Security Council decides to send peacekeeper advance party to Yugoslavia. Baker visits four CEI republics.

Dec. 16: Under pressure from Germany, EC foreign ministers decide to recognize independence of Croatia and Slovenia on Jan. 15. European Space Agency orbits two satellites with Ariane rocket in Guyane. Norway first country to recognize independence of Russia.

Dec. 17: Gorbachev and Yeltsin agree to dissolve USSR on Dec. 31, thereby eliminating Gorbachev's own post.

Dec. 19: NATO Council receives report from Baker on USSR dissolution and weapons control. Yeltsin assumes control of Soviet Foreign Ministry, KGB, Parliament and presidential office. Paul Keating succeeds Bob Hawke as Australian premier.

Dec. 20: Suspension of GATT Uruguay Round. First meeting of North Atlantic Cooperation Council brings together NATO, former WTO and Baltic governments to discuss conversion of military production to peacetime uses. All Soviet republics except Georgia sign expanded Commonwealth agreement. Civil conflict in Georgia. Yugoslav federal premier Ante Markovic resigns. Bosnia and Herzogovena (BH) and Macedonia accept EC independence recognition conditions. South African constitutional conference opens. Acting Soviet Premier Anton Silayev appointed Russian representative to EC.

Dec. 23: EC FMs recognize Russia as USSR successor state.

Dec. 24: Supreme Soviet dissolves itself.

Dec. 25: President Gorbachev resigns; US recognizes new independent states.

Dec. 26: First free election in an Arab country gives victory to FIS in Algeria.

Dec. 28: CIS defense ministers meet in Moscow; dispute over Black Sea fleet.

Dec. 29: CIS leaders meet in Minsk to complete policies and structures.

Dec. 31: El Salvador peace agreement at UN, final achievement for Perez de Cuellar.

1992

Jan. 1: International Space Year opens. Boutros Ghali UN Secretary-General. Portugal succeeds Netherlands in EC chair. Croatia and Serbia accept Vance UN peace plan.

Jan. 2: Price liberalization in several CIS republics.

Jan. 6: Gamsakhurdia flees Georgian capital, Tbilisi.

Jan. 7: Casualties in Tbilisi. Five EC peacekeepers killed in Yugoslavia.

Jan. 9: EC conference on Yugoslavia resumes in Brussels.

Jan. 11:   President Chadli Benjeddid of Algeria resigns, leading to army takeover and election annulment.

Jan. 13:   In Poland, first Solidarity strike since fall of communism, protesting energy price rises.

Jan. 14:   Egon Klepsch (German CDU) elected president of European Parliament, succeeding Enrique Baron Crespo (Span.Soc.).

Jan. 15:   EC countries, Austria, Switzerland, Vatican recognize Croatia and Slovenia. State visit by Mitterrand to Luxembourg. EP blocks EC aid to Morocco, Syria.

Jan. 16:   Gibraltar election returns Soc. Labor Party to power; leader Joe Bassano resists Spanish consultative role agreed by UK. Exiled 27 years, Mohammed Boudiaf returns to Algeria to head State Council.

Jan. 17:   Marie-Anne Isler-Béguin (F) elected 1st Green Party (ecologist) VP of European Parliament.

Jan. 19:   Incumbent Jelio Jelev (UDF) wins Bulgarian presidential election with 53.3% in 2nd round. UN advance guard deployed in Yugoslavia.

Jan. 20:   Finno-Russian treaty of cooperation signed.

Jan. 21:   Opposed by Slovak deputies, federal parliament in Prague rejects Havel proposal for national referendum on future of Czechoslovak federation.

Jan. 22:   Washington conference on aid to ex-USSR (47 countries, 7 IGO's) creates Frankfurt airlift. EC Commission issues directives against state monopolies in gas, electricity.

Jan. 23:   Creation of Euro-Hermespace to develop ESA shuttle.

Jan. 24:   Civil war in Georgia after Gamsakhurdia return. Russia-Ukraine tension over Crimea and Black Sea fleet. SA President Frederik De Klerk announces Blacks will participate in referendum on provisional government.

Jan. 27:   ASEAN meets in Bangkok to consider end of Cold War. Turkey bombs PKK in SE Turkey.

Jan. 28:   In State of the Nation address Bush proposes further disarmament: reduction of US naval missiles against CIS land-based MIRV's .

Jan. 29:   Yeltsin accepts, suggests dismantling SDI and reducing nuclear warheads to 2500 from 10000. Czechoslovak parliament denies Havel extra powers. Renewed fighting in Ngorno-Karabakh: 47 die in helicopter crash. French armaments administrator Yves Sillard proposes WEU European Armaments Agency (EAA), replacing SCA.

Jan. 30:   In Prague, CSCE admits all CIS states to membership, Croatia, Slovenia as observers; modifies unanimity rule for "very serious" cases. Yeltsin visits London. In Singapore, ASEAN creates 6-nation free-trade area, to be phased in over 15 years. Resignation of Andorran parliament blocks sovereignty negotiations.

Jan. 31: In New York, at 1st Security Council summit, Yeltsin proposes nuclear powers cooperate in joint SDI defense.

Feb. 3: Conference of Black Sea states at Istanbul. Conference of non-aligned countries in Larnaca, Cyprus. UN human rights commission (Geneva) warns against racism. Armenia and Azerbaijan agree to negotiate on Ngorno-Karabakh, with observers from CSCE, EC and US. At Davos world economic forum EC Commissioner Sir Leon Brittan proposes GATT work out global competition rules. Brit. Con. Sir Geoffrey Finsberg President of Council of Europe assembly.

Feb. 4: At Council of Europe, Lech Walesa accuses West of selling to Poland without investing. Finnish PM Paavo Vayrynen announces Finland's intention to join EC.

Feb. 6: Albert Reynolds Irish PM, succeeding Charles Haughey (both Fianna Fail). Yeltsin state visit to France; Mitterrand renews European confederation proposal.

Feb. 7: TEU signing in Maastricht. Bosnian - H. leaders agree to "mini peace conference" under Lord Carrington.

Feb. 8: 8th quadrennial session of UNCTAD, in Carthagena, Colombia, studies life expectancy, literacy and other aspects of Third World human development. Winter Olympics in Albertville, France.

Feb. 9: Council of Europe Sec. Gen. Catherine Lalumière meets Bush in Washington to discuss wider role in guaranteeing minority rights.

Feb. 12: Delors submits post-Maastricht 5-year budget to EP.

Feb. 14: CIS Minsk summit fails to agree on retaining unified Red Army.

Feb. 16: First ECO summit, meeting in Teheran, admits Azerbaijan, Turkmenia and Uzbekistan. Milan Babic, president of Krajina, disavowed by own parliament.

Feb. 17: Lyon chosen as headquarters of Euronews, 13-station consortium for 24h international service.

Feb. 21: Security Council decides to send 14,000 peacekeeperss to Croatia and Bosnia-Herzegovina.

Feb. 22: Premier Eddie Fenech Adami and governing Nationalist Party win Maltese general election (51.8%) over Labour Party (46.5%), opposed to EC membership.

Feb. 23: Conservative demonstration in Moscow. In Glasgow, John Major rejects Scottish devolution, declaring choice is between union and independence. Governing NSF suffers setback in Romanian local elections.

Feb. 25: Polish zloty devalued 12%.

Feb. 27: Finland announces decision to apply for EC membership. 49th Ariane space launch in Kourou puts Japanese and Arab League satellites in orbit.

Feb. 28: Hunger riots in Albania crushed by military; new mass exodus threat closes port of Durres. CSCE adopts Ngorno-Karabakh peace plan.

Feb. 29:	At academic conference "Tribes and Europe" Mitterrand warns of new regional conflicts, renews proposal for all European confederation.
March 2:	8 CIS republics and San Marino admitted to UN, now numbering 175 states.
March 3:	Bosnian Serbs boycott referendum; Muslims and Croats favor independence. Hungarian constitutional court rejects law permitting prosecution of communist-era crimes.
March 4:	CSCE completes 3 years of "confidence-building" negotiations, setting limits on military manoevers. WHO reports 75% of deaths have environmental causes.
March 6:	Azeri President Moutalibov resigns following Baku street demonstrations and "uncontrollable" fighting in Ngorno-Karabakh. Bosnian Serb leader Radovan Karadzic calls for 3 ethnic republics. Jean-Luc Dehaene (CVP) Belgian premier.
March 7:	Slovak Christian Democrats split: new federalists (KDH) and separatists (SKDH) led by premier Jan Carnogursky and Jan Klepac, respectively. Yugoslav army attacks Osijck; Belgrade rally demands Milosevic resignation.
March 8:	NYT leaks Pentagon paper on opposing "exclusively European" defense systems.
March 10:	NACC advocates CSCE conciliation in Ngorno-Karabakh. Boutros Ghali appoints Cyrus Vance to peacemaking mission in Azerbaijan. Schevardnadze president of new Council of State in Georgia. US makes new UR proposals to EC, enlarging "Green Box".
March 11:	EC, US, Japan and Russia agree to set up International Center for Science and Technology (ICST) in Moscow to stem weaponist brain-drain. OECD research ministers also discuss flight of scientific personnel from eastern Europe, propose agency to fund research. OECD also proposes clearing house to exchange ideas on research planning and financing in OECD countries.
March 15:	Swiss President René Felber says Federal Council favors EC membership. In Catalonia CIU (Nat. coalition) wins 3rd successive election; separatist ERC gains seats.
March 16:	Acting Azeri President Iacoub Mamedov proposes summit to Armenian president Levon Ter-Petrossian.
March 18:	Finnish parliament approves EC application. EC mediator gains acceptance of a federal Bosnia-H. composed of 3 ethnic cantons. Yeltsin appoints himself defense minister, creates Russian army. By 68.73% majority SA whites "close book" on Apartheid.
March 22:	CIS summit in Kiev agrees on intervention force but leaves doubts on Ukraine remaining a member. WHO and UNICEF call for immediate health assistance to ex-USSR. Opposition Democratic Party, led by Sali Berisha, wins Albanian general election.

March 23: CS parliament rejects Slovak independence motion.

March 24: CSCE 4th plenary session opens in Helsinki. Slovenia and Croatia become full members. N-Karabakh conference called for. EC recognizes Georgia. Enzo Friso elected Sec. Gen. of ICFTU at Caracas world congress. Turkish ultimatum to Kurdish separatists.

March 25: Council of Europe bioethics conference, Madrid. ECHR condemns France for refusing official recognition of a sex change.

March 30: UK Lib. Dem. leader Paddy Ashdown takes election campaign to France to emphasize importance of European issues. King Juan Carlos of Spain repeals 1492 declaration of Jewish expulsion. ECHR condemns France for not responding "within a reasonable period" to case of haemophiliac infected by AIDS-tainted blood. Russian IMF accession terms (3% participation) agreed. Soviet debt rescheduled by 17 creditor countries.

March 31: EC agriculture ministers reject GATT arbitration conclusions on oleaginous crop support.

April 1: 16 of 18 Russian republics sign federation treaty; Chechen-Ingush and Tatarstan decline.

April 2: Following Socialist defeats in regional and local elections, Pierre Bérégovoy succeeds Edith Cresson as French premier. At EC conference ex-Yugoslav republics agree to resume trade exchanges.

April 7: EC Council decides to review Blue Europe fisheries policy

May 1: CSCE "confidence-building" restrictions on military manoevers enter into force.

May 13: Jersey, CI, parliament decides to review constitutional links with UK.

May 15: Security Council demands withdrawal of Serbian and Croatian troops from Bosnia-H. Popular Front opposition deposes President Moutalibov (again) in Azerbaijan. In Baltics Mitterrand demands Russian troop withdrawal. Thatcher denounces "centralized superstate" ambitions of EC Commission in Hague speech.

May 16: Swiss referendum favors World Bank and IMF membership.

May 17: Swiss Federal Council votes for EC application.

May 18: Security Council recommends UN membership for Croatia and Slovenia. Klaus Kinkel succeeds Dietrich Genscher as German FM.

May 19: Washington visit of Nursultan Nazarbaev, president of Kazakhstan, gives hope of US ratification of START, held up pending settlement of nuclear weapons control issues in Russia, Ukraine, Belarus and Kazakhstan. Drought threatens Africa with famine.

May 21: EC agreement (Italy dissenting) on CAP reform. House of Commons 1st reading approves Maastricht treaty. In La

Rochelle summit France and Germany confirm joint military force open to other nations.

May 22: In London James Baker hints at military action against Serbia. Bosnia-H., Croatia and Slovenia join UN.

May 23: Kosovo Albanians hold clandestine election, favor independence.

May 25: Luigi Scalfaro (Chr.Dem.) elected Italian President on 16th vote of electoral college. Thomas Klestil (People's Party) elected Austrian President by 57%.

May 29: Sarajevo in flames; Security Council votes sanctions against Serbia. Turkey opens bridge to Nakhitchevan, Azeri enclave.

June 1: Resignation of Georgi Metiouchin, Governor of Russian Central Bank.

June 2: Denmark rejects Maastricht treaty in national referendum by 50.7% to 49.3%, about 46,000 votes.

June 3-14: UNCED Earth Summit in Rio de Janeiro.

June 5: Czechoslovak general election; separatists win in Slovakia.

June 6: Waldemar Pawlak succeeds Jan Olszewski as Polish PM.

June 8: Security Council decides to send 1000 Blue Helmets to hold Sarajevo airport.

June 11: Russian privatisation law sets October deadline for share sales.

June 12: France halts Hades nuclear missile production.

June 16: Bush-Yeltsin Summit in Washington agrees major ICBM cuts, including MIRV's and SDI cooperation. Sali Berisha warns Bush a Serbian move against ethnic Albanians could trigger Balkan war. Croatia and Bosnia-H. form alliance. Opposition demonstrations in Belgrade.

June 18: Irish referendum approves Maastricht treaty by 68%. French farmers demonstrate against CAP reform. Giuliano Amato Italian PM. Islamic Conference in Ankara threatens military intervention in Sarajevo.

June 19: WEU Council approves new emergency intervention role. Concil of Europe conference on technical aid to Eastern Europe suggests international corps of experts. GATT suspends Yugoslav membership.

June 20: Commission proposals on EC reform and enlargement submitted to FM's in Luxembourg. Klaus and Meciar agree to divide Czechoslovakia; Havel demands referendum. In policy change, Yeltsin ready to intervene in ethnic conflicts in ex-USSR to protect Russians. Ukrainian Cossacks renounce 1654 allegiance to Russia.

June 21: Bosnia-H. declares war on Serbia.

June 23: Versailles parliamentary Congress adds provision for European union to French constitution (592 votes to 73). McDonalds opens outlet at Pompeii.

June 24:	EC FM's approve directive on working week and shop opening hours with UK derogations. Azeri-Armenian peace meeting in Minsk. Labor Party wins Israeli elections.
June 25:	BSEC treaty signed in Istanbul. Carrington "summit" in Strasbourg fails to find Yugoslav peace formula.
June 26:	EC Lisbon summit favors EFTA-country accessions before 1996 constitutional conference. Delors reappointed. Warning to Serbia.
June 28:	On WW1 anniversary, Mitterrand makes surprise visit to Sarajevo.
June 29:	OAU summit in Senegal. Algerian president, Ahmed Boudiaf assassinated. Estonians approve new constitution.
June 30:	Ulster Unionists meet with Irish government for first time since 1922. Fidel Ramos succeeds Corazon Aquino as Philippine President. Abdou Diouf (Senegal) OAU president
July 2:	Luxembourg parliament ratifies TEU. Death of Maurice Le Lannou, European geographer.
July 4:	Slovaks block Havel presidential re-election bid.
July 6-8:	G7 in Munich makes no progress on Uruguay Round; major loan to Russia.
July 9:	CSCE summit in Helsinki. WEU coordinates Serbia policy, sending fleet to implement naval blockade.
July 10:	ESA spacecraft Giotto flies past Grigg-Skellerupp's comet. Helsinki CSCE summit creates post of High Commissioner for National Minorities. Hanna Suchoka Polish PM. Ariane orbits Eutelsat 11-54, covering all Europe, and Indian satellite.
July 14:	First CIS "peacemakers" in South Ossetia, Georgia, on non-member territory.
July 15:	US millionnaire Milan Panic PM Yugoslavia (Serbia-Montenegro)
July 16:	Slovak parl't declares independence; Havel resigns. 50th anniversary deportation Paris Jews (Vél.d'Hiv.). Arkansas Gov'r Bill Clinton US Dem. presidential candidate.
July 17:	Belgian parl't approves TEU. EFTA-Israel pact on industrial and processed farm goods, fish and marine products. Portugal threatens to block ASEAN-EC agreement unless Indonesia improves human rights. EC-US pact on limiting gov't aid to civil aircraft constructors.
July 18:	Romanian PNL leader Radu Campeanu proposes ex-King Michael as presidential candidate. Death of Victor Louis.
July 19:	Baker and Rabin give new impetus to Middle East peace negotiations.
July 20:	In *Le Figaro* Milosevic denies Serbian involvement in Bosnia-H. conflict. COE Sec. Gen. Catherine Lalumière visits 5 ex-USSR republics.

July 21:   Death of Pierre Uri, French economist, "behind scenes" architect of Paris and Rome treaties.
July 23-24: 2nd Ibero-American summit, Madrid.
July 25:   UK broadens EC international conference on Yugoslavia to include UN, CSCE.
July 27:   French astronaut Michel Tognini takes off from Russian space center, Baïkonour, with 2 Russian astronauts.
July 29:   Erich Honecker returned to Germany for trial.
July 31:   Russ. mission joins with Space Station Mir. Nicolier (CH) and Malerba (I) take off from Cape Canaveral in US shuttle Atlantis to launch ESA satellite Eureca. EC Commission endorses Swedish membership. Main-Danube canal open.
Aug. 2:   ESA satellite Eureca launched by NASA shuttle. President Tudjman of Croatia re-elected.
Sept. 16:   UK, Spain leave ERM.
Sept. 20:   French referendum on TEU (51.05% yes).
Sept. 27:   Romanian presidential and parliamentary elections.
Sept. 30:   EC finance ministers reject "two-speed" monetary union.
Oct. 1:   Russia distributes 10,000—ruble privatization vouchers to all citizens. US Senate ratifies START.
Oct. 3:   Mozambique peace settlement signed in Rome. Governing party wins first free election in Angola over UNITA. Conflict in Abkhazia, Georgia. Clinton endorses NAFTA with reservation on environmental standards and retraining. Itamar Franco succeeds impeached Fernando Collar de Mello as Brazil's acting president.
Oct. 8:   NAFTA treaty initialled in San Antonio, Texas.
Oct. 9:   Death of Willy Brandt.
Oct. 11:   Ion Iliescu re-elected Romanian President.
Oct. 12:   Columbus quincentenary.
Oct. 16:   European Council in Birmingham reviews "lesson" of TEU ratification, reaffirms subsidiarity principle.
Oct. 19:   German "greens" leader Petra Kelly found dead. Yugoslav leader Dobrica Cosic and Bosnian Alija Izetbegovic agree to reverse ethnic expulsions.
Oct. 20:   Izetbegovic agrees to division of Bosnia-H into 10 autonomous regions.
Oct. 26:   Constitutional referendum in Canada defeated.
Oct. 28:   Italy ratifies TEU.
Oct. 29:   Croat ethnic cleansing of Muslims in Prozor; Zagreb sends back Bosnian refugees.
Oct. 30:   Russia suspends troop withdrawals from Baltic states. ECHR tells Ireland it cannot ban information on abortion abroad.
Nov. 3:   Arkansas governor Bill Clinton wins US presidential election.
Nov. 4:   Russia ratifies START, signed July 1991. EC Commission approves negotiations with Finland. Suchoka visits Bonn.

Nov. 6:	In absence of GATT agreement US sets high tariffs on white wine, rapeseed oil and gluten, with 30-day stay; France particularly affected.
Nov. 7:	Death of Alexander Dubcek.
Nov. 13:	Spain's 200,000 Muslims and 12,000 Jews achieve legal status with catholics, ending 1492 discrimination.
Nov. 16:	Former communist Democrat Labor Party wins Lithuanian elections.
Nov. 20:	Greece 10th WEU member; WEU and NATO ships blockade Yugoslavia. Norwegian parliament votes to re-apply for EC membership. Peseta and Escudo devalued 6%, stays in ERM.
Nov. 21:	EC and US agree on farm products in Uruguay Round; negative reaction in France.
Nov. 30:	Russian supreme court upholds Yeltsin's CP ban at national level.
Dec. 3:	Danish reject proposals for softening TEU.
Dec. 6:	By 50.3 to 49.7% and 16 cantons to 7, Swiss electorate rejects membership in EEA, effectively also putting hold on Switzerland's application for EC membership.
Dec. 9:	Operation "Restore Hope" lands in Somalia.
Dec. 11, 12:	Edinburgh summit of European Council agrees concessions to Denmark on single currency, defense and EC citizenship. EC budget compromise set. Institutional *status quo* confirmed.
Dec. 13:	Liechtenstein endorses EEA.
Dec. 14:	Stockholm CCSE conference; US Sec. of State Eagleburger calls for war crimes trials for Yugoslav conflict. Viktor Chernomyrdin Russian PM in People's Congress power struggle.
Dec. 17:	NAFTA signed; Bush envisions extension to South America. NATO willing to enforce Serbian no-fly embargo in Bosnia.
Dec. 18:	FRG ratifies TEU.
Dec. 31:	SEA elimination of obstacles to free movement of goods and services across EC frontiers.

1993

Jan. 1:	SEA single market. Treaties of European Union (12), EEA (18) and social rights (11) scheduled to enter into force, but subject to clarification after Danish rejection. Denmark succeeds UK in EC chair. Birth of Czech Republic and Slovakia as separate states.
Jan. 3:	Yeltsin and Bush sign START II in Moscow.
Jan. 20:	Bill Clinton first US Democrat president in 12 years. Bosnian Serbs accept Owen/Vance EC/UN peace plan.

1994

ESA spacecraft Ulysses flies past Sun's north pole.

1995

Jan. 1:   EC Commission's term extended to 5 years.
? :   Ulysses flies past Sun's south pole.

1996

EC constitutional conference.
Jan. 1:   Earliest date for TEU establishment of single currency
(UK participation subject to parliamentary approval).

1997

July 1:   TEU latest date for EC central bank.

1999

Jan. 1:   Latest date for single currency.

2002

ESA Rosetta launch to collect comet samples.

Appendix II

Acronyms

Acronyms are normally given in English only. Cross-references are supplied when a foreign abbreviation is equally common or more frequently used e.g. (CERN - ECRN; FEOGA - EAGGF) or when a special acronym is employed, e.g. EAEC - EURATOM.

- A -

A - Austria
AAA - Agricultural Adjustment Act, 1933 (US)
ABC - Atomic, biological and chemical (weapons, WEU)
ABM - Anti-Ballistic Missile (treaty)
ACA - Agency for Control of Armaments (WEU)
ACE - Actions by the Community relating to the Environment (EC)
ACP - Africa, Caribbean, Pacific development (EC)
Acquis communautaire - consolidated policy binding on all EC members, including new ones.
AFCENT - Allied Forces Central Europe (NATO)
AFP - *Agence France Presse*
AFTA - ASEAN Free Trade Area
ALB - Albania
AMCO - African-Malagasy Common Organisation
AND - Andorra
APDCVT - see FORCE
APEC - Asia Pacific Economic Cooperation
APVTTC - see EUROTECHNET
ARION - Study visits scheme for education specialists (EC)
ASEAN - Association of South-East Asian Nations
ASQ - Agencies for Security Questions (WEU)
Atlantic Alliance - see NATO
AUS - Australia
AWACS - Airborne Warning and Control System (mil.)

- B -

B - Belgium
Baltic states - Estonia, Latvia, Lithuania
BBCC - Ball-Bearing Coordination Centre (CMEA)
BENELUX - Belgium, Netherlands and Luxembourg (customs union)

BG - Bulgaria

BH - Bosnia Herzegovina

BIRD - International Bank for Reconstruction and Development (World Bank or IBRD)

Blue Europe - see CFP

BRD - *Bundesrepublik Deutschland*, see FRG

BSEC - Black Sea Economic Cooperation

BSI - British Standards Institution

BTO - Brussels Treaty Organisation

- C -

CAF - Committee on Agriculture and Fisheries (EFTA)

CAN - Canada

CAP - Common Agricultural Policy (EC)

CAP 2 - Reformed CAP (1992)

CC - 1. Consultative Committee (EFTA); 2. Conciliation Committee (EEA); 3. *Corps consulaire*

CCC - see CDCC

CCMTS - Committee on Cooperation in Material and Technical Supply (CMEA)

CCPA - Committee on Cooperation in Planning Activities (CMEA)

CC - PU - see SCUP

CCT - Common Customs Tariff (see CET)

CD - 1. Conference on Disarmament (see CDE); 2. *Corps diplomatique*

CDE - Conference on Security and Confidence Building Measures and Disarmament in Europe.

CDCC (formerly CCC) - Council for Cultural Cooperation (Council of Europe)

CDPE - Steering Committee for the Conservation and Management of the Environment and Natural Habitats (SCCMENH, Council of Europe)

CDU - Christian Democratic Union (FRG)

CEDC - Central European Development Corporation

CEDEFOP - European Centre for the Development of Vocational Training (EC)

Cedex - Special post box (business mail, France)

CEET - Common Effective External Tariff (AFTA)

CELAD - European Committee on the Fight against Drugs

CENELEC - European Committee for Electro Technical Standardisation (ECETS)

CENTO - Central Treaty Organisation

CEPES - European Centre for Higher Education (Bucharest, UNESCO)

CEPT - 1. Common Effective Preferential Tariff (AFTA); 2. see ECPT

CERI - Centre for Educational Research and Innovation (OECD)

CERN - European Centre for Nuclear Research

CET - Common External Tariff (EC, GATT)

CFE - Conventional Forces in Europe (treaty)

CFP - Common Fisheries Policy (EC)
CH - Switzerland
CHC - Cultural Heritage Committee (CDCC)
CHG - Council of Heads of Government (CIS)
CHS - Council of Heads of State (CIS)
Chunnel - Channel Tunnel
CIA - Central Intelligence Agency (US)
CI - Channel Islands
CICR - see ICRC
CIDREE - Consortium of Institutions for Development and Research in Education in Europe (UNESCO)
CIENS - Cooperative Index of European and National Standards
CIF - Cost, Insurance, Freight (shipping)
CIS - Commonwealth of Independent States
CISL - see ICFTU
CIU - Convergence and Union (Catalonian nationalist coalition)
CLRA - Conference of Local and Regional Authorities (Council of Europe)
CM - 1. Council of Ministers; 2. Committee of Ministers
CMEA - Council for Mutual Economic Assistance (COMECON)
CMP - Committee of Members of Parliament (EFTA)
COCE - Committee on Origin and Customs Exports (EFTA)
COCOM - Coordinating Committee on Multilateral Export Controls (technology transfer, NATO)
COE - Council of Europe (not usually abbreviated)
COMECON - see CMEA
COMETT I and II - Community Programm for Education and Training in Technology (EC)
Common Market - see EEC
Con. - Conservative Party
CORDEE - Cooperation for the Renewal and Development of Education in Europe (UNESCO)
CP - Communist Party
CPE - Centrally planned economy
CR - Croatia
CRE - Standing Conference of Rectors of European Universities
CRS - *Compagnies Républicaines de Sûreté* (French national guard)
CS - Czechoslovakia
CSBM - Confidence and Security-Building Measure
CSCE - Conference on Security and Cooperation in Europe
CSFR - Czech and Slovak Federal Republic (official name of Czechoslovakia)
CSP - Cereal Substitution Product (EC)
CSTC - Committee on Scientific and Technical Cooperation (CMEA)
CTBT - Committee on Technical Barriers to Trade (EFTA)
CTE - Committee of Trade Experts (EFTA)
CU - Cuba
CVD - Countervailing duty (EC, EFTA, GATT, US)

CVP - Flemish Catholic People's Party
CY - Cyprus

- D -

D - Germany
DAC - Development Assistance Committee (OECD)
DARA - *Deutsche Allraum Agentur* (German Space Agency)
DC - 1. Defence Committee (WEU); 2. Defense Council (CIS); 3. District of Columbia (US)
DDR - see GDR
dis. - Disarmament
DK - 1. Denmark; 2.Danish Krone
DM - German mark
DOD - Department of Defense (US)
DOM - *Département d'Outre-Mer* (French overseas department)
DPA - German Press Agency
DRG - Defence Representatives Group (WEU)

- E -

E - Spain
EAA - European Armaments Agency (proposed for WEU)
EAC - European Astronauts Centre (ESA)
EAEC - European Atomic Energy Community (EURATOM)
EAEG - East Asian Economic Group (proposed)
EAGGF - see FEOGA
EBLUL - European Bureau for Lesser Used Languages (Dublin)
EBRD - European Bank for Reconstruction and Development (EC)
EC - 1. European Community (ECSC, EEC and EAEC after fusion); 2. Economic Committee (EFTA); 3. Examining Committee (EFTA)
EC 92 - Single EC market after Dec. 31, 1992
ECB - European Central Bank (TEU)
ECC - European Campaign for the Countryside (Council of Europe, 1987-1988)
ECCA - European Center for Conciliation and Arbitration (CSCE)
ECDVT - See CEDEFOP
ECE - Economic Commission for Europe (UN)
ECES - see CENELEC
ECHR - European Court of Human Rights (Council of Europe)
ECJ - European Court of Justice (EC)
ECLA - European Conference of Local Authorities (Council of Europe): see also SCLRAE
ECM - European Committee on Migration (Council of Europe)
ECNR - see CERN
ECO - Economic Cooperation Organisation (Turkey, Iran, Pakistan)
ECPT - European Conference of Posts and Telecommunications (CEPT)

ECSC - European Coal and Steel Community
ECU - European Currency Unit (EC)
ECY - European Conservation Year (Council of Europe, 1970)
EDC - European Defence Community (proposed)
EEA - European Economic Area (formerly European Economic Space, EC and EFTA)
EEC - European Economic Community
EEP - Export Enhancement Program (US Ag.)
EES - European Economic Space (see EEA)
EFTA - European Free Trade Association
EIB - European Investment Bank (EC)
EINEC - see EURYDICE
EIR - see IRL
EIS - European Information System (EC)
ELDO - European Launcher Development Organisation
ELLAS - see GR
EMA - European Monetary Agreement (EC)
EMCF - European Monetary Cooperation Fund (EC)
EMI - European Monetary Institute (TEU)
EMS - European Monetary System (EC)
EMU - European Monetary Union (TEU)
ENVIREG - Regional anti-pollution program (EC)
EP - European Parliament, or European Parliamentary Assembly (EC)
EPA - see EP
EPC - European Patent Convention
EPU - European Payments Union (OEEC)
EPO - 1. European Patent Office; 2. see EUROPOL
ERASMUS - European Action Scheme for the Mobility of University Students (EC)
ERC - *Esquerra Republicana de Catalunya* (Catalonian independence party)
ERCA - see EUREKA
ERDF - European Regional Development Fund (FEDER in French)
ESA - 1. European Space Agency; 2. EFTA Surveillance Authority (proposed)
ESCB - European System of Central Banks (EC)
ESD - European Schools Day
ESDA - European Security and Defence Academy (proposed for WEU)
ESF - European Social Fund (EC)
ESPRIT - EC research program in information technology
ESRO - European Space Research Organisation
ESSR - European Source of Synchotron Radiation
ESTEC - Technical and Research Centre (ESA)
EUDISED - European Documentation and Information System for Education (CDCC)
EURATOM - see EAEC
EUREKA - European Research Coordination Agency (EC)
EUROFED - Proposed European bank (TEU)

EUROPOL - European Police Office (TEU)

EUROTECNET - Action program in vocational Training and Technological Change (EC)

EURYDICE - Education Information Network in the European Community

EWC - European Water Charter (Council of Europe)

EYC - European Youth Centre (Council of Europe)

EYE - European Year of the Environment (EC, 1980)

EYF - European Youth Foundation (Council of Europe)

- F -

F - France

FEOGA - European Agricultural Guidance and Guarantee Fund (CAP/EC)

FAO - Food and Agriculture Organisation (UN)

FDP - Free Democratic Party (FRG)

FEDER - see ERDF

FF - 1. French Franc; 2. Fianna Fail party (IRL)

FIS - Islamic Salvation Front (Algeria)

FISC - see ICFTU

FL - 1. Liechtenstein; 2. Foreign language

FM - Foreign Minister

FOB - Free on Board (shipping)

FORCE - Action Program for the Development of Continuing Vocational Training (EC)

FORPRONU - Peacekeeping force in ex-Yugoslavia (UN)

FOVU - Steering Committee for Nordic Cooperation on General and Adult Education (NC)

FRG - Federal Republic of Germany

FTA - Free Trade Area (EFTA and GATT)

- G -

G7 - Seven most industrialized nations (CAN, F, FRG, I, JN, UK, USA)

GATT - General Agreement on Tariffs and Trade

GB - Great Britain (UK)

GBA - Alderney (UK)

GBG - Guernsey (UK)

GBJ - Jersey (UK)

GDP - Gross domestic product (econ.)

GDR - German Democratic Republic

GNP - Gross national product (econ.)

GMT - Greenwich mean time (UT)

GO - Governmental organization

GR - Greece

Green Box - Payments to farmers not subject to progressive reduction (GATT/UR)

Green Europe - see CAP
GWh - Million watt-hours

- H -

H - Hungary
Hermes - ESA shuttle
HS - Holy See (Vatican)

- I -

I - Italy
IAEA - International Atomic Energy Agency (UN)
IASS - Institute for Advanced Security Studies (WEU)
IATA - International Air Transport Association (employers)
IAU - International Association of Universities
IBEC - International Bank for Economic Cooperation (CMEA)
IBRD - see BIRD
ICAO - International Civil Aviation Organisation (UN)
ICRC - International Committee of the Red Cross / Crescent (CICR)
ICBM - Intercontinental Ballistic Missile
ICE - International Conference on Education (UNESCO)
ICFTU - International Confederation of Free Trade Unions (Brussels, CISL)
ICONE - see CIENS
ICSEM - International Commission for the Scientific Exploration of the Mediterranean (CIESM)
ICST - International Centre for Science and Technology (Moscow, OECD)
IDA - International Development Association
IDF - Industrial Development Fund for Portugal (EFTA)
IEA - International Energy Agency (OECD)
IEC - International Electrotechnical Commission
IFCTU - International Federation of Christian Trade Unions (FISC)
IFHR - International Federation for Human Rights
IGC's - Intergovernmental committees (for speeding up EC integration before 1993)
IGO - Intergovernmental organization
IIB - International Investment Bank (CMEA)
ILO - International Labour Office (or Organisation)
ILY - International Literacy Year (UNESCO, 1990)
IMF - International Monetary Fund
IMM - International Money Market
IMP - Integrated Mediterranean Programs (EC)
INF - Treaty on land-based Intermediate-Range Nuclear Forces (dis.)
INR - Institute for Nuclear Research (CMEA)
INRLC - see MERCATOR

INTERMETALL - CMEA research institute on metals
INTERPOL - International Police Organisation
IOC - International Olympic Committee
IOM - 1. Isle of Man; 2. International Office of Migration (UN)
IPO - see INTERPOL
IRA - Irish Republican Army
IRBM - Intermediate Range Ballistic Missile
IRL - Ireland (EIR)
ISL - Iceland
ISO - International Standardization Organization
ITO - International Trade Organisation (proposal replaced by GATT)
IUCN - International Union for the Conservation of Nature

- **J** -

JN - Japan
JRC - Joint Research Centre (EURATOM)

- **K** -

KDH - Christian Democratic Party (Slovakian federalist)
km^2 - square kilometer

- **L** -

L - Luxembourg
Lab. - Labour Party (UK)
Lib. Dem. - Liberal Democratic Party
LDC - Less developed country
LINGUA - Program for the quantitative and qualitative improvement of foreign language competence (EC)
LF - Luxembourg franc
LHC - Large Hadron Collider (CERN)
Lib. - Liberal Party
LINGUAPAX - UNESCO program for foreign language teaching
LN - 1. Liechtenstein; 2. League of Nations
LRINF - Longer-range INF
Ltd - Limited liability company (= US Inc.)

- **M** -

M - Malta
Maastricht treaty - see TEU
MBFR - Mutual and Balanced Force Reduction (treaty)
MC - Monaco
MCPP - see MEDSPA
MEDSPA - Mediterranean coastal protection program (EC)
MEP - Member of the European Parliament (EC)

MERCATOR - Information network on regional languages and cultures (EC)
MEX - Mexico
MFN - Most favored nation clause (GATT)
MIL - military
MIRV - Multiple-warhead intercontinental re-entry vehicle (nuclear missile)
MIT - Massachusetts Institute of Technology (US)
MLF - Multilateral Force
MOD - Ministry of Defence
MON - Mongolia
MPLA - Popular Movement for the Liberation of Angola
MTFF - Man-tended free flyer (ESA)

- N -

N - Norway
NAA - North Atlantic Assembly (NATO parliamentarians' unofficial body)
NAC - North Atlantic Council (NATO)
NACC - North Atlantic Cooperation Council (NATO with CIS and former
  WTO members)
NAFTA - North Atlantic Free Trade Area
NASA - National Aeronautics and Space Administration (US)
NATO - North Atlantic Treaty Organisation (Atlantic Alliance)
NATUROPA - European Information Centre (and Review) for Nature
  Conservation (Council of Europe)
NC - Nordic Council
NCA - Nordic Central Agreement (NC)
NEA - Nuclear Energy Agency (OECD)
NEICS - Network of national information centers on academic mobility and
  the equivalence of diplomas (CDCC)
NGO - Non-governmental organization
NL - Netherlands
NNA - Neutral and non-aligned states
NNP - Net national product (econ.)
NNPT - Nuclear Non-Proliferation Treaty (dis.)
Non-proliferation treaty - see TNPNA
NORDEK - Nordic common market (proposed, NC)
NORDMAL - Action program for language cooperation (NC)
NPT - Non-Proliferation Treaty (nuclear weapons, dis.)
NSF - National Salvation Front (former communists, Romania)
NSS - Steering Committee for Nordic Educational Cooperation (NC)
NYT - New York Times
NZ - New Zealand

- O -

OAS - Organization of American States
OAU - Organisation for African Unity

ODS - Civic Democratic Party (Czechoslovakia)
OECD - Organisation for Economic Cooperation and Development (formerly OEEC)
OEEC - Organisation for European Economic Cooperation
OIEC - Organisation of International Economic Cooperation (proposed, CMEA)
OPEC - Organisation of Petroleum Exporting Countries
OTA - Optical telescope assembly (ESA)

- **P** -

P - Portugal
p.a. - per annum, yearly
PAC - see CAP
Paris treaty - see ECSC
PC - Political Committee
PE - Portuguese escudo
PETRA - Action Programme for the Vocational Training of Young People (EC)
PHARE - Program of Western economic aid for the reconstruction of Central and Eastern Europe (G7 initiative coordinated by EC)
PKK - Kurdistan Workers Party (Turkey)
PL - Poland
PNL - National Liberal Party (Romania)
PO - Post Office
Plaid Cymru - Welsh National Party
PQ - Province of Quebec
PM - Prime Minister
PRC - People's Republic of China
PRI - Peace Research Institute (FRG)
PSOE - Spanish Socialist Labor Party
PTT - Postal, telephone and telecommunications administration(s)

- **R** -

ROC - Republic of China (Taiwan)
ROM - Romania
Rome treaties - see EEC and EURATOM
RPIT - see ESPRIT
RPR - Rally for the Republic (French Gaullist)
RUNP - Romanian United National Party

- **S** -

S - Sweden
SA - South Africa
SAC - 1. Standing Armaments Committee (WEU); 2. Strategic Air Command (NATO)

SACEUR - Supreme Allied Commander, Europe (NATO)
SCCMENH - see CDPE
SCMM - Steering Committee on Mass Media (Council of Europe)
SALT - Strategic Arms Limitation Treaty
SAM - Surface to air missile
SCA - Standing Committee on Armaments (WEU)
SCLRAE - Standing Conference of Local and Regional Authorities of Europe (Council of Europe; formerly European Conference of Local Authorities)
Scot. Nat. - Scottish National Party
SCUP - Standing Conference on University Problems (CDCC)
SDI - Strategic Defense Initiative (Star Wars, US)
SDP - Social Democratic Party
SDR - Special Drawing Rights (IDF for Portugal, EFTA and IMF)
SEA - Single European Act (EC)
SEATO - South-East Asia Treaty Organisation
SEP - Socialist Unity Party (GDR)
SF - Finland
SHAPE - Supreme headquarters, allied powers, Europe (NATO)
SHERPAS - Officials who prepare ministerial or summit meetings
SKDH - Slovakian Christian Democratic Party (separatist)
SL - Slovenia
SM - San Marino
Soc. - Socialist Party
Soc. Dem. - Social Democratic Party
Solidarnosc - Solidarity (PL)
SP - Peseta (Spanish currency)
SRINF - Shorter-range INF
sq.m. - square mile
SS - Social Security
Star Wars - see SDI
SSC - Superconducting Super Collider (US)
START - Strategic Arms Reduction Treaty (succeeding SALT I and II, dis.)
Stasi - East German secret police (*Staatsicherheitsdienst*)
STSP - Solar Terrestrial Science Program (ESA/NASA)
SU - Soviet Union (see USSR)
SWG - Special Working Group (WEU)

- T -

TAC - 1. Total Allowable Catch (CFP/EC); 2. Technological and Aerospace Committee (WEU)
TBT - Technical Barrier to Trade (GATT, EC, EFTA)
TEU - Treaty of European Union (Maastricht treaty)
TIR - Transports Internationaux Routiers (international road transport agreement)

TNPNA - Treaty on the Non-Proliferation of Nuclear Armaments (non-proliferation treaty)
TPA - Third Party Access (electricity grid, EC)
TR - Turkey
TRIPS - Trade-Related Intellectual Property Rights (EC/GATT)

- U -

u.a. - Unit of Account
UDF - 1. Union for French Democracy; 2. Union of Democratic Forces (BG) 3. United Democratic Front (H)
UDR - Union for Democratic Reform (BG)
UK - United Kingdom
UN - United Nations
UNCED - UN Conference on Environment and Development (Rio-de-Janeiro, 1992)
UNCTAD - United Nations Conference for Trade and Development
UNESCO - United Nations Educational, Scientific and Cultural Organisation
UNHCR - High Commission for Refugees (UN)
UNICE - Union of Industrial and Employers' Confederations of Europe
Union - several connotations, especially "European Union" approved in Maastricht, Dec. 1991
UNITA - Union for the Total Independence of Angola
UNO - United Nations Organisation
UPU - Universal Postal Union
Uruguay Round - Multilateral free trade negotiations started in Montevideo (GATT)
US - United States
USA - see US
USSR - Union of Soviet Socialist Republics (Soviet Union)
UT - Universal Time (see GMT)
UU - Ulster Unionist Party

- V -

VAT - 1. Value-added-tax; 2. Vatican (see HS)
VN - Vietnam
VP - Vice-President

- W -

Warsaw Pact - see WTO
WCC - World Council of Churches (Geneva)
WCEFA - World Conference on Education for All (UNESCO)
WEU - Western European Union
WFTU - World Federation of Free Trade Unions
WHO - World Health Organisation (UN)
WIPO - World Intellectual Property Organization

World Bank - see BIRD
WTO - Warsaw Treaty Organisation (Warsaw Pact)
WW1 - First World War
WW2 - Second World War
WWF - World Wildlife Fund

- Y -

Y - Yemen (People's Republic)
YU - Yugoslavia

Select Bibliography

Activities of OECD in 1988, Paris, Organization for Economic Cooperation and Development, 1989; *ibid. 1989*, 1990.

Agriculteurs français, Les, Le Monde Dossiers et Documents, Nr 197, Paris, Le Monde, 1992.

"ASEAN's Leaders tout Free Trade in Self-Defense", in *Asian Wall Street Journal*, New York, Jan. 28, 1992, p. 1.

"ASEAN Nations agree to create Free Trade Area", in *Asian Wall Street Journal*, New York, Jan. 29, 1992, p. 1.

Baranowsky, Vladimir, "The Treaty on the Elimination of Intermediate-Range and Shorter-Range Missiles", in Institute of World Economy and International Relations, USSR Academy of Sciences, *Disarmament and Security: 1987 Yearbook*, Moscow, Novosti Press, 1988.

Bray, Nicholas, "Bank of England seeks Power at Home, Influence in European Monetary Union", in *The Wall Street Journal*, New York, October 10, 1991.

Brugmans, Henri, *L'Europe prend le large*, Recherches européennes, Collection du Collège d'Europe, Vols I, II, Paris, Librairie Générale du Droit et de la Jurisprudence, 1961.

Brugmans, Henri, *Prophètes et Fondateurs de l'Europe*, Bruges, Collège d'Europe, 1974.

Carrol, John E. (ed), *International Environmental Diplomacy*, New York, Columbia University Press, 1990.

Chatham House Study Group, *Britain in Western Europe: WEU and the Atlantic Alliance*, London and New York, Royal Institute of International Affairs, 1956.

Common Agricultural Policy for the 1990's, A Luxembourg, Office for Official Publications of the EC, 5th ed., 1989.

Common Fisheries Policy, The, Luxembourg, Office for Official Publications of the EC, 1986.

Cook, Don, *Forging the Alliance, NATO 1945-1950*, London, Secker and Warburg, 1989.

Council of Europe (*et al.*), introduction by Stephen Jones, *European Cooperation on Education*, Strasbourg, Standing Conference of European Ministers of Education, 1991.

Council of Europe Newsletter, Documentation Centre for Education in Europe, Strasbourg, Council of Europe, 1991 (periodical, ref. ISSN 0252-0591).

De Cecco, Marcello and Giovannini, Alberto, *A European Central Bank*, New York, Cambridge University Press, 1989.

Delors, Jacques, *Le Nouveau concert européen*, Paris, Jacob, 1992.

De Staercke, André, and others, *NATO's anxious Birth*, London, Hurst, 1985.

Duverger, Maurice, *Le lièvre libéral et la tortue européenne*, Paris, Albin Michel, 1990.

Economic and Monetary Union, Luxembourg, Office of Official Publications of the EC, 1990.

EEC Agricultural Policy and the Environment, London, Agra Europe, 1988, VI.

EFTA, Geneva, European Free Trade Association, 1987.

El-Agraa, Ali (ed.), *The Economics of the European Community*, 2nd. ed., Oxford and New York, Philip Alan / St. Martin's Press, 1985.

Energy in the European Community, 4th ed., Luxembourg, Office of Official Publications of the EC, 1991.

Environment: Directory of Community Legislation in Force, Luxembourg, Office of Official Publications of the EC, 1992.

Environmental Policy in the European Community, Luxembourg, Office for Official Publications of the EC, 1992.

ESA Annual Report '90, Paris, European Space Agency, 1991.

European Community and its Eastern Neighbours, The, Luxembourg, Office for Official Publications of the EC, 1990.

European Community and the Energy Problem, The, Luxembourg, Office of Official Publications of the EC, 1983.

Europe without Frontiers: Completing the internal Market, Luxembourg, Office of Official Publications of the EC, 1989.

Eyskens, Mark, ed. Sherwen, N. and Jochmans, F, *From Détente to Entente*, Brassey's Atlantic Commentaries, Nr 4, Brassey, London, 1990.

Far Eastern Economic Review, July 25, 1991.

Focus, GATT Newsletter, Nr 67, Geneva, General Agreement on Tariffs and Trade, Dec. 1989.

Forman, Craig, "EC Leaders move toward Unity on Currency, but Discord remains", in *The Wall Street Journal*, New York, Dec. 10, 1991.

Fourth environmental Action Programme with Evidence, House of Lords, Select Committee on the EC, session 1986/87, London, HMSO, 1987;

General Agreement on Tariffs and Trade, The, Geneva, General Agreement on Tariffs and Trade, 1986.

Gill, Stephen (ed.), *Atlantic Relations: Beyond the Reagan Era*, Hemel Hempstead (UK), Harvester Wheatsheaf and New York, St. Martin's Press, 1989.

Giovannini, Alberto and Mayer, Colin, *European financial Integration*, New York, Cambridge University Press, 1991.

Gorbachev, Mikhail, *Address to the Supreme Soviet on visits to GB, FRG and France*, Moscow, Novosti Press, 1989.

Gorbachev, Mikhail, *Perestroïka: New Thinking for our Country and the World*, New York, Harper and Row, 1987.

Gorbachev, Mikhail, *Visit of Mikhail Gorbachev to France: Documents and Materials*, Moscow, Novosti Press, 1989.

Grosser, Alfred, *The Western Alliance: European-American Relations since 1945*, London, Macmillan, 1980.

Gunther, John, *Inside Europe Today*, 2nd version, New York, Harper Brothers, 1961.

Hackett, Clifford, *Cautious Revolution: the European Community arrives*, New York and London, Praeger, 1990.

Heseltine, Michael, *The Challenge of Europe: Can Britain win ?* London, Pan, 1991.

Heywood, Robert W., *European Community: Idea and Reality*, San Francisco, EM Text, 1990.

Histoire de l'Europe (collective authorship), Paris, Hachette and Council of Europe, 1992. Also published in Germany, Greece, Netherlands and Portugal.

Hopkins, Raymond, *Global Food Interdependence: Challenge to American Foreign Policy*, New York, Columbia University Press, 1980.

House, Karen and Revzin, Philip, "Germany's Kohl shapes its new Policies", in *The Wall Street Journal*, New York, Feb. 7, 1992.

Hufbauer, Gary, *Procedures for Monitoring and Disciplining Government Aids*, EFTA Occasional Paper Nr 30, Geneva, EFTA Economic Affairs Department, 1989.

Hughes, Rachel, "A European Germany", in *Europe*, Nr 304, New York, 1991.

Jakobson, Max, *Finland: Myth and Reality*, Helsinki, Otava, 1987.

Johnson, Stanley and Corcelle, Guy, *L'autre Europe "verte": la politique communautaire de l'environnement*, Paris, Nathan, 1987.

Jopp, Mathias and others, *Ten Years of the CSCE Process: Appraisal of and Prospects for all-European Détente and Cooperation*, Frankfurt, Place Research Institute, 1985.

Jordan, Robert (ed), *Europe and the Superpowers: Essays on European International Politics*, New York, St. Martin's Press, 1991.

Jouanneau, Daniel, *Le GATT*, Collection "Que sais-je", Paris, PUF, 1987.

Kerr, Anthony J.C., *The Common Market and how it works*, Oxford and New York, etc., Pergamon Press, 1983.

KPMG - Peat Marwick, *World*, special EC edition, New York, KPMG - Peat Marwick, 1989.

Krugman, Paul, *EFTA and 1992*, EFTA Occasional Paper Nr 23, Geneva, EFTA Economic Affairs Department, 1988.

Lodge, Juliet (ed), *The European Community and the Challenge of the Future*, New York, St. Martin's Press, 1989.

Lory, Marie-Joseph, *Douze leçons sur l'Europe, 1914-1947*, Cahiers de Bruges, Collège d'Europe, Bruges, de Tempel, 1968.

Louis, André, "The ECU and its Role in the Process towards Monetary Union", in *European Economy*, Nr 48, Luxembourg, Office of Official Publications of the EC, September 1991.

Lucas, Michael R., *The Western Alliance after INF: Redefining US policy towards Europe and the Soviet Union*, Boulder and London, Lynne Rienner Publishers, 1990.

Lustiger, Jean-Marie, *Nous avons rendez-vous avec l'Europe*, Paris, Mame, 1991.

Mathieu, Jean-Luc, *La Communauté européenne: marché ou état ?*, Paris, Fernand Nathan, 1990.

McLachlan, Donald, see Chatham House Study Group.

Mink, Georges, *Europe de l'est: la transition*, Problèmes politiques et sociales, Nr 636, Paris, La Documentation française, 1990.

Molle, Willem, *The Economics of European Integration*, Aldershot (UK) and Brookfield (US), Dartmouth, 1991.

Möttölä, Kari and Patomäki, Heikki (ed), *Facing the Change in Europe*: EFTA countries' Integration Strategies, Helsinki, The Finnish Institute of International Affairs, 1989.

NATO Secretary-General, *The North Atlantic Treaty Organization: Facts and Figures*, 11th ed., Brussels, NATO Information Service, 1989.

National Food Review (periodica)l, Vol. 13, Washington, US Department of Agriculture, Jan. 1990.

Naturopa (Periodical), European Information Centre for the Conservation of Nature and Natural Resources, Strasbourg, Council of Europe.

OECD, Paris, Organisation for Economic Cooperation and Development, 1985.

Paarlberg, Don, *Farm and Food Policy: Issues of the 1980's*, Lincoln, University of Nebraska Press, 1980.

Pelkmans, Jacques, "ASEAN and EC 1992", in *National Institute Economic Review*, November 1990.

Pontillon, Robert, "Une Europe de la défense", in *Le Monde*, Paris, July 11, 1990.

Pulzer, Peter, "Head over Heart for Europe", in *The London Review of Books*, London, Mar. 21, 1991.

"Resolution of the Council on EC environment Policy (C 328)", *in Official Journal of the EC*, Luxembourg, Office of Official Publications of the EC, December, 1987.

Riding, Alan, "Europeans accept a single currency and Bank by 1999", in *The Wall Street Journal*, New York, Dec. 10, 1991.

Salsa, Claudia Pasqualini, *Il diritto dell' ambiente*, Milano, Ed. del Sole 24 ore, 1988.

Schiavone, Giuseppe, *The Institutions of COMECON*, New York, Holmes and Meier Publishers, Inc., 1980.

Schoutete, Philippe de, *La Coopération politique européenne*, Paris, Fernand Nathan, 1980.

Shapiro, Alan C., *Multinational Financial Management*, Boston, Allyn and Bacon, 1989.

Shea, Jamie, ed. Sherwen, Nicholas, *NATO 2000: A political Agenda for a political Alliance*, Brassey's Atlantic Commentaries, Nr 3, London, Brassey's, 1990.

Shennan, Margaret, *Teaching about Europe*, London and Strasbourg, Cassell-Council of Europe, 1991.

Single European Act, The, Luxembourg, Office of Official Publications of the EC, 1987.

Staercke, André and others, *NATO's anxious Birth*, Hurst, London, 1985.

Starkey, Hugh (ed), *The Challenge of Human Rights Education*, London and Strasbourg, Cassell-Council of Europe, 1991.

Tendron, Georges, "Man and his Environment", in *Naturopa*, Nr 41, Strasbourg, Council of Europe, 1982.

Thomas, Hugh, *Ever closer Union: Britain's Destiny in Europe*, London, Hutchinson, 1991, pp. 96.

Thurow, Lester, Head to Head: the coming economic Battle among Japan, Europe, and America, New York, William Morrow & Co, 1992.

Trente ans de Communauté européenne, Le Monde Dossiers et Documents, Nr hors série, Paris, Le Monde, 1987.

Urjewicz, Charles, *La Crise des nationalités en URSS*, LDF Problèmes politiques et sociaux, Nr 616, Paris, La Documentation française, 1989, pp. 64.

Vandermeersch, Dirk, "The SEA and the Environmental Policy of the EEC", in *European Law Review* (periodical), 1987, 12/06.

Wallace, Helen and Wessels, Wolfgang, *Towards a new Partnership: the EC and EFTA in the wider western Europe*, EFTA Occasional Paper Nr 28, Geneva, EFTA Economic Affairs Department, 1989.

Weiss, Julian, "Another Single Market", in *Europe*, May 1990, pp. 23, 24.

Western European Union Committee for Parliamentary and Public Relations, *Preliminary draft Manual*, Paris, Western European Union, 1989.

"West Europeans gather to seek a tighter Union", in *New York Times*, December 8, 1991.

Whiteney, Craig, "Britain's Way: a qualified Agreement", in *New York Times*, New York, Dec. 11, 1991.

Zwass, Adam, *The Council for mutual economic Assistance: the thorny Path from political to economic Integration*, Armonk, N.Y. and London, M.E. Sharpe, Inc., 1989.

Index

Z

X

Y

174 CC FS 952 ICI
01/18/96 32550 SELE
INFORMATION CONSERVATION, INC.